Fundamentals of System-on-Chip Design on Arm® Cortex®-M Microcontrollers

Fundamentals of System-on-Chip Design on Arm® Cortex®-M Microcontrollers

RENÉ BEUCHAT, FLORIAN DEPRAZ,
ANDREA GUERRIERI, SAHAND KASHANI

arm Education Media

Contents

Contents

Preface

The exponential increase in computing power the world has witnessed since the introduction of general-purpose computing to the public is nothing short of phenomenal. Few endeavors undertaken by humanity can claim similar growth. Media outlets are quick to publicize computational advances achieved by newly released high-performance systems as large figures lend themselves to making eye-catching headlines. Yet, this public-facing side of today's computing landscape represents only a fraction of the computers currently running on our planet.

The ever-increasing market penetration of the internet has promoted the development of countless "smart devices", i.e., devices that are connected to the internet and which leverage this connectivity to provide functionality that would not be possible without network access. The web of internet-connected devices in this category forms a network called the "Internet of Things" (IoT). IoT devices are connected to the internet by means of a small computer that is typically hidden within the device. Since the computers in IoT devices are not directly user-facing, most people don't realize the sheer number of them that exist in everyday equipment. Examples of IoT devices include voice-controlled home assistants, intelligent doormats that can tell how many people have come in and out of a shop, and smart fridges that do grocery shopping for you on the internet. Consumer-grade devices are not the only IoT devices on the market; countless industrial applications of internet-connected machines can also be found. For example, it is now common for machines in a factory to be interconnected via the internet for continuous monitoring and automated maintenance. In essence, IoT devices allow for more direct integration of the physical world into the digital one, so as to minimize the amount of menial and repetitive human interaction with the objects around us.

The computers inside IoT devices are not full PCs, as including one in an IoT device would make the device both voluminous and expensive. IoT devices are instead populated with **embedded systems**, i.e., small computers that are specialized for the appliances in which they are embedded (hence the name). Embedded systems predate general-purpose computers and have only recently become internet-connected. Indeed, the vast majority of current appliances on the market are from the pre-IoT era and are basically standalone devices that were once programmed and released into the field, never to be touched again. Nevertheless, appliances show their age quickly and most usually get replaced every few years. In fact, most newly released appliances leverage internet connectivity to offer some form of intelligence. As a result, the market will inevitably be flooded with billions of IoT devices in the near future. A huge opportunity exists for developers to come up with creative applications that leverage these distributed embedded systems in ways that are as yet unforeseen. However, such a future can only be possible if more developers become familiar with how embedded systems are put together in order to make best use of their abilities.

Organization of this Book

This book aims to provide readers with an understanding of the fundamental building blocks of modern embedded systems that lie at the heart of billions of IoT devices. Teaching a course on embedded systems for over 40 years has exposed us to the various difficulties encountered by students while learning this topic. Writing this book is our attempt to provide a central support for conveying the field of embedded systems in the way we believe it should be taught.

This book describes systems that have matured considerably over the past 40 years. One of the biggest differences between today's embedded systems and those of yore is the fact that we now live in a world where devices can no longer afford to take up a large footprint. As a result, the industry has steered heavily towards the design and fabrication of energy-efficient systems on a chip (SoC), i.e., systems in which a single chip integrates most components needed to run a computer. SoCs have taken a prominent role in modern embedded systems and are likely to remain the dominant architecture of IoT devices for the foreseeable future. This book covers embedded systems built around Arm Cortex-M processor cores, a popular CPU architecture often used in modern low-power SoCs that target IoT applications. Though we illustrate modern SoCs using Arm's Cortex-M core, the main principles used in such systems can be used to build SoCs with other processor cores as well.

A processor core by itself is not enough to build a SoC and many programmable interfaces are needed to support interaction with other devices through various communication protocols. No modern SoC would be useful without support for such protocols and we put a large emphasis on covering the most common ones in this text. We mostly cover these protocols at the logic level, but a select few also involve dabbling in electrical concerns.

The book is organized as follows.

- Chapter 1 introduces embedded systems from a high-level hardware and software perspective. We cover basic systems built on microcontroller-based architectures before moving to SoC-based designs.

- Chapter 2 is a theoretical chapter that goes over the basics of chip design, a multi-faceted task that involves technology, logic, power, reliability, and configurability aspects. We also provide a brief overview of processor architecture and the characteristics of integrated circuits.

- Chapter 3 details the heart of many modern IoT devices, namely the Arm Cortex-M processor architectures and instruction sets. This is a heavy chapter that covers the processor's interrupt and exception handling mechanisms, its memory protection unit, and the Arm® TrustZone® technology used to provide software with secure access to the hardware. Additionally, we detail the Arm Cortex Microcontroller Software Interface Standard (CMSIS), a software interface with generic code that can enforce portability between different Cortex-M cores. The final section takes a more practical approach by looking at a development kit from Texas Instruments, the MSP432P401R.

- Chapter 4 steps back from the processor core and looks at how one would approach the task of interconnecting the various components in a SoC. This chapter incrementally introduces the core principles needed to build a modular interconnect through a case study where we build one such interconnect from scratch. The principles covered here can then easily be applied to a variety of real-world interconnect designs.

- Chapter 5 drills into applications of the theory developed in Chapter 4 by studying some system interconnect protocols used on actual Cortex-M processors: the AMBA® AHB-Lite, APB, AXI4, and AXI4-Lite protocols.

▦ Chapter 6 focuses on how a SoC interfaces with the external world, i.e., with devices that are not integrated within the SoC. This chapter is protocol-heavy. We start with an overview of external bus architectures before diving into the details of various serial protocols and data coding techniques. We finish this chapter with a presentation of multiple network-based communication protocols.

▦ Chapter 7 covers the most common peripherals integrated in a modern SoC and the programmable interfaces that can access them. We go over the general block diagram and typical register control interface of GPIO controllers, timers, analog-to-digital converters (ADC), and various serial communication interfaces. This chapter concludes with a case study in which we explore the different programmable interfaces that are included with the Arm Cortex-M1 DesignStart processor core.

▦ Chapter 8 continues with a detailed coverage of memories used in modern SoCs. These include various static/dynamic, volatile/non-volatile, and on-chip/off-chip memories.

▦ Chapter 9 closes our discussion on hardware with a brief overview of SoC-FPGA devices. These are modern SoC designs that tightly couple an FPGA with a SoC to create a powerful medium for integrating custom logic with SoC systems.

▦ Chapter 10 concludes this book with a discussion of software programming concerns, particularly with respect to the environment in which programs are run (whether bare-metal or under the control of an operating system). This chapter also details some classical scheduling algorithms routinely found in real-time operating systems used on SoCs.

The material covered in this book can be considered fundamental background for any student intending to major in computer engineering. It is also valuable for any student whose interests lie at the intersection of computer science and electrical engineering.

Finally, it is important to state what this book is not. The systems described and used for illustrative purposes in this book are complex and are often detailed in reference manuals that are multiple thousands of pages long. This book does not aim to be a substitute for such reference manuals, and readers who wish to know specific details of the devices covered in this book should refer to the manuals accordingly. Our goal is instead to convey core principles to the reader, because once such principles are acquired, their application in different devices becomes just a matter of extensive engineering.

Target Audience

This book is written with a second undergraduate course in digital design in mind. We assume readers are familiar with the basics of computer science and have taken a first programming course in C. Knowing how various types of numbers are represented in a computer is particularly important to understanding the topics covered in this book. Embedded systems heavily rely on protocols to communicate with sensors and many of these protocols depend on signals exhibiting a certain electrical property. We therefore assume that readers have taken a primer on electronics. Finally, embedded systems are clocked digital systems and we expect readers to be comfortable with digital design.

The appendix covers all prerequisite material and can be used as a reference whenever needed. Experienced readers may freely skip this section, but we do recommend going through it as a refresher.

Target Platform

This textbook is about the main principles behind how microcontrollers work and it is, therefore, more of a theoretical than a hands-on book. However, we do take a more practical approach in some chapters (e.g., Chapter 3), as well as in the additional material and exercises hosted on https://github.com/Introduction-To-System-On-Chip. These exercises use the MSP-EXP432P401R low-cost development board from Texas Instruments. The QEMU simulator is also used in some exercises.

A Note for International Readers

In this book, the point (.) is used as a decimal separator:

$$0.5 \times 2 = 1$$

The comma (,) is used to improve the readability of numbers greater than 999:

$$999 + 1 = 1,000$$

$$99,999 + 1 = 100,000$$

These conventions are typical in English writing, but may be unfamiliar to some international readers. We hope they do not cause confusion.

Acknowledgments

When asked to reflect on their experience writing a book, all authors seem to paint a similar portrait: the task was a long and laborious one that took multiple years to complete. It is easy to think that such tales are vastly exaggerated and, in fact, we held that very opinion when we started writing this book. People tend to believe they are gifted with the ability to perform tasks better than others would; however, one needs to put oneself in the other person's shoes before coming to such conclusions. We certainly did not do so. In particular, we had somehow forgotten to account for the fact that we all had day jobs and any progress on this book would need to be made after working hours, a time where one is particularly unproductive. We nevertheless thought we could easily do this. Well, let's just say that writing a book is an extremely humbling experience ...

This book would not have been possible without the help of many people. The writing process would not have started without the original outreach of Jialin Dou, from the Arm University Program, who helped us shape the general outline of the text. However, the process would perhaps never have ended without regular probing from Liz Warman, Director of Educational Content and Technology at Arm. This book went through numerous delays, including a significant one due to the global COVID-19 outbreak that turned everyone's life upside down in 2020. Liz was our principal contact person at Arm and was always very supportive of our other increased work obligations during the pandemic. We'd like to thank her for her incredible patience, without which this book would not have come to an end. We'd also like to give special thanks to Mark Radford, who tirelessly helped give this book a consistent narrative. His heroic copy-editing passes have been critical to put this book in the form you see today. We also thank Alison Sage and Beth Dufour for shouldering the administrative tasks that arose in the late stages of the writing process, allowing us to concentrate on the writing.

The authors would like to thank EPFL for its institutional support. Finally, we thank Arm for its commitment to broadening the reach of education by agreeing to provide open access to this book for all students to enjoy.

The authors

I want to thank all the students who followed my courses throughout the 35 years I have been teaching at the university; they are my motivation for getting up and going to work. I would like to thank Professor Jean-Daniel Nicoud, the inventor of the Smaky computers in Switzerland and my main professor in this field of micro-computing. His teaching mindset and the enthusiastic way in which he communicated with his students inspired me and I strived to follow a similar approach: working with passion, without counting the hours spent on the job, and enjoying the challenge of solving complex engineering tasks along the way. My sincere thanks to my friends, former students, and work colleagues – Sahand, Andrea, and Florian – who co-authored this book with me. Working together has been a fantastic experience. Finally, I'd like to thank my close family, in particular my wife Yannik, who accepted the countless nights and weekends I spent working on this book.

René Beuchat

Acknowledgments

I deeply thank my wife, Eliéva Pignat, for her help, time, and endless support during this journey. I also wish to express my gratitude to René Beuchat for being a great teacher and helping me discover embedded systems during my studies, but also for the opportunity to be a co-author on this book. I want to add a special word to my parents and brother for being so supportive. Finally, thanks to Jonathan Gleize for his useful feedback and for being such a great friend over the years.

Florian Depraz

First, I would like to thank my co-authors for supporting each other to keep writing this book in this tough time. A particular thanks to René, an exemplary colleague and teacher. A special thanks to Professor Paolo Ienne, director of the Processor Architecture Laboratory at EPFL, for his encouragement to work on this book, Giovanni De Micheli, director of EPFL's Integrated System Centre, and Philippe Flückiger, director of EPFL's MicroNanoTechnology Centre, for their support. I would also like to thank all the colleagues who surrounded me in my early career, and especially those with whom I worked side-by-side in the crucial years of my professional growth. Finally, I would like to thank all my family and friends, always close even if geographically distant. Without all of them I would not be the person I am today. Writing this book doesn't mean that my learning journey with electronics is done. I will always consider myself a newbie in front of the magnificence of semiconductors. As Einstein said, "Once you stop learning you start dying", this is really my favorite dictum.

Andrea Guerrieri

I would like to thank René Beuchat, my past instructor and now co-author, for instilling his passion for teaching in me and believing in my educational ability to help write parts of this book with him. It was a bumpy ride, but I'm glad to say the experience was worth it. I would also like to thank my PhD advisor, Professor James Larus, for the openness he expressed towards my taking part in this book adventure despite having a full-time job as a graduate student at the same time. James' advice and his encouragement to work on this book as a contribution to the academic community helped me develop my pedagogical skills in ways that would not have been possible in the standard graduate school curriculum. Few people knew I was participating in this book and I'm thankful to be surrounded by friends and family whose excitement upon hearing of the news helped boost my morale and finally conclude the writing process.

Sahand Kashani

Author Biographies

 **René Beuchat** has been an associate Professor at HEPIA – the Geneva School of Engineering, Architecture and Landscape – since 1987 and has worked at EPFL – the Swiss Federal Institute of Technology in Lausanne – since 1981 after receiving his BSc and MSc from both schools. The two engineering universities are quite complementary as the first focuses on developing students' industrial and practical skills, while the second pursues a more academic and research-oriented curriculum. The schools have changed significantly since René joined over 35 years ago, a time when computer science didn't even exist as a faculty. René studied a joint electrical and mechanical engineering curriculum in his first year, a track with a very broad curriculum. He then continued with an electrical engineering specialization, mainly in low-power design intended for digital circuits and electronics. Microprocessors such as Motorola's M6800 and Zilog's Z80 appeared around that time and formed René's first experience with the fantastic world of computer science. René has continued working at HEPIA and EPFL since then, and will most certainly do so until his retirement. He participated in the exciting adventure of designing the Smaky family of microcomputers in Lausanne, where he mainly worked on networking aspects. Teaching has been a big part of his work throughout the years. René is a firm believer that cutting-edge technology can only be taught with personal experience and, as a result, participated in many research projects and collaborations with dozens of companies and universities. He has also supervised a few hundred student research projects, mainly through industrial collaborations in the field of embedded systems, networking, and FPGAs. René married a wonderful woman with whom he had two beautiful children and now has the joy of being a grandpa.

 **Andrea Guerrieri** is a senior research engineer and lecturer working for EPFL and HEPIA, with more than 15 years of experience in the field. At a young age he was curious and passionate about electronics, studying and building small electronics devices at home by himself. In 2006, after receiving a high school diploma in Electronics and Telecommunications from Istituto Tecnico Industriale Majorana (Italy), he started working in PB Elettronica (Italy). During these years, he had the chance to sharpen his skills in designing electronics and embedded systems, challenging himself while surrounded by a team of experts driven by the same commitment and passion. While a full-time employee in PB Elettronica, he received his BSc and MSc degrees in Electronic Engineering respectively in 2010 and 2015 from Politecnico di Torino, becoming the Principal Engineer responsible for the development of the company's flagship products. In 2017 he moved to Switzerland, joining the Processor Architecture Laboratory at EPFL, where he leads and participates in cutting-edge research projects. Recent projects involve reconfigurable systems-on-chip exploiting dynamic partial reconfiguration of FPGAs for future space missions, exoplanet observation, and post-quantum cryptography for nano-satellites, presented in international venues for ESA and NASA. Today, Andrea is a member of IEEE, author and co-author of multiple technical papers, and a reviewer for prestigious international conferences and scientific journals. He is also co-author of Dynamatic, the first dynamically scheduled high-level synthesis compiler, and recipient of the Best Paper Award at the International Symposium on Field-Programmable Gate Arrays (FPGA 2020), the premier conference for presentation of advances in FPGA technology, held in Seaside, California (USA).

 **Florian Depraz** is an embedded software engineer who graduated from EPFL in 2018. During his studies, he mostly worked on FPGAs and embedded systems. Interested in teaching and enabling people to develop their ideas, he became a course assistant and member of the LauzHack hackathon committee. Florian went to the UK and worked for three years at Arm in the Open Source Software department, contributing to projects for robotic and automotive platforms. He then decided to return to Switzerland and now works as an engineer within the Kudelski Group to build safer products for the IoT field.

 **Sahand Kashani** received his Master's in computer engineering from EPFL in 2017. He is currently a PhD candidate in the School of Computer and Communication Sciences at EPFL. His research focuses on rethinking the traditional FPGA compiler flow to improve hardware design productivity for modern compute-intensive FPGA workloads. Sahand is a former student of René's and has been working with FPGAs for over seven years. He is an avid systems geek and enjoys transmitting his passion for digital design and reconfigurable computing to students.

List of Figures

List of Tables

Chapter 1

A Memory-centric
System Model

In this first chapter, we will review the basics of a computer system. The main elements are the same for everything from a mainframe to a low-cost control system. Most differences depend on the scale of the system, such as its size, power consumption, and computing power. This chapter gives an overview of these universal architectures, which we also find in a system on a chip (sometimes "system-on-chip"), abbreviated SoC. An overview of the Arm processor family will help to explain the different terminologies in relation to the Cortex-M line. The chapter will address the following questions and more.

1. *Where can we find microprocessors in the world today and in the near future?*
2. *What are the basic elements involved in every computer architecture?*
3. *What is an embedded system?*
4. *What is a SoC?*
5. *What are the elements of a SoC?*
6. *What is the difference between a processor and a microprocessor?*
7. *What are the main elements found in a processor?*
8. *What is a microcontroller?*
9. *How do we start a new design for an embedded system?*
10. *What elements must be taken into account to realize such a design?*
11. *Where are the instructions to execute?*
12. *What kind of memories are available for an embedded system design?*
13. *What is the internal architecture of SRAM memory?*
14. *What are the main functions of a memory management unit (MMU)?*
15. *What are the main principles around the interrupt controller, the source of interrupts, and programmable interfaces?*
16. *For the core software, do we want to use a kernel, an operating system or nothing (bare metal)?*
17. *What is the CMSIS standard library and why should we use it?*
18. *Do we want to build everything from scratch ourselves?*
19. *Does high-level programming exist for this kind of processor?*

Since the mid-1970s, computers have been brought into personal use and into people's homes thanks to the invention of the microprocessor, starting with the Intel 4004. Microelectronic science has progressed to achieve almost unbelievable capacities in terms of the number of transistors that could be made available on a chip, and their size has decreased to just a few nanometers today. At the beginning of the 1980s, all of the basic components of a computer were integrated onto a single chip containing a microprocessor, memory, and programmable interfaces to communicate with the external world.

A system on a chip (system-on-chip) is basically everything required to implement a computer incorporated into a single chip.

In this chapter, the hierarchy of a modern computing environment is described, from world-spanning global systems to the small, single pieces of equipment found in a smartphone, a personal computer or a unit in the so-called Internet of Things (**IoT**). Everything can be interconnected.

1.1 Global Computing Systems

Nowadays, computing is pervasive throughout the entire world, with wide area networks, cloud computing, global servers, portable computers, tablets, and smartphones everywhere (see Figure 1.1). The expansion of the Internet of Things is one of the new technology revolutions, as well as the way human lives are increasingly integrated with computing capabilities. Evolution is also occurring rapidly in the fields of robotics, autonomous cars, and artificial intelligence, with many areas of research and numerous new industrial products.

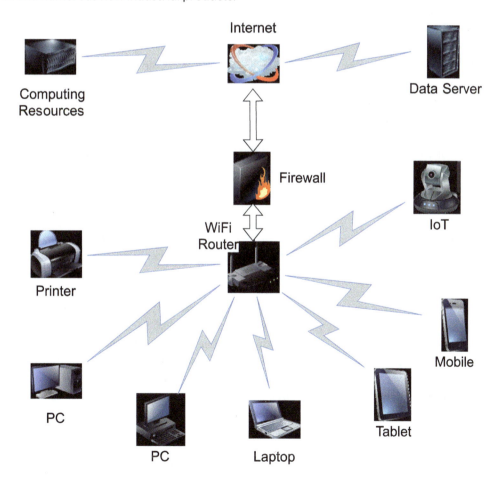

Figure 1.1 High-level component view of a global computing system

However, the majority of this technology is hidden from the average human user. Large servers are housed in dedicated buildings with cooling systems, and may be placed underground or even under the sea! Typically, they will have thousands of processing units in the form of microprocessors together with huge amounts of memory and specific accelerators such as graphics processing units (GPUs) or field-programmable gate arrays (FPGAs) for specialized operations.

1.2 General Computer Architecture

What is a computer architecture? It is, at the hardware level, a system composed of three basic elements:

- **processor(s)** or **microprocessor(s)** for data management and program execution

- **memories** for code storage, data storage, and operational storage (e.g. stack, heap)

- **I/O devices** for communication with internal facilities and the external world through **programmable interfaces**.

Connections between these elements are realized through three main **buses**:

- The **address bus** derives from the requestor unit, as the processor, and is used to specify which requestor unit to access and which element within this unit.

- The **data bus** is used to transfer information (data) between a requestor unit and a completer unit.

- The **control bus** is used to specify what to do: the direction of data transfers (reading or writing) from the requestor unit's point of view and when to do it in terms of timing.

The resulting hardware bus system also requires other mandatory functions and signals, including a clock to synchronize data transfers, a reset to initialize the system, power supply lines, and interrupt lines.

The first generation of computers were based on vacuum tubes. Large rooms were necessary to accommodate them, and their power supplies were huge; it was also necessary to replace the tubes on a frequent basis. Following the invention of the transistor, a new generation of computers was made possible, which were more reliable and faster. These were subsequently replaced by incorporating many transistors into a single circuit: the **integrated circuits** of the 1960s. This gave rise to a computing unit known as a **processor**, which used many components, which could take the form of complete boards or even occupy entire rooms. With the increase in transistor density, all of these parts became available on a single chip of silicon or "die": the **microprocessor**.

Figure 1.2 is a general view of a modern computer architecture, showing its basic elements. For the programmable interfaces, three simple examples are illustrated, providing an interface for display devices or different data sensors/actuators, a network (e.g. Ethernet) interface, and the control of a motor.

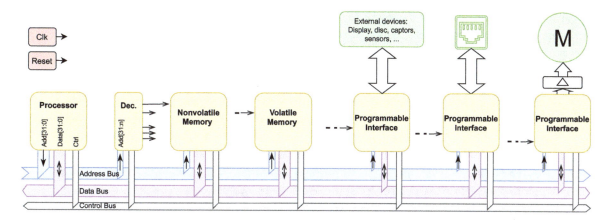

Figure 1.2 General computer architecture with minimum of elements (global hardware view; Dec. = Decoder)

The processor provides an address to select a device and indicates a memory position or programmable interface internal register. The control bus is used to provide the direction of the access, as either read or write. The decoder receives the upper part of the address and can select a specific unit of memory or a programmable interface to access; it generates a signal (called Chip Select) to enable exclusive access to one device at a time.

The selected device will accept the data provided by the processor (in a write cycle) or provide the data requested on the data bus (for a read access). The direction of write or read is always taken from the point of view of the requestor, here the processor.

The view in Figure 1.2 lacks any detail of the signals used or the pin connections. These elements are very specific to the actual devices involved. Physically, the buses consist of many wires. They transport information at specific times and, in general, synchronously via clock signals. They are defined by specifications and all the elements on the bus need to respect the defined protocols in terms of the logic levels (voltages) and timing used on the bus.

In a general computer, all of the electronic elements are specific and separated in different integrated circuits. However, increasing miniaturization means that most, if not all, of them can now be made available in a single die: a **microcontroller**.

Arm's Cortex-M is a **microprocessor** that forms the basis of many microcontrollers on the market today. It is not the only one and most processor manufacturers now offer different families of related products, more or less specialized. Such processor architectures include x86, AVR, PIC, RISC-V, ARC, and MIPS32, among the best known.

Arm has developed its microprocessors as an IP (intellectual property) architecture and sells them to hundreds of manufacturers, who use them to develop their own microcontrollers with specific programmable interfaces and memories. They are able to take advantage of the availability of a wide range of shared resources, such as development tools, languages and their compilers, operating systems, debuggers, and so on.

In terms of the **organization of this book**, Chapter 2 introduces the microelectronics needed to realize an integrated circuit, and Chapter 3 introduces the architecture of the Arm Cortex-M processor. The internal buses will be studied in Chapter 4 in terms of general interconnections, and the specific Arm buses will be considered in Chapter 5.

Chapter 6 describes many of the hardware signals and standard protocols used in the embedded-system world, and Chapter 7 explains how a variety of programmable interfaces work and how to control them.

More detail of memory elements and how they work is provided in Chapter 8, while Chapter 9 introduces the FPGA-SoC system, which offers engineers a more sophisticated system with which to design their own system architectures for very specialized systems.

Finally, Chapter 10 deals with elements of software development, including an introduction to real-time operating systems (RTOS).

1.3 Embedded System Architectures

An embedded system is a specialized computer designed for a specific application. Such systems are usually designed with a large market in mind to reduce the cost of production, and are designed from the hardware level up to the software level. They are produced with or without an operating system or a real-time kernel and have the same general architecture as seen in Figure 1.2. However, while the global view is similar, the details are different.

A similar case is that of a specialized system that needs very high computing power and is subject to constraints in execution time, having a limited window to respond to the events requiring computation. Nevertheless, all are based on a common architecture, but with different scales in terms of power consumption, calculation capabilities, memory capacities, and interface availabilities. As of 2020, the number of interconnected processors is still increasing, and they can be located on a single chip (multicores), on a board (multiprocessors), or distributed either locally or across the world.

Examples of embedded systems can be found all around us:

- coffee machines with panels for control of the machine

- anti-lock braking systems (ABS) on cars

- sports watches with health sensors

- cameras

- automated heating systems with temperature sensors and regulators

- hard disk drives

- mobile (or static) robots.

However, the hardware alone is not enough. On top of it, we must have a software application based on a kernel and/or simplified operating system (often called a real-time operating system or RTOS) that manages all of the resources, access to peripherals, memory access and protection, time management, and the scheduling of tasks. Above this low-level software may sit libraries of useful functions, such as graphical user interfaces (GUIs) for the display of information and user interaction, implementations of network communication protocols, and signal processing.

On the uppermost level are the applications themselves, as shown in Figure 1.3; the hierarchy allows any level to call a lower level as needed. A final and important part of the architecture is support for debugging and interactive control with the help of specialized hardware and development/debugging tools.

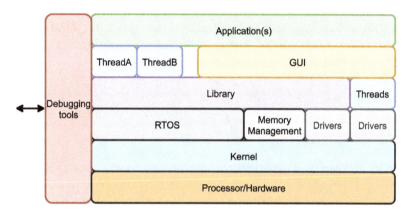

Figure 1.3 Software levels in an embedded system

More information on RTOSs can be found in Chapter 10. A true embedded system is represented by the full interconnection of the software and hardware elements: the system cannot exist without both parts.

1.4 Embedded System-on-Chip Architectures

A system on a chip is "simply" every element of a computer on a single integrated circuit. However, in general, SoCs cannot accommodate enough memory for a full operating system such as Linux or Android and, thus, some external memory must be provided, often on top of the SoC itself. A few gigabytes are usually added in this way. At present, this technique is used in the Cortex-A processor family, but why not in the Cortex-M family too in the near future?

High-end SoCs can include graphics processing units (GPUs), wireless modules for Wi-Fi, Bluetooth, and LoRa, and environmental and medical sensors.

Microcontrollers started with Texas Instruments' TMS1802NC (1971) of the TMS 0100 family, and later Intel's famous i8048 (1976) followed by the i8051 (1980), still available today as an 8-bit microcontroller and a leader for many years in this area of electronics. There are now many actors in the marketplace. Many of them provide their own proprietary architecture for their processors and/or the accompanying programmable interfaces. But almost all offer the Arm architecture in their portfolio as well. Why? Well, let's consider the perspective of a typical user: the designer or architect of a new product.

He or she is part of a large company with an existing investment in development tools and knowledge that it cannot afford to change for every project. Once a processor family has been selected, it will be used for many years. If the company offers different architectures but maintains compatibility at the processor level, it will be easier to adapt and evolve if the same basic knowledge and development tools can be applied.

Many manufacturers offer tools that can be used for all of their different processors, whether or not they have the same processor architecture: the user is happy and can move between them to use the one most compatible with a specific application. Similarly, many manufacturers make the same or very similar programmable interfaces available with many different processors and memory configurations. Thus, we have different layers of "users":

- **Application users** want a finished product, powerful in terms of what they want to do with it. In general, other than a few real enthusiasts ("geeks") they don't care about the technology, although if it's a smartphone many want the latest one!

- **Product designers** are expected to realize a product, based on what is available on the market, as an integrated circuit. They can choose from thousands of devices from hundreds of manufacturers. The levels of performance and integration depend on what is available. This kind of user is working at the level of the printed circuit board (PCB).

- **Designers of the SoC** itself, who may work in many different companies, depending on the company manufacturing the microcontrollers. They receive a request for a new product and must realize it on the basis of different criteria. These could include the choice of processor, the type and quantity of memory, the programmable interfaces that must be added, the accelerators that are needed, and so on. They may be engineers who specialize in designing integrated circuits and who are required to design a particular circuit, such as a specific sensor with processing and communication capabilities.

- **IP designers** of the processor architecture who need to create a new generation of it or develop specialized modules. The resulting designs will be sold to the existing integrators of the microprocessors (the product and SoC designers).

- At the lowest level of integration, we have the **founder companies**, who must provide the best capabilities in terms of the (greatest) number of transistors and/or (smallest) size associated with the lowest price and power consumption.

Today, one of the main actors in microprocessor IP is Arm with its Cortex families, A, R, and M. The last of these is the one specifically considered in this book. Many versions of the architecture are available and provided by Arm as ready-to-manufacture IP (intellectual property), with all of the elements of a computer available on a single die. The microcontroller manufacturers must add the programmable interfaces and select the appropriate options from those on offer.

To provide additional approaches to design, modules with "standard" connectors are available on the market with many features and components already incorporated; these may be referred to as **CoMs** (computers on modules) or **SoMs** (systems on modules). Some well-known examples include Arduino, Raspberry Pi, BeagleBoard, Toradex and iWave, and many manufacturers provide development kits that allows users to start using their microcontrollers before selecting a specific microprocessor and its PCB.

1.5 Elements of SoC Solutions

When an engineer has to design a new SoC solution and has considered the relevant issues highlighted in the previous section according to what the product is required to do, they need to think about the key elements to be used and/or developed.

First, it is usually nice to establish a first working system as a prototype to verify the functionality of the expected device. This is sometimes termed the minimum viable product (**MVP**). For this, a first version created with a software design kit (**SDK**), rather than any hardware, can be very useful and is recommended. This can enable verification of the amount of memory needed for the project, the response time of the system, and much other useful information besides. The final product will not rely on an SDK but an SDK will aid in its design.

If it's too much work to design a specific PCB for the product, it's possible to go with a CoM- or SoM-based system instead.

To start a new system design or integration, an engineer must ask questions about the:

- computing power needed, which will largely depend on the algorithm(s) used in the application and any additional units/devices required

- electrical power needed, which will depend on the application, where the system will be located and what power sources will be available

- use of battery power or mains/external power

- bandwidth of the data to be managed and/or transferred, and the number of operations per second involved

- communications needed:

  - wireless/RF (e.g. Bluetooth, Wi-Fi, LoRa, SigFox, ZigBee, GSM, 3G, 4G, 5G, etc.)

  - cabled (e.g. Ethernet 10/100/1G, CAN bus, USBxx, etc.)

- memory type and size that will be needed or could be expected

- extension connectors:

  - standard (PCIe, VME, etc.)

  - serial (UART, USB, etc.)

  - proprietary

  - for debugging (JTAG, SWD, etc.)

- devices to include, such as accelerometers, cameras, sensors, temperature monitors, current monitors, etc.

- aids to testing/monitoring hardware:

  - test points for oscilloscopes and logic analyzers

  - ways to view power consumption, voltage levels and ripple (voltages/currents)

  - LEDs

  - serial interfaces (UART, SPI, i^2c, etc.)

  - button for Reset.

There are obviously a lot of questions, and this book is intended to help you answer many of them. As a minimum, you will be aware of the potential problems and well-positioned to try to find appropriate solutions. Asking the right question helps to find an initial answer, and eventually the right answer.

Remember, you must read the full documentation and datasheets carefully to see how components are actually working. Occasionally, the documentation has errors but, equally, sometimes features have simply changed!

1.5.1 Processor Cores

There are many microprocessor families available on the market. One of the main selection criteria is the size of the data bus, in terms of 4, 8, 16, 32 or 64 bits of data path. Another is the size of the address bus needed to access the volume of memory that will be required.

Many well-known architectures have been developed since the 1970s, now half-a-century ago. As an engineer or future engineer, it is nice to be familiar with at least some of them. They can have a general-purpose or specialized architecture:

- i86 family (e.g. many/most PCs)

- Arm family (e.g. Raspberry Pi)

- PIC

- AVR (e.g. Arduino)

- i8051-based

- RISC V

- MSP430

- Xtensa (e.g. ESP32)

- DSP

- instruction set extensible.

There are also specialized extensions, such as:

- floating-point units (FPUs)

- graphics processing units (GPUs)

- memory management units (MMUs)

- cryptography extensions (e.g. AES).

There are likely to be others in the near future; for example, artificial intelligence accelerators. In terms of SoC design, there are also extensions in the form of programmable interfaces of many kinds, and extensions for FPGAs and complex programmable logic devices (CPLDs).

What is the minimum number of units inside a processor? Figure 1.4 is a block diagram of a very simple processor architecture. Almost all processors have this as a minimum. Let's consider its elements in more detail.

The job of a processor is to manipulate data. To do this, it executes a program, which is simply a list of basic instructions. Many such instructions are available on all processors, in the form of simple arithmetic and logical operations. The unit that executes these is the arithmetic and logical unit (**ALU**) and the operations are the classical ADDition, SUBtraction, sometimes MULtiplication and DIVision, logical AND, OR, EOR (exclusive OR, sometimes named XOR), and NOT, together with SHIFTing and ROTation. These latter two can function in a single cycle or on multiple cycles via a **barrel shifter**.

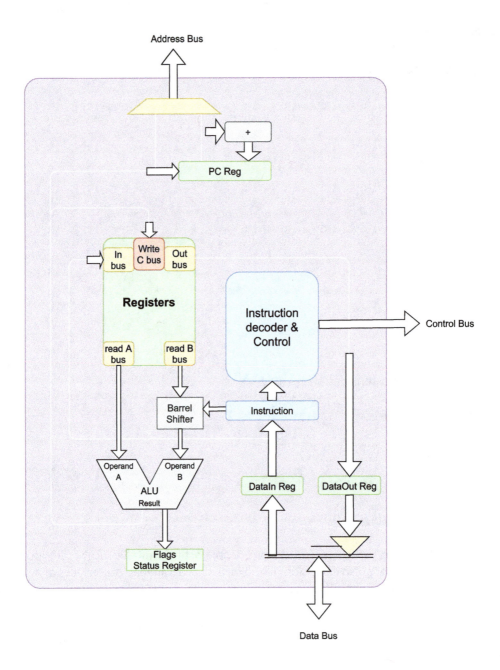

Figure 1.4 Simple processor architecture

1.5.2 Registers and the Control Unit

To save and execute the operations, registers are used as sources and destinations for data. These could be simple and unique, as was the case for the very first processors, in which they were termed the accumulator. In modern processors there may be 16, 32 or even more (see, for example, Figure 1.5). Indeed, depending on the mode of the processor, many banks of registers might exist. To write or read the content of these registers, access is realized through one or more internal data buses.

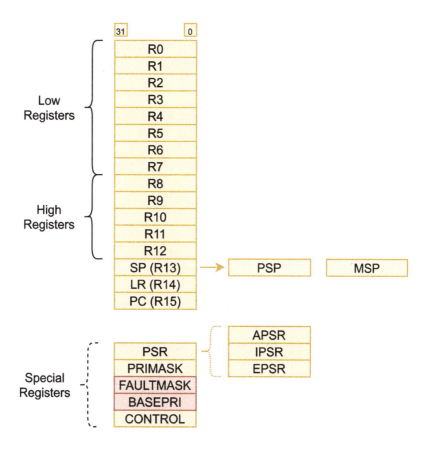

Figure 1.5 View of a processor's internal registers, here the Cortex M0

One particular register is the **flags** register or status register (see, for example, Figure 1.6). This holds the status of some of the operations from the ALU, mainly the arithmetic ones. In general, signed operations are done on signed numbers using two's complement operations (consult Annex 1 for a refresher on binary numbering). Almost all processors use the following status **flags**:

- **N** for **negative**. This is the most significant bit of the result. If equal to 1, it means that the number is negative, otherwise it is positive and coded in two's complement signed numbers.

- **Z** for **zero**. This means that the result has all bits set to 0 and the value of the register equals 0.

- **C** for **carry**. When two binary numbers are added or subtracted, we can have a carry. It's like having one more bit in the result register. This supplementary result bit becomes the carry flag.

- **V** for **oVerflow**. When a signed operation involves two signed numbers, if two positive numbers are added and the result is negative, it's an error and the V flag is activated. Similarly, when two negative numbers are added, and the result is positive. Strange? Yes, in the decimal world with unlimited digits, this does not occur. But in a processor, the number of bits in a number is always limited (e.g. to 8, 16, 32 or 64).

■ **Q** is a flag introduced with saturated arithmetic. Instead of having an overflow, the operation provides the biggest positive number as the result or the minimum negative one. The result is not correct but is better than that attainable with just the overflow flag. The Cortex-M3 processor saw the introduction of this flag.

It is the responsibility of the programmer to test whether an overflow or a carry has occurred and validate or invalidate the result accordingly.

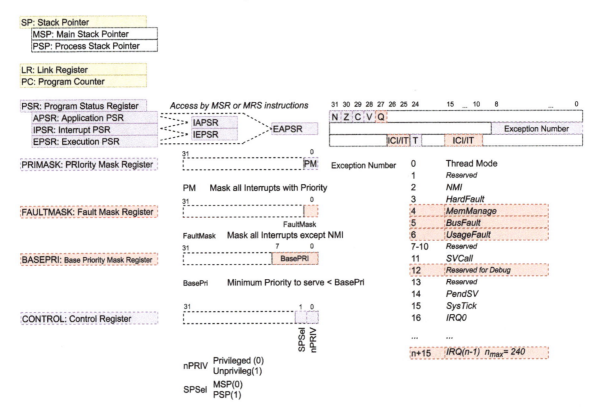

Figure 1.6 Status register and some specific registers

The instructions are coded in memory as binary code. They have a specific format and depend on the processor family. A given binary code can only be executed on a specific processor architecture. In general, every new processor family adds some instructions or changes the coding, or even the entire instruction set. We refer to this as the instruction set architecture (**ISA**). It is usually the intellectual property of the company that defined it. More information about the ISA of the Arm family, and especially the Cortex M, will be covered in Chapter 3.

The code is held in a memory external to the processor itself, but it can be on the same die. To access the current code, it is necessary to know where the next instruction is, read it, decode it and execute it. A specific register is used to provide this address and is called the program counter (**PC**). Its content is passed to the external address bus to select the instruction from the memory. Usually, the next instruction is at the next address. The PC is automatically incremented according to the size of the instruction.

When the program has a branch (or a jump), the new address must be loaded from the code of the instruction or the content of a global register or via some other operation. The PC receives a new value, which is the address from which to read the next instruction.

The data retrieved from the memory is passed to the **instruction register** to be decoded by the **instruction decoder and controller**. This very important part, also termed the **control unit**, decides what to do, which registers to access, controls the external control bus and all the internal sequences, and specifies the ALU operation to execute. In this simple scheme, reading and writing memory or the programmable interface is done at the execution stage.

In a very simple processor, every step of an instruction is completed before a new one is started, as shown in Figure 1.7. However, this is not very efficient in terms of its use of internal resources.

Figure 1.7 A sequence of decoded instructions from loading (fetch) to execution

A better approach is to do what is called **pipelining**; as soon as an instruction has been fetched into the internal instruction register, a new instruction can be fetched while the first one is being decoded. As soon as this decoding has finished its execution will start, and decoding of the new instruction can be started, as represented in Figure 1.8. A new instruction can be loaded in each cycle, and its result will be available two cycles later, but the frequency of the cycles will effectively be higher, as four instructions can be completed in the time previously taken to complete two.

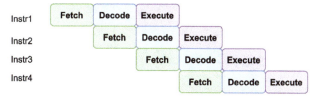

Figure 1.8 Pipelining of fetch, decoding and execution instructions

However, this kind of parallelism does leave some problems to be solved. For example, if a program branch or jump instruction has to be executed, the address of the next instruction will only be known when the execution of the previous one has completed; in this case, the next fetch needs to be delayed, breaking the pipeline or cancelling the sequence, as illustrated in Figure 1.9.

Figure 1.9 Instr2 involves a program jump and breaks the pipeline

Nevertheless, the gain from pipelining is positive because programs have many more continuous instructions than jumps. Some methods exist that can avoid completely breaking the pipeline, but we will just describe the standard features for now.

To transfer **data in** and **out** of the processor, two specific buffers access the external data bus. Sometimes a bidirectional buffer is used, with a tri-state buffer allowing the direction of transfer to be differentiated. The data can be an instruction, an access to a variable in memory, or an access to a programmable interface; anything that can provide or receive data.

When both instructions and data are made available through the same pairing of address bus and data bus, the architecture is described as **von Neumann** (named after a mathematician who, in 1945, was a reporter for a committee on computer architecture that proposed the main concepts of this architecture: an ALU, a control unit, memory, and input/output mechanisms). This architecture uses a **unified memory space**, holding both instructions and data. The same bus is shared for reading instructions and accessing data. Using a common bus reduces the physical lines, and allows the shared bus to be wide, but the transfers of instructions and data must be sequential, creating a bottleneck and reducing throughput.

Together, Figures 1.4 and 1.10 represent such a von Neumann architecture. Physically, the memories can be different but the same physical buses are used in a uniform way.

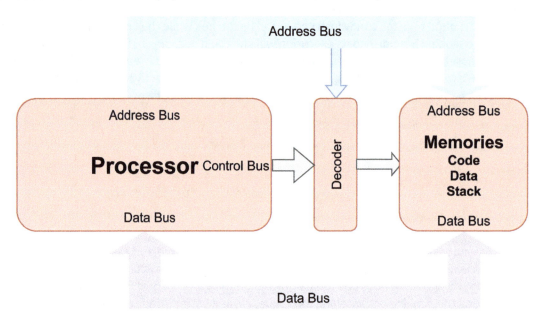

Figure 1.10 Organization of memory and buses in a von Neumann architecture

An alternative architecture, more powerful in terms of compute efficiency, is the **Harvard** architecture, represented in Figure 1.11. Here, the address and data buses are doubled up to separate access to instructions and data, which has a cost in terms of complexity and physical lines. However, it allows the reading of a new instruction to be done at the same time as a data transfer.

In operation, the instruction data bus is unidirectional, from memory to the processor. This means that a way needs to be found to load the code into memory if it is nonvolatile memory, but this is an implementation detail.

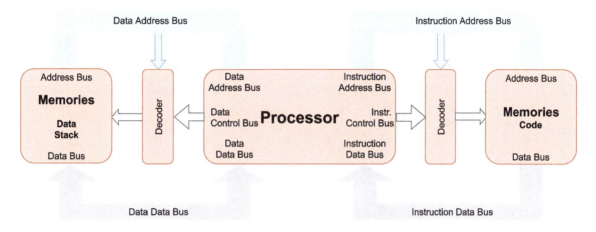

Figure 1.11 Organization of memory and buses in a Harvard architecture

Today, both architectures are in common use, as we will see in Chapter 3. However, before this, more description of the basic elements of a processing system are required.

1.5.3 Memory

As we saw in the previous sections, a processor needs to have memories for both the code and the data. A further specific area is used for a **stack**, a special form of data memory into which the processor can PUSH data to store it and POP data to recover it. We will consider this in more detail in due course, but we first need to have a model of memory, starting with a high-level model before moving to the level of the transistor.

A memory can be viewed as a large number of separate drawers, each with its own identification number, starting from 0 and increasing thereafter. Thus, a position in memory can be seen as a specific drawer and inside this a set of boxes represent the bits of information, an empty box representing a binary 0, and a full box a binary 1. If all of the drawers are housed in a single cabinet, this represents the memory chip. It is selected by a signal, the chip select (CS), which can be seen as the key to locking or unlocking the door of the cabinet.

A simple model of a cabinet with drawers is presented in Figure 1.12. By convention, a write access is done by a requestor unit, going from the processor to the memory, and a read access reads the content of one position in memory. For most memory, the reading is nondestructive, which means that the data is retained in that memory position after it has been read. In the illustration, access is made to drawer "01001" (in binary) and something placed inside it.

The next step is to create what is called a **memory map**, a model of the memories available on a system. Regardless of whether the memory is internal or external to the microcontroller, the memory map model will be the same.

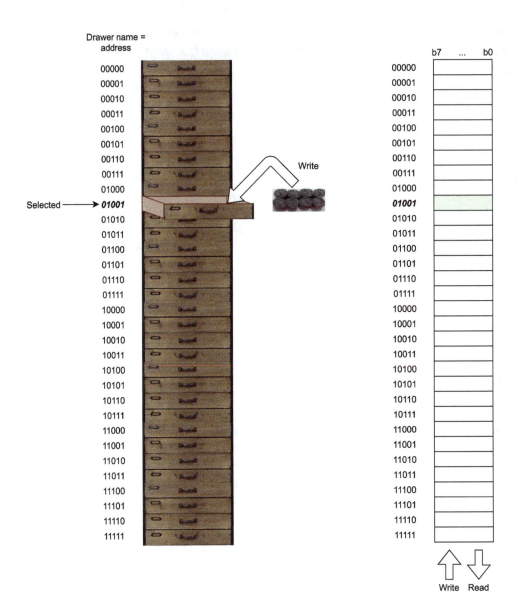

Figure 1.12 Memory model with drawers in a cabinet

To design a SoC or to understand how it is designed, we must determine what information is required in terms of access to the available memory:

- First, what is the available **address space** (the range of memory addresses that can be accessed)? This will depend on the number of address lines provided by the processor. Thus, 24 address lines provides a maximum of 2^{24} memory positions, or 16 mebibytes (MiB) of memory space; for a 32-bit address space, there are 2^{32} memory positions → 4 gibibytes (GiB) of memory space, based on the notion that an address represents one byte in memory.

▨ What is the width of the data bus? Common sizes are 8, 16, or 32 (or even more) bits. As of today, most modern processors, including the Cortex-M, use 16 or 32 bits.

▨ What type of memory should be used? Volatile or nonvolatile? Static or dynamic? Asynchronous or synchronous?

▨ What control signals are needed?

▨ Will the processor be required to start executing code following a Reset? If so, then nonvolatile memory will be required.

Once these questions have been answered, we can start the memory mapping, as follows:

▨ When the processor starts running at Power Up or after a Reset, it needs to execute code to start the system. This code needs to be immediately available and is called the **boot(strap) code**. Depending on the processor used, the **Reset vector**, the address at which to start a program at Power Up or Reset, and the exception vector table (to handle startup issues) will start at the address **0x0000 0000**; thus nonvolatile memory is needed. For some other processors, this address will be at a different location. Taking Figure 1.13 as an example, let's select nonvolatile (flash) memory of 4 MiB on a 16-bit data bus.

▨ Next, the system in this example needs to have a few megabytes of static memory (SRAM) that can be read from and written to. Let's select 8 MiB of SRAM, giving a memory space of 0x80 0000 bytes.

▨ We will assume that this hypothetical microcontroller has a 16-bit-wide memory bus, with separate access to the lower byte (LB; d7..d0) and the upper byte (UB; d15..d8). Thus, nonvolatile memory of 4 MiB (assuming an 8-bit byte) is represented by two memories of 2 MiB each organized on an 8-bit data bus, or one single device of 2 mebi-words of 16-bit width.

▨ Another thing that we need to know, and which depends on the microcontroller manufacturer, is where the programmable interfaces will be mapped: in the memory space, or in a specific input/output (IO)-space? Does the processor have specific hardware lines and specific instructions for their use? In the case of the Arm Cortex-M, this mapping is in the same memory space and, generally, in the upper address range.

▨ We also need to know whether the external architecture conforms to von Neumann or Harvard. For external memory access it is typically von Neumann, even if it is using a Harvard architecture internally.

▨ To make decoding more straightforward, the starting address of a memory is a multiple of its size.

▨ An address is treated as a byte address on almost all systems. If the bus width is 16 bits, the address bit0 is equal to 0 for an aligned memory address.

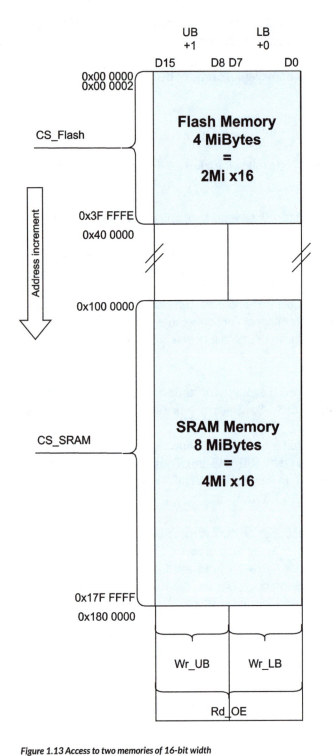

UB: Upper Byte D15..D8
LB: Lower Byte D7..D0

4 MiBytes ==> $2^2 * 2^{20}$ Bytes

=> 2Mi words of data of 16 bits width

=> 21 address lines to select all the memory positions

8 MiBytes ==> $2^3 * 2^{20}$ Bytes

=> 4Mi words of data of 16 bits width

=> 22 address lines to select all the memory positions

Figure 1.13 Access to two memories of 16-bit width

If we take the example shown in Figure 1.13, we can see the flash (nonvolatile) memory starts at address 0 (0x00 0000); the lowest address is at the top and the address increments downwards. The data bus is 16-bits wide, the address increment is two bytes at a time from one row of memory to the next and, in this organization, it is in **little-endian** format: the lowest address is on the lower part of the bus. Thus, in Figure 1.13, on the same row the even address is on the lower, right-hand side of the bus (bits d7..d0), while the offset (+1) is on the left-hand side (bits d15..d8).

The chip select (CS) signals depend on the highest part of the address bus. For many microcontrollers, this is simply a programmable interface to initialize the correct base address for all the available memories.

For read access, even if the memory needs to be read a byte at a time, access is only available for the full width of the data bus: the processor must simply ignore any unnecessary data provided.

However, for write access it is mandatory to select only the specific part of the memory (and data bus) to be written to, that is, the upper byte or the lower byte. Otherwise, incorrect information is likely to be written into an unintended part of the memory. Special (byte-enable) signals are provided by the processor to control this.

For a 32-bit data bus, four byte-enable signals are needed: **BE3** for b31–b24; **BE2** for b23–b16; **BE1** for b15–b8; **BE0** for b7–b0, assuming a little-endian convention. For a **big-endian** processor, the order will be reversed: **BE0** for b31–b24; **BE1** for b23–b16; **BE2** for b15–b8; **BE3** for b7–b0.

More design characteristics in relation to memory are explored in Chapter 8.

1.5.4 Memory Classes

When memory is needed, there are many different models to choose from. An initial high-level classification is needed, starting with whether the memory is volatile or nonvolatile (see Figure 1.14):

- **Nonvolatile memory.** When power goes down, the content of the memory is not lost and is available again at power up. This is mandatory for boot code used when a processor starts or restarts.

  - □ **ROM:** Read-only memory; the content of this memory is defined during the manufacturing of the device. In the case of error, the chip is effectively rendered unusable.

  - □ **PROM:** Programmable ROM; the content can be programmed with a specific piece of hardware called a memory programmer. The content can only be programmed once.

  - □ **EPROM:** Erasable PROM; like a PROM, could be programmed through specific programmer hardware, but a quartz window was installed on the top of the device and it was also possible to erase the memory via UV light, although it was necessary to remove the device from its board for erasure and reprogramming (which needed 12.5, 21 or 25 V depending on the specific device). A specific variation was a plastic case without the capability of erasing the memory, called OTP (One-Time Programmable).

□ **EEPROM** (or **E²PROM**): Electrically erasable PROM; as an advance on EPROM, one could now program the memory directly on the board and rewrite its content by electrical erasure byte by byte. Low density and expensive, but still used today inside some microcontrollers for memory of limited size.

□ **Flash Memory:** EEPROM-based and representing a major step forward in the embedded system world, NAND-type flash memory can be erased in blocks (the NOR-type works at word-level) and rewritten *in situ* using an appropriate protocol and a standard voltage. Commonly available in sizes of many gigabytes, it is routinely used in USB memory sticks and SD cards for cameras, and can be used by almost all microcontrollers.

□ **FRAM:** Ferroelectric random-access memory; a promising technology announced several years ago, that was expected to replace SRAM and flash memory, but competitive pressures from the latter have hindered FRAM development and it is not yet available at low cost and high density, although is available on some microcontrollers for easily modified nonvolatile memory.

□ **MRAM:** Magnetoresistive RAM; as with FRAM, a promising technology that has, to date, lost out to the burgeoning flash memory market and is not widely used/available.

□ **PRAM:** Phase-change RAM; utilizing changes in electrical resistance on CD/DVD-type media, PRAM promises larger capacities than either FRAM or MRAM, and has been made available for a few microcontrollers.

□ **ReRAM:** Resistive RAM; similar to PRAM in using electrical resistance changes, here in a dielectric.

□ **FeFET:** Ferroelectric field-effect transistor memory; a new hope for high-density and fast nonvolatile memory based on permanent electrical field polarization. Its evolution is worth following.

▣ **Volatile memory**. Represented by traditional random-access memory (**RAM**) (but note that nonvolatile memory forms also now offer random access [NVRAM], as described above). When power goes down, the content of volatile memory is lost. It can be static or dynamic. If the latter, it is necessary to periodically refresh the memory content.

□ **SRAM:** Static RAM; this is the basic form of volatile RAM, available up to a few megabytes. Four transistors are needed to memorize a bit of information, plus two more to access the content during read or write access.

□ **SSRAM:** Synchronous SRAM, in which access is synchronized via a clock.

□ **DRAM:** Dynamic RAM; the main idea behind DRAM is to make use of a memory element based on a single transistor to memorize and access a bit of information. The performance gain is huge (approximately fourfold compared to SRAM) but it is necessary to refresh the full memory every few milliseconds! Access is conducted in two steps: selection of a row of bits and then of the column in the selected row. The data is arranged in a matrix-like format.

☐ **SDRAM**: Synchronous DRAM; uses the same principle as DRAM but with clock-controlled synchronous access.

☐ **DDR SDRAM**: Dual data rate SDRAM (DDR[1], DDR2, DDR3, DDR4, DDR5); improves SDRAM performance by accessing memory on both (the rising and falling) edges of the clock signal. For the same clock frequency, the data transfer rate is doubled.

☐ **GDDR (SDRAM)**: Graphical DDR; very similar to DDR, but with special functions to improve local access and the performance of GPUs.

☐ **LPDDR**: Low-power DDR; a version of DDR (SDRAM) with significantly lower power consumption, aimed at mobile computers (tablets and smartphones).

☐ **QDR (SDRAM)**: Quad data rate; uses two clocks and separate read and write buses to achieve faster transfer rates than DDR, and is aimed at high-speed communications and networking.

Volatile memory can be further classified according to whether data access is synchronous or asynchronous:

▪ **Asynchronous**: No clock is used. The RAM family has some devices without a clock; they conduct asynchronous access.

▪ **Synchronous**: Memory access is clock-based; more recent RAM solutions use a clock to synchronize data transfers.

Data access to transfer addresses and data can be done in parallel or in serial:

▪ **Parallel data access:** In a parallel bus, all of the address and data lines are available, which enables the processor to execute code and access data directly with a very fast transfer rate between memory and the processor; less than ten nanoseconds for transfer of an entire (multi-bit) word. Note that some devices multiplex these lines.

▪ **Serial data access**: When the number of lines used to transfer addresses and data must be limited, serial access to memory (one bit at a time) is a sensible option. Memories used on SD cards and USB sticks use this approach. Information transfer is done with a serial bus in the form of SPI (Serial Peripheral Interface) or a QSPI (Queued SPI) controller. Alternative protocols include USB (fast) and I2C (low-speed protocol for multiple peripherals).

Addressing can also be approached in two different ways:

▪ **Parallel addressing for direct access**: To access a memory position the full address is transferred in parallel (to cover many bits of the address). Sometimes the address is provided in two steps as for DRAM (see above): first to specify the row address, then the column address.

▪ **Streaming access**: The first address accessed in memory is transferred, after which the address is automatically incremented, and the data is transferred to/from the next contiguous address, and so on.

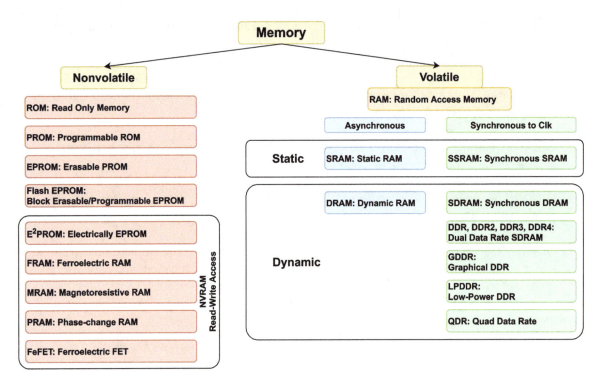

Figure 1.14 Classification of memory as volatile/nonvolatile

1.5.5 Internal Memory Organization

To better understand the internal function of memory, we will consider an SRAM chip, internal to a microprocessor, as illustrated in Figure 1.15.

The memory cell is represented by two inverters (realized by two transistors each) in a loop. Two transistors are used as a gate to transfer the data bit from two vertical lines, D and $\overline{D}$. When reading, these two passing transistors are selected on a row by a decoder, controlled by the address of the memory position to access. For a read access, the direct and complementary values are connected to a differential amplifier to provide the DataOut signal. The output is available in the case of a read cycle.

For a write cycle, the same process occurs but in reverse. The DataIn signal is activated inside the vertical lines by strong buffers. The inverted pair receives the new D and $\overline{D}$ value to write. There will be a short circuit if the value to be written and the one already in the cell have opposite levels. However, the transistors are designed to support this. The value to be written always wins via stronger transistors. When the chip is no longer selected, the passing transistors are closed, and the inverter pair keeps the value memorized.

The same architecture is available for each data bit of the memory, selected by a unique address. If the external data bus does not have separate DataIn and DataOut physical lines, the bits are connected on a bidirectional data bus.

To obtain a data bus with a width larger than 1 bit, multiple identical areas are added with the same selection line; in Figure 1.15, the data bus has a width of 8 bits.

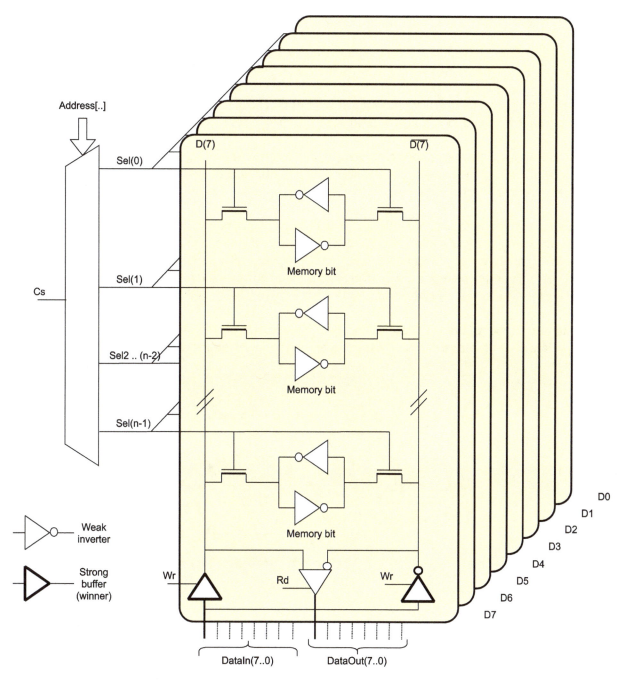

Figure 1.15 *Organization of an internal SRAM*

1.5.6 Interrupt Controllers

We now return to the processor. It executes the instructions that are provided from memory and read sequentially from the address provided by the PC register.

The instruction address provided by the PC register is automatically incremented by the size of the instruction code (16 bits and 32 bits are commonly used but this can vary and will depend on the specific processor). Some instructions provide branches or indirection in the code execution.

However, what happens if we have specific instructions that need to be executed as a result of an external request or an error in code execution, or if we need to respond to an external event?

Such requests are called **exceptions** or **interrupts**. The term **exception** is generally used for any kind of special request (from hardware or software); the term **interrupt** generally refers to a request that originates from **hardware**.

The sources of potential hardware interrupts are all of the programmable interfaces that the processor is serving; for example, a serial interface that is ready to send or receive a piece of data, a change to a parallel general-purpose input/output (GPIO) pin level, a packet of data being received on a network, a timer that detects a specific time value, and so on. An error detected on a programmable interface can also generate an interrupt.

In general, the processor needs to detect and identify the source of the interruption to go to an appropriate piece of software to handle the request and to do something with the associated data.

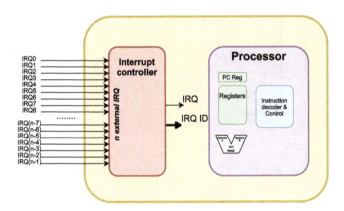

Figure 1.16 Simplified interrupt controller

An interrupt controller is a unit that receives external interrupts and generates an interrupt request (**IRQ**) to the processor. Figure 1.16 illustrates a simplified connection between an interrupt controller and the processor. In the case of hardware interrupts, n external interrupt requests can be generated. The interrupt controller is associated with a mechanism that allows the discovery of the highest-priority request, in the form of an interrupt request ID or identifier. This information is often referred to as a **vector**. Sometimes, the interrupt controller is treated as an internal element of the processor itself; in other architectures it may be a programmable interface under the control of the processor.

Figure 1.17 shows the minimum configuration required to manage an IRQ within a programmable interface. This configuration is used on the majority of programmable interfaces to generate a physical interrupt request to a processor. The names may change, but the functionality remains the same.

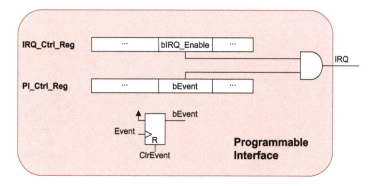

Figure 1.17 *Interrupt request from a programmable interface*

Thus, we have two internal registers with one bit on each:

- **bEvent** in a control register, here named **PI_Ctrl_Reg**, of the programmable interface is activated when a hardware event occurs. The processor can read this bit and through polling is able to see if/ when the associated event has occurred.

- A second register, here called **IRQ_Ctrl_Reg**, has a bit (**bIRQ_Enable**) that is used as a mask to allow the physical activation of an **IRQ** to the processor or to an intermediate interrupt controller if bEvent is activated.

To acknowledge the interrupt, an action needs to be taken by software, usually in the interrupt handler function of the program (firmware/driver). This will also depend on the programmable interface to activate the **ClrEvent** signal, as shown in Figure 1.17. Two main approaches are used:

- bEvent is cleared by a direct write to PI_Ctrl_Reg. Read the specific documentation carefully because for some programmable interfaces the bit is cleared by writing a '0' and in others a '1' must be written!

- Writing directly to the register (R) that generated the event. Again, the specific documentation should be consulted.

The IRQ output of the programmable interface is connected to the processor (inside the microcontroller) through a specific unit: the interrupt controller, as depicted in Figures 1.16 and 1.18. The interrupt controller can have different capabilities depending on the processor family. Chapter 3 will go into more detail for the Cortex-M family.

The idea behind this unit is to be able to receive many sources of hardware- or software-generated exceptions. If several are provided at the same time, arbitration is necessary. This could be done by the processor, but it is more efficient to do it through hardware. It will depend on a number of parameters, such as whether a higher-priority interrupt is already running, selection of the highest-priority waiting request, and so on. If a new interrupt is valid, the processor core is requested to service it and receives a vector associated with the request. This vector indicates where the processor must go in the program: the address of the IRQ handler.

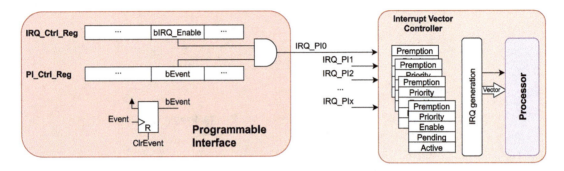

Figure 1.18 *Interruption from programmable interface to processor via interrupt vector controller*

On all processors there is a way to mask all interrupts (or almost all) with a single global mask. This is the **PRIMASK**, bit0 on the Cortex-M processor.

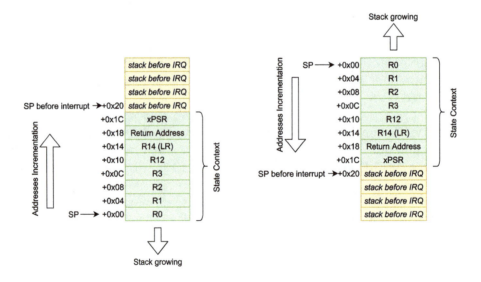

Figure 1.19 *Saving automatically on the stack after an IRQ on a Cortex-M processor*

On the Cortex-M processor, an automatic saving of some registers is done when an interrupt request is accepted. Figure 1.19 shows the saved registers on the stack. We need to carefully review a processor's documentation to see how its stack is filled. The left-hand side of the figure shows a stack with addresses incrementing from the bottom to the top. The stack itself grows in the opposite direction, from the highest address to the lowest, a convention used in most processors. The right-hand view represents exactly the same process, but the addresses are incrementing from the top to the bottom. Note that this is just a visual representation of the direction of the memory address incrementation, and does not reflect the data filling the memory in a different order.

1.5.7 Memory Protection Unit (MPU)/Memory Management Unit (MMU)

When a processor executes a program, it can do it with or without an operating system. It can do it as a single (sequential) program or through many pseudo-parallel tasks, often called **threads**. This is a way to allocate a small portion of the processor's time to many pieces of code at almost the same time: each thread is given the "impression" of running in isolation.

When a system is simple, the basic approach of having everything, such as resources, memories, interrupt service, and so on, in a single "space" is the easiest way to work. As a system becomes more complex, with multi-tasking and different "task spaces" that need to be protected from each other, so specific hardware becomes necessary.

One such simple example is the **memory protection unit** (MPU), which in fact protects both memory and programmable interfaces because they use the same access mechanism. The MPU separates the memory address map into zones and can limit access to these zones accordingly. The MPU is explained in more detail in Chapter 3.

A more sophisticated version of the MPU is the **memory management unit** (MMU). Its primary function is to receive a virtual address from the processor and generate a physical address. It uses internal tables to convert the address and provide the real one, which is passed to the decoder, memories and programmable interfaces. Figure 1.20 places the MMU in a global system context.

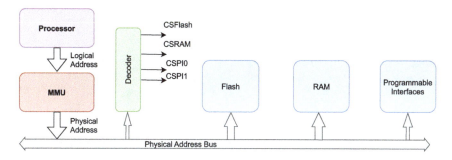

Figure 1.20 *Place of an MMU in a processor system*

In this view, the processor generates and manipulates a **logical** address. This address is the input to the MMU. Through tables associated with task management, the MMU generates the **physical** address used by the rest of the circuit. As already indicated, this approach is used for more complex systems, based on operating systems such as Linux. MMUs are typically available on larger computers and in the Arm Cortex-A family, but is not currently used in the Cortex-M family.

The second task performed by an MMU is the **protection** of different memory areas and programmable interfaces dependent on the running task and privilege of the processor at the time. Some memory areas can be accessed by some parts of the code and some areas cannot. This is the same functionality that is available in the **MPU** (as described above); the latter is an optional element on some Cortex-M processors and is implementation-dependent according to manufacturer.

The third and final capability of an MMU is to provide **virtual memories**, which is a means of delivering more logical address space than the physically available memory space!

How does this work? Let's consider the MMU representation in Figure 1.21, in which we have an area of memory used for program access through the Program Counter (PC) register. We can see that we have a logical memory space that is bigger than the physical memory available. When the PC accesses an address in the region of the logical memory space marked ①, the MMU translates this logical address (LA) to a physical address (PA) in the physical memory. While the PC only accesses this region, everything is fine. However, as soon as the PC ventures into the next region of the logical memory space ②, there is no corresponding physical memory available on the other side of the MMU. In this situation, the MMU generates an exception, the faulty instruction is suspended, and a piece of low-level software is run to save the current state of the physical memory to an external device (it could be a disk drive, flash memory or some other high-capacity memory store), and replace it with an image of the physical memory corresponding to ② loaded from the external memory store. The MMU memory map is updated to reflect the new LA → PA mapping and the instruction that caused the exception must be rerun.

These swapping operations are done by the processor in a memory that must always be available. It is a neat feature but it has a cost: the time to swap the data between physical memory and the external memory store. In general, such swaps are not done on large areas of memory but using small pages of a few kilobytes. It is not suitable for real-time systems!

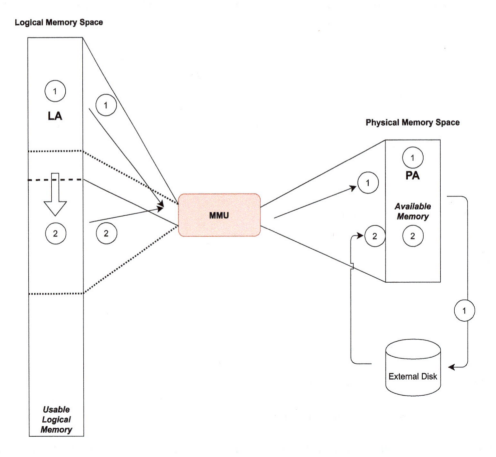

Figure 1.21 *MMU with virtual memory*

To sum up, an **MMU** has the capability to:

1. translate logical addresses into physical addresses

2. enable protection of memory areas

3. allow virtual memory of greater size than the available physical memory.

Because the first and last of these functions are not useful for microcontrollers, they are not implemented in this kind of integrated circuit. However, more powerful and power-hungry processors, which typically operate at a higher frequency, do implement an MMU. Only the second of these functions is useful for the complexity of the microcontroller class, and this is available in the more limited form of an **MPU**.

1.5.8 Interconnects

Inside and outside of the microcontroller, a lot of interconnections are needed to transfer addresses and data, as well as the control signals to synchronize the transfers. Chapter 4 is dedicated to explaining the main principles of these interconnections, and Chapter 5 covers the specific buses (AMBA AHB, APB and AXI) used in the Cortex-M family.

All of these buses are parallel buses involving many wires. A classical data bus is 16 or 32 bits wide but could be as large as 128 bits or even more. A wider bus means a higher data transfer rate for any given frequency of operation.

We have already seen that there are two main processor architectures available: von Neumann and Harvard. The former having a unified memory space for instructions and data transfers, while the latter has separate functionalities with separate address and data buses.

When the instruction and data buses are common, fewer wires are used but it is necessary to do sequential transfers to read an instruction and to access data memory. With a Harvard architecture, both can be done at the same time, giving better performance but a higher cost in terms of die area. It is the designer's responsibility to establish the correct balance between the resources needed and the performance expected, that is, to select the appropriate processor architecture.

Considering interconnectivity means ensuring that we have an overall view of all of the elements of a system, the bandwidth that will be required, and the bandwidth that will be available within our design.

In more powerful systems, another unit not yet discussed is the direct memory access (**DMA**) controller. This unit can work in parallel with the processor to access the data memory and to handle some data transfers and operations. In high-end devices, a DMA controller is often incorporated into specific programmable interfaces. In other implementations, it can be a generic unit handling many sources/destinations of data: memories and programmable interfaces. As a requestor unit, it will have a lot of wires for all of the available address/data and control buses.

If this kind of unit is in use, some decisions must be made, mainly as to whether data transfers for the processor can be done at the same time as the DMA controller is operating or whether the two must act sequentially. This can have a big impact on the overall performance and on the integrated circuit area needed.

The responsibility for such architectural decisions is mainly that of the microcontroller manufacturer. It must propose what it thinks is the best architecture for the best performance and the lowest price and power consumption.

For the purposes of this book on Arm Cortex-M processors, the **AMBA** (Advanced Microcontroller Bus Architecture) bus family is the one used. AMBA specifications are royalty-free, platform-independent and can be used with any processor architecture. The use of AMBA facilitates right-first-time development of multiprocessor designs with large numbers of controllers and peripherals. Widespread adoption means that AMBA has a robust global ecosystem of partners that ensures compatibility and scalability between intellectual property components from different design teams and vendors. Many other bus designs exist that use similar principles and are available on the market, for example:

- **Wishbone** (OpenCores)

- **Avalon** in FPGAs (Intel)

- **Open Core Protocol** (Accellera)

- **CoreConnect** (IBM).

The AMBA bus has gone through several different generations (AMBA 2, 3, 4, 5) and variations, including **AHB** (AMBA High-performance Bus), **APB** (Advanced Peripheral Bus), **AXI** (Advanced eXtensible Interface) and **CHI** (Coherent Hub Interface), which is used in high-performance, fully coherent multi-core systems.

Prior to AMBA 2, it was not possible to have concurrent access by two managers at the same time. An arbiter provided exclusive bus access to one manager unit at a time. However, through matrix organisation of the manager bus, many managers can now use the AHB or AXI bus architectures to perform concurrent transfers as long as they are accessing different subordinates, meaning they can run at higher frequencies.

The idea behind all of the buses mentioned above is the easier interconnection of interfaces, processors, accelerators, and memories. This allows designers (companies) to develop modules that are certified for one or more such buses. Integrators of specific bus architectures can then buy these modules and assemble their own SoC. These standards make it a lot easier to build a plug-and-play system that works first time.

These buses are designed for local connections between tens of units, with very few managers. For multi-core systems, new technologies are in development such as the network-on-a-chip (**NoC**), the idea being to have serial high-speed connections inside an integrated circuit, as we would have on a larger scale with lots of computers connected together. This is not something currently offered by the Cortex-M family, but look again in a few years' time…

1.6 System Architecture and Complexity

Divide and conquer! After an overview of the different parts of a processor core from a system point of view, we will now look at the two simplest Cortex-M components, M0 and M0+, and their different levels of integration. As we have seen, different manufacturers can design microcontrollers with their own architecture for the processor and programmable interfaces, or they can adopt a standardized architecture provided by specialized companies such as Arm and use a processor such as the Cortex-M, the more powerful Cortex-A, or the faster Cortex-R for real-time applications.

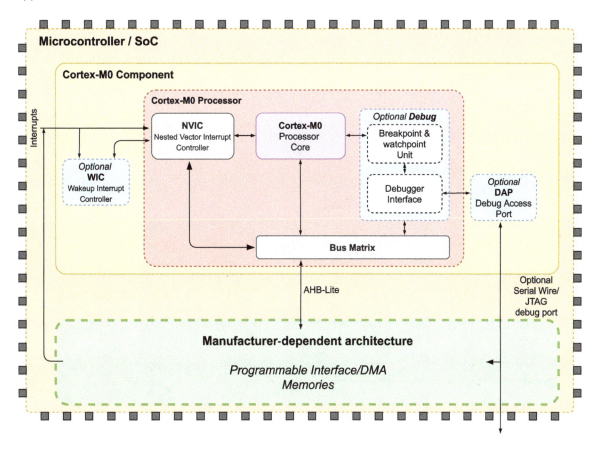

Figure 1.22 Microcontroller based on Cortex-M0

Once the main processor family has been selected, more detailed choices need to be made regarding power consumption, computing power and, of course, price. If we take the example of a simple low-power Cortex-M0 or Cortex-M0+ processor, there are many options available for the overall component configuration.

Thus, Figure 1.22 represents an overall view of a microcontroller/SoC based on a Cortex-M0 microprocessor. The overall configuration is realized by a manufacturer, the main architecture is provided by Arm. There are two principal areas containing various lower-level elements:

- The Cortex-M0 component, including:

  - Cortex-M0 processor, composed of:

    - Cortex-M0 processor core

    - nested vector interrupt controller

    - optional debug units:

      - breakpoint and watchpoint unit

      - debugger interface

    - bus matrix

  - optional elements, including:

    - wakeup interrupt controller

    - debug access port (Serial Wire or JTAG).

- The manufacturer-dependent component, including:

  - memories

    - Flash

    - RAM

    - reprogrammable nonvolatile (option)

    - clock generation

  - all programmable interfaces

  - internal bus architecture.

There are many options for the microcontroller designer and some headaches for a system designer who needs to select a specific microcontroller for their application design. Let's look at the higher level of complexity involved with a **Cortex-M0+**-based microcontroller, as shown in Figure 1.23. We can see that it has a few new optional units, principally an **MPU** for protection of areas in the processor component, but also a micro trace buffer (**MTB**) and a bus extension for a single-cycle I/O port.

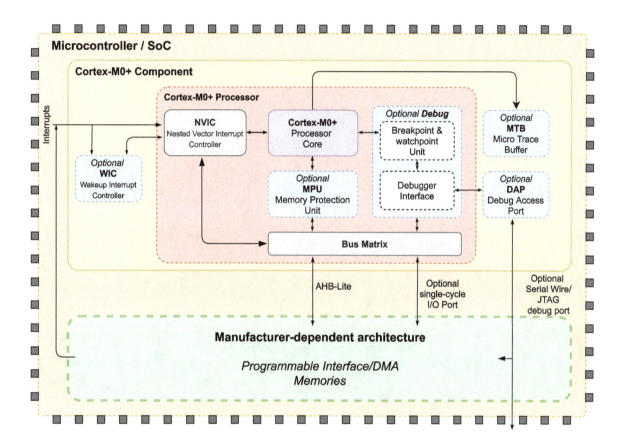

Figure 1.23 Microcontroller based on Cortex-M0+

The Cortex-M0 and -M0+ offer the lowest power consumption of the Cortex-M family, but with lower performance and a minimal instruction set. We can go much further with the Cortex M3, M4, M4F, M23, M33, M7, M55 and some forthcoming Cortex-M components, but complexity increases too with additional features, starting with the M3 core, and then the optional IEEE-754 32-bit floating-point unit (**FPU**) of the M4, shown in Figure 1.24. Here, the compiler uses the associated instructions to perform floating-point operations much faster.

We can see that a lot of additional debugging facilities can now be included in the Cortex component, a valuable feature for program tracing. All the optional parts shown in Figure 1.24 depend for their implementation on the manufacturer so, again, it is necessary to be very familiar with the full documentation of the specific device used.

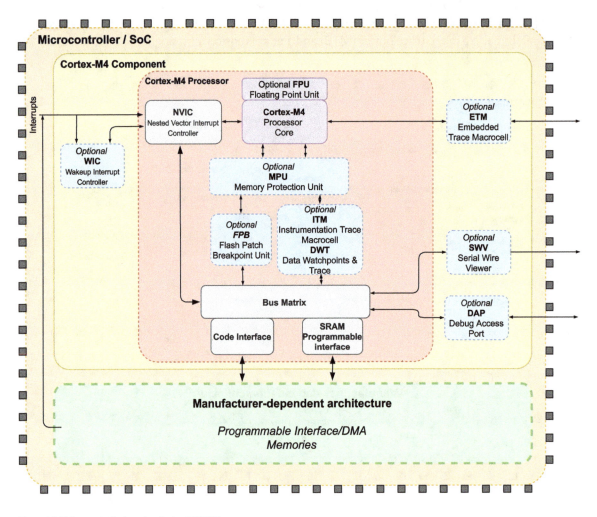

Figure 1.24 Microcontroller based on Cortex-M4/M4F

As new generations of processors evolve, their complexity generally increases. Different internal architectures are used, and different processors are offered to the integrating manufacturers. Arm proposes many architectures for use with the different processors in the Cortex-M family (as summarized in Table 1.1):

■ Arm v6-M on Cortex-M0/M0+

■ Arm v7-M on Cortex-M3

■ Arm v7E-M on Cortex-M4

■ Arm v8-M (with TrustZone) on Cortex-M23/M33

■ Arm v8.1-M on Cortex-M55.

For this class of processor, the register width is 32 bits. For the more powerful Cortex-A family, the register size is usually 32 bits too, but a new generation is proposed with the AArch64 architecture that would be 64-bits wide.

Table 1.1 Comparison of Cortex-M processors

Cortex -M	Architecture	Arch. Type	MPU	Caches	Pipeline	FPU	DSP	Interface	Security	Max no. IRQs
M0	Arm v6-M	von Neumann	-	-	3	-	-	AHB-Lite	-	1..32
M0+	Arm v6-M	von Neumann	option	-	2	-	-	AHB-Lite Optional single-cycle I/O port	-	1..32
M3	Arm v7-M	Harvard	option	-	3	-	-	AHB-Lite APB	-	1..240
M4	Arm v7E-M	Harvard	option	-	3	option	DSP	AHB-Lite APB	-	1..240
M7	Arm v7-M	Harvard	option	I / D	3..6	option	DSP	AXI AHBS/AHBP TCM	-	1..240
M23	Arm v8-M	Harvard	option	-	3		DSP	AMBA 5 AHB 5 Optional single-cycle I/O port	TrustZone	1..240
M33	Arm v8-M	Harvard	option	-	3	option	DSP	AMBA 5 AHB 5	TrustZone	1..480
M55	Arm v8.1-M	Harvard	option	-	4	option	DSP/SIMD Helium custom instruction	AXI5, M-AXI AHB5, S-AHB AHB5, P-AHB	TrustZone	1..480

TCM: Tightly coupled memory

1.7 Software for Embedded System Development

When it is time to develop software for the embedded system world, many questions must be answered.

If we want to develop an application for an embedded system based on the Cortex-M family, how do we start? First, we should understand that we are doing **cross-development**. This means that the software is developed on a workstation such as a PC, and downloaded to the memory of the embedded system through a serial link, often a JTAG or Serial Wire Debug (SWD) link through a USB interface on the PC.

Many development tools exist for the Cortex families. As a minimum, we need a text editor, a compiler and/or an assembler, a linker and a way to download the code in memory. This was the way programs were developed 50 years ago and is still in use today.

Another obligatory tool is a **debugger**, to be able to start a program running, to insert breakpoints to stop the program at key places, to advance step by step through the code, to examine memory, to disassemble the program code, and to look at the internal registers of the processor and the programmable interfaces. Ideally, we'd also like a way to measure power consumption.

Many companies provide integrated development tools with a color-coded editor keyed to the programming language used. For this class of processor, assembly-level programming is quite often used at the outset, but C/C++ is clearly the principal language for microcontrollers. Tools that support MicroPython are also becoming commonly available too; it's an interpreted language, so is a little bit slower but easier to use.

Development tools like this are often based on an environment called Eclipse. This is an open source development tool originally developed by IBM and subsequently placed in the public domain. The GNU compiler and debugger tools, **gcc** and **gdb**, are freely available and very often included in development tools.

Many other tools are offered by specialized tool vendors; for example, Keil, Altium TASKING, SEGGER, Arm Development Studio, Emprog ThunderBench, Green Hills MULTI, IAR Embedded Workbench, Lauterbach TRACE32, as well as the Mbed development platform. In general, they are not available free or else they have limits placed on the amount of code they can handle, but they can be very powerful and universal, supporting almost every processor manufacturer.

Some component manufacturers make their tools freely available, at least for a limited size of software. Examples include: Code Composer Studio from Texas Instruments; LPCXpresso, MCUXpresso, and Kinetis Design Studio for NXP processors; STM32Cube tools for ST processors.

Once we have addressed the development tools, the outstanding software-related question to answer when developing an embedded system is whether or not we want to use an **operating system** (OS):

▪ If yes, which category:

☐ Hard real-time?

☐ Soft real-time?

☐ Not real-time?

☐ Linux-based (typically requires a higher processor class, such as Cortex-A)?

▪ If, instead, we opt for **bare-metal** coding (executing instructions directly on the hardware), do we want:

☐ Our own fully home-grown bare-metal solution?

☐ To make use of available code libraries?

☐ To use a scheduler kernel?

Using an operating system or a kernel should be given serious consideration; after some initial learning time, it will make the development process easier and faster. Many operating systems and kernels are available on the market. One particular example is the Cortex Microcontroller Software Interface Standard (**CMSIS**), a vendor-independent hardware abstraction layer for microcontrollers that are based on Arm Cortex processors. This helps in the use and programming of the low-level elements of the microcontrollers. It is standardized and used by almost all manufacturers and development tool systems. Many other companies offer certified operating systems for real-time microcontroller-based applications; examples include µC/OS-III, Keil RTX, and FreeRTOS.

More on this entire topic can be found in Chapters 3 and 10.

1.8 Summary

In the course of this introductory chapter, we have surveyed the various topics that will covered by this book, starting from a very high-level view of a computer system with servers, clouds and internet access for PCs and IoT devices. All of these elements make use of processors of differing complexity.

We have given a view of the different levels found in an embedded system in the form of a microcontroller based on a processor, memories, and programmable interfaces. We have looked at the principles of interrupts and memory management and protection, and have provided basic information about interconnections. We have introduced the Cortex-M microprocessor family and briefly outlined its evolution from Cortex-M0 to Cortex-M7.

The next chapter introduces microelectronics and the basics of chip design.

Chapter 2

Basics of Chip Design

This chapter explains how to design a system on a chip (SoC), starting with the example of designing a SoC for an outdoor surveillance system. It introduces the fundamental principle of trade-offs, the difficulties that a designer may encounter, and the many choices that need to be made during the process. In particular, it highlights why work on specifications is critical to a proper understanding of the requirements of a system, and will address the following questions, amongst others.

1. What does it mean to design a SoC?

2. What is inside a SoC and how are the components linked?

3. How is a list of requirements and specifications translated into a design?

4. How do we balance expectation and reality? Is the desired design feasible?

5. What would be a typical SoC solution for an outdoor surveillance system?

6. Latency: How long does an instruction take to be processed?

7. Throughput: How many instructions can be processed per second?

8. IPS, FLOPS, clock speed: How is the performance of a pipeline calculated?

9. What is the optimum pipeline design?

10. What is a chip die?

11. What are the costs associated with the manufacture of chips?

12. Why do so many similar components exist on the market? Why are they not identical?

13. What is meant by the term "scaling"?

14. Why is scaling necessary?

15. What are the advantages and disadvantages of scaling?

16. What are the limits of scaling?

17. What do we mean by power consumption? Where does it originate?

18. What factors affect power consumption in a SoC?

19. What can the SoC designer do to model and control power consumption?

20. How are the power, performance and area of a SoC related?

21. What techniques can be used to optimize a SoC for area?

22. What techniques are available to optimize a SoC for performance?

23. What techniques can be used to optimize a SoC for power consumption?

24. What is meant by the term "reliability"?

25. What factors affect the reliability of a SoC?

26. *What can the designer do to improve the reliability of a SoC?*

27. *What can be configured in a SoC?*

28. *What are the benefits of configuring IP blocks?*

29. *Which elements of a Cortex-M SoC are configurable?*

2.1 Defining Requirements and Specifications

Before starting any development, several questions need to be addressed for the system to be defined clearly. A first idea of "what is to be designed" can then be produced. For example, for an external surveillance system, which we expect to design here, we could have these ideas:

▨ Working environment from −20 to 50 °C

▨ Memory storage

▨ The application will use a 4G antenna to send data

▨ The application will do some processing on the image acquired from the camera.

This list might lead to the following initial system requirements for the chip:

▨ Incorporate an imaging processor

▨ A flash controller is required to store image data

▨ An internal modem will be needed to connect through the cellular network

▨ Incorporate an integrated SIM card for cellular communication.

To establish the full specifications of the SoC, we need to answer several further questions:

▨ **Where will the system be used?**

Perhaps the system is expected to be used at room temperature and will not be guaranteed if used in extreme conditions, this being the case for many electronic devices. For instance, a smartphone is not expected to work at −50 °C or, at least, its performance is not guaranteed. However, some devices are used in extreme environments such as space or extreme cold and this might affect the way they are produced, because the entire system may need to be resistant to these physical constraints. It may mean that some specialized technology must be used, which, of course, increases the cost of production. In our example, the surveillance system is expected to be used in a normal environment from −20 °C to 50 °C. This is a typical temperature range for most systems and should not require specialized technology.

■ **What are the consequences if the system fails?**

The consequences of a system failing can be varied, from insignificant to life-threatening. For instance, if a smartphone fails, a reboot is usually all that is needed. Of course, it is annoying to have to reboot a phone and it is not a good business plan to irritate your customers in this way, so should be avoided as far as possible. Nevertheless, the consequences are relatively minor.

However, in the case of a system that helps a plane to land, a failure may have catastrophic consequences. The same is likely to be true of a system that detects obstacles in an autonomous car, or a life-supporting medical device. Such systems are termed safety-critical.

Safety-critical applications might have to meet specific requirements and certifications, for example, ISO 26262. They can require redundancy of some system components to ensure a failsafe protocol or to offer greater reliability. This is quite common in the automotive world, where components are duplicated to ensure that the final output is valid. Section 2.7 goes into more detail about system reliability.

In the example of the surveillance system, a priori, it could endure failure without being too dangerous to anyone. Of course, failure should be avoided as much as possible and good behaviors should be pursued if and when it does occur (for instance, avoiding loss of existing video recordings). It is also important to establish all of the safety norms and certifications needed in this domain before embarking on the design.

■ **Does the system need to do real-time processing?**

Real-time processing means that the response to some input needs to be time-bounded. Examples would include systems in a car such as the anti-lock braking system or the airbag system. Real-time processing is not necessarily about eliminating the delay in a response but about being certain that a response will be given within a specific amount of time.

Real-time systems may require special software provisions, such as the use of a real-time operating system (RTOS) instead of a normal one (Chapter 10 explores the goals of an RTOS). An RTOS enables more control of the time that is taken to handle an event. This software choice may also have a direct consequence on the hardware because if an RTOS is going to run on the chip, it may be worth adding a cache or a memory protection unit to ensure that the different running tasks do not corrupt each other's memory (see Chapter 3 for more details about protecting the memory). This could also be used to protect some peripherals from being accessed for tasks that they are not designed to support.

Our surveillance system is not real-time because it is not sensitive to delay. In terms of the video recordings that will be stored on a device, it does not matter if they are saved after a short delay or a long delay as long as they are stored at some point. Of course, for live surveillance video that is to be viewed by a human, the delay has to be minimized, although humans cannot perceive small differences in time or can accommodate some video lag such that the system is unlikely to require real-time processing.

■ What computing power does the system need? How fast does it need to be?

The questions of power consumption and processor speed are tightly bound, and it is why both questions often need to be answered together and trade-offs made accordingly. Will the system work with a battery or will it be attached to a constant energy source? If the device is to function on a battery, a low-power SoC would need to be designed to make the battery last longer. If very fast computation needs to be done, a specialized hardware unit may need to be added to the system.

Hardware units designed for a specific purpose can offer a fast and low power-consuming solution. However, a design that is flexible enough for use in many different applications is often more complex to build and test. The alternative, a software implementation, can be more flexible but results in slower execution and higher memory consumption. In the case of our surveillance application, using a digital signal processor (DSP) or an image-processing component could reduce the computing time by offloading the graphical operations.

As technology has evolved, it has become possible to put more transistors into a chip of the same size. This means more blocks can be added to a chip. Of course, this comes at a cost because the technology involved is usually more expensive and can require adjustments to the design of the system; for example, if the transistors are smaller and closer together, additional electronic constraints may arise. Section 2.5 provides more information about some of the different technologies available nowadays.

For our surveillance system, we expect to be connected to a power supply by cable and not to have any real issue of power consumption. However, performance will be important, and handling video is quite demanding. For security purposes, it may be sensible to incorporate a battery and a low-power mode such that in the case of a short-lived mains power failure the system could still record.

Another consideration concerns the capability of the hardware versus what the software is expected to do. For example, the inclusion of a floating-point unit (FPU) is costly in terms of space and might not be necessary in many applications. If the need for floating-point operation is only intermittent, an FPU could be emulated in software instead, even if it adds more processing time. However, for machine-learning applications, a DSP and floating-point unit would be essential to avoid the use of a slow software emulation.

■ What kind of connectivity will the system need?

The external connectivity of a system (e.g. Wi-Fi, Bluetooth Low Energy [BLE], 4G) can have a significant impact on its design because it will necessitate the addition of another radio component. In some cases, a coprocessor is added to handle such connectivity. This is the case for the Murata Type 1SC chip, which has an STM32L4 SoC together with a baseband CPU connected to a Long-Term Evolution (4G LTE) modem with an integrated SIM card.

Other connectors may also be useful, such as JTAG, UART, I2C, HDMI, USB, Ethernet, and so on. These will often depend on the external devices (e.g. GPS, accelerometer, gyroscope, temperature sensor, storage memory) connected to the system. A JTAG interface can be used to debug and program; a UART is often used to establish a headless connection with the board (i.e. a connection with just a terminal and no graphical interface). Would it also be useful to connect a screen, a mouse, and/or a keyboard to the system?

This raises the question of what type of input/output (I/O) the system will expose outside the chip for communication. The size of a chip is heavily affected by the number of I/O exports because the pins used to connect the chip to other components will have to be accorded sufficient space between them to be soldered. Section 2.3 briefly touches on the subject of chip packaging (e.g. shrink small-outline packages [SSOPs], thin small-outline packages [TSOPs]).

In our surveillance system example, 4G communication is expected, to transmit the video to an appropriate (work)station. Thus, a modem needs to be included in the design and a decision made as to whether to use a coprocessor. Depending on the video quality required, the throughput that must be supported by the communication can be determined. Having other port types such as HDMI (to connect a screen), USB (to connect a mouse, keyboard, etc.), UART (to connect to the system) and Ethernet could also greatly assist in developing and debugging the solution.

These requirements can be separated into a number of areas: Connectivity, Safety, Security, Power, and Performance. Answering the related questions will help to select or implement the elements or "blocks" that will comprise the final solution. The trade-offs considered should focus not just on size and power but also on cost and time to produce a custom SoC. Adding more IP (intellectual property) blocks implies more cost in licensing and/or engineering but should improve performance. The questions listed above are, of course, a non-exhaustive list and other questions may need to be included depending on the target system. Before starting the development, it is very important to be clear about what is needed and what is not needed. While software is relatively flexible and can be adapted quite quickly and cheaply to a new requirement, hardware can be very expensive and very hard (or even impossible) to change.

2.1.1 Choosing IP Solutions

Once we have a clear idea of what the system requires, the development starts by deciding where the different parts will be gathered. Designing a system on a chip is basically done by combining different blocks together. The high-level blocks that are typically needed in a SoC are as follows: processing elements, memory, interconnects, clock management, and peripherals. They are often broken down according to the following categories:

- **System components**. All the modules needed to make the chip work. This will be all the clock-related parts, from oscillators to clock divider, and how the clock is propagated through the system using it. These parts can also contain the analog components needed to regulate the voltage of the chip.

- **Digital system components and peripherals**. These will include the processor, the interconnect buses (e.g. AHB, APB, explained in later sections), digital peripherals such as UART, I2C, and SPI, and all the different system blocks that can be used to help the system work faster and/or more safely. These might include memory controllers, random-number generators, cryptography engines, a memory protection unit (MPU) and/or a TrustZone controller.

- **Memories**. Data storage can either be volatile, meaning that the data is not retained once the chip is powered down, or persistent, meaning that the data will remain intact following a reboot or power-down.

- **Processing elements**. This covers all of the components that will be used to process data or software, and can include processors, DSPs and various accelerators.

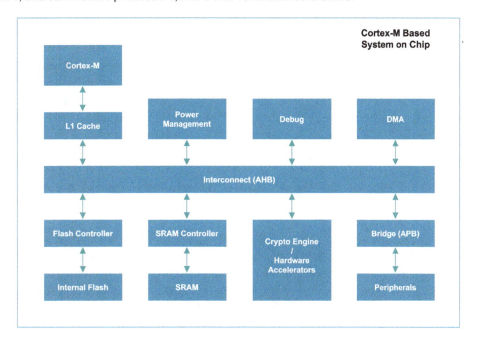

Figure 2.1 Example of a system on a chip showing the different blocks involved

The blocks needed to create a SoC can be designed from scratch or bought as IP (intellectual property) blocks from vendors. Figure 2.1 shows the typical blocks that need to be connected in order to produce a SoC. While all of these blocks could come from the same vendor, in some cases this is not possible.

Although the blocks shown in the figure are typical of a SoC, how do we know exactly which are needed for our design and whether others are also required? These questions should be answered through the design requirements and specifications.

Design requirements derive from the expected purpose of the system that needs to be built. These can include the power, size, power consumption, or even the final price of the chip. Requirements drive the cost of manufacturing and the technology that needs to be involved. The requirements provide information about which components should be implemented in hardware and which in software.

Development time also needs to be considered when it comes to the final cost. Most of the chips from the various vendors come with examples of programs for them that ease development. Software is a crucial part of SoC development because it is used to control the hardware and the interfaces exposed. Vendor code examples show how to use different peripherals and how the hardware can be controlled. Buying products from vendors that do not provide examples or good support may, a priori, be cheaper but the repercussions on the development time may be so considerable that the overall cost of the solution is higher.

While SoC design requirements are largely concerned with hardware constraints, the specifications describe the necessary functionalities of the product.

In terms of terminology, it is worth reiterating that a CPU is a single processor core for general-purpose applications. It cannot operate on its own because it needs inputs, outputs and peripherals and must have memory associated with it in order to function. Confusion arises between the definitions of microcontroller unit (MCU) and system-on-chip. In general, an MCU is composed of a CPU with small amounts of memory, I/O and peripherals and is used for basic control applications. A SoC is considered to be more complex because it can include elements such as GPUs, DSPs, image processors, and neural networks and is considerably larger from the point of view of memory and peripherals.

During design, the following question should be asked: **Is a custom SoC needed? If it is, how customized should it be?**

There are plenty of existing SoCs available from different vendors. However, some may have IP/peripherals that will not be used by the anticipated application, leading to unnecessary space and "dead" silicon. Furthermore, they may have been built in a technology that makes them large by today's standards. In some cases, they might not have been designed to incorporate a specific component that will be required, which implies that this latter must be added separately to the final board or emulated in software.

Creating a custom SoC should be considered to reduce the system to a bare minimum and keep both space and power consumption low. In addition, incorporating all of the necessary components within a single customized SoC makes the solution harder to reverse engineer and better protects the device from attacks or illicit copying.

Customization of a SoC can be done at multiple levels: from designing every single component afresh to integrating existing components from different vendors. Designing individual components can be a challenging process depending on their complexity and the knowledge it demands. It will need the implementation of a common interface to communicate with the other components of the system, and also requires the necessary software tooling and engineering time. Designing a complex block like the CPU from scratch would demand very considerable effort and expertise.

In general, most system designs use intellectual property (IP) blocks that are linked together using design tools. These blocks are defined in a hardware description language (HDL; e.g. VHDL, Verilog) that describes the circuit of each block and how it will behave. Computer-based electronic design automation (EDA) tools are used to write and debug the register transfer language (RTL) in the course of the simulation, validation, and implementation stages; for example:

- Cadence Encounter RTL Compiler

- Cadence Virtuoso

- Synopsys Design Compiler.

Catalogs of IP blocks from the likes of Arm, Cadence and OpenCore can be used for the design of a SoC. Table 2.1 contains a non-exhaustive list of such blocks.

Table 2.1 IP block examples

Interconnects	Interconnect family provides on-chip AMBA connectivity for components implementing any combination of AMBA AXI, AHB, AHB-Lite, APB and APB3 interfaces
Memory controllers	Memory controllers including dynamic and static memory controllers
System controllers	System controllers including interrupt controllers, DMAs, color LCDs, level-2 cache controllers, TrustZone controllers
Programmable interfaces	Peripherals including GPIOs, UARTs, synchronous serial ports, keyboard/mouse, smart cards, real-time clocks, external buses, test peripherals

All of the IP block catalogs provide the specifications of the components, providing information on:

- how to connect the component to a system (which interconnects it is compatible with)

- how the component can be configured and the list of registers exposed by its programming interface

- the type of delivery: whether it is in the form of RTL code or an already synthesized block

- the test bench used to validate the design.

If a block is not taken as an IP block from a third-party vendor and must be designed, one needs to know how it will be connected to the system. Because different types of interconnect exist, the new block will need to implement the correct signals and the correct interface to receive write and read commands. Once this is done, the next step is to create the programming interface for the component. This involves the list of registers that must be configured so that it can be used. Eventually, once the block has been designed and verified, it can be incorporated into the overall system design.

2.1.2 Choosing a Processor

As previously indicated, software is just as important as the underlying hardware. Coding is based on assembly language (assembler) to make it more readable for the programmer. However, in practice, assembler has to be translated into opcode commands that the processor can understand. Processors can only understand the opcodes for which they have been designed, meaning that, for example, an Arm core would give an undefined behavior if a program that was compiled for an Intel processor was run on it instead.

Thus, the first step necessary is to define the different instructions to be supported and the associated opcode that the processor will understand. This is termed the instruction set. If we use as an example the ADD assembler instruction that takes data from a register, adds an operand and puts the result into another register, the instruction will look like this for Arm:

```
ADD r1, r2, #4
```

However, for MIPS it will look like this:

```
addi $1, $2, 4
```

Meanwhile, for the TI MSP430 processor, because the relevant instruction only accepts two operands, register R2 must serve as both the input and the output for the ADD instruction:

```
ADD.W #4, R2
```

As described above, the processor does not actually understand this assembly language syntax, which is only used to make it more readable to humans. The translations of these instructions that will be understood by the processor are given in the following examples.

Arm Thumb assembler	0b 0001 1101 IISS SDDD

The Arm assembler instruction is translated to a 16-bit binary value, where 0001 110 is the opcode indicating that the operation to be executed is an ADDition between a register and an "immediate" value, III are three bits for the immediate value, SSS are three bits to indicate the source register, and DDD are three bits to indicate the destination number.

In our example, the source register is R2, the destination register is R1 and the immediate value is 4, as indicated by the colors such that the instruction would be translated into 0b 0001 1101 0001 0001.

MIPS assembler	0b 0010 00SS SSSD DDDD IIII IIII IIII IIII

The given MIPS instruction is translated into a 32-bit binary value, where 0010 00 is for the selection of the instruction ADD with an immediate, SSSSS are five bits to select the source register (for $2 it will be 0b 00010), DDDDD are the five bits to select the destination register (for $1 it will be 0b 00001), and the last bits, represented by IIII IIII IIII IIII, are used to represent the immediate value in 16 bits. Finally, in the case of the example, the instruction is translated into 0b 0010 0000 0100 0010 0000 0000 0000 0100.

TI MSP assembler	0b 0101 IIII 0111 RRRR

The given TI assembler instruction is translated into a 16-bit binary value, where 0b 0101 selects the ADD instruction and the following 0111 selects the parameters of the instruction (addition in 16 bits with an immediate value), IIII are four bits for the immediate value (in our case they are 0b 0100), and RRRR selects the register, which is both the source and the destination. The example instruction is therefore translated into 0b 0101 0100 0111 0010.

The second step required is to define all of the information that will be needed by a programmer, such as the list of registers that can be used, and the list of instructions to control the processor. This is the instruction set architecture (ISA). Its purpose is to provide an interface for the programmer to make use of the hardware. Most processors fall into one of two major categories, according to the instruction set they use: the Complex Instruction Set Computer (CISC) and the Reduced Instruction Set Computer (RISC). In the SoC market, RISC processors predominate because this kind of ISA requires a simpler level of hardware support, and there are a multitude of different ISAs provided by different vendors (e.g. Arm, TI, MIPS).

Note: Because Arm licenses its ISA to others, there are several companies that implement their own processor on the basis of this architecture; for example, Qualcomm's SnapDragon SoC family (based on ARMv8-A and ARMv7-A). However, even if the implementation is different, the common ISA means that a SnapDragon programmer can use the same instructions and registers when writing software for a Cortex-A (and vice versa).

In the case of the Cortex-M family, SoC vendors typically take an Arm processor or implement their own. This is partially due to the difference in ecosystems between the M and A classes. For microcontrollers (the M class), many vendors provide the necessary toolchains and specific APIs for programming the processor. However, for the A class, there are only a few software stacks (e.g. Linux) that are widely used; supporting different ISAs would be very complex and would require inordinate effort.

In the microcontroller world, vendors such as Altera, Xilinx, and Texas Instruments (TI) implement their own processors, although TI also provides Arm-based systems (such as the MSP432). See Table 2.2 for some examples of such implementations and their characteristics.

Table 2.2 Examples of non-Arm-based cores

Name	Description
TI MSP430 Microcontroller	Microcontroller
	16-bit RISC architecture
	Clock supports frequencies up to 16 MHz
	16 registers
	27 instructions
Altera Nios II	Soft processor (running on FPGA)
	32-bit RISC architecture
	32 registers
	Relatively similar to MIPS instructions
Xilinx MicroBlaze	Soft processor (running on FPGA)
	32-bit RISC architecture
	Clock supports frequencies up to 235 MHz
	32 registers
	Implements its own instruction set

Name	Description
T8051 Microcontroller Cadence	Microcontroller
	8-bit RISC architecture
	32 registers
	Intel MCS 51 instruction set
R8051XC2 Microcontroller	Microcontroller
	8-bit RISC architecture
	32 registers
	Clock supports frequencies up to 400 MHz
	Intel MCS 51 instruction set

In the embedded world, there are multiple different needs, depending on the intended application of the chip. A system that is used in a microwave oven does not need to be large. Most of the time, it will only have to control a screen and some buttons to start the desired cooking program. On the other hand, a system in a car to monitor the brakes and feed back real-time information might require more power from the processor. This is the reason why the Arm Cortex-M family offers so many different processors; each of them targets a specific group of applications. However, if the end-application uses Linux or another heavy operating system, then a more advanced core such as that of the Cortex-A family will be needed to provide the underlying hardware support, such as an MMU and memory virtualization.

In this context, the members of the Cortex-M family and their relevant characteristics are summarized below. Because each is different, it is important to know the specification of the SoC design that is going to be built to make a good choice. The family can be divided into three: those with the v6-M architecture suitable for low-power applications; those with the v7-M architecture if more performance is needed; those with the v8-M architecture if security needs to be included. The v8-M processors also have newer accelerators that can make them a good choice for performance reasons. More details are given in subsequent chapters.

V6 processors:

- **Cortex-M0:** the smallest Arm processor with the lowest amount of power.

- **Cortex-M0+:** similar to the Cortex-M0 but with a smaller pipeline; it also adds a memory protection unit and has two execution modes.

- **Cortex-M1:** again, similar to the Cortex-M0 processor, but optimized for FPGA applications; it embeds a special type of memory to ease integration with FPGAs.

V7 processors:

- **Cortex-M3:** for applications that need more complicated data processing,

- **Cortex-M4:** similar to the Cortex-M3 but can have a single-precision floating-point unit (FPU); it is also more suitable for signal processing

- **Cortex-M7:** similar to the Cortex-M4, but can support double-precision floating-point operations; it is optimized for performance.

V8 processors:

- **Cortex-M23:** can be used for constraint applications; it embeds the TrustZone IP for security applications.

- **Cortex-M33:** can be used for similar applications to the Cortex-M4 where TrustZone IP is also required.

- **Cortex-M35P:** similar to the Cortex-M33 but is made more tamperproof.

- **Cortex-M55:** similar to the Cortex-M7, it again adds TrustZone for additional security, and offers high performance, making it suitable for machine-learning and DSP operations.

Once the processor has been implemented or acquired from a specific vendor, it needs to have other components added to form an entire system. System creation is easier if most parts are taken from vendors, because their components have already been proven in other systems, and they usually offer the possibility of customizing the component too. Using IP blocks that have already been tested is less time-consuming. Indeed, as you might imagine, it is a big challenge for a single team to take on the design of an entire SoC from scratch.

2.1.3 Testing and Validating the Design

When designing a SoC, it is obviously useful to be able to test its functionality to see how the different IP blocks will interact with each other. It is also good to get an indication of the expected performance of the design by running software to try out the components. Arm offers a way to configure a SoC from a catalog of already implemented IP blocks and test its behavior through a simulator. The tool is called **Fast Model** and is designed for easy prototyping. Components can be written in C and integrated with each other through LISA (Language for Instruction Set Architecture) code. An integrated development environment (IDE) exists to connect the blocks with each other for the simulation (see Figure 2.2).

The main aim of this simulator is to provide an accurate view of a system and enable the user to develop software before the chip has been manufactured. During the simulation, it is possible to profile the running software and analyze the registers of the various components. This approach has limitations because software cannot emulate the associated hardware with complete accuracy, and it can make the system seem extremely slow. However, the benefit of using Fast Model is the ability to inspect the internal registers through the debugging interface, and it is also possible to log specific traces or bus accesses. This simulator is widely used for testing the expected behavior of a system before it is produced.

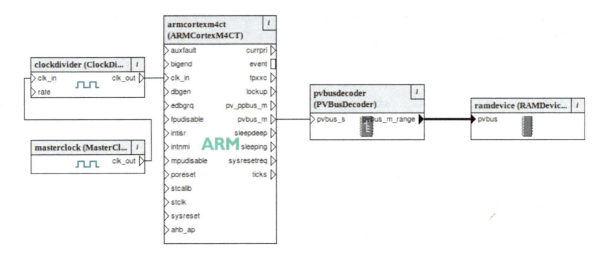

Figure 2.2 Screenshot of Fast Model diagram for Cortex-M4

FPGA prototyping can also be used. However, the debug environment for this is different, which makes it harder to look inside the system without impacting the runtime. However, while a simulator will execute the register transfer level (RTL) code of a system sequentially, the FPGA prototyping will execute in parallel, which offers better performance and a more accurate view than running on a simulator because it is closer to the hardware that will actually be used.

Once the production of the chip has started, the design cannot be updated. If the system exhibits issues that are not related to its manufacture, it is almost impossible to patch and the batch has to be thrown away. This means that verification of the design and implementation of the system must be conducted during development. Test-benchs are used to check the behavior of the blocks using simulators to test the HDL (e.g. ModelSim, Incisive Enterprise Simulator, Riviera-PRO). Signals are simulated and the results are analyzed to check the timings of the system and its responses.

Tools that are used to translate HDL into transistors also give validation of the maximum clock rate that can be used and of the electrical constraints.

To conclude, in order to produce a SoC, the first step is to produce the global design by defining the specification of the system. The requirements will help to deduce which blocks are needed to achieve the expected behavior of the system in relation to the key constraints (i.e. final size, cost, and performance of the chip). In terms of the selection of IP blocks, this can either be done through a catalog of existing components or the IP needed can be designed and implemented. Choosing them from a catalog might incur a fee but implementing them oneself will also cost time and require design knowledge.

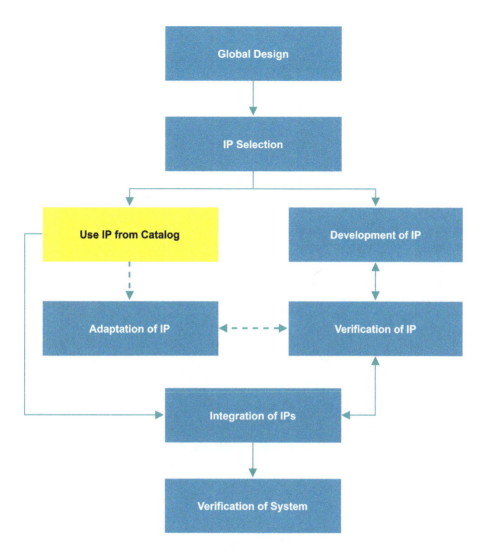

Figure 2.3 Steps in designing a SoC

Once the list of requisite IP blocks is available, they must be linked together, with or without the help of a third party that will validate the functionality of the design. The design must have the expected behavior in terms of the timing between the different components and the voltage regulation. If the target chip has one or more buses that implement a protocol (such as AMBA), these need to be functionally tested. Some test-benches are able to validate such behaviors. Then, verification of the SoC when running the expected software can be done using either a simulator or FPGA prototyping to check that all of the constraints have been respected. Once all of these steps have been validated, production of the final design of the chip can be initiated. Figure 2.3 illustrates this process. Designing a SoC is always a trade-off between power, size and cost:

- Size can be reduced by using fewer components, but performance may be degraded; a more up-to-date technology could be used but it might be more expensive to produce

■ Adding more computing power increases the size of the chip and increases its overall power consumption

■ Designing the chip components will demand significant effort in terms of validation and development; buying IP blocks from third parties might be more expensive but offers a shorter time-to-market.

2.2 Cycle Time: Definition, Optimum Pipeline, Performance

In this section, we describe the pipelining of a processor and explain how its performance is measured.

When someone wants to buy a new computer or SoC, their initial approach may be to look at the maximum clock speed to compare the performance of different options. So how do we increase the clock speed of a processor and what are the consequences for its performance? Is it really true that "The higher the clock speed, the better"?

2.2.1 Basic Concepts of Pipelining

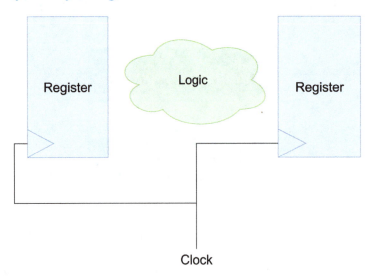

Figure 2.4 Basic pipelining concept showing two registers directed by one clock breaking down a logic block

In simple terms, the clock speed of a processor is constrained by the delay in propagation of logic between two registers. Taking the illustration in Figure 2.4, the clock speed should be slow enough to allow the output of the first register to propagate through the gate of the logic block and reach the second register. The clock "slack" is defined as the difference between the clock period and the longest path (critical path) that the clock needs to support. If the clock slack is positive, it means that the clock speed could be increased; if it is negative, it means that there is a timing violation. Indeed, it means that the time for the logic to reach the second register is longer than the time for the clock to change from 0 to 1.

The delay in a logic gate depends on several factors, including the technology used. The more logic gates that are placed in serial with one another, the more time is required for information to flow from its entrance to its output from the last gate. Two consecutive clock cycles need to be staggered sufficiently for the propagation of logic to occur for the slowest path of logic gates. In order to increase the speed of the clock, the solution is to divide the logic work done into additional pieces separated by registers, as shown in Figure 2.5, thereby reducing the longest path between any two registers; propagation is then faster and the clock speed can be increased.

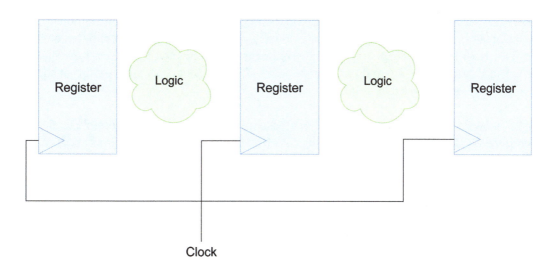

Figure 2.5 Three-stage pipeline

A processor typically implements five main blocks of logic, as shown in Figure 2.6.

- **Fetch** is the part that retrieves the next instruction to be processed in the processor's memory. Usually, the instruction to be fetched is the next in line because a program is sequential, but sometimes a jump occurs and the address of the next instruction needs to be computed, as is the case for code branches.

- **Decode** is the part that decomposes the instruction into smaller pieces to extract information from it. For instance, exactly what type of computation needs to be performed? An addition? A logical shift? Which registers need to be read and which written? All of this information and more is contained in the instruction.

- **Execute** is the part that involves the Arithmetic Logic Unit (ALU) and everything that enables computation; it receives the information about which operation to execute from the Decode stage.

- **Memory (access)** is the part in which any data is read from or written to memory, as required.

- **Write Back** is the part in which the results of the instruction are available and are written back into the registers.

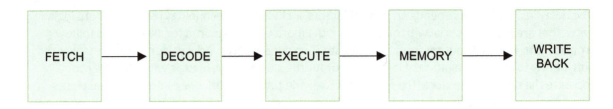

Figure 2.6 Logic blocks of a typical processor

Processor architectures make use of the simple pipelining trick of dividing logic into simpler stages. For the relatively simple processors of the SoC industry, pipelines usually consist of between three (e.g. Arm Cortex-M3) and six (e.g. Arm Cortex-M7) stages. More complex processors typically have between 8 (e.g. Arm Cortex-A7) and 14 (e.g. Intel i3, i5, i7) stages, but processors exist that support up to 31 stages (e.g. Pentium 4 Cedar Mill).

Figure 2.7 shows a simplified five-stage RISC processor pipeline. Note that it is possible to divide things differently; for instance, the Execute logic is often particularly heavy and it may be a good idea to divide this across two stages.

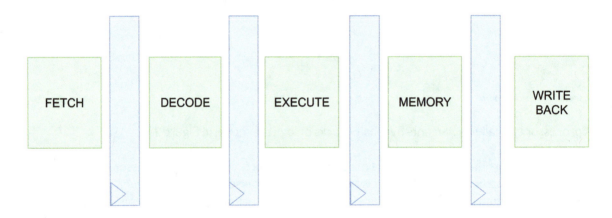

Figure 2.7 Five-stage RISC processor pipeline

If we can increase the clock speed simply by adding pipeline stages, why not simply create processors with hundreds of stages? As usual, in the SoC world, trade-offs have to be made when it comes to choosing the depth of a pipeline. To understand such choices better, we need to understand the pros and cons of pipelining.

2.2.2 Pipeline Latency and Throughput

When a collection of logic gates is divided into two pipeline stages, two clock cycles (versus one without pipelining) are now required to execute the same amount of logic. However, the clock speed cannot be exactly doubled because of the extra timing constraints imposed by the additional registers. These registers also consume energy and space in the processor. The clock speed can only be increased if the longest logical path is reduced such that adding stages with near-empty logic does not help to increase the clock speed. In addition, adding elements to the processor will definitely not simplify it. It will increase the complexity and the overall amount of logic, which increases the risk of design error, increases the time needed to develop and test, which ultimately leads to increased expense!

Running at the maximum possible clock speed is not always desirable. Using a high clock speed complicates the routing of the clock. It may require that the voltage supply is increased to sustain the clock rate, which increases the power consumption of the CPU. In general, we find that power consumption increases linearly relative to clock rate and quadratically relative to voltage. This latter is particularly significant because power consumption is a critical concern in SoC architecture, which is why one may choose not to use the maximal clock rate allowed by the design.

If pipelining a processor allows the clock speed to be increased but ultimately increases the time taken to fully process one instruction while also increasing power consumption and design complexity, why is every processor manufacturer using it? Is it only a marketing ploy?

The time that is taken for one instruction to be processed is called the latency and, yes, in this case if the clock speed is increased the number of pipelining levels increases. However, the goal of a performant processor is not to process one instruction as fast as possible, but rather to process a lot of instructions as fast as possible (literally millions). A second measure that is used for performance is called throughput. Throughput is the number of instructions that can be processed per second and it is what pipelining is all about. It is frequently referred to in terms of IPS (instructions per second) or MIPS (millions of instructions per second).

To better understand this concept let us take a simplified example where a clock is running at 1 Hz (one clock cycle per second). Without a pipeline (see Figure 2.6), the first instruction takes one clock cycle to process (so one second). The second instruction also takes one clock cycle, and so on. Overall, the latency is 1 second because one instruction needs 1 second to be processed, and the throughput is one instruction per second (1 IPS).

Now, if we consider a processor with a two-stage pipeline, the clock speed can be increased twofold, which means the clock runs at 2 Hz (two clock cycles per second). For the sake of simplicity, we consider an ideal case in which the clock speed can be doubled when the pipeline is doubled. In reality, this will not be exactly the case because it would have meant that the longest path had been cut precisely in half (unlikely) and we had neglected other timing constraints that may have appeared in the design (e.g. additional registers).

Figure 2.8 illustrates the processing of four instructions in a two-stage pipeline processor. At time 0, the four instructions are waiting in memory to be processed. At clock cycle 1, the first instruction enters the first stage of the pipeline. At clock cycle 2, the first instruction moves into the second stage of the pipeline and the second instruction can enter the first stage of the pipeline such that the two instructions can be processed in parallel. At clock cycle 3, the third instruction can enter the pipeline while the second instruction is in the second stage, and so on.

At the finish, two cycles have been needed to process each instruction at a rate of 2 Hz, which means the latency is one second, as was the case without pipelining. However, with pipelining, instructions can be processed in parallel. Thus, if processing of the first instruction is completed after 1 second, processing of the second instruction starts at 0.5 seconds and finishes at 1.5 seconds, while processing of the third instruction starts at 1 second and completes at 2 seconds, and so on. If we discount the very first instruction, thereafter two instructions are processed every second and the throughput is 2 IPS.

Therefore, in an ideal world, the throughput is proportional to the pipeline depth. However, in the harsh reality of life, things are not that simple, as we shall see.

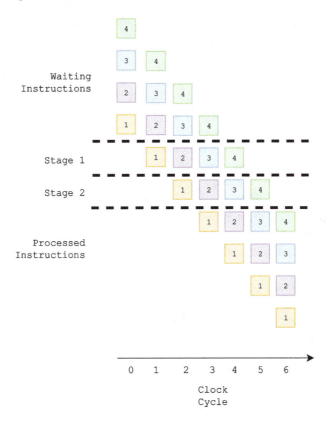

Figure 2.8 Ideal execution of four instructions (numbered 1, 2, 3 and 4) in a two-stage pipeline in six clock cycles

2.2.3 Effects of Pipeline Hazard and Data Dependencies of Throughput

In the preceding example, processing of the second instruction started before the first instruction had completed because the hardware logic was idle. However, what happens if the second instruction depends on the result of the first, which is often the case in programming? Let us consider the two instructions shown below: the first adds the contents of r1 and r2 together and stores the result in r0; the second instruction logically left-shifts the register r0 by one.

```
add r0, r1, r2
lsl r0, r0, #1
```

It is expected that the result of the first instruction will be known before the second instruction starts, meaning that execution of the second instruction must be stalled until the result of the first instruction is known. Such data dependencies are known as read-after-write (RAW) dependencies. It is why, in this case, the second instruction cannot start after 0.5 seconds as in the preceding example, and must start after 1 second.

Figure 2.9 shows a pipeline execution in which instructions are dependent on each other's results. As per the previous example, the first instruction starts to be processed at clock cycle 1 and moves into the second stage at clock cycle 2. However, this time the second instruction cannot start at clock cycle 2 because it needs the results of the first instruction which is still being processed in the second stage of the pipeline. The crossed grey box indicates that no instruction is processed in the first stage of the pipeline during this clock cycle. In the figure, the pipeline is underutilized because only one instruction can enter the pipeline at a time. Things that require the pipeline to be stalled in this way are called hazards. In this example, the hazard was due to data dependencies (also called data hazards) but other hazards exist, such as control hazards, which are caused by the resolution of a branch and may take several cycles. While the branch is unresolved, the processor does not know which instruction is next in line for processing. Stalling the pipeline until the hazard is resolved is one solution, which is also referred to as pipeline bubbling. Other more advanced solutions exist to resolve hazards; for instance, branch prediction, speculative execution (famous because some processor designs had associated vulnerabilities exploited by Meltdown and Spectre attacks), and out-of-order execution.

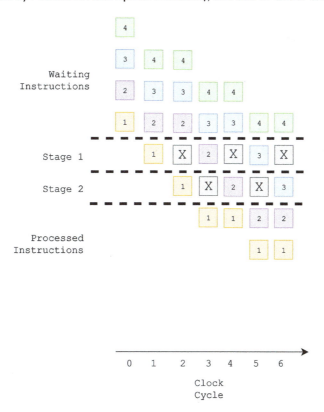

Figure 2.9 Two-stage pipeline with bubbling due to data dependency (indicated by X)

If all of the instructions being executed had similar dependencies, the throughput in the case of this simple two-stage pipeline processor would be 1 IPS. Because this is not the case in practice, the real throughput of this processor will be somewhere between 1 IPS (the worst case) and 2 IPS (the best case). The deeper the pipeline, the longer the hazard resolution. Indeed, the result of one instruction may only be available several clock cycles later. One solution for empirically computing the performance of this or any other processor is to run standard benchmarks, which are sample programs having known numbers of instructions, and measure the time required to process them.

One further measure for the performance of a pipeline is called instructions per cycle (IPC), which indicates the number of instructions that a computer can process in each cycle. This measure shows how efficient a pipeline is. If no hazard occurs, the pipeline would have an IPC equal to one because a new instruction is processed every cycle, as illustrated earlier in this chapter. The longer the pipeline takes to resolve hazards, the lower the IPC. The combination of the IPC with the clock speed gives the throughput of the pipeline.

In summary, having a shallow pipeline (only a few stages) leads to low clock speeds and underutilization of the hardware, but having a deep pipeline leads to poor IPC due to hazard resolution. The optimum pipeline is one that balances the highest clock speed with the fastest possible hazard resolution (the highest IPC).

2.2.4 Other Performance Considerations

One other parameter that plays an important role in processor performance is the hardware available to it. In particular, the hardware available in the Execute stage. Once again, trade-offs have to be made between very efficient and specialized hardware in a processor and the space and power it consumes. For instance, multiplication can be performed with specialized hardware, in which case the multiplications would be very fast (a few clock cycles), or it can be done with software, because multiplication is just a series of additions. With software, one multiplication may take many clock cycles to resolve; the hardware solution is therefore faster but requires specialized hardware, which will cost in terms of price, space and power consumption.

Another example of such hardware is that dedicated to the rapid processing of floating-point (non-integer) numbers, termed a floating-point unit (FPU). Not all processors have such hardware because this kind of operation is not universal. However, processors that do not have an FPU must emulate the calculation in software, which is very slow. As before, whether or not to include such a unit depends on price, space and power consumption trade-offs.

In fields such as scientific computational research, floating-point numbers are very heavily used. This is why the performance measure of floating-point operations per second (FLOPS) is often preferred over IPS/MIPS.

2.3 Die Area and Cost: Processor Area, Area of Peripherals, Interfaces

Constructing a SoC involves a complex and heavily articulated design flow. It needs highly skilled human resources, and requires the application of the most advanced design tools and technologies. Within the long list of elements involved, one of the key aspects, if not the most important, to take into account in the early stages of SoC development is the final target cost. This represents the market price, the final bill when the chip has been manufactured. An ideal SoC design achieves the lowest cost-to-performance ratio, which is the factor that largely determines the quality of the final product. In this section, rather than the factors affecting the development costs, we will focus our attention on the costs of manufacture. In particular, we want to introduce the relationship between the cost and the physical area of the processor, the peripherals and the interfaces: a good SoC designer must be aware of the impact that the die area can have on the fixed and variable costs of SoC production.

2.3.1 Basics of Chip Manufacturing

To describe the factors affecting the manufacturing costs we need to introduce some common terms and basic definitions associated with this area.

■ **Wafer**

A wafer is a thin slice of semiconductor material, such as crystalline silicon, used for the fabrication of integrated circuits. A wafer contains multiple dies, as shown in Figure 2.10.

Figure 2.10 Wafer (source: archive of EPFL's Center of MicroNanoTechnology. cmi.epfl.ch)

▣ Die

The die identifies the small block of semiconductor material on which a given functional circuit is fabricated. Figure 2.11 shows a chip die.

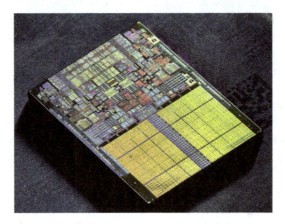

Figure 2.11 Chip die (source: https://www.flickr.com/photos/sic66/46279234254 Martijn Boer, 2018. Reproduced under the terms of the Creative Commons Public Domain Mark 1.0 licence, https://creativecommons.org/publicdomain/mark/1.0/)

▣ Yield

The yield represents the ratio of the number of dies that can be sold to the number of dies that can be manufactured from a given wafer.

▣ Silicon Technology Process

The silicon technology process identifies the set of manufacturing rules and characteristics for the production of a specific semiconductor device. Among these characteristics is the size of the gate length used in the transistor, which has been used to identify different generations of technology process, also referred to as technology nodes. These are typically identified as 28 nm, 14 nm, 7 nm, and so on.

Now that we have introduced the basic terms, we can proceed to analyze the costs that will affect the SoC.

2.3.2 System-on-Chip Costs

The total cost of a SoC can be represented by the following equation:

$$SoC_{costs} = design_{costs} + die_{costs} + testing_{costs} + packaging_{costs}$$

As previously indicated, we will discuss here only the costs related to the manufacture of the SoC.

The die size of a SoC, expressed in mm², depends on the technology used. As indicated above, a wafer will contain multiple dies, and the die number (dies-per-wafer) represents the ratio of the size of the wafer to the size of a die within it:

$$\#die = wafer_{size} \div die_{size}$$

From a purely mathematical perspective, we can enlarge the wafer to produce more dies, while enlarging the die size means obtaining fewer dies from the same wafer. While the first of these holds in practice, the second does not. The important piece of information missing from the equation is the effect of the die size on the yield. At the end of the manufacturing process, not all of the dies in a wafer will be usable. Manufacturing defects can occur during fabrication, mainly due to the advanced technology process being highly sensitive to impurities.

What is the relationship between SoC complexity and the yield? Complex SoCs integrate more functions, which involve larger die areas. Because a defective die will not be usable in realizing the final chip, they must be discounted. Furthermore, the probability of a defect occurring is proportional to the area of the die; hence, the relationship between die area and yield. Sometimes, for very expensive chips, a defective die can be fixed using advanced laser-based techniques, but this is not the case for low-cost microcontrollers. Achieving the maximum yield is not the main goal. Die area reduction and optimization can reduce the final cost of the SoC, but there are also other aspects to be taken into account, like the spacing between the die and its interfaces. Another factor affecting the yield is the design process. In fact, the yield can vary significantly depending on the silicon technology process used.

2.3.3 Processor Area, Area of Peripherals, Interfaces

The processor is the main component of the SoC. It represents the central core for managing all of the operations and the functionality of the chip. However, the area occupied by the processor is often not the dominant part of the die. Besides the processor, SoCs contain peripherals such as embedded memory, memory controllers, communications, and analog interfaces, as illustrated in Figure 2.12. All of these components must be taken into account to estimate the final target price of the SoC. First, because they occupy die area, thereby affecting the die size and yield; second, because they often require larger numbers of external pins and different "packaging".

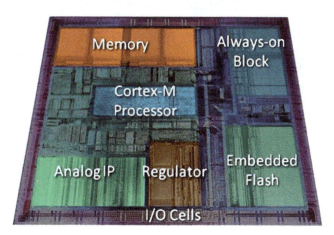

Figure 2.12 SoC internal blocks on a die (source: Reproduced with permission from Arm Ltd)

2.3.4 Memory Costs

The memory embedded in a SoC plays an important role in the overall costs of SoC fabrication. Although the physical structure of an SRAM cell is very regular and relatively simple in respect to other more complex IP blocks, larger memory requires a larger area with a proportionate effect on the die area. The impact on the final SoC cost can sometimes be very large, ranging from a few pennies up to several dollars. For this reason, chip manufacturers usually sell several versions of the same component differentiated only by the amount of embedded RAM and/or flash memory. Why is the size of the embedded memory so important for the final application? The answer is simple: the larger the memory, the more functions you can integrate into your software; adding more features to your final application makes it more competitive in the market.

2.3.5 Packaging

Packaging represents another aspect in the final cost of the chip. In this case, the costs are related to the manufacturing process used. Beyond a minimum package size as a result of die area and the number of I/Os required, the dimension of the final chip is a marketing decision driven purely by market needs.

Thus, the same SoC can be found on the market in different packaging. Depending on the final application purpose, it can be more convenient to adopt one specific package rather than another; for example, for thermal dissipation or resilience to vibration. On the other hand, sometimes it is good to have all of the pins exposed for debugging purposes or reworking. Figure 2.13 shows some examples of a few chip packages.

Figure 2.13 Different chip packages (source: Viswesr, 2011. Reproduced under the terms of the Creative Commons Attribution Share-Alike Licence, CC BY-SA 3.0 <https://creativecommons.org/licenses/by-sa/3.0>, via Wikimedia Commons.)

2.3.6 Technology Costs

All of the assumptions expressed thus far imply the implementation technology to be a fixed constant. Needless to say, the technology process used to design a SoC also affects its development and manufacturing costs. The semiconductor foundries or fabrication plants, also known as fabs, represent the industry that realizes the physical chips. Examples of such foundries include TSMC, GlobalFoundries, Samsung, Intel, and ST Microelectronics. Different technologies imply different levels of complexity and different manufacturing costs in consequence.

In the following section, we will explore device scaling to explain the reasons, advantages and disadvantages associated with the scaling of transistor size.

2.4 Scaling: Ideal versus Practical

The term scaling refers to the geometric reduction of the transistor, the small brick comprising the SoC. Since the invention of the MOSFET (metal-oxide semiconductor field-effect transistor) in 1959, the size of transistors has reduced exponentially over time, while the quantity of transistors integrated into a single chip has grown in the opposite direction. This trend that has seen transistor size reduction and integration into semiconductor chips is also referred to as Moore's law. To understand where we are today and where we are going, let us start from the beginning.

2.4.1 Historical Context

In 1947 at Bell laboratories, John Bardeen, Walter Brattain and their supervisor William Shockley built the first functioning point-contact transistor, shown in Figure 2.14: "We have called it the transistor, because it is a resistor or semiconductor device which can amplify electrical signals as they are transferred through it from input to output terminals".

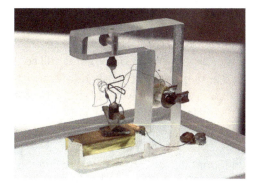

Figure 2.14 First contact transistor (source: Unitronic, 2013. Reproduced under the terms of the Creative Commons Attribution Share-Alike Licence, CC BY-SA 3.0 <https://creativecommons.org/licenses/by-sa/3.0>)

After ten years, Jack Kilby at Texas Instruments realized the first prototype of an integrated circuit, built on top of a germanium slice with gold wires (see Figure 2.15). The invention of the transistor earned Bardeen, Brattain and Shockley the Nobel Prize in Physics in 1956, while Kilby received the Nobel Prize in Physics in 2000 for the invention of the integrated circuit.

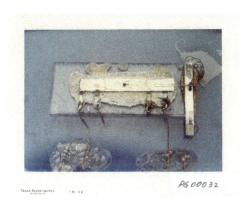

Figure 2.15 First integrated circuit (source: Jack Kilby's Integrated Circuit, 1987.0487.320 Photo: courtesy of National Museum of American History, https://americanhistory.si.edu/collections/search/object/nmah_689592. Reproduced with permission from Texas Instruments.)

Subsequent to the invention of the point contact transistor, Bell Labs developed the bipolar junction transistor (BJT), which was used to build early integrated circuits. However, the electrical characteristics required to make the bipolar transistors work, and the associated power consumption, limited the maximum number of transistors that could be integrated into a single chip. These characteristics made the BJT more suitable to power applications, usually in discrete packages, as opposed to integrated circuits. In the 1960s, MOSFETs appeared on the market, having the main advantage of consuming almost zero control current in a steady state, and greatly enhancing the feasibility and capability of integrating multiple devices in a single chip. In 1963, Frank Wanlass at Fairchild Semiconductor described the first logic gates using MOSFETs. This logic gate was built using nMOS and pMOS transistors, and was given the name complementary metal-oxide semiconductor, or CMOS. The first prototype was not integrated in a single chip but built using discrete components; its ultra-low power consumption compared to bipolar transistors was immediately evident, consuming only nanowatts of power, six orders of magnitude less. Later, with the technological advance of the silicon planar process, integrated circuits built using MOSFETs became even more attractive for their simplicity and low cost. Of course, this was quite a lengthy process; the first commercial CMOS integrated circuits used only pMOS transistors and suffered from poor performance, yield, and reliability. Processors using only nMOS transistors became common in the 1970s. However, while nMOS processors were less expensive, nMOS logic gates still consumed power when idle. This became a major issue in the 1980s as hundreds of thousands of transistors were integrated in a single die. In consequence, CMOS processors were widely adopted and have essentially replaced nMOS and bipolar processors for nearly all digital logic applications.

2.4.2 Moore's Law

In 1965, Gordon Moore, co-founder of Intel, observed that plotting the number of transistors that could be most economically manufactured on a chip over time produced a straight line on a semilogarithmic scale. At the same time, he found transistor count was doubling every 18 months or so. This observation has been called Moore's law and has subsequently become something of a self-fulfilling prophecy. Moore's law is driven primarily by the scaling down of the size of transistors and, to a lesser extent, by building larger chips, as illustrated in Figure 2.16. The integration levels of chips have been classified as small-scale, medium-scale, large-scale, very large-scale and ultra-large-scale. Chips with small-scale integration (SSI), such as the 7404 inverter, have fewer than 10 gates, with roughly half-a-dozen transistors per gate. Medium-scale integration (MSI) chips, such as the 74161 counter, have up to 1,000 gates. Large-scale integration (LSI) chips, such as simple 8-bit microprocessors, have up to 10,000 gates.

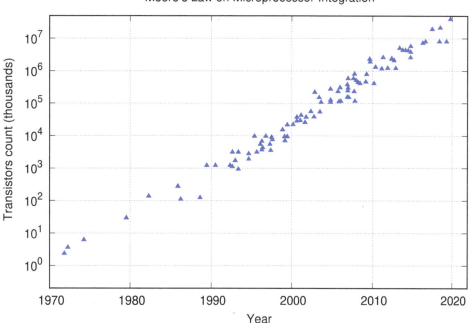

Figure 2.16 Illustration of Moore's law

It soon became apparent that new levels would have to be named every five years if this trend continued and thus the term very large-scale integration (VLSI) is now used to describe most integrated circuits from the 1980s onward. VLSI extends to 100,000 gates, beyond which ULSI is the better term. Current SoCs can edge into the VLSI range.

> "The complexity for minimum component cost has increased at a rate of roughly a factor of two per year. Certainly, over the short term, this rate can be expected to continue, if not to increase. Over the long term, the rate of increase is a bit more uncertain, although there is no reason to believe it will not remain nearly constant for at least 10 years. That means by 1975, the number of components per integrated circuit for minimum cost will be 65,000."

> Gordon Moore [1]

A corollary of Moore's law is Dennard's scaling law: as transistors shrink, they become faster, consume less power, and are cheaper to manufacture. Figure 2.17 shows the associated trend of advancement in CPU design, device integration, power consumption, and performance.

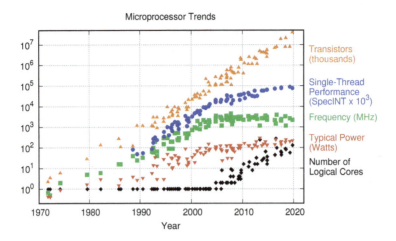

Figure 2.17 Microprocessor Trend. Original data up to the year 2010 collected and plotted by M. Horowitz, F. Labonte, O. Shacham, K. Olukotun, L. Hammond, and C. Batten. New data collected for 2010-2019 by K. Rupp. Reproduced with permission from K. Rupp under the terms of the Creative Commons Attribution 4.0 International Public License, CC BY 4.0, https://creativecommons.org/licenses/by/4.0/.

2.4.3 Technological Limits

Even though an individual CMOS transistor uses very little energy each time it switches, the enormous number of transistors switching at very high rates have once again made power consumption a major design consideration. Moreover, as transistors have become increasingly small, they cease to turn off completely; small amounts of current leaking through each transistor now lead to significant power consumption when multiplied by millions or billions of transistors on a chip. In the CMOS manufacturing process, feature size refers to the minimum dimension of a transistor that can reliably be built. The IEEE's International Roadmap for Devices and Systems (IRDS) introduces a new process generation (also called a technology node) every two to three years with a 30% smaller feature size that allows twice as many transistors to be packed into the same area. Feature sizes are generally specified in microns (10^{-6} m), while feature sizes smaller than 0.18 µm are expressed in nanometers (10^{-9} m). Besides such scaling, the IRDS also defines new types of manufactory processes to improve the yield and performance, while reducing the production cost. A recent process, named SOI (silicon-on-insulator), illustrated in Figure 2.18, and successor to the traditional bulk process, offers several advantages, allowing the reduction of some intrinsic limits such as the latch-up phenomenon, an electrical defect that can damage the device.

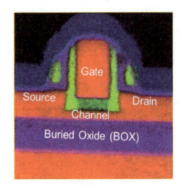

Figure 2.18 Silicon-on-insulator (source: https://www.st.com/content/st_com/en/about/innovation---technology/FD-SOI/learn-more-about-fd-soi.html © STMicroelectronics. Image reproduced with permission of STMicroelectronics.)

These new devices have already been adopted by the industry, and are usually referred to as advanced CMOS technologies. Among these we can find ultra-thin-body fully depleted (UTB FD), and FinFETs, or multi-gate (MG) MOSFET, such as the tri-gate transistor.

Figure 2.19 shows the structure of a FinFET transistor, in which it is possible to observe the 3D structure typical of this device (the 'fins' formed by the source and drain give it its name). The tri-dimensional structure of a FinFET enables more accurate control of the channel current within the same planar area, improving the maximum channel current and reducing leakage. Furthermore, the FinFET structure alleviates the short-channel effects (SCEs) that affect MOSFETs with sub-micron gate lengths, such as threshold voltage roll-off, sub-threshold slope/swing, and drain-induced barrier lowering (DIBL). Given the focus of this book, we have no space for further detail but would redirect the curious reader to an advanced microelectronics book for more information on this topic (see [2]–[5]).

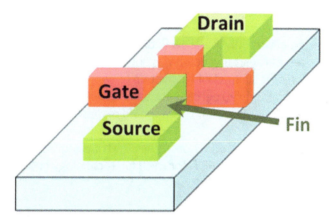

Figure 2.19 FinFet structure (source: Irene Ringworm, 2007. Reproduced under the terms of the Creative Commons Attribution Share-Alike 3.0 licence, CC BY-SA 3.0 <http://creativecommons.org/licenses/by-sa/3.0/>, via Wikimedia Commons)

Although the scaling of CMOS technology seems to have come to an end, advancement development of tri-dimensional structures like silicon nanowires (NW) and gate-all-around (GAA) transistors are still keeping Moore's law alive. Also, the combination of these advanced tri-dimensional structures opens great opportunities for the development of innovative devices. For example, the EPFL's experimental device MG-SiNW FET (multi-gate silicon nanowire FET) offers the capability of changing the MOSFET channel polarity at runtime, making it able to behave as nMOS or pMOS, depending on the bias voltage applied to the polarity gate (PG).

Currently, lithography limits are imposing constraints on the accuracy of device miniaturization. In fact, while technology nodes have always represented the points that mark technology advancement, today they are becoming less and less meaningful as a standalone parameter. In April 2020, the IRDS proposed the introduction of a three-number metric that combines contacted gate pitch (G), metal pitch (M), and the number of layers in a chip (tiers, T), simply GMT, to represent the advancement of technology. Another metric that can be adopted to describe future progress is the LMC, which characterizes the density capability of a chip, in terms of logic (L), memory (M), and interconnects (C).

2.4.4 An Overview of Today's Technology

Having introduced the progress made in chip production from a technology perspective, it is worth looking at what is happening in the industrial world as of today; we will take as reference points three of the principal actors in the marketplace: TSMC, Intel, and Samsung.

TSMC: TSMC's current state-of-the-art process technology is represented by its 5 nm FinFET. Its predecessor, 7 nm or N7, started production in 2017, and customers started using it to make chips in 2018, with more customers and chips coming onboard in 2019. TSMC's second generation of 7 nm technology entered production in 2018, and represented the first industrial adoption of EUV (extremely ultraviolet) process technology. TSMC announced a 5 nm technology node in the second quarter of 2019, which offers even more performance and size reduction. Production of this technology was scheduled for the beginning of 2020. However, this was apparently not the last node achievable with EUV, and TSMC has already scheduled the production of a 3 nm FinFET in its roadmap.

Intel: Intel's first 10 nm product was only made available in June 2019. The company is continuing to develop technology processes for scaling down this node. During an investors' meeting in 2019, it announced a 7 nm node, which it claimed will deliver up to twofold scaling and an increase in performace per watt of approximately 20 percent, for which it will also adopt EUV lithography. Its roadmap also includes the 5 nm and the 3 nm. These should respectively be ready by 2024 and 2027.

Samsung: Samsung is pioneering the introduction of the new transistor structure gate-all-around (GAA) and multi-bridge channel FET (MBCFET) for the 3 nm technology node. For this new node, they foresee the delivery of manufacturing by 2022.

On the Arm website, the page for each Cortex-M processor reports various benchmarks and the area of the IP block depending on the process technology used. Taking the example of the Cortex-M0, which is a small processor with a small number of gates, and using the 40LP (40 nm low-power) process technology, the total area of the block will be just 0.008 mm^2! This technology is relatively old, dating from 2008 if we use TSMC's roadmap as a guide. If we take the example of a more recent core, the Cortex-M33, then, according to the website, using 16FFC (16 nm FinFET compact) process technology means the area can again be just 0.008 mm^2. Even though the Cortex-M33 has many more gates than the Cortex-M0, it is possible to accommodate far more transistors in the same chip area using a more recent technology.

2.4.5 Beyond CMOS

Moore's law has become a self-fulfilling prophecy as every company strives to keep up with its competitors. Obviously, this scaling, known as "More Moore", cannot go on forever because transistors cannot be reduced to sizes smaller than atoms. At some point, a change of paradigm, "More than Moore", will be necessary if the evolution of computation technology is to advance much further. Examples of post-CMOS technology include quantum cellular automata (QCA) and nano-magnetic logic (NML). Some of these are a long way away from industry adoption, but this is not true for all of them. In terms of the exploration of these new technologies, the IRDS plays a reference role for the research and standardization of such new devices.

2.5 Power

The main difference between an embedded SoC and the classical CPU used in laptops and desktop – more than the integration of extra peripherals such as GPIOs, SPIs, and UARTs – is its power consumption. This fundamental factor is often a critical aspect in designing SoCs, given their deployment in low-power embedded applications, often battery-operated. However, power consumption is not easy to estimate at design time. Let us start this section dedicated to power consumption by explaining the most commonly used metrics for it:

- **Delay** (seconds)

  Performance metric, it represents the delay in executing a task caused by the circuit.

- **Energy** (joules)

  Efficiency metric, it describes the effort needed to perform a task.

- **Power** (watts)

  Performance metric, it represents the energy consumed per unit time.

- **Power–Delay Product** (Power × Delay) (joules)

  Measures the efficiency of performing an operation (typically a switching event) in a given technology.

- **Energy–Delay Product** (Power × Delay^2) (joule·seconds)

  A combined performance and energy metric, capturing the trade-off between the two and often used to indicate the merit of a given design.

2.5.1 CMOS Power Consumption

By design, CMOS circuits should not consume power when they are inactive (static). The basic CMOS component is the inverter, which is composed of pMOS and nMOS transistors, connected respectively to V_{dd} and to ground (*Gnd*), as shown in Figure 2.20. As a quick reminder of MOSFET behavior, the nMOS transistor is active when the voltage on the gate is high, while the pMOS transistor is active when the gate voltage is low. Looking at the equivalent representation using a MOSFET, it is easy to see that in the steady state there is no (static) current from V_{dd} to Gnd because the activities of the pMOS and nMOS transistors are mutually exclusive because they are driven by the same voltage.

So from where does the power consumption originate? It derives mainly from the state transitions $0 \rightarrow 1 / 1 \rightarrow 0$, and from second-order effects. There are two types of power consumption source: dynamic and static. While the former is proportional to the switching activity and the frequency of logic operations, the latter is independent of both and is a technology factor. In all cases, in CMOS circuits the contribution of dynamic power is an order of magnitude larger than that of static power.

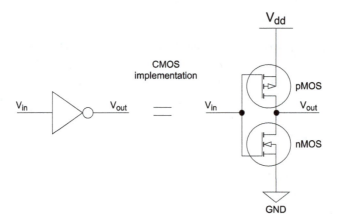

Figure 2.20 CMOS implementation

2.5.1.1 Dynamic Power

To explain dynamic power consumption, it is worth taking as a reference the circuit of a CMOS inverter. Let us analyze what happens during its transition. Imagine a regime in which the input voltage V_{in} is 0 V. In this situation, only the pMOS transistor is active, because on its gate there is 0 V. Now the transition begins, and V_{in} rises from 0 V to 3.3 V, with a slew rate of 1 V/μs. This means that the voltage increase is not instantaneous but takes a few microseconds to reach the upper value.

During this transition, there is a moment in which both MOSFETs are active, creating a current flow between V_{dd} and *Gnd*. This current is called a short-circuit current. The peak of the current is exactly in the middle of the transition, the moment at which both transistors are most active, represented in Figure 2.21. However, the energy dissipated by this current is very low, because of its very short duration. Now let us observe another aspect. It is easy to see that during the commutations from $0 \rightarrow 1$ and from $1 \rightarrow 0$ there is a charge and discharge of the output capacitance C_{load}, as shown in Figure 2.22. This capacitance, termed load capacitance or output capacitance, is the electrical equivalent of the input capacitance of the gate of the MOSFET connected in a cascade.

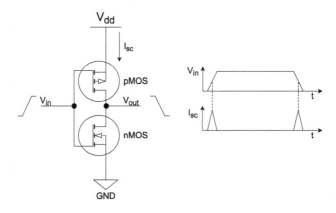

Figure 2.21 Transition in CMOS Inverter

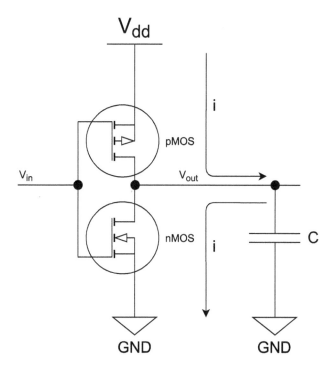

Figure 2.22 Load capacitance effect

The energy-per-transition dissipated from the capacitance is calculated with the following equation:

$$E = \int_0^{V_{dd}} C_{load} \cdot V_{dd} \frac{dV_c}{dt} \, dt = C \cdot V_{dd}^2$$

Hence, the fundamental formula to calculate the dynamic power consumption of the CMOS is:

$$P_{dyn} = f \cdot C \cdot V_{dd}^2$$

To recap, therefore, the factors affecting dynamic power consumption are

▦ supply voltage

▦ switching capacitance

▦ operating frequency.

However, in a CMOS circuit not every clock cycle involves a transition in the logic gate, because sometimes its value can remain stable for multiple cycles. A further parameter is missing from the formula above that can take this aspect into account, termed the:

▦ switching activity factor, α.

We use this parameter to complete the previous formula:

$$P_{dyn} = f \cdot C \cdot V_{dd}^2 \cdot \alpha$$

2.5.1.2 Static Power

We indicated above that dynamic power should be much more significant than static power, which would ideally be equal to zero. From a high-level perspective, static power consumption can be regarded as a technology consideration. In fact, it is widely dependent on the particular technology node in use and the parasitic effect, which are becoming more significant as we migrate to sub-micron devices. Static power consumption is calculated with the following equation:

$$P_{static} = V_{dd} \cdot I_s \, (e^{-\frac{qV_T}{KT}} - 1)$$

where V_{dd} is the operating voltage, I_s is the current, q is the electronic charge (1.6×10^{-19}), K is the Boltzmann constant (1.38×10^{-23}), T is the temperature, and V_T is the diode voltage, dependent on temperature.

For further details of the physical model of current leakage and the parasitic effect, we redirect the reader to advanced microelectronics texts [2]–[5]. However, we would like to mention here some of the factors that affect static power consumption; for example, reverse-biased p-n junction current, sub-threshold leakage, gate-induced drain leakage (GIDL), punch through, and gate tunneling. Another important factor is temperature: in sub-micron technologies, static power consumption can be significantly affected by the temperature.

2.5.1.3 Putting It All Together

In the preceding paragraphs, we have defined where the contributions of static and dynamic power consumption originate. Now, let us try to put all of this together. We have said that dynamic power consumption derives from transitions as a result of two factors: the charging and discharging of output capacitance, and the short-circuit current. We also said that static power consumption derives from leakage and second-order effects.

The overall power consumption of a CMOS circuit can be calculated using the following formula:

$$Power = P_{dyn} + P_{static} = f \cdot C \cdot V_{dd}^2 \cdot \alpha + I_{sc} \cdot f \cdot V_{dd} + I_{leakage} \cdot V_{dd}$$

where:

- f is the operating frequency

- α is the switching activity factor of the circuit

- C is the load capacitance

- V_{dd} is the operating voltage

- I_{sc} is the short-circuit current

- $I_{leakage}$ is the leakage current.

Glitches, which are spurious transitions due to unbalanced propagation delays in combinational components, occur especially in arithmetic operations, such as multiplication. In general, power consumption due to spurious glitches is around 15–20% of the total dynamic power. For instance, the estimated power consumption of a 16 × 16 multiplication is 43 mW, excluding glitches. Including the glitches in the total count as transitions, power consumption rises to 1138 mW. This is one of the reasons why eliminating glitches is one of the key methods in reducing power consumption.

2.5.1.4 Relationship between Power and Delay

From the mathematical equation above, we can see that the relationship between the supply voltage and dynamic power consumption is a quadratic one, thanks to the V_{dd}^2 factor in the equation. Nevertheless, in some conditions, the propagation delay can increase if the supply voltage goes down, due to the threshold voltage level of the MOSFET, the time required to charge and discharge the output capacitance, and other second-order effects, constraining the maximum operation frequency of the circuit. In this book, we will not go into the physical details to explain this relationship, but we would like to make the reader aware of this. For this reason, the energy–delay product often represents a more useful performance metric than the power–delay product.

2.5.2 Power Consumption Estimation

Power consumption estimation is one of the most difficult and time-consuming activities in the SoC design flow. Obtaining power consumption estimates that reflect practical reality requires very accurate simulation of the final circuit implementation, taking into account all of the parameters involved, including the technology used, capacitance and temperature. These aspects mean that power estimators cannot be simple digital simulators, because they have to take into account many physical parameters beyond the functional behavior alone. To recap, power consumption estimation involves the correlation of switching activity, switching capacitance, operation frequency, and power supply.

So how do we estimate power consumption? There are two possible approaches: a simulation-based approach and a probabilistic approach, the first based on simulation of the circuit, the second achieved through mathematical analysis of the circuit. Simulation-based methods, also called dynamic methods, can provide better results in terms of accuracy, assuming the estimation is done using accurate models and accurate simulations (e.g. using SPICE simulation engines). On the other hand, they are very time-consuming and require complete information about the input pattern. Probabilistic methods, also termed static methods, are simpler and faster in execution, only requiring information about the probability of the input pattern, but with a reduction in accuracy. Figure 2.23 shows the two different flows involved in these two estimation approaches.

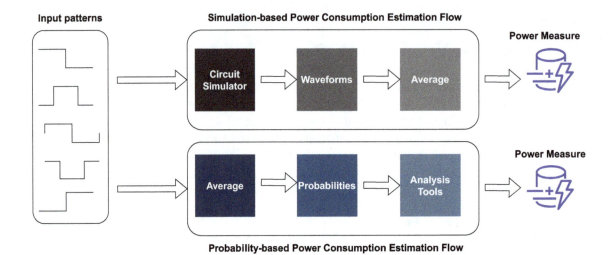

Figure 2.23 Power consumption estimation methods

2.6 Power/Performance/Area Trade-offs

One of the big trade-offs in designing digital circuits is in the relationships between power, performance and area, commonly referred to by the acronym PPA (power, performance, area). In the previous section, we introduced power consumption and its relationships to the operating frequency and switching activity of the circuit. Now, let us try to understand the reasons why these three PPA elements are related and why they represent a design trade-off, as captured in Figure 2.24.

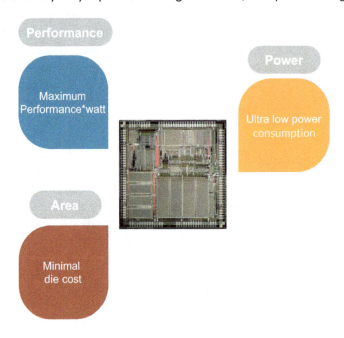

Figure 2.24 Power, performance and area trade-offs

When designing a digital circuit capable of executing a given mathematical function, the designer has plenty of flexibility when it comes to implementing this operation in hardware. All of the associated decisions can be made a function of the performance requirement(s). For example, designing for the highest possible throughput might mean that the circuit should be able to produce one output each clock cycle. Therefore, to execute this function and be able to compute a result every clock cycle requires that all of the necessary operations be completed in one clock cycle. On the other hand, if this level of throughput is not needed, the component can easily be shared to perform the same operation in two different moments in time, a technique known as "resource sharing".

Thus far, we can readily conclude that the relationship between PERFORMANCE and AREA is inversely proportional: more resources involve more (chip) area but confer higher throughput; fewer resources mean less area and a lower throughput. But what about POWER? Well, as the reader can deduce from both the preceding example and the previous section, POWER consumption is directly proportional to the PERFORMANCE, due to the volume of transistor switching that simultaneously increases power consumption too. However, we will see in due course that this relationship does not always hold true. Below we will introduce some basic techniques to optimize a SoC in order to meet the design needs, starting from some practical intuitions. After each technique, we will summarize the advantages and disadvantages that derive from the adoption of the optimization.

2.6.1 Optimizing Performance

SoC performance optimization might appear easy at first glance if the designer has infinite resources available to them. However, in the real world resources are limited and the SoC designer must try to achieve the best performance with the resources available for a given application. Recall the relationship between the die area and chip costs introduced in the previous sections. As an example, imagine designing a circuit to address the following equation:

$$y = (a * b) + (c * d) + e$$

This function consists of two multiplications and two additions. Depending on design constraints, these two operations can either be executed using two homogeneous arithmetic components Mul1, Mul2 and Add1, Add2, or the two multiplications can be executed by the same execution unit Mul1, and the additions by Add1. These can be regarded as the hardware resources needed for this function.

2.6.1.1 Parallelization

In general, parallel processing is the main approach to speeding up performance in hardware execution. Parallelization consists of replicating the same hardware unit multiple times. Using this technique, multiple outputs can be computed in parallel within the same clock period, reducing the overall execution time and achieving maximum throughput. In this case, the effective throughput is increased by the level of parallelism. We will see later how parallelization techniques can also be used to reduce power consumption by introducing more complex clock-management circuitry. A parallelized version of our circuit is represented in Figure 2.25. Because the operations performed by the multiplier and the adder are independent of each other, they can be parallelized by increasing the number of execution units from one to two.

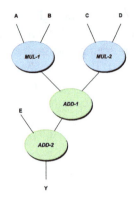

Figure 2.25 Fully parallelized circuit

Advantages:

▪ maximizes throughput.

Disadvantages:

▪ area increases.

2.6.1.2 Pipelining

Another commonly used technique to increase performance is called pipelining. The timing theory and the benefits deriving from the adoption of pipelining have already been explained in Section 2.2. Here, we focus only on one specific use case. Pipelining involves adding flip-flop registers, also called pipe registers, in between functional units of the circuit. In this technique, the scope of the pipelining is to reduce the critical path by introducing registers along its length. This allows the maximum clock frequency of the circuit to be increased, enabling higher performance. However, the addition of pipe registers introduces an overhead in clock-cycle latency, which can affect the total execution time. Figure 2.26 represents the pipelined version of our circuit.

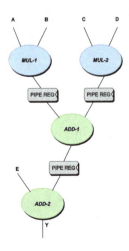

Figure 2.26 Pipelined circuit

Advantages:

▤ allows the operation frequency to be increased.

Disadvantages:

▤ increases latency (clock cycles).

2.6.2 Optimizing Chip Area

Area optimization implies the execution of the same computation using the minimum number of resources but, given a fixed technology, it is not always straightforward to optimize a design for area without affecting the timing and lowering throughput. While a designer might speed up a circuit by adding computational resources, in this case we are seeking to minimize them. As previously indicated, the principal technique used for optimizing a design in terms of area is resource sharing, which means sharing the same component for use at different moments of time. Figure 2.27 represents the application of the resource-sharing technique to our circuit.

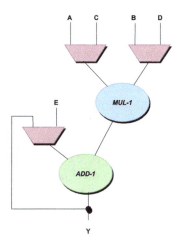

Figure 2.27 Shared circuit operation

In practice, sharing a resource is not as simple as shown here. It implies the addition of some extra logic to control the operations and fetch back the results. Indeed, scheduling operations can become very difficult for some complex circuits.

Advantages:

▤ reduces overall area.

Disadvantages:

▤ limits throughput

▤ needs control/arbitration circuitry.

2.6.3 Optimizing Power Consumption

Over the years, power consumption optimization has almost become a discipline and research topic in its own right. Multiple techniques and methods, some of them highly advanced, have been developed to both predict and reduce power consumption in CMOS devices [6]. In this book we introduce some techniques to reduce dynamic power consumption, having explained previously that static power consumption can be regarded as a technological factor, rather then being fixed by design. Thus, let us recall the dynamic power consumption equation, in which we can see the elements affecting it:

$$P_{dyn} = f \cdot C \cdot V_{dd}^2 \cdot \alpha$$

Given this equation, where can the SoC designer take action to reduce dynamic power consumption without affecting performance?

2.6.3.1 Clock Gating

At first glance, the first intervention the designer can make to reduce power consumption is to reduce clock frequency. However, this will slow down the circuit. The same goes for the supply voltage: we have already described the relationship between voltage and delay in which the delay can increase if the voltage drops. The power consumption derives from the transition between states, which is represented by the switching activity factor, α. Each non-necessary transition avoided can be a potential energy saving. How can unnecessary transitions be reduced inside a SoC? The most widely used technique is called "clock gating" (CG), which consists of masking the clock gate using a logic gate in order to block the propagation of the clock signal into the unused circuits. Adopting this technique allows the clock and all the transitions inside a circuit to be halted, dynamically and for a specific amount of time, eliminating their dynamic power consumption contribution. If used well, clock gating facilitates a significant reduction in the dynamic power consumption of the whole chip. Figure 2.28 illustrates the working principle of clock gating, although it does not represent an appropriate implementation of it.

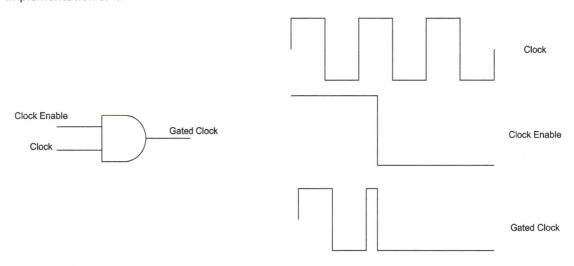

Figure 2.28 Working principle of clock gating (not an appropriate implementation!)

However, the benefits of clock gating don't come without costs. The introduction of a combinational logic in the clock path introduces skew and other timing problems, which can affect the timing integrity of the system. For this reason, special blocks have to be used when the clock-gating technique is applied. These special blocks include a sequential element beyond the logic gate, making the circuit synchronous. An appropriate clock-gating cell is shown in Figure 2.29. Moreover, if clock gating is to be applied to other IP blocks too, each should have its own enable signal and dedicated clock-gating cell, as illustrated in Figure 2.30.

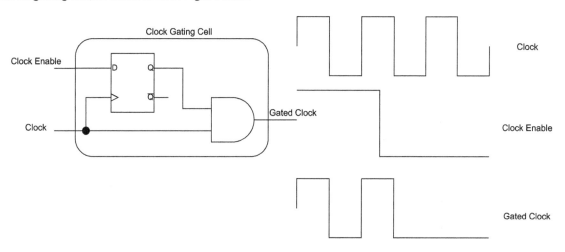

Figure 2.29 Clock-gating cell

Advantages:

- significantly reduces power consumption.

Disadvantages:

- requires extra logic

- adds skew to the clock signal.

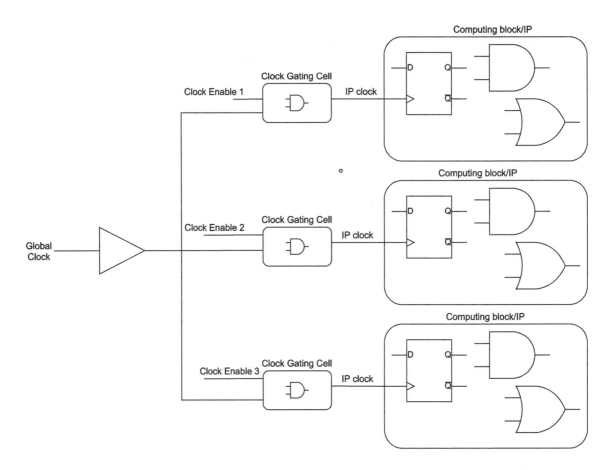

Figure 2.30 Distributed clock gating

2.6.3.2 Pipelining for Low Power

Several other techniques can be applied at the RTL with the aim of reducing unnecessary transitions. For example, adding pipe registers reduces the risk of glitches occurring, and consequently reduces unnecessary transitions. The technique is known as "glitch removal". Furthermore, pipelining can be used more directly to reduce power consumption. Thus, adding pipe registers shortens the critical path, which means increasing the clock slack, which is the time remaining before a timing violation would occur. More slack allows the voltage of the circuit to be reduced, in turn reducing power consumption: in this case, pipelining helps not by reducing switching activity but by reducing the supply voltage.

2.6.3.3 Parallelization for Low Power

The parallelization technique described above to increase performance can also be applied for reducing power consumption. In this case, the parallelized resources can effectively be run at a lower clock frequency without affecting the throughput. For example, parallelizing by a factor of two allows the clock frequency to be reduced by the same factor. However, the load capacitance will increase by the same factor too, nullifying the effect of frequency reduction. Thus, the real contribution to power reduction derives from a reduction in the supply voltage. Assuming all previous considerations remain valid, if the supply voltage reduces in this way the user can achieve a power lowering of up to 15%.

2.6.3.4 Optimization at FSM Level

At finite state machine (FSM) level, there are a number of different elements that can affect power consumption; for example, the state encoding. Binary coding consumes more energy than one-hot encoding, which consumes more than Gray (reflected binary) coding where there is only one bit changing state. Moreover, the state assignment should be done with the goal of minimizing the Hamming distance, which represents the number of bits that change per transition. Another thing that can be optimized at FSM level are the "don't care" conditions in the Karnaugh map, leaving a previous state unaltered if it avoids a pointless transition.

2.6.3.5 Other Optimizations

All of the optimizations described thus far have to be applied at design time. There are also advanced techniques that can reduce power consumption at runtime. Dynamic voltage and frequency scaling (DVFS), for example, consists of changing the operating voltage and frequency, lowering the power consumption when high performance is not needed. However, this technique also has consequences at design time, increasing the complexity because the designer should analyze all of the effects that this might have on the timing within the circuit. In fact, advanced techniques such as DVFS make circuits extremely sensitive to metastability, due to the fact that changing the voltage changes the internal thresholds of transistors for commuting states. For a detailed explanation we direct the reader to a more advanced text [6].

2.7 Reliability

2.7.1 Reliability Basics

What does the use of the term reliability mean in the context of SoC? In basic terms, reliability refers to the resistance of a device to failure. However, in this context, the real question concerns how a device can fail in the execution of operations. To address this question, let us introduce the topic by first defining some terminology: that is, failure, error, logical fault and physical fault. Thus, **failure** is a deviation from a design specification. The source of a failure can be generic, from an impromptu physical phenomenon to a design bug. An error is triggered by a failure that results in an incorrect signal value. A **logical fault** is an error that manifests itself as an incorrect logical result, while a **physical fault** is a failure caused by an aspect of the environment, such as aging, radiation, temperature or temperature cycling. In the following section we will discuss why it is important to evaluate this aspect at design time, depending on the final target application.

2.7.2 Critical Applications

Nowadays, processors and SoCs are everywhere, from smartphones and washing machines, to cars, trains and aircraft (see Figure 2.31). By definition, the required levels of reliability will be different in a smartphone and an aircraft.

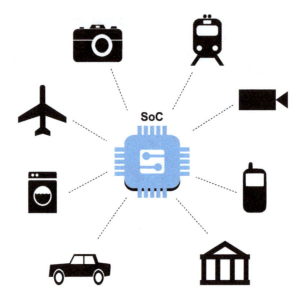

Figure 2.31 SoC-based devices

Where is the boundary between a critical application and a non-critical one? What differentiates a critical system is that its failure can have serious consequences, such as human injury or death, financial loss or environmental damage. Three different categories are commonly defined: safety-critical, mission-critical and financial-critical. The meaning of these categories is implicit within their titles. Examples of safety-critical devices are automotive, aerospace and medical equipment. Examples of mission-critical applications are sea and space exploration machines, while the simplest example of a financial-critical system is the IT system of a bank. In this book, we seek to help the reader understand what factors must be considered and what techniques can be applied when designing a SoC to make it suitable for a critical application.

2.7.3 Sources of Failure and Reliability Factors

The factors involved in the reliability of systems are distributed between the hardware and the software, from the most basic transistor at the technology level up to the operating system and the programmed code. However, in this chapter, we focus attention on the hardware components that affect reliability, particularly at CPU level. In this context, the main factors that affect reliability are technology process (i.e. transistor size), die area, and clock frequency. To explain further, smaller transistors are more susceptible to radiation effects, because the electrical charge required to modify the state of a transistor is smaller too. On the other hand, big and complex circuits involve more transistors switching at the same time, which increases the statistical probability of a fault. Finally, the contribution of operating frequency is crucial: increasing clock frequency makes digital circuits more subject to metastability and thus to fault.

2.7.4 Techniques and Applications

So how can we improve reliability when designing a SoC? Fault-avoidance techniques can be applied at different levels: in software, in hardware, in memory. Not all failures or errors produce faults and, indeed, not all faults result in incorrect program execution. If a fault is detected quickly enough it can be recovered from. How can a fault be recognized during execution? Below, we will describe some techniques that can be used to recognize and recover from such faults; for example, using redundant instructions or triple modular redundancy (TMR) can enable recovery via error-correcting codes, program rollback or functional reconfiguration. At the CPU level, the most commonly used techniques are lockstep, split-lock and redundant execution.

2.7.4.1 Lockstep

Lockstep is a technique used to detect and recover from soft errors in CPUs. The basic principle of lockstep is the parallel execution of the same instruction on two different cores, in which a monitoring system detects any execution mismatches by checking the memory. If the monitor detects a mismatch, it raises an error, triggering a recovery procedure called rollback. Figure 2.32 illustrates the working principle of lockstep.

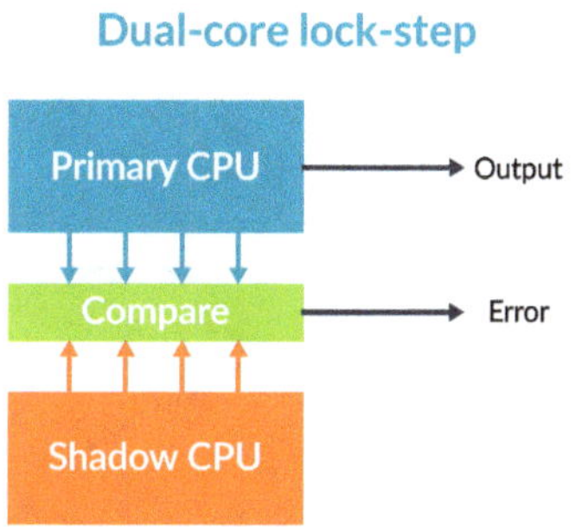

Dual-core lock-step

Primary CPU → Output

Compare → Error

Shadow CPU

Figure 2.32 Dual-core lockstep principle (source: Reproduced with permission from Arm Ltd)

2.7.4.2 Redundant Execution

In redundant execution, two copies of the application are run in parallel and a third, independent processor (a "safety island") compares the results. The main difference between this and the lockstep approach is the instruction-level accuracy. While lockstep requires a monitor to check the results cycle by cycle, in redundant execution the processors are not monitored step by step. This approach increases the degree of freedom for the development and also opens the system up to virtualization, as shown in Figure 2.33. However, it does increase the complexity of the overall system.

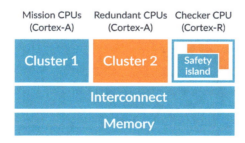

Figure 2.33 Redundant execution (source: Reproduced with permission from Arm Ltd)

2.7.4.3 Split-lock

Split-lock represents a trade-off of the two preceding techniques, adding in the flexibility missing from classic lockstep systems. Depending on the criticality of the application, a system can be configured either in split-mode, in which the CPUs are running independently and executing different tasks, or in lock-mode, in which the CPUs are executing the instructions in full lockstep; it also offers the potential for operation to continue (albeit in a degraded mode) in the event of one CPU failing.

2.7.5 Certification

In order to guarantee the level of safety in critical systems, a set of standards have been developed by international organizations. As mentioned earlier in the chapter, depending on the level of criticality of the system the requirements can be different. For this reason, there exist different certifications, typically organized by field of application. The list of such certifications is very long. Some examples include MIL-STD-882E (military), DO-254 (aviation), IEC 62304 (medical), and ISO 26262 (automotive), as shown in Figure 2.34. These certifications are undertaken by accredited certification bodies, sometimes referred to with the acronym CB. Typically, these CBs are overseen by an accreditation body (AB), usually one per country. An example is the American National Standards Institute (ANSI), the accreditation body for the United States.

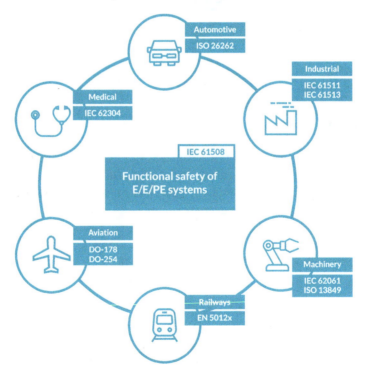

Figure 2.34 Certification standards for electrical/electronic/programmable electronic (E/E/PE) systems (source: Reproduced with permission from Arm Ltd)

2.7.5.1 Arm Safety Ready Portfolio

Arm's Safety Ready portfolio is a collection of products developed with expedited certification in view. It includes IP, tools, and methodologies to help users in the certification of their final products. Details of these products can be found within Arm's online resources at www.arm.com.

The list of currently available products forming this portfolio includes the following Cortex-M-class devices:

▤ Cortex-M0+ + Software Test Library

▤ Cortex-M3 + Software Test Library

▤ Cortex-M4 + Software Test Library

▤ Cortex-M7

▤ Cortex-M23

▤ Cortex-M33.

2.7.6 Reliable SoC Example: ARM Cortex-R5

The Cortex-R5 processor is a mid-range CPU for use in deeply-embedded, real-time systems. It implements the ARMv7-R architecture, and includes Thumb-2 technology for optimum code density and processing throughput. The pipeline has a single ALU but implements limited dual-issuing of instructions for efficient utilization of other resources such as the register file. A hardware Accelerator Coherency Port (ACP) is provided to reduce the requirement for slow software cache maintenance operations when sharing memory with other requestors. Interrupt latency is kept low by interrupting and restarting multiple load-store instructions, and by use of a dedicated peripheral port that enables low-latency access to an interrupt controller. The processor has tightly-coupled memory (TCM) ports for low-latency and deterministic accesses to local RAM, in addition to caches for higher-performance access to general memory. Error-checking and correction (ECC) is used on the Cortex-R5 processor ports and in Level 1 (L1) memories to provide improved reliability and address safety-critical applications. Many of these features, including the caches, TCM ports, and ECC, are configurable so that a given processor implementation can be tailored to the application for efficient area usage. Figure 2.35 shows the internal blocks of the ARM Cortex-R5. More detailed information can be found in the Cortex-R5 Technical Reference Manual (available at [7]).

Figure 2.35 Arm Cortex-R5 internal blocks (source: Reproduced with permission from Arm Ltd)

Figure 2.36 illustrates the triple-core lockstep (TCLS) implementation of the Cortex-R5. Three cores share both data and instruction cache, and the blocks that make up the TCLS Assist Unit are also shown: resynchronization logic, error detection logic, and majority voter.

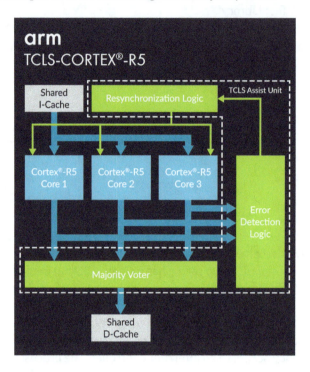

Figure 2.36 Triple-core lockstep (TCLS) implementation in Arm Cortex-R5 (source: Reproduced with permission from Arm Ltd)

2.8 Configurability

Looking at some of the latest devices in the embedded world, we can see that a new kind of system application has started to become prevalent. These applications monitor sensors and perform some processing of the data collected, sometimes using artificial intelligence. In addition, more chips are being designed to handle cellular data, which requires more computing power and energy. Technology evolves and so do the applications that use it. If we take the example of a simple washing machine; in the past, it only had three or four programs and the microcontroller used was fairly simple. Today, it usually has an LCD screen, may be connectable to Wi-Fi, and probably has some storage dedicated to storing new programs. It may even be firmware-upgradable.

Configurability of a chip can happen at multiple levels. One basic approach is to use an FPGA that is connected to an interconnect. Depending on the application, an FPGA may be reprogrammed in order to assist the processor. Another way to configure a chip is at design time, with IP blocks being configured according to the application. For example, a processor can be configured to have more functionality and thus to support a wider range of instructions. IP blocks can also be configured through software, not only to enable or disable them, but also to adjust their behavior. In this section, we explain the concepts behind chip configurability.

2.8.1 Configuration through FPGA

While it is possible to allow software within a system to evolve over time, it is not possible to update the hardware inside a chip without remanufacturing it. However, hardware components such as FPGAs are reprogrammable through software. Of course, they have a limited number of cells that can be used and not all functional designs can be accommodated. In addition, FPGAs are slower, bigger, and consume more power than a classic accelerator. This is mostly because they can be reprogrammed and require more hardware to support this functionality. Despite such drawbacks, they are still commonly used to allow programmers to deploy applications that can evolve over time.

In some cases, an FPGA alone is used, and connected through peripherals. The FPGA is programmed to run a synthesized SoC composed of a soft-core processor (for example, the Nios II from Altera, or the MicroBlaze from Xilinx) and peripherals connected through a bus. This will constitute a full-blown SoC as defined at the start of this chapter, but it will be running on an FPGA. This means that the entire system can be reprogrammed and updated, making it far more flexible than a hard-core SoC implementation.

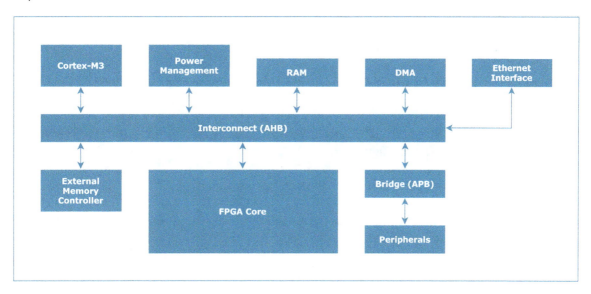

Figure 2.37 Example of a SoC with FPGA core

In other cases, the FPGA is connected to a classic processor core such as a Cortex-M and is used as an accelerator to off-load the processor. This is the case for the SmartFusion SoC FPGA from Microsemi. A Cortex-M3 core is connected to an FPGA in a similar chip configuration to that illustrated in Figure 2.37. All the other components are fixed (e.g. RAM, DMA) and only the FPGA can be reprogrammed. This chip can be found in Microsemi's SmartFusion evaluation kit (A2F-EVAL-KIT-2), which can have different peripherals and in which the FPGA has access to components such as buttons, LEDs, I²C, and an Ethernet port. The FPGA can be reprogrammed depending on the application that will run on the system. For example, it could be used to control the LEDs and the buttons or to filter the packets received from the Ethernet connector.

2.8.2 Hardware Configuration through Software

Most IP blocks are usually made as generic as possible so that they can operate in different modes. For example, a Direct Memory Access (DMA) controller will have to be configured before use to establish the source and destination addresses and the number of bytes to move. Similarly, it should be possible to configure the direction (either input, output or both) and to enable or disable interrupts for each of the ports in a GPIO controller. This is done through the programming interface of the IP block and many other things can be configured:

- interrupts can be enabled or disabled for specific peripherals

- caches can be disabled (or enabled)

- clock sources for peripherals and the processor can be configured

- SPI communication can be made half- or full-duplex

- UARTs can be configured for setting up baud rate, word length, etc.

- memory regions can be configured in the Memory Protection Unit.

As a more specific example, for a Real-time clock (RTC) component we might have the following registers:

- RTC_VALUE to set the time of the RTC: once the clock is started, reading this register will give the number of seconds since last configuration

- RTC_ALARM to set a time value that might generate an interrupt if the RTC_VALUE reaches it

- RTC_CTRL to enable or disable the clock and to enable or disable the interrupt when the time set in the RTC_ALARM register is reached.

These registers will have to be configured in the software in order to achieve the desired behavior when an application is running.

A chip can be designed to be more flexible in order to be used for more applications. This may mean that it can accommodate additional hardware in support of other system functions. For example, more I^2C or SPI interfaces might be added to enable more sensors to be connected to the chip. A SoC can be designed to have extra components such as a second processor, accelerators, and various peripheral controllers that will not be used by all of the applications that might be run on it. When these components are not needed, they can be disabled through a control register. The benefit is that a single SoC can be used for multiple different applications:

- Application A has to connect three sensors that are interfaced using I^2C and needs a UART for serial communication.

▪ Application B has to connect to a flash memory using SPI and has one sensor needing I²C.

▪ Application C needs four GPIOs for use as analog inputs for an ADC component and UART.

Because I²C needs two signals, a UART needs two signals and SPI needs four signals, a SoC could be designed to implement the layout shown in Figure 2.38, in which GPIOs can be configured according to the functionality needed by the application. This configuration, in which a pin can have multiple alternative functionalities, is known as GPIO multiplexing.

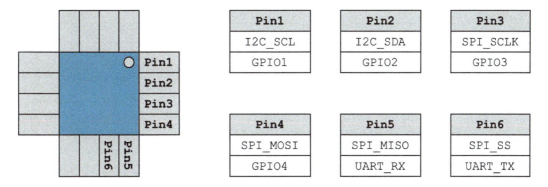

Figure 2.38 Example of GPIO multiplexing

However, if a GPIO is exposed to too many peripherals, conflicts may occur. As an example, consider the STM32F722IC chip from ST Microelectronics that can have up to three I²Cs, five SPIs, eight UARTs and three ADCs with 15 channels. All of the associated controllers will export signals through pins that will be connected to peripherals. In this case, and in most cases, the number of pins exposed for the chip is not sufficient for all of the peripherals to be enabled at the same time. This means that some GPIO pins can have multiple purposes, and sometimes two different GPIO pins might be configured for the same functionality.

Thus, in the ST SoC referred to above, the $UART_1$ receive signal (RX) can be connected to either PB7 or PA10. However, PB7 can also be configured as an SDA signal for I^2C_1 or even be used as an input/output pin. PA10 can also be used as a USB pin. If neither PB7 nor PA10 are available, because they are in use for another function, then $UART_1$ cannot be configured, because its RX signal is essential.

Note, however, that in some cases all of the peripherals can be instantiated on any of the GPIO pins of the chip; for example, the Nordic nRF9160 chip allows the programmer to decide on the GPIO pins to be associated with each peripheral without any conflicts.

2.8.3 IP Block Configuration during Chip Design
Another way to view configurability is to look at the different options available for a specific IP block. Looking at the Cortex-M family (see Table 2.3), we can see that different components can be added depending on the specific processor, with some having more features available at design time than others.

Table 2.3 Component options for Cortex-M processors

Cortex processor	M0	M0+	M1	M3	M4	M7	M23	M33	M35P
Bit-band memory	No	No	No	Optional	Optional	Optional	No	No	No
MPU	No	Optional	No	Optional	Optional	Optional	Optional	Optional	Optional
Security	No	No	No	No	No	No	Optional	Optional	Optional
Instruction cache	No	No	No	No	No	Optional	No	No	Optional
Data cache	No	No	No	No	No	Optional	No	No	No
Floating-point	No	No	No	No	Optional	Optional	No	Optional	Optional
Hardware divider	No	No	No	Yes	Yes	Yes	Yes	Yes	Yes
Configurable instructions	No	No	No	No	No	No	Yes	Yes	Yes

Let's assume the Cortex M7 is to be used in a system. The processor does not have an MPU and floating-point unit and these features are now needed for more advanced applications, so are added in. While the power consumption and size of the Cortex-M7 will increase in consequence, the design of the system will remain the same.

By applying the same idea to configurable instructions, it is possible for a chip designer to enable additional instructions to be accelerated within the Cortex-M (only for the v8M architecture). These instructions can be programmed and grouped with the aim of reducing program size and increasing performance. Figure 2.39 illustrates the creation of a new instruction that regroups multiple single instructions. The instruction simply checks whether a given register value contains a power of two. The assembly instruction behavior is translated into hardware logic using a register transfer language (RTL). Such custom instructions can then be used like normal instructions, but will be executable within one pipeline cycle. Typically, such instructions might be bit-field manipulations or comparisons.

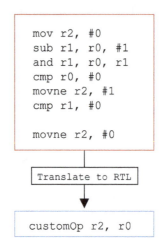

Figure 2.39 Example of a configurable instruction (checks whether a given register contains a power of two)

All of these configurations can only happen during the design phase; otherwise, the chip will have to be remanufactured.

References

[1] G. E. Moore, "Cramming more components onto integrated circuits," *Electronics*, vol. 38, no. 8, Apr., 1965.

[2] J. E. Ayers, *Digital Integrated Circuits: Analysis and Design*, CRC Press, 2010.

[3] J. M. Rabaey, A. Chandrakasan, and B. Nikolic, *Digital Integrated Circuits*, Pearson, 2003.

[4] W.-K. Chen, Ed., *The VLSI Handbook*, 2006.

[5] N. Weste and D. Harris, *CMOS VLSI Design: A Circuits and Systems Perspective*.

[6] J. Rabaey, *Low Power Design Essentials, Springer*.

[7] developer.arm.com

Chapter 3

The Arm Cortex-M
Processor Architecture

This chapter focuses on the specifics of the Cortex-M processor family. The architectures are explained, including the instruction sets for the different variants, together with the programmer's model (in essence, the registers) and the memory model, and then considers how these are manipulated. The chapter goes on to look at exceptions and interrupts and their handling mechanisms, before considering the software (CMSIS) that is required and available to drive all of this. We follow this up with an account of two of the options that are most commonly seen on the Cortex-M – the memory protection unit (introduced in Chapter 1) and the TrustZone security extension – before concluding the chapter with a case study that looks at how all of this is implemented on a real-life SoC. In the course of the chapter, we will seek to answer the following questions, among others:

1. *How have the Arm processor families evolved over time?*

2. *What is the intended purpose of the Cortex-M family as a whole?*

3. *What are the main similarities and principal differences within the Cortex-M family?*

4. *What are the different flavors of the Cortex-M and when did they appear?*

5. *What are the different flavors of the Cortex-M used for?*

6. *What is delivered in a Cortex-M processor?*

7. *What architecture is associated with the various Cortex-M flavors?*

8. *What is an Instruction Set Architecture and does it differ between families?*

9. *What instructions are supported by the various Cortex-M flavors?*

10. *How are the 16-bit instructions of Thumb encoded?*

11. *How is memory characterized?*

12. *Why is it necessary to have different types and attributes for memory?*

13. *What is a memory model for a processor?*

14. *How is a Cortex-M processor initialized?*

15. *How is the required software code placed in memory?*

16. *What is necessary to boot a Cortex-M system?*

17. *Why is it useful to have a shared, common software base?*

18. *Why is memory management necessary?*

19. *What is a Memory Protection Unit (MPU)?*

20. *What are memory regions?*

21. *What happens if two memory regions overlap?*

22. *How is an MPU configured?*

23. *What mechanisms are needed to make a system more resilient to attack?*

24. *What is TrustZone and how can it be configured?*

25. *How do you secure an application?*

26. *In a TrustZone-enabled Cortex-M, how does the software support the hardware?*

27. *How do you exchange data with a board?*

28. *How do you process and store this data?*

29. *Which RTOSs are supported for a board?*

30. *Where can I find the tools necessary to program a board?*

3.1 Processor Architecture: Functional versus Architectural View

3.1.1 Arm Families: A Bit of History

The Arm story started in 1985 when Acorn Computers sought to make a follow-up to its very successful BBC Micro home computer and decided to make its own RISC-based processor, launched in 1987, which became known as the Acorn RISC Machine (ARM), used 3 μm technology and had a frequency of 6 MHz. In 1990, Acorn Computers established a joint venture called ARM Holdings with Apple Computer and VLSI Technology to make a chip for Apple's first handheld computer (the Newton), and in 1994, Texas Instruments realized the first ARM7 device, used in the Nokia 6110 GSM phone, and the beginning of 165 licenses and 10 billion chips. Arm-based chips were subsequently used as the basis for Apple's iPod, iPhone and iPad and at time of writing, more than 160 billion Arm-based chips have been sold worldwide.

The Cortex-M, -A and -R processor families followed and introduced a new class of performance and applications, and 2020 brought the next-generation Cortex-X1 architecture, offering more powerful computing to customers, and more processor customization via the new Arm-v8.2 architecture. This is targeted at the ever-evolving smartphone market and uses the new 5 nm process technology and a clock frequency of 3 GHz, quite something in comparison to the original 3 μm and 6 MHz of 1985!

Table 3.1 provides a rough indication of how the Arm architectures and processors have evolved over time; it can be seen that the two do not shadow one another directly.

Table 3.1 Evolution of Arm architectures

Arch. Name	Processor / Core	Date	Notes
ARMv1	Arm1	1985	First Arm prototype
ARMv2	Arm2	1986	Coprocessor introduction
			3-level pipeline, 24-bit addressing (16 registers of 32 bits, thus 64 MiB addressable)
ARMv2a	Arm3 Arm250	1989	Cache added
ARMv3	Arm6, Arm7	1991–1994	MMU added 32-bit addressing T - Thumb state M - long multiply support Interface FPU, 4K cache
ARMv4	StrongArm Arm7TDMI Arm8 Arm8TDMI	1993 →	T - Thumb
ARMv5	Arm7EJ, Arm9E, Arm10E, Arm1020, XScale, FA626TE, Feroceon, PJ1/Mohawk	1998 →	E - Enhanced DSP instructions, saturated arithmetic J - support for Jazelle, java byte code execution acceleration
ARMv6	Arm11	2002 →	Include T, E and J extensions MMU Multiprocessor facilities Support for 64-bit buses Mixed-endian support
ARMv6-M	Cortex-M M0, M0+, M1	2007	**Introduction of low-end product to Cortex-M family;** lowest power consumption
ARMv7-A	Cortex-A A5, A7, A8, A9 MPCore, -A5, A7, A12, A15	2005 →	**Start of Cortex-A family** Multicore Arm & Thumb instructions Virtual address support Thumb-2
ARMv7-R	Cortex-R R4, R5, R7	2011	**Start of Cortex-R family** Arm & Thumb instructions Physical address only
ARMv7-M	Cortex-M M3	2004	**Start of Cortex-M family** Thumb instruction set only
ARMv7E-M	Cortex-M M4, M7	2010 →	Enhanced DSP instructions, saturated arithmetic

Arch. Name	Processor / Core	Date	Notes
ARMv8-A ARMv8.0-A	Cortex-A A32, A35 A53, A57, A72, A73 Apple	2011–2019	32-bit architecture 64-bit architecture Multicore
ARMv8-R	Cortex-R R52, R53, R82	2016 →	AArch64
ARMv8-M Baseline	Cortex-M M23	2016	TrustZone on Cortex-M
ARMv8-M Mainline	Cortex-M M33, M35P	2016 →	TrustZone on Cortex-M FPU Coprocessor
ARMv8.1-A	Qualcomm/Cavium	2017 →	AArch64
ARMv8.1-M	Cortex-M M55	2020	New capabilities for AI (Artificial Intelligence) Helium instructions
ARMv8.2-A	Cortex-A A55, A65, A75, A76, A77, A78 Qualcomm/Samsung/ Fujitsu/HiSilicon/Apple	2017 →	AArch64
ARMv8.2-A	Cortex-X1	2020	Processor customization
ARMv8.3-A	Apple	2017 →	AArch64
ARMv8.4-A	Apple	2019 →	AArch64

With simple processors, such as 8-bit and 16-bit microcontrollers, knowing the detail of the architecture is important for the programmer. A lot of applications have been designed in assembly language, even for 32-bit processors. The Cortex-M0 and -M0+ can be managed at this level. However, for higher levels of complexity a more efficient programming language, such as C, and some form of operating system are advisable. Thus, although it is perfectly feasible to program the Cortex-M family in C either without an operating system (bare-metal) or with an RTOS kernel, the Cortex-A family almost always uses an operating system such as Linux, Android or iOS. CMSIS is a set of low-level C functions that provide access to hardware as well as many libraries for the use of complex units targeted at digital signal processing (DSP), machine learning, and neural networks, as well as communication mechanisms such as TCP/IP, Bluetooth, and Wi-Fi. It is extremely useful, and very widely adopted for use with Cortex-M microcontrollers.

At the higher levels of development, it is not necessary to work directly with the processor or programmable interface registers, but it is still useful to understand the low-level architecture. This knowledge is important when debugging code, particularly when a disassembler is being used, and if we have to optimize a particular function to get the best possible performance from it.

In this section, we recap the various evolutions of the Arm processor families, and in the following section we review the high-level architecture of the Cortex-M as it appears in 2020 and the different variants available in terms of its components (as introduced in Chapter 1). The internal architecture is not detailed, but the blocks available for the given architectures are shown.

We also take an initial look at the instruction set architecture of Thumb-2. The ISAs of Arm processors have undergone many evolutions since their earliest beginnings, Thumb-2 being the instruction set for the Cortex-M. Depending on the precise architecture used, we will see that the number of available instructions varies.

3.1.2 Arm Architecture Evolution

After more than 35 years of evolution, many architectures have been designed and sold by Arm as IP (intellectual property). Most of them can be complemented and optimized for specific products. For the Cortex-M family alone, around 40 companies are producing chips based on the processor architecture. Table 3.2 shows the variety of different options and characteristics associated with the different Cortex-M models. In addition to these, some high-security architecture extensions have been made available in the form of the SC000 and SC300 SecurCore processors, built on the Cortex-M3 and intended for smartcard applications. Section 3.2 goes into more detail about the different members of the Cortex-M family.

Table 3.2 A comparison of Cortex-M processor characteristics and options

Feature	Cortex-M0	Cortex-M0+	Cortex-M1	Cortex-M3	Cortex-M4	Cortex-M23	Cortex-M33	Cortex-M35P	Cortex-M55	Cortex-M7
ISA (instruction set architecture)	v6-M	v6-M	v6-M	v7-M	v7E-M	v8-M Base	v8-M Main	v8-M Main	v8.1-M Main	v7-M
	Thumb, Thumb-2	Thumb, Thumb-2	Thumb, Thumb-2	Thumb, Thumb-2	Thumb, Thumb-2	Thumb, Thumb-2	Thumb, Thumb-2	Thumb, Thumb-2	Thumb, Thumb-2	Thumb, Thumb-2
DMIPS/MHz range	0.87–1.27	0.95–1.36	0.8	1.25–1.89	1.25–1.95	0.98	1.5	1.5	1.6	2.14–3.23
CoreMark®/MHz	2.33	2.46	1.85	3.34	3.42	2.64	4.02	4.02	4.2	5.01
Pipeline Stages	3	2	3	3	3	2	3	3	4	6
Memory Protection Unit	-	Option	-	Option	Option	(2x) Option	(2x) Option	(2x) Option	(2x) Option	Option
Maximum MPU Regions	-	8	-	8	8	16	16	16	16	16
Trace (MTB or Embedded Trace Macrocell [ETM])	-	Micro Trace Buffer (MTB) option	-	ETMv3 option	ETMv3 option	MTB or ETMv3 option	MTB and/ or ETMv4 option	MTB and/ or ETMv4 option	ETMv4 option	ETMv4 option
Digital Signal Processing	-	-	-	-	Yes	-	Option	Option	Option	Yes
Floating-point Hardware (SP = single-precision)	-	-	-	-	Scalar SP	-	Scalar SP	Scalar SP	Scalar Vector	Scalar
SysTick Timer	Option	Option	Option	Yes	Yes	Yes (2x)	Yes (2x)	Yes (2x)	Yes (2x)	Yes
Built-in Caches	-	-	-	-	-	-	-	Option I-Cache	Option I/D-Cache	Option I/D-Cache
Tightly Coupled Memory	-	-	Yes	-	-	-	-	-	Option	Option

Feature	Cortex-M0	Cortex-M0+	Cortex-M1	Cortex-M3	Cortex-M4	Cortex-M23	Cortex-M33	Cortex-M35P	Cortex-M55	Cortex-M7
TrustZone for Arm-v8-M	-	-	-	-	-	Option	Option	Option	Option	-
Coprocessor Interface	-	-	-	-	-	-	Option	Option	Option	-
Bus Protocol	AHB-Lite	AHB-Lite Fast I/O	AHB-Lite	AHB-Lite APB	AHB-Lite APB	AHB5 Fast I/O	AHB5 APB	AHB5 APB	AXI5 AHB TCM	AXI4 AHB-Lite APB TCM
Wake-up Interrupt Controller	Yes	Yes	-	Yes	Yes	Yes	Yes	Yes	Yes	Yes
Integrated Interrupt Controller (NVIC)	Yes	Yes	Yes	Yes	Yes	Yes	Yes	Yes	Yes	Yes
Maximum # Interrupts	32	32	32	240	240	240	480	480	480	240
Hardware Divide	-	-	-	Yes	Yes	Yes	Yes	Yes	Yes	Yes
Single-cycle Multiply	Option	Option	-	Yes	Yes	Yes	Yes	Yes	Yes	Yes
Dual-core Lock-step Support	-	-	-	-	-	Yes	Yes	Yes	-	Yes
Arm Custom Instructions	-	-	-	-	-	-	Yes	-	Yes	-
Common Criteria Certification	-	-	-	-	-	-	Yes	Yes	-	-

To summarize Table 3.2, the Cortex-M0/M0+/M1 have the Arm-v6-M architecture, the Cortex-M3/M4/M7 have Arm-v7-M, the Cortex-M23/M33/M35P have Arm-v8-M and TrustZone, the Cortex-M55 has Arm-v8.1-M, and the SecurCore SC000 and SC300 have Arm-v6-M and Arm-v7-M, respectively, and anti-tampering hardware. An IEEE 754-compliant single-precision floating-point unit and a DSP (Digital Signal Processor) extension are both options for the higher-end processors, according to manufacturer choice, with the latter providing support for the following operations:

- single-cycle 16/32-bit MAC (Multiply and Accumulate)

- single-cycle dual 16-bit MAC

- 8/16-bit SIMD (Single Instruction Multiple Data) arithmetic

- hardware divide (2–12 cycles).

According to software development toolmaker Keil, more than 7,600 different devices were built on the Cortex-M family in 2020; Table 3.3 shows a list of the device manufacturers and the numbers of devices involved.

Table 3.3 Number of devices proposed by manufacturers based on Cortex-M, by processor (total mid-2020: 7627)

Manufacturer	# Devices	M0	M0+	M1	M3	M4	M7	M23	M33	M35	M55
ABOV	20	11			9						
Active-Semi	17	11				6					
Ambiq Micro	10					10					
Amiccom	5	5									
Analog Devices	15	3			11	1					
APEXMIC	16		2		14						
Arm	63	2	3	1	3	4	6	3	13	4	2
Atmel	129		7		40	16	66				
AutoChips	46		20		26						
Cypress	507		4		243	260					
Dialog Semiconductor	15	10	1						4		
EtaCompute	3				3						
GigaDevice	160				41	119					
Goodix	18	18									
HDSC	75		75								
Holtek	215		215								
Infineon	183		143			40					
Lapis Semiconductor	2		2								
Maxim	16				4	12					
MediaTek	2					2					
Microchip	291		147		40	76		12			
Microsemi	6				6						
MindMotion	89	58			23						
Nordic Semiconductor	18	9				7			2		
Nuvoton	744	478				169		71			
NXP	865	165	170		79	410	14		13		
Redpine Signals	4					4					
RelChip	1	1									
Renesas	37				2	29		5			
Silicon Laboratories	1861				456	1050		123			

Manufacturer	# Devices	M0	M0+	M1	M3	M4	M7	M23	M33	M35	M55
Sinowealth	1				1						
SONiX	60	60									
STMicroelectronics	1541	114	242		227	683	239		36		
Texas Instruments	350				219	131					
Toshiba	232	19			132	81					
Unisoc	1					1					
XMC	2		2								
Zilog	7	2			5						

Source: Arm Keil (www.keil.com/dd2/).

Some manufacturers place several Cortex-M cores on the same die to create multiprocessor systems with a variety of capabilities. For example, many use a Cortex-M0 or M0+ for very low power management and when more powerful computing is needed, a better performance processor is woken up! This is an intriguing approach to handling the performance/power trade-off.

The same approach can be used with higher-end application processors such as the Cortex-A family, which can be allowed to sleep most of the time while a Cortex-M is used to support low-frequency activity and minimize power consumption. This is particularly suited to smartphone applications, where users want fast interaction when using the phone, often to watch videos or play games, but also want battery charge to last at least a full day. Thus, when not in use, the smartphone can "sleep" and a small low-power Cortex-M processor can monitor the receipt of a message or phone call. The future of embedded artificial intelligence and deep learning appears to lie in a similar approach. For example, NXP's new-generation i.MX 8M Plus chip, which is targeted at these areas, incorporates four Cortex-A53 processors, a Cortex-M7 secondary core for low-power management, and many accelerators. Meanwhile, NXP's i.MX8 chip family offers six Cortex-A processors for high performance and two Cortex-M processors for low power consumption when idle.

These high-end components are beyond the scope of this book, but we can see that the Cortex family offers great potential via its Cortex-A/Cortex-M multicore capabilities with their relatively high performance and low power consumption. Thus, the use of heterogeneous multiprocessors is clearly one way to design embedded systems that avoid using a high-performance processor to consume a lot of energy doing small tasks that can be done by a smaller, more power-efficient core.

3.1.3 References
More information about the evolution of the Arm architecture and the chips that have been built on it can be found on **WikiChip**, a wiki-style resource that describes itself as "the preeminent resource for computer architectures and semiconductor logic engineering, covering historical and contemporary electronic systems, technologies, and related topics" [1]. A good starting point for ARM-related information is en.wikichip.org/wiki/arm.

3.2 Cortex-M Processor Families

To give a large choice of capabilities for designing a SoC, Arm offers three separate Cortex families, of differing classes and characteristics, that can be integrated into a SoC, as shown in Figure 3.1. The processors in the Cortex-M family are the Arm cores that have been optimized for size and low power consumption. They have a more limited instruction set than the other two families. Within this M-class family, there are, in turn, a range of cores tailored for differing and/or specific applications. This section reviews these processors and their potential application.

Cortex-A	Cortex-R	Cortex-M
High Performance	Responsive and reliable	Small and low power Embedded Application
Rich OS (Linux, Windows)	RTOS	RTOS / Baremetal
Large instruction Set	Reduced instruction Set	Limited instruction set

Figure 3.1 Cortex families for system-on-chip design

3.2.1 Cortex-M Flavors

The different members of the Cortex-M family can be classified according to their architecture, as shown in Figure 3.2. Higher architectural levels can generally be interpreted as adding more functionality, bringing additional instructions and units to the core. The Arm-v6-M architecture has always been designed for low power consumption. The list of instructions is limited to the 16-bit Thumb instruction set to optimize the size of the final application. However, cores with this architecture deliver lower benchmark results for similar reasons.

In terms of the Arm-v7-M architecture, cores can have either this architecture or, if they have the DSP extension enabled, they will have the Arm-v7E-M architecture. Similarly, within the Arm-v8-M architecture, there is both a baseline version, which implements a subset of the full Arm-v8-M architecture, and a mainline version that has the full set of features. The baseline version provides a smaller number of gates and has a simpler instruction set, and its goal is to get closer to the Arm-v6-M architecture but with enhancements that make it more secure and faster than the latter. There is also an updated version of the Arm-v8-M architecture, called Arm-v8.1-M, which incorporates the Helium extension that enables vector instructions and improves performance.

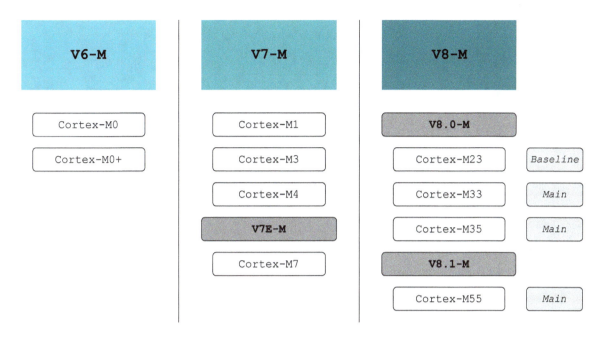

Figure 3.2 Cortex-M family classified according to architecture

3.2.2 Benchmarking

The data represented in Figure 3.3 is extracted from the information provided by Arm about the different Cortex-M processors. It shows the different sizes (using the same [40LP] process technology) and comparative performance of the cores. The metric used for performance is called CoreMark, from the Embedded Microprocessor Benchmark Consortium (EEMBC). The latter provides test suites that determine the performance of a system on the basis of processing time. The higher the score, the better. Benchmarking is a popular way to compare different systems because they will all produce a score that can be compared directly. The specific workload in this particular benchmark incorporates profiles of typical code used in a variety of algorithms that are commonplace in embedded systems:

- matrix manipulation

- math operations

- pointer manipulations

- cyclic redundancy checks.

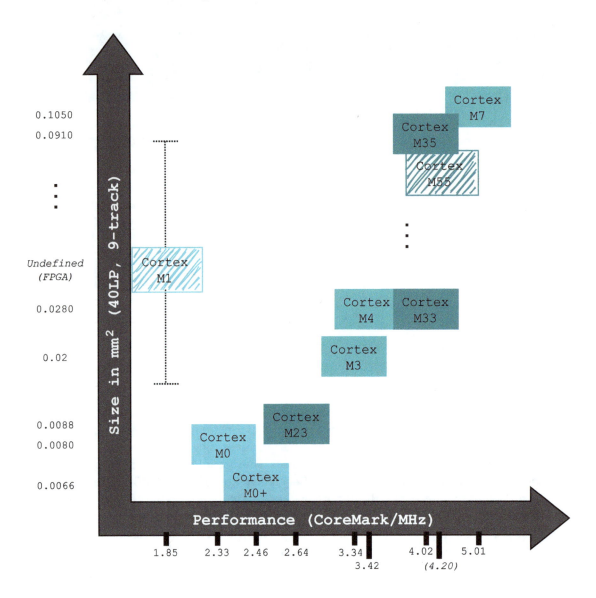

Figure 3.3 Benchmark performance versus size for the Cortex-M family, color-coded by architecture (light blue – v6-M; mid-blue – v7-M; dark blue – v8-M)

Because there is no system that operates with a standalone Cortex-M (it needs other peripherals in order to operate), the tests must be run on SoCs provided by several different vendors (see Table 3.4). At the time of writing, benchmarks for the Cortex-M35 and -M55 processors were only available via software emulation. In addition, because the Cortex-M55 had not yet been released, its precise core size could not be confirmed, while Arm does not publish a core size for the Cortex-M1 because it is supposed to be used in FPGAs, meaning that the design is not meant to be on a chip as such. The benchmark results are publicly available and can be accessed on the EEMBC website: www.eembc.org. Furthermore, the source code of the CoreMark benchmark is open and can be accessed on its GitHub website (github.com/eembc/coremark), meaning that a specific test can be reproduced to validate a result, or other chips can be benchmarked to the same standard.

Table 3.4 Microcontrollers and chips used in Cortex-M benchmarks

Cortex-M Core	Vendor	Chip
M0	ST Microelectronics	STM32F051C8
M0+	Microchip Technology	ATSAML21J18B
M23	Microchip Technology	ATSAML11E16A
M3	ST Microelectronics	STM32L152
M4	ST Microelectronics	STM32L476
M33	NXP Semiconductors	LPC55S69JBD100
M7	ST Microelectronics	STM32F746NGH6

3.2.3 Instruction Set Architectures

Arm offers the following instruction sets for the Cortex-M architectures:

▪ **Thumb(-1)** instructions. All basic processor operations can be handled through this set even though it is relatively small (56 instructions). Intended for general data processing and I/O control.

▪ **Thumb-2** instructions. This set expands the Thumb instruction set by adding more instructions for data processing. It also supports conditional branch instructions that depend on the result of the previous instructions, and exclusive instructions for use when there are multiple requestors in the system.

▪ **DSP** extension instructions. This set includes single instruction, multiple data (SIMD) and multiply–accumulate (MAC) instructions that are heavily used in audio and multimedia applications.

▪ **Single-precision floating-point** instructions

▪ **Double-precision floating-point** instructions. These involve 64-bit precision, rather than 32-bit.

▪ **Helium technology** extension instructions. This is an extension to the Arm-v8.1-M architecture to support scalar and vector instructions. For example, if we need to add 8 bytes to 8 other bytes, this can be achieved as a single vector instruction instead of having to use 8 instructions that add one byte to another in turn.

▪ **Custom** instructions that can be added at design time to make a specific function more performant.

Figure 3.4 illustrates the possible ranges of Cortex-M instructions, depending on the core involved. However, because some elements are optional (such as TrustZone for v8-M or floating-point units for the Cortex-M4 and -M7), some implementations of the cores listed will not support all of the instructions that are, theoretically, available to them. Because it is not within the scope of this book to detail the instructions one by one, this picture principally serves to illustrate how many instructions have been added as the Cortex-M family has evolved.

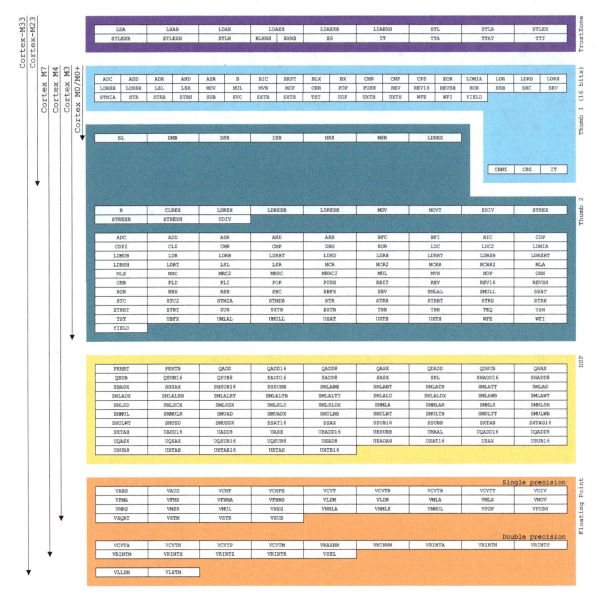

Figure 3.4 Principal instruction sets supported by different Cortex-M processors

3.2.4 Cortex-M Microarchitecture

A processor on its own is not enough for instructions to be executed: as a minimum, an interface to access memory and other peripherals is needed too. If we look at the components inside the various Cortex-M microcontrollers (see Figures 3.7 to 3.11), we can see that, in addition to a CPU, there is always a nested vectored interrupt controller (NVIC), a wake-up interrupt controller, and a bus of some form. Most other components are optional and can be added at design time if needed.

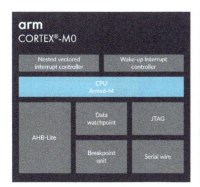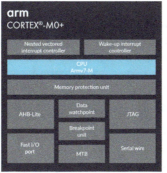

Figure 3.5 Simplified view of Cortex-M microcontrollers, Arm-v6-M architecture (source: Reproduced with permission from Arm Ltd)

With a small three-stage pipeline based on a von Neumann bus architecture, no privilege-level separation and no memory protection unit (MPU), the Cortex-M0 is a small and inexpensive processor. The Cortex-M0+ is an upgrade, having privilege-level separation and an optional MPU. It also has an optional single-cycle I/O interface for connecting peripherals that need low-latency access, and a low-cost instruction-trace feature called the Micro Trace Buffer (MTB). The Cortex-M1 is very similar to the M0 processor but is optimized for FPGA applications. It provides a tightly-coupled memory (TCM) interface to simplify memory integration within the FPGA and delivers a higher clock frequency too. However, because the Cortex-M1 is intended to be incorporated as a soft-core within an FPGA chip, rather than as a (hard-core) chip in its own right, it does not have a wake-up interrupt controller.

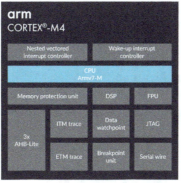

Figure 3.6 Simplified view of Cortex-M microcontrollers, Arm-v7-M architecture (source: Reproduced with permission from Arm Ltd)

In the Arm-v7-M family (Figure 3.6), we can see that more debugging units are available, and a memory protection unit can be added (and usually is). This architecture is used for applications that perform more complicated data processing. The Arm-v7-M instruction set provides more addressing modes, conditional execution, bit-field processing, and fuller multiply support. Thus, even with a relatively small Cortex-M3 processor, a relatively high-performance system is available.

If DSP-intensive and/or single-precision floating-point processing are needed, the Cortex-M4 processor is more suitable than the Cortex-M3 because it supports 32-bit SIMD operations and an optional single-precision floating-point unit (FPU). However, if size is not a dominant issue and performance is the main factor, the Cortex-M7 should be chosen. It offers a six-stage pipeline and superscalar design, allowing execution of up to two instructions per cycle. It has all the characteristics of the Cortex-M4 but the FPU can be configured to deliver double-precision. It is also designed to work with a high-performance and complex memory system through its support of instruction and data caches and TCM.

 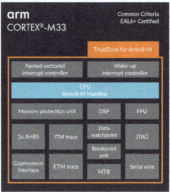 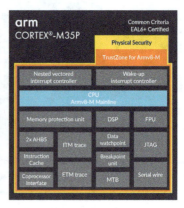

Figure 3.7 Simplified view of Cortex-M microcontrollers, Arm-v8-M architecture (source: Reproduced with permission from Arm Ltd)

All Cortex-M processors with the Arm-v8-M architecture (see Figure 3.7) offer the option to add TrustZone support for the additional security increasingly demanded by modern applications. The other principal difference from the Arm-v7-M architecture is the change in bus from AHB-Lite to AHB5. For constrained embedded systems that need more advanced security than is offered by the Arm-v6-M architecture, the Cortex-M23 processor with a TrustZone extension is a suitable choice. It is designed to provide a more up-to-date architecture than that of Arm-v6-M but to maintain the small size and low power consumption of the latter. Given the same options, the Cortex-M33 has a similar footprint to that of the Cortex-M4; however, it offers a coprocessor interface to support the offload of processing from the main processor. Finally, in this group, the Cortex-M35P processor offers all of the facilities of the Cortex-M33, but with the addition of anti-tampering features to prevent physical security attacks (e.g. side-channel and fault-injection attacks), together with an optional instruction cache.

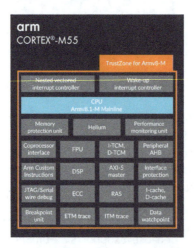

Figure 3.8 Simplified view of Cortex-M microcontroller, Arm-v8.1-M architecture (source: Reproduced with permission from Arm Ltd)

The most powerful Cortex-M processor yet, with TrustZone support and a Custom Instruction module (see Figure 3.8), should be available in 2021. The Cortex-M55 is optimized for machine-learning applications while having the same characteristics as the Cortex-M7 and additional instructions to offer excellent performance despite its small core size. Besides its support for custom instructions, what differentiates it most is its support for Helium vector technology and the performance monitoring unit that is added.

A further special case of the Cortex-M architecture is represented by the SecurCore SC000 and SC300 processors (see Figure 3.9), specifically designed to provide anti-tampering support in the context of secure credit card applications. These are based on the Cortex-M3 and provide either the Arm-v6-M (SC000) or Arm-v7-M (SC300) architecture.

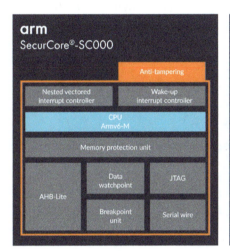 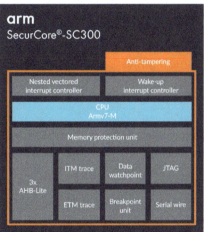

Figure 3.9 Simplified view of SecurCore SC000 and SC300 Cortex-M3-based processors, Arm-v6-M or Arm-v7-M architecture (source: Reproduced with permission from Arm Ltd)

3.2.5 Architectural Configuration

The configurations of the different Cortex-M processors allow vendors to create designs tailored to their needs. If an application needs a degree of computational power but is not performing any floating-point operations, then there is no need to have an FPU. If size is an important factor and the application has already been debugged and used in other cores, then an instruction-trace function like the MTB would consume unnecessary space. When designing a system based on a Cortex-M core, each manufacturer must decide which of the various optional functionalities must be incorporated/ enabled (or not):

- Data endianness: this is decided at design time and cannot be modified thereafter.

- SysTick timer: an optional 24-bit system timer that is present in most Cortex-M processors.

- Bit-banding: creates an area in memory that can be manipulated at bit level via a single word-aligned instruction.

- Memory protection unit (MPU): used to provide additional protection to the system; more explanation is provide later in this chapter.

- Tightly-coupled memory (TCM): fast memory inside the chip to reduce latency of access compared to traditional RAM.

- User/privilege support: some Cortex-M processors do not need to provide user support and only run in privileged mode.

- Caching structures: a data cache, an instruction cache, or both may be provided.

- Floating-point support: if required, single- (32-bit binary) and double- (64-bit binary) precision FPUs are available in the Arm-v7-M and Arm-v8-M architectures.

- Trace debugging support: this provides enhanced features for monitoring core execution and enables a debugging interface.

- DSP support.

- Number of interrupts to be supported: the limits on this vary according to the Cortex-M version: up to 32 (for the Cortex-M0, -M0+ and -M1), up to 240 (for the Cortex-M3, -M4, -M7 and -M23), and up to 480 (for the Cortex-M33 and -M35P).

- TrustZone security: Restricts access to the different peripherals and memories. Further details are provided later in this chapter.

3.2.5.1 Power Management

For low-power systems, it is important that the hardware layer provides the capability to limit or prevent current consumption when there is nothing to be done. However, when sleeping, the system must also have a mechanism to wake up if needed. There are two elements involved in this:

- An always-on power management unit that clamps or gates off unused parts of the integrated circuit in terms of power and/or clocks, while maintaining key processor state and register data. It also has a wake-up function connected to peripherals that are not put to sleep and can still trigger interrupts.

- A Sleep-On-Exit configuration that lets the core return to its sleep state once such an interrupt has been serviced, thus allowing a low-power application to be entirely interrupt-driven.

3.2.5.2 Debug and Trace

CoreSight is an Arm architectural framework for processors and software tools that is designed to enable enhanced debugging and tracing within SoCs to assist in identifying software issues. The resulting debug and trace functionality depends upon chip and tool designers adhering to this framework in their implementations. Typical actions enabled by the debugger might be: stopping, restarting and resuming core processing; executing instructions one at a time; reading or updating memory between instructions. Hardware breakpoints can be set to halt execution at a specific code location; data watchpoints can be used to inspect a specific variable or memory address over time and be notified once it changes. However, only a limited number of these are available in a system:

- Watchpoints: up to two for Cortex-M0/M0+ and -M1, compared to as many as four for all of the other Cortex-M processors.

- Breakpoints: up to four for Cortex-M0/M0+, -M1 and -M23, and up to eight for all other Cortex-M processors.

Trace functionality is essential both for debugging applications and for profiling. One issue in using breakpoints and halting execution is that it can serve to obscure bugs or even prevent them from appearing because the timings involved are no longer the same as in a standard execution. However, having a stream of data (a trace) that contains the instructions executed with the times taken is less intrusive and better reflects a real scenario.

The CoreSight architecture specifies a set of components for use in SoC subsystems in support of the collection of debug and trace information in a standardized format. These include control components, trace sources (to generate trace data), trace sinks (to store and output trace data), and debug ports and access ports.

Many of the wider set of debugging tools that are available are also able to support Cortex-M debugging, through either JTAG or Serial Wire Debug (SWD) interfaces, which are provided via the CoreSight-specified Debug Access Port (DAP) component. SWD exposes only one pin outside the chip for data tracing, and is a low-cost solution that incurs a relatively small overhead.

CoreSight-compliant systems can include the following trace sources (amongst others):

- Data Watchpoint and Trace (DWT): offers a way to monitor events for profiling the core. In addition, exception and data traces can be extracted along with the current number of cycles. In addition, it can sample the Program Counter to see the current instruction being executed.

- Instrumentation Trace Macrocells (ITMs): used to create logs with timestamps from the data extracted from the DWT. They can also be used by software to write data for output by the debugger.

- Embedded Trace Macrocells (ETMs): give a cycle-accurate instruction trace. They stream all the instructions executed to profile the code and know which lines were executed when. This can also be achieved in software; however, in this case, annotations must be added to the code to produce the results; using a hardware unit is less intrusive.

The traces thus generated can be linked and passed to trace sinks such as:

- Trace Port Interface Units (TPIUs): take ETM and ITM outputs and format data packets into a Single Wire Output (SWO) that can be streamed over a single trace pin (hence the name), or format an instruction trace for the Trace Port Analyzer that interfaces with a debugger. This stream of instructions is relatively fast, and requires a higher bandwidth than can be achieved with SWO, hence its use of five pins rather than just one.

- Embedded Trace Buffers (ETBs): can be used in place of a TPIU. Instead of streaming data to a connected debugger, the debug data is streamed to an on-chip memory that can be accessed later, the advantage being that no additional pins are needed. However, the size of the memory limits the number of bytes that can be stored, meaning that the debugger needs to regularly read the buffer to release memory.

Debuggers are hardware extensions that are plugged into the exposed interface of a chip. They usually support SWO and Trace Port, and often ETB- or MTB-enabled tracing, and are sold with graphical interfaces to format the data transmitted by the core and simplify analysis. All of the debug functionalities outlined above are optional: thus, a Cortex-M core might have a DAP that supports SWD, or JTAG, or both of these, or neither of them.

3.3 Arm Cortex-M Programmer's Model

In simple terms, a programmer's model represents all of the elements of a computer that can be affected by the execution of instructions in the processor. Logically, these are the state variables or, in physical terms, the registers on which a computer's set of instructions can act.

3.3.1 Instruction Set Architecture

Every processor family has a specific instruction set that defines its architecture. The original Arm instruction set had a 32-bit coding. However, for many existing applications based on smaller instruction sets this represented the loss of significant amounts of memory space to "inefficient" instruction coding. Therefore, a second, 16-bit instruction set, called Thumb, was defined with fewer capabilities but a better memory footprint. To be more efficient, both instruction sets were made available and can run the same program but in different processor states. More recently, the Cortex family introduced a new version of Thumb, Thumb-2, which allows a genuine mixture of 16- and 32-bit coding: the best of two worlds in a single coding system.

As described in Chapter 2, there are two main processor types: CISC and RISC. CISC processors are designed to reduce the number of instructions in a program by having multiple operations done as one. They also support some direct operations on memory during the course of instruction execution, rather than having to load or store data beforehand. Another CISC characteristic is that instructions might not have the same length, meaning that there can be instructions of 1, 2, or up to 16 bytes. The drawback of CISC processors is that the maximum clock frequency is limited to tens of megahertz because operations in the pipeline can take a long time to execute or might need additional cycles, and thus the critical path for the clock is increased. In addition, CISC's complex instruction set also increases the complexity of the hardware, because the decoding and execution of instructions is more complex. Processor families such as the 68000 (Motorola), i8086 (Intel) and Z80000 (Zilog), to name a few, are based on the CISC model.

Arm (and some other companies) preferred to take another direction with a reduced instruction set and instructions of mostly the same size. In a RISC processor, instructions can only operate on internal registers. First, an instruction must fetch data from the external memory with a LOAD instruction, then perform the necessary operations using internal registers, before using a STORE instruction to place the result back into memory. In this way, data transfers to and from the external world and manipulation of data in the internal registers are separate pieces of work done by different units, making it easier to realize more efficient logic and pipelining. The addressing modes to access data are very simple, as only the following are allowed:

▨ access to internal registers

▨ immediate value load

▨ relative or branched program counter (PC)-based access to memory

▨ indexing in registers for use as memory pointers.

Thus, in a RISC architecture, it is usually necessary to have three instructions for an addition: loading the operand into a register, executing the ADD instruction, and storing the result to memory. Within a CISC processor, this can be done through a single instruction.

Over the course of several Arm generations, there have been two instructions sets, ARM and Thumb. ARM used fixed 4-byte instruction encodings, whereas Thumb encodings were variable between 2 or 4 bytes. The main difference between them is that many ARM instructions are conditional, the execution depending on flags, which is not the case for the Thumb instruction set. However, Thumb-2 introduced a conditional execution element (if-then[-else] or IT) to the Thumb instruction set that made it almost equivalent to ARM. The Thumb-2 instruction set is backwards compatible with the Thumb instruction set.

To summarize, the following are now available on a Cortex-M processor:

▨ 32-bit instructions to provide:

   ☐ support for exception handling in Thumb state

   ☐ access to coprocessors

   ☐ DSP and media instructions

   ☐ more efficiency than 16-bit instructions to improve performance

- 16-bit IT (if-then) instructions for potential execution of 1 to 4 instructions following a Thumb conditional

- 16-bit Compare and Branch if Zero (**CBZ**) (or Non-Zero [**CBNZ**]) instructions to improve code size

- 16-bit Thumb coding for smaller code footprint.

As processor complexity has increased, the three main Arm families (A, R, and M) have been subject to a number of changes in ISA name, as outlined below:

- **T32** – this is the Thumb instruction set used on the Arm-M family as well as Arm-A and Arm-R, and is the only set available across all Cortex families

- **A32** – used on the Arm-A and Arm-R families; previously known as the ARM instruction set

- **A64** – instruction set for 64-bit data, although instruction encoding is 32-bit; this is a new instruction encoding for when a processor is in an **AArch64** execution state on the Arm-v8 architecture (not covered in this book). Note that the same architecture also supports an **AArch32** execution state, in which it will only run the A32 or T32 instruction sets.

- **Advanced SIMD** – an extension for the Arm-v7 and Arm-v8 architectures (not covered in this book) that adds 32 new 64-bit registers for AArch32, or 32 new 128-bit registers for AArch64, to support single instruction, multiple data (SIMD) arithmetic.

- **Floating Point** – an instruction set extension provided directly or as an option on some architectures starting with Arm-v7. It shares the same extension register set (not covered in this book) as that outlined above for SIMD.

At any given time, a processor that can support more than one instruction set will be in one execution state or another; if it is in the A32 state, it cannot execute T32 instructions and vice versa. To specify which instruction set to assemble, the Arm or THUMB directives are used. These do not change the execution state of the processor, just the ISA to use. A change of execution state is achieved (on the appropriate architecture) through a specific branch or jump instruction using **BL** <label> or **BLX** <Rm> (or **BXNS/BLXNS** for Secure and Non-secure states; see the section on TrustZone for more on this).

The next section gives details of the coding of the Thumb-2 instruction set. Other Arm instruction sets will not be covered, although the concepts explained are generally applicable to these other ISAs too.

Remember, the availability of some instructions depends on the manufacturer implementation, as well as selection from among the various options provided by Arm, which have increased in complexity with the additional improvements and additions to the architecture. To illustrate this:

- The first simple Cortex-M0 processor with the Arm-v6-M architecture has documentation (Architecture Reference Manual, Arm DDI 0419C [ID092410]) of around 430 pages.

- For the Arm-v7-M (Architecture Reference Manual, Arm DDI 0403E.d [ID070218]), documentation runs to around 860 pages.

- The Arm-v8-M (Architecture Reference Manual, DDI 0553B.l [ID30062020]) documentation is more than 2000 pages.

The current set of Arm architectures are as follows:

- **Arm-v7-M:**

  - for systems supporting only the Thumb instruction set, and where overall size and deterministic operation for an implementation are more important than absolute performance

  - where Arm-v7-M to Arm-v6-M compatibility is not an architectural requirement; many of the system-level registers defined to support Arm-v7-M features are reserved in Arm-v6-M; software must treat values read from such reserved registers as UNKNOWN.

- **Arm-v6-M:**

  - is a subset of Arm-v7-M and provides:
    - a lightweight version of the Arm-v7-M programming model
    - the Debug extension that includes architecture extensions for debug support
    - Arm-v6 Thumb 16-bit instruction set compatibility at the application level
    - an optional Unprivileged/Privileged extension
    - an optional Protected Memory System Architecture (PMSAv6) extension

  - Note: Arm-v6-M is upwardly compatible with Arm-v7-M, meaning that application-level and system-level software developed for Arm-v6-M can execute unmodified on Arm-v7-M.

- **Arm-v8-M:**

  - Implements a programmers' model designed for low-latency interrupt processing, with hardware stacking of registers and support for writing interrupt handlers in high-level languages.

  - Supports a variant of the T32 instruction set.

3.3.2 Processor Modes

The Arm architecture supports different levels of execution privilege. The privilege level depends on the processor mode. There are two processing modes in all Arm-v6-M and Arm-v7-M architectures (and Arm-v8-M architectures can have four processing modes in conjunction with the TrustZone extension):

- **Thread** mode: the normal mode when the processor executes a program.

- **Handler** mode: the exception-handling mode, always involving **privileged** software execution.

3.3.3 Register Set

The register set for the Cortex-M family is almost identical for all family members, thus minimizing any differences in software support. The principal differences revolve around some elements of the ISA and the physical resources available in the form of specialized units, buses, caches, debugging facilities, and an MPU.

3.3.3.1 Principal Registers

Chapter 1 briefly described the register architecture of the Cortex-M. There are sixteen 32-bit-wide general-purpose registers in which most of the processor's work is carried out, as follows:

- **R0–R7** are the lower registers: eight registers with their numbering selection done on three bits of coding

- **R8–R12** are the next in a further group of eight, also general purpose and termed the higher registers

- **R13** has the specific function of **Stack Pointer** (**SP**) because the v6-M and v7-M architectures have two working modes, two SP registers are available: **MSP** (Main SP) and **PSP** (Process SP). Similarly, for the v8-M architecture, there are four available. These registers are banked and the SP updated according to the mode in which the core is working.

- **R14** is used as a **Link Register** (**LR**) and receives the return address of a call to a subroutine or function by a **BL** (branch with link) instruction; at the end of the subroutine or function, an equivalent return instruction (branch with exchange) must be performed: BX <LR>.

- **R15** is the **Program Counter** (PC), which contains the address of the next instruction to be loaded and executed.

In general, R13, R14, and R15 are referred to in terms of their specific functions (**SP**, **LR**, and **PC**). Together, these 16 registers are sometimes referred to as the Arm **core registers** (**R0–R15**).

In addition to these general-purpose registers, there exist a smaller number of **special registers**, used to store a variety of information about the status of the processor, including its execution state:

- **PSR** is the Program Status Register, with some masked versions (or subsets) of it available as shortcuts depending on the flags used, for example:

  - ☐ **APSR**: Application PSR

  - ☐ **IPSR**: Interrupt PSR

  - ☐ **EPSR**: Execution PSR

- **PRIMASK** is the Priority Mask Register, used to manage the prioritization scheme for exceptions and interrupts

- **CONTROL** is the Control Register, used to identify specific control modes and the current stack.

The core and special registers described above are closely coupled to the processor; all other registers are memory-mapped. This means that they appear to the programmer in the same way as programmable interfaces with specific addresses.

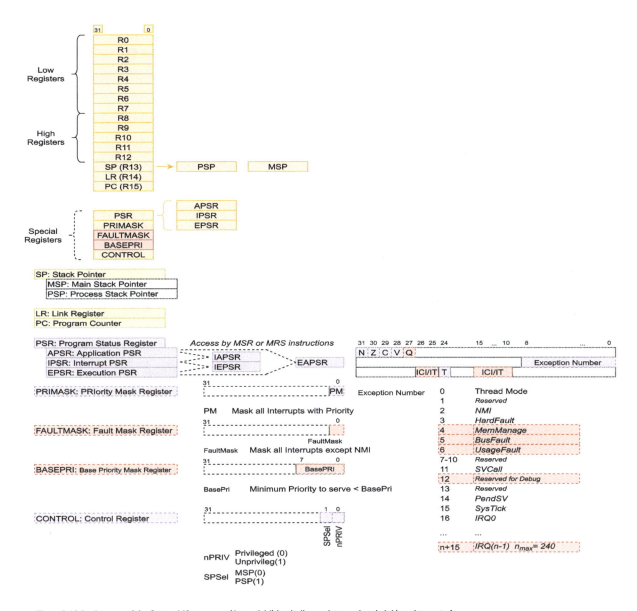

Figure 3.10 Register set of the Cortex-M0 processor (Arm-v6-M) (excluding registers colored pink); register set of Cortex-M3 and Cortex-M4 processors (Arm-v7-M) includes those in pink.

When programming in C or other high-level languages, and for application design, it is not essential to be familiar with the internal architecture and register set because such concerns are handled automatically by the compiler. However, these registers are referenced in the set of assembly instructions and might need to be inspected for debugging purposes. Similarly, if we want to go into more detailed levels of software optimization, and/or it becomes necessary to exert closer control of the underlying hardware, then a good knowledge of the processor and microcontroller architectures is a must.

Figure 3.10 illustrates the register set for the Cortex-M0 processor (Arm-v6-M). Additional registers for Arm-v7-M and the Cortex-M3 and -M4 processors are shown in pink (excluding any registers associated with the optional SIMD or floating-point instruction set extensions, where available). In the figure, the special registers are shown in violet: they are accessible via the **MSR** and **MRS** special-register instructions (see below).

3.3.3.2 Stack Pointer
An Arm-v6-M processor implements two stacks:

▩ the Main stack, SP_main or **MSP**

▩ the Process stack, SP_process or **PSP**.

The active stack pointer will be one of these two banked stack pointers, SP_main or SP_process. When the processor is in Handler mode, it uses SP_main. In Thread mode, it can use either, dependent on the value of the CONTROL.SPSel bit in the special-purpose CONTROL register. A processor reset selects and initializes **SP_main**.

For maximum portability across other profiles, Arm strongly recommends that software treats stack pointer (R13) bits [1:0] as Should Be Zero or Preserved (SBZP). Writing a non-zero value to bits [1:0] results in UNPREDICTABLE behavior. Reading bits [1:0] returns zero.

3.3.3.3 Program Status Register
The Program Status Register is a single 32-bit register with several aliases (or sub-registers), **APSR**, **IPSR** and **EPSR**, each providing a (mutually exclusive) view of a different subset of its contents, the layout of which are shown in Figure 3.11 (xPSR is a generic term for the program status register):

▩ The Application PSR holds flags that can be written by application-level (i.e. unprivileged) software.

▩ The Interrupt PSR holds the current exception number if the processor is executing an exception handler; otherwise, its value is zero.

▩ The Execution PSR holds bits pertaining to the current execution state of the processor.

Application software can use the **MRS** and **MSR** instructions to access either the complete **PSR**, any one of its sub-registers, or any two of its sub-registers in combination. More details of these instructions are provided in subsequent sections.

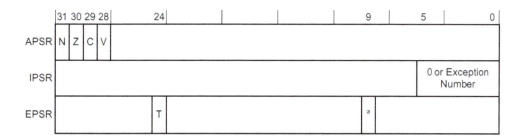

Figure 3.11 xPSR register layout

In an Arm-v7-M architecture that can incorporate the optional DSP SIMD extension (e.g. the Cortex-M4), four bits [19:16] of the **APSR** register are employed to indicate the result of an associated operation on either a byte or half-word, and are referred to as GE[3:0], that is, Greater than or Equal.

3.3.4 Addressing Modes

The Thumb-2 instruction set supports a limited amount of operand access. As a RISC processor, all operations are done with internal registers, with the most extensive being the three internal registers available to ADD or SUB instructions. Depending on the **ISA**, these three separate registers are only available from the set of lower registers **R0..R7** in 16-bit Thumb-2 encoding. For the ADD instruction that follows, Figure 3.12 shows the ALU and the registers used for the operation, together with the **APSR** register that is updated according to the result of the ADD (thanks to its S suffix) and any flags triggered.

```
ADDS    R7, R2, R4      // R7 ← R2 + R4, flags updated
```

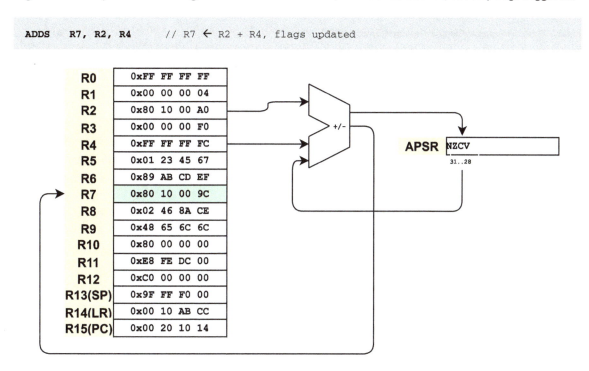

Figure 3.12 Addition (ADD) (or subtraction [SUB]) instruction with two source registers and one destination register (R0–R7 only)

If the carry must be added (see Figure 3.13), only two registers can be specified, one source and one destination. In this case, the common register need only be specified once, in the left-hand position:

```
ADCS    R2, R2, R7      // R2 ← R2 + R7, flags updated
ADCS    R2, R7          // R2 ← R2 + R7, flags updated, equivalent, same encoding
```

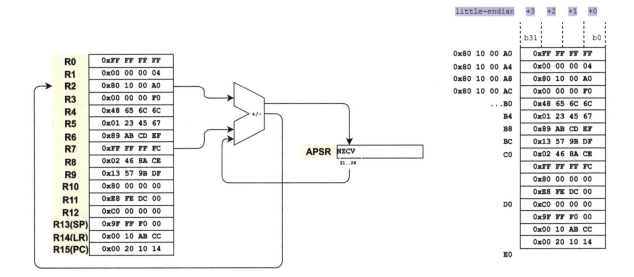

Figure 3.13 Add with carry (ADC) instruction using two registers in R0–R7 range

Arm processors support the following data types in memory:

- byte: 8 bits

- half-word: 16 bits

- word: 32 bits

- double-word: 64 bits.

As we have seen, processor registers are 32 bits in size. The Thumb instruction set contains instructions that support the following data types in registers:

- 32-bit pointers: a register in which the content is the address of a position in memory

- unsigned or signed 32-bit integers

- unsigned 16-bit or 8-bit integers, held in zero-extended form

- signed 16-bit or 8-bit integers, held in sign-extended form

- unsigned or signed 64-bit integers held in two registers.

To transfer data between the processor's registers and memory, indirect access with an index can be used. Two registers are added together and the result is an address, which is where the processor can either write data (STORE) or read and transfer data to an internal register (LOAD). The store can be of 8-bit, 16-bit or 32-bit width. Figure 3.14 illustrates the transfers for the following instructions (the destination address is computed via the addition of the contents of **R1** and **R2**):

```
STRB    R5, [R2, R1]    // Byte transfer, 8 bits
STRH    R5, [R2, R1]    // Half-word transfer, 16 bits
STR     R5, [R2, R1]    // Word transfer, 32 bits
```

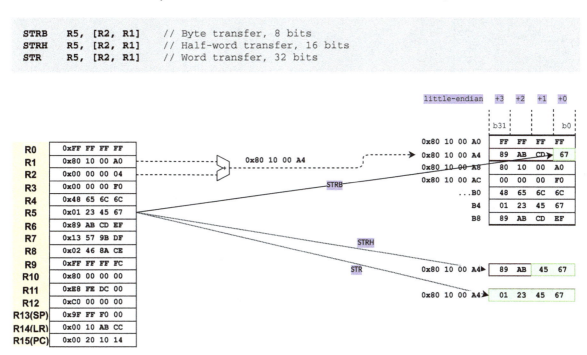

Figure 3.14 STORE in memory from register using indirect indexed addressing mode [R2, R1] and three different data sizes

For the LOAD instruction from memory into a register, bytes and half-words can be treated as unsigned or signed. In the destination register, the value is *always* updated over 32 bits, which is the width of the register. Figure 3.15 illustrates the loads listed below, with different sizes and unsigned or signed where appropriate. For unsigned loads, the data is zero-extended. For signed loads, the final value is extended; this means that if the number in the most-significant bit (MSb) is 1, all bits before it are set to 1 rather than 0.

```
LDRB     R3, [R2, R1]    // LoaD into Register a Byte, with zero-extension to 32 bits (unsigned)
LDRH     R4, [R2, R1]    // LoaD into Register a Half-word, with zero-extension to 16 bits (unsigned)
LDR      R5, [R2, R1]    // LoaD into Register a word, exactly as per memory (signed or unsigned)
LDRSB    R6, [R2, R1]    // LoaD into Register a Signed Byte, with sign-extension to 32 bits (signed)
LDRSH    R7, [R2, R1]    // LoaD into Register a Signed Half-word, with sign-extension to 32 bits
                         // (signed)
```

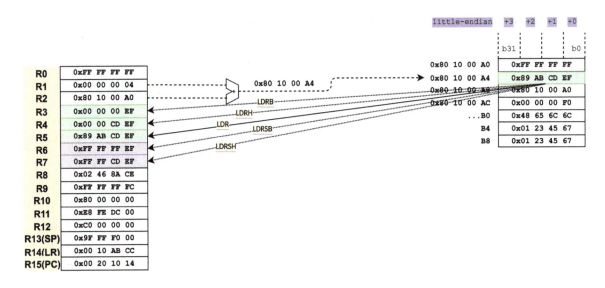

Figure 3.15 LOAD variants in terms of size and whether signed or unsigned

When a register is used as a pointer to a memory position, the index can be another register of 32 bits too, as in the earlier example. However, it can also be a *positive* value with a limited range coded on 5 bits, which means its value will lie between 0 and 31 ($2^5 - 1$). The (immediate) value coded in the instruction indicates a shift of 0, 1, or 2 units depending on the size of the transfer. In the following instruction examples, the index is 4 and the results in the registers are represented in Figure 3.16.

```
STRB    R6, [R1, 4<<0]  // Byte store, 8 bits
STRH    R6, [R1, 4<<1]  // Half-word store, 16 bits
STR     R6, [R1, 4<<2]  // Word store, 32 bits
```

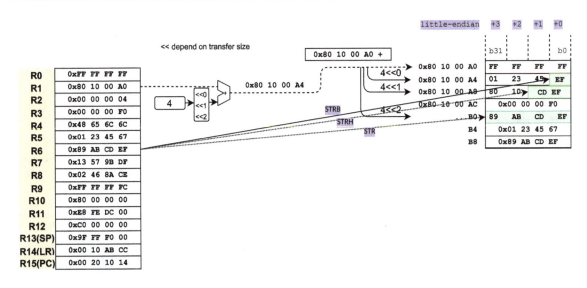

Figure 3.16 STORE instructions with indexed-plus-immediate (0, 1 or 2) destination accesses

It is sometimes necessary to be able to load a constant value into a register, that is, an immediate value (one derived from the instruction itself rather than from memory or a register). The size of the Thumb-2 instruction coding does not allow for 32-bit values. A **MOV** instruction supports values encoded in 8 bits, meaning that the immediate can range from 0 to 255 and is zero-extended when placed in the destination register (Rd). The optional **S** suffix stipulates a flag update on the result of the operation (as illustrated in Figure 3.17).

```
MOV{S} <Rd>, #<const>
```

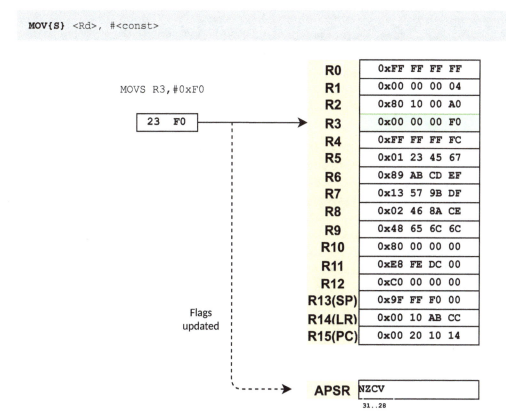

Figure 3.17 MOVS instruction moves an 8-bit zero-extended value into a register (in the range R0..R7) and updates flags

If the immediate value must be bigger, it can be placed in memory as a constant and accessed with addressing relative to the **PC**. The pseudo-instruction **LDR <Rd>, <label>** (see Figure 20) is constructed for this purpose as follows: a value is saved in code memory by the assembler as a word and loaded into a register by an access relative to the **PC**. The **PC** address used is the one next to the instruction currently being executed, because of the way the system increments the **PC** for relative address use.

LDR <Rd>, <label>	0	1	0	0	1	Rd	**PC-relative imm8 * 4** **(0 to 1023)**

Figure 3.18 Load address relative to PC

It is instructive to look at the Arm assembly code that is generated by this **LDR** instruction by using a Linux *readelf* command, as shown below. The first column is the address; the second is the corresponding data in hexadecimal, and the third is the opcode translated into human-readable code. Note that the data is only 2-bytes long, corresponding to the size of a typical Thumb instruction. It is possible that the data contained is actual data, that is, it does not translate into an instruction, or the instruction deduced in the third column is unknown, or by chance it corresponds to some operation. In this example, the address 0x0000_059C is not an instruction, but has the value 0x2000_0008, which translates to movs.

```
00000576:    4909              ldr       r1, [pc, #0x24]
00000578:    9800              ldr       r0, [r13]

. . .

0000059c:    0008              movs      r0, r1
0000059e:    2000              movs      r0, #0
```

1. When translated, the opcode at address 0x0000_0576 is 0x4909 = 0b0100_1001_0000_1001, which corresponds to the instruction Load to PC-relative (0b0100_1), using register r1 (0b001) as destination and the immediate value 0b0000_1001 = 0x9. When added to the **PC**, this immediate is multiplied by 4 for memory alignment. So, the final address is the content of the **PC** plus (0x9 × 4) = PC + 0x24.

2. The value [pc, #0x24] gives 0x0578 + 0x24 = 0x059C, which means that the result of the load is the content of address 0x059C, which is **0x2000_0008.** While the instruction currently being executed is still that in 0x0000_0576, the PC has already been incremented by 2 to get the next instruction.

3.3.5 Thumb-2 Introduction

Arm-v6-M supports the 16-bit Thumb instruction set from Arm-v7-M, including a small number of 32-bit instructions (**BL, DMB, DSB, ISB, MRS,** and **MSR**) introduced to the architecture as part of the Thumb-2 technology in Arm-v6T2. Thumb-2 allows the intermixing of 32-bit instructions with the older 16-bit Thumb instructions. This facilitates maximum compatibility when running programs for the older architecture on the newer one.

The big difference between Thumb-2 and the 32-bit ARM ISA is that almost all of the instructions in the latter are conditional, which is not the case with the 32-bit instructions of Thumb-2. However, a new IT (if-then) instruction in Thumb-2 gives it similar conditional functionality to that of the ARM ISA.

Many Thumb-2 instructions have a mandatory or optional **S** letter at the end of their mnemonic, such as **ADD/ADD**S. This stipulates that the instruction should modify the flags after execution, according to the result. Without the S, the flags are not changed. However, we need to be mindful that some instructions modify the flags even without an explicit S; examples being **CMP** and **TST**.

In the Thumb-2 instruction set, some instructions are limited to accessing the lower register set (**R0–R7**) only. It is easy to understand why this is the case for the 16-bit instructions, in which **Rm** (operand), **Rn** (source) and **Rd** (destination) are all coded with just 3 bits. With 4-bit coding, all 16 registers become addressable. However, using the **R13 (SP)** and **R15 (PC)** registers could produce unpredictable results because it might alter program execution.

A few instructions have two source register operands, Rn and Rm, and a destination register, Rd. For an instruction in which one register serves as both source and destination, it need be written only once, as the first of the instruction operands. The first operand is always the destination of the instruction's result. In the code descriptions that follow in this section, parameters in {} are optional (the brackets are not included when the instruction is actually written).

In Unified Assembler Language (UAL) code, the user can leave the assembler to select the best instruction to generate, but can (try to) force the selection by specifying the optional {<q>} instruction suffix as either **.N** (Narrow, for 16-bit encoding) or **.W** (Wide, for 32-bit encoding).

Some instructions can provide an immediate value in 3, 5, 7, 8, 10 or 11 bits. Most of the time the value is positive only and is extended to 32 bits via zero-extension on the left of the resulting value. Sometimes, it is a signed value and the most-significant bit (MSb) of the value is sign-extended to 32 bits.

Figure 3.19 shows the detailed 16-bit coding of some instructions on Thumb-2 (Tables 9 and 10 do likewise in more detail for Arm-v6-M Thumb-2 instructions coded in 16 and 32 bits, respectively). In fact, some upper bits of the 16-bit codings specify that a 16-bit extension follows this instruction and needs to be used to complete the instruction code.

	15	14	13	12	11	10	9	8	7	6	5	4	3	2	1	0
Shift by immediate, move register	0	0	0	opcode [1]		imm5					Rm			Rd		
Add/subtract register	0	0	0	1	1	0	opc	Rm			Rn			Rd		
Add/subtract immediate	0	0	0	1	1	1	opc	imm3			Rn			Rd		
Add/subtract/compare/move immediate	0	0	1	opcode		Rdn			imm8							
Data-processing register	0	1	0	0	0	0	opcode				Rm			Rdn		
Special data processing	0	1	0	0	0	1	opcode [1]		DN	Rm				Rdn		
Branch/exchange instruction set [3]	0	1	0	0	0	1	1	1	L	Rm				(0)	(0)	(0)
Load from literal pool	0	1	0	0	1	Rd			PC-relative imm8							
Load/store register offset	0	1	0	1	opcode			Rm			Rn			Rd		
Load/store word/byte immediate offset	0	1	1	B	L	imm5					Rn			Rd		
Load/store halfword immediate offset	1	0	0	0	L	imm5					Rn			Rd		
Load from or store to stack	1	0	0	1	L	Rd			SP-relative imm8							

Figure 3.19 Detailed bit coding for some 16-bit Thumb-2 instructions

The key to Figure 3.19 is as follows:

▪ Rm   operand source

                ☐ 3 bits: **R0..R7**, 0b000..0b111

                ☐ 4 bits: **R0..R14**, 0b0000..0b1110

        ☐ **R15 (PC)**, 0b1111, special use!

        ☐ **R13 (SP)**, bits [1..0] must be 00 or UNPREDICTABLE result

▦ Rn	operand source, 3 bits
▦ Rd	result destination, 3 bits
▦ Rdn	operand and destination of the result, 3 bits
▦ imm3	#immediate value in 3 bits
▦ imm5	#immediate value in 5 bits
▦ imm8	#immediate value in 8 bits
▦ PC-relative imm8	access relative to **PC** + #immediate value in 8 bits
▦ SP-relative imm8	access relative to **SP** + #immediate value in 8 bits
▦ B	word (0) or byte (1) size
▦ L	load (1) or store (0) direction
▦ DN	bit associated with Rdn (3-bit coding) to make full set of 16 registers (**R0..R15**) available
▦ opc/opcode	more sub-codes in this group
▦ (0) or (1)	bit must have this value or UNPREDICTABLE instruction will be executed.

In Tables 9 and 10, we can see the bit-level detail of the instructions of the Thumb-2 coding, although some instructions are not described here. The coding is mainly in 16 bits, but is in 32 bits for a few instructions. Every fetch (instruction load) is done in 32 bits because:

▦ the processor might be fetching two instructions at a time, meaning that there is no need to fetch the next instruction because it is already available, or

▦ the instruction is a 32-bit instruction and there is no special case, or

▦ the 32-bit data contains a 16-bit instruction, followed by the first 16 bits of a 32-bit instruction. On the next access, the remaining 16-bit extension of the latter is fetched.

The fetching unit takes care of these different possibilities so that the instructions are correctly presented to the processor.

Table 3.5 16-bit Thumb instruction codings in Arm–v6-M

Group	Instruction	15	14	13	12	11	10	9	8	7	6	5	4	3	2	1	0
32-bit instruction	First part of the code;	1	1	1	0	1											
	next 16 bits – rest of the 32-bit ARM instruction	1	1	1	1	0											
Shift, Add, Sub, Move, Compare		0	0														
	Shift by immediate, move register	0		Op0	Op1		imm5					Rm			Rd		
	LSLS{<q>} <Rd>,<Rm>,#<imm5> MOV{S}{<q>} <Rd>,<Rm>			0	0	0	#1-31 If #0 → MOVE instruction					R0..R7			R0..R7		
	LSRS{<q>} <Rd>,<Rm>,#<imm5>			0	0	1	If #0 → #32					R0..R7			R0..R7		
	ASRS{<q>} <Rd>,<Rm>,#<imm5>			0	1	0	If #0 → #32					R0..R7			R0..R7		
	ROR			0	1	1	If #1..31 → ROR					R0..R7			R0..R7		
	RRX			0	1	1	If #0 → RRX, shift #1					R0..R7			R0..R7		
	Add/subtract register	0	0	0	1	1	0	opc	Rm			Rn			Rd		
	ADD{S}{<q>}{<Rd>,}<Rn>,<Rm> ADDS <Rd>,<Rn>,<Rm>			0	1	1	0	0	R0..R7			R0..R7			R0..R7		
	SUBS{<q>}{<Rd>,}<Rn>,<Rm>			0	1	1	0	1	R0..R7			R0..R7			R0..R7		
	Add/subtract immediate	0	0	0	1	1	1	opc	imm3			Rn			Rd		
	ADDS{<q>}{<Rd>,}<Rn>,#<const>			0	1	1	1	0	#0..7			R0..R7			R0..R7		
	SUBS{<q>}{<Rd>,}<Rn>,#<const>			0	1	1	1	1	#0..7			R0..R7			R0..R7		
	Add/subtract/compare/ move immediate 8 bits	0	0	1	Op1		Rd			imm8							
	MOVS{<q>} <Rd>,#<const>			1	0	0	R0..R7			#0-255							
	CMP{<q>} <Rn>,#<const> Update flags!			1	0	1	Rn (R0..R7)			#0-255							
	ADDS{<q>}{<Rd>,}<Rn>,#<const>			1	1	0	Rdn (R0..R7)			#0-255							
	SUBS{<q>}{<Rd>,}<Rn>,#<const>			1	1	1	Rdn (R0..R7)			#0-255							
Data processing		0	1														
	Data processing register	0	1	0	0	0	0	opcode				Rm			Rdn		
	ANDS{<q>} {<Rd>,}<Rn>,<Rm> ANDS <Rdn>,<Rm> (AND)		AND	Rdn	↓	Rm AND Rdn	Update Flag	0	0	0	0	R0..R7			R0..R7		
	EORS{<q>}{<Rd>,}<Rn>,<Rm> EORS <Rdn>,<Rm> (Exclusive OR)		Exclusive OR	Rdn	↓	Rm EOR Rdn	Update Flag	0	0	0	1	R0..R7			R0..R7		
	LSLS{<q>} <Rd>,<Rn>,<Rm> LSLS <Rdn>,<Rm> (Logical Shift Left)		Logical Shift Left	Rdn	↓	Rdn SL Rm	Update Flag	0	0	1	0	R0..R7			R0..R7		

	15	14	13	12	11	10	9	8	7	6	5	4	3	2	1	0
LSRS[<q>] <Rd>,<Rn>,<Rm> / LSRS <Rdn>,<Rm>	LSR	Logical Shift Right	Rdn	↓	Rdn SR Rm	0 → Update Flag	0	0	1	1	R0..R7			R0..R7		
ASRS[<q>] <Rd>,<Rn>,<Rm> / ASRS <Rdn>,<Rm>	ASR	Arithm. Shift Right	Rdn	↓	Rdn SR Rm	MSb → Update Flag	0	1	0	0	R0..R7			R0..R7		
ADCS[<q>]{<Rd>,} <Rn>,<Rm> / ADCS <Rdn>,<Rm>	ADD Carry	Add+ Carry	Rdn	↓	Rdn + Rm +C	Update Flag	0	1	0	1	R0..R7			R0..R7		
SBCS[<q>]{<Rd>,} <Rn>,<Rm> / SBCS <Rdn>,<Rm>	Sub Carry	Sub+ Carry	Rdn	↓	???	Update Flag	0	1	1	0	R0..R7			R0..R7		
RORS[<q>] <Rd>,<Rn>,<Rm> / RORS <Rdn>,<Rm>	ROR	Rotate Right	Rdn	↓	Rdn ROR Rm<7:0>	Update Flag	0	1	1	1	R0..R7			R0..R7		
TST[<q>] <Rn>,<Rm> / TST <Rn>,<Rm>	TST	Test	-	↓	Rm AND Rdn	Update Flags	1	0	0	0	R0..R7			R0..R7		
RSBS[<q>]{<Rd>,} <Rn>,#<cst> / RSBS <Rdn>,<Rm>,#0	RSB	Reverse Sub	Rdn	↓	#0-Rm	Update Flag	1	0	0	1	R0..R7			R0..R7		
CMP[<q>] <Rn>,<Rm>	CMP	Compare	-	↓	Rdn-Rm +C	Update Flags	1	0	1	0	R0..R7			R0..R7		
CMN[<q>] <Rn>,<Rm>	CMN	Compare Negative	-	↓	Rm-Rdn +C	Update Flags	1	0	1	1	R0..R7			R0..R7		
ORRS[<q>]{<Rd>,} <Rn>,<Rm> / ORRS <Rdn>,<Rm>	ORR	OR	Rdn	↓	Rm OR Rdn	Update Flag	1	1	0	0	R0..R7			R0..R7		
MULS[<q>]{<Rd>,} <Rn>,<Rm> / MULS <Rdn>,<Rm>,<Rdn>	MUL	Multiply	Rdn	↓	Rm * Rdn	Update Flag	1	1	0	1	R0..R7			R0..R7		
BICS[<q>]{<Rd>,} <Rn>,<Rm> / BICS <Rdn>,<Rm>	BIC	Bit Clear	Rdn	↓	Rdn AND NOT Rm	Update Flag	1	1	1	0	R0..R7			R0..R7		
MVNS[<q>] <Rd>,<Rm> / MVNS <Rdn>,<Rm>	MVN	Move NOT	Rdn	↓	NOT Rm	Update Flag	1	1	1	1	R0..R7			R0..R7		
Special data processing	0	1	0	0	0	1	opcode	0	DN	Rm				Rdn		
ADD <Rdn>,<Rm>	ADD	Rdn 0..7 && Rm 0..7	Rdn		Rdn+ Rm	R0: R14	0	0	0	0	R0	...	R7	R0	...	R7
UNPREDICTABLE → use other binary coding		Rdn 0..7 && Rm 0..7 || R15 → UNPREDICTABLE					0	1		R0	R8	...	R14	R0	...	R7
CMP <Rdn>,<Rm>		Rdn 0..7 && Rm 0..7 → UNPREDICTABLE / R15 → UNPREDICTABLE				Update Flag	0	1			R0	:	R14	R0	...	R7
CMP <Rdn>,<Rm>		R15 → UNPREDICTABLE					0	1			.	:	R14	R8	:	R15

Instruction	15	14	13	12	11	10	9	8	7	6	5	4	3	2	1	0
MOV <Rdn>,<Rm>						1	1	0	MSb Rdn							
BX <Rm>		R15 → UNPREDICTABLE	PC	↓	Rm		1	1	0		R0	:	R14	(0)	(0)	(0)
BLX <Rm>	Branch & Link	If R15 → UNPREDICTABLE	PC LR, LSb=1	↓	Rm PC-2		1	1	1		R0	:	R14	(0)	(0)	(0)
Load from literal pool — LDR <Rd>,<label>	0	1	0	0	1	Rd	PC-relative imm8*4 → 0..1020									
Load/store — Load/store register offset	0	1	0	1	opcode			Rm			Rn			Rd		
STR $<Rd>$,[$<Rn>$,<Rm>]	Rd	→ .32	[Rn+Rm]		0	0	0									
STRH $<Rd>_t$,[$<Rn>$,<Rm>]	Rd	→ .16	[Rn+Rm]		0	0	1									
STRB $<Rd>_t$,[$<Rn>$,<Rm>]	Rd	→ .8	[Rn+Rm]		0	1	0									
LDRSB $<Rd>_t$,[$<Rn>$,<Rm>]	Rd .32	← .S8	[Rn+Rm]		0	1	1									
LDR $<Rd>_t$,[$<Rn>$,<Rm>]	Rd .32	← .32	[Rn+Rm]		1	0	0									
LDRH $<Rd>_t$,[$<Rn>$,<Rm>]	Rd .32	← .16	[Rn+Rm]		1	0	1									
LDRB $<Rd>_t$,[$<Rn>$,<Rm>]	Rd .32	← .8	[Rn+Rm]		1	1	0									
LDRSH $<Rd>_t$,[$<Rn>$,<Rm>]	Rd .32	← .S16	[Rn+Rm]		1	1	1									
Load/store word/byte immediate offset	0	1	1	B	L	imm5 (0..31) → 0..31 *Size					Rn			Rd		
STR $<Rd>_t$,[$<Rn>$,{#<imm5>]]	Rd	→ .32	[Rn+ imm5*4]	0	0											
LDR $<Rd>_t$,[$<Rn>${,#<imm5>]]	Rd .32	← .32	[Rn+ imm5*4]	0	1											
STRB $<Rd>_t$,[$<Rn>$,#<imm5>]	Rd	→ .8	[Rn+ imm5*1]	1	0											
LDRB $<Rd>_t$,[$<Rn>${,#<imm5>]]	Rd .32	← .8	[Rn+ imm5*1]	1	1											
Load/store half-word immediate offset	1	0	0	0	L	imm5 (0..31) → 0..31 *Size					Rn			Rd		

	15	14	13	12	11	10	9	8	7	6	5	4	3	2	1	0
STRH <Rd>h,[<Rn>,[#<imm5>]]	Rd	→ .16	[Rn+ imm5*2]	0	0											
LDRH <Rd>,[<Rn>,[#<imm5>]]	Rd .32	← .16	[Rn+ imm5*2]	1	1											
Load/store with stack	1	0	0	1	L	Rd		SP-relative imm8 (0..255) → 0..1020								
STR <Rd>,[SP,#<imm8>]	Rd	→ .32	[SP, imm8*4]	1	0											
LDR <Rd>,[SP[,#<imm8>]]	Rd .32	← .32	[SP, imm8*4]	1	1											
Generate PC-relative address	1	0	1	0	0	Rd		imm8 (0..255) → 0..1020								
ADR <Rd>, <label>	ADR[<q>]	<Rd>, <label>				<Rd> ←		PC-relative address (provided by this label)								
ADR <Rd>,<label>	Rd .32	← .32	[PC+ imm8*4]		0	Rd		imm8								
Generate SP-relative address	1	0	1	0	1	Rd		SP + #imm8*4								
ADD <Rd>,SP,#<imm8>	ADD[<q>]	<Rd>,SP, #const				<Rd> ←										
ADD <Rd>,SP,#<imm8>	Rd .32	← .32	[SP+ imm8*4]	0	0											
Miscellaneous 16 bits	1	0	1	1	opcode											
ADD SPSP,#<imm7>					0	0	0	0	0	imm7 (0..127)*4						
SUB SPSP,#<imm7>					0	0	0	0	1							
SXTH <Rd>,<Rm>	Rd .32	← .S16	Rm		0	0	1	0	0	0	1	Rm			Rd	
SXTB <Rd>,<Rm>	Rd .32	← .S8	Rm		0	0	1	0	0	1	1	Rm			Rd	
UXTH <Rd>,<Rm>	Rd .32	← .16	Rm		0	0	1	0	1	0	1	Rm			Rd	
UXTB <Rd>,<Rm>	Rd .32	← .8	Rm		0	0	1	0	1	1	1	Rm			Rd	
PUSH <registers>	{LR,R7,R6,R5,R4,R3,R2,R1,R0} lowest Add SP ← SP-4*NbReg				0	1	0	R14 /LR	<register_list> : {LR,R7,R6,R5,R4,R3,R2,R1,R0}							
CPS<effect> <iflags> CPSIE CPSID	IE/ID: Interrupt Enable/ Disable	PRIMASK. PM		im=0 im=1	0	1	1	0	0	1	1	im	(0)	(0)	(1)	(0)
Privileged execution																
REV <Rd>,<Rm>	Reverse Byte Order	Rd31-24 Rd23-16 Rd15-8 Rd7-0	←	Rm7-0 Rm15-8 Rm23-16 Rm31-24	1	0	1	0	0	0	0	Rm			Rd	

Instruction	15	14	13	12	11	10	9	8	7	6	5	4	3	2	1	0
REV16 <Rd>,<Rm>	Reverse Byte in Half-word	Rd31-24 Rd23-16 Rd15-8 Rd7-0	←	Rm23-16 Rm31-24 Rm7-0 Rm15-8	1	0	1	0	0	1		Rm			Rd	
REVSH <Rd>,<Rm>		Rd31-8 Rd7-0	←	SignExt (Rm7-0) Rm15-8	1	0	1	0	1	1		Rm			Rd	
POP <registers>	{PC,R7,R6,R5,R4,R3,R2,R1,R0} lowest Add SP ← SP+4*NbReg			Add	1	1	0	R15/ PC	<register_list> : {PC,R7,R6,R5,R4,R3,R2,R1,R0}							
BKPT #<imm8>	Info for debugger				1	1	1	0	imm8							
Hint instructions					1	1	1	1	opA				opB			
NOP	No Operation								0	0	0	0	0	0	0	0
YIELD	Yield								0	0	0	1	0	0	0	0
WFE	Wait For Event								0	0	1	0	0	0	0	0
WFI	Wait For Interrupt								0	0	1	1	0	0	0	0
SEV	Send Event causes an event to be signaled to all CPUs within a multiprocessor system								0	1	0	0	0	0	0	0
Store multiple registers	1	1	0	0	0	Rn	<register_list> : {R7,R6,R5,R4,R3,R2,R1,R0}									
STM <Rn>!,<registers>	If!, Rn ← Rn+4*NbReg Store <registers> R0..R7 in [Rn++]															
Load multiple registers	1	1	0	0	1	Rn	<register_list> : {R7,R6,R5,R4,R3,R2,R1,R0}									
LDM <Rn>!,<registers>	LDMIA If!, Rn ← Rn+4*NbReg Load <registers> R0..R7 from [Rn++]															
Conditional branch, and supervisor call	1	1	0	1	Condition				imm8							
B{cond} <label>	Conditional Branch PC + -256...+254 (even)				0b0000...0x1101											
BEQ <label>	Equal Z==1				0	0	0	0	SignedExt(imm8 *2) → -256...+254							
BNE <label>	Not Equal Z==0				0	0	0	1	SignedExt(imm8 *2) → -256...+254							
BCS / BHS <label>	Carry Set / Higher or Same C==1				0	0	1	0	SignedExt(imm8 *2) → -256...+254							
BCC / BLO <label>	Carry Clear / Lower C==0				0	0	1	1	SignedExt(imm8 *2) → -256...+254							
BMI <label>	Minus, Negative N==1				0	1	0	0	SignedExt(imm8 *2) → -256...+254							
BPL <label>	Plus, Positive or Zero N==0				0	1	0	1	SignedExt(imm8 *2) → -256...+254							

Instruction	15	14	13	12	11	10	9	8	7 6 5 4 3 2 1 0
BVS <label>	Overflow V==1				0	1	1	0	SignedExt(imm8 *2) → -256...+254
BVC <label>	No overflow V==0				0	1	1	1	SignedExt(imm8 *2) → -256...+254
BHI <label>	Higher (unsigned) C==1 and Z==0				1	0	0	0	SignedExt(imm8 *2) → -256...+254
BLS <label>	Lower or same (unsigned) C==0 or Z==1				1	0	0	1	SignedExt(imm8 *2) → -256...+254
BGE <label>	Greater than or equal (signed) N==V				1	0	1	0	SignedExt(imm8 *2) → -256...+254
BLT <label>	Less than (signed) N!=V				1	0	1	1	SignedExt(imm8 *2) → -256...+254
BGT <label>	Greater than (signed) Z==0 and N==V				1	1	0	0	SignedExt(imm8 *2) → -256...+254
BLE <label>	Less than or equal (signed) Z==1 or N!=V				1	1	0	1	SignedExt(imm8 *2) → -256...+254
BAL <label>	Always: Coding never used in Arm-v6-M				1	1	1	0	
UDF #<imm8>	UNDEFINED				1	1	1	0	imm8
SVC #<imm8>	Supervisor Call, Exception SVCall HardFault				1	1	1	1	imm8
Unconditional branch					0	imm11			
B <label> BL <label>	1	1	1	0	SignedExt(imm11 *2) → -2048...+2046				

Notes:

Specifies optional assembler qualifiers on the instruction; the following qualifiers are defined:

■ .N (narrow) specifies that the assembler must select a 16-bit encoding for the instruction; if this is not possible, an assembler error is produced

■ .W (wide) specifies that the assembler must select a 32-bit encoding for the instruction; again, if this is not possible, an assembler error is produced.

In more recent architecture variants (but not in Arm-v6-M), the Thumb instruction set supports additional conditional execution capabilities (not listed in this table):

■ a 32-bit conditional branch with a larger branch range

■ Compare and Branch on Zero (CBZ) and Compare and Branch on Non-Zero (CBNZ) instructions

■ an If-Then (IT) instruction.

3.3.6 Specialized Thumb-2 Instructions

Table 3.6 provides bit-level details for the 32-bit instructions used in the Arm-V6-M architecture, most of which are specialized instructions for various forms of program, register, and memory control. The instructions are represented by means of two rows; in each case, the first row is the first 16 bits (31:16), and the second row is the last 16 bits (15:0).

Table 3.6 32-bit (2 × 16-bit) Thumb instruction codings in Arm-v6-M (for Cortex-M0/M0+)

	15	14	13	12	11	10	9	8	7	6	5	4	3	2	1	0
32-bit instructions First part of the code; next 16 bits – rest of the 32-bit ARM instruction	1	1	1	0	1											
	1	1	1	1	0											
	1	1	1	1	1											
1st 16 bits	1	1	1		Op1											
2nd 16 bits	op															
UNDEFINED on Arm-v6-M	1	1	1	0	1											
UNDEFINED on Arm-v6-M	1	1	1	1	1											
UNDEFINED on Arm-v6-M	1	1	1	1	0											
	0															
Arm-v7-M	1	1	1	1	0											
	0															
Branch and miscellaneous control	1	1	1	1	0			Op1								
	1	Op2														
UDF.W #<imm16>	1	1	1	1	0	1	1	1	1	1	1	1	imm4			
Undefined ZeroExtend(imm4:imm12)	1	0	1	0	imm12											
BL <label>	1	1	1	1	0	S	imm10									
PC +/- 16 MiB	1	1	J1	1	J2	imm11										
next_instr_addr = PC; LR = next_instr_addr<31:1> : '1'	PC + (SignExt(S:I1:I2:imm10:imm11:'0') → 32					I1 = NOT(J1 EOR S), I2 = NOT(J1 EOR S) *Historical reason*										
Miscellaneous control instructions	1	1	1	1	0	0	1	1	1	0	1	1	(1)	(1)	(1)	(1)
	1	0	(0)	0	(1)	(1)	(1)	(1)	op							
Move to Special Register MSR <spec_reg>,<Rn> Rn {13,15} → UNPREDICTABLE SYSm not in the list → UNPREDICTABLE	1	1	1	1	0	0	1	1	1	0	0	(0)	Rn {0..12, 14}			
	1	0	(0)	0	(1)	(0)	(0)	(0)	SYSm (see Table 10)							
Move to Register from Special Register MRS <Rd>,<spec_reg> Rd {13,15} → UNPREDICTABLE	1	1	1	1	0	0	1	1	1	1	1	(0)	(1)	(1)	(1)	(1)
SYSm not in the list → UNPREDICTABLE	1	0	(0)	0	Rd				SYSm (see Table 10)							
DSB #<option> Data Synchronization Barrier	1	1	1	1	0	0	1	1	1	0	1	1	(1)	(1)	(1)	(1)
	1	0	(0)	0	(1)	(1)	(1)	(1)	0	1	0	0	Option 1 1 1 1			
DMB #<option> Data Memory Barrier	1	1	1	1	0	0	1	1	1	0	1	1	(1)	(1)	(1)	(1)
	1	0	(0)	0	(1)	(1)	(1)	(1)	0	1	0	1	Option 1 1 1 1			
ISB #<option> Instruction Synchronization Barrier	1	1	1	1	0	0	1	1	1	0	1	1	(1)	(1)	(1)	(1)
	1	0	(0)	0	(1)	(1)	(1)	(1)	0	1	1	0	Option 1 1 1 1			

3.3.6.1 Special Register Instructions (MSR and MRS)

The syntax for the **MSR** and **MRS** special register instructions shown in Table 3.6 includes a <spec_reg> argument that compiles to a numeric value in the SYSm field of the instruction encodings, as shown in Tables 3.7 and 3.8.

Table 3.7 Special register field encoding, SYSm, Arm-v6-M and Arm-v7-M

Special register	Contents	SYSm value (decimal)	SYSm value (8-bit binary)
APSR	Application Status Register: the flags from previous instructions	0	0b00000:000
IAPSR	Composite of the IPSR and APSR sub-registers	1	0b00000:001
EAPSR	Composite of the EPSR and APSR sub-registers	2	0b00000:010
XPSR	Composite of all three PSR sub-registers (APSR, IPSR and EPSR)	3	0b00000:011
IPSR	Interrupt Status Register	5	0b00000:101
EPSR	Execution Status Register: the EPSR bitfield exhibits read-as-zero (RAZ) behavior	6	0b00000:110
IEPSR	Composite of the IPSR and EPSR sub-registers	7	0b00000:111
MSP	The Main Stack Pointer	8	0b00001:000
PSP	The Process Stack Pointer	9	0b00001:001
PRIMASK	Register to mask out configurable exceptions: raises the current priority to 0 when set to 1. This is a 1-bit register.	16	0b00010:000
CONTROL	The CONTROL register	20	0b00010:100
-	Reserved		Other values

Note: Binary values shown split into the fields used in the instruction operation pseudocode, SYSm<7:3>:SYSm<2:0>.

Table 3.8 Additional special register field encoding, SYSm, Arm-v7-M only

Special register	Contents	SYSm value (decimal)	SYSm value (8-bit binary)
BASEPRI_MAX	On reads, acts as an alias of BASEPRI: on writes, can raise BASEPRI but is ignored if it would reduce it	18	0b00010:010
FAULTMASK	Register to raise priority to the Hard Fault level	19	0b00010:011
-	Reserved		Other values

3.3.6.2 Barrier Instructions (DMB, DSB and ISB)

The following instructions (see Table 3.6) provide varying forms of memory synchronization:

- **DMB** (Data Memory Barrier) instruction acts as a memory barrier. It ensures that all explicit memory accesses that appear in program order before the **DMB** instruction are observed before any explicit memory accesses that appear in program order after the **DMB** instruction. It does not affect the ordering of any other instructions executing on the processor.

- **DSB** (Data Synchronization Barrier) instruction acts as a special kind of memory barrier. Instructions in the program that follow it have to wait until its completion; the instruction completes only when the following are true:

  - [ ] any explicit memory access made before this instruction is complete – all LOADs and STOREs – have finished

  - [ ] all cache and branch predictor maintenance operations before this instruction have completed.

- **ISB** (Instruction Synchronization Barrier) instruction flushes the pipeline in the processor, so that all instructions following the ISB are only fetched from cache or memory after the instruction has completed. It ensures that the effects of all context-altering operations, such as those resulting from read or write accesses to the system control space (SCS), that completed before the **ISB** instruction are visible to the instructions fetched after the **ISB** instruction. The **ISB** instruction also ensures that any branches that appear in program order after it are always written into any branch prediction logic with the context that is visible after the **ISB** instruction. This is required to ensure correct execution of the instruction stream.

3.4 Memory Model

In the Cortex-M family, the address space of the external bus is unified via a von Neumann architecture, even if the internal architecture conforms to Harvard.

Depending on the address, different area and access capabilities are available. As a deliberate feature, the peripheral area, where the programmable interfaces are selected, is NOT cacheable: it is mandatory that the last real value of the different registers is read and not an old cached value.

Thus, for the different regions of memory, the possible **memory types** are:

- **Normal**: The processor can re-order the transactions for purposes of efficiency, and perform speculative reads.

- **Device**: The processor preserves the order of transaction access relative to the Device or Strongly Ordered memories.

- **Strongly Ordered**: The processor preserves the order of accesses relative to all other transactions.

The different ordering requirements for Device and Strongly Ordered memories mean that the memory system can buffer a write to Device memory, but must not buffer a write to Strongly Ordered memory.

Note that some memory regions cannot be used to provide Device-type memory for code execution.

3.4.1 Bit-banding

Another feature of the Cortex-M memory model is bit-banding. The idea of bit-banding is to enable the modification of individual bits in a region of memory, often necessary in the context of managing peripherals, in a single machine instruction. Otherwise, an entire word would have to be read into a register, the relevant bit updated therein, and written back, involving three instructions and running the risk of a conflict if, for example, an interrupt makes a change to a different bit in the original word while the copy is in the register. Bit-banding resolves this by using only the least-significant bit (0) of a word in memory to change a single bit in another memory area.

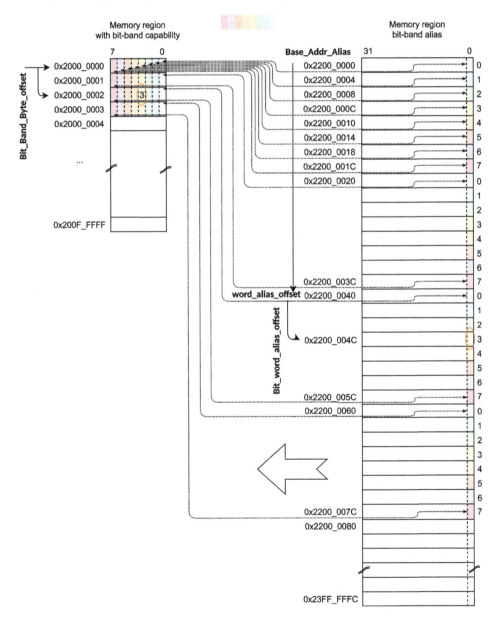

Figure 3.20 Example of bit-banding in SRAM

This bit-level access is provided to a 1 Mb region of "bit-banded" memory by reserving a 32 Mb area of "**alias**" memory and mapping between the two. Then, by reading a 32-bit word from the alias memory using a standard instruction, we can gain access to 1 bit of the bit-banded memory. If we write to bit 0 of a word in the alias memory the result is an atomic read-modify-write of the corresponding bit within the bit-banded region by means of a standard memory instruction. The bit-banded memory can be accessed as normal memory at the level of bytes, half-words or words, but using the alias memory means that a standard write instruction can also change a single bit of the bit-banded memory. Figure 3.20 shows a representative example of this mapping for SRAM, and Table 3.9 shows a worked example of access, as read or write, to the bit-banded SRAM address 0x2000_0002:3 through the alias address 0x2200_004C, based on this figure.

Note that the Cortex-M3, for example, can bit-band two such 1 Mb areas of memory, one in internal SRAM and one in the peripherals region. Thus, individual bits within the peripheral address range from 0x4000_0000 to 0x400F_FFFF can be accessed via the alias area 0x4200_0000 to 0x43FF_FFFF.

Table 3.9 Application of bit-banding (see Figure 3.20)

Name	Example	Value	Comment
Bit-banded area			
Base_Address_Bit_Band	0x2000_0000	Base address of the bit-banded memory to access	e.g. MSP432P401R
Bit_Band_Byte_offset	2	Address = **Base_Address_Bit_Band** + **Bit_Band_Byte_offset** → 0x2000_0000 + 2 → 0x2000_0002	The byte that needs to be changed. The offset address in the bit-banded memory, as a byte address, in which to change the bit.
bit_number	3	0..7 in the bit-banded region	The bit that needs to be changed: 1 bit in bit-banded memory → 4 bytes in alias memory
Alias area			
Base_Addr_Alias	0x2200_0000	0x2200_0000	Base address of the alias memory
Word_alias_offset	Bit_Band_Byte_offset * (4 * 8) → 2 * 32 → **0x40**	The offset in the alias memory of the target byte	Offset of the bit-banded byte in alias memory: 4 bytes/word * 8 bits/byte
Bit_word_alias_offset	bit_number * 4	Offset of the bit in the alias word memory: 3 * 4 → 0xC	4 bytes/word
Bit_Word_Offset	Word_alias_offset + Bit_word_alias_offset	0x40 + 0xC → 0x4C	Offset in alias memory
Bit_Word_Addr	Base_Address_Bit_Band + Bit_Word_Offset	0x2200_0000 + 0x40 → 0x2200_0040	Final address in alias memory to write the bit to change in bit-banded memory

Note: 1 bit (in bit-band memory) → 1 word (in alias memory) → 4-byte address increment

To summarize the address calculation involved in bit-banding:

Alias_Address = Base_Addr_Alias	(0x2200_0000)
+ Word_alias_offset	(Bit_Band_Byte_offset * [4 * 8])
+ Bit_word_alias_offset	(bit_number * 4)

3.5 Exceptions and Interrupts

Systems implemented with the Arm-v6-M base architecture have only one mode and all instructions are executed at privileged level. In Arm-v7-M, both unprivileged and privileged software execution modes exist (in Thread mode; Handler mode is always privileged). However, an optional Unprivileged/Privileged Extension allows Arm-v6-M systems to use the same privilege levels as Arm-v7-M.

Priority of execution in Arm-v6-M and Arm-v7-M systems is controlled by priority levels. Every exception has a priority level associated with it, as does the current execution stream within the processor. An exception that has a higher priority level than the latter will preempt it, effectively taking control of the processor. Arm-v6-M systems have a 2-bit priority field, supporting 4 levels of priority; Arm-v7-M systems have an 8-bit priority field, allowing up to 256 levels of priority to be defined. Alternatively, some of the 8 priority bits in an Arm-v7-M system can be used to establish configurable priority groupings. (Note that the 2-bit priority field in Arm-v6-M systems corresponds to the two most-significant bits of the Arm-v7-M's 8-bit priority field.)

In Arm-v7-M systems, exception priority can be changed dynamically through PRIMASK, FAULTMASK and BASEPRI registers. In Arm-v6-M systems, only the PRIMASK register can be used for this purpose.

As a minimum, six exceptions are supported on all Cortex-M systems: Reset, Non-Maskable Interrupt (NMI), HardFault, SVCall, PendSV and SysTick. Thus:

- **Reset**: This defines the routine that a processor runs following a system reset.

- Non-Maskable Interrupt: A specific hardware interrupt with the highest priority after Reset and unmaskable, that is, it cannot be disabled. Often used as a panic interrupt on power-down detection.

- **HardFault**: This serves as a generic fault for all classes of fault that cannot be handled by any of the other exception mechanisms, typically those caused by the execution of instructions (i.e. software).

HardFault is the only handler for such faults in Arm-v6-M systems, but Arm-v7-M and Arm-v8-M systems also support three finer-grained exceptions:

- **MemManage**: This handles memory protection faults as determined by the Memory Protection Unit.

- **BusFault**: This handles memory-related faults other than those handled by the MemManage fault, for both instruction and data memory transactions. Typically, these faults arise from errors detected on the system buses.

- **UsageFault**: This handles non-memory related faults caused by instruction execution, for example, when a code is sent to the processor but is not applicable to it. This could be a bad configuration of the development tools or a bad selection of the processor architecture to use, such as selecting a Cortex-M4 instruction set for compilation and trying to run it on a Cortex-M0, which supports a more limited set of instructions. Unaligned addresses and division by zero can also be configured to generate UsageFaults.

Each of these built-in exceptions has a predefined Exception Number (see Table 3.10), which maps to an offset within the Vector Table where each entry contains a 32-bit address that acts as the entry-point for the code that must be executed when that particular exception occurs. This table starts at address 0x0000_0000, with entry point 0 being reserved for the value of the Main stack pointer (**SP**) to be used following a reset.

On some implementations, the base address of the Vector Table can be changed. When the table is in nonvolatile memory, it is not efficient to have a dynamic software-based interrupt initialization: it must be done at compile time instead.

Table 3.10 Exception numbers and priorities on Arm-v6-M and Arm-v7-M

Exception number	Exception	CMSIS interrupt number	Priority
0	Not an exception, but **SP** initial value		
1	Reset		−3
2	**NMI** (Non-Maskable Interrupt)	−14	−2
3	**HardFault**	−13	−1
4	**MemManage** (Arm-v7-M/Arm-v8-M)	−12	Programmable
5	**BusFault** (Arm-v7-M/Arm-v8-M)	−11	Programmable
6	**UsageFault** (Arm-v7-M/Arm-v8-M)	−10	Programmable
7			
8			
9			
10			
11	**SVCall** (Supervisor Call)	−5	Programmable
12	Debug Monitor (Arm-v7-M/Arm-v8-M)	−4	
13			
14	**PendSV**	−2	
15	SysTick (option)	−1	Programmable
16	External Interrupt 0 (device-dependent)	0	Progr. in NVIC
17	External Interrupt 1 (device-dependent)	1	Progr. in NVIC

Exception number	Exception	CMSIS interrupt number	Priority
18	External Interrupt 2 (device-dependent)	2	Progr. in NVIC
...	External Interrupt ... (device-dependent)		Progr. in NVIC
Max	External Interrupt N-1 (device-dependent)	N-1	Progr. in NVIC

The exceptions and interrupts shown in Table 3.10 have either a fixed priority or a programmable one. Note that the lower the priority value (e.g. −3 for Reset), the higher its actual priority. All other exceptions/interrupts can have their priority changed in the System Control Space (SCS).

3.5.1 System Control Space (SCS)

We have seen that the Cortex-M processor has a set of closely coupled general-purpose registers (R0..R15) and special registers (for flags, control) available through specific instructions. Other registers must be memory-mapped as programmable interfaces within the Cortex-M component.

The System Control Space (SCS) is a 4 kiB address region of mapped memory that is reserved for system control and configuration, as shown in Table 3.11. The System Control Block (SCB), see Table 3.12, is located within the SCS and contains information associated with the exception model. Also located within the SCS are the registers used by the Nested Vector Interrupt Controller (NVIC) that, as we saw in Chapter 1, provides the integrated interrupt control that is a key characteristic of the Cortex-M processor family.

Table 3.11 System control space (SCS) for Arm-v6-M

Address	Group	Description
0xE000_E000 – 0xE000_E00F	System control and ID registers	Includes the Auxiliary Control register
0xE000_ED00 – 0xE000_ED8F		**System Control Block**
0xE000_EF90 – 0xE000_EFCF		IMPLEMENTATION-DEFINED
0xE000_E010 – 0xE000_E0FF	SysTick	Optional System Timer
0xE000_E100 – 0xE000_ECFF	NVIC	**Nested Vector Interrupt Controller**
0xE000_EDF0 – 0xE000_EEFF	Debug	Debug control and configuration; applies to Debug Extension only
0xE000_ED90 – 0xE000_EDEF	MPU	Optional MPU (Protected Memory System Architecture)

Table 3.12 System control block (SCB) summary for Arm-v6-M (Arm-v7-M [v7] additions shown in pink)

Address	Name	Type	Reset value	Description
0xE000_E008	**ACTLR**	RW	IMPLEMENTATION-DEFINED	Auxiliary Control Register, **ACTLR**
0xE000_ED00	**CPUID**	RO	IMPLEMENTATION-DEFINED	CPUID Base Register
0xE000_ED04	**ICSR**	RW	0x0000_0000	Interrupt Control State Register, **ICSR**
0xE000_ED08	**VTOR**	RW	0x0000_0000	Vector Table Offset Register, **VTOR**

Address	Name	Type	Reset value	Description
0xE000_ED0C	**AIRCR**	RW	bits [10:8] = 0b000	Application Interrupt and Reset Control Register, **AIRCR**
0xE000_ED10	**SCR**	RW	bits [4,2,1] = 0b000	(Optional) System Control Register, **SCR**
0xE000_ED14	**CCR**	RO	bits [9:3] =0b111_1111	Configuration and Control Register, **CCR**
0xE000_ED18	*SHPR1*	*RW*	*0x0000_0000*	*System Handler Priority Register 1, **SHPR1** (v7)*
0xE000_ED1C	**SHPR2**	RW	SBZ (Should Be Zero)	System Handler Priority Register 2, **SHPR2**
0xE000_ED20	**SHPR3**	RW	SBZ (Should Be Zero)	System Handler Priority Register 3, **SHPR3**
0xE000_ED24	**SHCSR**	RW	0x0000_0000	System Handler Control and State Register, **SHCSR**
0xE000_ED28	*CFSR*	*RW*	*0x0000_0000*	*Configurable Fault Status Register (v7)*
0xE000_ED2C	*HFSR*	*RW*	*0x0000_0000*	*HardFault Status Register (v7)*
0xE000_ED30	**DFSR**	RW	0x0000_0000	Debug Fault Status Register, **DFSR**
0xE000_ED34	*MMFAR*	*RW*	*UNKNOWN*	*MemManage Fault Address Register, **MMFAR** (v7)*
0xE000_ED38	*BFAR*	*RW*	*UNKNOWN*	*BusFault Address Register, **BFAR** (v7)*
0xE000_ED3C	*AFSR*	*RW*	*UNKNOWN*	*Auxiliary Fault Status Register, **AFSR** (v7)* *IMPLEMENTATION-DEFINED*
0xE000_ED40 -				
0xE000_ED84	-	-	-	*Reserved for **CPUID** registers, the CPUID Scheme (v7)*
0xE000_ED88	*CPACR*	*RW*	*UNKNOWN*	*Co-Processor Access Control Register, **CPACR** (v7)*
0xE000_ED8C	-	-	-	*Reserved (v7)*

Within the system control block, the Vector Table Offset Register, **VTOR**, allows the vector table to be relocated anywhere on a 32-bit-based address. The following is an example of **VTOR** initialization via the **SCB**:

```
SCB->VTOR = (uint32_t) &(__VECTOR_TABLE[0]);
```

The address of the table must be a multiple of its byte size. By default, a (16+16)*4 area for 16 external interrupts → 128 bytes. With the maximum of 496 interrupt sources available on some devices (+16 for exceptions) → 512 entries in the table, *4 → 2 kiB.

All the external interrupts are routed through the Nested Vector Interrupt Controller (**NVIC**). First and foremost, this enables the source of the interruption to be identified, as well as management of associated priorities and authorizations. Using this facility, the processor can branch to and execute the appropriate interrupt service routine, or handler. Table 3.13 shows all of the NVIC registers available to configure external interrupts for the Arm-v6-M and Arm-v7-M architectures. The main difference is that while Arm-v6-M is limited to a maximum of 32 interrupts, Arm-v7-M supports up to 15 times more (496), depending on the version and the manufacturer implementation. Note, however, that the **NVIC_IABR** register is not available at all in Arm-v6-M architectures.

Table 3.13   NVIC registers for Arm-v6-M (Arm-v7-M [v7] additions shown in pink)

Address	Name	Type	Reset value	Description
0xE000_E100	**NVIC_ISER**	RW	0x0000_0000	Interrupt Set-Enable Register
0xE000_E104– 0xE000_E13C	*NVIC_ISER1–* *NVIC_ISER15*	RW	0x0000_0000	*Interrupt Set-Enable Registers (v7)*
0xE000_E140– 0xE000_E17F	-	-	-	Reserved
0xE000_E180	**NVIC_ICER**	RW	0x0000_0000	Interrupt Clear-Enable Register
0xE000_E184– 0xE000_E1BC	*NVIC_ICER1–* *NVIC_ICER15*	-	0x0000_0000	*Interrupt Clear-Enable Registers (v7)*
0xE000_E1C0– 0xE000_E1FC	-	-	-	Reserved
0xE000_E200	**NVIC_ISPR**	RW	0x0000_0000	Interrupt Set-Pending Register
0xE000_E204– 0xE000_E23C	*NVIC_ISPR0–* *NVIC_ISPR15*	-	0x0000_0000	*Interrupt Set-Pending Registers (v7)*
0xE000_E240– 0xE000_E27F	-	-	-	Reserved
0xE000_E280	**NVIC_ICPR**	RW	0x0000_0000	Interrupt Clear-Pending Register
0xE000_E284– 0xE000_E2BC	*NVIC_ICPR0–* *NVIC_ICPR15*	-	0x0000_0000	*Interrupt Clear-Pending Registers (v7)*
0xE000_E2C0– 0xE000_E2FC	-	-	-	Reserved
0xE000_E300– 0xE000_E33C	*NVIC_IABR0–* *NVIC_IABR15*	RO	0x0000_0000	*Interrupt Active Bit Registers (v7)*
0xE000_E340– 0xE000_E3FC	-	-	-	Reserved
0xE000_E400– 0xE000_E41C	**NVIC_IPRn**	RW	0x0000_0000	Interrupt Priority Registers, NVIC_IPR0 – NVIC_IPR7
0xE000_E420– 0xE000_E5EC	*NVIC_IPR8–* *NVIC_IPR123*	-	0x0000_0000	*Interrupt Priority Registers (v7)*
0xE000_E5F0– 0xE000_ECFC	-	-	-	Reserved

The definitions of these registers are in the CMSIS header files, which are, specifically:

- ■ ***core_cm0.h*** for the Cortex M0

- ■ ***core_cm0plus.h*** for the Cortex M0+

- **core_cm1.h** for the Cortex M1

- **core_cm3.h** for the Cortex M3

- **core_cm4.h** for the Cortex M4

- **core_cm7.h** for the Cortex M7

- **core_cm23.h** for the Cortex M23

- **core_cm33.h** for the Cortex M33

- **core_cm35p3.h** for the Cortex M35P

- **core_cm55.h** for the Cortex M55

- **core_sc000.h** for the Cortex SC000

- **core_sc300.h** for the Cortex SC300

- **core_ARMv8MBL.h** for the Cortex Arm-v8-M baseline

- **core_ARMv8MML.h** for the Cortex Arm-v8-M mainline.

A sample extract of one such file is shown in Figure 3.21.

```
/**
  \ingroup    CMSIS_core_register

  \defgroup   CMSIS_core_base      Core Definitions

  \brief       Definitions for base addresses, unions, and structures.
*/

/* Memory mapping of Cortex-M0 Hardware */

#define SCS_BASE            (0xE000E000UL)                          /*!< System Control Space Base Address */
#define SysTick_BASE        (SCS_BASE +  0x0010UL)                  /*!< SysTick Base Address */
#define NVIC_BASE           (SCS_BASE +  0x0100UL)                  /*!< NVIC Base Address */
#define SCB_BASE            (SCS_BASE +  0x0D00UL)                  /*!< System Control Block Base Address*/

#define SCB                 ((SCB_Type      *)    SCB_BASE   ) /*!< SCB configuration struct */
#define SysTick             ((SysTick_Type  *)    SysTick_BASE ) /*!< SysTick configuration struct */
#define NVIC                ((NVIC_Type     *)    NVIC_BASE  ) /*!< NVIC configuration struct */
```

Figure 3.21 Example of register base address mapping in CMSIS header file (extract)

3.5.2 Interrupt Mechanisms

When entering into an exception state, the processor automatically goes into Handler mode and saves its current context onto a stack pointed to by one of the stack pointers, where its context is determined by the contents of registers **R0–R3**, **R12**, **LR (R14)**, and **xPSR**, together with a Return Address to go back to after execution of the exception (as illustrated in Figure 1.19).

On many processors, a specific RETURN instruction exists to return from exceptions. However, here the idea is to use a common approach for both a normal return from a branch and link, and for an exception return. Thus, a special code is saved as the Return Address on the stack.

An exception return occurs when the processor is in Handler mode and either a **POP** or a **BX** instruction loads the Return Address into the Program Counter (**PC**). The processor intercepts this value and bits [3:0] define the required exception return behavior, as shown in Table 3.14. The processor takes the **LR** value from the appropriate stack as the next instruction to execute.

Table 3.14 Exception return behavior

Value placed in PC by POP or BX	What happens?
0xFFFFFFF1	Return to Handler mode.
	Exception return gets state from the **Main** stack;
	on return, execution uses the **Main** stack.
0xFFFFFFF9	Return to Thread mode.
	Exception return gets state from the **Main** stack;
	on return, execution uses the **Main** stack.
0xFFFFFFFD	Return to Thread mode.
	Exception return gets state from the **Process** stack;
	on return, execution uses the **Process** stack

If the processor has a floating-point unit and is running floating-point instructions at the time of an interrupt, the **FPSCR** register, followed by registers **S15** to **S0**, will be automatically saved to the stack as well, prior to the saving of **xPSR** and the regular processor registers shown in Figure 1.19.

Beyond these registers, it is the responsibility of the programmer to ensure that any other registers are saved too, through assembler or the compiler.

In Figure 3.22, the different registers used for exceptions are schematized. The NVIC Interrupt Priority Register is available for every source of interrupts and allows specific priority levels to be assigned to them. Many interrupt sources can have the same priority level and then the priority is based on the interrupt-entry pin levels: the lower the value, the higher the priority. The predefined Reset, NMI and HardFault interrupts have negative priority levels and thus have the highest priority. A higher-priority interrupt can interrupt a lower one, creating nested interrupts.

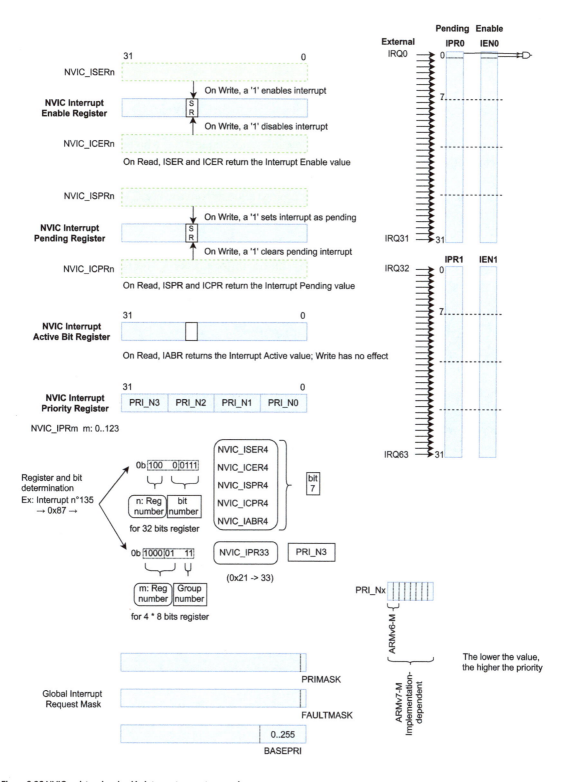

Figure 3.22 NVIC registers involved in interrupt request processing

For the processor to execute an interrupt:

■ The source of a hardware interrupt must be activated and unmasked at the programmable interface itself.

■ This unmasked activation will generate a pending interrupt in the NVIC.

■ In due course, the NVIC checks whether the new interrupt request has a higher priority than the one, if any, currently being processed; if it does, the request is forwarded to the processor.

■ The processor compares the priority of the incoming request from the NVIC with the 8-bit base priority mask (**BASEPRI**) to see whether it is higher than the one currently being serviced (remember: higher priority = smaller value).

■ Finally, the processor allows the request if the 1-bit exception mask register (**PRIMASK**) is at '0'; the latter can be manipulated with **MSR/MRS** instructions in privileged mode.

3.6 Arm CMSIS and Software Drivers

As we have seen, Arm offers multiple Cortex-M variants, each of which can be configured with smaller or greater numbers of units (for example, the MPU is optional). Most of the time, the different cores share similar functionality and code can be reused between them. For example, the general registers, the SysTick timer option, and the NVIC are usually present in all Cortex-M cores. Without a defined standard, everyone would have to implement their own source code for their chosen configuration. This exercise would be time-consuming and if the source code was not shared would have to be done by every SoC programmer. Fortunately, the Cortex Microcontroller Software Interface Standard (CMSIS) is a project developed by Arm to solve this. It provides a generic code library that can be reused across Arm cores to promote code portability.

This section starts by considering how a Cortex-M core actually starts (boots) before jumping into its application code. It then focuses on CMSIS and how it helps in the configuration of the various internal registers and units of Cortex-M processors. The exercises at the end of the section are focused on developing and running applications on the basis of this CMSIS standard.

3.6.1 Core Boot
At boot time, a Cortex-M processor needs the following:

■ the starting address of the stack pointer

■ a Reset Handler.

When the processor starts, it must configure the stack pointer register and execute the instructions that are defined in the Reset Handler. The information necessary for this is stored in a structure called the Vector Table. The first entry in the vector table points to the initial address of the main stack, and the others are 32-bit values containing the addresses of specific handlers, starting with the Reset Handler. The number of entries depends on the Cortex-M implementation and the included extensions (e.g. MPU, FPU, etc.) that will benefit from a handler for exceptions or interrupts.

The address of the vector table is implementation-specific and defined according to the processor concerned. The information can be found in the generic User Guide or Technical Reference Manual of the corresponding family and there are some distinctions:

- For Cortex-M0 and -M0+, the start address of the vector table is 0x0000_0000.

- For Cortex-M3, -M4, and -M7, the start address is defined by the **VTOR** (vector table offset register), which defaults to 0x0000_0000, but can be used to reallocate the vector table to another location.

- For Cortex-M processors with the Arm-v8-M architecture, the vector table is duplicated if the (TrustZone) security extension is implemented. This means that there is one table for the secure state and another for the non-secure state. The Reset Handler entry is only present in the secure table because, on reset, the processor always boots in the secure state. The secure vector table also contains a Secure Fault entry.

If the vector table is not available at startup, because it is corrupted or at another location or not implemented, the processor starts and tries to fetch it to access the Reset Handler and execute it. This will result in an unpredictable behavior because it will depend on the content of the memory and how it is interpreted as an instruction. The same thing happens if the **VTOR** address has been modified to point to an invalid location. The next time the system catches an exception, or an interrupt happens, the processor will execute whatever instruction it interprets in the entry for the corresponding handler.

In its boot sequence, the processor copies the value of the stack pointer (at the address contained in **VTOR** or 0x0000_0000, depending on the architecture) to the **SP** register (**R13**) and sets the program counter register (**R15**) to the address contained in the Reset Handler entry. This handler is responsible for system initialization and for calling the main function. When the vector table is created in C or assembler, it needs to be placed in the correct location. This is the goal of the linker script, which puts the vector table symbol at the top of the .text section (or similar) which has to be placed at the expected address in the compiled binary code.

3.6.2 Peripheral Registers

Throughout this book, various hardware registers are described by which to configure the different components of the SoC system (e.g. MPU, clock, TrustZone, SysTick, etc.). These registers are located at specific addresses, and may contain several flags, each at a different offset, such as:

| MPU Base Address | 0xE000ED90UL |
| SysTick Base Address | 0xE000E010UL |

The descriptions and addresses of the different registers that are software-programmable are found in the corresponding Technical Reference Manual of the Cortex-M processors. If a program needs to access a field from a register, it needs to:

- Look at the address of the register or use the corresponding assembly code to access it. Thus, the SysTick **VAL** register is at address 0xE000E018UL. To access the **APSR**, the **MRS** instruction must be used, and the C code may be different, depending on the compiler used:

Arm C Compiler (ArmCC)	GNU C Compiler (GCC)
`register uint32_t __regAPSR __ASM(„apsr");` `return(__regAPSR);`	`__ASM volatile ("MRS %0, apsr" : "=r"` `(result));`

- Look for the required field size and offset in the documentation.

- Create code to extract the field, usually done via bit masking.

While this can be done, it is hard work because there are many different components and registers. Furthermore, if every programmer was to write their own implementation to access these registers, it would take time to understand the corresponding code because everyone writes code in their own style, giving rise to multiple pieces of code with differing syntax but the same functionality.

Fortunately, a job of standardization has already been done through CMSIS. CMSIS is a hardware abstraction layer (HAL) that was open-sourced in 2008 and is now widely used. Making the code available online and free to use means that there are many contributors and users of the code, which helps to reduce the possible errors. The large online community ensures that there is good support to resolve issues, and potential fixes can be uploaded to the source code. The overall goal is to reduce the effort of programming a Cortex-M-family processor by providing all of the files and libraries necessary to configure it. In addition, because there are already multiple different implementations of the Cortex-M, this abstraction makes it easier to program them, with the same code reusable for different targets, even if they are not from the same family. Many chip vendors now integrate CMSIS into their codebases.

One purpose of CMSIS is to provide support for interfacing the processor and its peripherals. It helps maintain code reusability even if the core is updated. Figure 3.23 shows the architecture of the main CMSIS components and how it serves to interface the application to the microcontroller components. In brief, CMSIS can be divided into three parts:

- Libraries that provide code implementations and definitions used as-is by applications.

- APIs that are defined to give generic access to system components. These are effectively standardized definitions that when implemented provide a consistent software interface for a given type of component. If this layer is implemented, it means that the same code can be reused even if the underlying hardware changes.

■ Configuration files that describe the peripherals inside a system.

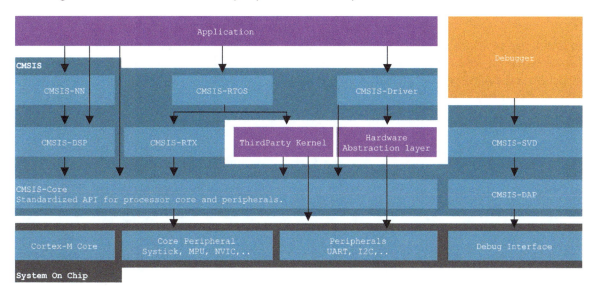

Figure 3.23 CMSIS architecture and its interactions with the application and the hardware (source: CMSIS Version 5.7.0 by Arm Ltd. The CMSIS is provided free of charge by Arm under the Apache 2.0 License. https://arm-software.github.io/CMSIS_5/General/html/LICENSE.txt)

CMSIS is mainly written in C, with some parts in assembler. The language choice arises because most microcontrollers are still programmed largely in C. Besides historical reasons, this is because C does not add too much overhead to the final code and makes it easy to access different parts of memory to setup registers. Using C++ with structures such as arrays, vectors or maps requires more code for the same functionalities. In the following sections, we will outline each of the CMSIS components shown in the figure.

3.6.3 CMSIS-Core

CMSIS-Core for the Cortex-M (there is a separate version for the Cortex-A) implements the basic run-time system for a Cortex-M device and gives the user access to the processor core and the device peripherals. To use CMSIS-Core, a number of files must be added to the embedded application: a startup file (which sets up the main stack pointer, reset handler, and key interrupt and exception vectors), two system configuration files, and a device header file.

Depending on the configuration flags set in the device header file, code of the overall library is either enabled or disabled when the corresponding header file from ./CMSIS/Core/Include is added to the project. Thus, the device header file will include a file with a name starting with the prefix core_ and ending with the Cortex-M name; for example, the corresponding file to be included in the device header file for a Cortex-M33 is core_cm33.h [2].

During compilation, the header file checks that all of the expected macros (see below) for the corresponding family are properly defined. If a flag is undefined and is expected, the compiler issues a warning and sets it to a default value, usually disabling the functionality. Finally, the header file checks that there is no discrepancy in the configuration; for example, that there are no SIMD or floating-point instructions if a DSP or FPU have not been enabled; otherwise it issues an error.

In addition to sanitizing the flags, the header file configures all of the base addresses of the components that are on the system and defines structures for all the registers. For example, the structure of the APSR register is defined as follows:

```
typedef union {
    struct
    {
        uint32_t _reserved0:16;     /*!< bit:  0..15  Reserved */
        uint32_t GE:4;              /*!< bit: 16..19  Greater than or Equal flags */
        uint32_t _reserved1:7;      /*!< bit: 20..26  Reserved */
        uint32_t Q:1;               /*!< bit:     27  Saturation condition flag */
        uint32_t V:1;               /*!< bit:     28  Overflow condition code flag */
        uint32_t C:1;               /*!< bit:     29  Carry condition code flag */
        uint32_t Z:1;               /*!< bit:     30  Zero condition code flag */
        uint32_t N:1;               /*!< bit:     31  Negative condition code flag */
    } b;                            /*!< Structure used for bit access */

    uint32_t w;                     /*!< Type used for word access */
} APSR_Type;
```

The following macros are also provided to retrieve a field of the corresponding register; they are usually named *<REGISTER_NAME>_<FIELD>_Pos* to obtain the appropriate position of a field, and *<REGISTER_NAME>_<FIELD>_Msk* to obtain the relevant mask of the field:

```
#define APSR_N_Pos31U                        /*!< APSR: N Position */
#define APSR_N_Msk (1UL << APSR_N_Pos)       /*!< APSR: N Mask */

#define APSR_Z_Pos30U                        /*!< APSR: Z Position */
#define APSR_Z_Msk (1UL << APSR_Z_Pos)       /*!< APSR: Z Mask */

#define APSR_C_Pos29U                        /*!< APSR: C Position */
#define APSR_C_Msk (1UL << APSR_C_Pos)       /*!< APSR: C Mask */

#define APSR_V_Pos28U                        /*!< APSR: V Position */
#define APSR_V_Msk (1UL << APSR_V_Pos)       /*!< APSR: V Mask */

#define APSR_Q_Pos27U                        /*!< APSR: Q Position */
#define APSR_Q_Msk (1UL << APSR_Q_Pos)       /*!< APSR: Q Mask */

#define APSR_GE_Pos16U                       /*!< APSR: GE Position */
#define APSR_GE_Msk (0xFUL << APSR_GE_Pos)   /*!< APSR: GE Mask */

...
```

Finally, the content of the fields of the APSR register can be retrieved using the following code:

```
/* Get the content of the register APSR into the corresponding structure */
APSR_TYPE aspr = __GET_APSR();

/*
  * Access to the 32-bit raw data of the register. Getting the corresponding field can
  * be done using the masks and position defined
  */
uint32_t w = aspr.w;
uint32_t zeroFlag = (aspr.b.N & APSR_N_Msk) >> APSR_Z_Pos;

/* ACCESS INDIVIDUAL FIELDS LIKE aspr.b.N */
uint32_t negativeFlag = aspr.b.N
```

A number of different function types are also implemented via CMSIS-Core (see next section):

▨ Get and Set functions for special registers. These functions are implemented in different files that are included according to the compiler being used (e.g. ArmCC, Clang, GCC), because the syntax to access the registers depends on the specific toolchain.

▨ Functions that take a specific component address to form an operation; for example, FPU and MPU macros that take the form of an address cast to the corresponding type (FPU_Type or MPU_Type).

3.6.3.1 Device Templates

As part of CMSIS-Core, Arm provides device template files for all of the supported Cortex-M processors, and various compilers (i.e. ArmCC, GCC, and IAR). These include register names for the core peripherals (e.g. FPU, PMU, MPU, SIMD, TrustZone), and functions to access the core peripherals, as well as generic startup and system configuration code.

For each available processor family, CMSIS offers the following structure under the folder ./Device/ARM to help kick off the programming effort:

▨ M core folder (e.g. ArmCM0 for Cortex-M0, ArmCM33 for Cortex-M33, etc.)

   ☐ /Include: Contains header files that configure the presence or absence of core peripherals.

   ☐ /Source:

      • Compiler-specific folders for linker and assembly code to start the board. This defines the Reset Handler and the vector table.

      • Generic files in C for these same definitions (described below), but also containing definitions of initialization functions for the core peripherals present/enabled.

The different Cortex-M classes are configurable, and some optional features can be added at design time. This means that CMSIS should be able to hide functionality that is not available; for example, if there is no MPU, there is no need to add the corresponding code. In the include directory Device/ARM/<Cortex Name>/Include [3] of the project, it is possible to edit a header file to reflect a core's specific configuration.

Here is a part of the file showing the different flags that can be set for the Cortex-M33 in Device/ARM/ARMCM33/Include/ARMCM33.h [4]:

```
#define __CM33_REV         0x0000U      /* Core revision r0p1 */
#define __SAUREGION_PRESENT    1U        /* SAU regions present */
#define __MPU_PRESENT          1U        /* MPU present */
#define __VTOR_PRESENT         1U        /* VTOR present */
#define __NVIC_PRIO_BITS       3U        /* Number of Bits used for Priority Levels */
#define __Vendor_SysTickConfig 0U        /* Set to 1 if different SysTick Config is
                                            used */

#define __FPU_PRESENT          0U        /* no FPU present */
#define __DSP_PRESENT          0U        /* no DSP extension present */
```

Different flavors of the header file exist for a given Cortex processor; for example, the file ARMCM33_DSP_FP_TZ.h defines the flags __FPU_PRESENT, __DSP_PRESENT.

The Cortex-M0 has fewer configuration options available than the Cortex-M33. The following default configuration for a Cortex-M0 system can be found in Device/ARM/ARMCM0/Include/ARMCM0.h [5]:

```
#define __CM0_REV          0x0000U      /* Core revision r0p0 */
#define __MPU_PRESENT          0U        /* no MPU present */
#define __VTOR_PRESENT         0U        /* no VTOR present */
#define __NVIC_PRIO_BITS       2U        /* Number of Bits used for Priority Levels */
#define __Vendor_SysTickConfig 0U        /* Set to 1 if different SysTick Config is
                                            used */
```

CMSIS also goes further by providing the code to initialize a core by defining the vector table and providing templates for the setup of different components of the system. It also provides a linker script that can be adapted depending on requirements. There are multiple compilers on the embedded system market, which use different syntax or attributes to generate binaries. CMSIS provides code versions suitable for the three most popular ones: IAR, GCC, and ArmCC.

ArmCC and GCC have different ways to represent the file used to deploy the code into memory. Respectively, they are referred to as "scatter scripts" and "linker scripts". Because of their differing syntaxes, these files are obviously different; however, both define:

- RAM/ROM base and end addresses

- address location of the vector table

- where the different segments of the code are loaded: instructions, data, Secure Gateway veneers (for TrustZone)

- configuration of the Stack and Heap start and limit addresses.

These settings indicate to the linker where to place the different parts of the code, so that once the binary is loaded into memory, all segments are at the correct location. It is important to note that the base addresses of the memories (i.e. RAM, ROM, etc.) depend on the particular system and may well be adapted.

The corresponding C-based startup file for a Cortex processor simply defines the vector table along with the reset vector. Except for the first entry, which is the location of the stack pointer start address, the table is simply a list of pointers. The vector table is defined as follows for all Cortex-M processors, although they can have slight variations (for example, in the number of interrupts supported):

```
extern const VECTOR_TABLE_Type __VECTOR_TABLE[496];
const VECTOR_TABLE_Type __VECTOR_TABLE[496] __VECTOR_TABLE_ATTRIBUTE = {
    (VECTOR_TABLE_Type)(&__INITIAL_SP), /* Initial Stack Pointer */
    Reset_Handler, /* Reset Handler */
    NMI_Handler, /* -14 NMI Handler */
    HardFault_Handler, /* -13 Hard Fault Handler */
    MemManage_Handler, /* -12 MPU Fault Handler */

  ...


    Interrupt8_Handler, /* 8 Interrupt 8 */
    Interrupt9_Handler /* 9 Interrupt 9 */

    /* Interrupts 10 .. 480 are left out */
};
```

where the symbol _INITIAL_SP derives from the scatter/linker script. Except for the Reset_Handler function, all handlers are weakly defined, meaning that they can be overwritten by a function that has the same name. If they have not been redefined in this way, the default implementation is used.

The following set of source code examples give a definition for the Reset Handler and the HardFault handler only; all the other handlers are aliased to the same function, called Default_Handler, which is an infinite while-loop:

```
void <name>_Handler (void) __attribute__ ((weak, alias("Default_Handler")));
void HardFault_Handler (void) __attribute__ ((weak));

void Default_Handler(void)
{
    while(1);
}
```

Thus, the definition of the Reset_Handler function consists of setting the stack limit, calling the SystemInit function, and calling the entry point for the main function:

```
__NO_RETURN void Reset_Handler(void)
{
    __set_MSPLIM((uint32_t)(&__STACK_LIMIT));
    SystemInit(); /* CMSIS System Initialization */

    __PROGRAM_START(); /* Enter PreMain (C library entry point) */
}
```

The definition of the HardFault handler also consists of a simple infinite while-loop (which can be redefined/overwritten to give more specific instructions):

```
void HardFault_Handler(void)
{
    while(1);
}
```

3.6.4 CMSIS-Driver

As can be seen in Figure 3.23, the hardware abstraction layers (HALs) for other (non-core peripheral) devices are not part of CMSIS. This is because these devices are vendor-specific implementations and CMSIS can only provide code to abstract the different generic hardware that the underlying core supports, such as SysTick, NVIC, SAU (TrustZone), Debug, Trace, MPU, and FPU. Other components are not necessarily Arm-branded and depend on the vendor implementation, which means that the register map, for instance, will differ according to the design selected during manufacture.

However, device HALs from vendors do provide access to the other system peripherals that are assembled around the core, such as DMA controllers, GPIOs, and serial communications units (USART, I²C, SPI).

Nevertheless, CMSIS provides some generic definitions in the driver specification that can be used to interface a device. This means that an application can either call the vendor-specific functions to configure a device or use a generic interface from CMSIS. Where it uses its own implementation, the application cannot be used directly on another device supported by a CMSIS driver but having a different device interface. This is the same logic as applies to middleware libraries. CMSIS-Driver provides a generic interface for the following drivers:

- Serial protocols: I²C, SPI, USART

- Communication: Ethernet, Wi-Fi

- Transfer: USB, CAN

- Memory: Flash, NAND, MCI, storage controllers

- Audio: Serial Audio Interface (SAI) (supporting I²S and other protocols)

- Virtual I/O (VIO).

3.6.5 CMSIS-DSP

CMSIS also offers a library of software in support of DSP applications on Cortex-M processor-based devices; a suite of more than 60 common signal processing functions divided into various categories:

- Basic math functions

- Fast math functions

- Complex math functions

- Filters

- Matrix functions

- Transform functions

- Motor control functions

- Statistical functions

- Support functions

- Interpolation functions.

The library has separate functions for operating on 8-bit, 16-bit, and 32-bit integers, and 32-bit floating-point values. The functions are designed for DSP applications that make heavy use of mathematical operations within signal-processing algorithms (e.g. fast Fourier transforms, finite impulse response filters). For each of the underlying operations, the library makes use of the best instruction available depending on the elements present in the Cortex-M, using either Helium instructions, DSP instructions or SIMD instructions.

3.6.6 CMSIS-NN
Similarly, CMSIS offers a library of software kernels aimed at maximizing the performance and minimizing the memory footprint of Cortex-M processor cores when running neural network (NN) applications. NNs are based on a group of algorithms that are designed to recognize patterns, and are used to classify data on the basis of a trained model or to identify similar features among data to group them. With the boom in Internet of Things (IoT) devices and associated data collection, having a way to process the sensed information on the spot can be better than having to send it to a remote server for processing. It certainly means that less data has to be transferred. As an example, instead of sending many bytes-worth of values, the device might simply return the overall classification of the values. This is particularly relevant where images are involved. Thus, a microcontroller connected to a camera might process the content of a recorded video "on the fly" and only send a specific alert to a server if it spotted something of interest.

There are some limitations in having a NN software library on a small controller because of power and memory footprints. The library offers wrapper functions that are based on the DSP/SIMD instructions of the core that are essential for NN algorithms. If a Cortex-M core does not support those instructions, it needs more time to obtain the results. SIMD instructions are present in the Cortex-M4, Cortex-M7, Cortex-M33, Cortex-M35P and Cortex-M55, but not in the other Cortex-M processors. Thus, if the library was used to compile NN-related code for a Cortex-M0, -M0+ or -M3, all NN instructions would be executed in software instead of making use of hardware accelerations, making the program far slower.

The library can only be used for the classification of an input. It cannot be used for training a model because it would take too much time on an embedded system; a pre-trained model needs to be fed into the library.

The CMSIS-NN library is divided into several functions, each covering a specific category of NN activity:

- Convolution functions

- Activation functions

- Fully connected layer functions

- Pooling functions

- Softmax functions

- Support (e.g. basic math) functions.

The library has separate functions to operate on different weight and activation data types, including 8-bit and 16-bit integers (q7_t and q15_t, respectively). Each implemented function is separated into one source file (*.c), and all the functions are then included in one top-level file.

3.6.7 CMSIS-RTOS

CMSIS provides a common API for real-time operating systems (RTOSs), together with a reference implementation of this API in support of the RTX RTOS extension, designed for Cortex-M processor-based devices. The RTOS kernel can be used to create applications that perform multiple tasks simultaneously. These tasks are executed by threads that operate in a quasi-parallel fashion, enabling flexible scheduling of system resources such as CPU and memory, and the RTOS provides methods for communication between threads. In fact, CMSIS provides two versions (v1 and v2) of the RTOS library, principally because the modifications needed to support the TrustZone security partitioning introduced with Arm-v8-M were too consequential for maintenance of a single version. Both can be used to create tasks and provide a generic interface so that other implementations can be used beneath. Although CMSIS supports RTX as a reference implementation, the RTOS API can be ported in support of other RTOSs; for example, this has already been done for FreeRTOS.

3.6.8 CMSIS-Zone

Embedded systems frequently integrate specific hardware for access protection or system isolation. For example, a Cortex-M33 processor-based system may incorporate a:

- SAU (Secure Attribution Unit): To create a Secure execution partition with controlled access from a Non-secure execution partition (see Section 3.9 for more details of the SAU).

- MPC (Memory Protection Controller): To control system-wide access to memory (again, more detail can be found in Section 3.9).

- PPC (Peripheral Protection Controller): To control system-wide access to peripherals (again, more detail can be found in Section 3.9).

- MPU (Memory Protection Controller): To prevent illegal access to some memory regions (depending on state; see Section 3.8 for more details of the MPU).

Embedded systems may also integrate multiple processors that must also share system resources (memory and peripherals).

Configuring resources such as memory regions is hard without a graphical interface to visualize the final result. The main purpose of the CMSIS-Zone helper is to assist in managing this complexity by creating the correct initialization code for all of these units, so that resources are correctly assigned or partitioned amongst them (into project and/or execution zones). This tool is based on an Eclipse package and generates the necessary outputs according to the given configuration. The file produced is partition_*.h and is similar to the following code, in which the function TZ_SAU_Setup does all of the necessary initialization of the SAU regions, depending on the macro defined:

```
#define SAU_INIT_CTRL 1
#define SAU_INIT_CTRL_ENABLE 1
#define SAU_INIT_CTRL_ALLNS 0
#define SAU_REGIONS_MAX 8 /* Max. number of SAU regions */

#define SAU_INIT_REGION0 1
#define SAU_INIT_START0 0x00000000 /* start address of SAU region 0 */
#define SAU_INIT_END0 0x001FFFFF /* end address of SAU region 0 */
#define SAU_INIT_NSC0 1

...

__STATIC_INLINE void TZ_SAU_Setup (void)
{
    ...
}
```

3.6.9 CMSIS-SVD

Debugging is an important part of software development. It is very rare that an application works first time and, even if it does, it is sometimes necessary to debug it after an unexpected behavior occurs. Standard debuggers cannot have any awareness of the current structure and configuration of a Cortex-M system. A view is required that describes the different parts so that the debugger can adapt accordingly, and possibly provide a graphical representation too.

The CMSIS System View Description (SVD) format formalizes the description of the system contained in a Cortex-M processor-based microcontroller; in particular, the memory-mapped registers of peripherals. The resulting CMSIS-SVD XML files are developed and maintained by silicon vendors, while tool vendors use them to provide device-specific debug views of peripherals in their debuggers, giving the programmer a global view of the system being programmed. This type of file gives information about the:

- Core: endianness, core peripherals, allocated SAU regions and configuration:

```
<cpu>
<name>CM33</name>
<revision>r0p0</revision>
<endian>little</endian>
<!-- Configuration of the optional components -->
<mpuPresent>true</mpuPresent>
<fpuPresent>false</fpuPresent>
<vtorPresent>true</vtorPresent>
<nvicPrioBits>3</nvicPrioBits>
<vendorSystickConfig>false</vendorSystickConfig>
<!-- Number of SAU regions that are configured -->
<sauNumRegions>1</sauNumRegions>
<!-- Configuration of the SAU regions -->
<sauRegionsConfig enabled="true" protectionWhenDisabled="s">
  <region enabled="true" name="SauRegion0">
    <base>0x00000000</base>
    <limit>0x001FFFE0</limit>
    <!-- secure / non-secure callable -->
    <access>c</access>
  </region>
</sauRegionsConfig>
</cpu>
```

- The memory addressing (byte or word addressable), and the size of the bus:

```
<addressUnitBits>8</addressUnitBits>   <!-- byte addressable memory -->
<width>32</width>                      <!-- bus width is 32 bits -->
```

- The default behavior of the peripheral's registers:

```
<!-- this is the default size (number of bits) of all peripherals  and registers -->
<size>32</size>
<!-- default access permission for all subsequent registers -->
<access>read-write</access>
<!-- by default all bits of the registers are initialized to 0 on reset -->
<resetValue>0x00000000</resetValue>
<!-- by default all 32Bits of the registers are used -->
<resetMask>0xFFFFFFFF</resetMask>
```

- Peripherals (e.g. timers, UARTs, SPI, I²C) and associated register fields (the code shown defines an EXAMPLE peripheral and creates an instance named EXAMPLE0 at location 0x40040100: it has only one CTRL register, at offset 0 with a reset value of 0, which is composed of two fields, EN and RST):

```xml
<peripherals>
    <peripheral>
      <name>EXAMPLE</name>
      <version>1.0</version>
      <description> Peripheral Example</description>
      <groupName>EXAMPLE</groupName>
      <baseAddress>0x40000000</baseAddress>
      <size>32</size>
      <access>read-write</access>

      <addressBlock>
        <offset>0</offset>
        <size>0x04</size>
        <usage>registers</usage>
      </addressBlock>

      <registers>
        <!-- CTRL: Control Register -->
        <register>
          <name>CTRL</name>
          <description>Control Register</description>
          <addressOffset>0x00</addressOffset>
          <size>32</size>
          <access>read-write</access>
          <resetValue>0x00000000</resetValue>
          <resetMask>0xFFFFFFFF</resetMask>

          <fields>
            <!-- EN: Enable -->
            <field>
              <name>EN</name>
              <description>Enable</description>
              <bitRange>[0:0]</bitRange>
              <access>read-write</access>
              <enumeratedValues>
                <enumeratedValue>
                  <name>Disable</name>
                  <description>Unit is disabled</description>
                  <value>0</value>
                </enumeratedValue>
                <enumeratedValue>
                  <name>Enable</name>
                  <description>Unit is enabled</description>
                  <value>1</value>
                </enumeratedValue>
              </enumeratedValues>
            </field>
            <!-- RST: Reset -->
            <field>
              <name>RST</name>
              <description>Reset</description>
              <bitRange>[1:1]</bitRange>
              <access>write-only</access>
              <enumeratedValues>
                <enumeratedValue>
                  <name>No_Action</name>
                  <description>Write has no effect</description>
                  <value>0</value>
                </enumeratedValue>
              <enumeratedValue>
                  <name>Reset</name>
                  <description>Reset the unit</description>
                  <value>1</value>
```

```
            </enumeratedValue>
          </enumeratedValues>
        </field>
      <fields>
    </register>
  </registers>
</peripheral>

<!-- EXAMPLE0 -->
<peripheral derivedFrom="EXAMPLE">
  <name>EXAMPLE0</name>
  <baseAddress>0x40040100</baseAddress>
</peripheral>
</peripherals>
```

3.6.10 Exercises

For some exercises in Chapter 3, the code is based on QEMU and is already configured with CMSIS. More details can be found in the corresponding README of the exercise.

QEMU is an open-source machine emulator used to emulate an Arm-based system named lm3s6965. More information on this device can be found on the Texas Instruments website [6]. This is a Cortex-M3-based chip (Arm-v7-M architecture) that has an MPU.

The goal of the exercises in this section is to apply the theory we have covered.

Using the project **QEMU_lm3s6965evb** on GitHub (github.com/Introduction-To-System-On-Chip), access the corresponding section (3.6) and jump to the corresponding exercise. The code is already configured with a version of CMSIS.

You will see more details on the purpose of the vector table and how to adapt it in a program. You will first experiment to find out what happens if this table is badly configured. You will then have a quick look at the RTOS provided by CMSIS and instantiate a new task that will print some data to the terminal.

3.7 Memory Protection Unit

Let us consider a typical program that attempts to connect to a cloud-based service (e.g. hosted by Microsoft Azure or Amazon Web Services). It will need some private assets to authenticate to the associated server, typically involving one or more cryptographic libraries (e.g. mbedTLS, OpenSSL) and some code to access the internet (e.g. lwIP, network stack). What would happen if some parts of this application were to be illicitly manipulated to dump the full memory and to retrieve its contents? It would mean that all the security keys used to connect to a provider could be exploited.

Likewise, within an application, intentional or unintentional buffer overflow can also occur; a function might be pushing so much data into a buffer that it causes the program to crash, erasing some of the memory that stores the return address of the function, or some data that is to be used later.

These examples illustrate why a system might need to protect its memory by using a Memory Protection Unit (MPU) to make it more robust. The first part of this section shows where this unit sits within a system and its purpose, and continues with the specific example of the Arm MPU and the memory layout of a SoC. While there are multiple types of MPU on the market, they all offer the same functionality and the concepts behind their configuration are similar. The section ends with an example of how to program this unit for a Cortex-M core, and how to diagnose issues if something goes wrong, before concluding with some practical exercises.

3.7.1 Purpose of the Memory Protection Unit

A memory protection unit is a hardware block located immediately adjacent to the processor of a SoC. It monitors the addresses requested by the core. Depending on the address, the range accessed, the type of access (i.e. read or write), and the configuration of the associated memory regions, the MPU allows or does not allow the transaction. As illustrated in Figure 3.24, the MPU creates a bridge between the core and the overall memory range, which also includes peripheral accesses. Any violation triggers an interrupt specific to the MPU, with a number of registers configured to indicate what went wrong.

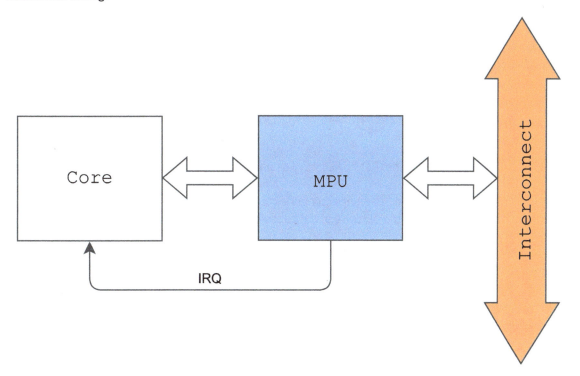

Figure 3.24 Location of the MPU in a system

Even if the memory address space remains simple in a SoC, a programmer might want to divide it into different regions so that different code running in different modes do not interfere with each other. Memory can also be designated as "read-only" or "execute never", among others, in order to protect peripherals. To operate in a safer way, the memory of a system needs protection to restrict access to data according to the mode in which the processor is running. If there is no protection of any kind, the memory could be written to, read from, or executed throughout its entire address space.

For small applications, this might not be an issue because the "surface of attack" will be relatively small. However, if the application is complex and an attacker finds some way to read the memory or inject some malicious code by re-writing part of the instructions in memory, then the system would be compromised.

Typical SoCs run multiple tasks and use a small OS (usually referred to as an RTOS for microcontrollers) to schedule them (see Chapter 7 for more details about RTOSs). The OS code (aka kernel image) always runs in privileged mode because it needs access to all of the SoC registers. Other tasks run in user mode to restrict access to the system registers and do not have the permissions necessary to update the MPU's configuration registers. Otherwise, any task would be able to update the unit.

Figure 3.25 depicts an example in which memory for an RTOS supporting multiple tasks has been split into several areas, and a set of MPU regions (0 to 5) has been defined that could be accessed by a task running within the OS. At startup, the kernel defines all of the MPU regions that it needs, depending on the tasks that are created:

- Region 5 has been configured to give access to an area of shared memory available for all of the tasks but only with read access

- Region 4 provides access to the code needed by Task 2 for execution

- Region 3 does likewise for the Task 1 code

- Region 2 provides access to the (RTOS) kernel code and cannot be accessed by regular (user) tasks

- Region 1 gives access to some I/O device components, such as an accelerator or gyroscope, that are only accessible by Task 2 for the purpose of data acquisition

- Region 0 controls access to specific I/Os that are only used by the kernel; this might be timer resources or storage devices

- There is no MPU region defined for the areas of memory shown in the figure in gray; this means that, depending on the MPU configuration, access will either trigger a fault or will default to the permissions associated with a predefined background or default region specification.

From the perspective of Task 2, only regions 1, 4 and 5 can be accessed, while access to regions 0, 2 and 3 is prevented. Because the MPU cannot differentiate which task (e.g. Task 1, Task 2) is being executed from a hardware perspective, the kernel must adjust the MPU regions by enabling, disabling or updating them accordingly during context switches of the tasks.

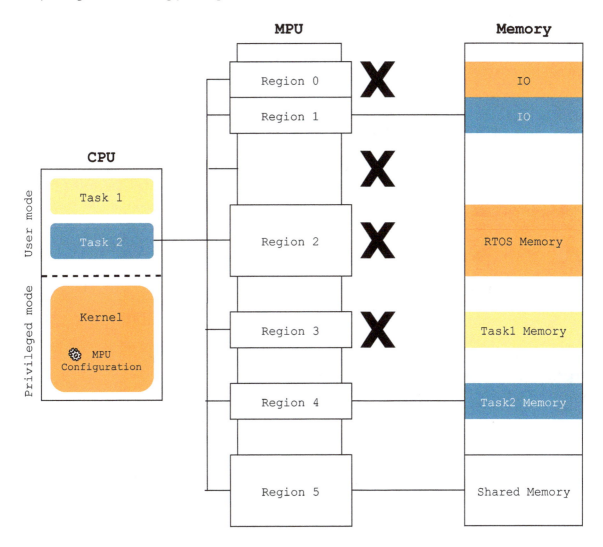

Figure 3.25 Memory-split example for an RTOS supporting multiple tasks from the perspective of task 2

Protecting access to specific memory locations in this way is extremely useful; however, the MPU can also be used to do more. Memory should be protected to keep trusted and secure assets safe, but the MPU can also be used for attack detection or to make a system more reliable by stopping a task from accessing a part of the memory that it is not supposed to. All memory regions should not be handled in the same way by the processor. This is why there are different types of memory within a system; for example, a specific address range might not need to be cached, or the accesses to read or write an area of memory should not be reordered.

This means that it is possible to define how a memory area should behave. For instance, it defines whether there is a caching mechanism and if the access order can be altered. This configuration of the memory is necessary because the processor might redefine the order of accesses to memory if there is no conflict and there are no dependencies. This is called out-of-order (OoO) execution. Even if the assembly instructions are in order in the code memory, the processor might execute them in a different order. In some cases, it is necessary to indicate to the processor that access to a range of memory cannot be reordered because accessing memory can have side effects on a specific mapped device.

Let us assume, as an example, that the address range 0x100_0000 to 0x100_0010 is mapped to an UART device. This unit might have a read-only register ACK mapped at address 0x100_0000. Reading this register might erase and update a DATA register at address 0x100_0004. The load instruction that accesses DATA and then accesses ACK should not be reordered to avoid losing the original contents of DATA. Furthermore, if these address contents were to be cached, then the cache might store the initial value of DATA and thus prevent the UART controller from seeing its actual value. A more specific example is given in this chapter to explain how a region can be configured.

3.7.2 The Arm MPU

An MPU can be implemented by different IP blocks (such as the Altera Nios II). However, we will focus here on the Arm one because it is used in most Cortex-M SoCs. Nevertheless, the functionality is the same and all Cortex-M MPUs are usually programmed in the same way.

In an Arm-based SoC, there is a default memory map. This partitions the memory into seven distinct **regions** with different attributes, as illustrated in Figure 3.26, and is applied when:

▨ there is no MPU

▨ the MPU is disabled

▨ the MPU is enabled and the address accessed is not inside a partitioned area of memory (i.e. a region)

▨ the vector table is accessed on exception.

As can be seen in Figure 3.26, accessing an address does not necessarily mean accessing RAM or another memory store. Sometimes, a read or write to a specific address range will be redirected to a peripheral such as a UART or some other memory-mapped peripheral device. In this context, the MPU can be used to redefine the default memory mapping to:

▨ divide and create new memory partitions called regions

▨ update memory types and attributes

▨ trigger a fault when an access violates a rule.

Note: As described in the TrustZone section that follows, although the MPU can control memory access it is not responsible for applying security rules. The Secure and Non-secure worlds each have an MPU implemented that can be configured separately.

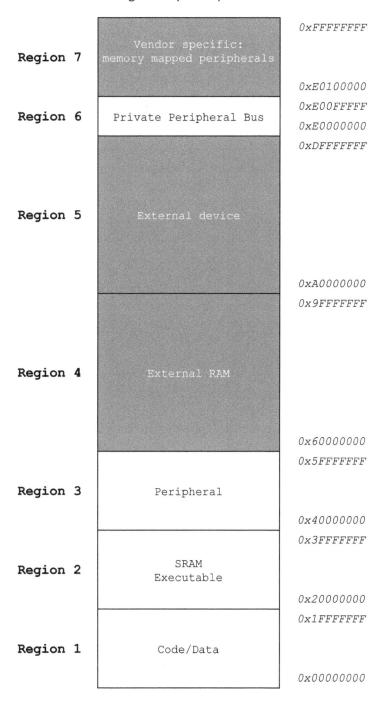

Figure 3.26 Default memory map in Cortex-M based systems

3.7.3 Region Memory Types

The configuration of MPU regions is based on memory types. As we saw in Section 3.4, there are three types of memory:

- **Normal**. In "normal" memory, the processor can perform out-of-order execution or speculative reads because there are no side effects associated with access to that specific part of memory. If a read transaction is repeated or if additional memory locations are fetched, there is no impact: write transactions can be buffered or repeated without side effects. Accesses can be restarted or merged with others. This type of memory is usually chosen for instructions and data for RAM and ROM memories.

- **Device**. In "device" memory, the order of access must be preserved because reordering it can have an impact: two consecutive reads or writes may not return the same value if their order is reversed. Thus, accesses are conducted sequentially according to the program order. However, the memory system can choose to buffer all the write accesses, which can occur in the interconnect or within the processor. This means that a memory transaction might be marked as complete even if it has not reached the peripheral/memory. This type of memory is generally used for memory-mapped peripherals and input/output locations.

- **Strongly Ordered**. "Strongly ordered" memory is very similar to "device" memory, the difference being that there is no buffering of the writes. Accesses are only considered to be complete once they have reached the peripheral/memory. Accesses to strongly ordered memory are identical in effect to executing a data memory barrier (**DMB**) instruction, then performing the memory access, and then instigating a further **DMB** instruction.

In addition to these three types, memory can also be classified as:

- **Shareable**: Indicates that a range of memory is shared between multiple processors.

- **eXecute Never (XN)**: The processor cannot execute any code held in this memory range. If it tries, a fault exception is generated.

- **Bufferable**: Indicates that writes can be buffered in a small cache before they are actually sent to the target location in memory. This means that if multiple writes are buffered, only one write may subsequently be sent to memory.

- **Read(able)**: The memory contents are readable (e.g. via a LOAD instruction).

- **Write(able)**: Values can be written into the memory location (e.g. via a STORE instruction).

As we have seen, memory types can be used to control the ordering of memory accesses for a specific address range. If there are additional requirements (e.g. potential contention between two peripherals), explicit memory barriers must be introduced to enforce them.

For the assembler code shown below, the accesses to memory that would result from the use of different memory types (via regions) for each of the two addresses (A and B) are shown in Table 3.15:

```
LDR r0, <address A>
LDR r1, <address B>
```

We can see from the table that in all the combinations in which the result is "No order defined", the second load could be executed before the first load.

Table 3.15 Memory access order for consecutive reads, according to region type

A \ B	Normal	Device Non-shared	Device Shared	Strongly Ordered
Normal	No order defined	No order defined	No order defined	No order defined
Device Non-shared	No order defined	A before B	No order defined	A before B
Device Shared	No order defined	No order defined	A before B	A before B
Strongly Ordered	No order defined	A before B	A before B	A before B

In terms of the default memory mapping for the Cortex-M shown in Figure 3.27, the memory types used for the various regions, together with their attributes and functions, are represented in Table 3.16 (where the memory is divided into segments of 512 MiB each). We can see that there are predefined regions for RAM, peripherals, and system registers.

Note: Region 7 cannot have its eXecute-Never field modified.

Table 3.16 Region attributes for default memory mapping

Region number	Size (MiB)	Memory Type	Attributes	Purpose
1 Code/Data	512	Normal Executable	Write Through	Stores the code and the data; this region is executable
2 SRAM	512	Normal Executable	Write Back Write Allocate	Same as Region 1
3 Peripheral	512	Device Execute Never	None	Used for all the peripherals of the system; there is a bit-banded area used to write specific bits
4 External RAM	512	Normal Write Back	Write Back/Through Write Allocate	Used for the same purpose as Region 1

Region number	Size (MiB)	Memory Type	Attributes	Purpose
5 External Device	512	Device Execute Never	None	Used for the external device memory
6 Private Peripheral Bus	512	Strongly Ordered Execute Never	None	Includes all the system control registers; for example, the MPU
7 Device	512	Device Execute Never	None	Implementation-specific depending on the vendor

3.7.4 MPU Region Overlapping

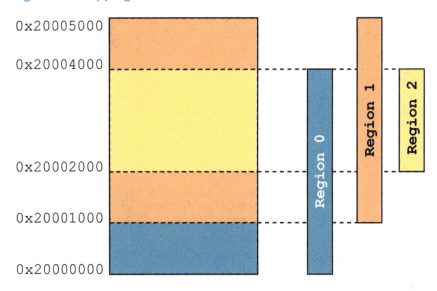

Figure 3.27 Overlapping of three different regions

In the Arm-v6-M and Arm-v7-M architectures, the MPU supports the overlapping of regions. The highest region number in the overlap is used to prioritize the characteristics applied to an address in the overlapping range. Thus, in Figure 3.27, three regions are defined, and they all overlap. The accesses between 0x2000_2000 and 0x2000_4000 are overseen by the Region 2 memory regime because it has higher priority than Regions 1 or 0. For the range 0x2000_1000 to 0x2000_2000, the memory attributes will be those of Region 1. The effect is independent of the attributes set for the separate regions. A typical scenario might involve Region 0 giving full access to both privileged and unprivileged (user) modes, but Region 2 giving full access only to privileged mode, with user mode restricted to read-only access. Another similar application of region overlapping might provide stack protection in the case of overflow.

3.7.5 MPU Configuration Registers
The MPU can be enabled in the following Cortex-M processors: -M0+, -M3, -M4, -M7, -M22, and -M33. However, their detailed implementation differs, as shown in the corresponding versions of their

Generic User Guides; for example, they support differing numbers of regions, as listed in Table 3.17. Nevertheless, for all of these devices, the addresses of the registers used to configure the MPU are the same: see Table 3.18.

Table 3.17 MPU regions supported by Cortex-M processors

Cortex Processor	No. of MPU Regions
M0+	0 or 8
M3	8
M4	8
M7	8 or 16
M22 & M33	0 or 8

Table 3.18 MPU configuration registers

Register Name	Access	Address	Function
MPU_TYPE	RO	0xE000_ED90	Gives the numbers of regions that can be configured
MPU_CTRL	RW	0xE000_ED94	Enable or disable the MPU
MPU_RNR	RW	0xE000_ED98	Select the region to be configured
MPU_RBAR	RW	0xE000_ED9C	Set the base address of the region selected
MPU_RASR	RW	0xE000_EDA0	Set the size and attributes of a region (NOT in Arm-v8-M)

Thus, it is possible to inspect the **MPU_TYPE** register, illustrated in Figure 3.28, to establish whether there is an MPU and how many regions can be configured. C code to print the content of the **MPU_TYPE** register is shown below:

```
uint32_t* mpuType = 0xE000ED90;
sprintf(printBuffer, "%08x", *mpuType);
printf("%s\n", printBuffer);
```

In Figure 3.28, the IREGION field is for the instruction region and the DREGION field for the data region. However, the regions are unified between instruction and data access, and there is no distinction between them. The values of the IREGION (absent in the Cortex-M23 & Cortex-M33) and SEPARATE fields of the **MPU_TYPE** register are therefore always 0. The DREGION field contains the overall number of regions, which means that each region definition applies to both instruction and data accesses.

The definition of each region consists of a base address, its attributes and its size, and also its memory type and access control. A region's base address must always be aligned to its size.

At least one region must be defined before the MPU is enabled. If this is not the case, the MPU must be enabled with the PRIVDEFENA field, which enables privileged software access to the default memory map. If unprivileged access is attempted to an address that does not fall into a region, an abort is generated. When the system starts, there is no region configured.

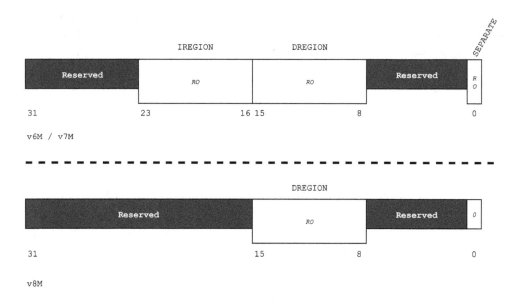

Figure 3.28 Fields of the MPU_TYPE register (above: Arm-v6-M & Arm-v7-M; below: Arm-v8-M)

The **MPU_CTRL** register (see Table 3.18) is illustrated in Figure 3.29 and allows the MPU to be enabled by writing to the ENABLE field, as well as keeping the MPU enabled during the handling of HardFault, NMI and FAULTMASK exceptions by setting the HFNMIENA field.

Figure 3.29 MPU_CTRL register fields

The region number register (**MPU_RNR**; see Table 3.18) is shown in Figure 3.30; writing to the REGION field of this register indicates which region is going to be configured in the subsequent register entries.

Figure 3.30 Region number register (MPU_RNR)

Figure 3.31 illustrates the region base address register (**MPU_RBAR**; see Table 3.18). The fields of this register allow the base address of a region to be configured; the precise function depends on the underlying architecture. The region to be configured is that defined in the **MPU_RNR** register. However, in the Arm-v7-M architecture, it is possible to change the region being configured by setting the VALID field in the **MPU_RBAR** register and selecting the region in its REGION field (this feature has been removed in the Arm-v8-M architecture).

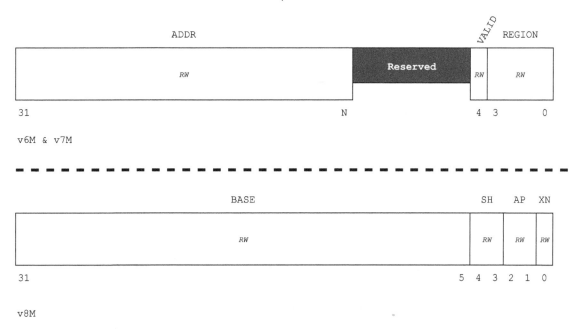

Figure 3.31 Fields of the region base address register (MPU_RBAR) (above: Arm-v6-M & Arm-v7-M; below: Arm-v8-M)

In the Arm-v8-M architecture, the base address is written in the BASE field of the **MPU_RBAR** register; the SH field is used to indicate whether the region is shareable, AP is used to indicate the access permissions, and XN is used to indicate whether the region is execute-never.

In the Arm-v6-M and Arm-v7-M architectures, the size and the attributes of the region are configurable via a separate **MPU_RASR** register (absent in the Arm-v8-M architecture), shown in Figure 3.32 (and Table 3.18). The fields can be written to as follows to configure the region specified in the **MPU_RNR** register:

▪ **XN**: indicates whether the region is execute-never

▪ **AP, TEX, C** and **B**: specify the access permissions

▪ **S**: indicates whether the region is shareable

▪ **SRD**: indicates whether each of the region's (eight) potential sub-regions (see below) is disabled (the least-significant bit of the field controls the first sub-region, the most-significant bit controls the last)

- **SIZE**: specifies the size of the region

- **ENABLE**: enables/disables the region.

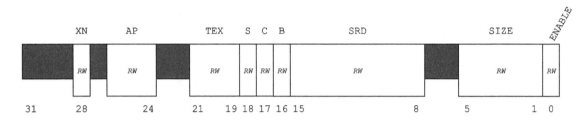

Figure 3.32 MPU region attributes and size register (MPU_RASR) fields (not in Arm-v8-M)

In Arm-v8-M processors, there is no **MPU_RASR** register; it has been replaced by the **RLAR** register. Instead of specifying the size of the region, this register contains the limit address of the region, while the attribute configuration is done via the **MPU_MAIR0** and **MPU_MAIR1** registers, as defined in Table 3.19 and illustrated in Figure 3.33.

Table 3.19 MPU region limit address and memory attribute indirection registers (Arm-v8-M only)

Register Name	Access	Address	Function
MPU_RLAR	RW	0xE000_EDA8	Set the region limit address
MPU_MAIR0	RW	0xE000_EDC0	Set region attributes
MPU_MAIR1	RW	0xE000_EDC4	Set region attributes

In the Arm-v8-M architecture, the limit address of the region is written in the LIMIT field of the **MPU_RLAR** register. Here, an attribute can be associated (via the ATTRINDEX field) with the attribute indices from **MPU_MAIR0** and **MPU_MAIR1** and the region can be enabled by setting the ENABLE field.

In some architectures (but not Arm-v8-M), each MPU region can be divided into eight non-overlapping **sub-regions** of equal size. This adds granularity within a region, allowing individual sub-regions to be enabled or disabled:

- If the relevant bit of the 8-bit SRD field in the **MPU_RASR** register (see Figure 3.32) is 0 (the default value), that particular sub-region address range has the attributes defined for the region of which it is a part;

- If the relevant SRD bit is 1, that particular sub-region address range is not treated as part of the region; if no other enabled region overlaps this disabled sub-region, and an access attempt is unprivileged or the background region is disabled, the MPU issues a fault.

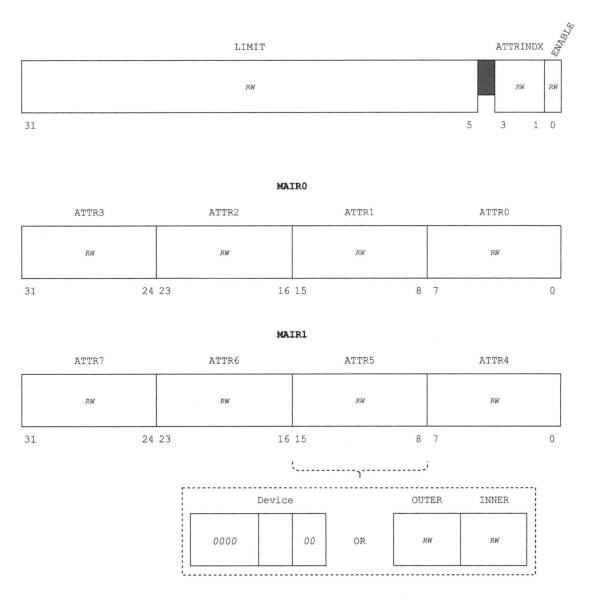

Figure 3.33 Fields of region limit address (MPU_RLAR) and memory attribute registers (Arm-v8-M only)

3.7.6 MPU Configuration Process

Figure 3.34 shows a comparison of two pieces of code used to configure the MPU. That on the left uses CMSIS while the one on the right accesses the registers using bit-level operations and bit masks in C. Because CMSIS offers helper functions to configure the MPU, we can see that this example is more user-friendly.

CMSIS for Arm-v7-M Architecture	C Equivalent (Example)

<pre>ARM_MPU_Disable();</pre>	<pre>volatile uint32_t* registerAddr;
	uint32_t registerValue = 0;
	
	registerAddr = 0xE000ED94U;
	*registerAddr = 0x0;</pre>

<pre>ARM_MPU_SetRegionEx(
  0UL   /* Region Number */,
  0x00000000UL   /* Base Address */,
  ARM_MPU_RASR(
    0UL   /* DisableExec */,
    ARM_MPU_AP_FULL /* AccessPermission */,
    0UL   /* TypeExtField */,
    0UL   /* IsShareable */,
    0UL   /* IsCacheable */,
    0UL   /* IsBufferable */,
    0x00UL   /* SubRegionDisable */,
    ARM_MPU_REGION_SIZE_128KB /* Size */));
 	
ARM_MPU_Enable(
  MPU_CTRL_PRIVDEFENA_Msk
   | MPU_CTRL_HFNMIENA_Msk
   | MPU_CTRL_ENABLE_Msk);</pre>
	<pre>registerAddr = 0xE000ED98U;
	*registerAddr = 0;
	
	registerAddr = 0xE000ED9CU;
	*registerAddr = 0x00000000UL;
	
	registerAddr = 0xE000EDA0U;
	registerValue = 0b10000 << 1;
	registerValue |= 0b11 << 24;
	registerValue |= 0b0 << 28;
	registerValue |= 1 /* Enable Region */;
	*registerAddr = registerValue;
	
	registerAddr = 0xE000ED94U;
	*registerAddr = 0x7;</pre>

Figure 3.34 Comparison of code to configure the MPU using CMSIS (left) and a C equivalent (right) in Arm-v7-M architecture

Figure 3.35 shows the equivalent CMSIS code to configure the MPU for the Arm-v8-M architecture. For the Non-secure MPU, the functions will be identical but are suffixed with _NS.

```
ARM_MPU_Disable();

ARM_MPU_SetMemAttr(
  0                    /* Index */,
  ARM_MPU_ATTR(
    ARM_MPU_ATTR_NON_CACHEABLE |
    ARM_MPU_SH_NON     /* Outer */,
    ARM_MPU_ATTR_NON_CACHEABLE |
    ARM_MPU_SH_NON     /* Inner */));

ARM_MPU_SetRegion(
  0UL                  /* Region number */,
  ARM_MPU_RBAR(
    0x00000000UL       /* Base Address  */,
    0UL                /* Is Shareable */,
    0UL                /* Read Only */,
    1UL                /* Non Privileged */,
    0UL                /* eXecute Never */),
  ARM_MPU_RLAR(
    0x1FFFFUL          /* Limit address */,
    0UL                /* MAIR index */));

ARM_MPU_Enable(
  MPU_CTRL_PRIVDEFENA_Msk
   | MPU_CTRL_HFNMIENA_Msk
   | MPU_CTRL_ENABLE_Msk);
```

Figure 3.35 CMSIS code example for configuring MPU in Arm-v8-M architecture

As already described in the preceding section on CMSIS, it is possible to create equivalent C code from scratch to perform MPU configuration. However, as can be seen in the Arm-v7-M versions in Figure 3.34, the latter provides greater opportunity for error and may not be as generic as the CMSIS version.

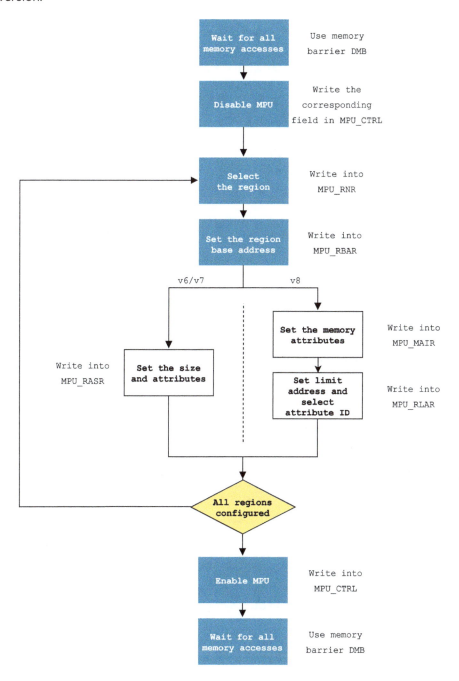

Figure 3.36 Flowchart for MPU configuration of Cortex-M processors

Figure 3.36 presents a flowchart that explains how to configure the MPU and in which order the registers need to be written. While configuring the MPU, no memory access (other than that required to configure the MPU) can be allowed. Indeed, trying to access the memory at this moment would result in undefined behavior. It is why it is important to use memory barriers before and after the configuration to prevent this happening. The MPU is first disabled by resetting the ENABLE field of the MPU_CTRL register. The region to be configured is selected by writing to the MPU_RNR register. The base address can then be defined in the **MPU_RBAR** register. Depending on the architecture, the size and attributes of region are configured either in the **MPU_RASR** register (Arm-v6-M and Arm-v7-M) or by using **MPU_MAIR0/1** and **MPU_RLAR** (Arm-v8-M architecture). Several regions can be configured in turn by following this scheme. When all the regions are ready, the MPU can be enabled by setting the ENABLE field of the **MPU_CTRL** register.

3.7.7 MPU Diagnostics

If a permission violation is detected, the MemManage handler entry is called from the vector table. If this specific vector entry is not enabled, a HardFault is generated instead.

If this happens, it is possible to retrieve the address that generated the fault and the reason for it by accessing the Memory Management Fault Address and Status Registers (**MMFAR** [or **MMAR**] and **MMFSR**).

Note: This is not available in the optional MPU of the Cortex-M0+.

The cause of the fault can be:

- An instruction access violation: this occurs when an address is fetched to execute an instruction.

- A data access violation.

- A fault on unstacking for a return from an exception.

- A fault on stacking for an exception.

- A fault during floating-point lazy state preservation; this can only happen on those Cortex-M processors (e.g. -M4, -M7, -M23 and -M33) that can have an FPU.

The **MMFAR** contains the 32 bits of the relevant address if the MMARVALID bit of the **MMFSR** field is set to 1, which means that the **MMFSR** status register should be read before the **MMFAR** address register to ensure that the value contained in the latter is valid. The **MMFSR** is contained in the 8 least-significant bits of the Configurable Fault Status Register (**CFSR**) and can be accessed as a sub-register; it gives the reason for the fault.

Inspection of these fields can be done in software, as illustrated by the CMSIS library extract shown in Figure 3.37.

```
if (SCB->CFSR & SCB_CFSR_MMARVALID_Msk)
{
  logPrint("Attempt to access address\n");
}
if (SCB->CFSR & SCB_CFSR_DACCVIOL_Msk)
{
  logPrint("Operation not permitted\n");
}
if (SCB->CFSR & SCB_CFSR_IACCVIOL_Msk)
{
  logPrint("Non-executable region\n");
}
if (SCB->CFSR & SCB_CFSR_MSTKERR_Msk)
{
  logPrint("Stacking error\n");
}
logPrint("MMFAR 0x%x\n", SCB->MMFAR);
```

Figure 3.37 Example of MPU debugging code accessing MMFAR and MMFSR fields

These registers can only be accessed in privilege mode. However, because this register is often used when an exception occurs, the processor will be in this mode.

Obtaining the control register and checking the nPRIV field gives information about the privilege level when the fault occurred. In CMSIS this is achieved as shown below:

```
logPrint("Control register 0x%x\n", __get_CONTROL());
```

Using a debugger like (GNU) gdb, it is possible to see the exception and to inspect the registers for fault analysis. Using print commands is discouraged in exception handlers; however, inside a gdb session, a breakpoint can be inserted into the **MemManage_Handler** function, as shown in Figure 3.38, to enable analysis of the significant registers.

```
(gdb) b MemManage_Handler
## Set a breakpoint in the handler and stop the execution when the program reaches it
(gdb) info reg
## Will print all the registers r0 to r15
(gdb) print/x *(uint8_t *)0xE000ED28
## Will print the MMFSR field
(gdb) p/x *(uint32_t*)0xE000ED34
## Will print the MMFAR that could contain the address causing the fault
```

Figure 3.38 Using gdb to print registers for debugging purposes

3.7.8 Fault Handling

Detecting an MPU fault is great; it means that the system can react if something unexpected happens. However, there are different ways to tackle such events, depending on the application. Usually, all of the information necessary to track an issue (mainly, the state of the system) is logged:

■ Processor register dump: As described in the previous section, the contents of the processor registers can help isolate the issue.

■ Configuration of the MPU regions: This can be retrieved by reading all of the MPU registers one by one and dumping their contents.

The logging can be done by writing into a specific storage memory or by sending through a serial interface or over the internet. The logs generated can subsequently be used by programmers to reproduce and resolve the access violation that generated the fault.

After fault logging, the system needs to make a decision: either to shutdown and restart the application, or to continue with its execution. The choice usually depends on the severity of the error. If the application must be restarted, then the system might need to have a form of soft exit in which, for example, some components are disabled or some additional contextual data, such as the time, is stored.

With an RTOS, the faulty task can be terminated and started again. All allocated memory needs to be released. If other tasks were depending upon or associated with the faulty process, they must be restarted too. This will be an implementation-specific procedure that will vary according to the application involved.

3.7.9 Exercises

Visit GitHub (github.com/Introduction-To-System-On-Chip/QEMU_lm3s6965evb) and complete the exercises for this section (3.7). This project needs some setup, as explained in the associated README file.

Table 3.20 Region configurations for MPU exercises

Region	Base Address	Limit	Size (KiB)	Attributes
7	0x2002_8000	0x2002_FFFF	16	Privileged and Unprivileged Read Only
6	0x2002_4000	0x2002_7FFF	16	Privileged Read/Write; Unprivileged Read Only
5	0x2002_0000	0x2002_3FFF	16	Privileged Read/Write
4	0x2001_8000	0x2001_FFFF	16	Privileged Read Only
3	0x2001_4000	0x2001_7FFF	16	Full access
2	0x2001_0000	0x2001_3FFF	16	No access
1	0x2000_0000	0x2000_FFFF	64	Full access (RAM with stack and heap)
0	0x0000_0000	0x0000_1FFF	128	Full access (ROM)

A useful aspect of QEMU is that it can print logs when a process catches an exception: Figure 3.39 indicates the logs that will be printed if a violation is detected.

Taking exception 4 [Data Abort] ...with CFSR.DACCVIOL and MMFAR 0x20010000 ...taking pending nonsecure exception 4	Exception taken from a data violation; this means the program is inside the MemManage_Handler
Taking exception 16 [Semihosting call] ...handling as semihosting call 0x4	Exception taken to print the log, this can be ignored in the context of the current exercise.

MemManage_Handler:
  control 0x0
  mmfar 0x20010000
  LR 0xfffffff9
	Log printed by the function logPrint inside the handler.

Figure 3.39 QEMU log prints when a memory access violation is detected (left) and explanations (right)

When the system starts, it runs in privileged mode. In the main function, the nPRIV field from the **CONTROL** register is checked and should have a value of 0. The function accessRegionsMPU initiates read and write accesses for the following addresses: 0x2001_0000U (Region 2), 0x2001_4000U (Region 3), 0x2001_8000U (Region 4), 0x2002_0000U (Region 5), 0x2002_4000U (Region 6), and 0x2002_8000U (Region 7).

3.7.9.1 Exercise

In the exercises, we will experiment with the configuration of the MPU and understand how to debug it if a fault occurs. The main goal is to understand the different types of instructions that can trigger a fault when the MPU is set up.

As the previous section was on CMSIS, we will also compare defining our own function to configure the MPU with using CMSIS predefined functions.

3.8 Arm TrustZone IP

3.8.1 Introduction

Small processors are used throughout the IoT domain but are also commonplace in the automotive and robotic domains. If we consider the current marketplace, we can see that manufacturers are using SoCs for more and more connected applications, including:

- Smart locks

- Smart lighting and heating systems

- Cameras

- Sensor acquisition (e.g. Smart meters).

During their lifetimes, many systems are now required to store certificates, private keys, and various other sensitive assets to provide protection against attackers or to avoid data leakage. Such assets might be used for the authentication of a device, for encryption and decryption of data, but also to ensure that the code being run is legitimate.

Most applications need multiple libraries to handle functions such as storage and communication (e.g. Bluetooth, Wi-Fi, LTE). The more code a system contains, the more scope there is for error. Isolation is the key to making a system more secure. This means that a system needs to be separated into different elements to make it more resilient to errors: if one such element falls vulnerable to an attack or has a bug, it should not impact the rest of the SoC.

In this section, we review the different elevation levels, also called privilege levels, used in support of such isolation. The concepts will be explained through the TrustZone technology for Cortex-M and how it can be configured. TrustZone effectively builds hardware-enforced isolation into the CPU. However, other implementations of this approach (for example MultiZone for RISC-V) follow similar principles.

Increased security can be achieved by adding more privilege levels. For Cortex-M processors, only two levels of privilege were available for the Arm-v6-M and Arm-v7-M architectures:

- an unprivileged mode, also called Thread mode (for running applications)

- a privileged mode, also called Handler mode (for handling exceptions).

This basic separation allows the critical aspects of system operation (e.g. task handling through an RTOS, exception handling) to be handled within a mode that has more control of the system registers. Indeed, the goal is to forbid direct application access to some processor peripherals such as the MPU. While we have seen in the previous section that the MPU provides some level of access control to memory, this has its limitations. For example, it cannot be used to prevent code running in privileged mode from updating the configuration of the MPU regions.

Systems need protection to avoid any data leakage that could allow an attacker to gain access to the device and trigger unexpected behavior. This is particularly acute for SoCs because many of the associated devices operate via remote communication mechanisms such as Wi-Fi or Bluetooth and so can be accessed remotely as well as physically.

To address this, the Arm-v8-M architecture offers an optional security extension, named **TrustZone**, which adds two further privilege levels, as illustrated in Figure 3.40:

- Non-secure mode, also called Non-trusted mode (Normal)

- Secure mode, also called Trusted mode (Protected)

Software running in the "Secure" part of a system is considered to be "trusted". It has access to more system resources and security assets. At the same time, the overall attack surface is reduced because access to critical code from the "Non-secure" world is restricted and protected. A related aspect is that the Secure software codebase should also be small (in comparison to an RTOS) to avoid a large attack surface that would offer more potential exploits.

Typically, the Secure world consists of:

▨ secure boot functions and secure handlers for any security faults that may arise

▨ cryptography operations

▨ access to specific peripherals, such as accelerators (using the Arm CryptoCell security extension)

▨ sensitive data and associated storage

▨ an updated library system.

On the other side, the Non-secure world will typically consist of:

▨ application code

▨ RTOS

▨ drivers.

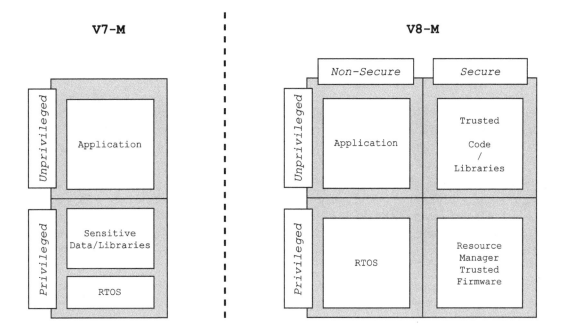

Figure 3.40 Cortex-M privilege levels

TrustZone adds new instructions to partition Secure and Non-secure software, providing better software containment. While Secure code can call all the locations of the Non-secure code, the Non-secure code can only call a predefined subset of the functions located in the Secure code. There are a fixed number of entry points, known as Secure Gateways, that act as anchors through which the Non-secure code can make calls to the Secure code. Whenever Non-secure code calls a Secure function, its input is not trusted. This reflects a baseline principle whereby the Secure side should never trust the Non-secure side. However, as we will see later, calls between the Non-secure and Secure worlds are transparent to the Non-secure components; they still behave like basic function calls.

3.8.2 Hardware Modifications for TrustZone

Some elements of the Cortex-M hardware have to be modified to support these two Secure and Non-secure worlds.

In terms of the general-purpose registers, the main and process stack pointers (register **R13**) need to be duplicated (banked). This banking is handled by the hardware when there is a change in the security state of the CPU or during a switch between application and exception modes. When accessing the **SP**, the hardware takes care of managing the access to the appropriate register, according to which "side" is being executed. Table 3.21 and Figure 3.41 illustrate the stack pointer (**R13**) registers for the **MSP** and **PSP**, depending on the security and execution state of the core.

Table 3.21 Banking of register R13 (stack pointer) depending on core state

State	Register R13
Non-secure application code	PSP_NS
Non-secure exception code	MSP_NS
Secure application code	PSP_S
Secure exception code	MSP_S

All other general-purpose registers (including the floating-point registers if the FPU is enabled) are not modified and remain common between the two security states. This means that the software must ensure that data is not leaked by writing garbage values into the registers when switching states.

In terms of the special registers (accessed through **MSR**, **MRS**, and **CPS** instructions), several of these have to be security-banked in a similar fashion to the stack pointer(s) because they are specific to the context of the processor: **CONTROL, PRIMASK, BASEPRI, FAULTMASK, MSPLIM,** and **PSPLIM**. Thus, for example, the special **CONTROL** register contains the SPSEL field, which gives information about which stack pointer is selected for the current state of the core.

The processor can run in either Secure or Non-secure mode. As will be explained in Chapter 5, the AMBA bus protocol has been extended to incorporate the HNONSEC signal, which communicates the security status of each transaction submitted to the bus.

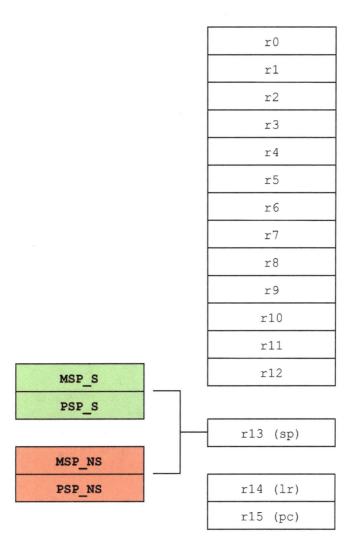

Figure 3.41 TrustZone general-purpose register banking

Using TrustZone, physical memory can now be configured in one of three states:

■ Non-secure: Can be accessed from all processor modes.

■ Secure but Non-secure Callable: Non-secure code can branch to a Non-secure Callable (NSC) memory region which contains special anchors (or Secure Gateways) for the purpose. A Secure API in the NSC region then invokes the appropriate function of the Secure library and once the code has been executed, the Secure library returns control to the Non-secure world.

■ Secure only: Only accessible from the Secure processor mode.

How are these secure memory regions defined (and how do these anchors work)? The MPU is not responsible for managing this: it only checks other access control attributes, as described in the preceding section. Instead, these secure regions are managed via additional hardware: the Security Attribution Unit (SAU) and the Implementation-Defined Attribution Unit (IDAU). The purpose of these units (jointly referred to as the attribution unit) is to assign the appropriate security attribution to specific address ranges and to generate a HardFault as necessary if/when breaches occur [7]:

▪ An IDAU is a specific piece of external hardware that defines a view of the memory layout when the system boots. It must be implemented by the SoC manufacturer to provide a default view at system startup because the SAU is only configurable through software. Up to 256 regions can be configured by an IDAU. If an IDAU is not present, the necessary SAU-based configuration must be done in the bootloader instead.

▪ Configuration of the internal SAU is done in software by writing into the different system registers. The SAU only supports a maximum of eight memory regions. If there is no IDAU present, there is no security until the SAU has been enabled/configured (the SAU is disabled on Reset).

The IDAU offers finer-grained granularity for defining memory regions in comparison to the small number of software-configurable regions enabled by the SAU. However, whereas the SAU is software-configurable, the IDAU configuration is fixed at design.

For instructions, the attribution unit will assign an ascending security status of Non-secure (NS), Non-secure Callable (NSC) or Secure (S), depending on the address involved and the regions configured. For data, the attribution unit checks the current security state of the core and returns a security attribute accordingly (NS or S). If the core is running in a Non-secure execution state and the data accessed is identified as Secure, a HardFault is generated.

Figure 3.42 depicts the units responsible for determining the address security type. The final attribute output by the joint attribution unit will be a combination of the region configurations of the SAU and the IDAU. If the two units differ in their attribution, the more restrictive of them is output. Table 3.22 shows the outcomes from various combinations of SAU and IDAU attributions.

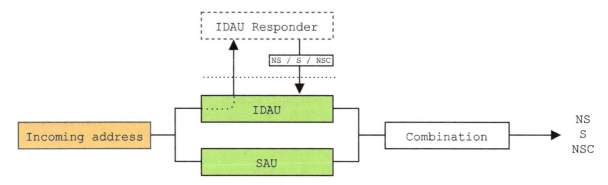

Figure 3.42 Security assessment of an address

Table 3.22 SAU and IDAU attributions and combined outputs

SAU	IDAU	Result
Unset	Secure	Secure
Unset	Non-secure	Non-secure
Secure	Unset	Secure
Non-secure	Unset	Non-secure
Secure	Non-secure	Secure
Non-secure	Secure	Secure
Unset	Unset	Default

As indicated above, the SAU is disabled at reset and must be programmed before activation. The registers available for this purpose are shown in Table 3.23, and perform similar functions to those used in MPU configuration. By default, the SAU marks all memory regions as Secure. If a region is to be Non-secure or Non-secure Callable, it must be configured by updating these registers, which can only be performed with secure privileged access. A fault is generated by any other form of attempted access.

Table 3.23 Registers available for SAU configuration

Register Name	Full Name	Description
SAU_CTRL	Control Register	For enabling and configuring the unit
SAU_TYPE	Type Register	Gives the number of regions configured
SAU_RNR	Region Number Register	Selector of the region to be configured
SAU_RBAR	Region Base Address Register	For setting the base address of the region
SAU_RLAR	Region Limit Address Register	For enabling the specific region, setting the security attribute, and giving the end (limit) address of the region

The SAU control register (**SAU_CTRL**, represented in Figure 3.43) has a single-bit field ALLNS (All Non-secure) that provides information on how the SAU should assign the memory when the SAU is disabled. If this bit is set to 1, all memory is designated as Non-secure. Otherwise, the memory is effectively designated as Non-secure Callable. The other relevant field of this register is the single-bit ENABLE, which can be used to enable and disable the SAU. The default value for **SAU_CTRL** is 0x0000_0000.

Figure 3.43 SAU_CTRL register fields

The SAU type register (**SAU_TYPE**, represented in Figure 3.44) indicates the number of regions available via the field SREGION. This is an 8-bit field, so a maximum of $2^8 = 256$ regions can be configured. However, a system designer can decide how many regions are needed and might specify a lower number. This register is Read Only because this is a hardware design choice; it cannot be updated through software.

Figure 3.44 SAU_TYPE register field

Just as for the MPU, there is an SAU register (**SAU_RNR**, represented in Figure 3.45) that contains the current number of the region that is to be configured (via **SAU_RBAR** and **SAU_RLAR**; see below); this REGION field is the same size as the SREGION field in the **SAU_TYPE** register.

Figure 3.45 SAU_RNR register field

The five least significant bits of the base and limit address registers (**SAU_RBAR** and **SAU_RLAR**, represented in Figures 3.48 and 3.49) are always forced to values of 0b00000 and 0b11111, respectively. This means that a region is always $2^5 = 32$-byte aligned, and the minimum size of a region is 32 bytes. The **SAU_RLAR** register has two other fields:

- NSC – set to 1 if the associated region is Non-secure Callable

- ENABLE – set to 1 if the associated region is enabled; otherwise, the register has no effect.

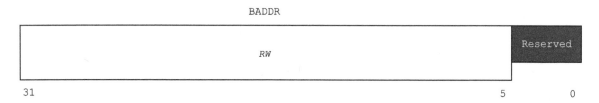

Figure 3.46 SAU_RBAR register fields

Figure 3.47 SAU_RLAR register fields

This means that writing the following code will create and enable a secure region starting at 0x000_15E0 (the five least-significant bits are masked to 0 and not written to the register) and finishing at 0x0002_001F (although the register fields BADDR and LADDR will contain 0x0000_1500 and 0x0000_2001, respectively):

```
SAU_RNG->REGION = 0;
SAU_RBAR->BADDR = 0x01500;
SAU_RLAR->LADDR = 0x02001;
```

Figure 3.48 shows a pseudocode example of how to configure the regions in the SAU and the resulting memory layout; the eventual assignment reflects the adjudicated outcome of the differing priorities indicated by the SAU and IDAU configurations.

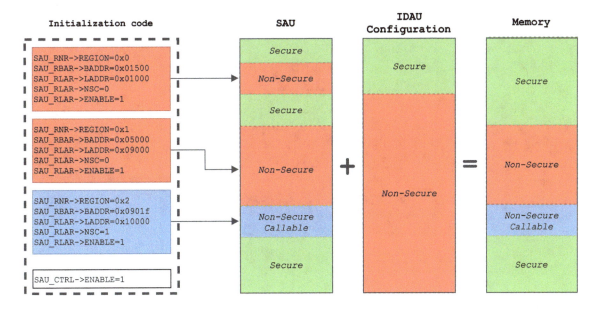

Figure 3.48 Example of IDAU and SAU memory configuration

While the combination of IDAU and SAU memory configuration offers good granularity, it may not be sufficient if the system has many peripherals or if the memory needs to be partitioned into many regions. To address this limitation, two more controllers are introduced, as depicted in Figure 3.49:

▦ Memory Protection Controller (MPC)

▦ Peripheral Protection Controller (PPC).

The MPC and PPC are placed in front of, respectively, the memory and the peripherals, and apply address aliases to change their effective addresses such that they appear in Secure or Non-secure addresses accordingly. The MPC and PPC are configured through registers and, for each block of addresses, control the state of the access (Secure/Non-secure) and either allow or prevent it as appropriate.

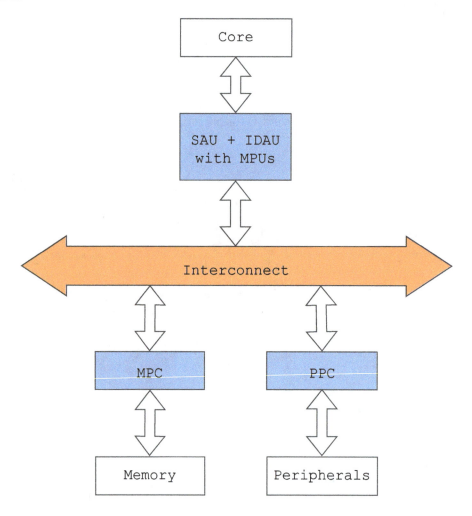

Figure 3.49 Memory and peripheral secure address aliasing using MPC and PPC

3.8.3 Switching Between Secure and Non-secure States

When a TrustZone-enabled system starts, it boots in the Secure privileged state and executes the Reset Handler. At this point, the SAU is initialized, and execution switches to the Non-secure code. The user application can then make calls to the Secure API if it needs to. This section explains how to jump between the two security worlds, and Figure 3.50 provides an overview of the process.

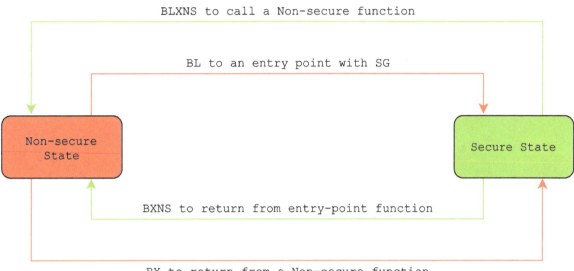

Figure 3.50 Switching between Secure and Non-secure states

3.8.3.1 Calling Non-secure Code from Secure Code

Secure code can call Non-secure code by using the new branch instructions, **BXNS** and **BLXNS**, as detailed in Table 3.24. If a regular branch instruction (**B, BL, BX, BLX**) is used, a fault is generated, depending on the version of the Arm-v8-M architecture in use:

■ Baseline: Secure HardFault

■ Mainline: SecureFault with the INVTRAN bit set to signal an invalid transition.

Table 3.24 Non-secure branching instructions

BXNS	The BXNS instruction causes a branch to an address and instruction set specified by a register and causes a transition from the Secure to the Non-secure domain. This variant of the branch instruction must only be used when additional steps, required to make such a transition safe, are taken.
BLXNS	The BLXNS instruction calls a subroutine at an address and instruction set specified by a register and causes a transition from the Secure to the Non-secure domain. This variant of the branch instruction must only be used when additional steps, required to make such a transition safe, are taken.

Before using these new branch instructions, the following steps must be followed to avoid data leakage/faults:

1. All non-banked general-purpose registers must be saved by pushing them onto the secure stack and then writing meaningless values into them (for example, 0). This step applies to registers **R0** to **R12** (and the **R14** link register if **BXNS**, rather than **BLXNS**, is used). Some of the registers may be used for holding arguments to the function but they should not contain sensitive information.

2. Non-banked system control registers such as **APSR** should be cleared.

3. The target address of the branch must be in the Non-secure code and its bit 0 set to 0b0.

This process is illustrated in the following code extract:

```
// Save registers to the stack
PUSH {r0-r12}
// Write the non-secure address to r0
LDR r0, =<Non-Secure address>
// Set all registers to 0
MOV r1, #0
MOV r2, #0
MOV r3, #0
MOV r4, #0
MOV r5, #0
MOV r6, #0
MOV r7, #0
MOV r8, #0
MOV r9, #0
MOV r10, #0
MOV r11, #0
MOV r12, #0
// Clear APSR
MSR APSR_nzcvq,r0
// Branch to Non-secure address contained in r0
BLXNS r0
```

When **BLXNS** is called, the function return address is in Secure code. A mechanism is needed to avoid having to send this confidential address to the Non-secure domain. When the **BLXNS** instruction is called, the link register (**R14**) is set to FNC_RETURN, which is a special value, while the return address is saved to the Secure stack. If the program counter (**R15**) is updated to FNC_RETURN (using **BX** or **LDR**) while the security state is Non-secure, the security state is updated to Secure and, at that point, the Secure stack can be read to retrieve the return address.

3.8.3.2 Calling Secure Code from Non-secure Code

To branch to Secure library code from a Non-secure state, two elements of configuration must be in place:

▪ Through the attribution unit (SAU and IDAU in combination), the target address must be configured as Non-secure Callable

■ The target address must be a Secure Gateway (**SG**) instruction, which indicates that the address is a correct location for the Non-secure code to branch to. If the target address does not contain an **SG** instruction, a fault is generated.

As illustrated in Figure 3.51, the Non-secure code can call the Secure function API using a standard branch instruction (e.g. **B, BL**) to a Secure Gateway instruction in the Non-secure Callable memory, indicated in the figure by an anchor. When executed from the Non-secure Callable memory, the **SG** instruction updates the security state to Secure and updates the least-significant bit of the link register (**R14**) to 0. Setting this bit to 0 is required when using a **BXNS** instruction to indicate that the return address is in Non-secure memory. The Non-secure Callable API function then branches to the Secure memory function. All of this processing is hidden from the Non-secure code: calling a valid Secure function appears identical to calling a normal function.

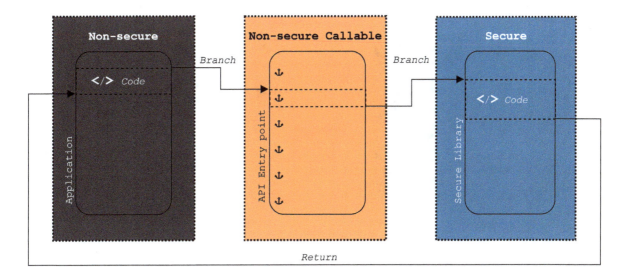

Figure 3.51 Branching from Non-secure to Secure code

Any direct branch to the Secure code from the Non-secure state results in the same faults as described above. Even if there is an **SG** instruction in the Secure code, the Non-secure state can never branch directly to this part of memory; it needs to access the Non-secure Callable part, which acts as a bridge.

3.8.4 Secure Applications
Creating the binary code for a Secure/Non-secure application implies a need for two projects, as illustrated in Figure 3.52. In this section, we explain how to develop the Secure application, before addressing the Non-secure application in the section that follows.

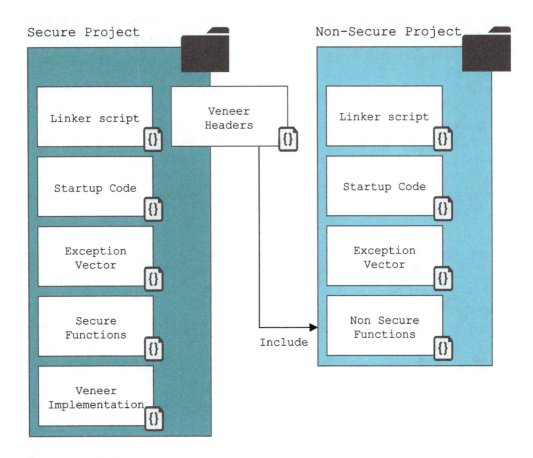

Figure 3.52 Typical project structure

Note: Some boards can only be programmed using one binary, whereas some boards can be programmed using a Secure binary and a Non-secure binary. In this latter case, the two binaries must be merged together.

The project files required for the Secure application are as follows:

▪ Linker script: contains the addresses where the different parts of the Secure code are stored. It also contains the address locations of the "veneers" (the anchors or Secure Gateways) that will be configured. Linker script usage has been outlined in the earlier section on CMSIS. The linker script code that is used to specify the location of the SG veneers in memory is shown below:

```
/** SG veneers placed in the section .gnu.sgstubs */
.gnu.sgstubs:
{
    . = ALIGN(32);
} > FLASH

_ld_veneer_base = ADDR(.gnu.sgstubs);
_ld_veneer_limit = .;
```

This code defines the region *.gnu.sgstubs*, which is 32-bit aligned and located in the flash memory. It also defines the variables *_ld_veneer_base* and *_ld_veneer_limit*. This region in memory must be configured as Non-secure Callable.

■ Startup file: contains the vector table, the startup code (reset handler) and all the code necessary to reach the Secure main function. More information about this file can be found in the previous section on CMSIS. The function of this file is not specific to the Secure domain and it should be just like that used for a normal application.

■ Main source file: contains the main function and the application code for the Secure side. The main function will configure the SAU and MPU regions if needed and branch to the Non-secure Reset Handler, as illustrated in the code below:

```
/* Non-secure callback functions typedef */
typedef void (*nsptr_void) (void) __attribute__((cmse_nonsecure_call));
int main(void)
{
  nsptr_void NonSecure_ResetHandler;
  /* Set Non-secure main stack (MSP_NS) */
  __TZ_set_MSP_NS(*((uint32_t *)(TZ_START_NS)));
  /* Get Non-secure reset handler */
  NonSecure_ResetHandler = (nsptr_void) (*((uint32_t *)((TZ_START_NS) + 4U)));
  /* Start Non-secure state software application */
  NonSecure_ResetHandler();

  /* Replace with your SECURE application code if the main returns */
  while (1)
  {
    __NOP();
  }
}
```

The first line of code in the sample above is a simple *typedef*, used in order to declare a function pointer that takes no arguments and returns nothing.Its given attribute (*cmse_nonsecure_call*) is understood by the compiler (if compiled with the *–mcmse* parameter) and implicitly indicates that the function is Non-secure, such that the compiler will add the necessary logic when the function is called. In this case, instead of using a classic branch instruction, the compiler uses the **BLXNS** instruction. This can be observed by checking the assembly code produced:

Address	OPCode	Meaning
296:	681c	ldr r4, [r3, #0]
298:	0864	lsrs r4, r4, #1
29a:	0064	lsls r4, r4, #1
29c:	0020	movs r0, r4
29e:	0021	movs r1, r4
2a0:	0022	movs r2, r4
2a2:	0023	movs r3, r4
2a4:	f000 f806	bl2b4 <__gnu_cmse_nonsecure_call>

As can be seen, the assembly code generated by the compiler does not branch directly using the **BLXNS** instruction. Instead, it first loads the address to branch to into register *r4*. Then it sets the least-significant bit of the address to 0 and moves the value into registers *r0*, *r1*, *r2*, and *r3*. Finally, it branches to the intrinsic function, which is located within the toolchain (see libgcc/config/arm/cmse_nonsecure_call.S). This is a Cortex-M Security Extensions (CMSE) wrapper for saving, clearing, and executing **BLXNS**, and restoring the caller's registers [8].

Before calling the Reset Handler of the Non-secure application, the main **SP** must be set and the address of the Reset Handler must be retrieved. As described in the previous section on CMSIS, the first element of the exception vector is the stack pointer (**MSP**) and the next is the Reset Handler. Once the base address of this vector is known, it is straightforward to obtain these two elements, as shown in the (colored) main source file code above.

- Secure function files: definition of the Secure functions that can be called from the veneers. This file contains functions which can be written without specific flags.

- Veneer files: contains the prototypes and definitions of the Secure Gateway functions that are stored in the Non-secure Callable region. These functions make the links to the Secure functions, as described above and illustrated in the code below:

```
#include "secure.h"      /* Header file with secure interface API */

/* Non-secure callable (entry) function */
int __attribute__((cmse_nonsecure_entry)) nsc_function(int x)
{
  return secure_function(x);
}
```

Again, the given CMSE attribute (*cmse_nonsecure_entry*) is understood by the compiler (if compiled with the *mcmse* parameter) and provides information to the toolchain that this function should be placed in the *.gnu.sgstubs* region, together with the necessary logic. Again, this can be observed by analysing the assembly code produced [9]:

```
/* Disassembly of section
 * gnu.sgstubs: */

00007c08 <nsc_function>:
7c08: e97f e97f sg
7c0c: f7f8 ba72 b.wf4 <__acle_se_nsc_function>
```

The disassembly shows that the first instruction is *sg*. As described above, this is the anchor that must be present. The second instruction is a simple branch to the function *__acle_se_nsc_function*, which wraps the function *nsc_function*, as shown in the code below:

```
000000f4 <__acle_se_nsc_function>:

/* Non-secure callable (entry) function */
    f4: b510          push {r4, lr}

/* Call to secure_function */
    f6: f240 23ad     movw r3, #685    /* Address of secure function: 0x2ad */
    fa: f2c0 0300     movt r3, #0
    fe: 4798          blx r3
/* Wrapper */
   100: 0001          movs r1, r0
   102: 0002          movs r2, r0
   104: 0003          movs r3, r0
   106: 4684          mov ip, r0
   108: bc10          pop {r4}
   10a: bc02          pop {r1}
   10c: 4686          mov lr, r0
   10e: f381 8800     msr CPSR_f, r1
   112: 470c          bxns r1
```

In this code, the return address contained in the link register (*lr*) is first saved onto the stack, then the address of the Secure function is stored in a register (*r3*) and branched into. Once the function returns, its return value stored in *r0* is copied to registers *r1, r2, r3, ip* (**R12**), and the link register (*lr*). This is done to erase all of the register values used in the function and avoid any leaking of information. The link register is popped back from the stack into *r1*, and the flag field from register **CPSR** (*CPSR_f*) is set to *r1* too. Finally, the code invokes a **BXNS** branch instruction to *r1* to return to the Non-secure address.

The disassembly of the *nsc_function* function is as follows:

```
000002ac <nsc_function>:
   2ac: 3003          adds r0, #1
   2ae: 4770          bx lr
```

This function adds 1 to *r0* and returns to the caller. The real address of the *nsc_function* is 0x2ac, but the *_acle_se_nsc_function* wrapper makes a branch to 0x2ad (which is 0x2ac + 0x001).

▪ The header file function should declare the prototypes of the Non-secure Callable functions (e.g. *nsc_function*) as extern, as shown below:

```
#ifndef VENEER_H_
#define VENEER_H_

/* Non-secure callable functions */
extern int nsc_function(int x);

#endif /* VENEER_H_ */
```

The entire process is represented in Figure 3.53.

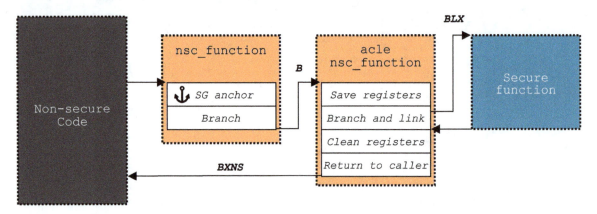

Figure 3.53 *Sequence call from Non-secure code to Secure function*

The Cortex-M Security Extensions (CMSE) need some flags to support the generation of the new instructions presented above. Currently, Arm Compiler 6 and GCC (version 6 or above) are compliant and can be used with CMSE.

When compiling, *include <arm_cmse.h>* and the compiler option *–mcmse* must be used. This enables the attributes shown below to be used in the C code:

```
__attribute__(cmse_nonsecure_call)
__attribute__(cmse_nonsecure_entry)
```

It also provides definitions for the intrinsics of the Test Target (TT) instruction, which queries the security state and access permissions of a memory location [10].

3.8.5 Non-secure Applications
A Non-secure application is composed of the following files:

■ Linker script: standard linker script containing the RAM/ROM addresses in which the Non-secure code is stored.

■ Startup file: very similar in content and function to the Secure startup file but for the Non-secure side.

■ Main source file: contains the main function and the application code for the Non-secure side.

■ Veneer header file: contains the prototypes of the Secure Gateway functions that are defined in the Secure project.

A Non-secure application does not need any special attributes to call Secure functions; they can be called seamlessly.

While building the Secure library, the *–mcmse* compiler flag is needed, as described both above and below. To share the veneers, a library must be created by adding the following parameters to the linker script:

```
--out-implib=secureapp-cmse-implib.lib
--cmse-implib
```

The library produced can be integrated into the Non-secure build using the following parameter:

```
-lsecureapp-cmse-implib.lib
```

Apart from adding this library and including the path to the veneer include file, the Non-secure project does not need any additional build options.

3.8.6 Arm-v8-M-based Boards
Arm-v8-M is a relatively new architecture for the Cortex-M. At the time of writing, there are only a small number of such chips available on the market. Table 3.25 lists some of the available chips that support TrustZone.

Table 3.25 List of chips/dev-boards with an Arm-v8-M core and TrustZone enabled

Board Name	Vendor	Cortex Processor
GD32E230	GigaDevice	M23
SAM L10/L11	Microchip Technology	M23
NuMicro® M	Nuvoton	M23
SmartBond DA1469x	Dialog	M33
nRF91	Nordic Semiconductor	M33
STM32L5 series	STMicroelectronics	M33
LPC5500 series	NXP	M33

Attackers can choose to attack anything but if a specific system is ubiquitous, it is likely to be a target. However, it is worth noting that few will try to breach a system if the time taken to obtain sensitive data is too long (effort versus reward). TrustZone memory isolation is done to make sure that sensitive data does not leak and key peripherals are manipulated safely. Manufacturers of new devices must make sure they are resilient against attacks and can be trusted by customers. The TrustZone for Arm-v8-M blog [11] is a good place to obtain news of vendor announcements in this area.

Many development boards already exist that enable experimentation with the new Arm-v8-M cores. Similarly, simulators such as Arm Fast Model or QEMU can be used to start programming or prototyping on this new architecture. The Arm MPS2+/MPS3 FPGA prototyping board contains an FPGA that can also be programmed with a subsystem provided by Arm [12].

Some of the development kits come packaged with specific IDEs (such as Arm DS-5, Keil, or Atmel Studio 7). These tools can help in the programming of the board and avoid programmer involvement in some of the more cumbersome steps. Various templates/examples [13, 14] are provided to simplify integration and implementation of Secure and Non-secure applications and hide some of the configuration steps (for example, configuring the Non-secure and Secure memory addresses, simplifying the configuration of the SAU regions).

3.9 Case Study: Arm Cortex-M4F-based MSP432 from Texas Instruments

This section explains how to program the MSP432-based development kit from Texas Instruments (TI). The board is a great starting point to understand what a hardware abstraction layer (HAL) is and what can be configured in a SoC. All of the tools described are free, and it is also possible to monitor the power consumption of the board. For more functionality, the board can be extended with BoosterPacks, which are pluggable boards that add extra features, such as Wi-Fi, to the MSP432.

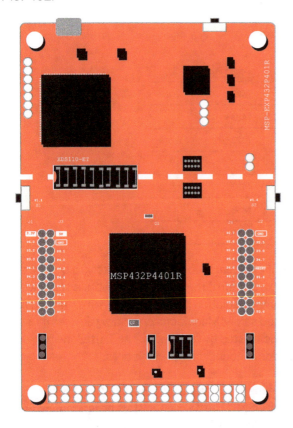
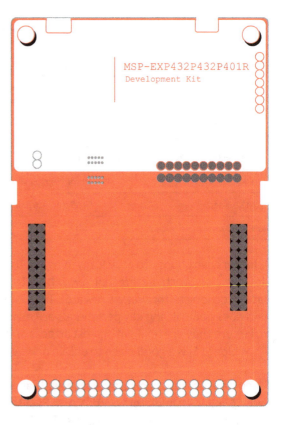

Figure 3.54 TI development kit MSP432

Most boards in the embedded marketplace have similar characteristics. This means that gaining knowledge of a specific board is likely to be applicable to others because the concepts are similar. This section is a more practical one, designed to link together many of the theoretical concepts (e.g. interrupts, GPIO, serial communication) explained in the preceding sections of the chapter.

The exercises described will demonstrate how to configure the MSP432 board and its components. They also provide an initial insight into how to use timers and interrupts to trigger or receive events.

3.9.1 Naming and Documentation

Each board manufacturer can produce many different chips with similar base components. In our case, the full chip name is MSP432P401RIPZ, as represented in Figure 3.54, where the standard prefix is MSP432. Within this chip category, there are many different flavors: MSP432P4011, MSP432P401VT, MSP432P4111, MSP432E401Y, MSP432P401M, and so on. The chip naming for this category is of the form **MSP432x401yzPZ**, as illustrated in Table 3.26.

Table 3.26 Naming code for the MSP432 chip family

Code	Description	Details
MSP432	Prefix	Name of the chip family
x	Power type	P: Low power consumption
		E: Higher power consumption with more components for communication (SPI, CAN, USB, Ethernet)
4	Max. frequency	48 MHz
0	Features	General-purpose chip
1	Peripheral	ADC peripheral
y	Memory size	R: 256 KiB of Flash, 64 KiB of SRAM
		M: 128 KiB of Flash, 32 KiB of SRAM
		V: 512 KiB of Flash, 128 KiB of SRAM
		Y: 1024 KiB of Flash, 256 KiB of SRAM
		1: 2048 KiB of Flash and 256 KiB SRAM
z	Temperature range	S: 0 °C to 50 °C
		I: –45 °C to 85 °C
		T: –40 °C to 105 °C
PZ	Chip packaging	LQFP-100

TI documentation for chips usually consists of two data sheets:

- A family reference manual that describes the core functionalities [15]. For example, it details the address map, the general-purpose registers, the system registers, and so on. This is a generic manual that can be used for all chips that embed the core concerned. For our development kit, the chip family name is MSP432P4xx. The "xx" suffix means that it covers all chips named thus with any combination of two numbers in their names in this position.

- A device-specific data sheet that ties the reference manual concepts to the device [16]. It specifies a chip's device pin-out mapping, the peripherals controller base addresses, and so on. In this specific case, the data sheet gives information for the MSP432P401R and MSP432P401M chips and their different package types.

Most of the time, both data sheets are needed if one is to program the chip properly. When using a board, the LaunchPad Development Kit user guide is often necessary to check what is connected; for example, external crystals for clock, components, and so on [17]. The board that we are going to use is the MSP-EXP432P401R.

Note: If you are interested in obtaining further information about this board, the book *Embedded System Design with the Texas Instruments MSP432 32-bit Processor* gives an extensive view of this chip [18]. However, the goal of this section is not to provide deep knowledge of the board, but rather to link together the different sections of this chapter by providing a practical example.

Low-level software development relies on writing the desired values in the correct memory space to communicate with the hardware resources. Most of the time, manufacturers provide a HAL library that allows rapid development by abstracting the low-level hardware considerations via high-level functions, as briefly described at the end of the previous section in relation to TrustZone. Here, we are going to use the TI HAL for the MSP432.

3.9.2 Description of the Development Kit

The development kit has two parts. One is the actual board with the MSP432 chip, which exposes some GPIOs, two buttons and two LEDs, as shown in the lower part of Figure 3.55. This part also has a JTAG, power supply and UART that are, by default, connected to the other part of the kit.

The different GPIO pins that are available can be configured according to the needs of the application running on the board. This is a typical example of GPIO multiplexing, as described in Chapter 2. The pins are named in the form PX.Y, where X indicates the GPIO port and Y the GPIO number. Figure 3.56 shows these GPIO pin names and their multiplexed configuration. For instance, pin P3.2 can serve two different alternative functions: it can be programmed to be either the RX signal of UART2 (RX2) or the SOMI (Slave-Out/Master-In) signal of SPI2 (SOMI2) or simply a GPIO pin.

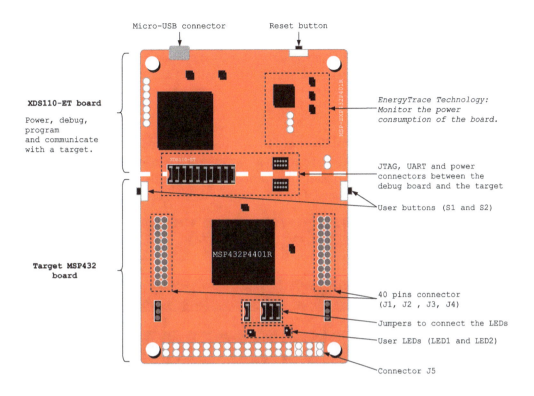

Figure 3.55 Representation of the MSP432 development kit

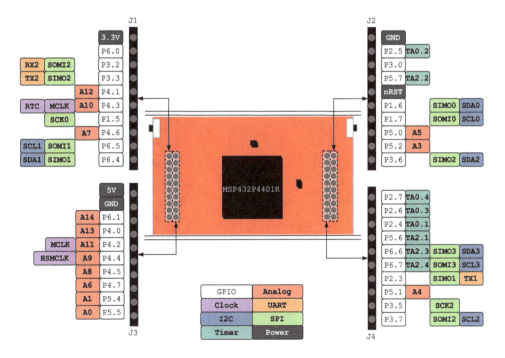

Figure 3.56 GPIO description and multiplexing on the MSP432

The other part of the kit (XDS110-ET), shown in the upper part of Figure 3.55, is for programming and debugging. It has a micro-USB connector that can be plugged into a computer to flash through JTAG, communicate with the UART and power the board. This second part also gives access to a real-time power consumption reading and states that can be analyzed with TI's EnergyTrace Technology to obtain information about the consumption of the board.

3.9.3 Inside the MSP432 Chip

The MSP432P401R is based on an Arm Cortex-M4. It has been conceived as a low-power chip that can deliver high performance for specific applications by virtue of the following modules: floating-point unit (FPU), hardware multiplier, digital signal processor (DSP), and encryption accelerator. It does not have any cache. The components of the chip are shown in Figure 3.57.

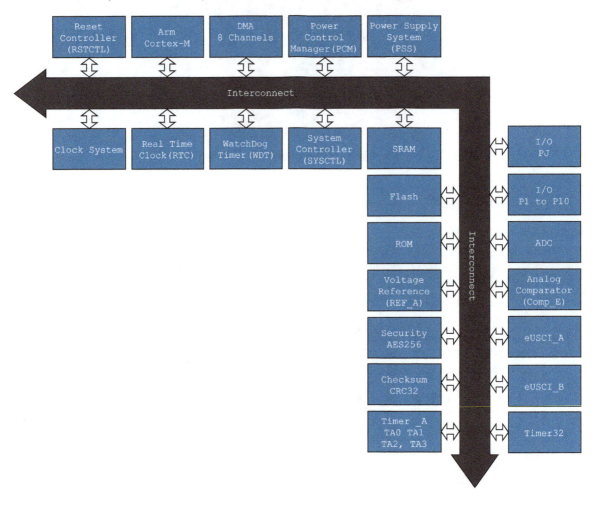

Figure 3.57 Components of the MSP432 chip

As indicated in Section 3.6, the Cortex-M4 can include optional component blocks. For this particular TI chip family, the specific Cortex-M4-based configuration is shown in Table 3.27.

Table 3.27 Specific configuration of the Cortex-M4-based MSP432 chip

Configuration	Value
No. of interrupts	64
Interrupt priorities	8
Memory protection unit	Yes
Floating-point unit	Yes
Bit-banding support	Yes
Endianness	Little
JTAG	Yes
Wake-up controller	No (TI custom-controller is used instead)

Referring back to Sections 3.5.1 and 3.6.2 on the subject of memory-mapping, Figure 3.58 shows the mapping of the peripheral region of memory in more detail. For each of the peripherals, the Technical Reference Manual referred to above defines the associated registers and describes how to configure them. For most peripheral components, there are four kinds of register:

* Configuration: usually contains CTL in its name

* Enable: usually contains EN in its name; used to start or stop a peripheral

* Status: usually contains STAT in its name; used to monitor the peripheral and to indicate the status of its different parts as appropriate

* Interrupt handling: usually contains I in its name; used to enable an interrupt (IE), obtain its status, and clear it.

The board supports CMSIS for configuration of the Cortex-M4. To configure the internal peripherals available, TI provides some CMSIS-like header files that define the associated registers, as shown in Figures 3.61, 3.62 and 3.63. Of course, it is also possible to write into the registers without these helper structures and macros. For each module, all of the registers are described in the MSP432 documentation. Make sure to check the value of the registers at startup: some of them have predefined values at reset (usually 0x0000_0000), but might also have some undefined values!

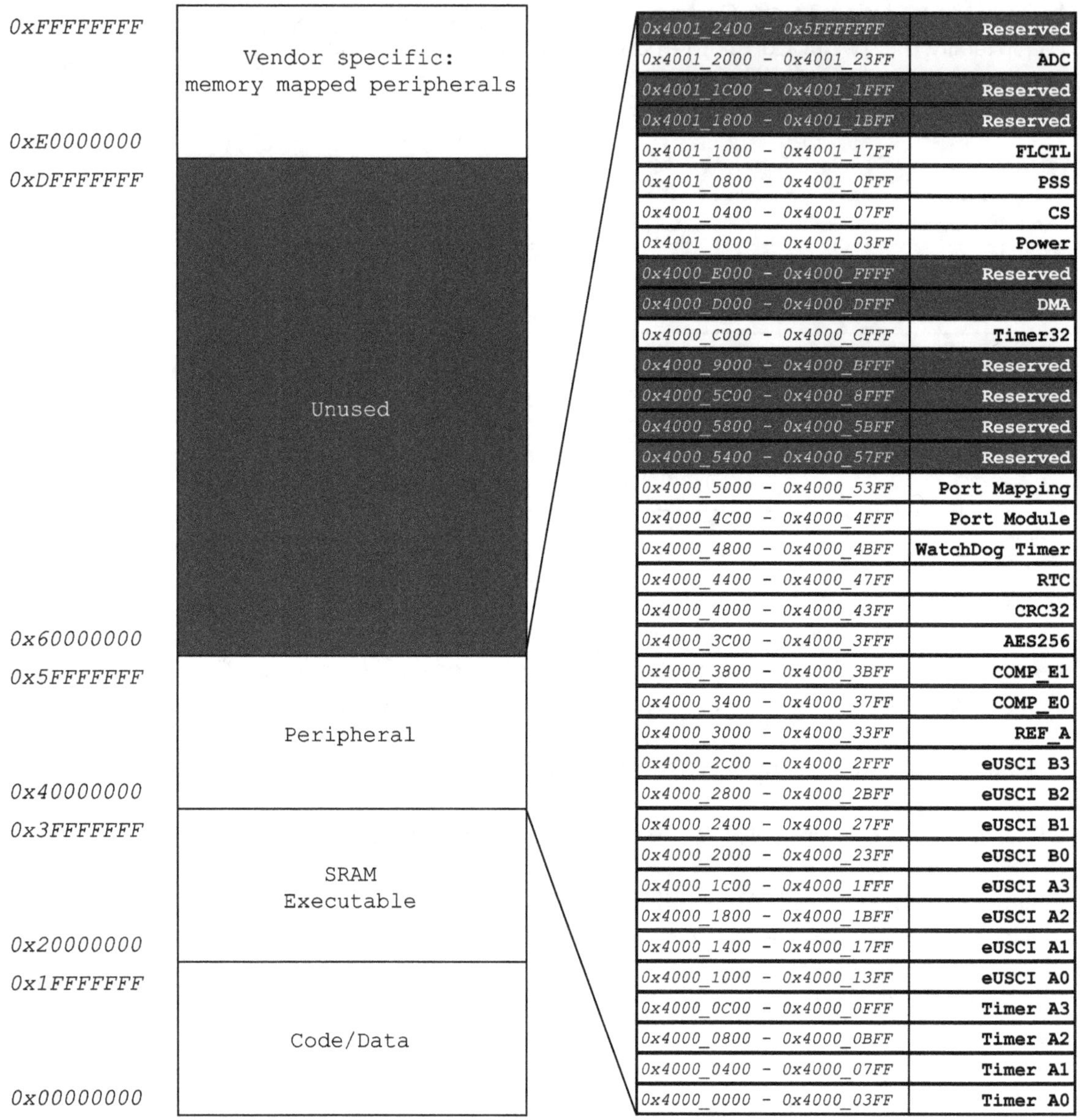

0x4001_2400 – 0x5FFFFFFF	Reserved
0x4001_2000 – 0x4001_23FF	ADC
0x4001_1C00 – 0x4001_1FFF	Reserved
0x4001_1800 – 0x4001_1BFF	Reserved
0x4001_1000 – 0x4001_17FF	FLCTL
0x4001_0800 – 0x4001_0FFF	PSS
0x4001_0400 – 0x4001_07FF	CS
0x4001_0000 – 0x4001_03FF	Power
0x4000_E000 – 0x4000_FFFF	Reserved
0x4000_D000 – 0x4000_DFFF	DMA
0x4000_C000 – 0x4000_CFFF	Timer32
0x4000_9000 – 0x4000_BFFF	Reserved
0x4000_5C00 – 0x4000_8FFF	Reserved
0x4000_5800 – 0x4000_5BFF	Reserved
0x4000_5400 – 0x4000_57FF	Reserved
0x4000_5000 – 0x4000_53FF	Port Mapping
0x4000_4C00 – 0x4000_4FFF	Port Module
0x4000_4800 – 0x4000_4BFF	WatchDog Timer
0x4000_4400 – 0x4000_47FF	RTC
0x4000_4000 – 0x4000_43FF	CRC32
0x4000_3C00 – 0x4000_3FFF	AES256
0x4000_3800 – 0x4000_3BFF	COMP_E1
0x4000_3400 – 0x4000_37FF	COMP_E0
0x4000_3000 – 0x4000_33FF	REF_A
0x4000_2C00 – 0x4000_2FFF	eUSCI B3
0x4000_2800 – 0x4000_2BFF	eUSCI B2
0x4000_2400 – 0x4000_27FF	eUSCI B1
0x4000_2000 – 0x4000_23FF	eUSCI B0
0x4000_1C00 – 0x4000_1FFF	eUSCI A3
0x4000_1800 – 0x4000_1BFF	eUSCI A2
0x4000_1400 – 0x4000_17FF	eUSCI A1
0x4000_1000 – 0x4000_13FF	eUSCI A0
0x4000_0C00 – 0x4000_0FFF	Timer A3
0x4000_0800 – 0x4000_0BFF	Timer A2
0x4000_0400 – 0x4000_07FF	Timer A1
0x4000_0000 – 0x4000_03FF	Timer A0

Memory map (left diagram):

- 0xFFFFFFFF — Vendor specific: memory mapped peripherals
- 0xE0000000
- 0xDFFFFFFF — Unused
- 0x60000000
- 0x5FFFFFFF — Peripheral
- 0x40000000
- 0x3FFFFFFF — SRAM Executable
- 0x20000000
- 0x1FFFFFFF — Code/Data
- 0x00000000

Figure 3.58 Peripheral memory map for the MSP432 chip

```
#define PERIPH_BASE     ((uint32_t)0x40000000) /*!< Peripherals start address */
#define PERIPH_BASE2    ((uint32_t)0xE0000000) /*!< Peripherals start address */
/*! Base address of module ADC14 registers */
#define ADC14_BASE      (PERIPH_BASE + 0x00012000)
/*! Base address of module AES256 registers */
#define AES256_BASE     (PERIPH_BASE + 0x00003C00)

/* Other module definition ... */

/*! Base address of module SYSCTL registers */
#define SYSCTL_BASE     (PERIPH_BASE2 + 0x00043000)
/*! Base address of module TIMER32 registers */
#define TIMER32_BASE    (PERIPH_BASE + 0x0000C000)
/*! Base address of module TIMER_A0 registers */
#define TIMER_A0_BASE   (PERIPH_BASE + 0x00000000)
/*! Base address of module TIMER_A1 registers */
#define TIMER_A1_BASE   (PERIPH_BASE + 0x00000400)
/*! Base address of module TIMER_A2 registers */
#define TIMER_A2_BASE   (PERIPH_BASE + 0x00000800)
/*! Base address of module TIMER_A3 registers */
#define TIMER_A3_BASE   (PERIPH_BASE + 0x00000C00)
/*! Base address of module WDT_A registers */
#define WDT_A_BASE      (PERIPH_BASE + 0x00004800)
```

Figure 3.59 CMSIS-like example of base address definitions for the peripherals in MSP432

```
typedef struct {
  __IO uint16_t CTL;          /*!< TimerAx Control Register */
  __IO uint16_t CCTL[7];      /*!< Timer_A Capture/Compare Control Register,
                                   CCTL_0 to CCTL_6 */
  __IO uint16_t R;            /*!< TimerA register */
  __IO uint16_t CCR[7];       /*!< Timer_A Capture/Compare Register */
  __IO uint16_t EX0;          /*!< TimerAx Expansion 0 Register */
       uint16_t RESERVED2[6];
  __I  uint16_t IV;           /*!< TimerAx Interrupt Vector Register */
} Timer_A_Type;
```

Figure 3.60 CMSIS-like example of timer register definitions in MSP432

```
#define TIMER_A0            ((Timer_A_Type *) TIMER_A0_BASE)
#define TIMER_A1            ((Timer_A_Type *) TIMER_A1_BASE)
#define TIMER_A2            ((Timer_A_Type *) TIMER_A2_BASE)
#define TIMER_A3            ((Timer_A_Type *) TIMER_A3_BASE)
```

Figure 3.61 CMSIS-like example of timer declarations in MSP432

All the modules of the system have a defined structure corresponding to the format <Module Name>_ Type (e.g. Timer_A_Type), and a base address of the form <MODULE_NAME>_BASE (e.g. TIMER_A0_ BASE). This is to help the programmer avoid having to redefine all the addresses and registers. The definitions can be found in the header file called *msp432p401r.h*. They match the base address of the peripherals as shown in the memory map above (Figure 3.59). For example, to update the CTL register of the TIMER_A0, the code below can be used:

```
TIMER_A0->CTL = /* Value ... */;
```

While it is possible to configure the components by manually updating the registers, TI offers utility functions that ease the setup. These functions are part of its *driverlib* library. This is a closed-source implementation, which means that while it is possible to access the documentation (to be found online; see [19]) and the prototype of the functions, their actual content remains obscure. This hardware abstraction layer is useful for fast configuration of the board. However, as will be discussed below, these functions can hide some of the steps that might be needed to achieve a desired behavior, making it hard to know which fields of the different registers are modified through the associated calls.

3.9.3.1 Clock System

Every SoC needs a way to configure clocks. This is a vital part of the chip because all of the digital components are driven through clocks. For some peripherals, specific frequencies are needed to achieve a desired timing. This is the case for the Real-Time Clock, from which it is necessary to produce a 1 Hz (1 tick per second) signal to count the number of seconds elapsed. For example, this can be done by using a crystal oscillating at 32.768 kHz or 2.097152 MHz, and performing a binary division by, respectively, 2^{15} or 2^{21}. A binary division is simple because it can be done using shift-right operators.

Having the ability to reduce or increase the frequency of the clock can reduce or increase power consumption as well as computational power. This is why it is useful to be able to configure the clocks of a system. However, as we explain below, depending on the oscillator, it is not always easy to achieve specific frequencies. In addition, some oscillators might offer great performance with a high speed but might not be reliable in terms of precision.

In the MSP432, multiple oscillators are available (five internal and two external), supporting a variety of frequencies, ranging from ~10 kHz to 48 MHz. Each of them has its own characteristics in terms of power, precision, configurability, and speed. The main reason for using external crystals is the higher accuracy that they can provide in comparison to internal sources; however, being outside the chips, the risk is that they could become disconnected. Fortunately, there is an *in-chip fail-safe* mechanism that monitors the input. If there is no signal coming from the external components, it is detected, and the corresponding internal source is used instead. Otherwise, the chip would become unusable until the crystal was operational again.

To achieve high-level clock frequencies (starting at 1 MHz), four of the available sources (oscillators) can be used:

■ Digitally Controlled Oscillator (DCO). This internal source can be configured to achieve different frequencies, and has been calibrated to provide frequencies of 1.5, 3 (default), 6, 12, 24 and 48 MHz. The main functionality of this component is that its frequency is configurable around each of these values through $2^{12} = 4096$ steps above and below the central calibrated value, as illustrated in Figure 3.62. The DCO is controlled through the **CSCTL0** register, where the DCORSEL field can be used to select the corresponding calibrated frequency; for example, CS_CTL0_DCORSEL_4 selects 24 MHz. The DCOTUNE field then determines the fine tuning of this frequency as required.

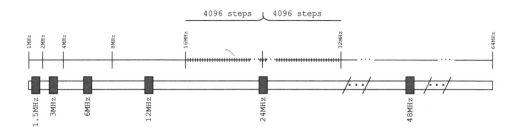

Figure 3.62 DCO frequency ranges

▣ High-Frequency eXTernal (HFXT) crystal oscillator. This is located on the board but is outside the chip. On this particular board, the crystal provides a 24 MHz frequency. However, crystals offering frequencies from 1 MHz to 48 MHz can be used instead.

▣ Low-power oscillator (MOD OSC). This typically operates at 25 MHz.

▣ Low-frequency oscillator (SYS OSC). This acts as a fail-safe for the external HFXT source and operates at 5 MHz.

The remaining three sources can be used to achieve lower-level clock frequencies, between ~10 kHz and 128 kHz:

▣ Low-Frequency eXTernal (LFXT) crystal oscillator. Again, this is located on the board but outside the chip. Here, it runs at 32.768 kHz but, depending on the crystal selected, can operate at a lower value.

▣ Very-low power/frequency oscillator (VLO). This typically operates at 9.4 kHz.

▣ Low power/frequency oscillator (REFO). This can be configured to run at 32.768 kHz or 128 kHz through an internal register. It is the fail-safe for the external LFXT source, in which event, it falls back to its lower frequency.

These oscillators feed the clock sources shown in Table 3.28 and can be assigned in support of the five different system clocks listed. Selection is via the different multiplexers controlled by register **CSCTL1**, as illustrated by the clock tree in Figure 3.63, where external sources are denoted by (!). Table 3.28 also shows that the system clocks can be selected as inputs for peripherals.

Table 3.28 System clocks and potential sources

System Clock Name	Description	Source	Divisible
MCLK	Master Clock	LFXTCLK	Yes (1, 2, 4, 8, 16, 32, 64, 128)
	Input for CPU and peripherals	VLOCLK	
		REFOCLK	
		DCOCLK (Default)	
		MODCLK	
		HFXTCLK	

System Clock Name	Description	Source	Divisible
HSMCLK	Subsystem Master Clock Input for peripherals	LFXTCLK VLOCLK REFOCLK *DCOCLK* (Default) MODCLK HFXTCLK	Yes (1, 2, 4, 8, 16, 32, 64, 128)
SMCLK	Low-speed Subsystem Master Clock Input for peripherals Max. frequency: half of HSMCLK's maximum frequency	HSMCLK	Yes (1, 2, 4, 8, 16, 32, 64, 128)
ACLK	Auxiliary Clock Input for peripherals Max. frequency: 128 kHz	*LFXTCLK* (Default) VLOCLK REFOCLK	Yes (1, 2, 4, 8, 16, 32, 64, 128)
BCLK	Backup Clock Input for peripherals Max. frequency: 32.768 kHz	*LFXTCLK* (Default) REFOCLK	No

Selection and configuration of the clocks is implementation-specific to the MSP432. This is done through the **CS** (Clock System) registers. For this specific component, it is necessary to write a specific value into the KEY field of the register, as shown below (providing additional security to make sure that the clocks are not unwittingly updated during execution):

```
CS->KEY = CS_KEY_VAL;          /* 0x695A to write, 0xA596 when read */
```

Setting the corresponding clock depends on the value of the different selectors of the multiplexers in the clock tree. This is controlled by register **CTL1**. For example, to assign:

- ACLK to REFO, the content of **CTL1** field SELA should be 2

- HSMCLK and SMCLK to DCO, the content of **CTL1** field SELS should be 3

- MCLK to DCO, the content of **CTL1** field SELM should be 3.

The **CTL1** register also configures the associated dividers of the clocks (DIVM, DIVHS, DIVS, DIVA). So, to have all the clocks running at the default frequency, without any division, **CTL1** should be configured as shown below:

```
CS->CTL1 = CS_CTL1_SELA_2 | CS_CTL1_DIVA_0 |
           CS_CTL1_SELS_3 | CS_CTL1_DIVHS_0 | CS_CTL1_DIVS_0 |
           CS_CTL1_SELM_3 | CS_CTL1_DIVM_0;
```

Using the TI *driverlib* it is possible to achieve the same default behavior with the following code (please note that the library automatically sets CS_KEY_VAL in the function *MAP_CS_initClockSignal* to modify the Clock System registers):

```
MAP_CS_initClockSignal(CS_ACLK,   CS_REFOCLK_SELECT, CS_CLOCK_DIVIDER_0);
MAP_CS_initClockSignal(CS_HSMCLK, CS_DCOCLK_SELECT,  CS_CLOCK_DIVIDER_0);
MAP_CS_initClockSignal(CS_SMCLK,  CS_DCOCLK_SELECT,  CS_CLOCK_DIVIDER_0);
MAP_CS_initClockSignal(CS_MCLK,   CS_MODOSC_SELECT,  CS_CLOCK_DIVIDER_0);
```

The clock signals can be output to some of the GPIO pins, such as MCLK(P4.3), HSMCLK(P4.4), and ACLK(P4.2). This can be used to monitor the speed or to provide a clock to another board, and is explained further in the GPIO section below.

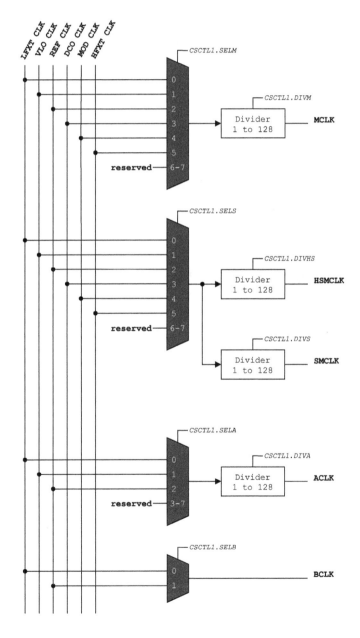

Figure 3.63 Clock tree assignment through the CSCTL1 register

3.9.3.2 Power

According to the TI documentation, the power consumption of the MSP432 is 80 µA per MHz and 660 nA when in standby operation. Running at a higher frequency makes processing faster but also means that power consumption is increased.

Most of the time, an embedded system is powered by battery. If it is to last longer, it cannot run all the time with all the peripherals activated and executing no-op (NOP) operations at a high frequency. The system should be able to deactivate all of the modules it does not need and enter a sleep state until it is required to do something. A wake-up of the processor can be triggered through:

- User operation: someone pressing a button.

- An external sensor/peripheral generating an interrupt detected through a GPIO: for example, a temperature sensor reaching a threshold, an inertial motion unit detecting a fall, and so on.

- An internal interrupt: from a timer or from an internal peripheral that has completed its processing.

TI's *driverlib* allows the power level of the board to be manipulated and switched to a low power consumption mode using the Power Control Manager (PCM) component by calling, for instance, PCM_gotoLPM3(); this function sets the power mode of the board to Low Power Mode 3. Depending on the selected mode, some peripherals and/or internal functions of the board are switched off to save energy.

Thus, after initializing all of the peripherals, a *main* function might set the power mode to low power while waiting on the next interrupt. This can be done by adding the code shown below to the end of the *main* function:

```
/* Going to sleep */
while (1)
{
    PCM_gotoLPM0();
}
```

3.9.3.3 Interrupts

As described in Chapter 1, interrupts (or interrupt service requests, IRQs) are used in a system to signal to the processor that a component needs some attention. The following steps should occur if the corresponding interrupt is not masked and the interrupt is enabled in the system:

- A unit in the system (e.g. Timer, GPIO, UART) raises an IRQ.

- The processor stops its current execution and enters interrupt mode.

- Depending on the number of the interrupt, the corresponding handler is called from the interrupt vector table.

- Within the handler, the source of the interrupt is checked and serviced accordingly. The same handler can be used for multiple units.

■ Once serviced, the interrupt request is cleared and the processor returns to execution of the original program.

```
/* Interrupt vector table. */
void (* const interruptVectors[])
  (void) __attribute__ ((section (".intvecs"))) =
{
    (pFunc)&__StackTop,     /* The initial stack pointer */
    Reset_Handler,          /* The reset handler         */
    NMI_Handler,            /* The NMI handler           */
    HardFault_Handler,      /* The hard fault handler    */
    MemManage_Handler,      /* The MPU fault handler     */
    BusFault_Handler,       /* The bus fault handler     */
    UsageFault_Handler,     /* The usage fault handler   */
    0,                      /* Reserved                  */
    0,                      /* Reserved                  */
    0,                      /* Reserved                  */
    0,                      /* Reserved                  */
    SVC_Handler,            /* SVCall handler            */
    DebugMon_Handler,       /* Debug monitor handler     */
    0,                      /* Reserved                  */
    PendSV_Handler,         /* The PendSV handler        */
    SysTick_Handler,        /* The SysTick handler       */
    PSS_IRQHandler,         /* PSS Interrupt             */
    CS_IRQHandler,          /* CS Interrupt              */
    PCM_IRQHandler,         /* PCM Interrupt             */
    WDT_A_IRQHandler,       /* WDT_A Interrupt           */
    FPU_IRQHandler,         /* FPU Interrupt             */
    FLCTL_IRQHandler,       /* Flash Controller Interrupt */
    COMP_E0_IRQHandler,     /* COMP_E0 Interrupt         */
    COMP_E1_IRQHandler,     /* COMP_E1 Interrupt         */
    TA0_0_IRQHandler,       /* TA0_0 Interrupt           */
    TA0_N_IRQHandler,       /* TA0_N Interrupt           */
    TA1_0_IRQHandler,       /* TA1_0 Interrupt           */
    TA1_N_IRQHandler,       /* TA1_N Interrupt           */
    TA2_0_IRQHandler,       /* TA2_0 Interrupt           */
    TA2_N_IRQHandler,       /* TA2_N Interrupt           */
    TA3_0_IRQHandler,       /* TA3_0 Interrupt           */
    TA3_N_IRQHandler,       /* TA3_N Interrupt           */
    EUSCIA0_IRQHandler,     /* EUSCIA0 Interrupt         */
    EUSCIA1_IRQHandler,     /* EUSCIA1 Interrupt         */
    EUSCIA2_IRQHandler,     /* EUSCIA2 Interrupt         */
    EUSCIA3_IRQHandler,     /* EUSCIA3 Interrupt         */
    EUSCIB0_IRQHandler,     /* EUSCIB0 Interrupt         */
    EUSCIB1_IRQHandler,     /* EUSCIB1 Interrupt         */
    EUSCIB2_IRQHandler,     /* EUSCIB2 Interrupt         */
    EUSCIB3_IRQHandler,     /* EUSCIB3 Interrupt         */
    ADC14_IRQHandler,       /* ADC14 Interrupt           */
    T32_INT1_IRQHandler,    /* T32_INT1 Interrupt        */
    T32_INT2_IRQHandler,    /* T32_INT2 Interrupt        */
    T32_INTC_IRQHandler,    /* T32_INTC Interrupt        */
    AES256_IRQHandler,      /* AES256 Interrupt          */
    RTC_C_IRQHandler,       /* RTC_C Interrupt           */
    DMA_ERR_IRQHandler,     /* DMA_ERR Interrupt         */
    DMA_INT3_IRQHandler,    /* DMA_INT3 Interrupt        */
    DMA_INT2_IRQHandler,    /* DMA_INT2 Interrupt        */
    DMA_INT1_IRQHandler,    /* DMA_INT1 Interrupt        */
    DMA_INT0_IRQHandler,    /* DMA_INT0 Interrupt        */
    PORT1_IRQHandler,       /* Port1 Interrupt           */
    PORT2_IRQHandler,       /* Port2 Interrupt           */
    PORT3_IRQHandler,       /* Port3 Interrupt           */
    PORT4_IRQHandler,       /* Port4 Interrupt           */
    PORT5_IRQHandler,       /* Port5 Interrupt           */
    PORT6_IRQHandler        /* Port6 Interrupt           */
};
```

Figure 3.64 Interrupt vector table

From an application perspective, an interrupt can be handled through a function called a handler. All of these are stored in the vector table as represented in Figure 3.64, which has been extracted from the TI sample code. (The name of the file is *startup_msp432p401r_gcc.c*, in the *gcc* folder of the base project examples.)

As their names suggest, all of these handlers correspond to a unit that can trigger an interrupt. The index of a handler in the vector table corresponds to the ID of the interrupt in the NVIC. For example, the handler for Timer A0 interrupts is *TA0_0_IRQHandler* and it has ID number 25 in the NVIC.

By default, all these functions are mapped to the Default Handler, which is an infinite while-loop. They are declared in the same file, as shown in Figure 3.64. The following code maps the interrupt handlers to the Default Handler, where the *weak* keyword means that the mapping can be overridden (redefined) by another function:

```
extern void <NAME>_IRQHandler     (void)
__attribute__((weak,alias(«Default_Handler»)));
```

If a unit has its interrupt enabled, the handler must have a proper (i.e. non-default) definition to make sure the correct behavior is implemented. If the handler has not been redefined by the user then the program will be blocked in the infinite loop as soon as the associated interrupt is raised.

Because there are a limited number of NVIC handlers, some are used for several interrupts. This is the case, for instance, for Port 1 of the GPIO. It can have multiple sources of interrupt (there being multiple pins that can trigger an IRQ). Once the handler has been called it is necessary to determine which interrupts are the triggers. The function *GPIO_getEnabledInterruptStatus* can be used to get the number of the I/O that needs to be serviced in *PORT1_IRQHandler* (it is also possible to read the IFG register from P1). For example, if both buttons on the board are mapped to this handler and there is an application that wants to increment a counter when P1.1 is pressed and to decrement the counter when P1.4 is pressed, it will have to call the function *GPIO_getEnabledInterruptStatus* and analyze the output for the port GPIO_PORT_P1. If it contains the GPIO_PIN1 bit, the counter is increased, whereas if it has the GPIO_PIN4 bit it will be decreased. The code below shows how to determine the interrupts in the IRQ handler:

```
/*
 * Redefine the IRQ Handler for PORT1 interrupts.
 */
void PORT1_IRQHandler(void)
{
    static uint32_t counter = 0;
    uint16_t status = GPIO_getEnabledInterruptStatus(GPIO_PORT_P1);

    /* status = P1->IFG; */
    if (status & GPIO_PIN1)
    {
        /* Only for the P1.1 (left button). */
        counter++;
    }
    else if (status & GPIO_PIN4)
    {
```

```
      /* Only for the P1.4 (right button). */
      counter--;
  }

  /*
   * Always clear the interrupt
   * otherwise the Handler will be called over and over.
   */
  GPIO_clearInterruptFlag(GPIO_PORT_P1, status);
  P1->IFG &= ~status;
}
```

In all cases, after the interrupt request is serviced, the interrupt needs to be cleared by way of acknowledgment; otherwise, it will be called repeatedly.

As previously described, it is necessary to enable interrupts so that the processor is notified of them. If the interrupts are disabled, the interrupts are masked and they are ignored. In the MSP432, three levels of enablement are required:

- First, for the unit within the module. Thus, for the GPIO, it is the corresponding pin that can trigger an IRQ (for example, Pin 1 of Port 1 for a left-button press); for Timer A, it is the instance of the timer (e.g. Timer A0, Timer A1, Timer A2). This is done using the function *<Module Name>_enableInterrupt()*. For instance, the code below shows how to enable the interrupts for Timer A0 and GPIO pin P1.1:

```
Timer_A_enableInterrupt(TIMER_A0_BASE);
GPIO_enableInterrupt(GPIO_PORT_P1, GPIO_PIN1);
```

This can also be done by writing directly into the corresponding register inside the module:

```
P1->IE |= BIT1;
```

- The second level of enablement involves telling the interrupt controller (NVIC) that the IRQ for the corresponding module should not be ignored. This is done by calling the function *Interrupt_enableInterrupt()*. The code below enables interrupts in the NVIC for Timer A0 and Pin 1 of GPIO Port 1:

```
Interrupt_enableInterrupt(INT_TA0_0)
Interrupt_enableInterrupt(INT_PORT1)
```

This uses the definition from the HAL in the TI library, but it can also be done through *NVIC_EnableIRQ()* from the CMSIS interface. All interrupt numbers have a definition in the form of a variable *INT_<Module Name>*.

- Finally, the processor must be enabled to receive and respond to interrupts. This is done through the function *Interrupt_enableMaster()*. The corresponding CMSIS function is *_enable_irq()*.

Interrupts can also be disabled at these same three levels, the corresponding functions being:

▨ *<Module Name>_disableInterrupt()* or by clearing the Interrupt Enable (IE) bit in the corresponding module

▨ *Interrupt_disableInterrupt()* or, through the CMSIS interface, *NVIC_DisableIRQ()*

▨ *Interrupt_disableMaster()* or, through CMSIS, *__disable_irq()*.

3.9.3.4 Timers

Timers are an essential component in embedded systems. Usually, there are multiple types of timer. They are used to control time in a system for:

▨ establishing a time difference between two measurements

▨ triggering an event at a specific time, e.g. sending data, sensing values

▨ generating interrupts after a predefined time has elapsed; this can be used to execute another task in an RTOS

▨ generating special outputs such as pulse-width modulation (PWM), to control a servo motor or reduce a voltage. This generally uses a function called 'output compare' to do something on a pin when the free-running counter of the timer reaches a programmed value. The action can be to do nothing, set the pin level, clear it or toggle the pin state

▨ as a complementary capability, catching the timer value on an external event as a rising edge, a falling edge, or both, on dedicated pins. This feature is called input capture. This can generate an interrupt where the time of the event is available in a specific register

▨ creating a "watchdog" timer.

A real-time clock (RTC) is a slow timer used to remember the current date (in terms of year, month, day, hours, minutes and seconds). The purpose is to trigger an interrupt at a specific time of day, such as reporting sensor values that have been gathered to a server at 4:00 pm every day. Compared to some other timers, it offers easy configuration to count the number of seconds or to create alarms, and has specific real-time applications such as setting alarms periodically throughout a day/month/year.

Within the Cortex-M4, there is an integrated timer called **SysTick**, which can be configured to generate an IRQ that can be processed in the *SysTick_Handler* function. This is an internal counter that can be programmed through CMSIS and has the same frequency as the MCLK system clock.

Reducing the average power delivered by an electrical signal via PWM is based on two characteristics: frequency and duty cycle. The frequency, which defines the period of the signal, depends on the application, for example:

- LEDs: lighting/flashing as required

- DC electric motors (such as fans): ~20 kHz

- Servo motors: ~50 Hz.

The duty cycle is simply the proportion of time that a signal is set to a digital 1 in relation to the period of the signal. Thus, in Figure 3.65, if the period is 4 ms and the signal is high for 2 ms at a time, it means that the duty cycle is 50%. As illustrated, the higher this value, the bigger is the average output voltage. To control the power delivered to a device via PWM, the frequency of the signal is held constant and the duty cycle is varied. Thus, the duty cycle controls the angle in a servo, or the rotation speed of a motor, or the light intensity of an LED. For an LED with no pull-up resistor, applying a low duty cycle decreases its intensity. While it is possible to create PWM via software, it is more reliable to use a timer: the frequency can be easily programmed, and counters can be used to trigger events.

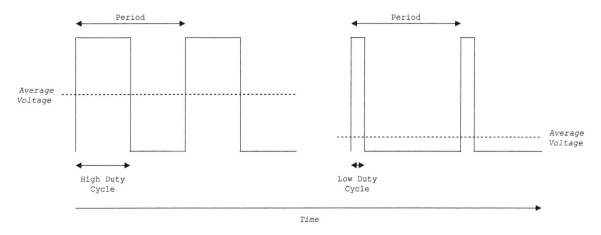

Figure 3.65 Timer signal period and duty cycle

Timers are basic units that increment a counter and generate interrupts when a value is reached. There are two kinds of timer modules in the MSP432:

- Timer_A, providing four timers (A0, A1, A2 and A3). These have 16-bit counter registers and can be closely configured through seven capture/compare registers that can be used to trigger interrupts at different times. Timer_A can also be programmed to run in different modes as explained later. The clock source can be ACLK, SMCLK or one of two external sources that can have their frequency divided.

- Timer32, providing two timers. It has a 32-bit counter. This type is simpler in terms of configuration and offers fewer possibilities than Timer_A. However, it can count to a higher value and can be configured through the MCLK clock source, which is its input (in the form MCLK, MCLK/16 or MCLK/256).

A watchdog timer acts as a countermeasure in the event of the program being executed stalling. It usually takes the form of a counter that is regularly reset to 0 by the system, after a given period. However, if the counter reaches a particular value, because the system is in a bad or conflicted state and cannot clear the counter, the watchdog is triggered to either restart the board or create an interrupt that will clear the task that has stuck in its execution. Hence, it is a fail-safe mechanism that is triggered if a program or IRQ has stalled or is taking too much time to complete.

In a debug session, when a program can be stopped for inspection, the watchdog functionality is usually disabled to avoid it automatically restarting the board because of the delay. For example, the code below can be written as the first *main()* instruction to disable the watchdog for debugging purposes:

```
/* Stop watchdog timer using TI's HAL */
WDT_A_hold(WDT_A_BASE);

/* Stop watchdog timer by writing to registers */
WDT_A->CTL = WDT_A_CTL_PW | WDT_A_CTL_HOLD;
```

3.9.3.5 General-Purpose Input/Output (GPIO)

Within a board, multiple pins are usually available to obtain inputs or outputs of various signals. These I/Os are divided into ports that group the associated pins together. They are used for communication or to control components (e.g. buttons, LEDs, other boards). Such pins are used for general purposes, meaning that it is possible to configure them according to need.

Configuring a GPIO means making decisions about the following characteristics:

- Input/output: The direction of the signal that will use the pin needs to be specified. For instance, a button might be connected to an input pin and an LED to an output pin.

- Pull-up/pull-down/no pull-up: There are internal pull-up and pull-down resistors that can be enabled by the software such that it is not necessary to add one when connecting a component to the board (for input pins only).

- Interrupt: As described earlier in this chapter, an interrupt can be enabled or disabled for a given GPIO port/pin.

- Interrupt trigger: It is possible to specify on which edge (rising or falling) of a signal an interrupt will be triggered.

- Alternate functions: It is possible to configure a pin to support a function other than simple I/O, e.g. I²C, SPI, UART, timers, ADC.

The GPIO module has a 16-bit data width and cannot be accessed via a 32-bit word. The HAL provides simple functions to help with programming the GPIO. For instance, to program a GPIO pin in input mode with a pull-up resistor, the function *GPIO_setAsInputPinWithPullUpResistor()* can be used. To select which edge triggers an interrupt, the function *GPIO_interruptEdgeSelect()* can be used.

Different GPIOs are available in the MSP432 and the ports can have different electronics to interface with alternative functions and the external world, and to support the assignment of various purposes to them. However, in general, there are limitations on how they can be used. Thus, a pin can only be assigned a function from a specific set of functions. For example, it is not possible to assign an I²C signal on just any pin: the signals of the I²C controller 1 (I2C1) are mapped to P6.4 and P6.5 and it is not possible to use other pins for this purpose. Furthermore, if these pins have already been programmed for SPI1 signals, it is no longer possible to use them for I2C1 signals.

To use the alternate function of a GPIO, the function *GPIO_setAsPeripheralModuleFunctionInputPin()* can be used as shown in the code below, where pins P6.4 and P6.5 are programmed to adopt the alternative function of providing SDA and SCLK signals for I²C communication:

```
GPIO_setAsPeripheralModuleFunctionInputPin(GPIO_PORT_P6,
    GPIO_PIN4 + GPIO_PIN5, GPIO_SECONDARY_MODULE_FUNCTION);
```

3.9.3.6 Other Components
Several more advanced components exist in the MSP432 board. The most popular are:

- Analog-to-Digital Converter (ADC): This component converts an analog input signal (a voltage) into a digital number that is proportional to the input. Several sensors exist that output analog signals. For instance, a temperature sensor might be connected to the GPIO pins of the board. The specifications and data sheet of the temperature sensor will indicate whether the temperature is output in analog format. If this is the case, the sensor needs to be connected to an ADC before the information obtained can be transferred to the CPU: the processor cannot handle analog signals. The specification of the sensor should also indicate how to convert the digital value to a meaningful value; for instance, a temperature.

- Enhanced Universal Serial Communication Interface (eUSCI): On the MSP432, the eUSCI component supports three modes of serial communication:

  - Universal Asynchronous Receiver-Transmitter (UART): often used for debugging. It allows a board to be connected to a PC and the output of a program to be logged.

  - Serial Peripheral Interface (SPI).

  - Inter-Integrated Circuit (I²C).

  Serial communication is very useful in embedded systems when it is necessary to connect with other boards or hardware. It provides a compact solution (i.e. it does not require many pins) for the transfer of information to one or more components. Pins are quite a limited resource on a board, which is why serial communication is so popular.

- Direct Memory Access (DMA) controller: This component enables access to memory independently of the CPU, and allows CPU time to be freed up accordingly. Indeed, memory access no longer requires the CPU at all. On the MSP432, the DMA component can work in several transfer modes:

☐ Memory-to-memory: data can be copied from one place in memory to another.

☐ Peripheral-to-memory: the output of a peripheral (for instance, an ADC) can be copied directly into memory.

☐ Memory-to-peripheral: memory content can be directly fed to a peripheral (for instance, using I²C).

3.9.4 Programming the MSP432 Board

To start the exercises and examples, first install Code Composer Studio (CCS). This is an IDE that can be used on most operating systems. The tool is based on Eclipse like much other development software, for example, STM32Cube (from ST Microelectronics) and DS-5 (from Arm). The installer is available on the Texas Instruments website along with some documentation for its setup [20].

To start with the examples, it is necessary to install the **SimpleLink MSP432P4** SDK from the Resource Manager. This can be done by selecting the corresponding board and in the Software tab, selecting the Install icon.

Once the software is launched, it asks for the workspace location where the projects will be instantiated.

Now, the example can be imported to the workspace. Go through **Windows > Show View > Others**. Search for *Project Explorer* and **Open**. After a right-click in the explorer, select **Import > CCS Projects**, search for the *baseProject* and click **Finish**.

This sample project configures a UART to print a string repeatedly and blinks an LED. Build the project by using **CTRL + B** or the Build icon. To flash the development board, click on the **Debug** icon. After a successful download, the CSS IDE should update the perspective to Debug.

In the console, you should have the same output from the debugger as shown in Figure 3.66.

```
CORTEX_M4_0: GEL Output: Memory Map Initialization Complete
CORTEX_M4_0: GEL Output: Halting Watchdog Timer
CORTEX_M4_0: WARNING: On MSP432P401R hitting a breakpoint cannot be detected by the
debugger when the device is in low power mode.

    Click the pause button during debug to check if the device is held at the
breakpoint.
```

Figure 3.66 Console output after successful flash and debug command

At this point, the program is stopped at a breakpoint. This means that the execution is stalled, and nothing will happen until it is resumed. To resume, either the **Continue** button needs to be pressed, or the **Step** button used to go through the instructions one by one.

The UART configured by the *baseProject* prints the string "Loop" over and over again through the same USB used for powering and programming the board. A serial communications emulator running on the cross-development station, such as PuTTY, Minicom or Tera Term, can be used with the following parameter settings to view the output from the board: 9600 8N1 (9600 baud/bits per second, 8 data bits, no parity bit and 1 stop bit).

To inspect the code and the status of the board, it is possible to inspect additional views through **Windows > Show View > Others**:

- **EnergyTrace:** Can be used to monitor the power consumption of the board and to get a graph over time of the current used. Once the program is flashed, open this view, and start the recording. You should see something similar to Figure 3.67, while blinking an LED should produce an output similar to that shown in Figure 3.68.

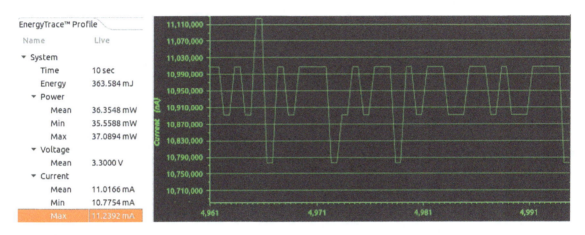

Figure 3.67 EnergyTrace profile and output

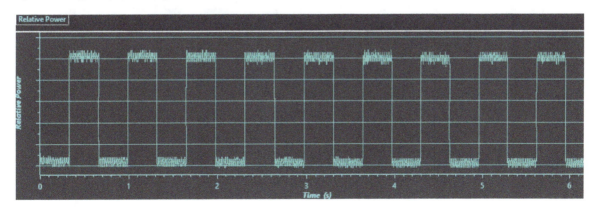

Figure 3.68 Power measurement over time (from CCS, blinking LED)

- **Disassembly:** As the title of this view suggests, it shows the compiled code as assembly instructions, and should appear similar to Figure 3.69.

■ **Memory Allocation:** This allows inspection of the built binary image and displays the number of bytes used by each function, as illustrated in Figure 3.70.

■ **Connected Target:** Indicates the boards that have been detected by the IDE. This is useful in debugging to establish that the board has been detected correctly.

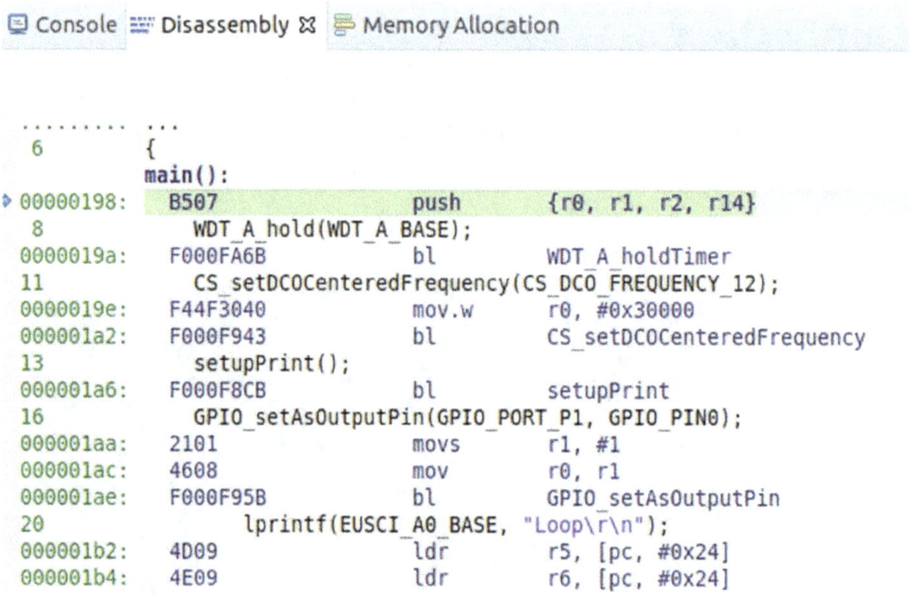

```
 Console    Disassembly    Memory Allocation

. . . . . . . . .  . . .
      6          {
                 main():
▸ 00000198:      B507              push        {r0, r1, r2, r14}
      8            WDT_A_hold(WDT_A_BASE);
0000019a:        F000FA6B          bl          WDT_A_holdTimer
     11            CS_setDCOCenteredFrequency(CS_DCO_FREQUENCY_12);
0000019e:        F44F3040          mov.w       r0, #0x30000
000001a2:        F000F943          bl          CS_setDCOCenteredFrequency
     13            setupPrint();
000001a6:        F000F8CB          bl          setupPrint
     16            GPIO_setAsOutputPin(GPIO_PORT_P1, GPIO_PIN0);
000001aa:        2101              movs        r1, #1
000001ac:        4608              mov         r0, r1
000001ae:        F000F95B          bl          GPIO_setAsOutputPin
     20            lprintf(EUSCI_A0_BASE, "Loop\r\n");
000001b2:        4D09              ldr         r5, [pc, #0x24]
000001b4:        4E09              ldr         r6, [pc, #0x24]
```

Figure 3.69 Disassembly instructions from Code Composer Studio

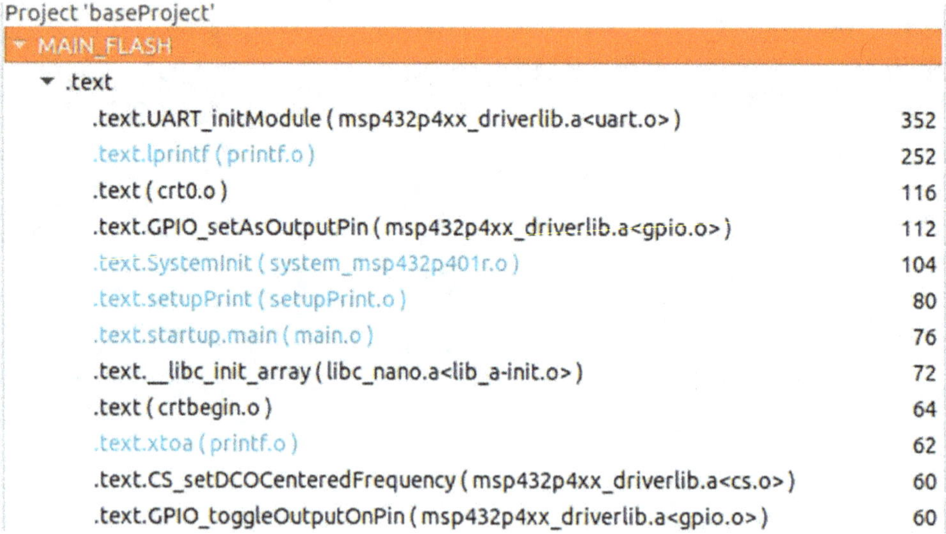

```
Project 'baseProject'
▼ MAIN_FLASH
    ▼ .text
        .text.UART_initModule ( msp432p4xx_driverlib.a<uart.o> )                    352
        .text.lprintf ( printf.o )                                                  252
        .text ( crt0.o )                                                            116
        .text.GPIO_setAsOutputPin ( msp432p4xx_driverlib.a<gpio.o> )                112
        .text.SystemInit ( system_msp432p401r.o )                                   104
        .text.setupPrint ( setupPrint.o )                                            80
        .text.startup.main ( main.o )                                                76
        .text.__libc_init_array ( libc_nano.a<lib_a-init.o> )                        72
        .text ( crtbegin.o )                                                         64
        .text.xtoa ( printf.o )                                                      62
        .text.CS_setDCOCenteredFrequency ( msp432p4xx_driverlib.a<cs.o> )            60
        .text.GPIO_toggleOutputOnPin ( msp432p4xx_driverlib.a<gpio.o> )              60
```

Figure 3.70 Memory allocation example from CCS

■ **Registers:** Lists all of the system registers with their associated descriptions, as shown in Figure 3.71. All of the register values can be inspected and even modified through the debugger. The registers of the peripherals (e.g. MPU, ADC, DMA, timer) can be monitored, along with the core registers of the processor. This is an extremely valuable tool for debugging! Being able to change a register on-the-fly is very useful in testing small changes.

Name	Value	Description
▾ ⨁ Core Registers		Core Registers
⬓ PC	0x000001CE	Program Counter [Core]
⬓ SP	0x2000FFF0	General Purpose Register 13 - Stack Pointer [Core]
⬓ LR	0x000001C9	General Purpose Register 14 - Link Register [Core]
▸ ⬓ xPSR	0x01000000	Stores the status of interrupt enables and critical processor status signals [Core]
⬓ R0	0x00000001	General Purpose Register 0 [Core]
⬓ R1	0x40004C02	General Purpose Register 1 [Core]
⬓ R2	0x0000FBF7	General Purpose Register 2 [Core]
⬓ R3	0x00011C37	General Purpose Register 3 [Core]
⬓ R4	0x0001869F	General Purpose Register 4 [Core]
⬓ R5	0x0000074C	General Purpose Register 5 [Core]
⬓ R6	0x40001000	General Purpose Register 6 [Core]
⬓ R7	0x00000000	General Purpose Register 7 [Core]
⬓ R8	0x00000000	General Purpose Register 8 [Core]

Figure 3.71 Debugger view of the MSP432 registers

■ **Expressions:** By right-clicking on a variable name and selecting **Add Watch Expression**, it is possible to monitor the value of the variable if it is in scope (can be found) and when the debugger is stopped. It is also a very valuable tool for checking on the value of a variable at any given moment.

3.9.5 Exercises

All of the exercises are available on Github (https://github.com/Introduction-To-System-On-Chip). The corresponding project is called MSP432. Here is a list of the topics covered:

■ Clock configuration: Set up the clocks through registers and then through the *driverlib* provided by TI. Which method is faster? Which is cleaner/easier to read?

■ Clock configuration: Try different clock settings for the MCLK. Use the DCO source and then the VLO source to compare the speed of execution of a program blinking a LED. Look at their relative power consumptions using EnergyTrace.

■ Timer: Measure the time difference between multiple instructions in milliseconds.

■ Timer: Trigger an interrupt every 5 seconds that blinks an LED.

■ GPIO: Get input from a button and configure an IRQ to switch an LED on and off.

- Timer + GPIO: Configure a PWM that outputs to an LED and can be updated through a button and, depending on the duty cycle, the LED intensity should vary.

- Inspect the different registers through the *gdb* (GNU debugger) interface.

References

[1]   *WikiChip Chips & Semi - Semiconductor & Computer Engineering*. [Online]. Available: en.wikichip. org/wiki/WikiChip

[2]   *ARM-Software/CMSIS_5*. [Online]. Available: github.com/ARM-software/CMSIS_5/blob/master/ CMSIS/Core/Include/core_cm33.h

[3]   *ARM-Software/CMSIS_5*. [Online]. Available: github.com/ARM-software/CMSIS_5/tree/master/ Device

[4]   *ARM-Software/CMSIS-_5*. [Online]. Available: github.com/ARM-software/CMSIS_5/blob/master/ Device/ARM/ARMCM33/Include/ARMCM33.h

[5]   *ARM-Software/CMSIS_5*. [Online]. Available: github.com/ARM-software/CMSIS_5/blob/develop/ Device/ARM/ARMCM0/Include/ARMCM0.h

[6]   *Texas Instruments Stellaris LM3S Microcontroller*. [Online]. Available: www.ti.com/product/ LM3S6965

[7]   *TrustZone® technology for ARM®v8-M Architecture*. [Online]. Available: static.docs.arm. com/100690/0100/armv8_m_architecture_trustzone_technology_100690_0100_00_en.pdf

[8]   Patchwork, *[7/8,V8M,arm-embedded] ARMv8-M Security Extension's cmse_nonsecure_call: use __gnu_ cmse_nonsecure_call*. [Online]. Available: patchwork.ozlabs.org/patch/603553/

[9]   Arm Keil, __attribute__((cmse_nonsecure_entry)) function attribute. [Online]. Available: www. keil.com/support/man/docs/armclang_ref/armclang_ref_pge1446817691182.htm

[10] *Arm Compiler armclang Reference Guide*. [Online]. Available: developer.arm.com/ documentation/100067/0611/Other-Compiler-specific-Features/TT-instruction-intrinsics

[11] Arm Community, *TrustZone for ARMv8-M blog*. [Online]. Available: community.arm.com/ developer/ip-products/processors/trustzone-for-armv8-m/b/blog

[12] Arm Developer, *Download FPGA images. [Online]*. Available: developer.arm.com/tools-and- software/development-boards/fpga-prototyping-boards/download-fpga-images

[13] *Microchip SAM L11 Security Reference Guide.* [Online]. Available: ww1.microchip.com/downloads/ en/AppNotes/SAM-L11-Security-ReferenceGuide-AN-DS70005365A.pdf

[14] *CMSIS-Zone Documentation.* [Online]. Available: arm-software.github.io/CMSIS_5/Zone/html/ index.html

[15] *MSP432P4xx SimpleLink™ Microcontrollers, Technical Reference Manual.* [Online]. Available: www. ti.com/lit/ug/slau356i/slau356i.pdf

[16] *MSP432P401R, MSP432P401M SimpleLink™ Mixed-Signal Microcontrollers.* [Online]. Available: www.ti.com/lit/ds/symlink/msp432p401r.pdf

[17] *MSP432P401R SimpleLink™ Microcontroller LaunchPad™ Development Kit (MSP EXP432P401R), User's Guide.* [Online]. Available: www.ti.com/lit/ug/slau597f/slau597f.pdf

[18] D. Dang, D. J. Pack, and S. F. Barrett, *Embedded systems design with the Texas Instruments MSP432 32-bit processor.* Morgan & Claypool, 2017.

[19] *Texas Instruments MSP432SDK Documentation.* [Online]. Available: dev.ti.com/tirex/content/ simplelink_msp432_sdk_1_30_00_40/docs/driverlib/msp432p4xx/html/driverlib_html/index. html

[20] *Texas Instruments Code Composer Studio (CCS) Integrated Development Environment (IDE).* [Online]. Available: www.ti.com/tool/download/CCSTUDIO.

Chapter 4

Interconnects

In Chapter 1, we briefly introduced the concept of an interconnect. Given that the design and implementation of a SoC is all about placing a number of individual components on a chip such that they will work together as an integrated system, the connections between these components are absolutely fundamental to its successful function. In this chapter, we will study this challenge in some detail, and will address the following questions, among others:

1. What is an interconnect and what are the defining characteristics of its underlying protocol?

2. What principle do interconnects use to enable timing interoperability between system components?

3. What are the trade-offs between shared-bus, and full and partial crossbar-switch topologies?

Our goal in this chapter is to introduce readers to the **system interconnect**, perhaps one of the most foundational elements in a system because it allows all of the subsystems to communicate with each other. An interconnect is defined by its **communication protocol**, a set of rules that two entities attached to the interconnect must adhere to in order for communication to take place. Real-world interconnects are complex and it is difficult to explain some of the design choices in their protocols once the sheer size of the interface they expose is in view. Therefore, this chapter takes an example-driven approach and considers the theoretical concepts needed to construct an interconnect's communication protocol. We start with a bare-minimum protocol and build upon it by increments until we obtain a communication protocol with sufficient functionality to satisfy the interconnect performance needed between a variety of subsystems. We will then return to consideration of commercial interconnects in the following chapter.

4.1 Introduction

The design and implementation of a complete SoC is a complex and time-consuming task that can easily involve the work of hundreds of engineers over many months or even years. The engineering effort behind the design of a SoC or, indeed, any circuit is significant due to the iterative nature of the steps that must be undertaken before a chip can be manufactured. Engineers have long acknowledged that the most time-consuming part of any project is testing, debugging, and verifying the functionality of the product under development. This statement holds true for both software and hardware projects, but is particularly significant in hardware development because, in general, engineers cannot "patch" an error in a system that has already been shipped without recalling the device. The cost of fixing a bug increases non-linearly with the lateness of the stage at which it is detected, and this encourages engineers to take extra care to fix errors as early as possible. If we detect an error in a later stage of the design process, we can attempt to solve the issue without reiterating the complete design chain. However, this is not always possible because the problem can reflect a deeper issue that we cannot solve at that stage alone. Such cases are likely to require higher-level changes in previous stages too, sometimes going all the way back to the digital design stage, and ultimately forcing us to revisit the entire design chain. Of course, finding one bug can often expose another one, and the design cycle can repeat multiple times before a problem can be considered solved.

The underlying cause of these recurring design fixes is the complexity of the system under development. As one can imagine, complex systems are harder to design and debug than simple ones because the time taken to debug and verify a design increases non-linearly with the complexity of the system. In theory, therefore, we should be trying to build systems that are inherently less complex so that we can better manage development time. However, at first glance it seems that each new generation of SoC supports ever more functionality, which suggests that our systems are *increasing* in complexity!

The key approach to taming design complexity in a large project is a technique you've probably tried when doing group work: divide-and-conquer in terms of the workload, and then attempt to merge the resulting pieces together. The analogy in hardware design is the decomposition of a monolithic system into a set of smaller subsystems such that each can be assigned to a different engineering team. The immediate advantage of this approach is that we have automatically reduced the size of the circuit that each team must manage, and we already know that smaller circuits tend to be less complex and easier to design and test. Now that we have a theoretical goal in mind, let us look at how we might advance towards it in practice.

First, how do we divide a monolithic SoC into subsystems? Our goal is to enable teams to work on the individual subsystems independently of one another, so it is important to choose system boundaries that enable this. In general, the easiest way is to take regions of the system specification that form well-defined abstractions and factor them out as independent components, as illustrated in Figure 4.1. For example, if a specification says the system needs an SPI communication interface to connect to external peripherals, then this is a perfect candidate for a dedicated subsystem. Alternatively, if the system needs a mechanism to move data between various endpoints in the SoC without consuming CPU cycles, then this functionality could be factored into another independent subsystem (a DMA controller). The main takeaway is to focus on high-level functionality and encapsulate it in a specialized component that a team can develop without having to worry too much about the rest of the system.

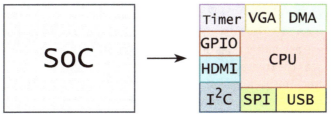

Figure 4.1 Breaking up a monolithic system into independent subsystems

Next, how do we merge all of these subsystems back together once they have been developed? We shouldn't forget that a SoC is intended to be a single and complete system on a chip, so its subsystems must have a way to communicate with one another or the functionality that each exposes would not be collectively available to the system as a whole. Thus, in technical terms, we also need to define what the **interface** between the various subsystems will be. This interface between the various subsystems is the one exposed by the **system interconnect**: a fundamental piece of system infrastructure, comprised of various buses, that handles data movement between entities in the system (see Figure 4.2). The interconnect is the foundation on which the rest of the system is built:

a "good" interconnect will achieve the performance goals of the designers while not getting in their way when it comes to implementing their subsystems independently. By contrast, a poorly designed interconnect will often cause designers to spend time finding workarounds to its limitations rather than working on the core logic of their designs. Thus, interconnects are fundamental to the flexibility, manageability, and performance of a system.

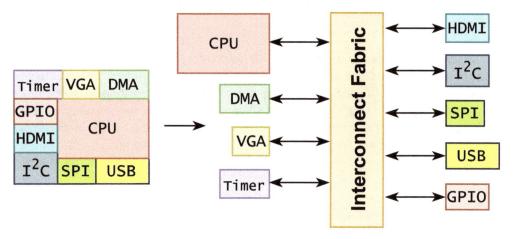

Figure 4.2 Merging subsystems through a system interconnect

4.2 Building an Interconnect Protocol

4.2.1 Defining the Entities that are Communicating

Before we dive into the theory behind interconnect protocols, we need to define some vocabulary. The role of an interconnect is to provide a communication channel through which two entities can interact. The interconnect enables this interaction when entities follow a set of rules defined by a communication protocol, and each message exchanged using this protocol is called a **transaction**. In all forms of communication there is always an entity that initiates the interaction and another entity that receives the message and either does or does not respond. In "interconnect-speak", we generally call the entity that initiates the transaction the **requestor**, and the entity on the receiving end of the transaction the **completer**. The background functions of the requestor and completer are irrelevant to understanding how the interconnect protocol allows these entities to communicate, so we omit any characterization of what these subsystems actually do.

To simplify our discussion, let's assume our system contains just two entities: a requestor (System X) and a completer (System Y), both driven by the same clock. Let's also disregard the intermediate interconnect fabric shown in Figure 4.2 and try to connect the requestor directly to the completer. Our running example therefore looks like the system shown in Figure 4.3. However, Systems X and Y were developed by independent teams and have been built very differently: System X uses a custom intra-system communication protocol (CX) between its three subsystems, whereas System Y uses a different custom internal communication protocol (CY) between its three subsystems. Thus, we encounter our first hurdle when we try to connect the two systems' internal interfaces together: they look completely different and are incompatible.

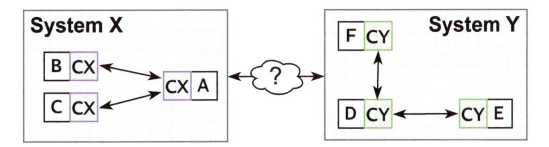

Figure 4.3 Two independent systems that need interconnecting, but protocols CX and CY are incompatible

The basic problem here is that the signals of the CX and CY protocols have different semantics and there is no clear way of connecting a signal from CX to a corresponding signal in CY (if such a signal even exists). If they are to communicate, Systems X and Y would need to share a common interface protocol, so we modify both systems such that they continue to use their custom interfaces for **internal** communication while at the same time exposing a common **external** interface that allows them to talk to each other. Each system is responsible for implementing some form of conversion between its internal interface and the common external one, but once this translation process exists, then any two systems that implement the external interface can communicate with each other. The system interconnect effectively defines the protocol of this externally visible interface. Figure 4.4 shows an example of such a system, in which Systems X and Y, respectively, expose a requestor and completer interface to a notional system interconnect. The requestor and completer interfaces both adhere to the same protocol and we represent this by assigning them the same color in the figure.

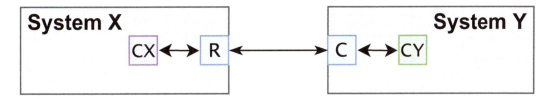

Figure 4.4 The system interconnect defines a common externally facing interface between systems

In the following sections we design a model interconnect protocol from scratch, incrementally adding features that will satisfy various communication requirements between different pairs of requestors and completers in a system. A crucial aspect of our protocol that needs to be stated at the outset is that it is **synchronous**. Thus, requestors and completers only recognize the interconnect on the **rising edge of the clock** and all decisions they take are based on what is seen at this clock edge.

4.2.2 Single-word Transactions

The simplest form of transaction that we need an interconnect protocol to support is the movement of a single word from a requestor to a completer, that is, a single-word write transaction. Let's consider what control and data signals an interconnect would need in order to provide such functionality. The first thing required is a mechanism via which the requestor can signal its intention to write to the completer. We can achieve this by transmitting a write bit, "WR", from the requestor to the completer. In parallel to the WR bit, the requestor has to send the data it wants to write to the completer and we can do this by transmitting a write data word, "WRDATA", from the requestor to the completer. Note that we use a 32-bit data bus in our examples, but an interconnect can generally handle data widths of any power of two. Our protocol interface now looks like the one shown in Figure 4.5, while Figure 4.6 shows a straightforward way in which the requestor could write to the completer using such signals.

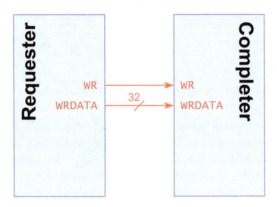

Figure 4.5 Interconnect interface for write transactions

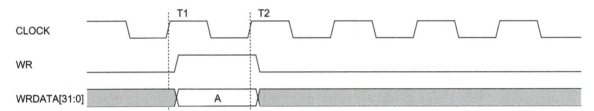

Figure 4.6 Write transaction

The timestamps in Figure 4.6 correspond to the following actions:

1. The write transaction starts when the requestor asserts a WR signal on the rising edge of the clock. Asserting the WR signal allows the requestor to signal its intention to write to the completer. At the same time, the requestor drives the WRDATA bus with the 32-bit value it wishes to write to the completer (0xA in this example).

2. The completer has seen the WR and WRDATA signals on the rising edge of the clock and has registered the transaction. The requestor can then safely deassert the WR and WRDATA signals. The WRDATA bus is grayed-out in all cycles in which WR is deasserted because its value will not be significant and the completer doesn't need to pay any attention to it.

This simple write transaction therefore has an end-to-end latency of one cycle. In theory, the protocol assumes that the completer can accept a new write transaction every clock cycle. We'll revisit this assumption later in the chapter.

Now let's consider how an interconnect protocol can support the movement of a single word in the opposite direction, from the completer to the requestor, that is, a single-word read transaction. Just as with the write transaction above, we need a mechanism by which the requestor can communicate its intention to read from the completer. We can achieve this by transmitting a read bit, "RD", from the requestor to the completer. We'll also need a bus through which the completer can provide the data to be read. Because we assume all buses to be unidirectional, the completer cannot reuse the WRDATA bus to transmit its data. Therefore, we add a second bus, which we name "RDDATA". Figure 4.7 shows what the interconnect protocol's interface looks like after these additions, and Figure 4.8 shows how we can use these signals to implement a simple read protocol.

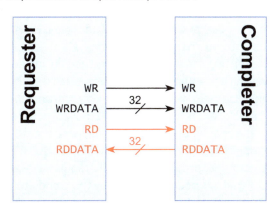

Figure 4.7 Interconnect interface for write and read transactions

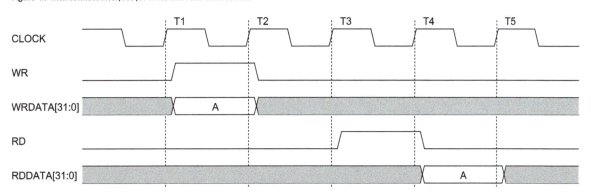

Figure 4.8 Write transaction followed by a read transaction

The timestamps in Figure 4.8 correspond to the following events:

1. A write transaction begins: the requestor asserts WR and drives WRDATA with the word (0xA in this example) that it wishes to transfer to the completer.

2. The write transaction ends with WR and WRDATA being deasserted, and the completer has registered the write operation.

3. A read transaction begins: the requestor asserts the RD signal on the rising edge of the clock and signals its intention to read from the completer.

4. The completer registers the requestor's RD signal on the rising edge of the clock and has thereby noted the requestor's intention to read. The completer then drives the RDDATA bus with the data to be read.

5. The requestor captures the data returned by the completer by registering the content of the RDDATA bus. This concludes the read transaction.

Notice that the requestor communicates its intention to read from the completer on a given cycle, C, but the data read from the completer is returned on cycle C+1. A natural question is why the completer would not be able to return the data on cycle C? In theory, nothing prevents an interconnect protocol from permitting read data to be returned during cycle C (and, in fact, many protocols do allow this); however, this would imply that the overall read operation is asynchronous and we have stated that the interconnect we are building is synchronous. Nevertheless, putting aside this synchronous aspect for the sake of argument, we note that asynchronous reads can involve long combinational paths between the requestor–completer pair, which could result in a lower overall clock frequency to adjust for long critical delays. To eliminate the critical delays introduced by such long combinational paths, interconnect protocols generally require at least a one-cycle latency for a read transaction after the RD signal has been registered by the completer. The end-to-end latency of a read transaction in our protocol is therefore two cycles (one cycle for the completer to register the RD signal sent by the requestor, and one cycle for the requestor to register the RDDATA bus content sent by the completer).

In this simple read protocol, communication between the requestor and the completer is made explicit through the RD signal, whereas the result coming back from the completer is implicit through the RDDATA bus (there is no extra control signal being propagated back by the completer to indicate when the data bus contains valid data). Implicit communication protocols have the downside that the requestor needs to be aware of what the latency of the completer is in advance so that it knows when to register the RDDATA bus content. For example, a completer that may only be able to respond to a read at cycle C+2 would be incompatible with a requestor that expects the RDDATA bus to contain valid data at cycle C+1. We will solve this issue later in the chapter through a technique that enables interoperability between any requestor–completer pair regardless of minor timing-related implementation differences.

4.2.3 Addressed Transactions

We've assumed until now that there is only is one location, that is, only one register, in the completer that the requestor can communicate with. Exposing a single register to a requestor, however, is rarely enough in reality and most completers would need to have multiple requestor-facing internal registers. For example, suppose the completer is a DMA controller with four registers that need exposing to the requestor: (1) a source address register, (2) a destination address register, (3) a command register, and (4) a status register. We could simply replicate all of the protocol signals shown in Figure 4.7 for each of the four registers exposed by the completer, but this would require a substantial amount of wiring. Instead, we propose to augment the protocol interface with an address bus, "ADDR", wide enough to address all registers exposed by the completer. Figure 4.9 shows what our protocol interface now looks like, and the waveform in Figure 4.10 shows how we can use the ADDR bus to index the completer registers in our protocol in support of two write and two read transactions.

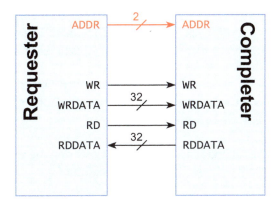

Figure 4.9 Interconnect interface for addressed write and read transactions

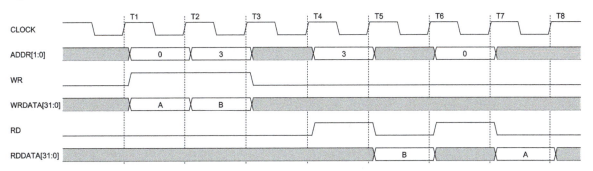

Figure 4.10 Addressed write and read transactions

The timestamps in Figure 4.10 correspond to the following events:

1. The WR signal, WRDATA bus, and ADDR bus are all asserted at the rising edge of the clock. This process begins a write transaction with payload 0xA and an address destination corresponding to register 0 in the completer.

2. The first write transaction terminates and the requestor immediately starts a new write transaction by keeping the WR signal asserted. The target address and payload have changed in this transaction and the requestor now intends to write data 0xB to register 3 in the completer.

3. The second write transaction finishes and the requestor deasserts the WR signal.

4. The RD signal and the ADDR bus are asserted on the rising edge of the clock. This process begins a read transaction for register 3 in the completer.

5. The RD signal and ADDR are deasserted as the completer will have registered the target register address at this clock edge and it is safe for the requestor to release them. In turn, the completer starts responding to the read request and returns the contents of register 3 on the RDDATA bus (0xB, written to register 3 earlier by the second write transaction).

6. The requestor concludes the first read transfer by registering the contents of the RDDATA bus and, thereby, retrieving the contents of register 3 from the completer. The requestor then re-asserts the RD signal and ADDR bus to start a new read transaction, this time for register 0 in the completer.

7. The RD signal and ADDR bus are deasserted as they have been captured by the completer. The completer then responds by returning the contents of register 0 on the RDDATA bus (0xA, written to register 0 earlier by the first write transaction).

8. The requestor concludes the second read transfer by registering the contents of the RDDATA bus and thus retrieving the contents of register 0 in the completer.

4.2.4 Burst Transactions

Suppose we want to read a large amount of information from the completer and transfer it to the requestor. For example, let's say the completer is a small on-chip memory with four 32-bit words of storage and that the requestor needs to read all four words back-to-back in rapid succession. Figure 4.11 shows what the timing of such read transactions would look like with our existing interconnect protocol.

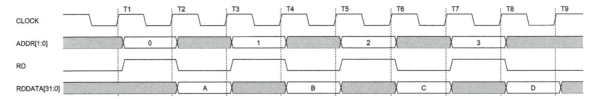

Figure 4.11 Back-to-back addressed read transactions

Two things need to be said about the waveforms in Figure 4.11. The first point of interest is that each transaction issues a sequentially increasing target index in the ADDR bus, which is incremented by one between successive transactions. The second point of note is that the data throughput on the RDDATA bus is low. Recall that we said earlier that the lowest end-to-end latency for a read transaction is two cycles. Given that a data word can be transferred between the requestor–completer pair every two cycles, the data throughput is therefore half the clock rate of the interconnect. Moreover, this is the best-case scenario and slower completers will have a proportionally smaller data throughput. In the general case of a completer with an N-cycle end-to-end read latency, the maximum data throughput will be:

$$\frac{1}{N} \times freq_{interconnect}$$

This throughput is, arguably, quite low and would not allow a requestor to rapidly collect data from a completer. Given that the content of the ADDR bus is the only requestor-facing differentiating factor between successive transactions, we argue that we could amortize the cost of transmitting this incremental address information if it were possible for the requestor to just transfer the address of the first register it wanted to read, and then somehow instruct the completer to auto-increment the address by itself for successive reads until a certain number of registers have been read. In this way, the requestor would just need to start one transaction and transmit a single target on the ADDR bus, and the completer then takes care of the rest with the requestor just needing to register the multiple successive results that will appear on the RDDATA bus. In the interconnect literature, this concept is referred to as a **burst transaction**; it is generally implemented by adding a "LENGTH" bus to the protocol to convey the length of the transfer in words that the requestor wishes to perform with the completer (single-word transfers are then treated as burst transfers with a LENGTH of 1). Figure 4.12 shows our protocol's interface augmented with this new bus. Note that our example uses a 4-bit-wide bus to describe the transfer length, which means we can specify transfers of up to 15 (0b1111) data words per transaction. Of course, wider sizes for the LENGTH bus are possible and it is not uncommon to see 10-bit-wide LENGTH buses in real protocols, allowing maximum burst lengths of 1023 (0b11 1111 1111) data words for a single issued address!

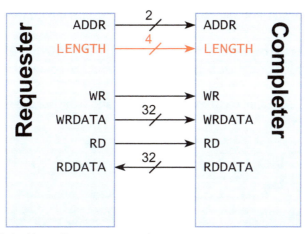

Figure 4.12 Interconnect interface for burst transactions

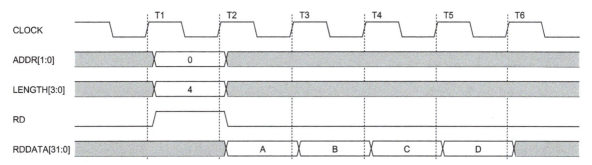

Figure 4.13 Burst-read transaction

Figure 4.13 shows the waveform of a four-word burst-read transaction; we describe its timestamps below:

1. The requestor signals its intention to start a burst-read transaction by asserting the RD signal, the ADDR bus, and the LENGTH bus. The ADDR bus contains the address of the *first* completer register the requestor wishes to read (0 in this example). The LENGTH bus contains a value greater than or equal to 1 and corresponds to the number of words the requestor wishes to read sequentially from the completer. The burst length in this example is four words.

2. The completer registers the burst-read transaction and the requestor can now deassert RD, ADDR, and LENGTH. The completer proceeds to drive the RDDATA bus with the contents of register 0.

3. The requestor registers the contents of register 0 from the RDDATA bus. The completer auto-increments the address register index and drives RDDATA with the contents of register 1.

4. The requestor registers the contents of register 1 from the RDDATA bus. The completer auto-increments the address register index and drives RDDATA with the contents of register 2.

5. The requestor registers the contents of register 2 from the RDDATA bus. The completer auto-increments the address register index and drives RDDATA with the contents of register 3.

6. The requestor registers the contents of register 3 from the RDDATA bus. This concludes the burst transaction because four words have been transmitted from the completer to the requestor.

Burst transactions can also be applied to write operations and an analogous example is shown in Figure 4.14.

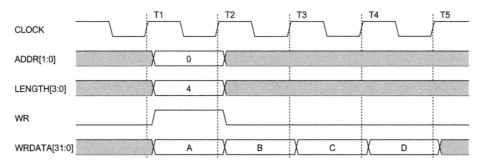

Figure 4.14 Burst-write transaction

We describe the timestamps for the four-word burst-write transaction in Figure 4.14 below:

1. The requestor signals its intention to start a burst-write transaction by asserting the WR signal, the ADDR bus, and the LENGTH bus. The ADDR bus contains the address of the *first* completer register the requestor wants to write to (0 in this example). The LENGTH bus is driven to a value of 4, so a total of four words will be transmitted from the requestor to the completer during the transaction. Finally, the WRDATA bus is driven with the value intended for completer register 0 (0xA in this example).

2. The completer has seen WR, ADDR, and LENGTH on the rising edge of the clock so the requestor can safely deassert these signals. The completer captures the first data word transmitted by the requestor on the WRDATA bus (0xA) and writes it to the register identified by the ADDR bus (0 for the first data element). At the same time, the requestor drives the WRDATA bus with the value intended for register 1 in the completer.

3. The completer auto-increments its register index and captures the content of the WRDATA bus into register 1. The requestor drives WRDATA with the value intended for register 2 in the completer.

4. The completer auto-increments its register index and captures the content of the WRDATA bus into register 2. The requestor drives WRDATA with the value intended for register 3 in the completer.

5. The completer auto-increments its register index and captures the content of the WRDATA bus into register 3. This concludes the burst transaction because four words have been transmitted from the requestor to the completer.

The larger the burst length, the more we amortize the "wasted cycles" during which the requestor sends control information to the completer (RD and ADDR in the case of read transactions, WR and ADDR in the case of write transactions). Burst transactions are foundational to the performance of an interconnect and are often used to transmit large amounts of data between systems in a SoC. Two of the more prominent examples are a CPU's cache controller doing a burst-write transaction to flush an entire cache line to memory, and the same controller performing a burst read to populate a cache line from memory.

4.2.5 Backpressure

4.2.5.1 Completer-to-requestor Backpressure

Until now, we've assumed that a completer can always accept a new transaction as soon as the previous one has been completed. However, in reality, a completer is often busy with some other internal workload that may require it to (temporarily) prevent a requestor from performing any writes or reads to its internal registers. In such cases, the completer needs a way to inform the requestor that it is not ready to accept any transactions and that the requestor must wait until the completer is in a state in which it can handle a transaction. The mechanism through which a completer communicates its unavailability to a requestor is referred to as **backpressure** and a requestor waiting on a completer's acknowledgement in this context is said to be **stalled**. Backpressure is generally implemented by a completer-to-requestor "READY" signal and a transaction starts only when WR/RD and READY are **both asserted in the same clock cycle**. Protocols that expose a READY signal in this manner are often referred to as **ready-valid interfaces** because a control signal on the requestor's side (WR/RD) conveys the *validity* of various buses (ADDR, LENGTH, WRDATA) while a control signal on the completer's side (READY) conveys the *readiness* of the receiving side. Figure 4.15 shows what our protocol interface looks like when augmented with such a completer-to-requestor READY signal.

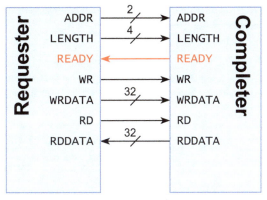

Figure 4.15 Interconnect ready/valid interface for managing completer-to-requestor backpressure

Backpressure is a simple concept, but it is clearly one of the most misunderstood mechanisms in the classroom because students often create requestors that stall indefinitely and can never start a transaction. It is useful to walk through the flawed reasoning that goes into the design of such stalled requestors in order to avoid it! Let's try to understand this through a role-playing case study. Suppose a requestor wishes to perform a write transaction to a completer. To simplify the discussion, let's assume the completer has only one target register and that it does not support burst transactions. In this scenario, the only signals of interest between the requestor and completer are, therefore, WR, WRDATA, and READY. Furthermore, suppose the completer needs two cycles end-to-end to perform a write operation, but that the requestor *does not know* this[1]. Figure 4.16 shows a timeline for our example.

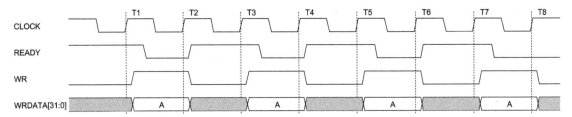

Figure 4.16 Indefinite stalling as a requestor attempts to perform repeated write transactions without success

The actions performed by the requestor and completer are best understood when considering the sequence of events shown in Figure 4.16 from the point of view of each entity, as captured in Table 4.1.

Table 4.1 Requestor and completer viewpoints in an indefinite stalling scenario (see Figure 4.16)

Time	Requestor's Point of View	Completer's Point of View
1–2	The requestor wants to start a write transaction on the rising edge of the clock at T1. It knows the completer may be busy, so it decides to check the READY signal to gauge its availability. The READY signal is asserted, so the requestor concludes the completer is available and starts the write transaction by asserting the WR and WRDATA signals.	The completer is READY on the rising edge of the clock at T1. However, after seeing the requestor's WR signal, it immediately deasserts READY because, as indicated, it needs two cycles to perform a write operation.
2–3	At the rising edge of the clock at T2, the requestor sees that WR is asserted but READY is now deasserted, so it concludes that the completer did not accept the write transaction. The requestor wishes to retry the transaction but it checks READY and, because it is deasserted, decides to postpone the write until further notice.	At the rising edge of the clock at T2, the completer has finished getting ready for the write and it decides to assert the READY signal again so that it is seen as available by the requestor at the next rising clock edge (at T3).
3–4	At the rising edge of the clock at T3, the requestor sees the completer's READY signal is asserted again so it decides to re-attempt its previously failed write transaction by asserting WR/WRDATA.	The completer, which had previously seen WR asserted, expected to accept a write transaction at T3, but WR is deasserted at the rising edge of the clock and the completer decides not to perform any write. However, during T3–T4, the completer sees WR is asserted, and because it needs two cycles to complete the write, it decides to deassert READY to notify the requestor to wait.

---

[1] This is a fair assumption because a requestor cannot be expected to know the implementation details of every completer it could potentially be connected to.

Time	Requestor's Point of View	Completer's Point of View
4–5	At the rising edge of the clock at T4, the requestor again sees that WR is asserted and READY is deasserted, so it again concludes that the completer did not accept the transaction.	At the rising edge of the clock at T4, the completer has finished getting ready for the write so it decides to assert the READY signal again so it is seen as available by the requestor at the next rising clock edge (at T5).

The back-and-forth between the requestor and the completer shown in Table 4.1 can continue indefinitely and the net result is that no transfer ever completes in its entirety. In fact, all transfers started by the requestor are seen by the completer, but because each entity only reacts to signals it sees at the rising edge of the clock and, at those specific times, we never have an instance in which both WR and READY are asserted simultaneously, we end up without any transactions being accepted by the completer. It should be clear that the root cause of this issue is a timing incompatibility between the requestor and the completer: the requestor expects that a write transaction that begins at cycle C will conclude at cycle C+1 if the completer is ready at cycle C. However, in our example, the completer needs two cycles to perform a write, which is incompatible with the requestor's expectation. We argue that this problem can be solved if the requestor *does not* check READY before deciding to assert WR.

Perhaps the easiest way to understand the sequence of events the requestor and completer are experiencing is to draw an analogy with a common problem you have probably faced on multiple occasions during your life. Have you ever walked down a street and noticed another person walking toward you on the same "lane"? A collision is inevitable if you get too close and it makes sense that you need to walk on separate lanes. You've probably tried switching lanes, only to find that the other person did exactly the same thing at the same time, so you decide to switch back, but you see the other person has reciprocated and is on your lane yet again! The process sometimes continues several times until it's too late and you actually bump into each other. The requestor and completer in our example are going through exactly the same (digitally equivalent) sequence of events: both entities decide to do something at the same time, not knowing for sure what the other is doing, only to realize that what they expected of the other did not occur. The message to take away here is that when two actors react simultaneously to their inputs, neither of them can guarantee what the next state of the other will be.

So what is the solution? Let's look back at our walking analogy for some inspiration again. We concluded that the problem was that both walkers decided to change lanes at the same time, so what if just one of the people decided to move instead? Indeed, if you decided that you were going to remain on your lane no matter what happens, then the other person would end up switching to the other lane and you would no longer collide. We can achieve the same effect between our requestor and completer by adding a new rule to our communication protocol: if a requestor wants to start a transaction, then it should assert its control signals and **keep them asserted** until the completer's READY signal is asserted, at which point the requestor and completer are both aware of each other's state and the requestor can safely deassert its control signals. The design choice to keep signals asserted until they are acknowledged by the other entity has two implications: (1) the requestor must *not* check the READY signal before deciding to assert its control signals because otherwise the completer may never know of the requestor's intention to start a transaction; (2) transactions **cannot be interrupted** once started because a requestor cannot deassert its control signals early, and all data words must be transmitted for both entities to acknowledge the transaction has finished. Figure 4.17 shows an example in which a write transaction and then a burst-write transaction use this protocol.

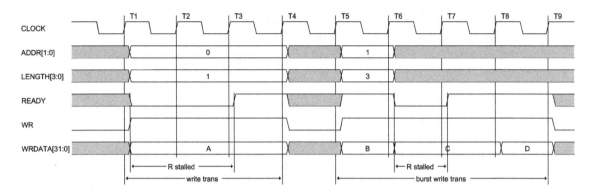

Figure 4.17 Simple/burst-write transactions with completer-to-requestor backpressure

The timeline of the events shown in Figure 4.17 is as follows:

1. The requestor decides to start a single-word write transaction to register 0 of the completer by asserting its control signals (ADDR, LENGTH, WR) and driving the WRDATA bus with the payload of the write (0xA). The requestor does not involve the READY signal in its decision to start a transaction.

2. At the next rising edge of the clock (T2), the requestor sees that the READY signal is deasserted, so it *keeps its control signals asserted*.

3. At the next rising edge of the clock (T3), the requestor sees that the READY signal is still deasserted, so it continues to *keep its control signals asserted*.

4. At the next rising edge of the clock (T4), the requestor sees that READY is finally asserted. This means the completer is ready and has accepted the transaction because WR and READY are both asserted at the same rising clock edge. This concludes the single-word write transaction.

5. The requestor decides to start a burst-write transaction to registers 1 to 3 of the completer by asserting its control signals (ADDR, LENGTH, WR) again and driving the WRDATA bus with the payload of the first write (0xB).

6. The READY signal is asserted at the rising edge of the clock and the completer registers the first write to register 1 with data 0xB. Because the transfer's base register index and length will have been registered by the completer, the requestor can now deassert the ADDR and LENGTH buses. However, it keeps the WR signal asserted and drives the WRDATA bus with the payload destined for register 2 in the completer (0xC).

7. The completer is busy and the READY signal is seen as deasserted by the requestor at the rising edge of the clock. The completer is therefore exerting backpressure on the requestor, which then decides to keep its WR control signal asserted and maintains the existing write payload on the WRDATA bus.

8. The completer asserts the READY signal and the requestor registers it on the rising edge of the clock. Because READY and WR are both asserted, the requestor concludes the completer has

accepted the write of value 0xC to register 2 (recall that the completer auto-increments the register index in a burst transaction). The requestor then maintains the assertion of WR and drives WRDATA with the payload destined for register 3.

9. The READY signal is asserted at the same time as WR on the rising edge of the clock, so the completer accepts to register 3 the final write of this burst transaction (with payload 0xD). This concludes the three-word burst transaction.

Notice that the requestor does not need to know any of the completer's latency-related implementation details because the backpressure mechanism automatically ensures that a requestor can communicate with any completer, no matter how long it might need before it accepts a transaction. In summary, a transaction must first be **accepted** by a completer before it can be executed. In a write transaction, this acceptance phase is conducted at the first rising edge of the clock where both WR and READY are asserted, with any additional control signals needed to characterize the transaction (ADDR, LENGTH) also being asserted at this time. The management of backpressure in accepting the transaction and on all following write cycles is therefore handled by the READY signal.

Now that we've dealt with completer-to-requestor backpressure for write transactions, let's turn our attention to backpressure applied to read transactions. We argue that accepting a read transaction can be done using the same approach as for a write transaction, that is, the requestor must assert RD and any additional control signals needed to characterize the transaction (ADDR, LENGTH) until both RD and READY are asserted on the rising edge of the clock. This handles the completer's acceptance of the transaction, but how can the completer exert backpressure on the requestor during the data transmission portion of the transaction? In a write transaction, data flows from the requestor to the completer and the WR signal conveys the **validity** of the WRDATA bus. For a read transaction however, the RD signal does *not* convey the validity of the RDDATA bus, but rather the validity of the control signals relevant to starting a transaction (ADDR, LENGTH). We need an additional completer-to-requestor signal to convey the validity of the RDDATA bus, so we add a "RDDATAVALID" signal to our protocol. Figure 4.18 shows our protocol augmented by this additional signal, and Figure 4.19 shows an example in which a read transaction and then a burst-read transaction use RDDATAVALID to exert backpressure on the requestor.

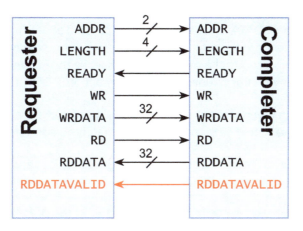

Figure 4.18 Interconnect interface for completer-to-requestor backpressure during the read data transmission phase

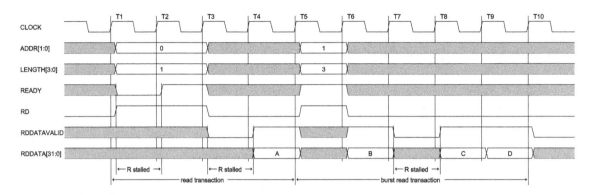

Figure 4.19 Simple/burst read transactions with completer-to-requestor backpressure

We detail the timeline of events shown in Figure 4.19 below:

1. The requestor starts a read transaction for register 0 of the completer on the rising edge of the clock by asserting the RD signal and any relevant control signals that convey information about the transaction (ADDR, LENGTH).

2. The completer has deasserted READY and is exerting backpressure on the requestor, so the requestor *keeps its control signals asserted*.

3. At the rising edge of the clock both RD and READY are asserted and the completer accepts the transaction. The requestor can now deassert all of its control signals. Because this is a read transaction, data is not yet available in this cycle and will arrive in a subsequent cycle (recall that the bus is synchronous).

4. The RDDATAVALID signal is deasserted at the rising edge of the clock: the completer is exerting backpressure on the requestor with respect to the RDDATA bus. Therefore, the requestor does not register RDDATA and simply waits until the next cycle.

5. The RDDATAVALID signal is asserted at the rising edge of the clock and the requestor uses this as a cue to register the RDDATA bus and receives the payload of register 0 (0xA). This concludes the single-word transaction in the example. The requestor then immediately starts a burst-read transaction for registers 1 to 3 of the completer by asserting the RD signal and any relevant control signals that convey information about the transaction (ADDR, LENGTH).

6. The RD and READY signals are both asserted at the rising edge of the clock and the completer accepts the burst transaction. The requestor can now safely deassert its control signals.

7. The RDDATAVALID signal is asserted at the rising edge of the clock and the requestor registers the contents of register 1 from the RDDATA bus.

8. The RDDATAVALID signal is deasserted at the rising edge of the clock: the completer is again exerting backpressure on the requestor with respect to the RDDATA bus. Therefore, the requestor does not register RDDATA and waits instead.

9. The RDDATAVALID signal is asserted at the rising edge of the clock and the requestor registers the contents of register 2 from the RDDATA bus.

10. The RDDATAVALID signal is asserted at the rising edge of the clock and the requestor registers the contents of register 3 from the RDDATA bus. This concludes the burst-read transaction because three words have been transmitted from the completer to the requestor.

Notice that the RDDATAVALID signal is irrelevant in the transaction-acceptance phase and we represent it accordingly in the waveform. Our protocol, with the incorporation of the READY and RDDATAVALID signals, can now enable completer-to-requestor backpressure for both write and read transactions.

4.2.5.2 Requestor-to-completer Backpressure

We've seen how a completer can exert backpressure on a requestor through the deassertion of the READY/RDDATAVALID signals, but how can a requestor exert backpressure on a completer? One may wonder why a requestor would ever need to do such a thing because, after all, shouldn't a requestor know what it wants to write to the completer before initiating a burst transaction? Well, perhaps this is the case when only a small amount of data needs transmitting, but if large amounts of data are involved some requestors may not know the extent of the payload they want to transmit at the outset. For example, consider the setup shown in Figure 4.20 in which a requestor uses a 16-entry internal FIFO buffer to store data that is to be sent to a completer, but where the requestor needs to perform a 64-word burst-write transaction. When starting the write transaction, the requestor does not know all 64 words that it will transmit to the completer; at most, it knows 16 of these words. However, the requestor also knows that the internal FIFO buffer it is using is going to be incrementally drained and refilled while data is being pulled from it onto the WRDATA bus and pushed to it from some downstream source inside the requestor. In effect, the requestor can perform a stall-free 64-word burst-write transaction *only* if the FIFO's source can supply new values every clock cycle. Of course, the requestor cannot guarantee this and an occasional cycle where no data is fed into the FIFO may occur. In such cases, the requestor needs to exert backpressure on the completer until a new word is available to be written. This is why some interconnect protocols also enable requestor-to-completer backpressure.

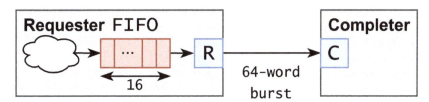

Figure 4.20 Requestor sourced by FIFO wishing to perform burst-write transaction

The question is whether we need additional signals in our protocol interface to support requestor-to-completer backpressure for write transactions? Thankfully, we can piggyback on the WR signal for this purpose and Figure 4.21 shows an example of how we can use WR to exert this backpressure during a burst-write transaction. The idea is that WR informs the completer of when there is valid data on the WRDATA bus. The requestor can therefore exert backpressure on the completer simply by deasserting WR in the middle of a transaction until such time as it has valid data to present on WRDATA again. In Figure 4.21, the requestor exerts backpressure on the completer at time T3 because the WR signal is deasserted while READY is asserted, thereby stalling the completer. However, at time T5 it is the completer that is exerting backpressure on the requestor because WR is asserted while READY is deasserted. To summarize, completer-to-requestor backpressure for write transactions is exerted via the READY signal, whereas requestor-to-completer backpressure is done directly through the WR signal.

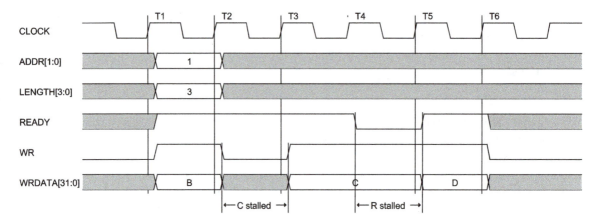

Figure 4.21 Burst-write transaction with requestor-to-completer backpressure

Let's now discuss requestor-to-completer backpressure in read transactions. In a similar way to writing, the requestor may need to exert backpressure on the completer during a burst-read transaction when it needs more time to consume a data word. Consider the setup shown in Figure 4.22 in which a requestor needs to perform a 64-word burst-read transaction, but only has a 16-entry FIFO buffer in which to store data words read from the completer. If the FIFO can be drained every clock cycle, then the requestor can perform a stall-free 64-word burst transaction. However, the requestor cannot guarantee this and an occasional cycle in which the FIFO is not emptied cannot be excluded, meaning that the requestor needs a way to exert backpressure on the completer to avoid losing data in such situations.

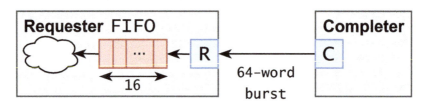

Figure 4.22 Requestor drained by FIFO wishing to perform burst-read transaction

However, unlike our approach to write transactions, we cannot piggyback on the RD signal for requestor-to-completer backpressure. Indeed, the RD signal conveys the requestor's intention to *start* a read transaction during the acceptance phase of a transfer. Asserting RD when all of the data words from the previous transaction have not yet been received would be equivalent to the requestor telling the completer it wanted to start a new transaction as soon as the current one had terminated[2]. Therefore, we must reserve the RD signal solely for the acceptance phase of a transaction and must add to our protocol a further signal, RDDATAREADY, to convey a requestor's availability during a read transaction. Figure 4.23 shows our protocol's interface augmented by this RDDATAREADY signal. Just as for completer-to-requestor backpressure, a data word is considered successfully transferred from the completer to the requestor when both RDDATAVALID and RDDATAREADY are asserted at the rising edge of the clock.

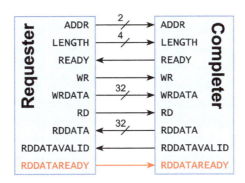

Figure 4.23 Interconnect interface for requestor-to-completer backpressure during the read data transmission phase

Figure 4.24 shows a scenario in which the requestor exerts backpressure on the completer during a burst-read transaction. On the rising edge of the clock at time T4, we see that RDDATAVALID is asserted and RDDATAREADY is deasserted, so the requestor is exerting backpressure on the completer and forcing it to *keep its RDDATAVALID and RDDATA signals asserted* until acknowledged by the requestor. The opposite occurs on the rising edge of the clock at time T6, where the completer exerts backpressure on the requestor by deasserting RDDATAVALID.

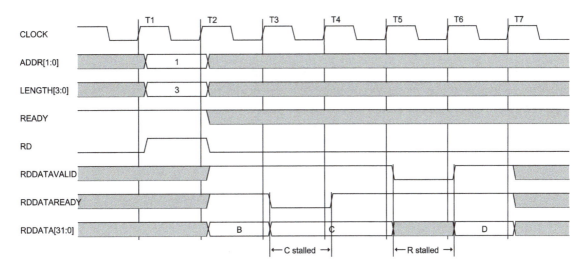

Figure 4.24 Burst-read transaction with requestor-to-completer backpressure

---

[2] Some protocols allow requestors to inform completers of future transactions such that they can prepare themselves and write/read data in a more efficient way. For example, consider a completer that, if given advance notice, could ensure that its internal buffers had enough space to avoid stalling during a burst-write transaction.

In summary, backpressure is the key mechanism that enables timing compatibility between communicating entities. An interconnect without backpressure support effectively constrains all requestors and completers to having identical timing, which in turn greatly limits the set of requestors and completers that can communicate with one another. We now have an interconnect protocol that allows requestors to perform addressed write or read transactions of varying lengths and protocol overheads. The protocol also allows either entity to temporarily stall the other in order to adjust for differences in timing or processing capacities. Figure 4.25 summarizes the interface for the resulting interconnect protocol.

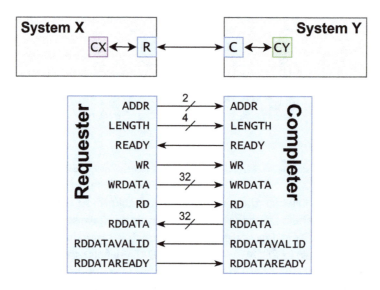

Figure 4.25 Final set of interconnect protocol signals

4.3 Interconnecting Multiple Requestors and Completers

The interconnect protocol that we have built in the previous section was incrementally developed using a two-entity system of directly connected components as its driving example. However, real systems rarely involve the cooperation of just two entities and we need to find a way to interconnect multiple requestor–completer pairs together. Let's therefore modify our driving example from a two-entity system to the three-entity system shown in Figure 4.26, where we have a requestor that

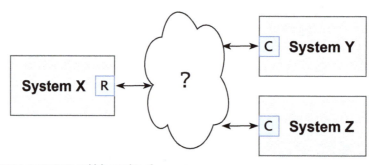

Figure 4.26 How do we connect a requestor to multiple completers?

needs to communicate with two completers. Thus we encounter our first hurdle when attempting to interconnect the three entities: the requestor only has one externally facing interface, but there are two completers, each with the same interface. The question is, how can we physically connect one set of wires and buses from the requestor to two sets of wires and buses, one for each completer?

Because every requestor interface can only be connected to a single corresponding completer interface, the first idea might be to simply require the requestor to have multiple interconnect interfaces, one for each completer with which it wishes to communicate. Figure 4.27 illustrates what a system that implements such an idea would look like. Although this resolves the initial communication issue, such an implementation comes with a number of significant disadvantages. The first is that the requestor would be much more complex to implement because it now has to manage multiple internal interfaces, each of which needs dedicated buffering and logic resources. The second disadvantage is that the requestor would only ever be able to interface with as many completers as it had interfaces, which could be extremely limiting because one rarely knows in advance how many peripherals might need to be connected to a given requestor. Simply consider the case in which the requestor is the CPU in a SoC. Many SoCs use the same CPU, but each SoC can have a highly variable number of peripherals attached to it. A small SoC would not want a CPU with many interconnect ports because it would consume more die area than necessary. Therefore, manufacturers would have to sell the same CPU with varying numbers of interconnect ports, which would arguably represent a huge amount of time and trouble for comparatively little benefit. We therefore need to find another way to connect a requestor to multiple completers.

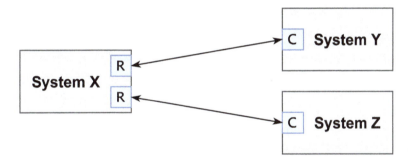

Figure 4.27 Adding an interconnect interface to System X for every completer to which it must connect

If having a single requestor manage multiple interconnect interfaces doesn't scale, and we can only connect one requestor interface to one completer interface, then we need to introduce something between the requestor and the completers to **multiplex** the requestor's access to them. This intermediate component is called the **interconnect fabric** and an example system with two requestors and four completers connected through such a fabric is shown in Figure 4.28. The interconnect fabric solves the requestor–completer connection issue by:

1. Associating every requestor with a completer port in the fabric and every completer with a requestor port in the fabric

2. Intercepting all of the transactions issued by the requestors and routing them to the appropriate target completer.

Note that up until now, we have been referring to the "interconnect" simply as a protocol because we were directly connecting a requestor and a completer. In reality, the interconnect consists of both the communication protocol *and* the interconnect fabric that provides the bridge between all of the requestors and completers. In a system like this with more than two entities, a requestor and a completer never communicate directly with one another, but rather always communicate with the interconnect fabric, which then ensures that any transactions are routed to their intended destination.

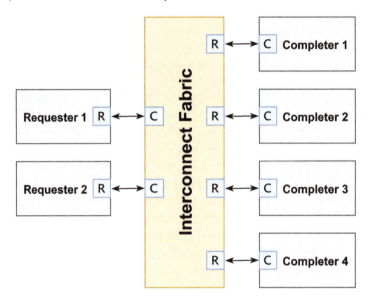

Figure 4.28 Interconnect fabric linking all requestors and completers

The interconnect protocol affects the *types of transactions* that can occur between a *given* requestor–completer pair, whereas the interconnect fabric's implementation affects the *communication patterns* that can occur among *different* requestor–completer pairs. The interconnect fabric is, therefore, a central part of a SoC and its implementation heavily influences the system's performance and flexibility. In the following sections we'll explore different interconnect fabric topologies and gauge their advantages and disadvantages. But before we talk about any topologies, we first need to expand the notion of addressing that we developed in the previous section to multi-completer systems.

4.3.1 Address Translation in Multi-completer Systems

While developing the protocol of our interconnect, we covered the concept of addressed transactions, that is, transactions in which a requestor can use the ADDR bus to ask that its write or read involves a specific register in the completer. Our protocol works well when a requestor is directly connected to a completer, but how would a requestor be able to address registers in different completers through the interconnect fabric given that the ADDR bus we used earlier was only wide enough to accurately capture the register indices of the single completer to which the requestor was connected?

It turns out that we can extend our previous addressing scheme to grant requestors access to multiple completers, simply by expanding the **address space** of the requestor and increasing the width of the requestor's ADDR bus until it is wide enough to identify the registers of all completer peripherals.

We can illustrate this idea through the example in Figure 4.29, which shows a hypothetical system containing one requestor and four completers, all connected to the interconnect fabric. For illustrative purposes, only the ADDR bus of each entity is shown, but keep in mind that each interface has the full set of signals defined by our protocol (ADDR, LENGTH, WR, RD, etc.). Notice that the first and second completers can support up to eight internal registers by virtue of their 3-bit ADDR bus, although they each physically contain fewer registers than this. Similarly, the third and fourth completers expose a 4-bit ADDR bus, supporting up to 16 internal registers in theory, but each containing fewer registers in practice. Adding up all of the completer-side registers gives a total of 30 (5 + 6 + 9 + 10) registers that the requestor could potentially address. We therefore set our requestors ADDR bus width to *at least* 5 bits so as to permit addressing for up to 32 registers. Because we'd like some spare capacity to allow for other peripherals to be added to the interconnect, we choose to go with a 6-bit requestor-side ADDR bus.

Interconnect fabric　　　　　　**Requester address space map**

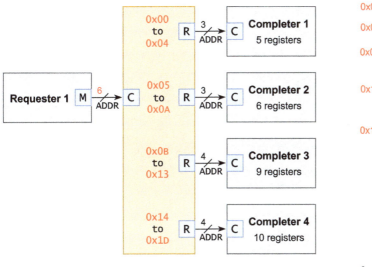
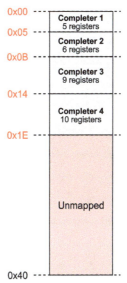

Figure 4.29 Addressing multiple completers with a tightly packed address map

In addition to simply extending the requestor's ADDR bus, we also need to decide where the various completers and their registers will be located in the requestor's address space. This location information, that is, the layout of the various completers as seen from the requestor's point-of-view, is defined in the requestor's **address map**. The right-hand side of Figure 4.29 shows a simple address map in which all of the existing completer registers are tightly packed in a contiguous region of the requestor's address space. Of course, there are many possible address map arrangements for a given system and our example just shows the first that might intuitively come to mind[3]. The only criteria for an address map to be valid is that each completer occupies a contiguous region of the requestor's address space and that no two completers' address mappings overlap.

---

[3] Later, we will consider whether this particular address map arrangement is conducive to efficient decoding in the interconnect.

Figure 4.30 illustrates the interconnect fabric's transaction routing functionality through a series of write transactions. We omit many signals from the timing diagrams to avoid excessive clutter, but keep in mind that all signals defined in our interconnect protocol are also present in parallel to those shown here. We also represent the interconnect's latency as ideal (i.e. with no delay) to prevent the waveform from becoming too wide, whereas a real protocol would use a synchronous design for better timing and would involve latency of at least one cycle between the requestor-side signal entering the interconnect fabric, and the translated completer-side signals exiting the fabric.

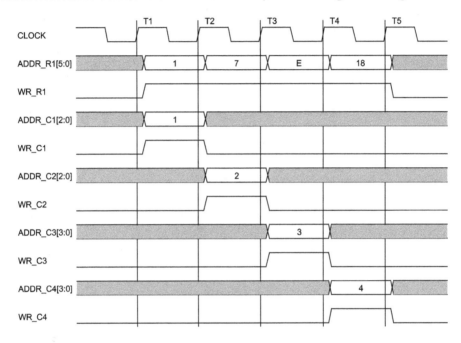

Figure 4.30 Interconnect address translation with a tightly packed address map

Let's detail the various events depicted in Figure 4.30:

1. The requestor issues a write transaction directed toward address 0x1. This corresponds to the region occupied by the first completer in the requestor's address map, more specifically to the register with index (0x1 – 0x0) = 1. The interconnect therefore asserts the first completer's WR signal as well as 0x1 on its ADDR bus.

2. The requestor issues a write transaction directed toward address 0x7. This corresponds to the region occupied by the second completer in the requestor's address map, more specifically to the register with index (0x7 – 0x5) = 2. The interconnect therefore asserts the second completer's WR signal as well as 0x2 on its ADDR bus.

3. The requestor issues a write transaction directed toward address 0xE. This corresponds to the region occupied by the third completer in the requestor's address map, more specifically to the register with index (0xE – 0xB) = 3. The interconnect therefore asserts the third completer's WR signal as well as 0x3 on its ADDR bus.

4. The requestor issues a write transaction directed toward address 0x18. This corresponds to the region occupied by the fourth completer in the requestor's address map, more specifically to the register with index (0x18 – 0x14) = 4. The interconnect therefore asserts the fourth completer's WR signal as well as 0x4 on its ADDR bus.

Notice that the interconnect only forwards a transaction to the intended completer; other completers will be oblivious to the fact that a transaction has occurred. But how does the interconnect determine which is the target completer of a given transaction? All interconnects contain an **address decoder**, which takes care of detecting this. The address decoder also contains some logic to offset requestor-provided addresses into values that are valid for the target completer's register range. We have a glimpse of this process in the explanation above of Figure 4.30, where we see the interconnect subtracting the base offset of each target completer from the requestor-side address. Figure 4.31 shows what the address-decoding logic for the tightly packed address map of Figure 4.29 would look like. For ease of representation, we only show the ADDR and WR signal logic in the interconnect, but similar logic exists for all of the other signals defined for our protocol's interface.

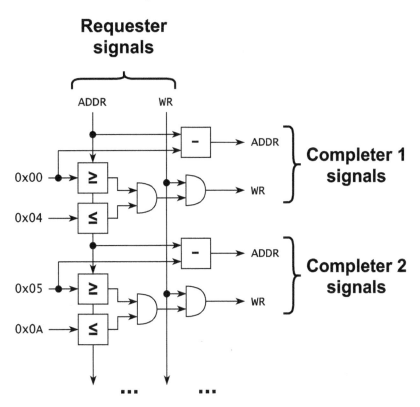

Figure 4.31 Interconnect fabric address-decoding logic for tightly packed address map

The address decoder detects the target completer by comparing the requestor-side address against the high and low offsets of each completer defined in the address map. If the input address is valid and falls within the defined region for a particular completer, then the interconnect enables that completer's WR signal. Though the address map layout we defined earlier is intuitively easy to understand, it has a non-negligible impact on the address-decoding logic in the interconnect fabric: decoding such a tightly packed address map requires comparators for both upper and lower bounds of each completer's assigned location in the address map, as well as a subtractor to correctly offset the address into each completer's domain. Furthermore, inequality comparators themselves are implemented internally as subtractors with some additional logic, so this arrangement ends up requiring three subtractors for each completer port of the interconnect. This results in a fairly long critical path from the requestor to the completers, which would cause the maximum achievable clock frequency supported by the interconnect to be fairly low. The clear message to take away from this is that the arrangement of the address map has a direct influence on the decoding logic needed in the interconnect.

The obvious question is whether we can find a more hardware-friendly implementation of the address-decoding logic, and the answer is most definitely yes! The trick is not to try and optimize the address-decoding logic itself, but rather to come up with an address mapping scheme that is more amenable to efficient hardware decoding. The address mapping schemes used in interconnects achieve this by taking advantage of the binary nature of computer number representations. The idea is to sufficiently distribute the completers within the address map such that the need for inequality comparisons and subtractors in the fabric's decoding hardware is eliminated. Figure 4.32 shows an example of the outcome of such an approach to address mapping.

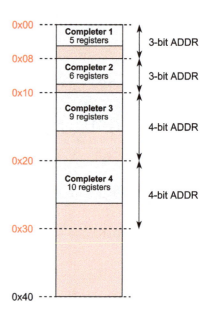

Figure 4.32 Addressing multiple completers with a decoding-friendly address map

What we've essentially done is to ensure that the completer boundaries within the requestor's address map are all multiples of powers of two. For example, the mapping of the first completer of Figure 4.32 starts at address 0x00 and lasts until 0x07, a region that can accommodate eight possible registers even though the completer only contains five. The address range from 0x05 to 0x07 is, therefore, an undefined region of the address space. Similarly, the mapping of the third completer starts at address 0x10 and lasts until 0x1F, a region of 16 possible registers, whereas in reality the completer only defines 9 such. The algorithm for placing completers in the address map now depends on the bit-width of each completer's ADDR bus rather than on the number of registers it defines internally. This address-mapping scheme permits the use of the simpler interconnect address-decoding logic shown in Figure 4.33.

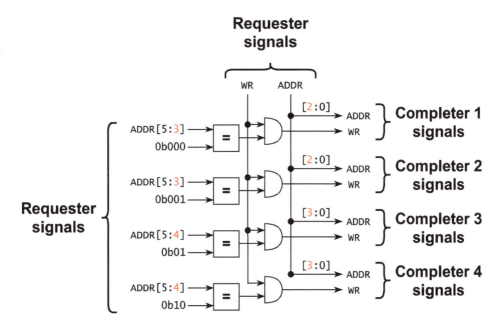

Figure 4.33 Interconnect fabric address-decoding logic for a decoding-friendly address map

Notice how the interconnect's decoding hardware no longer contains any subtractors, but rather just relies on indexing a subset of the wires in the ADDR bus, an operation that comes for free because no additional hardware is needed. This is due to the fact that subtracting a power of two from the requestor-side address is equivalent to just keeping the low-order bits of the ADDR bus, a trick that would not have been possible if the completers were not placed at multiples of powers of two in the address space. Furthermore, observe that we no longer need to perform inequality comparisons to determine the target completer of a transaction and can instead rely on a **longest-prefix** equality comparator. Students often wonder why the comparators for the different completers are of varying widths. The answer is that without a longest-prefix equality test, it would be possible for multiple downstream completers to match a given address provided by the requestor, and a transaction would therefore be routed simultaneously to more than one completer. Using a longest-prefix equality operator uniquely identifies the target completer and we can always find such a prefix if all the completers are placed at powers of two in the address space. Finally, an equality comparator can be implemented as a parallel reduction of XOR gates and has a shorter critical path than a subtractor that uses long carry-propagation chains. The critical path of the resulting address-decoding hardware is therefore very short and enables higher interconnect clock frequencies.

Figure 4.34 illustrates the interconnect fabric's transaction-routing capability in relation to the same four write transactions we saw in Figure 4.30, this time using our new address-decoding scheme.

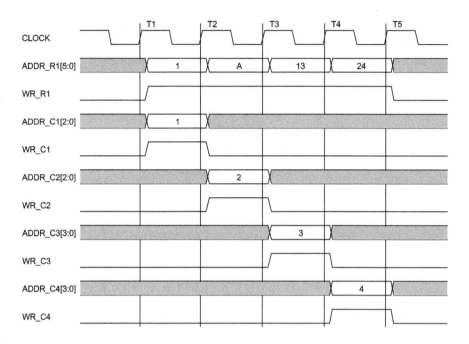

Figure 4.34 Address-translation waveform for a decoding-friendly address map

Let's detail the events shown in Figure 4.34:

1. The requestor issues a write transaction for address 0x1. This address corresponds to the region occupied by the first completer in the requestor's address map, more specifically to the register with index (0x1 − 0x0) = 1. Notice that this number is the same as the 3 low-order bits of the ADDR bus (0b000**001**).

2. The requestor issues a write transaction for address 0xA. This corresponds to the region occupied by the second completer in the requestor's address map, more specifically to the register with index (0xA − 0x8) = 2. Notice that this number is the same as the 3 low-order bits of the ADDR bus (0b001**010**).

3. The requestor issues a write transaction for address 0x13. This corresponds to the region occupied by the third completer in the requestor's address map, more specifically to the register with index (0x13 − 0x10) = 3. Notice that this number is the same as the 4 low-order bits of the ADDR bus (0b01**0011**).

4. The requestor issues a write transaction for address 0x24. This corresponds to the region occupied by the fourth completer in the requestor's address map, more specifically to the register with index (0x24 − 0x20) = 4. Notice that this number is the same as the 4 low-order bits of the ADDR bus (0b10**0100**).

It is therefore possible to create efficient address-decoding logic in the interconnect fabric by co-designing the address-mapping scheme with the hardware of the fabric itself. We conclude this section on address translation by noting that a requestor now sees multiple completers in its address space and must therefore ensure that no transaction it issues will transgress a given completer boundary. This cannot happen with a simple read/write transaction, but could occur in a burst transaction because the "metadata" of the transaction (the ADDR and LENGTH buses that are asserted by the requestor until the completer accepts the transaction) are only asserted at its outset. If the burst length is longer than the boundary of a given completer, then the register index-incrementing logic within that completer could overflow.

4.3.2 Arbitration in Multi-requestor Systems

We have discussed how the interconnect fabric enables a requestor to access multiple completers, but what about the situation in which a system contains multiple requestors? SoC systems often have multiple requestors such as CPUs and DMA engines, and it is not uncommon for multiple requestors to wish to communicate with the same set of completers. However, all requestors operate independently of one another and can issue transactions in parallel, including transactions in the same cycle destined for the same completer! Of course, each completer has only one interconnect interface port and more than one requestor cannot communicate with it at the same time. The interconnect fabric therefore needs to act as an **arbiter** and sequentialize the requestors' access to the completer. There are many ways to implement such arbitration logic and each variant results in a different interconnect fabric topology. In this section we'll examine a few common topologies and discuss some of their advantages and disadvantages.

4.3.2.1 Shared-bus Architectures

The simplest way to implement an interconnect fabric is to use a *shared-bus* architecture, that is, a fabric topology in which all requestors and completers share a single set of common interconnect protocol wires (ADDR, LENGTH, WR, RD, etc.) between them. Figure 4.35 depicts an example of such a shared-bus interconnect fabric.

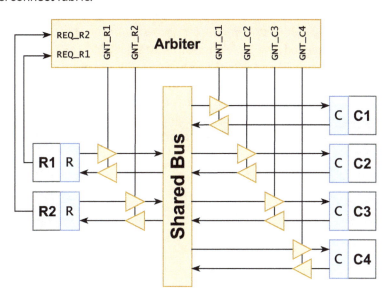

Figure 4.35 Shared-bus architecture with tri-state gates guarding access to a shared bus

Because requestors and completers share the same interconnect protocol wires, all requestor and completer interconnect interfaces have to be guarded by a tri-state gate because only a single requestor–completer pair can be connected to the bus at any given time. These tri-state gates are, in turn, under the control of a global arbiter, which grants a requestor access to the bus upon request. Note that our interconnect protocol does not contain any signals related to arbitration logic because the protocol gives each requestor the illusion that it is connected to a single completer, a situation in which arbitration logic is unnecessary. Therefore, we need instead to use an additional out-of-protocol signal between the requestors and the arbiter for this purpose (thus, shared buses use *requestor-side* arbitration). The arbiter receives all requestor requests and sequentially grants bus access by enabling the specific requestor and completer's tri-state gates.

Shared-bus architectures are relatively easy to implement, can operate at fairly high clock speeds, and are economical in terms of hardware resources. However, they have a major downside, because shared buses don't support any notion of concurrency. Indeed, requestors do not compete for access to specific completers, but rather for the shared bus in its entirety. Shared-bus architectures can therefore cause requestors in a systems to spend a significant amount of time waiting for access to the bus, and waiting times get worse the more requestors exist in the system, which is an unfavorable situation for SoCs, which often contain many independent accelerator units that act as requestors. Shared-bus architectures are, therefore, rarely used in SoCs.

4.3.2.2 Full Crossbar-switch Architectures

Figure 4.36 shows an alternative topology for the interconnect fabric: that of a *full crossbar switch*. A full crossbar interconnects all requestors to all completers by layering a *switch* in front of all of the completers. In the figure, these switches are shown as "SW" rectangles in front of each completer, while each circle represents a possible requestor–completer connection. White circles show inactive connections and yellow circles show active ones. A switch consists of an N-input arbiter, with N being the number of requestors in the system, and is typically implemented as a wide multiplexer. A full crossbar enables any particular requestor–completer pair to communicate at the same time as any other, with arbitration only needed if multiple requestors attempt to communicate with the same completer. The left-hand image in Figure 4.36 shows a case in which arbitration is unnecessary because both requestor–completer pairs are distinct, whereas the right-hand image shows a case in which arbitration through the completer-side switch is necessary because both requestors are trying to access the same completer at the same time. Full crossbar architectures enable maximum concurrency by using a fine-grained *completer-side* arbitration scheme and are often used in high-throughput interconnects.

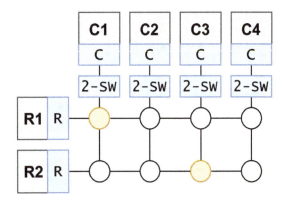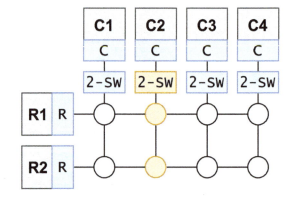

Figure 4.36 Full crossbar-switch architecture

In addition to supporting full concurrency, full crossbar switches do not require any extra out-of-protocol signals for arbitration purposes because each switch can see when multiple transactions are simultaneously directed at the same completer and can automatically provide backpressure on all requestors except the one that was granted access to the completer. Therefore, the interconnect protocol itself acts as the arbitration mechanism, while the arbiter design defines the arbitration policy (e.g. round-robin access to queued requestors, priority access for certain requestors, etc.).

However, full crossbars require significant resource in terms of die area, because the crossbar size grows quadratically with the number of requestors and completers in a system. In large systems, such a design can, therefore, be costly to implement.

4.3.2.3 Partial Crossbar-switch Architectures

Full crossbars are costly to implement partly because they allow requestors to communicate with any completer. However, in real-world SoCs, some requestors may only ever need connectivity to a subset of the system's available completers. For example, while a CPU may need to be connected to most peripherals, a DMA unit may only need interconnection with memories. Thus, in a full crossbar, some requestor–completer connections are never used and consume die area resource for no reason. In such cases, one can use a *partial* crossbar-switch architecture for the interconnect fabric instead of a full one.

Figure 4.37 shows an example of such an architecture, enabling interconnectivity between three requestors and four completers. Notice that each switch is sized in such a way as to only accommodate as many requestors as are physically connected to the completer it is protecting. For example, because all three requestors in our system can communicate with the first completer, we place a 3-input arbitration switch in front of that completer. By contrast, only the first and third requestors can communicate with the fourth completer, and therefore we place a smaller 2-input arbitration switch in front of this completer. Because the other two completers need only be reached by a single requestor, we can remove their switches altogether and save die area. Thus, partial crossbar switches offer all the advantages of full crossbar switches, while saving area by eliminating unneeded connectivity between certain requestor–completer pairs.

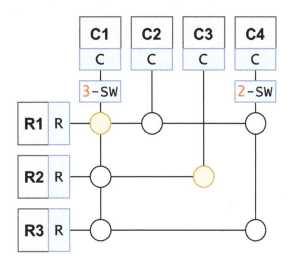

Figure 4.37 Partial crossbar-switch architecture

In summary, an interconnect is not only a protocol that allows a *given* requestor–completer pair to communicate, but also an intermediate fabric between requestors and completers that allows *different* requestor–completer pairs to support a variety of communication patterns.

4.4 Design Flexibility Enabled by the Use of an Interconnect

Until now we've incrementally added functionality to a single interconnect protocol to give component designers the choice of a wide range of different transaction types. Although a sophisticated interconnect protocol is arguably beneficial at a performance level, it certainly does not help beginners who are just starting to design components and wish to use the protocol. Indeed, there are far too many types of transfers and signals for a beginner to readily keep in mind, and building a component in an incremental fashion becomes difficult because one often doesn't know which signals to start with for an initial design that can be built upon.

Though interfacing with an interconnect may seem like a daunting prospect at first, we argue that this needn't be the case. The fact that the interconnect intercepts requestor-side transactions before routing them to completers is actually a great way to *simplify* component development because it offers completers the opportunity to *not* support the full set of signals defined by the protocol. Indeed, because the interconnect fabric is *generated* by a tool at design time to match the interfaces exposed by the requestors and completers, one can very well decide to create a completer with only a small subset of the protocol's signals, just enough to support development of the functionality required. For example, a simple completer component without burst-transaction support or any requestor- or completer-side backpressure management could easily look like the interface shown in Figure 4.38.

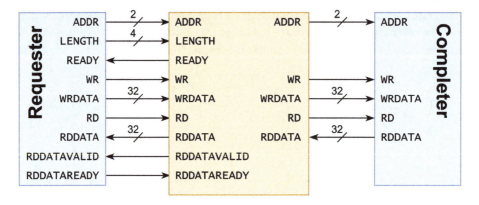

Figure 4.38 *Interface adaptation through the interconnect fabric*

Notice that the completer only uses the protocol signals that it needs, and it relies on the interconnect to *convert* requestor-side transactions to ones that are compatible with the completer. For example, if the requestor decides to start a burst-write transfer to this completer, the interconnect will be tasked with converting this into a series of transactions that the completer can understand; in this case, a series of single-word transactions.

Cambridge computing pioneer David Wheeler famously once stated that "all problems in computer science can be solved by another level of indirection". Although his statement has been positioned as the "fundamental theorem of software engineering", we argue that this principle can just as well be applied to hardware engineering. Indeed, an interconnect fabric could be generated that would transparently perform any of the following conversions for the component designer:

- burst-length adaptation

- requestor and completer clock domain crossings such that requestor and completer can run at different clock speeds

- bus-width adaptation between narrow and wide requestors/completers

- backpressure absorption

- latency adaptation

- … and many more!

We should also distinguish between the interface and the implementation of the interconnect fabric, because having an intermediate layer between communicating entities opens the door to multiple implementations of the former. In this chapter, we have developed examples in which internal communication in the fabric is done via parallel buses, but this need not be the case and some interconnects are implemented internally as a network-on-a-chip (NoC), or even as high-frequency serial interfaces that span entire chips. As far as component designers are concerned, the fabric itself is a black box having a number of properties, but its implementation is transparent to the functionality it exposes.

We therefore conclude this chapter by arguing that interconnects can greatly simplify subsystem design for the component designer by automatically taking care of any unimplemented protocol semantics.

Chapter 5

The Advanced Microcontroller
Bus Architecture (AMBA)

Having studied the principles behind interconnects in some detail in the course of Chapter 4, together with some of the common mechanisms underlying their implementations, we can now move on to consideration of real-world commercial interconnects. In particular, we will study those most commonly used in Cortex-M-based SoCs, namely APB, AHB-Lite and AXI, all of which form part of Arm's AMBA family of interconnects. Among the questions that we will endeavor to address in the course of the chapter are:

1. *What is AMBA and how does it fit within a system's overall design?*

2. *What are the relative advantages and disadvantages of the AHB and APB interconnects, and what trade-offs do these reflect?*

3. *How does AXI improve upon AHB (and APB)?*

4. *Does the apparent increase in complexity of AXI actually complicate or simplify system design?*

5.1 Overview

In Chapter 4 we learned about the basic mechanisms one needs in order to get two or more on-chip subsystems to communicate with each other, and we illustrated these by developing our own interconnect protocol. With the knowledge gained from this exploration, we now turn our attention to some real-world interconnect protocols. Note that such protocols are complex and one could write an entire book on this topic alone!

In fact, it is daunting to give a comprehensive description of any one protocol, let alone all of those in use in Arm-based SoCs. Instead, we adopt the following philosophy for this chapter: on encountering a new protocol, the key to understanding it is to have a big-picture idea of the principles used in achieving its design goals. Thus, we wish to give readers sufficient insight that, after reading this chapter, they will be able to:

■ relate the mechanisms used in real-world protocols to the conceptual ones we developed in Chapter 4

■ describe the main design choices that enable a protocol to achieve its performance/power goals

■ understand the limitations associated with the high-level design of each protocol.

There exist countless system interconnects in the real world because every processor architecture typically defines its own system interface and communication protocol. Table 5.1 lists a small sample of the many interconnects used in commercial products.

Table 5.1 Some prominent real-world interconnects

On-chip?	Origin	Acronym	Name
Yes	Arm	APB	Advanced Peripheral Bus
		AHB	Advanced High-performance Bus
		AXI	Advanced eXtensible Interface
		ACE	AXI Coherency Extensions
		CHI	Coherent Hub Interface
	Altera (Intel)	-	Avalon Bus
	IBM	-	CoreConnect
	ST Microelectronics	STBus	ST Bus
	OpenCores	-	Wishbone Bus
No	Intel	FSB	Front-Side Bus
		QPI	Quick Path Interconnect
		UPI	Ultra Path Interconnect
	AMD	HT	HyperTransport
		IF	Infinity Fabric
		-	Infinity Architecture

An on-chip interconnect is used to link functional blocks that all reside on the same chip, whereas an off-chip interconnect is used to link functional blocks distributed across several chips. Because they represent complete systems on a single chip, SoCs use on-chip interconnects.

In this chapter we will look into a small selection of interconnects defined by AMBA, the **A**dvanced **M**icrocontroller **B**us **A**rchitecture. AMBA was originally developed by Arm but has since become an **open standard** for interoperability between system interfaces. Despite its name, AMBA is not a single bus architecture, but rather a **family of on-chip** protocols, enabling interconnect designs with very different performance and power profiles. Although the AMBA acronym contains the word "microcontroller", the protocols it defines are not limited to such simple devices, nor just to bus interconnects. In fact, a variety of AMBA protocols extend far beyond microcontrollers and have been successfully used in systems that span a performance spectrum from low-power processors to high-end multi-processor systems. However, there are far too many protocols defined by AMBA for us to cover them all in an introductory text. Therefore, because of their prominence in many of today's SoCs, we focus our discussion on four of them:

▣ AMBA 3 AHB-Lite[1]

▣ AMBA 3 APB

▣ AMBA 4 AXI4-Lite

▣ AMBA 4 AXI4.

---

[1] Note that there exists a "full" variant of AHB-Lite, i.e. AHB, but the extra features provided by this extended interface can be implemented more efficiently by using the AXI protocol family. We will therefore discuss AXI4 in preference to AHB, and limit our presentation of the latter to its AHB-Lite variant.

The AHB-Lite and APB interfaces are used on most Cortex-M series processors, while the AXI4 family of interfaces are used on the majority of Cortex-A series processors but also on some higher-performance Cortex-M processors. In addition to being used on application-specific integrated circuits (ASICs), the AMBA protocols have also played an important role in the development of SoC-FPGA devices, that is, devices that contain both an Arm processor and an FPGA in a single chip. Indeed, most such devices use an AXI4 interconnect to provide multiple high-bandwidth communication channels between the CPU and the FPGA. These communication channels have allowed such devices to be very successful in a large set of edge-computing applications that require the presence of both a custom-built accelerator running on an FPGA and a high-performance processor for running an operating system.

However, before we dive any further into the details of these protocols, we start with a brief historical overview of AMBA.

5.2 History of AMBA

Let's start by taking a look at the different versions of AMBA to see how it has evolved over the years to meet the demands of new processors. Figure 5.1 shows a summarized timeline of AMBA's evolution since its inception.

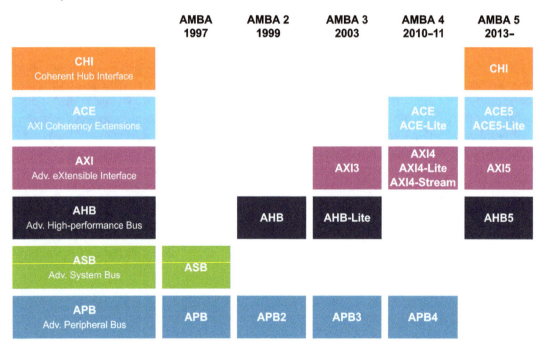

	AMBA 1997	AMBA 2 1999	AMBA 3 2003	AMBA 4 2010–11	AMBA 5 2013–
CHI Coherent Hub Interface					CHI
ACE AXI Coherency Extensions				ACE ACE-Lite	ACE5 ACE5-Lite
AXI Adv. eXtensible Interface			AXI3	AXI4 AXI4-Lite AXI4-Stream	AXI5
AHB Adv. High-performance Bus		AHB	AHB-Lite		AHB5
ASB Adv. System Bus	ASB				
APB Adv. Peripheral Bus	APB	APB2	APB3	APB4	

Figure 5.1 Evolution of the AMBA specifications

- **AMBA.** The first generation of AMBA was released in 1997 with the introduction of the Advanced System Bus (ASB) and the Advanced Peripheral Bus (APB). APB is a **state machine**-based communication protocol with a small and simple interface designed for low-bandwidth and low-power control access to, for example, register-based interfaces on system peripherals. A state machine-based communication protocol handles transfers in order, **one at a time** with each transfer taking **multiple clock cycles** to process at both communicating endpoints. Although APB is still widely used today and has undergone numerous revisions, ASB has been deprecated and superseded by more up-to-date protocols.

▨ **AMBA 2**. The second generation of AMBA appeared in 1999 and added the Advanced High-performance Bus (AHB) to the protocol family. AHB is a **pipelined** communication protocol: it splits each transfer into two independent phases and overlaps the execution of phases from adjacent transfers in order to increase bus utilization in comparison to a simple state machine-based communication scheme. AHB also allows larger bus widths than APB, thereby enabling higher data-transfer throughputs.

▨ **AMBA 3**. The third generation of AMBA, released in 2003, introduced AHB-Lite and the Advanced eXtensible Interface (AXI3[2]) protocols. AHB-Lite is a subset of AHB that simplifies bus design for systems with a single requestor, whereas AXI3 targets high-performance and high-clock-frequency system designs. Unlike APB and AHB, AXI3 no longer uses shared interface signals and instead creates dedicated signals for each type of transfer[3]. These dedicated signals are grouped together into multiple **channels**, one for each type of transfer, such that each channel can operate independently of the others. Having dedicated channels allows AXI3 to support simultaneous reads and writes, outstanding transfers, and out-of-order transactions.

▨ **AMBA 4**. The fourth generation of AMBA was released in 2010 with the introduction of the AXI4, AXI4-Lite, AXI4-Stream, and ACE protocols. AXI4 is a minor revision of AXI3, and AXI4-Lite is a trimmed-down version of AXI4 that targets simple control access to register-based interfaces on system peripherals (as per APB). AXI4-Stream, however, is quite unlike other AMBA interfaces because it is a point-to-point interface designed for *unidirectional non-addressed* data transfers from a requestor (called the "Transmitter") to a completer (called the "Receiver"). This is in contrast to all other AMBA protocols, which are memory-mapped designs and are used for *bidirectional addressed* transfers. Because of its point-to-point nature, AXI4-Stream interconnects have reduced signal routing and are particularly suitable for implementation on FPGAs. The AXI Coherency Extensions (ACE) protocol was released later in 2011 and extends AXI4 with additional channels for **hardware coherency**. Coherency allows multiple processors to share memory and enables heterogeneous architectures such as Arm's *big.LITTLE* processing. The corresponding ACE-Lite protocol enables one-way coherency that can, for example, allow an accelerator to read from the caches of a fully coherent ACE-enabled processor.

▨ **AMBA 5**. The fifth (and final, to date) generation of AMBA was released in 2013 and introduced the Coherent Hub Interface (CHI), as well as the AHB5 and AXI5 protocols. CHI enhances the ACE protocol via a **separation of the protocol itself from the physical transport layer**, which effectively renders it an architecture rather than just a protocol, and thereby allows different system implementations to make varying trade-offs between performance, power, and area. The AHB5 protocol builds upon the previous-generation AHB-Lite to complement the Arm-v8-M architecture and extend security foundations from the processor to the entire system. Finally, AXI5 extends

---

[2] The first release of AXI is commonly called AXI3 because it was released with the third revision of the AMBA specifications; there are no AXI1 or AXI2 protocols.
[3] For example, a single interface signal used for both read and write transfers.

the AXI protocol family with a number of performance and scalability features that align with, and complement, CHI.

Table 5.2 relates the Arm processor families to the AMBA protocols that they typically use.

Table 5.2 AMBA protocols supported by Arm processor families

AMBA protocol	Arm processor family[4]
APB	All Arm processors
AHB	Arm7, Arm9, Cortex-M
AXI	Cortex-A, Cortex-R
ACE	Cortex-A
CHI	Cortex-A

While the AMBA protocols do support the interconnection of arbitrary requestors and completers, they are predominantly focused on the requirements of processors. In consequence, some of these requirements end up propagating beyond the abstraction provided by the processor and into the interconnect's interface. This will become more apparent when we study the various signals exposed by the AMBA buses.

5.3 AHB-Lite and APB Interconnect Protocols

Let's kick off our discussion of AMBA with the AHB-Lite and APB protocols, two **memory-mapped** and **byte-addressable** protocols for connecting requestors to one or more completers. The AHB-Lite design makes it amenable to use in high-performance and high-clock-frequency systems, while that of APB makes it suitable for interfacing within low-power and low-performance systems. The most common AHB-Lite completers are high-bandwidth peripherals such as DMA engines and internal or external memory, whereas typical APB completers are peripherals such as timers, GPIO controllers, and I²C controllers.

Although an AHB-Lite interface *could* be used on low-performance completers, such devices would have simpler implementations by using APB instead. Thus, AHB-Lite and APB completers are often used together in a system to allow high-performance subsystems to communicate through AHB-Lite, while low-power subsystems interface with their higher-power counterparts using the slower APB protocol to save power. Figure 5.2 presents an overview of how such a combined AHB-Lite/APB system might appear, with interfaces depicted in pink being high-bandwidth components that use the AHB-Lite protocol, and interfaces colored green being low-bandwidth components that use the APB protocol.

Note that we have used the terms "requestor" and "completer" to refer to transaction initiators and responders until this point. Though some AMBA protocols generally adhere to this terminology, some also use more specific per-protocol names to refer to these system entities. We will therefore introduce and use the official AMBA names for each of these entities in the following sections.

---

[4] Note that these interconnect protocols can be used on any device that exposes the associated interface and need not be restricted to Arm-based processors; for example, the Xilinx Microblaze processor exposes an AXI3 interface.

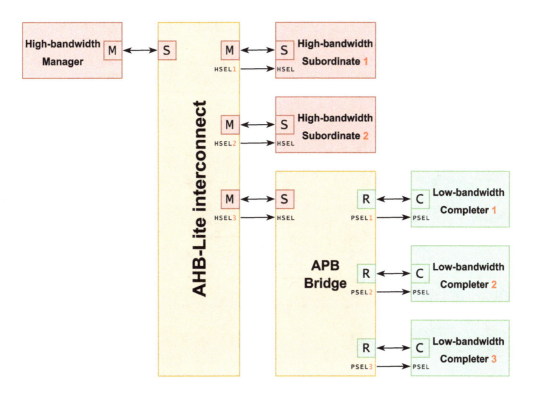

Figure 5.2 High-level overview of combined AHB-Lite and APB interconnects

5.3.1 AHB-Lite Interconnect Protocol

First, let's cover some terminology. The AHB-Lite interconnect protocol refers to a requestor as a **manager** and to a completer as a **subordinate**.

In keeping with our chapter's stated philosophy, let's start by discussing the principles used by AHB-Lite to achieve its design goal of providing a high-bandwidth communication interface for high-clock-frequency systems. It achieves this goal through a combination of logical and physical design choices:

- In Chapter 4 we explained how the use of bursts amortized the cost of performing multiple back-to-back bus operations. Indeed, without burst functionality, multiple back-to-back reads would achieve a bus utilization of 50% at best. In *logical* terms, AHB-Lite provides an alternative solution to this bus utilization challenge by allowing managers to issue bus operations in a **pipelined** fashion. Thus, each operation consists of two phases: (1) an address phase, and (2) a data phase. The phases of adjacent operations overlap and effectively enable up to 100% bus utilization, even for back-to-back reads. We'll look at this in more detail in due course when we describe the protocol's signaling behavior.

- Although pipelining definitely improves bus utilization, it is still not sufficient to support the high-bandwidth communication required by some high-performance peripherals. AHB-Lite addresses this in *physical* terms by allowing the use of **wide data buses** to increase bandwidth beyond what is achievable through increased bus utilization alone.

Now that we have a high-level idea of the principles behind AHB-Lite's design, let's have a look at the various signals exposed by its interface. Figure 5.3 shows an example system with an AHB-Lite manager on the left interconnected to a single AHB-Lite subordinate on the right. In the following sections, we'll introduce each of the signals shown but for now we will just make a few high-level observations before we look into any specifics.

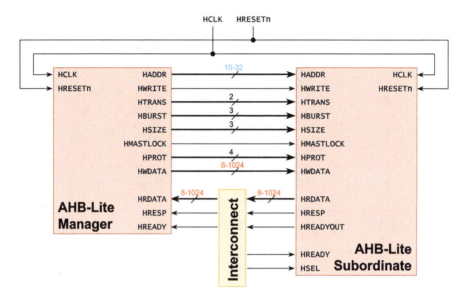

Figure 5.3 AHB-Lite manager and subordinate interfaces

- All AMBA protocols prefix their signal names with a protocol-specific character so that they are easier to identify in large, multi-protocol systems. In the case of the AHB-Lite protocol, this prefix is the letter 'H'.

- Both the manager and the subordinate are driven by the same clock signal. Indeed, AHB-Lite is a single-clock-edge design and all communication between entities on the bus is driven by the same clock domain. This does not mean that, internally, the managers and subordinates themselves cannot have multiple clock domains, but does mean that communication between them through the AHB-Lite interface is synchronous with the rising edge of the same clock signal. AHB-Lite also defines an **active-low** reset interface for each manager and subordinate through the HRESETn signal.

- The AHB-Lite protocol allows a range of data bus sizes to accommodate systems in need of higher throughput, and supports power-of-two bus sizes that range from 8 to 1024 bits.

- AHB-Lite has unbalanced signaling, with subordinates having two more signals to handle than managers (the HSEL and subordinate-side HREADY signals). This is somewhat atypical because one would usually expect subordinates to be easier to implement than managers, and to see this reflected in their protocol interface ports. In this case, the reason for this extra signaling is that multiple subordinates can be connected to the same manager and the AHB-Lite protocol designers decided to expose the extra signaling to handle this multiplicity on the subordinate side of the interconnect.

To gain a complete view of the protocol, let's lift the covers of the interconnect and see how managers and subordinates are wired together. To provide a consistent and non-simplistic frame of reference for our study, we will use the high-level system shown in Figure 5.4 as a running example for the rest of our discussion. This system consists of one manager and two subordinates connected through the interconnect. Figure 5.5, in turn, shows how the interconnect itself is implemented as defined by the AHB-Lite specification.

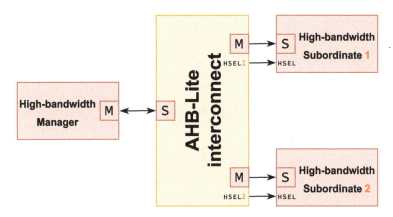

Figure 5.4 High-level overview of an AHB-Lite interconnect

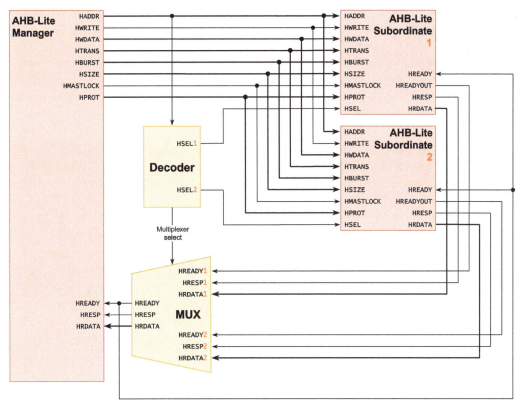

Figure 5.5 AHB-Lite interconnect with a centralized address decoder and a subordinate-to-manager multiplexer (MUX)

AHB-Lite is an unusual protocol because its specification not only defines how communication is performed through interface signals at the endpoints (the manager and the subordinates), but also **how the interconnect is implemented**. This greatly influenced the design of AHB-Lite, and also accounts for some of its weaknesses. Thus, the AHB-Lite specification **mandates** that systems with two or more subordinates must have a bus interconnect logic involving two elements: (1) a **centralized address decoder** that monitors the manager's address bus and enables a single subordinate-select signal, and (2) a **centralized subordinate-to-manager multiplexer** that routes traffic from the selected subordinate back to the manager. We stated earlier that AHB-Lite uses a pipelined operating model to enable high bus utilization. In order to support this pipelining scheme, the AHB-Lite specification further mandates that the address decoder be **combinational**, such that a new operation can be issued every cycle.

The structure of the AHB-Lite interconnect seen in Figure 5.5 actually allows us to infer many things about its functionality without even having to look at the detailed protocol waveforms associated with it:

- Knowing that there is only one address decoder and one multiplexer in the system explains why AHB-Lite is a single-requestor design, because it means that the interconnect can only monitor one address bus.

- The fact that the specification mandates the use of a multiplexer in the interconnect also means that AHB-Lite systems cannot be implemented using a shared tri-state bus and, therefore, they require dedicated wiring channels between the manager and the subordinates.

- Although the address decoder is combinational and therefore stateless, the multiplexer must be stateful. If it were stateless, then the path between manager and subordinate would also be combinational (i.e. based only on present inputs), something that we highlighted in Chapter 4 as a pitfall for interconnect design that greatly reduces achievable clock rates.

- Because an AHB-Lite manager *broadcasts* its outgoing signals to all subordinates, every subordinate effectively sees all operations on the bus. However, subordinates are designed to only sample the manager's control signals when their own decoder-generated subordinate-select signal, HSELx, is active.

- The only control-related subordinate-to-manager signals are HREADYOUT and HRESP. HREADYOUT is used to apply subordinate-side backpressure in AHB-Lite and is provided to the manager by the multiplexer through the HREADY signal[5]. Notice that HREADY is broadcast to both the manager and the subordinates. Because this backpressure signal is shared by all subordinates and the manager only sees a single HREADY signal, it means that a new bus operation cannot begin until the previous operation (to any other subordinate) has finished. Thus, all operations on the bus are performed in order, which is consistent with AHB-Lite's pipeline-based approach.

---

[5] An AHB-Lite subordinate exposes two "ready" signals on its interface: (1) HREADYOUT, a signal output by the subordinate to the multiplexer, and (2) HREADY, a signal output by the multiplexer to the manager and all subordinates. Unfortunately, these signals have very similar names in the AHB-Lite specification, despite working in opposite directions to one another.

5.3.1.1 Basic operations

Let's have a look at some transfer waveforms and introduce the signals used on the AHB-Lite interface more formally. We will start with the minimal signal set needed to understand each type of transfer, and we will then incrementally add new signals whenever new functionality is needed. An AHB-Lite **transfer** consists of two successive phases:

1. An **address phase** that lasts a single HCLK cycle, but which can be extended if stalled by the previous transfer's data phase.

2. A **data phase** that spans a single HCLK cycle, but which can be extended through a backpressure mechanism.

The key thing to understand is that bus communication is pipelined and the address phase of the *current* transfer therefore overlaps with the data phase of the *previous* transfer. The descriptions of the address and data phases given above imply that only the data phase can be stalled. However, because the address phase of the current transfer overlaps the data phase of the previous one, the net result is that the current transfer's address phase stalls if the previous transfer's data phase stalls. The waveform in Figure 5.6 shows what a simple stall-free back-to-back write transfer looks like using AHB-Lite when a manager attempts to perform the writes shown in Table 5.3.

Table 5.3 Target addresses and data payloads for back-to-back write transfers in Figure 5.6

Address	Data
0x0	0xA
0x4	0xB
0x8	0xC
0xC	0xD
0x10	0xE

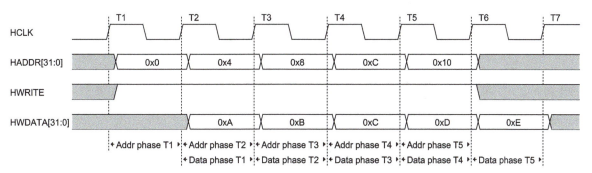

Figure 5.6 AHB-Lite back-to-back write transfers with overlapping address and data phases

We describe the cycle-level behavior of these write transfers below:

1. At time T1, the manager wishes to issue a write transfer. It therefore starts the *address phase* of the desired transfer at the rising edge of the clock and drives the HADDR bus and HWRITE signal

accordingly. The HADDR bus represents the target address of the transfer, while the HWRITE signal informs the subordinate of the manager's intention to write. In this example, the target address of the transfer is address 0x0. The end of the clock cycle concludes the address phase of this transfer.

2. At time T2, the manager starts the *data phase* of the transfer initiated at time T1, that is, it drives the HWDATA bus with payload 0xA corresponding to the data intended for address 0x0. At the *same* time, the manager starts the address phase for the *next* write transfer by asserting the HWRITE signal and driving the HADDR bus with the intended target address (0x4). The end of the clock cycle concludes the data phase of the transfer destined for address 0x0, as well as the address phase of the transfer targeting address 0x4.

3. At time T3, the manager starts the data phase of the transfer destined for address 0x4 by sending payload 0xB on the HWDATA bus. The manager also asserts the HWRITE signal and HADDR bus to start a new write transfer for address 0x8, and so on.

This overlapping sequence of address and data phases continues until five transfers from the manager to the subordinate have taken place. Because of the pipelined nature of the communication protocol, the data phases are always one clock cycle behind their corresponding address phases, and the five-word transfer of our example therefore takes a total of six clock cycles from start to finish. This concludes our overview of how simple write transfers are handled in AHB-Lite.

AHB-Lite read transfers are analogous to write transfers, the only difference being that a manager needs to convey its intention to read. In AHB-Lite, this control information is conveyed through the HWRITE signal for both write and read transfers: thus, a manager asserts HWRITE to signal its intention to write to a subordinate, while it simply deasserts HWRITE to signal its intention to read. Although the HWRITE control signal is thus shared between write and read transfers, the data buses are not and AHB-Lite has dedicated unidirectional data buses for the write (HWDATA) and read (HRDATA) payloads. Figure 5.7 shows what a typical five-word back-to-back read transfer would look like.

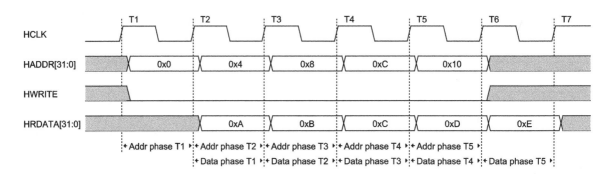

Figure 5.7 AHB-Lite back-to-back read transfer

As presented, our simple AHB-Lite transfer suffers from a design flaw because the set of signals we've introduced to date don't permit the bus to ever be idle. Indeed, because of the binary nature of the HWRITE control signal used to indicate both write and read transfers, every single clock cycle will indicate that either a write or a read transfer is taking place, and no idleness can be represented. Figure 5.8 shows an example of such a scenario, in which writes and reads are interleaved and it is impossible to identify any idleness on the bus. We use "Write/Read (xxx)" to indicate that a transfer intends to write or read to/from address (xxx), and "Data (xxx)" to refer to data for or from address (xxx).

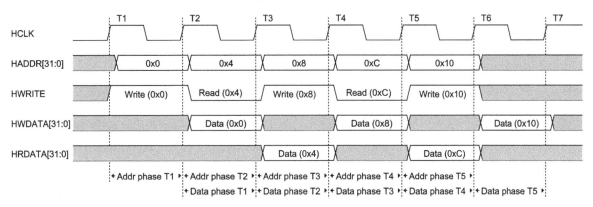

Figure 5.8 AHB-Lite transfers cannot idle without additional signaling

This is a great opportunity to introduce a new interface signal to our discussion of the AHB-Lite protocol, namely HTRANS. HTRANS is a 2-bit signal sent from the manager to the subordinate to indicate the *type* of transfer being requested. Table 5.4 shows its encoding and a summary of the four possible transfer types it describes. Note that some of the transfer types are concerned with AHB-Lite bursts, a subject we have not discussed as yet. We will therefore defer our discussion of these latter transfer types and focus on those relevant to our current discussion of idleness.

Table 5.4 HTRANS signal encoding

HTRANS	Type	Description
0b00	IDLE	Informs the subordinate that no data transfer is required in this transfer
0b01	BUSY	Allows managers to insert idle cycles in the middle of a burst and is therefore a mechanism for manager-to-subordinate backpressure
0b10	NONSEQ	Indicates that non-sequential transfer is required (i.e. a single transfer), or that this transfer is the first of a burst
0b11	SEQ	Indicates that the current transfer is one of the subsequent transfers of a burst

In effect, HTRANS allows the AHB-Lite protocol to bypass the binary-valued write-or-read meaning of the HWRITE signal through the use of a secondary transfer-type signal. The manager signals its intent to not perform any write or read transfer by sending IDLE on the HTRANS bus during a transfer's address phase. Alternatively, the manager can signal that a non-sequential transfer (i.e. not involving a burst) is required by sending NONSEQ on the HTRANS bus. Figure 5.9 shows an example in which HTRANS is used to avoid a transfer during a cycle between two reads. The detail of the event sequence, keyed by the rising clock-edge cycle times, follows.

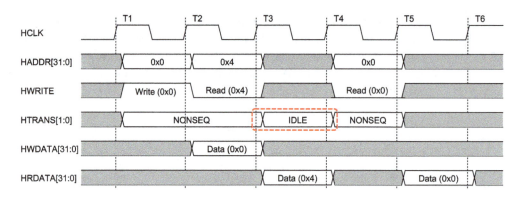

Figure 5.9 AHB-Lite idle transfers through HTRANS signal.

1. The manager starts the address phase of a transfer by driving the HADDR bus with the target address (0x0) and asserting the HWRITE signal to convey its intention to write. Because this is not an idle (or burst) transfer, the HTRANS bus is simultaneously driven to NONSEQ in order to convey that this is a non-sequential transfer. This concludes the address phase of the first transfer.

2. The manager starts the data phase of the previous write transfer to address 0x0 by sending its payload data (for 0x0) on the HWDATA bus. The manager also wants to start another transfer and therefore begins the address phase of a new transfer to address 0x4. However, this time the manager wishes to read, so the HWRITE signal is deasserted, but HTRANS is maintained at NONSEQ. This concludes the data phase of the first transfer and the address phase of the second.

3. The manager receives the result of the previous read transfer (from 0x4) on the HRDATA bus and concludes the data phase of the second transfer. The manager no longer wishes to write or read to the subordinate at this point and therefore starts the address phase of the next transfer by sending IDLE on the HTRANS bus. The subordinate then effectively ignores the HADDR and HWRITE signals upon seeing this IDLE signal. This concludes the address phase of the third transfer, a transfer during which no data will be exchanged.

4. The data phase of the previous IDLE transfer occurs, during which no payload is provided on HWDATA or received on HRDATA. This concludes the IDLE data phase. However, at this point the manager wishes to perform another read transfer and therefore starts the address phase of a new transfer (to address 0x0) by deasserting HWRITE and driving HTRANS to NONSEQ.

5. The data phase of the new read transfer takes place and the manager receives payload (from 0x0) on the HRDATA bus (i.e. the value it had written to the subordinate in its earlier transfer at T1).

5.3.1.2 Transfer-specific Data Widths

Let's now turn our attention to how the interconnect can provide functionality for higher-level elements of the computing stack. Suppose the AHB-Lite manager is a CPU with a 32-bit data bus and that it is executing instructions from a compiled C program. Furthermore, suppose the program is trying to write data to memory in 16-bit wide blocks, something that could easily be expressed in the C programming language. However, if we look at the CPU data bus width, we realize that transfers on the bus can only be done in 32-bit blocks. If narrow writes cannot be expressed on the bus, the CPU would only be able to emulate a 16-bit write on a 32-bit bus by reading a 32-bit word from memory, overwriting the target 16-bit subset onto that word, and then writing the whole word back to memory. This is extremely costly because it means that a narrow write would need three bus transfers when a native-width write could be done in just one. However, if the interconnect can provide some help with this, such operations would become much more economical to perform. AHB-Lite tackles this design problem by providing another control signal on its interface, HSIZE, a 3-bit signal that indicates the size of a single transfer in bytes. Table 5.5 lists the encoding of HSIZE as it is used to indicate the data widths involved.

Table 5.5 HSIZE signal encoding

HSIZE	Size (bytes)	Size (bits)
0b000	1	8
0b001	2	16
0b010	4	32
0b011	8	64
0b100	16	128
0b101	32	256
0b110	64	512
0b111	128	1024

The HSIZE bus is driven by a manager during the address phase of a transfer to indicate how many bits transmitted on the data buses must be sampled (in the case of a write transfer) or returned (in the case of a read transfer) by the subordinate. A manager can only stipulate a transfer size that is less than or equal to the native width of its data bus, because larger transfers (obviously) wouldn't physically fit on the bus. Thus, a manager with a 64-bit data bus can only use HSIZE encodings that represent 1, 2, 4, or 8 bytes per transfer. Figure 5.10 shows an example waveform of a how a manager with a 64-bit data bus can use the HSIZE bus to write a total of 21 bytes of data to a subordinate. Again, the detail of the event sequence, keyed by the rising clock-edge times, follows.

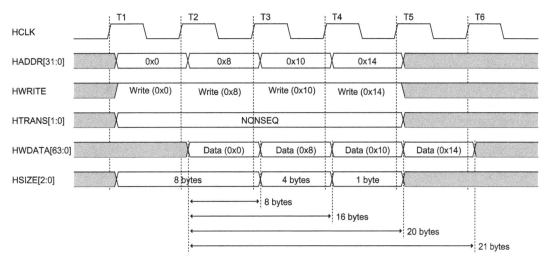

Figure 5.10 AHB-Lite write transfers for a 21-byte transfer to a subordinate

1. The manager starts the address phase of a write transfer to address 0x0. This is not a burst and HTRANS is therefore driven to NONSEQ. The fastest way to transmit 21 bytes through an 8-byte wide bus is to perform two 8-byte transfers, one 4-byte transfer, and finally one 1-byte transfer. The manager therefore drives the HSIZE bus to signal that it will put 8 bytes of data on the HWDATA bus for the subordinate to sample. This concludes the address phase of the first transfer.

2. The manager starts the data phase of the first transfer by driving the HWDATA bus with 8 bytes of data. This concludes the data phase of the first transfer. At the same time, the manager starts the address phase of the second transfer, to target address 0x8 (0x0 + 8). Again, it drives the HSIZE bus to signal that it will transmit 8 bytes of data on the HWDATA bus during this second data transfer, which concludes the address phase of this transfer.

3. The manager starts the data phase of the second transfer by driving the HWDATA bus with 8 bytes of data, concluding the data phase of the second transfer. It now starts the address phase of the third transfer, to target address 0x10 (0x8 + 8). Having decided that this transfer will be 4 bytes wide, it drives HSIZE to signal that 4 bytes of data will be sent on the HWDATA bus during the third data phase, concluding the address phase of the third transfer.

4. The manager starts the data phase of the third transfer by driving the HWDATA bus with 4 bytes of data. The data is placed in the low-order bits of the bus and the subordinate need only sample these low-order bits. This concludes the data phase of the third transfer. The manager also starts the address phase of the fourth transfer, to target 0x14 (0x10 + 4). Having already transmitted 20 bytes to the subordinate, the manager now drives HSIZE to signal that only 1 byte of data will be transmitted on the HWDATA bus during the fourth data phase. This concludes the address phase of the fourth transfer.

5. The manager starts the data phase of the fourth transfer by driving the HWDATA bus with 1 byte of data on the low-order bits of the bus. The subordinate uses the HSIZE bus value from the previous address phase to determine how much of the bus to sample and retrieves the low-order byte from HWDATA. This concludes the data phase of the fourth transfer, at which point 21 bytes of data have been transmitted from the manager to the subordinate.

The AHB-Lite bus thereby supports power-of-two data sizes ranging from 1 to 128 bytes for each transfer. This mechanism allows higher-level elements of the computing stack to efficiently make narrow transfers to devices over the bus. You may recall our earlier comment that AMBA buses tend to be CPU-focused and that some processor-specific requirements would, therefore, drive the design of the interconnect; the HSIZE bus is one such example.

5.3.1.3 Bursts

In Chapter 4 we introduced a **burst** as a mechanism for a series of bus transfers with consecutive addresses that is used to reduce the overhead of transmitting an individual address on the bus for every one of these back-to-back transfers. Reducing this address transmission overhead increases bus utilization, but such overheads don't really exist in a pipelined protocol such as AHB-Lite because the address and data phases of consecutive transfers overlap anyway. So why are "bursts" supported in the AHB-Lite protocol? The reason is that informing a subordinate that the next few transfers form a burst may allow the subordinate to prepare itself internally to handle such a workload, potentially avoiding any need to exert backpressure on the manager while doing so.

The AMBA protocols typically refer to each of a burst's individual bus transfers as a **beat**, and the AHB-Lite protocol defines multiple types of burst according to their number of beats (the burst length) and how addresses are incremented between each beat. This information is conveyed by a manager to a subordinate during the address phase of a transfer through the HBURST bus, involving a 3-bit signal that encodes one of eight supported burst types, as described in Table 5.6.

Table 5.6 HBURST bus encoding

HBURST	Name	Description
0b000	SINGLE	Single-beat burst
0b001	INCR	Incrementing burst of undefined length
0b010	WRAP4	4-beat wrapping burst
0b011	INCR4	4-beat incrementing burst
0b100	WRAP8	8-beat wrapping burst
0b101	INCR8	8-beat incrementing burst
0b110	WRAP16	16-beat wrapping burst
0b111	INCR16	16-beat incrementing burst

Note that the total amount of data transferred in a burst is defined by multiplying the number of beats by the amount of data in each beat (as conveyed through the HSIZE bus). This definition implies that HSIZE must remain constant throughout the burst and that the manager cannot change the data width between beats. The AHB-Lite protocol also requires that managers maintain the direction of a transfer constant throughout a burst: bursts can be composed of write transfers or read transfers, but not a combination. Although the AHB-Lite protocol defines eight types of burst, they all fall into one of two broad categories:

■ **Incrementing** bursts – The address of the next beat is computed as ($addr_{prev}$ + HSIZE), i.e. successive beats always have incrementing addresses.

■ **Wrapping** bursts – The address of the next beat is computed as ($addr_{prev}$ + HSIZE) mod (#beats × HSIZE), i.e. successive beats' addresses wrap when they cross an address (or block-size) boundary defined by the product of the number of beats (defined by HBURST) and the data width (in bytes; defined by HSIZE).

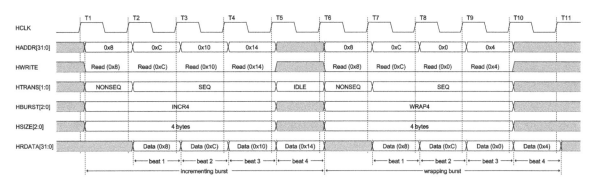

Figure 5.11 Four-beat incrementing burst (left) and wrapping burst (right)

We'll explain what wrapping bursts are actually used for shortly, but we first illustrate the operational difference between these two categories through the example in Figure 5.11, in which a manager performs a burst read starting from address 0x8 with two different types of 4-beat bursts. Thus, as keyed by the rising clock-edge time labels in the figure:

1. The manager decides it wants to read 4-byte blocks of data from the subordinate's memory at addresses 0x8, 0xC, 0x10, and 0x14. It chooses to perform an incrementing burst read over the bus because the addresses are increasing with a constant increment (i.e. the data width is identical for all transfers). Therefore, the manager starts the address phase of the first transfer in the burst, that is, a read transfer from address 0x8. Because this is a 4-beat *incrementing* burst with a size of 4 bytes, the HBURST bus is driven to INCR4 (0b011) and the HSIZE bus encoded with a 4-byte data size (0b010). Furthermore, given that this is the first transfer of the burst, the manager drives HTRANS to NONSEQ because this beat is non-sequential with respect to any previous transfer.

2. The manager starts the data phase of the first transfer and retrieves the read data from the HRDATA bus. At the same time it starts the address phase of the second transfer of the burst read, from address 0xC. Because this is the second transfer of the burst, the HTRANS type is set to SEQ. The HSIZE bus remains unchanged from the previous transfer because all transfers within a burst must use the same data width. This concludes the data phase of the first transfer and the address phase of the second one.

3. The manager starts the data phase of the second transfer and the address phase of the third transfer. Only the HADDR bus is changed, being incremented to match the target address of 0x10.

4. The manager starts the data phase of the third transfer and the address phase of the fourth transfer. Again, only the HADDR bus is changed, this time being incremented to 0x14.

5. The manager starts the data phase of the fourth transfer. This marks the end of the burst because 4 beats have occurred, as specified by the INCR4 burst type at time T1. In the course of this last clock cycle, the manager decides to finish the transfer and therefore issues an IDLE signal (on the HTRANS bus).

Between times T6 and T11, a second burst occurs, the only differences from the first being the burst type (WRAP4 instead of INCR4) and the addresses issued on the HADDR bus during the last two beats. This *wrapping* burst involves a 4-beat burst of 4-byte elements and, therefore, the address (or block-size) boundary around which to wrap is set to 4 × 4 = 16 bytes. The resultant wrapping behavior can be seen at time T8, where the previous address (0xC) is initially incremented by 4 bytes to 0x10, but is then wrapped back by 16 bytes to 0x0 before being issued on the HADDR bus. Overall, the effect is to read 4-byte blocks of data from the subordinate at addresses 0x0, 0x4, 0x8 and 0xC, but the reading order will be 0x8, 0xC, 0x0 and 0x4.

One may wonder what purpose wrapped transfers serve in a bus protocol? It turns out that this is another example of a CPU-specific optimization of AHB-Lite's protocol design. CPUs never interface directly with memory because the two device types differ greatly in speed, and thus direct interactions would easily cause bottlenecks for the processor. Instead, a CPU interfaces with a high-speed internal cache (local copy of frequently accessed memory) and only "interacts" with memory (also mediated via the cache) when this cache does not contain the requested data.

Let us consider a scenario in which the CPU asks for data from a target address, but a cache "miss" occurs because the data is not in the cache. The cache will then fetch a full, line-sized block[6] of data from memory, populate its internal cache line accordingly, and then return the specific word within this line that was requested by the CPU. To understand why a wrapping burst could be advantageous in this scenario, we need to look more closely at the cache's interaction with memory over the AHB-Lite interface. Thus, suppose the cache line is 16-words wide and that the cache uses an incrementing burst to populate this from memory: the incrementing burst will fetch this data from memory in order, from word 0 to word 15. If the CPU had asked for the last word in the cache line, it would need to wait for 16 transfers to occur on the bus before the cache actually contained the data corresponding to the requested address, forcing an unnecessary wait upon the processor. A wrapping burst solves this problem by decoupling the first access of the burst from its target memory region, effectively providing a mechanism for a manager to indicate which part of the data is most important to it and is needed first (hence it is sometimes referred to as a "critical-word-first" cache-fill scheme). The remaining transfers in the wrapping burst then take care of filling up the rest of the cache line.

Besides these defined incrementing and wrapping bursts, the AHB-Lite protocol also supports incrementing bursts of undefined length (identified by the INCR burst type [0b001] shown in Table 5.6). Such a burst is akin to a **streaming** workload, that is, a workload where the manager does not know the amount of data that is to be read or written in advance. An undefined-length burst must be explicitly stopped by a manager[7], but otherwise follows a similar pattern to other incrementing bursts, with the first transfer having type NONSEQ and all following transfers having type SEQ. The only difference is that the manager must drive HBURST to INCR (rather than INCRx). Undefined-length bursts are terminated either by sending IDLE on the HTRANS bus, or by driving HTRANS to NONSEQ (and thereby signaling the start of a new burst or single transfer). The introduction of an undefined-length burst type now creates two ways in which single-beat bursts can be accomplished: either by (1) issuing SINGLE on HBURST and NONSEQ on HTRANS, or (2) issuing INCR on HBURST, NONSEQ on HTRANS, and terminating the undefined-length burst after one transfer. Figure 5.12 shows an example of the two approaches to a single-beat burst, followed by an undefined-length burst terminated after three beats.

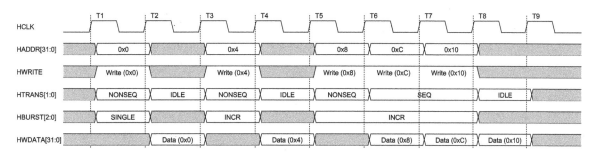

Figure 5.12 Two ways of encoding a single-beat burst, followed by an undefined-length burst lasting three beats

---

[6] The size of a cache line depends on the CPU, but is typically large enough to contain 4, 8, or 16 words' worth of data.
[7] Unlike all other burst types, in which the length of the burst is implicitly understood by both the manager and the subordinate by means of the burst-type identifier.

5.3.1.4 Backpressure

A general-purpose protocol must always support a backpressure mechanism that allows either endpoint to handle occasional throughput mismatches by stalling the other. The AHB-Lite protocol is no exception and provides support for bidirectional backpressure: subordinate-to-manager backpressure is achieved through the HREADY signal; manager-to-subordinate backpressure is achieved through the HTRANS bus. Note that HREADY is a dedicated subordinate-to-manager backpressure signal, whereas the HTRANS bus only provides manager-to-subordinate backpressure when driven to BUSY (Table 5.4 shows how BUSY is encoded on the HTRANS bus). The AHB-Lite protocol refers to a cycle during which no transfer occurs as a **wait state**.

We start by considering subordinate-side backpressure. Because of its pipelined design, AHB-Lite does not permit subordinates to directly extend the address phase of a transfer[8]. This means that only the data phase of a transfer can be stalled and subordinates must therefore be designed such that they can sample the various control signals generated during the address phase at all times. During a data phase, subordinates can deassert HREADY to insert wait states if they require more time to respond to a transfer, with the address phase of the next transfer only accepted when HREADY is high again.

Let's continue with manager-side backpressure. Because the address phase of a transfer cannot be stalled, manager-to-subordinate backpressure again only makes sense for the data phase. However, let's think about what type of transfer might be stalled by a manager. Would it make sense for a manager to support stalling of *all* the transfer types defined by HTRANS, that is, IDLE, NONSEQ, and SEQ? In fact, it makes little sense for a manager to stall an IDLE transfer because that would equate to the manager stalling itself, so we can readily rule out this option. With respect to the data-related transfer types, would AHB-Lite gain any advantage from allowing a manager to stall simple single-beat transfers represented by the NONSEQ type? The answer is also no here too, because managers should have enough internal resources to handle such small requests before issuing them, in order to avoid needlessly occupying a subordinate. Manager-to-subordinate backpressure therefore only makes sense for bursts in which a manager may run out of internal buffering space due to unexpected downstream stalls, a situation that only arises when larger data transfers are performed. The AHB-Lite protocol follows this reasoning and therefore only supports manager-side backpressure for bursts. The end result is that the protocol indirectly forces managers to follow a design in which back-to-back single-beat transfers are unstallable on the manager side and high bus utilization can be achieved (although this does not mean that such transfers cannot be stalled on the subordinate side).

Figure 5.13 illustrates examples of both types of backpressure mechanism at play during a 4-beat incrementing burst. Notice how, after the rising edge of the clock at time T3, the manager decides to backpressure the subordinate (perhaps due to a lack of space in its internal buffers) and therefore drives the HTRANS bus to BUSY and **holds its control and data signals**[9]. The subordinate reciprocates using the same technique and holds its HREADY and HRDATA signals constant. The backpressure is only stopped at time T4 when the manager drives HTRANS back to SEQ to continue the burst. Time T4 therefore marks the start of the first cycle during which the address phase with target 0x10 is

---

[8] As we discussed in Chapter 4, a backpressured entity must *hold its signals* until it is no longer being stalled by the other entity for reliable two-way communication to work. If a subordinate were permitted to stall the address phase and no address phase had yet been issued (which could occur at startup time, for example), then *technically* a manager would not be allowed to change its signals and the system would never progress.

[9] We explained this mechanism in Chapter 4 as being necessary for reliably implementing backpressure between two systems.

valid. The subordinate accepts this transfer to 0x10 at T5, but it also decides to backpressure the manager at this point by deasserting the HREADY signal and stalling the data phase. The manager maintains its control/data signals until T7 when HREADY has been reasserted and the address phase with target 0x14 is accepted.

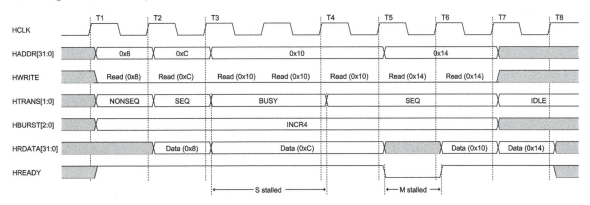

Figure 5.13 AHB-Lite backpressure mechanisms; the periods marked as stalls are wait states

5.3.1.5 Multi-manager Systems

We introduced AHB-Lite as being a single-manager communication protocol due to the presence of a single decoder and multiplexer in the interconnect. However, real systems often contain multiple managers in a configuration in which several of them need access to a common subset of subordinates. For example, systems commonly have a DMA engine to support efficient data movement between peripherals and memory, but the memory is typically shared with the processor in the system. AHB-Lite, despite technically being a single-manager design, can be used in a multi-manager system by separating each manager into a dedicated **layer** and constructing the system with an interconnection scheme that allows parallel access paths between managers and subordinates. This type of interconnect scheme is called **multi-layer AHB** and its simplest form is represented in Figure 5.14, by a hypothetical two-manager system in which we've identified the independent layers in red and blue.

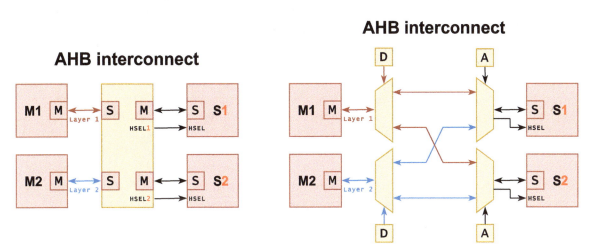

Figure 5.14 Multi-layer AHB interconnect block diagram

The D and A components in Figure 5.14 correspond to the standard decoder defined by the AHB-Lite protocol, together with an arbiter. Collectively, these two components allow parallel access paths from a single manager to multiple subordinates, and from multiple managers to the same subordinate. An AHB-Lite layer spans from its respective manager as far as, but not including, the rightmost multiplexer/demultiplexer used to provide a parallel access path to a shared subordinate. Each such layer is effectively a single-manager design based on the AHB-Lite protocol, so no arbitration or manager-to-subordinate multiplexing is needed within it and such tasks are instead handled externally by a subordinate-side arbiter and demultiplexer.

5.3.1.6 Locked Transfers

Until now, all of the subordinates that we've considered have been simple devices and have exposed a single AHB-Lite interface. However, some subordinates expose multiple bus interfaces and are called **multi-ported subordinates**. Exposing multiple ports essentially allows subordinates to support *concurrent* accesses by multiple managers and, as a result, increase overall system bandwidth (assuming the subordinate can keep up with all the managers). However, bandwidth requirements are not the only reason completers might have multiple ports. A single-port subordinate can only interface with multiple managers through a multiplexed interconnect, which effectively interleaves the managers' transfers to the subordinate. However, because of the pipelined nature of the AHB-Lite protocol, transfers can only be handled by subordinates in order and this interleaved handling of transfers can create performance issues for some high-throughput subordinates, particularly memory controllers. Indeed, internally, memory controllers group multiple requests to adjacent addresses together in order to minimize technology-dependent overheads such as DRAM row buffer switching. However, if the interconnect breaks up these related groups of transfers before sending them to the subordinate, the subordinate can no longer see a relationship between the transfers and therefore cannot optimize access to the underlying physical memory. For this reason, memory controllers implement a multi-ported AHB-Lite interface, allowing them to see concurrent accesses directly, retain the access order, and thus locally optimize access to physical memory.

Although multi-ported subordinates can enable higher performance, this doesn't come without its share of problems because AHB-Lite managers now need to consider how an interleaving of their transfers can affect the state of the subordinate. Let's take the common scenario of two CPUs trying to use a software lock in a high-level program to provide mutually exclusive access to some shared resource. A software lock is basically a number stored at a shared address in memory whose value identifies its current owner. The procedure for acquiring a lock involves reading its state, checking whether it is available and, if it is, overwriting its value with an identifier that is unique to the software thread. If a thread reads a lock and sees it is free, there is nothing to prevent another thread from overwriting the lock with its identifier before the first thread's write has managed to do so. The second thread would therefore assume it has acquired the lock, whereas in fact it now belongs to the first thread. The root cause of this subtle timing issue is that parallel threads are attempting to access and modify the same data without correctly synchronizing access to the resource and are therefore party to a **data race**. A data race can be prevented by ensuring that the read-modify-write operation on the lock resource is performed as a single indivisible step such that no thread can read the lock without witnessing any other thread's write of it.

The AHB-Lite protocol provides support for such indivisible operations through the use of a **locked transfer**, a *sequence* of bus operations that must be completed by a subordinate before it handles any other transfers. A manager can inform a subordinate that a sequence of transfers is indivisible by asserting the HMASTLOCK signal in its address phase. A subordinate can then ensure that no other operations are performed between the first and last transfers of the critical sequence, such that the whole sequence appears as a single operation. Figure 5.15 presents an example of how a locked transfer can be used to implement an indivisible read-modify-write sequence for acquiring a software lock: a manager asserts HMASTLOCK at time T1, and reads the value of the software lock; at time T2 it sees that the lock is free (unlocked), and at time T3 it writes to the software lock and then deasserts HMASTLOCK. Any manager that attempts a transfer during this sequence would be backpressured until the locked transfer has finished, thereby guaranteeing the first manager uninterrupted access to the subordinate throughout the locked transfer[10].

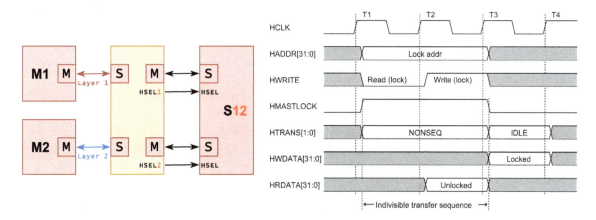

Figure 5.15 AHB-Lite locked transfer for indivisible transfer sequences

5.3.1.7 Transfer Responses
The AHB-Lite specification does not provide a mechanism for managers to cancel a transfer once it has started, and subordinates are therefore the only entities on the bus that can control the progression of an active bus operation. In general, bus transfers complete successfully, but occasionally some subordinates need to terminate a transfer early for peripheral-specific reasons. For example, a subordinate wouldn't be able to successfully complete a write transfer to read-only memory. However, subordinates cannot unilaterally terminate (or silence) a transfer because managers would then be unable to determine the state of the system. Indeed, managers are the only *active* entities in a system and should, therefore, always be able to determine the state of the subordinates if higher-level software is to implement functionality reliably. One approach to this would be for a manager to query a subordinate about its status after *every* transfer through *software*. Although this is a good practice in resilient programming, it is highly unlikely that all software will perform such checks consistently. A more dependable approach would be for the *hardware* to regularly report the status of a transfer to the manager. The AHB-Lite protocol provides one such consistent hardware mechanism through the use of **transfer responses**. A transfer response is a

---

[10] The manager-to-subordinate locking mechanism defined by AHB-Lite highlights the inefficiency of locked transfers in general. Indeed, the system could be stalled for a long period if there is a delay between the read and write parts of the sequence. More recent AMBA protocols and CPUs use *Exclusive Transfers* to implement read-modify-write sequences more efficiently. Exclusive transfers rely on a subordinate-side monitor to detect when multiple managers are accessing the same location and the system is only stalled if multiple managers attempt a transfer to the same location within the subordinate.

message that a subordinate automatically sends back to a manager after every transfer to signal its success or failure. In the AHB-Lite protocol, this message is conveyed through the HRESP signal and its encoding can be seen in Table 5.7. The HRESP signal is driven by the subordinate during the data phase of a transfer, and a transfer is considered successful when HREADY is asserted and HRESP is driven to OKAY. In the event of subordinate-side backpressure, HRESP must still be driven to OKAY by the subordinate because backpressure is not indicative of any error occurring.

Table 5.7 HRESP signal encoding

HRESP	Response	Description
0	OKAY	The transfer has completed successfully, or the subordinate needs additional cycles to complete the request (due to backpressure or outstanding beats in a burst).
1	ERROR	An error has occurred during the transfer and is signaled back to the manager so that it is aware of the failure. Errors are communicated over two clock cycles: during the first clock cycle, the subordinate holds HREADY low, before holding it high on the second clock cycle.

Figure 5.16 illustrates an example in which a manager issues transfer requests to a read-only memory (ROM). The first transfer occurs at time T1 with the manager starting a read transfer for address 0x0 in the ROM, which the subordinate sees at the rising edge of the clock at time T2. The read is successful and the subordinate responds with the payload data on the HRDATA bus and by driving HRESP to OKAY. This response is seen by the manager at time T3, when it starts a new transfer sequence by issuing a 4-beat incrementing burst write with base address 0x4. The subordinate sees the write transfer at time T4 and decides to return an error to the manager because a write has been attempted to read-only memory. Thus, the subordinate responds with an ERROR signal on HRESP and simultaneously deasserts HREADY to stall the manager. The manager *must* be stalled because it would otherwise have continued with the next beat of its burst. The manager sees the error response at time T5 and decides to cancel its 4-beat burst by issuing an IDLE transfer. The subordinate continues to drive HRESP to ERROR during this cycle because it also applies to the latest transfer, that is, the second beat of the erroneous burst.

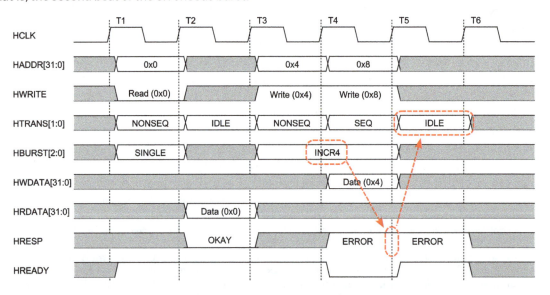

Figure 5.16 AHB-Lite error response and transfer cancellation

5.3.1.8 Protection Control

It is obvious that the bytes exchanged over a bus in a complex system are by no means the same, and often have different characteristics. For example, some bytes may correspond to instructions being fetched for a processor, while others may just be plain data. Similarly, some bytes may contain sensitive information and require better protection, whereas others may be more freely manipulated by intermediate interconnect infrastructure. To handle this heterogeneity in data characteristics, the AHB-Lite protocol provides a dedicated tagging mechanism by which data can be labeled appropriately while in transit through the interconnect. This mechanism is represented by the HPROT bus, on which a 4-bit signal is encoded where each bit represents a binary data tag. The HPROT bus is driven by the manager during the address phase of a transfer and Table 5.8 documents its encoding.

Table 5.8 HPROT bus encoding

HPROT[3]	HPROT[2]	HPROT[1]	HPROT[0]	Description
-	-	-	0	Instruction fetch
-	-	-	1	Data access
-	-	0	-	User-level access
-	-	1	-	Privileged access
-	0	-	-	Non-bufferable
-	1	-	-	Bufferable
0	-	-	-	Non-modifiable
1	-	-	-	Modifiable

The first tag (lowest bit) of HPROT represents whether the bytes being transferred correspond to an instruction fetch or a simple data access. The second tag marks the access sensitivity of the data being transferred. The third tag defines whether the transfer is bufferable: if a write transfer is marked as bufferable, then the interconnect is permitted to provide the manager with a subordinate transfer response immediately, and to temporarily buffer the transfer locally before forwarding it to the subordinate. Thus, only write transfers can be bufferable because reads cannot be handled by the interconnect without recourse to the subordinate. Finally, the fourth tag determines whether a transfer is modifiable: a transfer is considered modifiable if the interconnect can modify its characteristics while in transit.

This completes our brief overview of the main features offered by the AHB-Lite protocol: a protocol designed with high data throughput in mind; throughput that is achieved by a combination of wide data buses and a pipelined communication scheme that enables high bus utilization. We have also seen how the AHB-Lite protocol provides a myriad of associated features that enable variable-width data transfers, flow control, the ability to inform subordinates of an upcoming group of related transfers, atomic bus operations, data protection flags, and transfer status responses.

5.3.2 APB Interconnect Protocol

We introduced the AHB-Lite protocol as an interface suitable for high-throughput devices, but not all completers require a high-performance interface. Although the AHB-Lite protocol could be used for low-throughput completers, its comparative complexity would be of little benefit because such completers would not be able to handle pipelined transfers fast enough due to the characteristics of the peripherals involved. For example, it serves no purpose for a requestor to be able to send a few megabytes' worth of transfers per second to a completer if the downstream peripheral the completer represents can only ingest them at a speed of a few kilobytes per second. In these circumstances, low-throughput completers would frequently need to backpressure the requestor to ensure that the incoming and outgoing traffic at the completer remained manageable. Nevertheless, AHB-Lite communication would work fine and the requestor's transfers would be handled by the low-throughput completer appropriately. However, the main problem with using this protocol on low-throughput devices is that it needlessly complicates the design of such completers because *every* low-performance completer would need to implement the pipelined logic needed to correctly communicate with the requestor, despite probably having to exert backpressure on an almost continual basis to inhibit the speed afforded by such logic.

AMBA provides a solution to this problem with the **Advanced Peripheral Bus** (APB), a simpler interconnect protocol that is more suitable for low-performance devices thanks to a communication scheme that is low-throughput *by design* and thereby obviates completers from the need to implement sophisticated high-throughput interconnect logic. Thus, the APB protocol replaces the AHB-Lite pipelined communication protocol with one based on a **state machine** in which completers handle a *single* in-flight transfer one at a time, with *no overlap* between transfers (i.e. no pipelining). Thus, every transfer is handled over multiple clock cycles and bus throughput is reduced accordingly. Combined with a lower clock frequency, the APB bus thereby achieves low-throughput communication by design, and simplifies the implementation of completers that don't need the advanced features provided by the AHB-Lite protocol. The APB bus also features additional signaling that completers can use to reduce the amount of circuit switching done on large buses in between transfers, thereby reducing power consumption, and making the protocol particularly suitable for low-power completers.

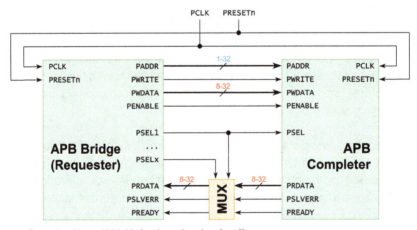

Figure 5.17 APB requester (instantiated by an APB bridge) and completer interfaces[11]

The APB protocol refers to a transaction initiator as a **requester**, and to a transaction responder as a **completer**. We will use these official names in the rest of our APB coverage. Figure 5.17 shows what the APB protocol's requester and completer interfaces look like in more detail (the APB bridge acts as a requester, as described below). Just as in the AHB-Lite protocol, both requester and completer are driven

---

[11] The multiplexer is actually unnecessary in a single-completer system, but is shown for completeness.

by the same clock and are therefore in the same clock domain. However, unlike the AHB-Lite protocol, APB exposes a symmetrical interface, with the requester and completer supporting the same signal set, many elements of which are closely related to their AHB-Lite counterparts. Nevertheless, overall, APB is a simpler design because it drops the HSIZE, HBURST, HPROT, HTRANS, and HMASTLOCK signals. Thus, the APB bus does not support variably sized data transfers, bursts, data tagging, requester-side backpressure, or locked transfers. Furthermore, because APB was designed to be used on simple register interfaces, it does not support wide data buses and restricts itself to widths of 8, 16, or 32 bits. A corollary of not supporting variably sized data transfers is that all APB entities in a system must share the same data bus width. The only new signal introduced by APB is the PENABLE signal.

Despite the similarities referred to above, the AHB-Lite and APB protocols have different signal sets and are thus incompatible. However, AMBA introduced an intermediate interconnect component, the **APB bridge**, to convert AHB-Lite transfers into APB ones. This bridge is basically an adapter that exposes an AHB-Lite subordinate interface on one side (not shown in Figure 5.17) and an APB requester interface on the other. All pipelined AHB-Lite transfers directed to the APB bridge from an AHB-Lite manager are automatically backpressured and handled over multiple clock cycles by the APB subsystem (consisting of the bridge and the low-throughput APB completers it interfaces with). The APB bridge then relays a response back to the AHB-Lite manager and releases its backpressure. The main advantage of using an APB bridge is that this interconnect component becomes the only APB element in a system that needs to implement a high-throughput AHB-Lite interface, thereby allowing the design of all of the low-throughput completers to be simpler because they can restrict themselves to implementing the APB protocol alone. Thus, the only APB requester in such a system is the APB bridge. Note that the APB subsystem can be clocked at a lower frequency than the AHB-Lite subsystem with which it interfaces in order to use less power. Thus, the APB bridge also acts as a potential clock-domain crossing region.

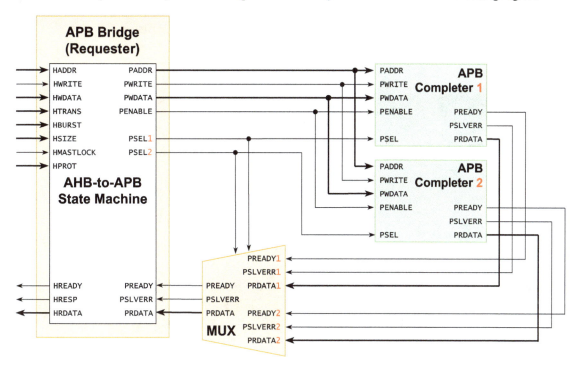

Figure 5.18 APB bridge interconnect block diagram

Figure 5.2 illustrated where an APB bridge fits within a larger overall system, and Figure 5.18 shows more detail of how its various signals interface with AHB-Lite and the rest of the APB subsystem in a hypothetical two-completer design. Much as with the AHB-Lite bus, most signals driven by the APB requester (i.e. the APB bridge, in this case) are broadcast to the completers and, therefore, all such devices see every operation on the bus. The APB bridge's state machine becomes responsible for selecting which target completer should handle the transfer. This completer selection process is performed through the generation of PSELx completer-select signals, which are sent to individual completers as appropriate, but also to a multiplexer which then forwards the selected completer's responses back to the state machine[12].

Figure 5.19 describes the three operating states of the APB state machine. The state machine resets to an IDLE state in which it waits for an AHB-Lite transfer. When the bridge receives such a transfer, the state machine then transitions to a SETUP state in which the PSEL signal corresponding to the target APB completer is asserted. This SETUP state gives the target completer the opportunity to prepare itself for the transfer and also serves to configure the multiplexer between the requester and the completers so that it will forward the selected completer's response(s) to the state machine once the transfer has occurred. The state machine then unconditionally transitions from the SETUP state to an ACCESS state in which both PSEL and PENABLE are asserted and the transfer occurs if the completer is ready to handle it, in which case the read data and the completer's transfer response are forwarded via the multiplexer to the state machine. The state machine remains in the ACCESS state for as long as is necessary for the completer to perform the transfer. There are two options at this stage: (1) if another AHB-Lite transfer is received by the APB bridge, then its state machine transitions back to the SETUP state in support of a further APB transfer (possibly to a different completer); (2) if no further AHB-Lite transfer is received, then the state machine transitions back to the IDLE state. Every transfer on the APB bus therefore takes at least two cycles, but possibly more depending on whether the completer applies any backpresure during the transfer.

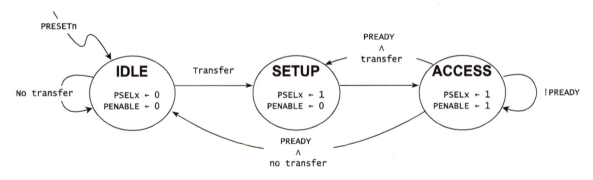

Figure 5.19 APB bridge state machine

5.3.2.1 Basic Transfers

Let's now look at what an actual APB transfer looks like. Figure 5.20 shows a sample execution of two APB read transfers. The first transfer starts with a SETUP state at time T1, where the requester asserts the PSEL signal and simultaneously drives the PADDR bus with the target address 0x0. The

---

[12] This multiplexer is stateless and is entirely controlled by the PSELx signals generated by the state machine.

requester also deasserts the PWRITE signal to convey that a read operation is requested. At the next rising edge of the clock, time T2, the state machine unconditionally enters the ACCESS state and, because the completer's PREADY signal is asserted and it is not applying any backpressure, the read data is placed on the PRDATA bus and the transfer concludes. At this point, there is no incoming transfer pending on the bus and so the state machine transitions to the IDLE state at time T3, marking the end of the first APB transfer. Notice that PADDR, PSEL, and PWRITE are all asserted during the SETUP and ACCESS states, while PENABLE and PREADY are only relevant in the ACCESS state.

The second transfer starts at time T4 with another SETUP state in which the requester again asserts the PSEL signal and this time drives the PADDR bus with the target address 0x4. The PWRITE signal is again deasserted to convey that a read operation is requested. At time T5, the state machine unconditionally enters the ACCESS state, but PREADY is deasserted by the completer as it applies backpressure, so the state machine remains in the ACCESS state until the rising edge of the clock at time T7 where PREADY is reasserted by the completer and it places the payload data on the PRDATA bus. The state machine transitions back to the IDLE state, and the second APB transfer concludes.

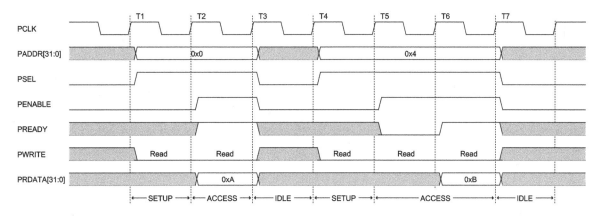

Figure 5.20 APB read transfers

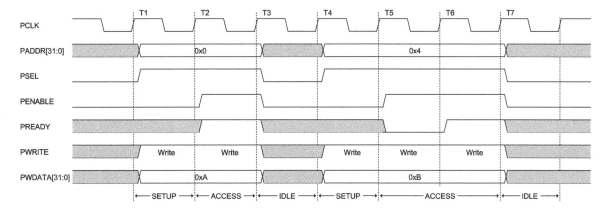

Figure 5.21 APB write transfers

In turn, Figure 5.21 shows an example of two APB write transfers. Write transfers have exactly the same timing as read transfers, the only difference being that the PWRITE signal is asserted to signal the intention to write instead of read. The PWDATA bus follows the timing of the PADDR and PWRITE signals and is also driven during both the SETUP and ACCESS states.

5.3.2.2 Low-power Transfers

As we saw in Chapter 2, chips consume power through a combination of static and dynamic power, but dynamic power is by far the more significant of the two. We also saw that dynamic power consumption is directly affected by the amount of circuit switching performed, so any attempt to reduce unnecessary switching in an interconnect can help reduce overall power consumption. Such extra switching is particularly prevalent between successive transfers in relation to large multi-bit buses.

To counter this potential design issue, the APB protocol allows some interface signals to remain *constant* between one transfer finishing and the next one beginning, in order to reduce any wasteful circuit switching. To have the most effect, the APB protocol allows the requester to apply this principle to the PADDR, PWDATA, and PRDATA buses, that is, all of the multi-bit buses of the interface that would most contribute to reducing dynamic power if switching was avoided. In addition, the PWRITE signal can also remain constant between transfers because the PSEL and PENABLE signals can be used to inform the completer of when PWRITE is valid, and thus the APB protocol can also eliminate a small amount of switching of this signal[13]. The APB protocol therefore replaces multi-bit switching between transfers with two single-bit switching operations on the PSEL and PENABLE signals instead, thus consuming less dynamic power.

Figure 5.22 shows an example of this principle applied to two write transfers that are identical to those shown in Figure 5.21, but which now avoid unnecessary switching of the PADDR, PWRITE, and PWDATA signals between transfers.

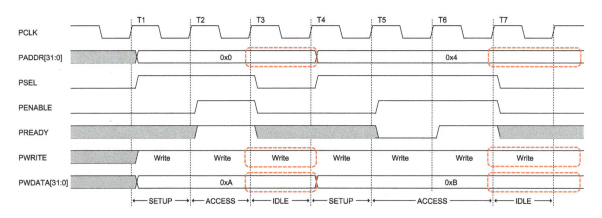

Figure 5.22 APB write transfers (low-power version)

---

[13] The savings are much smaller than for the PADDR, PWDATA, and PRDATA buses because PWRITE is only a one-bit signal.

5.3.2.3 Transfer Responses

Optionally, completers can signal if an error condition occurs during a transfer by using the PSLVERR signal, similarly to the use of the HRESP signal in the AHB-Lite protocol. This PSLVERR signal is not a prerequisite of APB completers, but could be useful for conveying information to the requester upon error so that it can react accordingly. The PSLVERR signal's value is only relevant on the last cycle of an APB transfer, that is, when PSEL, PENABLE, and PREADY are all asserted. An unasserted value for PSLVERR implies that the transfer was successful and no errors were reported, whereas an asserted PSLVERR during the last cycle of a transfer signals that an error has occurred.

Figure 5.23 shows an example of two read transfers in which the first succeeds and the second fails. The requester should disregard the PRDATA bus on the second transfer because it contains invalid data following the failure. Note that the APB protocol does not specify whether the state of the completer peripheral could have changed following the failed transfer. It is possible for a failed write transfer to have modified an internal register of the completer, or for a failed read transfer to have yielded invalid data on the PRDATA bus.

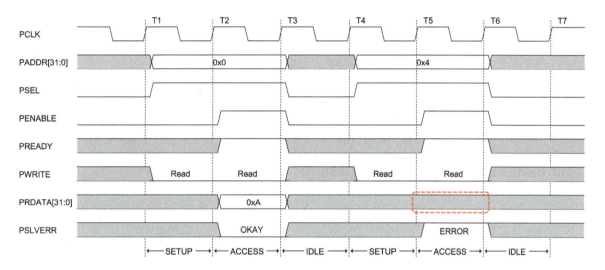

Figure 5.23 APB read transfers with different error responses

This concludes our coverage of APB, a simple protocol suitable for low-throughput control access to register-based interfaces. The protocol only provides support for single-beat transfers and completer-side backpressure, so components that don't need sophisticated features can be implemented easily without having their interconnect-facing interface needlessly complicate their design. In conjunction with AHB-Lite, the APB protocol allows designers to build efficient heterogeneous systems composed of high- and low-speed peripherals using interfaces best suited to each type of peripheral.

5.4 AXI Interconnect Protocol

The AHB protocol was AMBA 2's proposed interconnect for high-performance systems. Although AHB's performance was suitable for processors of its time, some of the design choices made ultimately became bottlenecks for new processors that relied on more aggressive techniques to achieve increased parallelism. Thus, over time, AMBA has evolved to match the needs of such processors by either revising existing protocols or introducing new ones. Following AMBA 2, AMBA 3 released two protocols: (1) AHB-Lite, already described above, which was a simplified variant of AHB and therefore shared similar weaknesses, and (2) AXI, a new protocol designed specifically to handle the needs of the new higher-performance processor segment.

AXI was a radically different design from the previous AMBA buses and learned many lessons from the limitations of AHB/AHB-Lite. In fact, AXI is arguably the most influential of all the AMBA protocols and paved the way for many of the protocols that followed. There are now several versions of AXI, the first being called AXI3 because it was introduced with AMBA 3. A minor revision of AXI3 was introduced with AMBA 4, named AXI4, and forms our focus for this section. In fact, AMBA 4 introduced four new protocols (AXI4, AXI4-Lite, AXI4-Stream, and ACE/ACE-Lite), but we will limit our coverage to just two of these:

1. AXI4 – a high-performance protocol designed for high-throughput devices;

2. AXI4-Lite – a lighter variant of AXI4, more suited to low-throughput devices.

In essence, AXI4 is intended to be the successor to AHB/AHB-Lite, while AXI4-Lite basically provides an APB-equivalent for the AXI4 protocol family. For brevity, we will refer hereafter to the AXI4 and AXI4-Lite protocols simply as "AXI" and "AXI-Lite"[14].

Note that the AXI bus is more complex than AHB-Lite and we remind readers that our intent is not to provide a comprehensive description of this (or any other) protocol, but rather to convey enough insight into its underlying design principles to instill an understanding of how it achieves its higher-performance design goals: let's get started!

5.4.1 AHB-Lite Performance Bottlenecks

As we indicated above, the AXI bus is more complex than that of AHB-Lite and this is reflected in the sheer number of signals exposed by its interface. Indeed, the AXI bus comprises more than 35 signals whereas the AHB-Lite bus only involves 15. It would make little sense to explain each AXI interface signal in turn because it wouldn't be immediately obvious why AXI adopted such a design. Instead, we approach AXI's architecture by reviewing the AHB-Lite interface and analyzing which of its design choices are responsible for inhibiting its performance. Once this analysis is complete, we can propose changes to AHB-Lite to increase its performance ceiling. Because these changes are essentially those adopted by AXI, it means we will have understood the principles behind AXI's architecture and how it emerged in its current form.

---

[14] Note that there is no AXI3-Lite protocol (AMBA 3 only released a "full" version of the AXI protocol).

We therefore start this section by outlining a simple example that we will use to drive the initial part of our discussion. This system is shown in Figure 5.24 and consists of a processor and a memory controller connected together through an AHB-Lite interconnect. We assume that all entities in the system have a 32-bit data bus and that the memory controller is single-ported for simplicity. As for the workload, we assume that the processor needs to compute a function $f(arg)$ for two values, x and y, and that these values are not in the processor's internal registers and must first be fetched from memory. This memory (external DRAM in the figure) is outside the processor and can only be accessed through the memory controller.

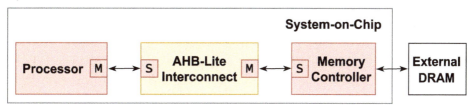

Figure 5.24 Example processor-to-memory system

5.4.1.1 Transfer Reordering

We first note that the function $f(arg)$ depends only on the value of arg, so both $f(x)$ and $f(y)$ could easily be computed in parallel by the processor if it has enough functional units to handle them simultaneously. This means that the end-to-end latency involved in the processor computing both functions largely depends on how fast it can obtain the data values x and y from memory. DRAM memories usually have a **row buffer** in which an entire row of data bytes, reflecting the most recently accessed addresses, are stored such that adjacent accesses to memory need not incur costly DRAM cell accesses. Thus, if an incoming address request falls into an address range whose data is currently stored in the row buffer, then this access can be serviced by the buffer instead of having to go to the DRAM cells and the data can be returned on the bus straightaway. Furthermore, memory controllers generally know what address range is currently contained in the external memory's row buffer and can therefore optimize accesses to the memory accordingly by **reordering** incoming requests from the processor to minimize row buffer switching before forwarding them to the external memory. Armed with this understanding of a memory's internal organization, let's look into the process of retrieving variables x and y from memory, subject to a particular row buffer state, to see how the system's performance is affected.

Thus, consider the scenario in which (only) variable y is in the DRAM row buffer and the processor is connected to the memory controller through an AHB-Lite interface. This interface only exposes a single address bus so the processor must decide on the order in which variables x and y will be requested on the bus. If the external memory receives a request for variable x before variable y, then the DRAM would incur two row buffer switches; however, if it receives a request for variable y before variable x, then only a single row buffer switch would be necessary because the first transfer, for variable y, can be serviced directly from the existing contents of the row buffer. Ideally, we'd like the processor to be able to send the two addresses in **any order** to the memory controller and have the memory controller reorder the requests to exploit its knowledge of the DRAM row buffer status (requesting variable y before variable x). Unfortunately, this is impossible with the AHB-Lite bus because of its pipelined nature: the address and data phases of successive transfers overlap and a new transfer's address phase cannot be accepted by a subordinate until the previous transfer's data phase has finished. This obliges the processor to wait until the data of its first transfer has arrived before sending out the request for the second. Under such conditions, the memory controller only ever has visibility of a single address window and so cannot reorder transfer addresses to optimize DRAM row buffer access; it has no option but to just forward each incoming request directly to memory, which can easily result in many unnecessary row buffer switches and significantly reduced system performance.

In this example, the root cause of the performance issue is that both the processor and memory controller are capable of reordering transfers[15], but the AHB-Lite link that connects them does not enable it. We illustrate this arrangement in Figure 5.25: the only way to incur minimal DRAM row buffer switches would be for the processor itself to keep track of the external memory's state and optimize its request ordering accordingly. However, it is not the job of the processor to keep track of this state because doing so would significantly complicate its design – it is far more appropriate that the memory controller should manage this.

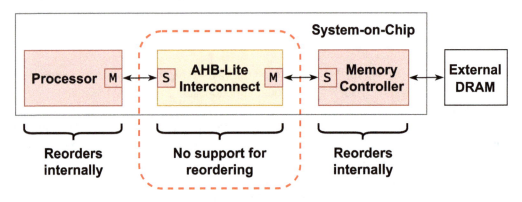

Figure 5.25 AHB-Lite cannot support transfer reordering because of its pipelined design

The performance issue described above can be solved if the interconnect allows entities on the bus to issue multiple transfers before receiving the result of any one in particular. In effect, this means there is a window of transfers between the communicating entities of size *greater than one*. An interconnect that supports multiple in-flight transfers in this way is said to support **outstanding transfers**. If, in addition, the interconnect also permits completers to respond to transfers in an alternative order to that in which they were received, then the interconnect is said to support **transfer reordering**. An interconnect that supports transfer reordering must also support outstanding transfers, but the reverse relationship need not apply[16].

However, we still need to discuss how to add such reordering support to an interconnect protocol in practice. Let's suppose we have such an an interconnect and look back at our example of a memory

---

[15] Processors internally reorder memory requests to extract more instruction-level parallelism from a program, and memory controllers internally reorder memory requests to optimize DRAM row buffer accesses.

[16] For example, if outstanding transfers are supported, but transfer reordering is not, then the memory controller could reorder requests when sending them to the external memory but must then put the responses back in order before returning them to the processor. This would help to reduce row buffer switches, but may not allow the processor to retrieve data any more quickly.

controller reordering a processor's request for variables x and y. If the memory controller returns the data for variable y before variable x, how would the processor know that the first data returned actually corresponds to variable y? Without any additional information it would be impossible for the requestor to know this. When transfers are always performed in sequence, the order in which data is received on the bus will be the same as that of the requests and the requestor can thereby associate the data with the corresponding request. However, in a system in which reordering can occur, the order in which data arrives at the requestor is no longer a reliable basis on which to associate the data with a corresponding request. Therefore, it is necessary for the requestor to perform this request-to-data association explicitly, which could be achieved if the requestor issues a **transfer identifier** with each request and the completer returns this same identifier to the requestor when responding to a request. This would ensure that the requestor can correctly associate any data or response received from a completer with its corresponding request.

5.4.1.2 Transparent Interconnect Pipelining

As SoCs become larger, it becomes inevitable that some entities will be distantly placed from each other on a chip and that the interconnect itself can become the critical path of the system. A classical digital design technique for breaking long combinational paths is to pipeline the paths to cut register-to-register delays until the target chip frequency is achieved[17]. Although pipelining *inside* a processor can allow it to achieve very high clock frequencies, a similar effect is not automatically realized when the approach is used on an interconnect's interface unless some precautions are taken.

Consider the simple write-only requestor–completer pair shown in Figure 5.26, in which all of the signals that link the two entities flow in a common direction, from the requestor to the completer. The left-hand side of Figure 5.26 shows the system's behavior with an unpipelined interconnect, while the right-hand side shows the same system's behavior with a (singly) pipelined interconnect. The waveforms under each interconnect configuration show how the interface's two signals are seen by the requestor (in red), and by the completer (in blue). Notice that both the pipelined and unpipelined variants of the interconnect keep all signals aligned, and the timing relationship between the signals as seen from each of the requestor and completer perspectives is the same.

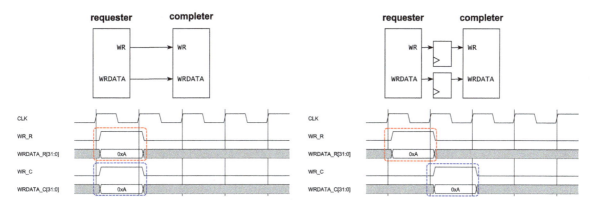

Figure 5.26 Unidirectional pipelining is well-defined

---

[17] Note that we refer here to *physical* pipelining, i.e. the act of adding registers to all wires and buses, and not to the *logical* pipelining of a protocol such as that provided by AHB-Lite.

Now consider the simple read-only requestor–completer pair shown in Figure 5.27, in which the read control signal (RD) flows from the requestor to the completer, but the data bus flows in the opposite direction, from the completer to the requestor. As before, the left-hand side of the figure shows the behavior of the system with an *unpipelined* interconnect, and the right-hand side shows the same system's behavior with a pipelined interconnect. In the unpipelined case, the read data is returned by the completer one cycle after the requestor asserts its read control signal. However, once pipelined, this relationship breaks and the requestor's view of the system becomes skewed because it only sees the read data three cycles after it asserted the read control signal. Thus, pipelining the interconnect as shown in Figure 5.27 is **not transparent** to the requestor, which means that the latter would have to be modified internally to accommodate the new signal timings provided by the pipelined interconnect.

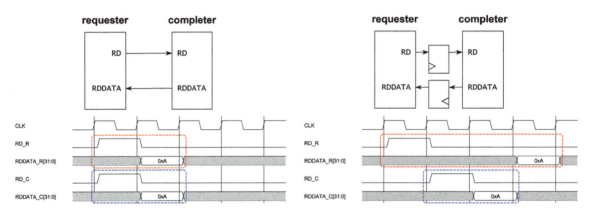

Figure 5.27 Bidirectional pipelining is ill-defined

By definition, a pipeline consists of a set of signals that travel in the same direction[18]. If all signals flow in the same direction, then adding a pipeline register to each signal can easily help achieve higher clock frequencies while at the same time guaranteeing that all signals remain aligned. This is the case for the unidirectional write-only system we saw in Figure 5.26. However, if a pipeline involves a set of signals that do not all flow in the same direction, then adding a register to each signal may help increase clock frequencies, but it also causes signals of opposing directionality to fall out of sync and no longer align. The AHB-Lite bus suffers from this precise problem because control and write data signals travel in one direction, but transfer status responses and read data travel in the opposite direction. It can therefore be difficult to optimize the clock frequency of an AHB-Lite interconnect if a manager and subordinate are distant from each other on a SoC die.

A solution to limited interconnect clock speeds would be, therefore, to separate the exposed signals of the interconnect's interface into distinct groups in which all the associated signals travel in the same direction. Such a design would permit each group to be pipelined independently to achieve higher transfer frequencies, while also guaranteeing that signals within the group do not fall out of alignment. The pipelining would thus be rendered **transparent** to the requester and completer, and could be configured automatically by electronic design automation (EDA) tools.

---

[18] The only signal in a pipeline that may travel in the opposite direction is a backpressure signal, responsible for stalling the pipeline.

5.4.1.3 Unaligned Transfers

Recall that the processor in our sample system of Figure 5.24 has a 32-bit data bus. Consider now how the processor could perform an unaligned narrow transfer such as the 16-bit write to address 0x1 shown on the left-hand side of Figure 5.28. Although the AHB-Lite protocol supports narrow writes, it requires that all transfers be to addresses that are aligned to the transfer's data width. Therefore, the processor cannot perform the 16-bit write transfer of our example because address 0x1 is *not* aligned to a two-byte boundary, but spans it. Instead, the processor must break its 16-bit transfer into two 8-bit transfers that *are* aligned, as shown on the right-hand side of Figure 5.28.

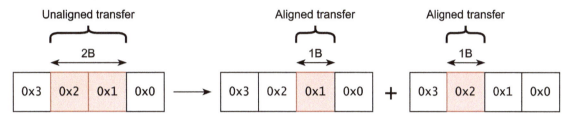

Figure 5.28 Unaligned 16-bit write transfer as a sequence of two aligned 8-bit AHB-Lite transfers

However, we note that the processor and memory controller share a 32-bit data bus and that the unaligned address range 0x1–0x2 sits within the larger aligned address range of 0x0–0x3. Therefore, in theory, it should be possible for the processor to directly write these 16 bits of data as a single 32-bit transfer if the interconnect has a way to mark which bits of the write data bus contain valid data. The interconnect could then transmit this data validity indicator to the completer, which will just update the marked data elements with the corresponding payload from the data bus.

Given that data in computing systems are typically manipulated in byte-sized blocks, it would make sense for the smallest granularity of data validity to be at byte-level too. Thus, we could replace the two 8-bit AHB-Lite transfers from our example with a single 32-bit transfer, as shown in Figure 5.29, by adding a 4-bit **byte-lane write strobe** to the interconnect [19]. Byte-level write strobes are economical to implement in an interconnect and allow requestors to perform unaligned bus accesses more efficiently.

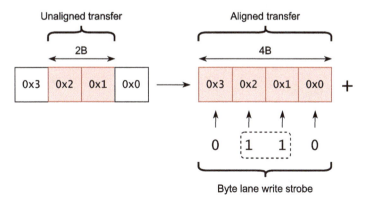

Figure 5.29 Unaligned write transfer as an aligned transfer and a byte-lane write strobe

---

[19] Note that a byte-lane strobe is only needed for write transfers because a requestor can always implement narrow reads internally by performing a full bus-sized read and then selecting the subset of bytes in which it is interested.

5.4.1.4 Simultaneous Read and Write Transfers

For the final part of our consideration of the significant limitations of the AHB-Lite interconnect, we use the example system shown in Figure 5.30, in which a DMA unit is required to copy the entire contents of one external memory to another.

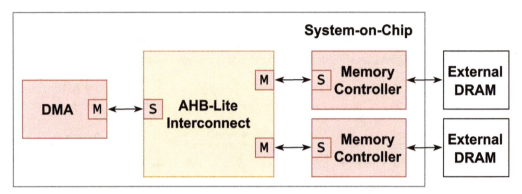

Figure 5.30 Half-bandwidth DMA streaming system with single AHB-Lite interface

Ideally, the DMA unit should be able to **stream** all of the data from the first memory to the second using the interconnect's **full bandwidth**, as represented in Figure 5.31. This would involve reading a block of data from the first memory and storing it in a buffer inside the DMA unit, and then starting to read the next block of data from the first memory while **simultaneously** writing the block stored in the DMA's internal buffer to the second memory; the process repeats itself until all the blocks have been transferred.

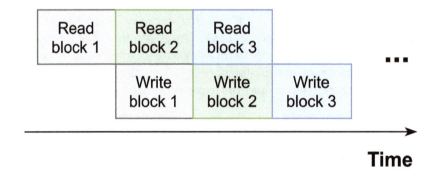

Figure 5.31 Idealized full-bandwidth streaming

However, such an execution regime is impossible with the AHB-Lite bus. Recall that the AHB-Lite interface exposes a single HWRITE signal whose polarity conveys whether the associated transfer corresponds to a read or a write. If the HWRITE signal is currently being asserted to issue a write transfer, the same signal cannot simultaneously be deasserted to issue a read transfer (as would be required by the scheme in Figure 5.31). A DMA unit with an AHB-Lite interface can thus read or write at any given time, but not both, and therefore can only achieve 50% of the interconnect's full bandwidth at best. Figure 5.32 shows what the execution of the memory copy actually looks like with an AHB-Lite interface.

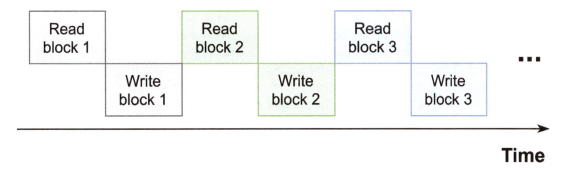

Figure 5.32 AHB-Lite half-bandwidth streaming

We could circumvent this half-bandwidth limitation by adding a second AHB-Lite interface to the DMA unit, as shown in Figure 5.33. Now, using one interface for reading and the second for writing ensures that the full interconnect bandwidth is utilized. However, we argue that replicating the AHB-Lite interface on the DMA unit is not the correct way to resolve this problem. As we stated in Chapter 4, a good interconnect design will achieve the performance goals of the designers while not getting in their way when it comes to implementing their subsystems independently, whereas a poorly designed interconnect will often force designers to spend time finding workarounds to its limitations. Replicating an AHB-Lite interface on a DMA unit to get around the half-bandwidth limitation of the interconnect is, therefore, not the way to go.

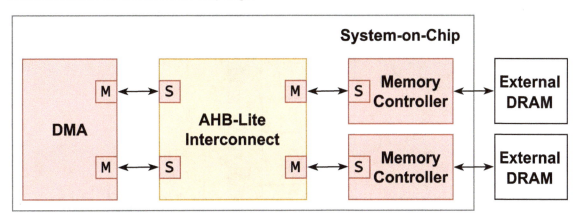

Figure 5.33 Full-bandwidth DMA streaming system with multiple AHB-Lite interfaces

Thus, to support full bandwidth utilization, an interconnect should provide **decoupled read and write interfaces** out-of-the-box if it is to be a truly high-performance interface suitable for a variety of systems.

This completes our survey of the major design flaws in AHB-Lite that need to be addressed within a better-performing successor. Now that we have a clearer view of the design choices that limit AHB-Lite's performance and the principles and approaches that could be used to address them, let's dig into how the AXI interconnect tackles these issues from a practical perspective.

5.4.2 AXI High-level Structure

As for our previous coverage of the AHB-Lite protocol, we start with some terminology. The AXI interconnect protocol uses the same terminology as AHB-Lite to refer to a requestor (the **manager**) and a completer (a **subordinate**). We now continue by discussing AXI's high-level design and how it enables **transparent** auto-pipelining of the interconnect to achieve higher clock frequencies than those available with AHB-Lite. As we discussed earlier, pipelining the interconnect is only transparent to a manager and subordinate if all of the signals in the pipeline flow in the same direction. To achieve this, AXI therefore decomposes its interface into five separate unidirectional **channels**. Each channel consists of multiple signals and conveys a specific type of information from the manager to the subordinate, or vice versa. These five AXI channels are responsible for conveying:

- write address/control information

- write data

- write responses

- read address/control information

- read data/responses.

Figure 5.34 provides a high-level overview of the AXI interconnect and its channels.

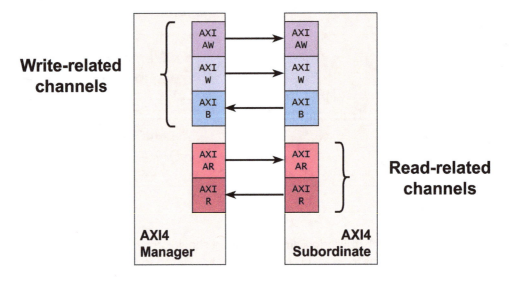

Figure 5.34 High-level AXI manager and subordinate interfaces with their five unidirectional channels

Table 5.9 lists the characteristics of each AXI channel. Just as with its predecessors, all AXI interface signals are named in such a way as to make them easier to identify, here beginning with a channel-specific prefix.

Table 5.9 The AXI interconnect's five unidirectional channels

Channel name	Source	Target	No. of signals	Channel prefix
Write Address	Manager	Subordinate	11	AW
Write Data	Manager	Subordinate	5	W
Write Response	Subordinate	Manager	4	B
Read Address	Manager	Subordinate	11	AR
Read Data/response	Subordinate	Manager	6	R

When first encountering AXI, students often expect the protocol to have just two channels: one for reading and one for writing. However, recall that the previous AMBA buses all provided a mechanism for a transfer response to be returned to the manager such that it can determine the success of an operation. The AXI protocol also provides support for transfer responses, which necessarily flow from the subordinate to the manager, and therefore have a directional conflict with the manager-originating nature of transfers. If the transfer responses shared the same channels as their transfer-related associates it would prevent automatic pipelining of the interconnect, which is why they are afforded a separate channel.

It is also common for students to wonder why there are three write-related channels when there are just two read-related ones. The reason is that data in a write transfer flows from the manager to the subordinate, but the response flows in the opposite direction, so a dedicated unidirectional channel is required for the write response such that it can be automatically pipelined if necessary. However, in terms of read transfers, data is already flowing from the subordinate to the manager and so the signals necessary for the response can simply be added to this read data channel because they flow in the same direction.

At this stage it is easy to see that AXI supports simultaneous write and read transfers because it exposes discrete channels for each transfer type. Thus, we have seen, just with our high-level view of the AXI interconnect, how the interface addresses two of the four AHB-Lite performance bottlenecks described in the preceding section: (1) support for simultaneous write and read transfers, and (2) transparent interconnect pipelining.

Next, we will look in more detail at the various channels to see how AXI solves the other two performance bottlenecks identified, that is, transfer reordering and unaligned transfers. But first, we need to describe the basic format of an AXI transfer.

5.4.3 Basic Transfers
The AHB-Lite protocol defined a strict one-cycle relationship between the address and data phases of a transfer. The AXI protocol relaxes this constraint and allows looser coordination between events occurring on the different channels. The most typical timing dependencies between channels for read and write transfers are shown in Figure 5.35, where the (red) numbers above each arrow indicate the overall

ordering of events. Note that there is no ordering of events between the three write-related channels (at the top of the figure) and the two read-related channels (at the bottom of the figure) and hence we can use the same initial value (i.e. 1) for the temporality of events that occur on both sets of channels.

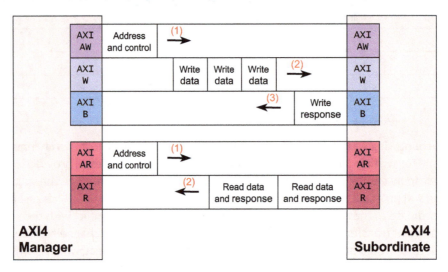

Figure 5.35 Typical AXI transfers and inter-channel event ordering

Thus, as illustrated in Figure 5.35, write transfers generally begin with the manager sending address and control information to the subordinate through the write address (AW) channel. Upon acceptance by the subordinate, the manager then sends the intended write data to the subordinate through the write data (W) channel. Finally, the subordinate responds with a **single** write response (on the B channel) to convey the success or failure of the **entire** transfer[20].

Read transfers start similarly, with the manager sending address and control information to the subordinate, now through the read address (AR) channel[21]. Upon acceptance by the subordinate, the manager then receives the read data and a transfer response for **each** beat of the transfer. This contrasts with write transfers, which involve a single response for the entire transfer. The reason for these beat-driven responses is that the manager needs to be notified if an error occurs during a read transfer so that it does not propagate the error downstream if, for example, it is consuming the received data and performing computations accordingly. In write transfers, it is the subordinate that decides whether a multi-beat write ends up changing the subordinate's state, so a single transfer response is sufficient to convey this information back to the manager.

Figure 5.36 delves into the channels of the AXI interface and shows all the signals that they support. In AXI, just as for its predecessors, a manager–subordinate pair is driven by the same clock. However, unlike its predecessors, AXI exposes a wholly symmetrical interface between the manager–subordinate pair because the two share the same signal set[22].

---

[20] Single-beat and multi-beat (i.e. burst) transfers both receive a single write response.
[21] The read address channel has an identical structure to the write address channel.
[22] Recall that AHB-Lite and APB both exposed asymmetric designs, in which managers/requesters and subordinates/completers had different interfaces.

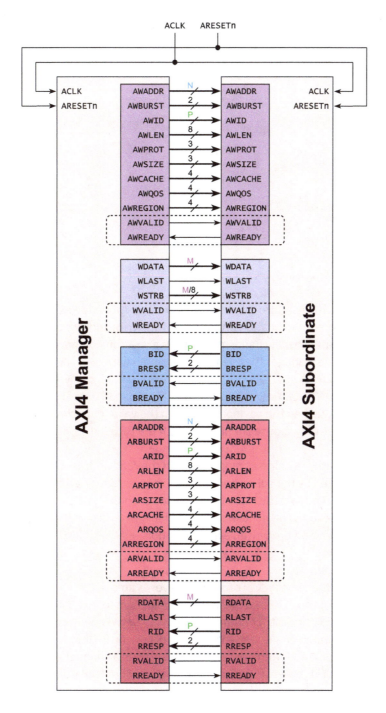

Figure 5.36 AXI manager and subordinate interfaces; flow-control signals are shown with a dashed border

Now that we have seen what signals each of the channels support, let's look at how simple write and read transfers are performed in AXI: the left-hand and right-hand sides of Figure 5.37 show, respectively, the waveforms of single-beat write and read transfers.

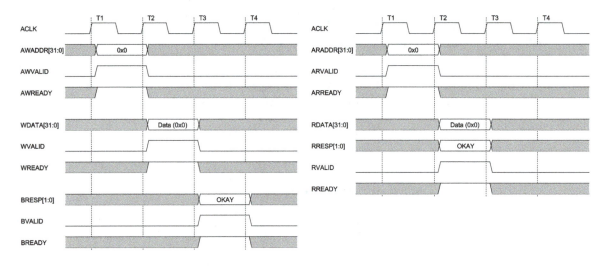

Figure 5.37 AXI single-beat write (left) and read (right) transfers

The write transfer begins with an address being issued on the write address channel through the AWADDR bus. The control information provided on this write address bus is accepted by the subordinate if the channel-specific handshake signals are asserted, that is, both AWVALID and AWREADY are high. The manager then sends its intended data over the write data channel, specifically through the WDATA bus. Like the write address channel, the write data channel has its own handshake signals (WVALID and WREADY) and the payload data is accepted when the handshake succeeds. Finally, when the payload data from the write data channel is accepted, a write response is sent over the write response channel through the BRESP bus.

The read transfer begins with an address being issued on the read address channel through the ARADDR bus. Once accepted by the subordinate, it returns the requested data over the read data channel through the RDATA bus. At the same time, a read response for this beat is returned on the RRESP bus. The standard ready-valid handshaking mechanism occurs on the read address and read data channels, much as it does on the write-related channels.

5.4.4 Elastic Inter-channel Timing

In Figure 5.35, we showed the most *typical* ordering of events among the various AXI channels for write and read transfers, but this does not mean that all transfers follow the same event sequencing. Indeed, we said that AXI avoids the strict timing relationship between interface signals imposed by AHB-Lite by relaxing the dependencies between events occurring in different AXI channels. What does this actually mean in practice? Remember that all signals in a channel are synchronous with their channel-specific valid signal. It is therefore correct to reason about the ordering of any combination of signals between channels by reasoning about the ordering of their corresponding valid signal.

Figure 5.38 attempts to explain the timing relationships between the read address channel and the read data channel, and the write address channel and the write data/response channels, for a *single* transfer. The figure uses single- and double-tipped arrows to represent the following semantics:

▪ A single-tipped arrow points to a signal that must be asserted **before or after** the signal at the start of the arrow.

▪ A double-tipped arrow points to a signal that must only be asserted **after** the assertion of the signal at the start of the arrow.

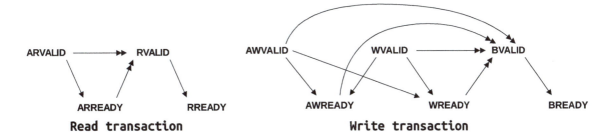

Figure 5.38 AXI protocol handshake dependencies, reproduced from AXI specification (source: Reproduced with permission from Arm Ltd)

Let's start with the relationship between the read address channel and the read data channel. Basically, a manager that asks to read something from a subordinate cannot expect to receive the data before the subordinate has seen the requested address. We therefore conclude that RVALID must come *after* ARVALID. However, there is no specific ordering defined for the ready and valid signals within a single channel and the ready signals can easily come before or after the corresponding valid signals.

Next, consider the relationship between the write address and write data channels. Here, the AXI rules differ from those of read transfers because the write data is permitted to arrive before the subordinate has accepted the associated control information from the address channel, as shown in Figure 5.39. This means that a subordinate can accept the payload of a write transfer before knowing where it should be written! However, the write response validity *always comes after* the validities of the write address channel and the write data channel.

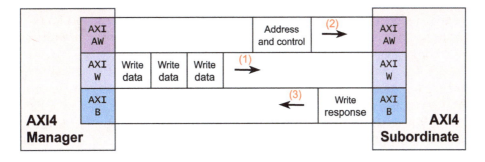

Figure 5.39 Alternative write-transfer ordering with write address following write data

Note, however, that it is uncommon for managers to drive the write data channel before the write address channel, and more common for these two channels to be driven concurrently or for the write data channel to be driven after the write address channel. Nevertheless, when developing managers and subordinates, it's important to be aware of AXI's relaxed channel ordering so that one constructs state machines that will handle the various channels in such a way that all orderings permitted by the interconnect are taken into account.

5.4.5 AXI Transfer-ordering Model

The dependencies shown in Figure 5.38 only apply to signals of the *same* transfer, and do not reflect any relationship between signals from *different* transfers. In particular, there is no relationship between the AxVALID (i.e. AWVALID or ARVALID) signal from one transfer (which conveys the manager's request for a fresh transfer) and the BRESP or RRESP signals of a previous transfer (which convey the "end" of that transfer). This means that a manager can request a new transfer just by asserting AxVALID and waiting for the subordinate to acknowledge the write or read address channel, without having received a response for any previous transfer. Thus AXI supports outstanding transfers.

The AXI interconnect also supports transfer identifiers, so that responses can be reordered by subordinates if necessary. Transfer identifiers are defined by the manager in the write/read address channel when issuing a transfer through the AWID or ARID buses. The transfer identifier is relayed to the subordinate by an intermediate interconnect component and the subordinate then reflects this identifier back to the manager when it replies so that the manager can associate the data received on the write response or read data channels with its original request. Write responses are identified via the BID bus and read responses via the RID bus. AXI has adopted a convention that transfers with the same identifier must be replied to in the order in which they were requested, but transfers with different identifiers can be replied to in any order. Thus, managers can enforce ordering if they so wish by assigning the same identifier to all transfers, or can enable reordering by assigning different identifiers to transfers.

However, if we look more closely at the complete set of interconnect signals shown in Figure 5.36, we can see that while the write address, read address, write response, and read data channels all contain a transfer identifier, the *write data channel* does not. In fact, AXI does not support write data interleaving because there is no mechanism by which a manager can determine whether or not a subordinate supports it[23]. It is also difficult for subordinates to reorder writes and much simpler for a manager to do so before it issues the requests on the bus. Therefore, AXI support for reordering among the write channels is limited to the write response channel (commensurate with its support for read response reordering).

We illustrate simple write and read response reorderings in Figure 5.40. For clarity, we assume that no backpressure is applied on the AXI channels, so the ready signals are assumed to be high and are not shown. The left-hand side of Figure 5.40 shows a waveform for a reordered write response. The write transfer begins at time T1 with the manager issuing a target address on the AWADDR bus and simultaneously assigning an identifier (0x1 in our example) to the transfer through the AWID bus. However, before receiving the corresponding write response, the manager issues a second target

---

[23] For the sake of completeness, note that AXI3 supported write interleaving and had a WID bus in the write data channel for this purpose. However, because, as stated, managers have no way of determining whether a subordinate supports interleaving, a manager needed to know in advance to which subordinates it could issue interleaved writes. This broke the modularity principle, with the manager needing to know subordinate implementation detail and unable to rely solely on the subordinate's interface for communication. Therefore, support for write data interleaving was dropped in AXI4.

address, at T2, with another identifier (0x2). In this example, the two transfer responses are reordered by the subordinate and returned at times T4 and T5. The read transfer shown on the right-hand side of Figure 5.40 follows a very similar sequence of steps, the only difference being that the read response is provided through the read data channel rather than a separate response channel.

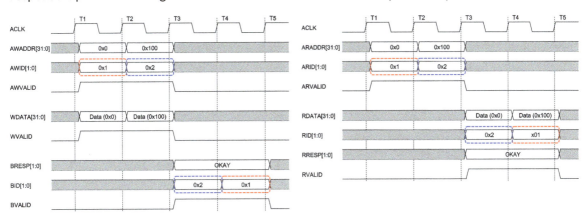

Figure 5.40 AXI single-beat write (left) and read (right) response reorderings

5.4.6 Unaligned Data Transfers Using Byte Strobes

AXI supports unaligned write transfers using the same byte strobe mechanism that we introduced earlier in this section. The write strobe is conveyed through the WSTRB signal in the write data channel, as represented in Figure 5.41. The write strobe has byte-level granularity and therefore has size $M/8$, where M corresponds to the width of the WDATA bus in bits.

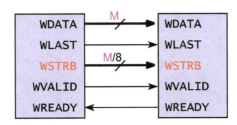

Figure 5.41 AXI write-channel byte strobe signal (WSTRB)

Figure 5.42 shows an example of the write strobe's operation when attempting to write a 16-bit payload to address 0x1. The example proceeds to first read the contents of the target memory location, then writes to the location with a narrow byte strobe, before reading the target address again to verify/illustrate the byte strobe's effect.

The AXI protocol requires that addresses issued on the write and read address channels be aligned to the data bus boundary. Thus, the example begins with a read transfer to address 0x0 (rather than the 0x1 target). The 32-bit word contained at this address is 0xFFFF_FFFF. A write transfer follows with payload data 0xDEAD_BEEF and a write strobe of 0b0110. Because only bits 1 and 2 of the write strobe are asserted, the subordinate will select the second and third bytes (i.e. bits 8–23) of the write payload 0xDEAD_BEEF as the data to be written (i.e. 0xADBE). Finally, reading back from address 0x0 returns 0xFFAD_BEFF and we can see that only the middle bytes of the original address content have been modified by the write transfer.

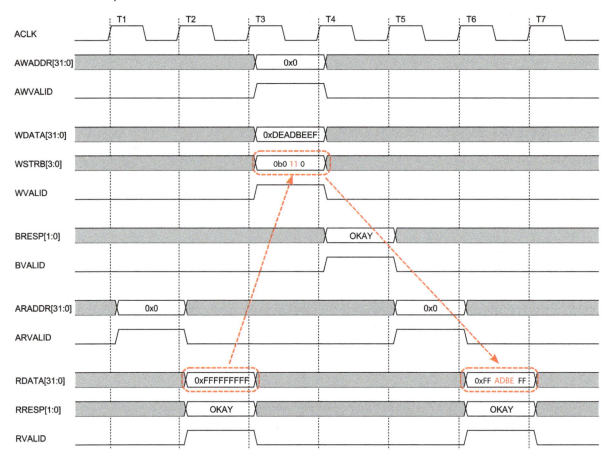

Figure 5.42 AXI unaligned write transfer

5.4.7 Bursts

The AXI protocol supports multiple types of bursts, some of which are already familiar from the AHB-Lite protocol. Three types of information are needed when requesting a burst transfer in AXI, all of which are communicated over the write and read address channels:

1. The burst **type** is communicated through the 2-bit AxBURST signal and can take the values INCR, WRAP, or FIXED. The INCR and WRAP burst types were already available in the AHB-Lite protocol and their functionality is unchanged in AXI, whereas the FIXED burst type is newly introduced with the AXI protocol.

   a. The INCR type corresponds to a simple incrementing burst and is the default type of burst, in which the addresses for successive beats simply increment.

    b. The WRAP type corresponds to a wrapping burst, which simply wraps around when incrementing over particular address (or block-size) boundaries, as we have already seen (Section 5.3.1.3).

    c. The FIXED type corresponds to a fixed burst. A fixed burst simply keeps the target address of successive beats constant and is most useful when trying to perform a burst to a fixed location in the address space, such as a FIFO buffer[24].

2. The burst **length** in beats is conveyed through the 8-bit AxLEN buses and allows managers to specify burst lengths of between 1 and 256 beats. Wrapped bursts are the exception here, and can only be used when the burst length is 2, 4, 8, or 16 beats and the start address is aligned to the size of each transfer. Wrapping bursts are primarily used for interfacing with a processor's cache, and 16 beats are generally more than enough to fill the cache lines typical of modern processors. Note that the AxLEN buses are zero-based and the value provided on the bus therefore corresponds to a transfer of AxLEN+1 beats. Thus, an AxLEN value of 0b1111_1111 corresponds to 256 beats.

3. The **byte size** of a beat is sent through the 3-bit AxSIZE buses. AXI retains the same beat size options as AHB-Lite, namely between 1 and 128 bytes, in power-of-two increments.

One improvement over AHB-Lite's handling of bursts is that AXI only requires the first address of a burst to be specified by the manager and it is then the subordinate's responsibility to auto-increment the address on successive beats. If the manager had to specify the address of each beat explicitly, then the address channel could not be used for conveying outstanding transfers because it would be busy sending beat addresses. Given a base address, the transfer type, the number of beats, and the size of each beat, subordinates have all the information required to automatically increment addresses as each beat is received.

Because the write data channel is designed to be independent of the write address channel, the write data channel includes a WLAST signal to inform the subordinate of the end of a write transfer. This signal is asserted on the last beat of a transfer and allows a subordinate's write data channel to identify the end of a transfer without having to be coupled to the write address channel. Similarly, the read data channel also supports an RLAST signal so that it too is decoupled from its corresponding address channel.

Finally, note that, unlike AHB-Lite, there is no burst transfer of undefined length in AXI. Such transfers are not typically performed by managers and subordinates that are using a memory-mapped interface, being favored instead by point-to-point connections between specific accelerators in a system. The AMBA 4 specification therefore chose to exclude undefined-length bursts from the AXI protocol and relocate them in a dedicated protocol more suited to such accelerators, the AXI4-Stream protocol. This latter is beyond the scope of our coverage and we refer readers to the AXI4-Stream specification for more details. Another advantage of transferring undefined-length bursts into another protocol is that there is less ambiguity in AXI's semantics because there is now only one way to specify each type of transfer, whereas AHB-Lite had "corner cases" in which the same type of transfer could be encoded in two different ways (for example, a single-word burst via type SINGLE or INCR).

---

[24] FIFOs normally expose a single address at which the next element in the buffer can be read from or written to. Fixed bursts are therefore particularly useful for rapidly filling or draining a hardware FIFO over the bus.

Figure 5.43 shows an example of a five-beat incrementing burst-write transfer at address 0x0, and Figure 5.44 shows a similar example for a burst-read transfer. Both examples first define the characteristics of the burst in their respective address channels by driving the AxADDR, AxBURST, AxLEN, and AxSIZE buses. Remember that the AxLEN bus is zero-based, and thus a value of 4 means that five beats are requested. Notice that an address for the transfer is only transmitted by the manager at the outset; thereafter, the subordinate automatically determines that successive words provided on the write data channel must correspond to an appropriately auto-incremented address. A similar process applies to read transfers.

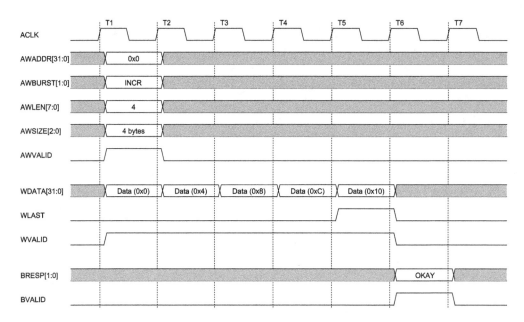

Figure 5.43 AXI burst-write transfer

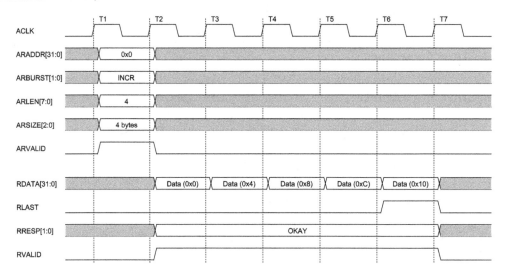

Figure 5.44 AXI burst-read transfer

5.4.8 Additional Signals

AXI defines a number of advanced signals that are beyond the scope of this introductory text. We provide brief descriptions here for reference, but we encourage readers to refer to the AMBA 4 specification for more details:

- Transfer responses in AXI have been extended from AHB-Lite's 1-bit signal to a 2-bit bus and can take one of four values (OKAY, EXOKAY, SLVERR, and DECERR) to convey more accurate status responses to the manager.

- The AXI protocol splits AHB-Lite's 4-bit HPROT bus into a 3-bit AxPROT bus and a 4-bit AxCACHE bus. The AxPROT signals basically convey the protection type of the transfer (effectively using the three low-order bits of HPROT), while the AxCACHE signals convey how transactions can progress through the system (whether they can be split into smaller pieces, buffered, etc.).

- AXI adds support for QoS in the interconnect, through the AxQOS buses. In basic terms, QoS allows an interconnect to assign priorities to different transfers from the same manager and gives the manager a finer-grained level of control over the performance of a system.

- AXI does not support locked transfers because implementing this feature has a significant effect on the complexity of the interconnect and on its ability to provide quality-of-service (QoS) guarantees[25]. Thus, AXI does not contain a mechanism to allow exclusive access to a subordinate and managers must rely on higher-level semantics such as software semaphores for this purpose.

- AXI supports the notion of a *region* in the address space through the AxREGION buses. Regions basically allow a subordinate to provide multiple logical interfaces via the same physical interface. For example, a subordinate might exhibit different behaviors in different regions by providing read-only access through one region, but read-write access via another region.

5.4.9 AXI-Lite Interconnect Protocol

The AMBA 4 specification introduced a "light" variant of AXI that is more suitable for control access to simple register-based interfaces. This lighter variant of AXI is called AXI-Lite and is the APB-equivalent of the AXI protocol family. That said, why would one use AXI-Lite given that APB already exists? Well, the main problem with APB was that a bridge is needed to translate pipelined AHB-Lite transfers into the non-pipelined state-machine-based APB protocol, because the two protocols were fundamentally incompatible. AXI-Lite eliminates the need for such a bridge by adopting the same interface as its higher-performance AXI counterpart and then removing the signals that are not needed for the type of transfers for which AXI-Lite is intended. Thus, AXI-Lite simplifies the designer's task compared to APB, because he or she need only be familiar with one protocol to connect all of the various subsystems in their SoC. We can summarize the AXI-Lite interface in a single phrase: it is a trimmed-down version of AXI that only supports full-width, in-order, aligned transfers of 32- or 64-bit size.

---

[25] AXI3 did have support for locked transfers through an AxLOCK signal, but this was dropped in AXI4.

The biggest changes in AXI-Lite compared to the full AXI interface are in the write and read address channels:

■ Because all transfers are only a single beat long, the AxLEN and AxBURST signals have been removed from the interface.

■ Similarly, AxSIZE has also been dropped because the size of a transfer can be determined by the physical width of the bus.

■ The AxID buses have been eliminated because register interfaces follow peripheral-specific behavior and accesses to the peripheral must be done in the same order as that requested by the manager to guarantee that the peripheral behaves as expected; thus, there is no need for reordering.

■ Because, by definition, single-beat transfers cannot be split and so cannot be buffered and responded to by the interconnect (rather than the subordinate), the AxCACHE buses have also been dropped.

■ Finally, quality-of-service, that is, prioritizing certain transfers over others, does not make sense for a register-based interface and the AxQOS buses have also been removed.

On the data channel side, the only change is the dropping of the WLAST and RLAST signals, no longer needed because all AXI-Lite transfers are a single beat in length.

The resulting AXI-Lite interface is shown in Figure 5.45; it is a very simple protocol to present because it just consists of a reduced set of the original AXI protocol signals. Everything else in relation to the protocol is, therefore, effectively identical, minus the functionality excluded by the removal of the various signals described above. Thus, the operation of the AXI-Lite protocol can be summarized with the single-beat transfer examples presented earlier in Figure 5.37. Translating a single-beat transfer from an AXI manager into an equivalent AXI-Lite transfer becomes trivial, because the wires missing in the AXI-Lite interface can simply be ignored by the AXI interconnect when forwarding the transfer to an AXI-Lite subordinate.

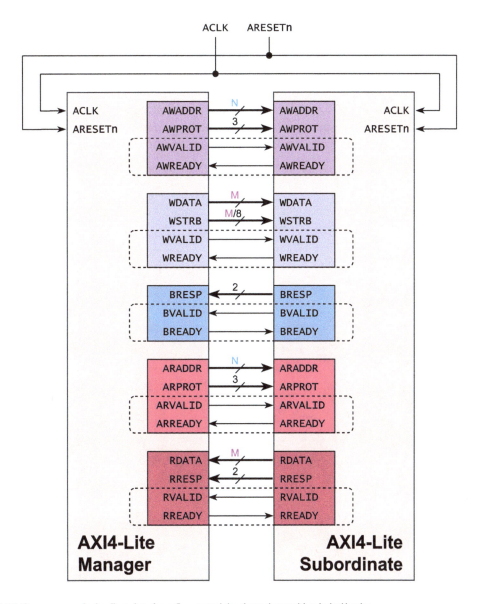

Figure 5.45 AXI-Lite manager and subordinate interfaces; flow-control signals are shown with a dashed border

5.4.10 Conclusion

In conclusion, the AMBA 4 AXI protocol family caters to the versatile interconnection needs of a SoC. On the one hand, the AXI protocol is a high-bandwidth interface that supports transparent pipelining, variably sized transfers, long bursts, transfer reordering, unaligned transfers, and many more features. On the other hand, its lightweight counterpart, the AXI-Lite interface, consists of a reduced set of AXI signals that makes it easy to implement simple control interfaces. Together, the AXI and AXI-Lite interfaces allow a designer to deal with just a single interconnect for all of their needs.

Finally, this is perhaps an appropriate place to convey a drop of wisdom. Looking back, it would be easy to be overwhelmed when first encountering an interface such as the AXI interconnect, boasting as it does such a large number of signals. However, once the principles behind its functionality and design are understood, the interconnect becomes quite simple to digest, especially given its symmetry and modularity. If there's one takeaway to give to budding engineers, it's not to learn things by heart but instead to always strive to understand the principles that lead to a particular object being designed as it is. Even the most complex designs can be readily understood through a principled approach and it is not uncommon for things to be much simpler than they first appear once this is adopted!

Chapter 6

Interfacing with the
External World

In the previous two chapters, we have studied the communications that must be managed within a SoC. However, given their typical deployment within embedded devices, another fundamental aspect of SoCs is their ability to interface with the world beyond the chip, sometimes referred to as "the real world"! In this chapter, we consider the basis of such connectivity, including the underlying mechanisms and protocols that are involved, before going on to review the vast array of potential communication forms and protocols, from serial wires to wireless networks (with a little bit of history too), that a SoC designer might have to take into consideration when it comes to implementing a SoC in a real-world situation.

This chapter will answer many questions that relate to the real world external to the SoC itself. Most of these connections are made through programmable interfaces. This chapter will answer the following questions, among many others.

1. *What are serial communications?*

2. *What are UARTs, the SPI, I²C, 1-Wire, and CAN physical connections?*

3. *How can we code bits in the physical world?*

4. *How can we recover a clock from a data stream?*

5. *What is the 8b/10b protocol and what is its coding?*

6. *What is bit stuffing?*

7. *What are the different USB standard and connections?*

8. *What were the RS-232, RS-422 and RS-485 specifications?*

9. *What are the debugging connections JTAG and SWDIO?*

10. *What are the wired and wireless Ethernet connexions?*

6.1 External Bus Architectures

Many microcontroller-based systems involve connections to the outside world, mediated by programmable interfaces, as illustrated in Figure 6.1. Having addressed the internal communications of SoCs in the preceding two chapters, we now turn our attention to these external communications. We start by studying serial connections and some of the basic bit-coding mechanisms used to transfer information over them, before looking at the physical and data-link layers of some widely used serial communication protocols. We will end by looking at some of the wireless, radio frequency (RF)-based connections that are now in common use too, considering the principles behind them and the scope and extent of the data transfers that they support.

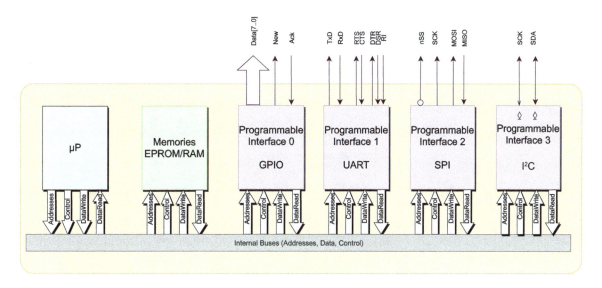

Figure 6.1 A general microcontroller schematic showing a variety of external connections

The microprocessor (µP) in a microcontroller makes use of one or more internal transfer buses. In the microcontroller of Figure 6.1, there are separate internal buses for addresses, data and control signals. Every device on the SoC that is associated with the microprocessor, whether (as in this case) they are memories or programmable interfaces, needs to be interfaced to these buses, which typically involve parallel, synchronous (clock-driven) communication, just as we have described in Chapters 4 and 5.

However, when a SoC needs to communicate with external devices, as is very often the case, such as captors, actuators, forms of external memory, or other computing systems, then further links are necessary and are very commonly implemented via serial, asynchronous communication, which dispenses with parallel buses in favor of a slower data rate and a minimal use of wires. This form of communication is the subject of this chapter.

Figure 6.2 is a high-level view of the types of device with which a SoC or microcontroller is likely to communicate on a serial level. The figure also provides an indication of the number of signals or wires that are involved in these various serial communications, which are obviously far fewer than would be involved in the parallel connections used for high-throughput comms within the SoC itself.

In practice, the microprocessor at the heart of a SoC will not have direct connections to these serial peripherals. Instead, there are specialized modules to handle the communications involved, and these modules are connected to the CPU via the same set of internal parallel buses as used for other SoC components. Thus, Figure 6.3 illustrates a specific SoC from the Cortex-M4F-based MSP432 family of Texas Instruments (as seen in Chapter 3's case study) in which two specific modules (ringed in blue in the figure) have been incorporated to handle external serial communications. Here, they are referred to as eUSCI_A and eUSCI_B modules and they allow many combinations of serial line configuration; moreover, they may be replicated many times on the same device.

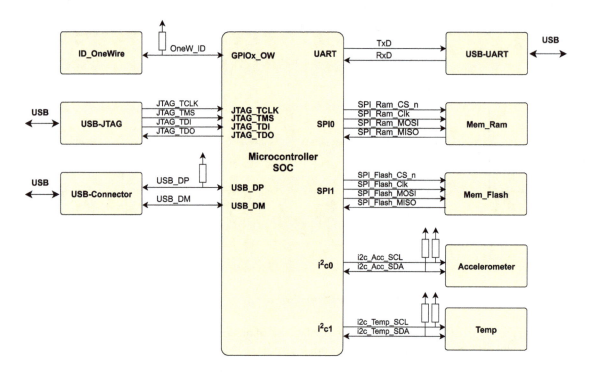

Figure 6.2 High-level view of serial links commonly used by SoCs

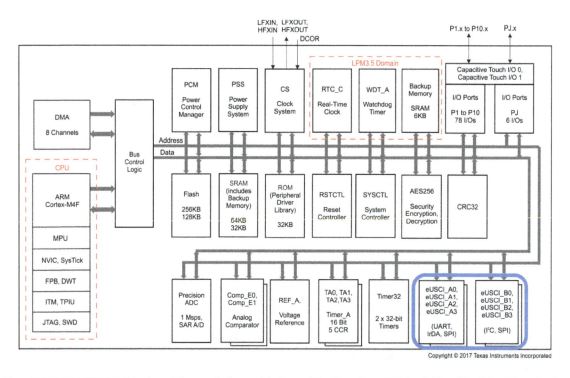

Copyright © 2017 Texas Instruments Incorporated

Figure 6.3 TI MSP432P401R SoC showing serial communications modules (source: https://www.ti.com/lit/ds/symlink/msp432p401r.pdf. Reproduced with permission from Texas Instruments.)

6.2 Serial Interfacing Techniques

When two systems must communicate, the number of wires involved is very significant to the interconnection. Transferring data one bit at a time in a serial manner is cost-effective in terms of wire cost, particularly when it comes to long-distance connections or, at the other end of the scale, the complexity and space involved in implementing them on a printed circuit board. With improvements in managing impedance, and the use of differential lines, high-speed serial communications devices can now enable links at speeds ranging from kilobits per second to tens of gigabits per second, depending on the protocols and physical layers involved.

When it comes to microcontrollers, as we have already seen, it is necessary to use specific programmable interfaces to customize the serial interfaces to match those needed by different peripherals, with the connections to these programmable interfaces using internal parallel buses for addresses, control and data. As illustrated in Figure 6.4, a programmable interface is seen from the microprocessor as a set of accessible registers, a subject that we will study in more detail in Chapter 7. Some of these registers are both readable and writable (specified as R/W) by the CPU, while others may be read-only (RO) or write-only (WO). All such programmable interfaces will be specific to the manufacturer and the particular SoC, so when using these devices, it's the programmer's responsibility to familiarize themselves with the specifics of the datasheets that pertain to the unit and/or peripheral concerned.

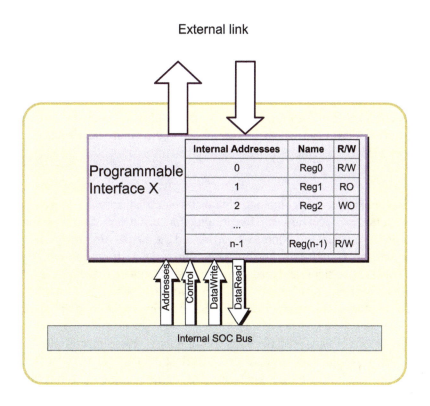

Figure 6.4 Block diagram of programmable interface and register model

6.2.1 The ISO Open Systems Interconnection (OSI) Model

Over the course of the next few sections, we will look at the development of some of the most commonly used serial links. However, before we go any further we should mention the Open Systems Interconnection (OSI) model. First developed in the 1970s to promote the characterization, standardization, and interoperability of communications functions for networks and computers, it was adopted and further developed by the International Organization for Standardization (ISO) in the 1980s. The model abstracts data flows into seven architectural layers, from the physical level of bit transfer to the application level of resource sharing and information exchange, to facilitate the description of data transfers, as shown in Table 6.1.

Table 6.1 OSI Model of ISO

Layer		Protocol data unit (PDU)	Function
Host layers	7. Application		High-level APIs, including resource sharing, remote file access
	6. Presentation	Data	Translation of data between a networking service and an application; including character encoding, data compression and encryption/decryption
	5. Session		Managing communication sessions, i.e. continuous exchange of information in the form of multiple back-and-forth transmissions between two nodes
	4. Transport	Segment, Datagram	Reliable transmission of data segments between points on a network, including segmentation, acknowledgement and multiplexing
Media layers	3. Network	Packet	Structuring and managing a multi-node network, including addressing, routing and traffic control
	2. Data link	Frame	Reliable transmission of data frames between two nodes connected by a physical layer
	1. Physical	Symbol	Transmission and reception of raw bit streams over a physical medium

Section 6.2 largely concerns itself with the lowest two layers of this representation, with some references to the network layer too, which we consider in slightly more detail in Section 6.3. Note that, in practice, not all layers are implemented in any given interconnection.

6.2.2 Morse Code

Historically, the first application of a combined digital and electrical connection was the use, in the 1840s, of the "Morse" protocol between two long-distance stations. What became known as Morse code, named after Samuel F. B. Morse who invented the single-wire telegraph, was based on two signs: a dot and a dash. A dot is one time unit in length, and a dash is three, with a single time unit left between consecutive signs, and three time units left between the characters formed from combinations of up to five signs (see Figure 6.5). Once a word has been thus formed, a gap of seven time units is left to the start of the next word. It is, in basic terms, a time-modulation protocol.

In Morse code, the number of signs used to codify the alphabet varies substantially. Thus, the letter "E" is just one dot, and a "T" is just one dash, whereas the less commonly used letters "J", "Q" and "Y" all involve differing orders of three dashes and a dot. The longest codification, in terms of time, is that of the number "0", involving five dashes. The code is optimized for the English language. In electrical terms, the code consists of just an open or closed contact on the line, translated into a sound at the receiver's end.

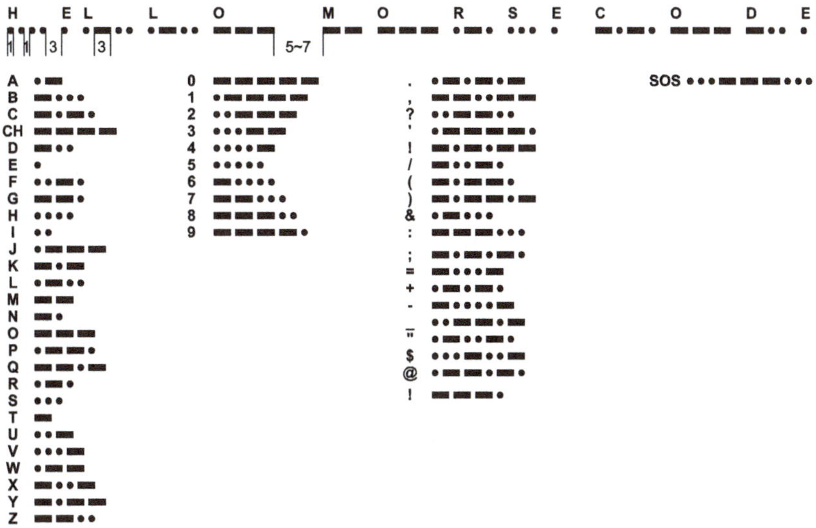

Figure 6.5 Morse codes

We can represent this time-based code in a binary format if we say that a dot will be represented by a '1', while a dash will be '111' because it is activated for three units of time, and the gaps or silences between codes, characters and words can be represented, respectively, as '0', '000', and '0000000'. Figure 6.6 shows an example of this coding, with inter-character spaces represented by "|" and inter-word spaces by "/".

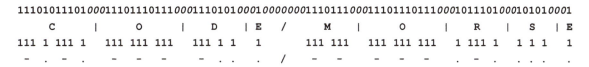

```
11101011101000111011101110001110101000100000001110111000111011101110001011101000101010001
     C      |     O      |    D    | E  /    M    |      O      |    R    |   S   | E
111 1 111 1   111 111 111   111 1 1   1      111 111   111 111 111   1 111 1   1 1 1   1
 -  .  -  .    -   -   -     -  . .   .  /    -   -     -   -   -    .  -  .   . . .   .
```

Figure 6.6 Example of Morse coding in binary format (with English translation)

6.2.3 Bit Coding

Morse code was a reasonably efficient coding but suffered from various drawbacks, particularly when considered for use in binary format in more sophisticated electrical equipment. For example, not all characters are of the same length, meaning that gap characters were a critical component yet represented a significant overhead within the code, and the code is optimized for the English language. Although Morse code still has residual uses, it has been superseded by a series of other coding systems, culminating in the **fixed-length ASCII** (American Standard Code for Information Interchange) code that was developed in the 1960s and remains by far the most widely used code today. This started as a 7-bit binary code, allowing 128 (2^7) characters to be defined, and was subsequently extended to a number of different 8-bit versions that support a variety of additional application- or language-specific character sets (there is more detail of ASCII in the Appendix).

In terms of the transmission of a binary code, at the physical electrical level, there are a large variety of different systems that can be used to represent the zeros and ones of the bit-encoded information, as illustrated in Figure 6.7 and explained in more detail in Table 6.2.

For data to be successfully transmitted on a line, there must be some form of synchronization between the transmitter and the receiver, to ensure that the receiver is sampling the line at the same rate as the sender is altering it, and at the optimal point to minimize interpretation errors. This is often referred to as a "**line code**" and will vary according to the transmission medium involved. One approach is to provide an explicit clock signal in association with the data itself, which is the case in, for example, the SPI protocol or I²C. Sometimes, the timing function is included within the data coding, such as in FM0 and FM1 where there is a transition between every bit and may be another transition in the middle of the bit depending upon whether a 0 or a 1 is being represented, or in the "self-clocking" Manchester code where there is always a transition in the middle of a bit.

In other protocols, the transmitter and receiver must agree on a specific data rate or discover it by analysis of the received data, as in UART transmission.

If a system is able to combine variations in levels, frequencies and/or phases, it gains the potential to encode more bits per unit of time.

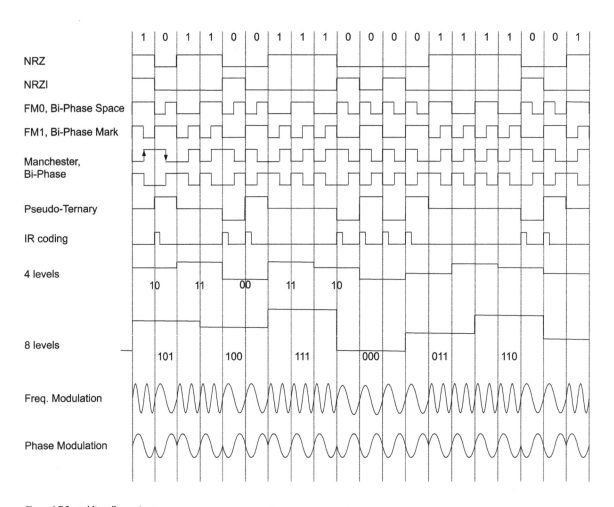

Figure 6.7 Some bit-coding systems

Table 6.2 Bit-coding system regimes/line codes

System	Description	Explanation
NRZ	Non Return to Zero	1 is represented by a high level; 0 by a low level
NRZI	Non Return to Zero Inverted	1 is represented by maintenance of the current level; 0 by inversion of the current level
FM0 or Bi-phase Space FM1 or Bi-phase Mark	Frequency Modulation	Always a transition **between** bits, plus a transition in the **middle** of the bit only if: - a 0 is to be represented (in FM0) - a 1 is to be represented (in FM1). Otherwise, no transition.
Manchester or Bi-phase		Always a transition in the **middle** of the bit: - first part, the transmitted value; - second part, the inverted value.
Pseudo-ternary		3 voltage levels: + / Gnd / – - 1 is always at Gnd - 0 alternates between + and – levels
Multi-level	Group of 2 bits → Group of 3 bits → Group even more bits together	Coding via 4 analog levels (00 ... 11) Coding via 8 analog levels (000 ... 111) Coding via 2^n analog levels
Frequency Modulation	Two different frequencies provide the distinction between a '0' and '1'	Grouping two bits together can be coded with four different frequencies
Phase Modulation	The same frequency is used, but a shift in the phase distinguishes '0' and '1'	Grouping two bits together can be coded with four different phases (0°, 90°, 180°, 270°) on a single time unit

6.2.4 Packet-based Protocols

At a higher level, it is necessary to synchronize the transmission of bit-coded data to the byte or word size used by the computing device, and ensure that the bits are concatenated and organized such that they can be correctly interpreted by the receiver. Thus, the resulting bytes are assembled into payload-containing messages that also include control information to form a "**packet**", as illustrated for two different protocols in Figures 6.8 and 6.9.

If data is to be transmitted over a network, in which there might be many potential recipients, then the intended recipient of a piece of data will generally be identified by an address at the start of the data packet, in the packet's "**header**". The address of the source of the packet is usually included too. Other parameters often follow before the actual data appears. A method for detecting or even correcting possible transmission errors is incorporated into the packet too, most commonly in the form of a "**checksum**" (the result of a pre-agreed calculation reflecting the content and position of the bits or bytes within the packet that can be performed by the recipient and compared to verify correct receipt). The most frequently used calculation is a polynomial division, known as a cyclic redundancy check (CRC).

To delimit the packet, various flags will precede and follow the useful information. These delimiters can, for example, enable a recipient to detect the start of a packet and to synchronize its internal clock for processing the packet.

In most packet-based protocols, the recipient will respond to the receipt of a packet with an **acknowledgement**, sometimes in the form of a simple character, but more often in a special packet, especially in higher-level protocols.

Figure 6.8 shows how data is packaged in the BISYNC protocol, which supports the transmission of **any** data character. The packet includes various delimiters and flags and a two-byte CRC checksum. If the data payload itself includes any of these "special" or reserved characters (e.g. SOH, STX, ETX, DLE), the protocol achieves this by preceding the character with the code for the DLE (Data Link Escape, 0x10) character, which will be removed on receipt (to transmit the DLE code itself, it must be sent twice in succession).

BISYNC Format

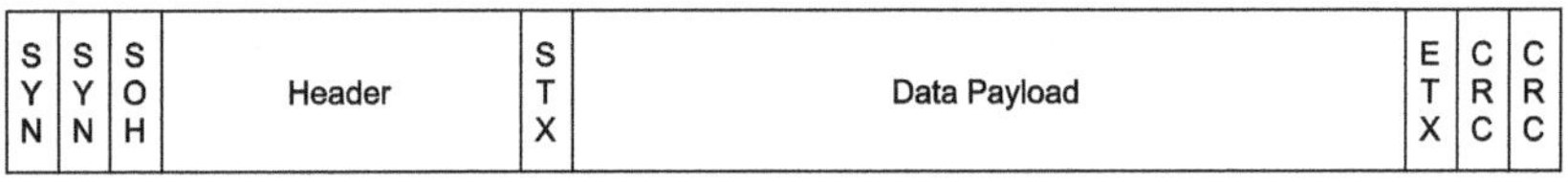

S Y N	S Y N	S O H	Header	S T X	Data Payload	E T X	C R C	C R C

SYN	Synchro	0001 0110	0x16
SOH	Start Of Header	0000 0001	0x01
STX	Start Of Text	0000 0010	0x02
ETX	End Of Text	0000 0011	0x03
CRC	Cyclic Redundancy Check (16 bits)	Polynomial Division on 16 bits	

Figure 6.8 Data packet for BISYNC protocol

Figure 6.9 shows the packet structure used in the SDLC/HDLC protocol. SDLC (Synchronous Data Link Control) was developed in the 1970s by IBM for its SNA (Systems Network Architecture) network protocol, before being modified by ISO to become the HDLC (High-Level Data Link Control). HDLC allows any number of bits in the data part, whereas SDLC constrains this to a byte-multiple. Again, a CRC-based checksum is used for error detection, typically in 16 bits but negotiable to 32 bits, and includes address, control, and data payload in its calculation.

SDLC/HDLC

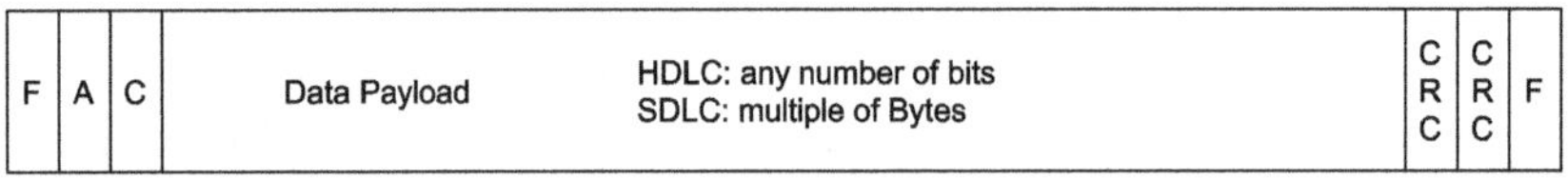

F	A	C	Data Payload	HDLC: any number of bits SDLC: multiple of Bytes	C R C	C R C	F

F	Flag of Synchronization	0111 1110	0x7E
A	Address of Destination	0000 0001	0x01
C	Control	0000 0010	0x02
CRC	Cyclic Redundancy Check (16 bits)	Polynomial Division on 16 bits	

Figure 6.9 SDLC/HDLC packet structure

6.2.4.1   Bit Stuffing

In SDLC/HDLC coding, a technique called "**bit stuffing**" is used to enable transmission of the full set of binary data. Thus, to avoid the interpretation of the bit sequence "0111 1110" (with six consecutive '1's) in the data payload as a packet synchronization (delimitation) **flag** (see Figure 6.9), each time five '1's appear consecutively, an additional '0' is automatically inserted by the sender. This '0' is then removed automatically by the receiver. This ensures that the flag pattern can never occur in normal data, so can be used as a marker for the start and end of a packet without any possibility of being confused with normal data. USB and CAN protocols, which we will look at later in this chapter, use bit stuffing in a similar manner.

Another approach to the suppression within the data field of what would otherwise be interpreted as a flag is to use an **escape code**, as in the BISYNC protocol where, for example, any occurrence of the (synchronization flag) code 0x7E in the data payload is replaced by the sender with 0x7D and 0x5E codes, with the 0x7D flag likewise replaced by 0x7D and 0x5D codes; the receiver then removes and replaces these codes accordingly.

A further application of bit stuffing is the limitation of run lengths in binary transmissions (run-length limitation or RLL), which is designed to limit the number of consecutive bits of the same value being transmitted in one go. For example, if a number of zero bits are transmitted consecutively, the absence of any voltage to sense over a prolonged period means that the receiver risks a loss of synchronization in relation to where one bit ends and the next begins. By using bit stuffing, patterns of one or more bits starting with a '1' are inserted into streams of zeros at specific intervals to enable synchronization to be maintained. Extended streams of binary ones are similarly "stuffed" with zeros to the same end.

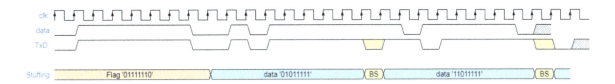

Figure 6.10 Bit stuffing after five consecutive '1's, with the exception of the initial message synchronization flag

Figure 6.10 presents an example of a bit-stuffed transmission, which illustrates bit stuffing in support of synchronization, with a '0' being inserted whenever five '1's have been transmitted: if the binary value 01111110 must be sent, the physically transmitted value will be 011111**0**10; if the value 01111100 is to be sent, the transmitted value will be 011111**0**00.

Two further approaches to **bit synchronization** that are used in various line codes are described in the following sections: data strobe encoding and paired disparity encoding.

6.2.5 Data Strobe Encoding

In some protocols, the data is transmitted in association with another wire called a "**strobe**". The main idea is that by application of a simple logical function a clock can be retrieved from the pair of wires (**Data + Strobe**) because the two signals are designed such that they never change their level at the same time. By performing a simple XOR function at the receiver end, a form of clock is recreated.

Figure 6.11 shows an example of this encoding.

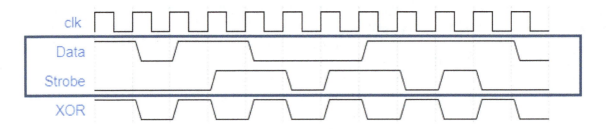

Figure 6.11 Bit synchronization via data strobe encoding

The *clk* signal shown at the top of the figure is used by the transmitter to synchronously generate the *Data* and *Strobe* signals. These have the property that either may change its logical value in one clock cycle, but never both; more precisely, the *Data* signal is transmitted as-is and the *Strobe* signal changes state *if and only if* the *Data* signal stays constant between two data bits. An XOR of the two signals at the receiver end enables construction of a local clock that echoes (but doesn't completely mimic) that of the transmitter and facilitates data recovery. Thus, it can be observed that the *Data* line must be sampled on both edges of the receiver's XOR-generated clock signal. This mechanism is used in, for example, the IEEE 1355, IEEE 1394 (FireWire) and SpaceWire interface standards.

6.2.6 Paired Disparity Encoding (8b/10b Protocols)
Most binary transmissions represent ones with a positive voltage and zeros with an equivalent negative voltage. The combination of these voltages over time represents the DC (direct current) voltage component of the associated signal. Because many electrical signals need to pass through electromagnetic fields (e.g. from transformers), the overall DC value of a signal should be null if the signal is to be successfully transmitted without degradation, especially over any significant distance. Thus, a **DC-balanced** signal is one in which the number of ones is balanced by the number of zeros, and **disparity** refers to the level of imbalance between the two in a bit pattern or signal. Unsurprisingly, the **running disparity** refers to the running total of the disparity of all previously transmitted bits.

If we look at the patterns of the line codes shown in Figure 6.7 above, we can see that some, such as the Manchester bi-phase code, exhibit good DC balance (i.e. have eliminated the DC component) while others do not, relying on other aspects for their accuracy/efficacy. There are a number of ways of *eliminating the DC component* from a signal. As described in Table 6.2, the Manchester code effectively achieves this by means of an inversion in level during the transmission of every single bit, which is known as a **constant-weight** encoding.

A common alternative to this approach is **paired disparity** encoding. The idea behind this is fairly simple: the disparity of each "codeword" is assessed; every codeword that averages to a negative disparity is paired with some other codeword that averages to a positive disparity, and the transmitter makes use of the running disparity to pick the codeword of the pair that will push the overall DC level back towards zero. The receiver is designed such that either codeword of the pair will decode to the same set of data bits.

In practice, this is achieved by taking the combination of source bits of the codeword and generating a longer code, with more bits, via a lookup table. Doing this at byte-level gives rise to **8b/10b coding** in which an 8-bit word becomes a 10-bit symbol, affording us 1024 (2^{10}) possible values with which to design our encoding. The 3b/4b and 5b/6b encodings behave similarly and, in fact, form the basis of the 8b/10b coding, as we will see. More complex 64b/66b and 128b/132b schemes, which provide statistical rather than strict bounds on DC balance, are also in common use but will not be described here.

In the example that we will consider here, two distinct cases of 8b/10b coding are defined, depending upon whether we are dealing with a data transfer or a control signal (e.g. start-of-frame, end-of-frame, and link-level conditions). For data, all 256 (2^8) possible 8-bit inputs give rise to valid codewords, whereas there are only 12 valid control commands.

The 8-bit source is split into two: the five lowest bits are encoded into a 6-bit group (the 5b/6b portion) and the three highest bits are encoded into a 4-bit group (the 3b/4b portion), and these two code groups are concatenated (in reverse) to form the 10-bit symbol that is transmitted on the wire. An example is shown in Table 6.3.

Table 6.3 8b/10b encoding generated from 3b/4b and 5b/6b elements

Value (Decimal/ Hexadecimal)	Value (Binary) 3 bits + 5 bits HGF EDCBA	10-bit Code abcdei fghj	Alternative 10-bit Code abcdei fghj
0 / 00	000 00000	100111 0100	011000 1011
1 / 01	000 00001	011011 0100	100010 1011
2 / 02	000 00010	101101 0100	010010 0011
3 / 03	000 00011	110001 1011	110001 0100
4 / 04	000 00100	110101 0100	001010 1011
5 / 05	000 00101	101001 1011	101001 0100
6 / 06	000 00110	011001 1011	011001 0100
7 / 07	000 00111	111000 1011	000111 0100
8 / 08	000 01000	111001 0100	000110 1011
9 / 09	000 01001	100101 1011	100101 0100
10 / 0A	000 01010	010101 1011	010101 0100

The data symbols are often referred to as D.x.y where x is the 5-bit element that ranges from 0 to 31 and y is the 3-bit element that ranges from 0 to 7. The 12 control (or special) symbols are referred to as K.x.y and have different encodings from any of the D.x.y symbols. The scheme is summarized in Figure 6.12.

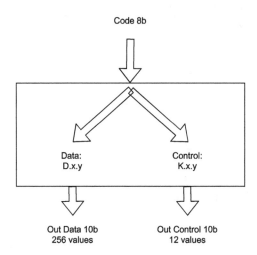

Figure 6.12 Principle of 8b/10b encoding with two coding cases: data and control

The lookup tables for the x (5b/6b coding) and y (3b/4b coding) elements of the data (D) and control (K) cases are set out below. Thus, Table 6.4 shows how the lowest 5 bits of a data source (EDCBA) are converted into a 6-bit code, and Table 6.5 shows how its highest 3 bits (HGF) are converted into a 4-bit code. The output gains two additional bits, and its order is effectively reversed, so that HGF_EDCBA becomes abcdei_fghj, where i and j are the additional bits added into each element of the original, which serves to ensure the uniqueness of the control symbols that are generated on a similar basis.

Table 6.4 5b/6b coding: 5 bits (32 inputs) → 6 bits (64 possible outputs of which 46 are used for D.x)

5b Input (Decimal/ Hexadecimal)	5b Input (Binary)	6b Output (Binary) (RDo: for this data) abcdei	
D.x	EDCBA	Input RDi = −1	Input RDi = +1
D.00 / 00	0 0000	10 0111 (RDo: +2)	01 1000 (RDo: -2)
D.01 / 01	0 0001	01 1101 (RDo: +2)	10 0010 (RDo: -2)
D.02 / 02	0 0010	10 1101 (RDo: +2)	01 0010 (RDo: -2)
D.03 / 03	0 0011	11 0001	
D.04 / 04	0 0100	11 0101 (RDo: +2)	00 1010 (RDo: -2)
D.05 / 05	0 0101	10 1001	
D.06 / 06	0 0110	01 1001	
D.07 / 07	0 0111	11 1000	00 0111
D.08 / 08	0 1000	11 1001 (RDo: +2)	00 0110 (RDo: -2)
D.09 / 09	0 1001	10 0101	
D.10 / 0A	0 1010	01 0101	
D.11 / 0B	0 1011	11 0100	

5b Input (Decimal/ Hexadecimal)	5b Input (Binary)	6b Output (Binary) (RDo: for this data) abcdei	
D.x	EDCBA	Input RDi = –1	Input RDi = +1
D.12 / 0C	0 1100	00 1101	
D.13 / 0D	0 1101	10 1100	
D.14 / 0E	0 1110	01 1100	
D.15 / 0F	0 1111	01 0111 *(RDo: +2)*	10 1000 *(RDo: -2)*
D.16 / 10	1 0000	01 1011 *(RDo:+2)*	10 0100 *(RDo:-2)*
D.17 / 11	1 0001	10 0011	
D.18 / 12	1 0010	01 0011	
D.19 / 13	1 0011	11 0010	
D.20 / 14	1 0100	00 1011	
D.21 / 15	1 0101	10 1010	
D.22 / 16	1 0110	01 1010	
D.23 / 17	1 0111	11 1010 *(RDo: +2)*	00 0101 *(RDo: -2)*
D.24 / 18	1 1000	11 0011 *(RDo: +2)*	00 1100 *(RDo: -2)*
D.25 / 19	1 1001	10 0110	
D.26 / 1A	1 1010	01 0110	
D.27 / 1B	1 1011	11 0110 *(RDo: +2)*	00 1001 *(RDo: -2)*
D.28 / 1C	1 1100	00 1110	
D.29 / 1D	1 1101	10 1110 *(RDo: +2)*	01 0001 *(RDo: -2)*
D.30 / 1E	1 1110	01 1110 *(RDo: +2)*	10 0001 *(RDo: -2)*
D.31 / 1F	1 1111	10 1011 *(RDo: +2)*	01 0100 *(RDo: -2)*

Table 6.5 3b/4b coding: 3 bits (8 inputs) → 4 bits (16 possible output values of which 14 are used for D.y)

3b Input (Decimal/ Hexadecimal)	3b Input (Binary)	4b Output (Binary) (RDo: for this data) fghj	
D.x.y	HGF	Input RDi = –1	Input RDi = +1
D.x.0	000	1011 *(RDo: +2)*	0100 *(RDo: -2)*
D.x.1	001	1001	
D.x.2	010	0101	
D.x.3	011	1100 *(RDo: 0)*	0011 *(RDo: 0)*
D.x.4	100	1101 *(RDo: +2)*	0010 *(RDo: -2)*
D.x.5	101	1010	
D.x.6	110	0110	
D.x.P7 *Primary*	111	1110 *(RDo: +2)*	0001 *(RDo: -2)*
D.x.A7 *Alternate*	111	0111 *(RDo: +2)*	1000 *(RDo: -2)*

If we study Table 6.4, we can see that each 5-bit input will generate two alternative 6-bit outputs. For any binary number with an even number of digits, every bit sequence of non-zero disparity will have a disparity that is a multiple of two; thus, for a 6-bit number, the possible disparities will be ±2, ±4 or ±6. Where one of these outputs has no disparity (i.e. equal numbers of ones and zeros), it is always used. Similarly, outputs with higher disparities than ±2 are always discarded, as shown in Table 6.6 (which also avoids the synchronization issues associated with long runs of ones and zeros described previously). Of the possible outputs that remain, the sender must select the alternative that, in conjunction with the second element of the encoding, will bring the running disparity back toward zero.

Table 6.6 Fourteen 6-bit codes unused due to high disparities (RDo = Running Disparity output)

Not Used	Not Used	RDo
000000	111111	−6, +6
011111	100000	−4, +4
101111	010000	−4, +4
110111	001000	−4, +4
111011	000100	−4, +4
111101	000010	−4, +4
111110	000001	−4, +4

In practice, the running disparity is assigned a starting value for each packet of −1, and each generated 10-bit symbol in the packet will either have no disparity or two alternatives with disparities of +2 and −2, respectively. In the latter case, it will be the alternative that will toggle the running disparity backwards or forwards between −1 and +1 that is selected for transmission, as illustrated in Table 6.7.

(In Table 6.4, RDi indicates the input or current value of the running disparity, and RDo indicates the running disparity associated with the particular bit sequence "output"; thus, when RDi is −1, the encoding with an RDo of +2 will be used, and when RDi is +1, the encoding with an RDo of −2 will be used.)

Table 6.7 Running disparity selection

RDi input	RDo of selected coding	New RD
−1	−2	Error
−1	0	−1
−1	+2	+1
+1	−2	−1
+1	0	+1
+1	+2	Error

Because the encoding makes more possible values available, the number of consecutive bits of one value can be kept low (as we have seen above), and so the protocol enables good bit synchronization/clock recovery.

Of the 64 possible values available as output from the 5b/6b encoding, 44 are used to code the D.x data. The 20 values that are not used can be applied to represent control characters instead. In practice, the 14 values rejected because of their high disparities (see Table 6.6) are ignored for this purpose, leaving 6 available for use in the x element of the 12 K.x.y control codes, defined as a whole in Table 6.8. None of the 10-bit control code encodings has a greater disparity than ±2, and there is no overlap with any of the data encodings. The encoding of the y element of these K.x.y control codes is shown in Table 6.9.

Table 6.8 The 12 K.x.y control codes, utilizing 5 different values of x

8b Input (Decimal/ Hexadecimal)	8b Input (Binary)	10b Output (Binary) (RDo: for this data) abcdeifghj	
K.x.y	HGF E DCBA y x	Input RDi = −1	Input RDi = +1
K.28.0 / 1C	000 1 1100	001111 0100 (RDo: 0)	110000 1011 (RDo: 0)
K.28.1 / 3C	001 1 1100	001111 1001 (RDo: +2)	110000 0110 (RDo: -2)
K.28.2 / 5C	010 1 1100	001111 0101 (RDo: +2)	110000 1010 (RDo: -2)
K.28.3 / 7C	011 1 1100	001111 0011 (RDo: +2)	110000 1100 (RDo: -2)
K.28.4 / 9C	100 1 1100	001111 0010 (RDo: 0)	110000 1101 (RDo: 0)
K.28.5 / BC	101 1 1100	001111 1010 (RDo: +2)	110000 0101 (RDo: -2)
K.28.6 / DC	110 1 1100	001111 0110 (RDo: +2)	110000 1001 (RDo: -2)
K.28.7 / FC	111 1 1100	001111 1000 (RDo: 0)	110000 0111 (RDo: 0)
K.23.7 / F7	111 1 0111	111010 1000 (RDo: 0)	000101 0111 (RDo: 0)
K.27.7 / FB	111 1 1011	110110 1000 (RDo: 0)	001001 0111 (RDo: 0)
K.29.7 / FD	111 1 1101	101110 1000 (RDo: 0)	010001 0111 (RDo: 0)
K.30.7 / FE	111 1 1110	011110 1000 (RDo: 0)	100001 0111 (RDo: 0)

Table 6.9 3b/4b coding, 3 bits → 4 bits, for K.x.y resulting codes

3b Input (Decimal or Hexadecimal)	3b Input (Binary)	4b Output (Binary) (RDo: for this data) fghj	
K.x.y	HGF	Input RDi = −1	Input RDi = +1
K.x.0	000	1011 (RDo: +2)	0100 (RDo: -2)
K.x.1	001	0110 (RDo: 0)	1001 (RDo: 0)
K.x.2	010	1010 (RDo: 0)	0101 (RDo: 0)
K.x.3	011	1100 (RDo: 0)	0011 (RDo: 0)
K.x.4	100	1101 (RDo: +2)	0010 (RDo: -2)
K.x.5	101	0101 (RDo: 0)	1010 (RDo: 0)
K.x.6	110	1001 (RDo: 0)	0110 (RDo: 0)
K.x.7	111	0111 (RDo:+2)	1000 (RDo: -2)

Figure 6.13 summarizes the transformations involved. In written form:

1. Take the 8 input data bits: *HGFEDCBA*.

2. Split this into two blocks: *HGF* and *EDCBA*.

3. Perform the 3b/4b and 5b/6b conversions on these two blocks accordingly.

4. Swap the positions of the two converted blocks => *iedcba* and *jhgf*.

5. Shuffle the bits in each block and concatenate them: *abcdei fghj*.

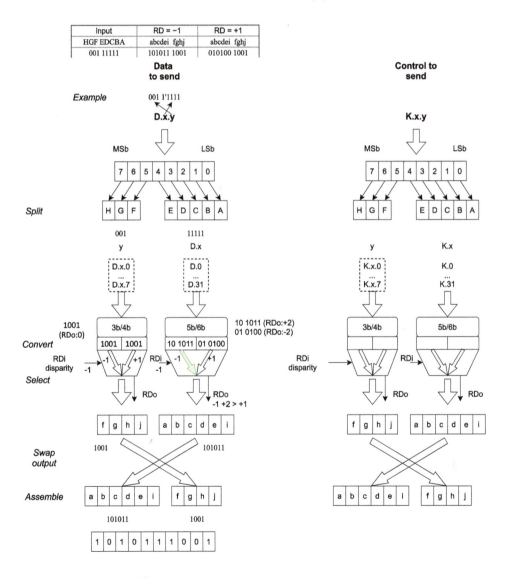

Figure 6.13 Transformation algorithm for 8b/10b coding

The 8b/10b encoding scheme has the following practical benefits:

▪ maintains a DC balance

▪ a maximum of five consecutive zeros or ones supports clock recovery and synchronization

▪ maintains a fixed encoded length, 10 bits, and therefore a fixed data rate

▪ supports both data and commands

▪ has a relatively simple, fast encoding/decoding scheme

▪ improves data reliability via several error-detection mechanisms, including:

  ☐ validation of correct codes (only 268 of the possible 1024 10-bit codes are used)

  ☐ validation of correct running disparity

  ☐ validation that consecutive numbers of ones or zeros do not exceed five in number, either within a code or between consecutive codes.

It should be emphasized that the 8b/10b encoding documented here represents one specific implementation of the scheme (as used by IBM) and the output of any given implementation would vary depending on how the state machine that manages the final bit-shuffling is defined. Thus, you must refer to the specification of each implementation if you want to know the exact mapping used for any given application.

Paired disparity encoding in general is used in a wide variety of well-known, high-data-rate communications, including gigabit Ethernet, Aurora, DisplayPort, FireWire, InfiniBand, PCI Express, Serial ATA, SSA, and USB 3.0.

6.2.7 UARTs

One of the most longstanding devices available in the computer world is the **Universal Asynchronous Receiver/Transmitter** (UART).

The basic purpose of a UART is to transfer one byte of information at a time along a single wire, which it does bit by bit. To this end, it will contain one or more shift registers, effectively used to disassemble the byte that arrives at the UART on a parallel bus into a series of sequential bits, with a remote UART reassembling the bits into a byte at the other end of the wire. To support synchronization at the byte or character level, the sender sets the line by default to a high level, indicating that it is idle. The first transition to a low level tells the receiver that transmission of a byte is starting. The duration of this so-called **start bit** is the 1-bit timing. The byte itself is then transmitted in a length of 5 to 8 bits (which might seem strange for a byte), representing the code for a character, typically using a 7-bit or 8-bit ASCII code (although some very old telex system protocols used as few as 5 bits in their character sets). A further bit may be added as a parity check (to maintain Even parity or Odd parity), before one or more **stop bits** complete the transmission, raising the line back to the idle level, as illustrated in

Figure 6.14. A new character can be transmitted as soon as the appropriate number of stop bits has been sent.

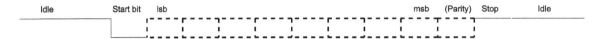

Figure 6.14 Asynchronous data transfer, least significant bit first, NRZ coding

When two UARTs want to communicate, it is necessary to select the same bit rate (in bit/s) at both the transmitter and the receiver because no clock is transmitted between the two. A programmable clock source must be supplied to each of the UARTs. Some parameters used to generate standard bit rates from three different quartz clock frequencies are presented in Table 6.10. With the exception of the 110 bit rate, all of those shown are either multiples or factor-of-two divisors of the classical default value of 9,600 bit/s. Some are in common use, as indicated in blue in the first column of the table, but the very old 110 bit rate and the others below 9,600 bit/s are seldom used any longer, and neither are those above 230,400 bit/s.

Table 6.10 Bit rate parameters for asynchronous transfer with different reference clocks

Bit Rate	Relation to 9600	3.6864 MHz	7.3728 MHz	8.0000 MHz	Real bit rate @ 8 MHz	Relative Error @ 8 MHz (%)
110	0.01146	33 512.73	67 025.45	72 727.27	110.0004	0.00
300	$1/32$	12 288.00	24 576.00	26 666.67	299.9963	0.00
600	$1/16$	6 144.00	12 288.00	13 333.33	600.0150	0.00
1 200	$1/8$	3 072.00	6 144.00	6 666.67	1 199.9400	0.00
2 400	$1/4$	1 536.00	3 072.00	3 333.33	2 400.2400	0.01
4 800	$1/2$	768.00	1 536.00	1 666.67	4 799.0402	−0.02
9 600	1	384.00	768.00	833.33	9 603.8415	0.04
19 200	2	192.00	384.00	416.67	19 184.6523	−0.08
38 400	4	96.00	192.00	208.33	38 461.5385	0.16
57 600	6	64.00	128.00	138.89	57 553.9568	−0.08
76 800	8	48.00	96.00	104.17	76 923.0769	0.16
115 200	12	32.00	64.00	69.44	115 942.0290	0.64
230 400	24	16.00	32.00	34.72	228 571.4286	−0.79
460 800	48	8.00	16.00	17.36	470 588.2353	2.12
921 600	96	4.00	8.00	8.68	888 888.8889	−3.55
1 843 200	192	2.00	4.00	4.34	2 000 000.0000	8.51
3 686 400	384	1.00	2.00	2.17	4 000 000.0000	8.51

In general, to control the UART bit rate, a programmable interface uses a clock frequency that is 16 times higher than the selected bit rate, to ensure data recovery with good accuracy (i.e. low relative error).

Thus, in summary, a UART character transmission consists of:

- start bit

- data bits (5 to 8)

- parity bit (optional, even/odd)

- stop bit (1, 1.5 or 2)

- speed determined by external selection.

The protocol described here is the one available on almost every microcontroller or SoC with what is sometimes called a transistor–transistor logic (TTL) level. They can be used over a short distance or on the same board between different components. The logical high voltage used by a UART reflects the power supply voltage associated with its integrated circuit, typically 3.3 V or 5 V (with the logical low voltage being 0 V). Such voltages are not really adequate for reliable data transmission over any significant distance and do not conform to any protocol as such. Thus, in practice, a serial link based on a UART will usually have some form of protocol-based line driver to convert these logical signals into a recognized standard such as the long-established RS-232, RS-422 or RS-485 transmission protocols, which define specific voltage levels, polarities, signal names, pinouts and connectors, and which we will study further in due course.

The UART interface use two lines for data transmission:

- TxD   Transmit Data

- RxD   Receive Data.

Two additional signals, RTS and CTS, allow synchronization of data flow between two systems. The initial application of these signals was in the RS-232 specification for controlling connection to analog telephone lines via a modem (short for MOdulator-DEModulator unit), where RTS was used by the sender to indicate that it had some data it wanted to send, and CTS was used by the receiver to respond with an all-clear for the transmission. As direct communication between computers overtook the use of modems, the use of these signals changed slightly, such that RTS became a hardware-based flow control signal used to indicate readiness to accept data. Once the serial line buffer is full and no more data can be accepted, RTS is deactivated. In most programmable interfaces these two signals are active low and, thus, often designated as nRTS and nCTS:

- nRTS Request To Send, active low

- nCTS Clear To Send, active low.

When two units are connected together, as illustrated in Figure 6.15, their TxD and RxD connections must be crossed, as should be their nRTS and nCTS signals. However, in some devices the meanings of TxD and RxD may be reversed, depending upon whether they adopt the viewpoint of a master (e.g.

microcontroller) or a slave (e.g. peripheral), so it is important to establish this before deciding whether the connection between the two does or does not require a "crossover".

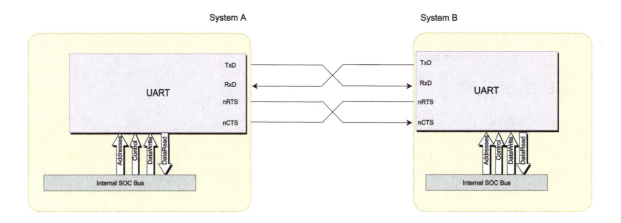

Figure 6.15 Connection between two units using UART protocol

The same can apply to the RTS and CTS lines, particularly in the context of whether they adopt an active-high or active-low polarity. The potential for misunderstanding if the configuration of the specific device is not fully researched is quite high, and a lot of bad connections are initially created as a result.

UART sampling of the RxD signal is illustrated in Figure 6.16. When the falling edge of the start bit is detected, a counter is started. When this counter reaches a value between 8 and 14, the RxD signal is sampled and, assuming that the start bit is verified, the counter is reset and the data is then sampled again every 16 counts, until all the bits have been sampled and the results stored to form the received data character. The value of the parity bit can be checked against the UART's internal calculation if necessary, and the module checks that the line turns idle again for the duration of the stop bit(s), when it can await the start of the next data character.

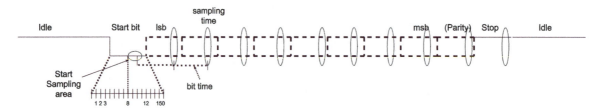

Figure 6.16 UART data sampling

6.2.7.1 RS-232

The RS-232 standard was introduced in 1960 and was designed to connect a piece of data terminal equipment (DTE) to a piece of data communications equipment (DCE), which would then transmit the data involved down a telephone line. At the far end of the line, another DCE would receive the data and pass it on to another DTE, again using the RS-232 standard. The DCE typically consisted of a modem, and the original DTE was a teletypewriter, which subsequently evolved into a computer terminal and then an actual computer. In its original form, the standard only needed to support a data rate that could accommodate the fastest someone could type on the DTE!

It is not surprising that the standard reflects this early history. The first role of the standard was to establish basic communication between the four pieces of equipment involved, as illustrated in Figure 6.17. In this instance, a terminal and a computer want to communicate with each other, via a pair of modems.

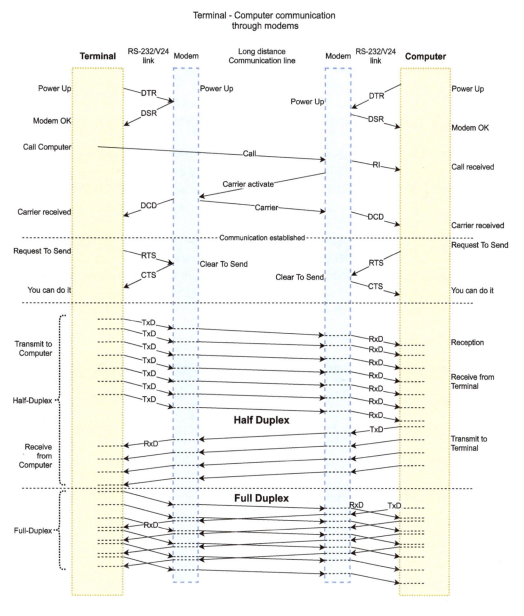

Figure 6.17 Data communication transfers between a terminal and a computer through a modem

Thus, both the terminal and the computer first activate the DTR (Data Terminal Ready) signal to tell their respective modems that they are ready for a communication. If the modems are ready too, they activate the DSR (Data Set Ready) signal in response. Note that RS-232 also supported another approach to establishing communication, in which an incoming "telephone call" from the remote modem would trigger the receiving modem to activate the RI (Ring Indicator) signal to inform the computer that it had a call.

Modems transfer data over a wire by generating and then modulating an analog carrier signal. When a remote modem detects this carrier signal it activates the DCD (Data Carrier Detect) signal, which informs the equipment to which it is connected (e.g. the computer or, more specifically, a UART within the computer) that the other equipment is online and ready to communicate.

As described previously, a further pair of signals, RTS and CTS, are used locally to synchronize the authorization of the data transfers, and data is now sent on the TxD line to the modem where it is modulated for analog line transmission (such analog lines supported a maximum signal frequency of around 3 kHz). The same occurs in the other direction. When only one piece of equipment can transmit at any given time, it is referred to as a half-duplex connection; when data flows concurrently in both directions (which can occur because TxD and RxD are separate circuits), it is a full-duplex connection. In the early days of RS-232, typical data rates were between 300 and 1200 bit/s. In France, the very popular MiniTel system that predated the Internet was a 75/1200 bit/s system, in which the transmission rate of 75 bit/s reflected the normal typing rate on a keyboard.

At its outset, RS-232 involved a physical connector with 25 pins (DB-25), which was also able to support a number of other standards/protocols, such as V.24. However, these connectors occupied a lot of space and, as we have seen, for most situations only eight signals, plus a signal ground, were necessary for successful RS-232 communication (see Table 6.11), leading to the introduction of a 9-pin (DB-9) RS-232 connector, as shown in Figure 6.18.

Table 6.11 RS-232 DB-9 signal names and directions

Pin	SIG.	Signal Name	DTE (PC)	DCE (modem)
1	DCD	Data Carrier Detect	in	out
2	RxD	Receive Data	in	out
3	TxD	Transmit Data	out	in
4	DTR	Data Terminal Ready	out	in
5	GND	Signal Ground	-	-
6	DSR	Data Set Ready	in	out
7	RTS	Request to Send	out	in
8	CTS	Clear to Send	in	out
9	RI	Ring Indicator	in	out

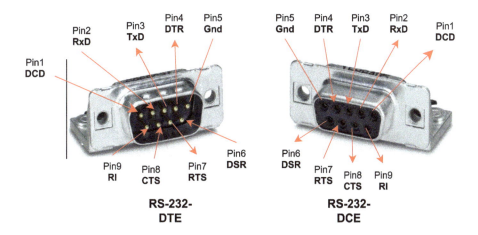

Figure 6.18 RS-232 DB-9 connector as DTE male connector and DCE female connector

As you might have noticed, the definitions of the two ends (DCE and DTE) of an RS-232 link are asymmetric, that is, the pin assignments are not identical, and a designer must decide whether their equipment will present a DCE or a DTE interface. Note too that a connector to a DTE device is typically male, and to a DCE device is typically female.

When an RS-232 connection does not involve a modem (as is usually the case nowadays) but two DTE-based computer systems, then it is necessary to cross the signals between them. This is commonly achieved by using a "**null-modem**" adapter. Figure 6.19 illustrates three of the possible ways in which this can be achieved, depending on the extent to which hardware-based flow control, or "**handshaking**", is implemented.

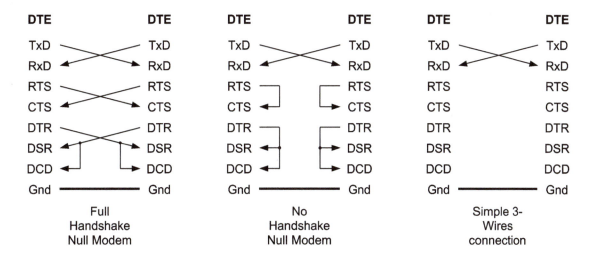

Figure 6.19 Null-modem options for back-to-back connection of two (DTE) computers

Thus, the Full Handshake option retains the full handshaking functionality of an equivalent modem-based configuration. The No Handshake option effectively disables hardware-controlled handshaking of data transfers by looping the relevant signals back on each other as appropriate. The simple 3-wire option is functionally similar to this, but means that the device to which this null modem is connected (e.g. a UART controller) must internally ignore or disable these flow control signals if communication is to occur.

In the world of personal computers (PCs), serial connections migrated to these 9-pin connectors and the 25-pin connectors were, instead, dedicated to the handling of parallel communication with printers. These days, very few PCs have RS-232 connectors of any sort; their role has been taken by the Universal Serial Bus (USB) connector.

Nevertheless, because of their simplicity and historical ubiquity, RS-232 interfaces are still used, particularly where a short-range, point-to-point, low-speed wired data connection is entirely sufficient, such as in industrial machines, scientific instruments, and networking equipment. Because these latter are common areas of application for SoCs, RS-232 remains of some relevance today, but is arguably of more significance in the present context as an illustration of the basic principles involved in the use of UARTs in microcontrollers to support serial communication.

The signals available on a full UART interface are:

- TxD Transmit Data

- RxD Receive Data

- nRTS Request To Send, active low

- nCTS Clear To Send, active low

- nDTR Data Terminal Ready, active low

- nDSR Data Set Ready, active low

- nRI Ring Indicator, active low.

As indicated, most of these signals are active low, but it is necessary to verify this for each programmable interface in use. As we have already seen, TxD and RxD are often the only two signals that are really used. If hardware-based data synchronization is required, nRTS and nCTS are employed too. The other signals are present for historical reasons, as previously described, and are seldom used today.

To connect a UART to an RS-232 line, some adaptations are necessary in terms of:

- Signal polarities

- Voltage levels.

As described in the previous section, the signal voltage used by a UART derives from the power supply of its integrated circuit, typically +3.3 V or +5 V. The RS-232 standard specifies considerably larger voltages, and negative ones too. A line driver therefore needs to be used to convert the UART's TTL-based communication into RS-232 communication, and meant that, for many years, PCs had to include ±12 V power supplies to support their RS-232 connectors. More specifically, in RS-232:

■ Logic level '0' is represented by a positive voltage between +3 V and +15 V, relative to the common Signal Ground pin, and is sometimes called the "space" state or condition

■ Logic level '1' is represented by a negative voltage between −3 V and −15 V, and is sometimes called the "mark" state or condition.

Technically, RS-232 components must be able to withstand open-circuit voltages of ±25 V. Figure 6.20 is a schematic of a UART-enabled DTE-to-DCE connection using line drivers (or level adapters), and Figure 6.21 illustrates the effect of UART to RS-232 conversion at the signal level.

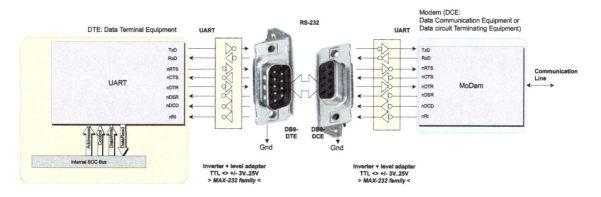

Figure 6.20 Block diagram of UART-to-modem RS-232 communication via level adapters

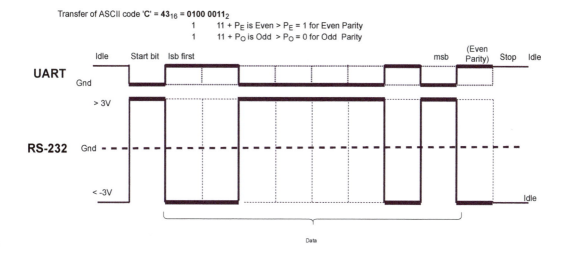

Figure 6.21 Example of UART and RS-232 signal transmission levels, using 8 bits, even parity, and 1 stop bit, for the letter 'C'

The voltages required to support the RS-232 standard are problematic for a small system. However, in the late 1980s, Maxim Integrated designed and produced an extremely useful chip (the "MAX232") that uses capacitors to invert and then double the TTL voltage of 5 V into RS-232-compatible voltages (±10 V, but more typically +7.5 V and −7.5 V).

A further significant feature of the chip was that it did not insist on the minimum RS-232 input voltages of ±3 V, but accepted standard TTL levels of 0.8 V and 2 V as indicators of '0' and '1' logic levels, which helped to protect the chip from high input voltages.

The basic version of the chip has two inverters (level adapters) acting in each direction, as shown in Figure 6.22, which enables straightforward integration of the basic RxD/TxD signals and an RTS/CTS handshaking protocol.

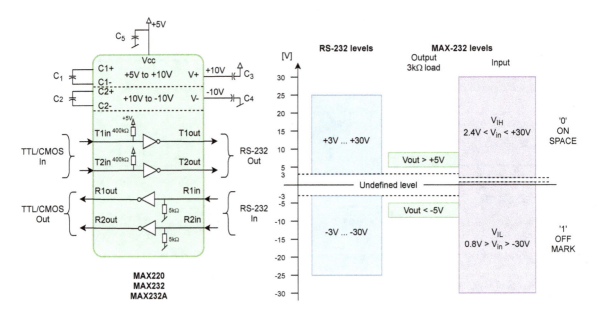

Figure 6.22 MAX232 and RS-232 signaling levels and data transmission

The MAX232 allowed a genuine RS-232 system to be readily implemented with a low component count, and extended the life of RS-232 by many years. Nowadays, these chips are offered by many manufacturers, with variants that support different voltages and greater numbers of inverters, which enables more of the RS-232 signals to be converted and supported. Thus, the MAX212 chip uses a smaller 3.3 V power supply and can convert three outgoing signals and five incoming ones, providing full modem-oriented RS-232 capabilities, and the MAX3237 does likewise but with five transmitters and three receivers. Schematics of these two chips are shown in Figure 6.23.

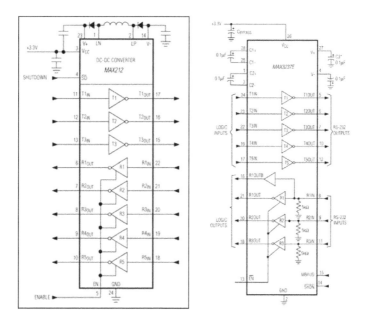

Figure 6.23 Full UART to RS-232 conversion via MAX212 (left) and MAX3237 (right) integrated circuits (source: Copyright Maxim Integrated Products (http://www.maximintegrated.com). Used by permission.)

As indicated above, few personal computers have RS-232 connectors these days. Thus, to communicate with boards such as the MAX232 via a PC will usually require a USB-to-UART/TTL or USB-to-RS-232 adapter (see Figure 6.24). The company FTDI was the first to implement a device that would handle such protocol conversions, and there are now many similar adapters on the market, many of which make use of the FTDI-232 chip family.

Figure 6.24 Asynchronous USB to RS-232 adapter

The simplest adapter (illustrated in Figure 6.25) has just three wires with voltage levels of 3.3 V or 5 V, depending on the model:

▨ Gnd (Blue)

▨ TxD (Output, Red) connected to RxD of UART

▨ RxD (Input, Green) connected to TxD of UART.

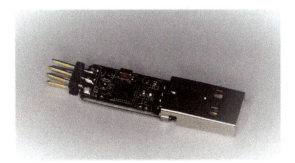

Figure 6.25 USB to UART adapter (USB-Serial-Cable-F)

The RS-232 specification cannot support connection lengths of more than 15 meters or so, unless very-low-capacitance wires are used. Newer specifications, such as **RS-422** and RS-423, were designed to improve on the asynchronous serial protocol of RS-232 while using the same form of connector; for example, RS-422 (see Figure 6.26) paired each data line with a dedicated return line (in a so-called "twisted pair") to create a differential signaling system that supported communication over greater distances (up to 1500 m) at higher speeds than RS-232. RS-422 retains some niche application, but for general use these protocols, like RS-232, have been superseded by USB-based connections.

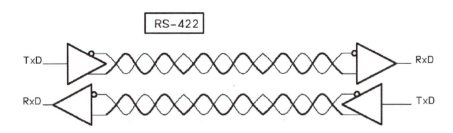

Figure 6.26 RS-422 connection

Although RS-232 may be in decline, the UART is not, and is an important part of a microcontroller for external serial communication. The signals used to establish such communication are largely obsolete but the basic mechanism involved has been retained in the form of commands sent in the serial stream, which means that an understanding of RS-232 provides important background knowledge when it comes to SoC-based serial communication.

6.2.7.2   RS-485

In addition to point-to-point connections, the RS-422 specification was also designed to support a **multi-drop** digital signaling circuit, or primitive form of network, involving one transmitter and "fan-out" to as many as ten receivers. In the 1980s, a more sophisticated serial communications standard, RS-485, was designed to use the same differential signaling approach to implement a true multi-drop, multi-point linear network that could support up to 32 devices (nodes or stations) with multiple transmitters as well as multiple receivers, as illustrated in Figure 6.27. Data speeds of up to 10 Mbit/s were achievable over distances of 10 m or less, and 100 kbit/s over distances of up to a kilometer.

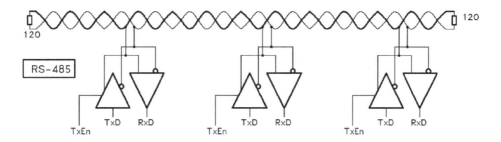

Figure 6.27 RS-485 interconnection topology

RS-485 is designed to be a "balanced" system. Thus, two wires are used to transmit the signal, with the signal on one wire being the exact opposite of the signal on the second wire: if one wire is transmitting a high, the other wire will be transmitting a low, and vice versa. Drivers are used to convert a single-level signal into these two differential signals, which typically involve a voltage of ±7 V (relative to the 0 to 5 V signal range of a UART).

A higher-layer protocol is needed to establish which node should be allowed to transmit, and this node then activates the corresponding TxEn (Transmit Enable) signal and transmits data on the TxD line, effectively implementing a half-duplex communication (four wires would be required for full-duplex comms). All of the receivers connected to the RS-485 "bus" will receive the data. If two or more transmitters try to take control of the bus at the same time, collisions will occur, but the drivers are designed in such a way that this will not be destructive for them. The differential twisted-pair lines are terminated by an impedance of 120 Ω at each end, in the form of a simple resistor, which inhibits signal reflections and reduces noise. When all of the nodes are quiet or unpowered, the undriven differential data lines can "float" such that noise may be interpreted as data; thus, pull-up and pull-down "biasing" resistors are also included in the termination as a fail-safe against such (tri-state) floating.

6.2.8 SPI

The Serial Peripheral Interface, SPI, is an interface specification for synchronous serial data transfer, using a clock. It was originally developed by Motorola in the mid-1980s. SPI implements a master–slave architecture with a single master and multiple slaves, selected by individual Slave Select (SS) or Chip Select (CS) lines.

SPI is a four-wire, full-duplex protocol involving four logic signals:

- **SCK**: Serial Clock (output from master)

- **MOSI** (or SIMO): Master Out, Slave In (data output from master)

- **MISO** (or SOMI): Master In, Slave Out (data output from slave)

- **CS** (or nCS): Chip Select (often active low, but depends on the slave device; output from master).

Data flow on the MOSI and MISO lines is bidirectional. If more than one slave is connected to the three basic lines (i.e. SCK, MOSI and MISO), then a separate physical CS line is used to select one at a time. The master also supports a further signal, for use when it acts as a slave:

- **SS** (or nSS): Slave Select.

Figure 6.28 illustrates the basic SPI architecture.

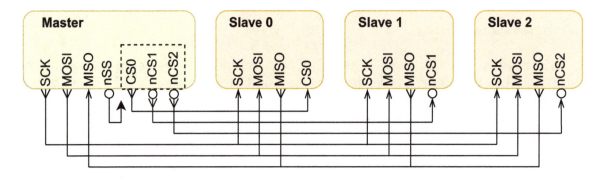

Figure 6.28 SPI device connections

The master must first configure the clock to a frequency supported by the slave(s). It can then activate the CS signal for the appropriate slave. Then, during each clock cycle, a full-duplex transmission occurs: on each clock edge the master transmits a bit on the MOSI line (which the slave reads) while the slave sends a bit on the MISO line (which the master reads). The most-significant bit is usually the first to be transferred, and this cycle continues until an entire byte has been exchanged. If more data needs to be exchanged, the relevant registers in the master and slave are reloaded and the process repeats until the transmission is complete. At this point, the master stops toggling the clock and deselects the slave. Figure 6.29 summarizes this data exchange.

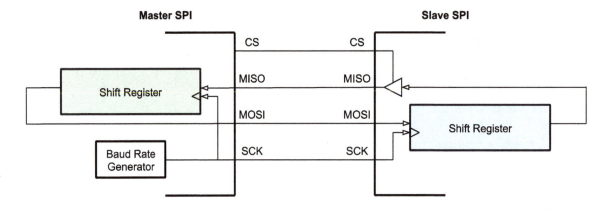

Figure 6.29 SPI master–slave data exchange

This regime applies even when transmission is unidirectional. Thus, if a read-only transmission is required, the master must send dummy data, and the master must discard the data it receives in the case of a write-only transmission.

Each device has its own specific protocol that must be used to access it. For many slave devices, the first data transmitted will be the address of an internal register in the slave, followed by the new data to write to that register.

As shown in Figure 6.28, the SCK, MOSI and MISO lines of all of the devices are typically connected together. For this to be successful, the MISO (output) line of every slave must have a "**tri-state**" configuration, which means that it can assume a high-impedance state in addition to the usual high and low logic levels. This effectively removes the output from the circuit (i.e. when it is not selected) and allows multiple devices to share the same line (as required on a bus that cannot listen to more than one device at a time). Unfortunately, some slave devices don't support this configuration and an external tristate buffer may be required. In this context, a designer must be very careful during the conception phase to verify the datasheets of all the components in use.

The master needs to provide a separate line for each slave it has to access (in the example shown in Figure 6.28, CS0, nCS1, and nCS2). Some of these lines will be active high (e.g. CS0) and some active low (e.g. nCS1 and nCS2), again depending on the specific component, so the designer must take care to employ the correct signal polarity. Unfortunately, manufacturers do not always use naming conventions that correctly indicate this; for example, naming a signal as CS and then indicating elsewhere in their documentation that the signal is active low! Designer beware!

If only one slave device is connected, it may be possible to activate the CS signal on a permanent basis, but this will again depend on the individual components.

Whenever data is sent synchronously, using a clock to drive it, some questions must be answered:

- What is the **polarity** of the clock signal used to time the sending and receipt of data: is the leading edge a rising edge or a falling one? Or what is the idle state of the SCK line, '1' or '0'? This is the polarity level.

- What is the **phase** of the data bits relative to the clock pulse: is data transmitted on the leading edge or the trailing edge? Or is it the first or second edge which samples the data?

In SPI, these parameters (CPOL and CPHA) are configurable at the master side (but are often predefined at the slave side), which adds more flexibility to the communication channel. Each parameter has two possible values, giving a total of four possible configurations, as described in Table 6.12. Of the four modes shown in the table, modes 0 and 3 are used most commonly. Figure 6.30 illustrates the transmission timings for a 16-bit data transfer, in terms of the two alternative clock polarities and the two possible phasings of the transfer.

Table 6.12 SPI clock modes

Mode	CPOL	Description	CPHA	Description
0	0	SCK idle state is 0	0	Data output is activated because CS is asserted. Leading (rising) edge of SCK drives registration of first data bit (indicated by red ellipse in Figure 6.30); the data must have been ready on the line before this leading edge. Next leading edge transfers the next bit and so on… The last leading edge completes the transfer.
1	0		1	Again, data output is activated because CS is asserted. Trailing (falling) edge of SCK drives registration of first data bit (indicated by blue ellipse in Figure 6.30); the data must have been made ready on the line by the leading edge that preceded it. Next trailing edge transfers the next bit and so on… For the last cycle, the data signal line is held valid until CS is deasserted.
2	1	SCK idle state is 1	0	As for Mode 0, but the leading edge of SCK is a *falling* edge.
3	1		1	As for Mode 1, but the trailing edge of SCK is a *rising* edge.

SPI is a *de facto* standard. It is not very sophisticated, but its simplicity and comparative flexibility have firmly established its use in many, if not most, SoC-based microcontrollers. Various derivative protocols exist, and the signal names are not always consistent. One poor example is the use of SDO (Slave Data Out) and SDI (Slave Data In) designations with directional changes for a master and a slave, which creates ambiguity that is absent from the MOSI/MISO naming convention.

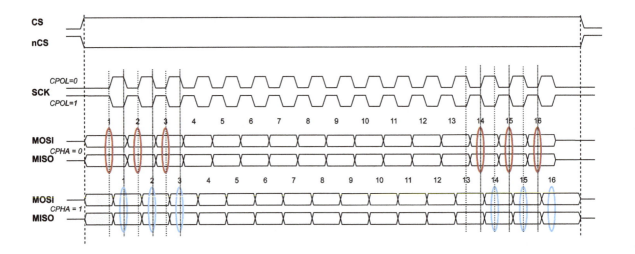

Figure 6.30 Alternative timings of SPI data transmission (16-bit transfer)

On some devices, SDI and SDO are combined, creating a half-duplex configuration for which three wires are sufficient (CS, SCK, and SDI/SDO), with data transfers using the bidirectional SDI/SDO signal alternately as required.

It is also possible to create a multi-master SPI architecture, as illustrated in Figure 6.31, in which some units can act as either master or slave. However, it requires additional wiring and a bespoke protocol to enable the SPI bus to be assigned to a specific master, given that only one can be active at any time and arbitration is therefore required. If a master is acting as a slave, the SS (Slave Select) input pin is used to select the device. As a master, it uses a port connection to select the appropriate slave, one pin for each slave in the form of a Chip Select signal. In the example of Figure 6.31, these Chip Select pins are active low as their names indicate (nCSx).

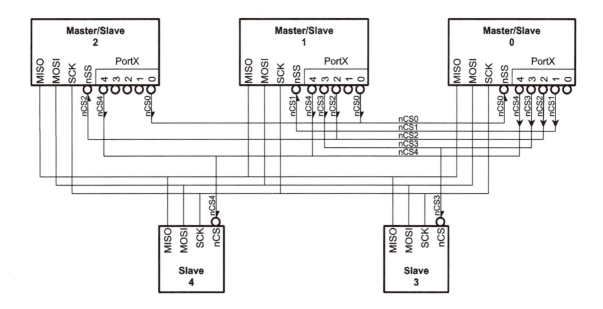

Figure 6.31 Multi-master SPI configuration

6.2.8.1 Quad SPI

One reason for the popularity of SPI is that its simplicity confers a small footprint in terms of die area, making it very useful on small boards. SPI is aimed at high-speed on-board communications with peripherals but can also handle simple external devices with low data transfer rates. The SPI bus is the basis of the communication used for the serial memories (of many gigabytes) used in cameras. However, its data transfer rate can be a limitation when it comes to moving large volumes of data around quickly; for example, from ROM or other memories.

There are two ways to speed up such transfers: either increase the bandwidth, or increase the bus width. In Quad SPI (QSPI) both are done. Thus, the clock frequency is increased to around 100 MHz, and the single MOSI signal is replaced with four serial I/O signals (typically sacrificing the MISO signal in the process and implementing a half- rather than full-duplex interface), hence the name Quad SPI. Figure 6.32 illustrates the change. Note that there is also an intermediate solution, Dual SPI, which just repurposes MOSI and MISO in a unidirectional, half-duplex configuration.

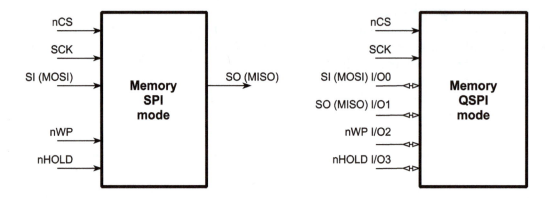

Figure 6.32 Memory device showing support for both SPI and QSPI modes

One of the ideas behind this approach is to retain compatibility with regular SPI, its MOSI/MISO line functions, and the number of pins on the device (unchanged in the two different modes shown in Figure 6.32). Thus, in the first phase of the (non-standard) Dual and Quad SPI protocols, a command is transferred by the master to the slave to enquire of its transfer capability in relation to these protocols. If the slave device agrees, the pin use can be changed and the next part of the transfer can be done with two or four bits of data in parallel, doubling or quadrupling the transfer rate.

In some devices, a specific command allows the fast quad mode to be retained until a further command rescinds the change.

6.2.9 I²C

I²C (I-squared-C), or "Inter-Integrated Circuit", is a synchronous serial communication bus protocol invented in 1982 by Philips, now known as NXP Semiconductors. It is slower than SPI but also physically simpler, only using two lines for data transfer and synchronization (making it a half-duplex protocol), and is widely used to connect peripherals to microcontrollers over short distances either within a board or between boards. I²C implements a packet-switched, multi-master and multi-slave bus and its main characteristics are:

▪ two lines for data transfer and synchronization: SCL (Serial Clock) and SDA (Serial Data)

▪ different transfer speeds:

☐ 100 kbit/s (standard)

☐ 400 kbit/s (Fast-mode)

☐ 1 Mbit/s (Fast-mode plus)

☐ 5 Mbit/s (Ultra Fast-mode, a write-only I²C subset)

▪ open-collector (open-drain) output using pull-up resistors, typically of 4.7 kOhms (push–pull amplifiers for the Ultra Fast-mode)

- target address + transfer direction form the first transmission

- acknowledged transfer

- SCL always controlled by the master.

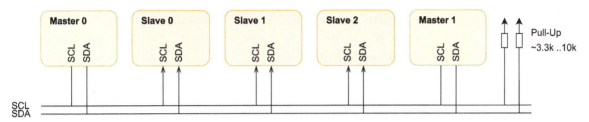

Figure 6.33 I²C connection

Before we describe the messaging design of I²C, it is necessary to have some definitions, as per Table 6.13.

Table 6.13 I²C system functions

Function	Description
Master	The unit that sends the SCL (clock) signal
	Starts and finishes a transfer
	Stops a transfer
	Transmits the data in a write transfer
	Receives the data in a read transfer
Slave	The unit that receives an address to be accessed
	Receives the data in a write transfer
	Transmits the data in a read transfer
Transmitter	Master or Slave, the unit that sends the data, and receives the acknowledgement
Receiver	Master or Slave, the unit that receives the data, and sends the acknowledgement

6.2.9.1   Data Transfers

Figure 6.34 illustrates the timing and signal relationship for a basic I²C data transfer:

- The default idle state of both lines (SCL and SDA) is high (logic level '1'), due to the pull-up resistor on each.

- It is a rule that, except for the **Start** and **Stop** signals (or a **Restart** condition), the SDA line can only change when the SCL line is low (logic level '0').

- Thus, a transaction is **Started** by the master driving the SDA line to ground (low, logic level '0') while SCL remains high.

- The master then drives the SCL line low before setting the appropriate SDA level for the first bit, which will be the most-significant bit (A6) of a 7-bit slave address.

■ The master then allows the SCL line to float and the pull-up attracts the signal level to high, before driving it low again and setting the SDA level for the next address bit (A5), repeating the process until reaching the least-significant address bit, after which it sets a Read/Write (R/nW) bit, in which high indicates 'Read', and low (hence the 'n' designation) indicates 'Write'.

■ If a slave recognizes its address it acknowledges it, driving SDA to '0' for a single bit, interpreted as an ACK. If no slave recognizes the address, the SDA line will float high by virtue of the pull-up resistors, amounting to a NACK (Negative Acknowledgement), and the master should halt the transfer by setting a Stop condition (see below).

■ Assuming successful address recognition, either the master will control the SDA line and send an 8-bit data byte (for a write transaction; see Figure 6.35) or the slave will do the same (for a read transaction; see Figure 6.36), although the master always controls the SCL signal. At this point, for data transmission, master and slave become transmitter and receiver (or vice versa).

■ For a write transaction, after 8 bits have been transmitted, the slave (in receiver mode) provides an ACK on the SDA line if the data has been accepted.

■ For a read transaction, after 8 bits have been transmitted, the master (in receiver mode) either provides an ACK if it wants to receive more data, or a NACK (NAK) if it's the last byte of the transfer.

■ To finish the transfer, the master sets a **Stop** condition by letting SCL float high, followed by SDA.

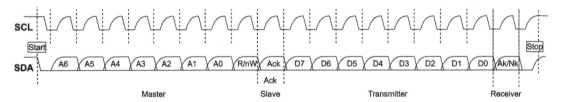

Figure 6.34 Timing of single I²C transfer

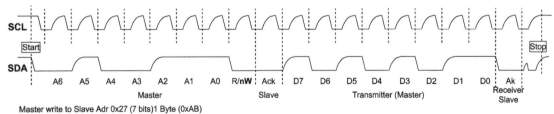

Master write to Slave Adr 0x27 (7 bits)1 Byte (0xAB)

Address
```
7 bits: 0x27 --> 010 0111 + R/nW
8 bits: 0x4E --> 0100 1110 (Write)
        0x4F --> 0100 1111 (Read)
```

Figure 6.35 Example of single I²C write transfer

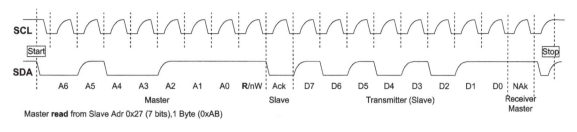

Master **read** from Slave Adr 0x27 (7 bits),1 Byte (0xAB)

Address
7 bits: **0x27** --> **010 0111** + R/nW
8 bits: 0x4E --> **0100 1110** (Write)
        0x4F --> **0100 1111** (Read)

Figure 6.36 Example of single I²C read transfer

If a master needs to transfer multiple data bytes, it starts as for a single transfer, but continues sending or receiving consecutive data bytes as represented in Figure 6.37.

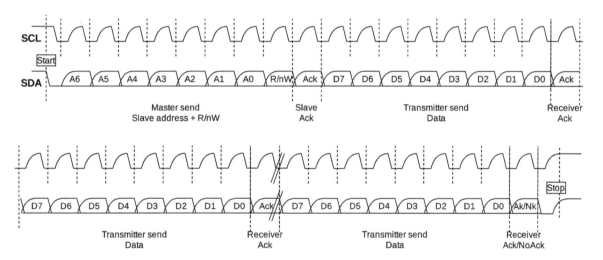

Figure 6.37 Timing of multiple I²C transfer

6.2.9.2   Arbitration

As already indicated, I²C is a multi-master bus protocol: many masters can access the same I²C bus. If one master is conducting a transfer, all of the others must give way. How is this governed? First, recall that the outputs are open-collector outputs such that only the low, logic level '0' state is an actively driven state, with the high, logic level '1' state being generated by the pull-up resistors.

Thus, if one master activates the SDA line (drives it low), it will be visible to all of the other masters, who must verify that the lines are in an inactive state (i.e. high) before starting a transfer. If a master starts a transmission with a Start sequence, all the others must wait until the completion of the transfer via a Stop.

What happens if two or more masters want to start a transfer at about the same time? I²C has an arbitration policy in which each master checks the level of the SDA data line and compares it with what it expects it to be; if the two levels are not the same, the master drops out. Let's assume that two masters simultaneously activate SDA, followed by SCL to Start a transaction, and so both believe they have the bus (the state of the SDA line will be what both expect it to be). They then start to transmit their data while checking the SDA line, and both will continue to do so until one transmits a '1' bit (logical high) and the other transmits a '0' bit (logical low). In this situation, the low will prevail (because it is actively driven, whereas the high is the result of the float created by the pull-up resistor), and the master that was expecting to see a high on the SDA line will drop out, leaving the other master to complete its transfer.

The same principle applies if more than two masters want to transfer data: eventually, only one will prevail. Figure 6.38 shows an example of SDA-based arbitration for two masters; in this instance, the arbitration occurs during specification of the slave address. If both masters had wanted to access the same device, the arbitration policy would continue to be followed until a difference on the SDA line occurred (e.g. in the data portion of the transfer) and the "losing" master then dropped out.

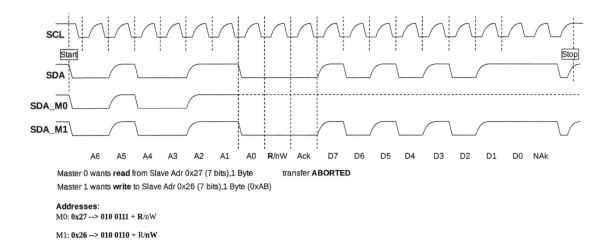

Master 0 wants **read** from Slave Adr 0x27 (7 bits),1 Byte transfer **ABORTED**
Master 1 wants **write** to Slave Adr 0x26 (7 bits),1 Byte (0xAB)

Addresses:
M0: **0x27 --> 010 0111 + R/nW**

M1: **0x26 --> 010 0110 + R/nW**

Figure 6.38 *I²C multi-master arbitration*

6.2.9.3 Addressing

As we have already seen, standard addressing in I²C involves 7 bits. Some device manufacturers specify this in terms of 7 bits (A6..A0) and a separate R/nW directional bit; others define it in terms of two distinct 8-bit addresses in which bit 0 is either odd ('1') to indicate read access or even ('0') to indicate write access (bits 7 to 1 being identical in both cases). For example:

- 7-bit address in A6..A0: 0b010 0111 (→ 0x27), followed by either '0' for write or '1' for read

- addresses in 8 bits of either 0b0100 1111 (→ 0x4F) for read or 0b0100 1110 (→ 0x4E) for write.

In practice, these are identical but appear different on the datasheet, which can cause confusion.

An extension to 10-bit addressing is available on some devices. In this case, two bytes are sent:

■ Byte 1: a fixed element of 5 bits '1111 0', followed by the 2 most-significant bits (9..8) of the 10-bit address, and then the R/nW field set to '0'

■ Byte 2: the remaining 8 bits (7..0) of the 10-bit address.

Each of these bytes must be acknowledged. Then, if the master wants to write data, it just continues with the data to be sent. However, if it wants to read data then it must trigger a **Restart** before resending the first byte (Byte 1) but this time with the R/nW field set to '1', whereafter it can continue as in a normal read transfer.

On a related note, some slave devices, such as EEPROMs, may support larger internal address spaces and the master may have to select which of the slave's possible internal addresses it wants to access or, more commonly, the starting address of a write to this larger address space. Using an approach analogous to 10-bit addressing, this can be achieved in I^{2}C by first sending the bus address of the slave, and following it with a write transfer that specifies the internal register or starting address within the component, after which the relevant data can be transferred (and acknowledged by the slave) until the Stop of the transfer, as illustrated in Figure 6.39.

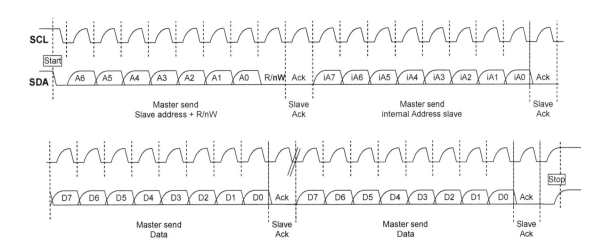

Figure 6.39 Multiple I^{2}C write transfer to a specific internal slave address

In this same scenario, if the master wishes to read rather than write data a similar approach is taken except that, after the device address and the starting internal register address have been sent, the master triggers a **Restart** and then specifies the bus address of the slave again but in Read mode. The data are then read from the slave, and acknowledged each time by the master until the last byte is reached, when it allows the SDA line to drift high (to NACK) to complete the transfer, as illustrated in Figure 6.40.

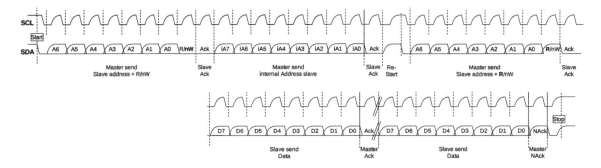

Figure 6.40 Multiple I²C read transfer from a specific internal slave address

Two small groups of I²C addresses (of the forms 0000 XXX and 1111 XXX) are **reserved** for specific purposes, as described in Table 6.14. For more details of the use of these, it is necessary to refer to the relevant device documentation. This leaves the standard address range available to I²C as 0b0000 101 to 0b1110 111.

Table 6.14 Reserved I²C addresses

Slave address	R/nW	Description
0000 000	0	General Call address; a second byte is transferred, e.g. for software reset: 0x06
0000 000	1	START byte, no acknowledgement allowed
0000 001	X	CBUS address, for compatibility between I²C and CBUS devices
0000 010	X	Reserved for other bus formats
0000 011	X	Reserved for future purposes
0000 1xx	X	High speed (HS)-mode master code
1111 1xx	1	Device ID
1111 0xx	X	10-bit slave addressing (as described above)

6.2.10 I²S

In the mid-1980s, Philips invented another, similarly named serial protocol, I²S (I-squared-S), or "Inter-IC Sound", designed to handle the digital audio data associated with CDs, DAT, and portable music players that were first popularized by Sony's Walkman. Despite the name, I²S is not related to I²C.

The purpose of this protocol was to transfer binaural or stereoscopic sound between two devices continuously, helping in the communication between a sound management chip and a processor (or microcontroller). No commands are transferred, only data.

The principal I²S characteristics are as follows:

- serial transmission on one data line (SD)

- synchronous with a clock signal (SCK), sometimes termed the "bit clock"

- indication of left or right stereo channel via a Word Select (WS) signal (not very descriptive, but is the reference name), sometimes referred to as the "left–right clock"

- a Master provides the clock (SCK) and word select (WS) signals; any unit can act as a master

- transfer functions:

  - one Transmitter of data

  - one Receiver of data

  - optionally, one Controller.

Given these definitions, the possible interconnection cases are depicted in Figure 6.41.

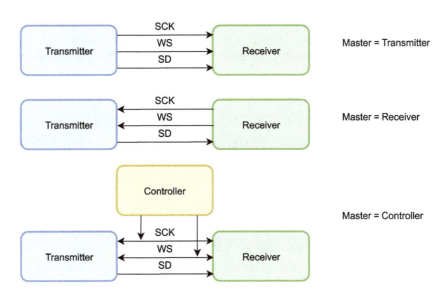

Figure 6.41 Different I²S configurations

We should note that the simple architectures in Figure 6.41 are those in common use. Designers can also add multiplexing and variants in support of multi-master or multi-slave configurations. However, to avoid short-circuits, only one signal of each type can be emitted.

The Word Select signal is used to indicate which of the two stereo channels is being transmitted:

- If WS = '0', data for the Left channel is being provided.

- If WS = '1', data for the Right channel is being provided.

Table 6.15 I²S clock frequencies (other common sampling rates are 8, 32, or 88.2 kHz)

$f_{sampling}$ [kHz] (= WS)	Bits/channel	No. of channels	Data rate [MHz] (≤ SCK)
44.10	16		1.41
	24		2.12
	32		2.82
48.00	16	2	1.54
	24		2.30
	32		3.07
96.00	16		3.07
	24		4.61
	32		6.14

The frequency of this "left–right clock" (WS) tick, or switching, reflects the sampling rate of the audio data; for example, for standard CD Audio it is 44.1 kHz. The data transfer rate, representing the minimum "bit clock" (SCK) frequency, will be the product of this sampling rate, the number of channels (typically two, left and right), and the number of bits per channel (or the "precision"), as shown in Table 6.15. As implied, the rate of the clock signal (SCK) provided by the master unit (commonly ~2.5 MHz) must be greater than or equal to the relevant data rate specified in the final column of the table.

If a mono (rather than stereo) transmission is required, then the WS "tick" for the unused channel has a duration of just one SCK cycle.

Figure 6.42 shows the timing of a standard I²S stereo transmission. The WS and SD signals are sampled and acquired at the rising edge of the SCK signal. The SD and WS can change between two SCK rising edges but only:

- after (i.e. > 0 ns) the rising edge of the SCK signal, and

- within the first 20% of the cycle associated with this rising edge.

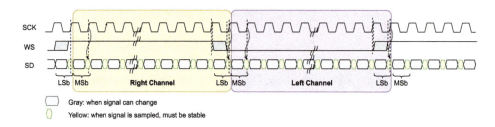

Figure 6.42 I²S timing diagram

In the case where the receiver is acting as the master, it transmits the SCK and WS signals. There is no negotiation between the transmitter and the receiver in I²S (and no error-detection mechanism) and, therefore, it is possible to have a transmitter that provides either more or fewer bits per "sampling" than the receiver is expecting. In the former case, the transmitter only sends data, most-significant bit (MSb) first, until WS changes (under the control of the receiver). The receiver will simply not receive the lowest bits (the least important audio information), and will start to synchronize on WS at the next rising clock edge. In the latter case, the transmitter will add '0'-value bits after the least-significant bit (LSb), until WS changes (again, under the control of the receiver), as illustrated in Figure 6.43. Because the extra "padded" bits are set to '0', they have no informational value and should not be problematic for the receiver.

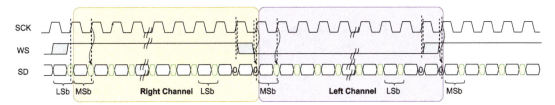

Figure 6.43 Padding of I²S transfer having fewer bits than the receiver is expecting

Because I²S does not provide provision for the transfer of control/status information, another bus, such as I²C, is commonly used to support such functionality.

Some audio interface chips use timings derived from the I²S standard, with either the MSb left-aligned to the WS change, effectively one clock cycle before that in I²S, or right-aligned, with the LSb always the last bit transmitted immediately before the WS change. However, they are not directly I²S-compatible.

6.2.11 1-Wire (One-Wire)

The 1-Wire bus was developed by the company Dallas Semiconductor, subsequently acquired by Maxim Integrated. It is a bus with only a single signal for data transfers, plus a ground wire (which allows a return current to flow through the data wire). 1-Wire is similar in concept to I²C but operates at lower data rates and over longer distances. 1-Wire has been designed for very-low-power slave devices and provides a simple communication bus design for microcontrollers that can be driven using only a single GPIO pin with tri-state capability (where the direction can be controlled), or with an open-collector (or open-drain) output and a pull-up resistor. A UART can also be used. The basic 1-Wire configuration is represented in Figure 6.44.

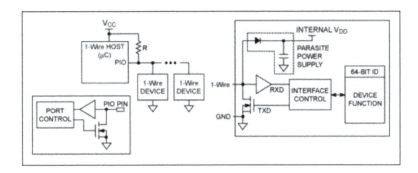

Figure 6.44 1-Wire master–slave configuration from Maxim datasheet (source: Copyright Maxim Integrated Products (http:// www.maximintegrated. com). Used by permission.)

Some 1-Wire slave devices derive their power supply from a third pin, but most obtain power from the data line itself (a "**parasitic**" power supply), which is typically held 'high' at 3 V or 5 V when the line is inactive. In this situation, an internal capacitor is charged through an internal diode, as represented in Figure 6.45. The discharge time of the capacitor must be long enough to cover the longest activation of the data line (when it is driven 'low', to '0', and there is no power supply), which is less than 1 ms.

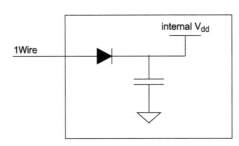

Figure 6.45 Parasitic power supply via diode and capacitor from 1-Wire signal line

1-Wire slave devices commonly take the form of temperature probes, timers, voltage and current sensors, battery monitors, and memories. The very popular **iButton**, which resembles a watch battery, is a portable, stainless-steel packaging of a 1-Wire low-density memory device, offering EEPROM, EPROM, NV SRAM (nonvolatile SRAM) or ROM functionality of up to 64 Kibits. An iButton can also provide RTC (real-time clock) capability (on the DS1904 model), while other iButtons can provide temperature measurement and/or data-logging facilities, making them suitable for temperature tracking.

Some 1-Wire devices offer a SHA-256 or SHA-3 authentication function with a symmetric key to protect their data, and an asymmetric protocol, using an ECDSA algorithm, is also available on some devices. There are also 1-Wire interface devices, providing connectivity from I²C to 1-Wire (DS2482-xx), from 1-Wire to I²C (DS28E17), and from UART to 1-Wire (DS2480B).

Every 1-Wire device has a unique factory-assigned 64-bit identifier, programmed into ROM, consisting of an 8-bit family number, specific to that type of device, a unique 48-bit identifier within the family, and an 8-bit CRC number for identity validation purposes. The 8-bit family identifier effectively places a limit on the number of different types of 1-Wire device that can exist. Nevertheless, their unique ID makes 1-Wire chips, especially in iButton form, particularly useful as electronic keys.

The basic elements of 1-Wire **communication** are represented in Figure 6.46 and are as follows:

- The idle data line high of a '1' is achieved via a pull-up resistor (R_{PU}), connected to V_{CC} (V_{PUP} in the figure) and operable in one of four different voltage ranges:

  - ☐ 1.71–1.89 V
  - ☐ 1.71–3.63 V
  - ☐ 2.97–3.63 V
  - ☐ 2.8–5.25 V.

- An open-collector transistor (or open-drain MOSFET) is used to briefly connect the pull-up resistor to ground and pull the data line low, to '0'.

- Only the master unit can activate the bus, pulling the data line low to '0'; however:

  □ if a slave has received a '0' from the master, it can keep the line low (legacy version of the protocol)

  □ a slave can also put the line low itself to send a "presence" pulse (current version of the protocol).

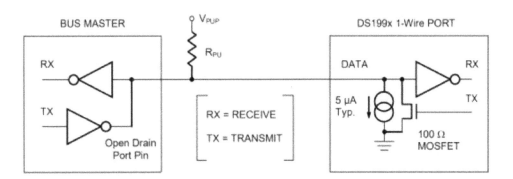

Figure 6.46 Simple master–slave 1-Wire bus connection from Maxim datasheet (source: Copyright Maxim Integrated Products (http://www. maximintegrated.com). Used by permission.

The 1-Wire **protocol** is simple and basically involves the following elements:

- an initialization phase:

  □ a Reset **pulse** is transmitted by the master, which elicits a **presence pulse** in response from every available device(s)

- a ROM-targeted command that specifies what action to take in relation to the slave ROM:

  □ **Read** the 8-bit family code, the unique 48-bit identifier, and the 8-bit CRC

  □ **Match** the ROM, allowing the master to address a specific device on a multi-device system: only the device with the specified address answers

  □ **Skip** access to ROM and go to the RAM component: if multiple devices are on the bus, many will respond!

  □ **Search** for all of the ROM-based identifiers in a multi-device system: this process requires many iterations to complete

- a memory function command

- data transmission.

The basic sequence of a **data transmission** involves a reset pulse followed by an 8-bit command, after which data is sent or received in groups of 8 bits:

▦ The reset pulse is sent by the master, which pulls the data line low for at least 480 μs, resetting every slave on the bus (see Figure 6.47).

▦ Once the master has released the bus, a slave indicates its presence by holding the line low for at least 60 μs.

▦ To send a '1', the master holds the line low very briefly (a pulse of 1 to 15 μs). To send a '0', it holds the line low for much longer (60 to 120 μs).

▦ The slave detects the falling edge of the pulse and reads the data line about 30 μs later, detecting that the line has either returned to high (a '1') or is still held low (a '0'), as represented in Figure 6.48.

▦ If the master wants to receive data (see Figure 6.49), it sends a brief (low) pulse of 1 to 15 μs to start each bit transfer: if the slave wants to return a '1' it does nothing and the pull-up resistor takes the line high, indicating a '1' by default; if the slave wants to return a '0' it pulls the data line low for a minimum of 60 μs.

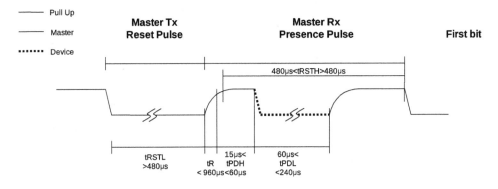

Figure 6.47 Reset sequence started by master; slave device returns presence pulse

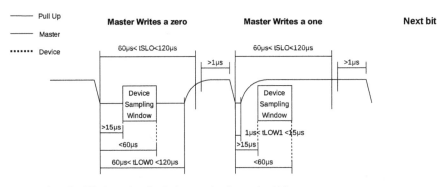

Sampling Window: when the device samples the received bit

Figure 6.48 1-Wire bit transmission, master to slave device

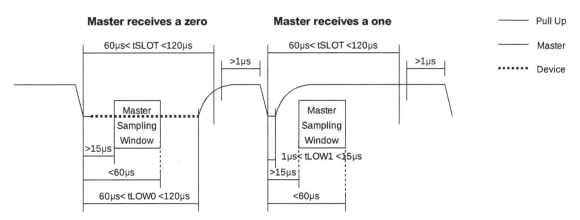

Master receives a zero

60µs< tSLOT <120µs

>1µs

Master
Sampling
Window

>15µs

<60µs

60µs< tLOW0 <120µs

Master receives a one

60µs< tSLOT <120µs

>1µs

Master
Sampling
Window

1µs< tLOW1 <15µs

>15µs

<60µs

Pull Up

Master

Device

Sampling Window: when the Master samples the received bit

Figure 6.49 1-Wire bit transmission, slave device to master

In a standard 1-Wire implementation, data rates of up to 16.3 kbit/s can be achieved. However, some chips offer an "overdrive" capability in which a transistor is used to moderate voltages and timings to accelerate the rising edge of the pulses and increase the effective data transfer rate at least five-fold (e.g. to 76.9 kbit/s). One such example is the Maxim DS28E05, illustrated in Figure 6.50.

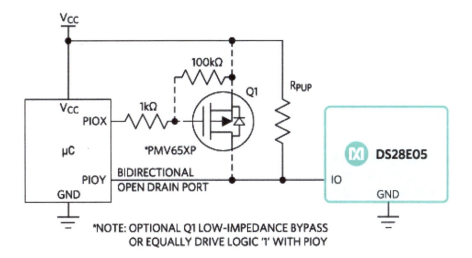

Figure 6.50 1-Wire overdrive power supply from Maxim datasheet (source: Copyright Maxim Integrated Products (http://www.maximintegrated.com). Used by permission).

Table 6.16 shows the comparable timings for 1-Wire functions in a regular 1-Wire device (from the Maxim DS199x family) and the overdriven DS28E05 chip. The parameter values reflect those represented in Figures 6.46 through 6.48, and the timings will vary depending on the particular circuit. With a longer slot time of 120 µs, the bit rate is limited to 8.3 kbit/s; with the minimum tSLOT (60 µs), the data rate increases to more than 16 kbit/s.

Table 6.16 Comparison of function timings for different 1-Wire devices

Function	Parameter	DS199x		DS28E05	
		Min [µs]	Max [µs]	Min [µs]	Max [µs]
IO PIN: 1-Wire Reset, Presence Detect					
Reset Low	tRSTL	480	960	48	80
Reset High	tRSTH	480		48	
Presence Detect	tMSP			8	10
Presence Detect High	tPDH	15	60		
Presence Detect Low	tPDL	60	240		
IO PIN: 1-Wire Write					
Write 0 Low time	tW0L	60	120	8	16
Write 1 Low time	tW1L	1	15	0.25	2
IO PIN: 1-Wire Read					
Read Low time	tRL	1	15	0.25	2 − δ
Read High time	tMSR			tRL + δ	2
Read Data Valid	tRDV	15	15		
Time SLOT					
SLOT	tSLOT	60	120		

6.2.12 CAN

Automotive electronics specialist Robert Bosch GmbH developed the serial message-based Controller Area Network (CAN) bus in the mid-1980s in conjunction with the University of Karlsruhe. Its main use is in real-time control of vehicles and robots, where it allows multiple microcontrollers/devices ("nodes") to communicate with one another without the need for a governing host computer, and with a minimum of interconnecting wires. Although Bosch makes the standard freely available, the protocol is not open, and a license is required to develop applications on it. CAN has also been normalized by the ISO, the most recent update being in 2016, in the 11898 standard, which currently exists in four parts:

■ ISO 11898-1 specifies the CAN data link layer and physical signaling

■ ISO 11898-2 specifies the "high-speed" CAN physical layer, for speeds up to 5 Mbit/s

■ ISO 11898-3 specifies the "low-speed, fault-tolerant" CAN physical layer, for speeds up to 125 kbit/s

■ ISO 11898-4 specifies time-triggered (rather than event-triggered) CAN communication.

The CAN data link layer is divided into two sublayers: LLC (Logical Link Control) and MAU (Medium Access Unit).

Bosch is still heavily involved in developing CAN, bringing forth CAN FD (Flexible Data) in 2012, which allows flexibility of data rates and message sizes, and speeds of up to 8 Mbit/s.

6.2.12.1 Architecture

Low-speed CAN operates on a linear bus, a star bus, or a group of star buses connected by a linear bus. High-speed CAN operates on a linear bus, which runs from one end of an environment to the other, and is the dominant form in automotive applications. The CAN bus consists of two wires (CANH and CANL) in a twisted pair. It works on the basis of differential signaling and must be implemented with appropriate resistances to inhibit signal reflection and force the lines back to their idle state. In a low-speed bus, fractional resistances are implemented at each node, but in the linear high-speed bus, as depicted in Figure 6.51, the bus is terminated with a 120 Ω resistor at each end.

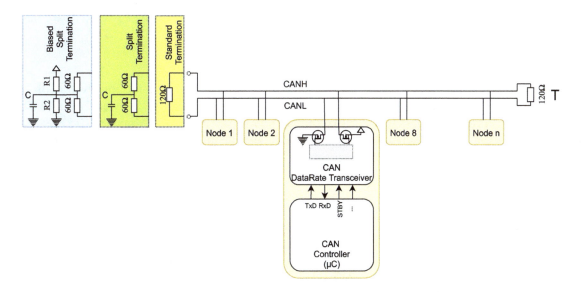

Figure 6.51 Nodes on a high-speed differential CAN bus showing alternative termination configurations

Each CAN bus node can act as a master and consists of three elements:

■ a CPU or microcontroller (µC in Figure 6.51) of some form

■ a CAN controller, often part of the microcontroller, which handles the logical (LLC) data link aspects of moving messages from the CPU on and off the CAN bus

■ a CAN transceiver, which handles the physical (MAU) data link aspects (i.e. the electrical level conversions) of moving the data stream on and off the physical CAN Bus.

In the standard approach to high-speed CAN bus termination (single 120 Ω resistors at each end, between the two lines), the bus floats between the nodes and ground, and can have different absolute levels between them, with line drivers implemented to accommodate this. If the bus is open on all the nodes, the two lines should have the same potential, around the middle voltage, but the most important thing is that their ΔV is low. A more stable configuration in electromagnetic terms, producing a better common-mode voltage (the average of the voltages on the two wires) when the lines are open/idle, is to implement a "split" termination in which two 60 Ω resistors are arranged serially with the common point connected to ground through a capacitor. This approach is more efficient and serves to reduce vehicle emissions. A further improvement of this approach is achieved by installing a voltage divider circuit and a capacitor at both ends of the CAN bus, in a so-called "biased split" termination, with the common-mode voltage determined by the R1/R2 divisor between V_{DD} and ground. These approaches are represented in Figure 6.51.

The CAN protocol that we describe in the remainder of this section is just one of several higher-level protocols that have built on the low-level physical and data link architecture described above. For example, CANopen specifies and implements the upper five levels (3 to 7) of the OSI model for a protocol aimed at embedded industrial automation. It can be used on network media other than the CAN bus, such as EtherCAT and Powerlink, and involves a master unit coordinating many slaves. More detailed information can be found in the appropriate reference documents.

6.2.12.2 Signaling

The CAN bus defines two physical states, termed **dominant** (active) and **recessive** (inactive/open). The differential signaling of the CAN bus is based on a conceptual AND. Thus, in high-speed CAN signaling, a device transmits a dominant (a '0') by driving the CANH wire up towards 3.5 V and the CANL wire down towards 1.5 V, creating a nominal 2 V differential between them. If no device is transmitting a dominant, the terminating resistors passively return the two wires to the recessive ('1') state with a nominal differential voltage of <0.5 V.

Low-speed CAN signaling operates on the same basis but involves larger voltage swings, with CANH driven up toward the power supply voltage (V_{DD}) of 5 V, and CANL down toward 0 V when a dominant ('0') is being transmitted. In the inactive recessive state (representing a '1'), these voltage levels are effectively reversed by the effect of the termination resistors, with CANH pulled to 0 V and CANL to 5 V. This regime allows the low-speed CAN bus to implement a simpler receiver, which need only look at the sign of (CANH – CANL) to determine the value of the signal being sent.

Figure 6.52 shows the simple transmission (on the TxD pin) of the sequence '101'. A '1' is represented by the recessive state and the CANH and CANL lines are both open and at the same voltage (ΔV ≈ 0 V). The transmission of the following '0' involves the dominant mode and thus the two transistors in the CAN transceiver are activated: CANH is connected to V_{DD} and CANL is connected to ground. These are strong levels (hence the term "dominant"). Receiving nodes have an internal comparator that monitors the (CANH – CANL) level and determines the logical level to send to the RxD pin.

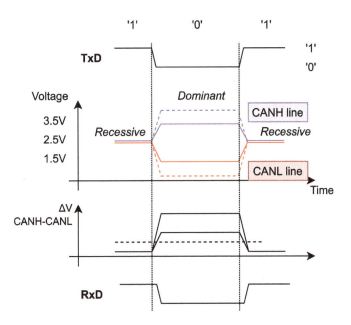

Figure 6.52 Recessive/dominant CAN bus differential AND-based signaling

6.2.12.3 Arbitration

Because many nodes can access the bus at the same time, a CSMA/BA (Carrier-Sense Multiple Access/Bitwise Arbitration) protocol is employed. First, the bus is monitored to see whether a transfer is currently in progress. If the bus is found to be in a recessive state for more than a few bits' duration, the node assumes that the bus is free and starts its transfer. If more than one node starts a transfer at the same time (by sending its ID on the bus), then bitwise arbitration of a form very similar to that described above for I²C kicks in, with each node continuing to transmit until a difference arises between their transmissions, at which point one or more nodes drop out, until eventually only one remains. In the I²C protocol, an actively driven low ('0') prevailed over a passive high ('1'); in CAN bus arbitration, a dominant ('0') signal similarly prevails over a recessive ('1') signal level.

The process is illustrated in Figure 6.53 for three nodes (stations) that start to send their ID on the CAN bus at the same time:

■ The first bit sent by all three stations is a dominant '0', and so they all continue.

■ Likewise, the second bit, which is a recessive '1' for all, so they continue again.

■ For the third bit, Station 1 wants to send a '1' and the other two stations a '0'; Station 1 sees the dominant level '0' on the bus does not match the '1' it attempted to send and so withdraws from the transfer.

■ Stations 2 and 3 continue until one of them wants to send a '1' and the other a '0'. The dominant '0' again prevails and, in this instance, Station 2 also withdraws from the transfer, leaving Station 3 to complete its transmission.

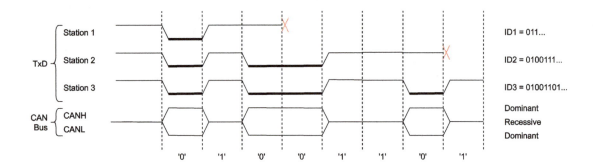

Figure 6.53 CAN bus arbitration between three nodes in the ID phase

6.2.12.4 Framing

The CAN protocol has four different frame types:

- Data – this frame is used to transmit data and is the predominant frame on the CAN bus.

- Remote – used (uncommonly) to request data from a remote source.

- Error – transmitted by any node that detects an error.

- Overload – specialized form of error frame.

Only the Data frame transfers data, with the other three frame types used for different types of signaling. A Data frame and a Remote frame are illustrated in Figure 6.54, but note that there is no data field in a Remote frame. When idle, the bus is in a recessive state.

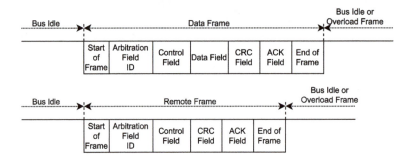

Figure 6.54 CAN Data and Remote frame formats

CAN frames can have one of two different formats, a base frame format and an extended frame format. The only difference between them is the length of the identifier used (which forms part of the "Arbitration Field" shown in Figure 6.54): 11 bits in a standard frame, 29 in an extended frame. An IDE bit indicates which of these is in use, and devices that support the extended frame format can also handle standard messages.

A more detailed view of a CAN frame (Data or Remote) is shown in Figure 6.55; note that the 1-bit RTR effectively forms part of the Arbitration field.

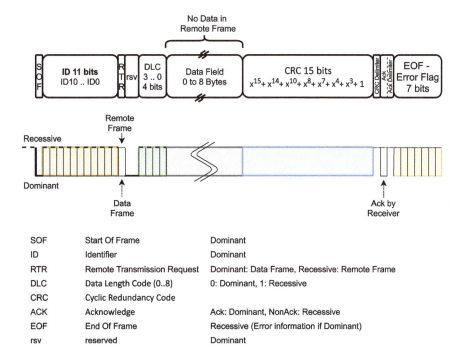

Figure 6.55 Standard CAN frame with 11-bit identifier, most-significant bit first

The standard CAN frame has eight basic elements:

■ The frame starts with a **SOF** (Start Of Frame) synchronization bit, in the form of a dominant line level.

■ The **ID** or **Arbitration** field follows, with the most-significant bit of the message's ID transmitted first. This ID will play the leading role in the arbitration process described above. If many nodes want to start a transmission simultaneously, and provides a mechanism for message prioritization.

■ An **RTR** (Remote Transmission Request) bit follows and indicates whether the frame is a data frame (level is dominant) or a remote frame (level is recessive).

■ The following 6-bit **Control** field starts with two reserved bits (both dominant) and then contains a 4-bit binary DLC (Data Length Code) indicator of the byte-length of the data field, with a value between 0 and 8. Thus DRDD → 0b0100 → 4. In a remote frame, lacking a data field, DLC takes the signed value of the associated data frame.

■ The **Data** field follows, containing between 0 and 8 bytes (i.e. 0..64 bits), depending on the DLC value, with the most-significant bit first for each byte.

■ The following 15-bit **CRC**, with an additional recessive bit as a concluding delimiter, is calculated on the (unstuffed) frame content, including the SOF, arbitration, control and data fields, and a blank (15 zeros) CRC placeholder. The CRC value is the remainder of the polynomial division that uses the following polynomial:

$$x^{15} + x^{14} + x^{10} + x^8 + x^7 + x^4 + x^3 + 1$$

- The **ACK** field consists of 2 bits, the ACK slot, and the ACK delimiter (a 1-bit recessive). The data sender sends a recessive bit in the ACK slot, and the receiver places a dominant bit in the slot as an acknowledgement of successful data receipt.

- An **EOF** (End of Frame) field containing 7 recessive bits is sent (without bit stuffing; see below).

An extended CAN frame is illustrated in Figure 6.56. The 1-bit SRR (Substitute Remote Request) occupies the position (but not the function) held by the RTR bit in the standard CAN frame and is recessive. The IDE (Identifier Extension) bit is also recessive, and an additional 18 bits of message identifier then follow.

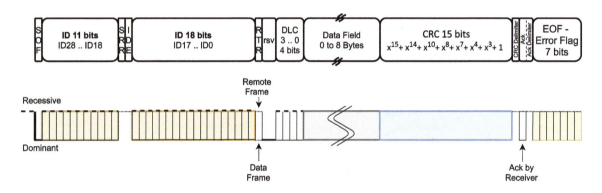

Figure 6.56 Extended CAN frame with additional ID bits (29 in total)

An **Error** frame does not conform to the same format as the Data and Remote frames (see Figure 6.57). It is transmitted whenever a node detects an error in a data or remote frame, and causes all of the other nodes on the CAN bus to send an error frame too. This prompts the original transmitter to retransmit its message.

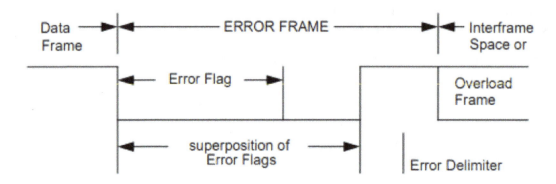

Figure 6.57 CAN Error frame

6.2.12.5 Bit Stuffing

As we have seen, data transfer on the CAN bus is of the type NRZ (Non Return to Zero) and there isn't a clock for bit synchronization. Therefore, in order to recover a clock function from the data, the number of consecutive bits of the same level must be sufficiently short to exhibit minimal timing variation. Thus, run-length limitation (RLL) bit stuffing, as previously described in the context of packet-based protocols, is applied to CAN transmissions that contain five consecutive bits of the same level (either ones or zeros): an additional bit of opposite value is inserted by the transmitter, and subsequently discarded by the receiver.

All fields of the CAN frame can be stuffed, with the exception of the CRC delimiter, ACK field, and EOF. The introduction of a stuffing bit can itself trigger a further instance of bit stuffing, as in the second example below:

- 1111 1001 0 → 1111 10001 0

- 1000 0001 1111 0000 01 → 1000 00101 1111 00000 1011.

6.2.13 Universal Serial Bus (USB)

Toward the end of the 1990s, UART-based transfers provided a data rate of 230,400 bit/s for point-to-point connections between systems. All personal computers had one or more RS232-style DB-9 connectors for various peripherals, while connections to a keyboard or mouse used connectors dedicated to the purpose, as did external disc extensions. In 1996, a consortium of seven manufacturers (Compaq, DEC, IBM, Intel, Microsoft, NEC and Northern Telecom) sought to simplify and standardize all of these different connections and protocols, and reduce the physical space they occupied on PCs, by introducing the Universal Serial Bus (USB) specification. Version 1.0 was little used, but two years later version 1.1 was taken up by Apple on its iMac, which became the first mainstream PC to dispense with legacy ports. Thereafter, the dissemination of the USB among PCs became very rapid.

The USB interface was designed to be self-configuring, requiring minimal user intervention to establish. Besides handling peripheral communication, it was also intended to supply electrical power (~ 5 V), although the maximum of 500 mA available on each connector limited this function to small devices unless an externally powered hub was used, which compounded transformer overheads.

A USB system consists of a host with one or more downstream ports, and thus multiple peripherals, and implements a tiered-star topology with a master/slave protocol to communicate with the peripheral devices, which cannot interact with one another directly. USB hubs may be incorporated into the network, splitting the USB connection into 4 or 8 ports that share the bandwidth of the original port. Hubs can be cascaded in a tree-like fashion in as many as five tiers to connect a maximum of 127 peripherals to a single host controller port.

There have been a number of versions of the USB standard (which have included redesignations of existing standards that can create confusion); they are summarized in Table 6.17.

Table 6.17 USB generations

Standard	USB 1.1	USB 2.0	USB 3.0	USB 3.1	USB 3.2	USB 4
Year	1998	2000	2008	2013	2017	2019
Transfer rate names	Low Speed (LS); Full Speed (FS)	High Speed (HS)	SuperSpeed (SS)	USB 3.1 Gen2	USB 3.2 Gen 2x1 (SuperSpeed USB 10Gbps); USB 3.2 Gen 2x2 (SuperSpeed USB 20Gbps)	
Re-named @USB 3.1			USB 3.1 Gen1			
Re-named @USB 3.2			USB 3.2 Gen 1x1 (SuperSpeed USB 5Gbps)	USB 3.2 Gen 1x2 (SuperSpeed USB 10Gbps)		
Max transfer rates (s⁻¹)	1.5 Mbit; 12 Mbit	480 Mbit	5 Gbit	10 Gbit	10 Gbit; 20 Gbit	40 Gbit
Connectors	Type-A Type-B	Type-A Type-B Mini-A Mini-B Mini-AB Micro-A Micro-B Micro-AB	Type-A SuperSpeed Type-B SuperSpeed Micro-A SuperSpeed Micro-B SuperSpeed			
			Type-C			

6.2.13.1 USB 1.1

The Universal Serial Bus really achieved commercial implementation with version 1.1. This involved half-duplex differential signaling on an unterminated single data pair, labelled D+ and D−, in a twisted-pair data cable with two power lines. Two speed modes were available: Low Speed (LS) at 1.5 Mbit/s, and Full Speed (FS) at 12 Mbit/s. This represented a significant improvement in comparison to existing UART speeds.

A USB host (the master/PC end) implements 15 kΩ pull-down resistors on both data lines; when no device is connected, this pulls both lines low, indicating the absence of any connection (or a reset). A USB device (slave/peripheral) pulls one of the data lines high with a 1.5 kΩ pull-up resistor, which overpowers one of the pull-down resistors in the host and sets the lines to an idle state:

- the D+ line is pulled up for Full Speed signaling

- the D− line is pulled up for Low Speed signaling.

This effectively allows the device to self-configure its speed of communication with the host. In combination with the (limited) power supply provided on the USB cable, this offered a new plug-and-play capability not previously available in the marketplace, and a variety of industries rapidly developed to take advantage of this facility. Thus, USB-connected mice, keyboards, joysticks, cameras, loudspeakers, printers, scanners, disk drives, CD/DVD readers and burners, and many others became available.

Another key aspect of the USB specification was that most of the application software needed to drive a USB-connected peripheral would reside on the host, and the relatively few PC operating systems in use (then and now) would be responsible for identifying a newly connected device and installing an appropriate driver for it. This meant that the vendor and product IDs used by the USB peripherals, and communicated to the host (along with various other descriptors in terms of communication and data formats), had to be standardized, but the devices themselves would otherwise be relatively simple to implement.

The USB 1.1 protocol used a NRZI-type format with specific SOF (Start Of Frame) and EOF (End Of Frame) delimiters and bit stuffing, and just two types of connector were supported, Type-A and Type B, illustrated in Figure 6.58.

Figure 6.58 USB Type-A plug (left) and receptacle (middle), and USB Type-B connector (right)

The pin functions for these two types of connector, plus some of those that followed (as documented in Table 6.17), are set out in Table 6.18.

Table 6.18 Pin functions for various USB connectors

Type A/B USB 1.x/2.0	Type-A	Type-B	Mini/Micro A/B	Mini-A	Mini-B	Micro-A	Micro-B
1	V_{BUS}		1		V_{BUS}		
2	D–		2		D–		
3	D+		3		D+		
4	Gnd		4		ID pin: Host		
			5		Gnd		

Type A/B USB 1.x/2.0	Type-A	Type-B	Mini/Micro A/B	Mini-A	Mini-B	Micro-A	Micro-B
USB 3.0	SS Type-A	SS Type-B				USB 3.0	USB 3.0 Micro-B
1	V_{BUS}					1	V_{CC}
2	D–					2	D–
3	D+					3	D+
4	Gnd					4	USB-OTG
5	StdA_SSRx–	StdB_SSTx–				5	Gnd
6	StdA_SSRx+	StdB_SSTx+				6	Tx–
7	Gnd_Drain					7	Tx+
8	StdA_SSTx–	StdB_SSRx–				8	Gnd
9	StdA_SSTx+	StdB_SSRx+				9	Rx–
						10	Rx+

6.2.13.2 Beyond USB 1.1

It was quickly recognized that 12 Mbit/s was not fast enough for data transfers to external disks or even devices such as printers and scanners, particularly given that as many as 127 devices had to share the bandwidth of a single PC USB port. Thus, in 2000, **USB 2.0** introduced a "High Speed" (HS) 480 Mbit/s bus together with, first, Mini and then Micro USB connectors. The latter was still in use until recently on smartphones, for data transfers and charging. A pull-up resistor on the D+ line of a device indicates that it can support the HS data rate of 480 Mbit/s, and then a software-configured status register confirms its capability to run faster.

For some devices, principally cameras, the fact that they had to act as a slave device was a limitation when one wanted to connect it directly to another USB device such as a printer, which led to the development in 2001 of the supplemental USB **On-The-Go** (OTG) protocol and connection, via which a device could act as either slave or master, depending on circumstance. Mini and, subsequently, Micro USB connectors incorporated an additional, fifth "ID" pin to support the function.

In 2008, **USB 3.0** introduced the SuperSpeed (SS) bus, offering data rates of up to 5 Gbit/s, and subsequent iterations of version 3.x improved this rate still further, as well as introducing name changes for marketing purposes, as summarized in Table 6.17. The SS speed improvements were achieved by introducing two extra differential pairs (one pair for TX, one for RX), enabling full-duplex communication and based on paired disparity encoding: 8b/10b for USB 3.0/3.1 (USB 3.2 Gen1x1 and Gen 1x2) and 128b/132b for USB 3.2 (Gen 2x1 and Gen 2x2). As a result, USB 3.0 SS connectors had five extra pins (the other being another ground), as shown in Table 6.18 and illustrated in Figures 6.59 and 6.60. The recently introduced **USB 4.0** uses a dual-lane function to offer a data rate of 40 Gbit/s.

Figure 6.59 SuperSpeed Type-A connector (male)

Figure 6.60 SuperSpeed Type-B plug (left); SuperSpeed Micro-B connector (right)

Roughly contemporary with, but distinct from, the introduction of USB 3.1 came the introduction (in 2014) of the **USB Type-C** connector, illustrated in Figures 6.61 and 6.62. One advantage of this connector is that it is fully reversible (rotationally symmetrical). It contains 24 pins in two rows of 12, and thereby supports both full-duplex communication and dual-lane operation, massively improving data transfer rates. Thus, there are two pairs of differential transmission lines, TX1+/TX1– and TX2+/TX2–, and a further two pairs of reception lines, RX1+/RX1– and RX2+/RX–, as well as the original D+/D– pair for backwards compatibility the Type-C connector also provides two configuration lines (CC1 and CC2, which can be used to determine the orientation of the cable as well as supporting power delivery functions; see below) and supports two further signals (SBU1 and SBU2) for sideband use. USB 4.0 makes use of the Type-C connector to support tunneling of USB 3.x, DisplayPort and PCI Express protocols. In addition, the Type-C connector also has four pairs of power (V_{BUS}) and ground pins (longer than the others, to ensure they connect first) to allow an improved, bidirectional power supply function to the bus-connected device, as described below, and a V_{CONN} power supply to support the electronics associated with the cable itself and non-bus-powered accessories.

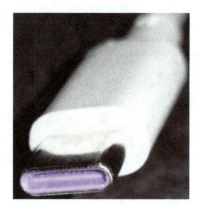

Figure 6.61 USB Type-C connector

	Long	Short	Short	Long	Short	Short	Short	Short	Long	Short	Short	Long
	A12	A11	A10	A9	A8	A7	A6	A5	A4	A3	A2	A1
Cable plug	Gnd	RX2+	RX2-	V_{BUS}	SBU1	D-	D+	CC	V_{BUS}	TX1-	TX1+	Gnd
	Gnd	TX2+	TX2-	V_{BUS}	V_{CONN}			SBU2	V_{BUS}	RX1-	RX1+	Gnd
	B1	B2	B3	B4	B5	B6	B7	B8	B9	B10	B11	B12

	A1	A2	A3	A4	A5	A6	A7	A8	A9	A10	A11	A12
Re-cept-acle	Gnd	TX1+	TX1−	V_{BUS}	CC1	D+	D−	SBU1	V_{BUS}	RX2−	RX2+	Gnd
	Gnd	RX1+	RX1−	V_{BUS}	SBU2	D-	D+	CC2	V_{BUS}	TX2−	TX2+	Gnd
	B12	B11	B10	B9	B8	B7	B6	B5	B4	B3	B2	B1

Figure 6.62 USB Type-C connector pin layouts

Many of the enhanced functions associated with USB 3.1/3.2 and USB 4.0, such as dual-lane operation, derive from exploiting the second set of pins in the Type-C connector, originally only intended to support cable reversibility and be otherwise redundant.

Figure 6.63 depicts almost all of the USB connectors that have been utilized since it was introduced.

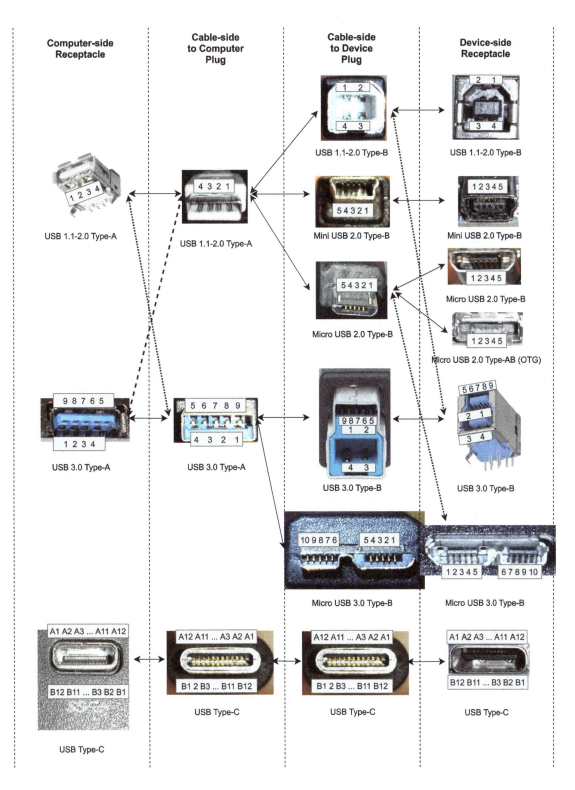

Figure 6.63 USB standard connectors from USB 1.1 to Type-C

6.2.13.3 Power Delivery

In 2012, USB added a new protocol extension, Power Delivery (PD), to standardize and extend the existing transmission of power through USB connections. PD defined five profiles, ranging from 5 V/2 A (10 W) to 20 V/5 A (100 W), the last of which was intended to be sufficient to recharge the batteries of higher-power devices such as laptops and tablets.

The Type-C connector, with its four pairs of power supply pins, has allowed further extension and refinement of the PD functions and specifications. In order to receive appropriate current from a host's V_{BUS} power supply, the CC1 and CC2 lines in a Type-C connector have pull-up resistors on the power-source end and pull-down resistors on the power-sink end. The values of these determine the outcome of an initial negotiation based on analog levels, and then a fixed V_{CONN} value is applied to the receptacle power source: the cable connects just one CC line and V_{CONN}. In standard PD mode, following this negotiation process, V_{BUS} can be at 5 V, 9 V, 15 V or 20 V, with currents ranging from 3 A to 5 A at the highest 20 V output.

An extension of PD, termed Programmable Power Supply (PPS), gives granular control of voltage and current, allowing for customized battery charging. The PD protocol is quite complex and its detail is beyond the scope of this simple introduction.

6.2.14 JTAG and SWD

6.2.14.1 JTAG

The Joint Test Action Group (JTAG) was formed in 1985 when surface-mounted devices (SMDs) started to be widely used on integrated circuits. These obscured many of the connections within a board and made it much more difficult to test it with the traditional tools/probes such as oscilloscopes or logic analyzers. The JTAG solution was to add a number of extra pins to every chip on a board, which would then be linked together in a daisy-chain or star topology (depending on the number of extra pins used), such that a single "JTAG port" or interface would give a test probe access to the "test access port" (TAP) of every chip on the board. By 1990, this "**boundary scan**" approach to testing had been adopted as the initial version of the IEEE 1149.x standards, and is now in almost universal use. IEEE 1149.1 defines the signals to control the physical protocol of the daisy-chained JTAG "bus", represented in Figure 6.64. The standard defines the signals for both debug and test systems (DTSs) and target systems (TSs).

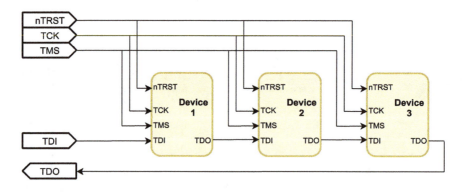

Figure 6.64 JTAG daisy-chain bus for testing of integrated circuit devices

Implementation of a JTAG interface requires four basic signals, together with an optional reset function:

■ TCK (Test Clock)

■ TMS (Test Mode Select)

■ TDI (Test Data In)

■ TDO (Test Data Out)

■ nTRST (Test Reset) – optional, active low.

The JTAG protocol conforms to a state machine that is dependent on the state of the TMS line. State transitions only occur on the rising edge of the Test Clock, and each state has a different name. The TMS line changes state on the falling edge of the Test Clock, and is sampled on its rising edge, as represented in Figure 6.65. The system can reside for as long as necessary in either of two possible initial states: Test-Logic-Reset, with TMS = 1 (indicated in green); Run-Test/Idle, with TMS = 0 (indicated in blue).

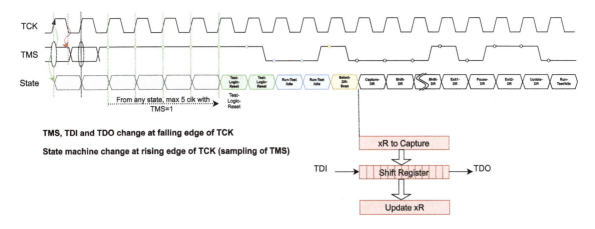

Figure 6.65 JTAG signal sequence to initiate a reset (TMS = 1 for five TCK cycles) and perform a data register scan

From this initial point, a JTAG controller can start sequences to exchange information with the target system. This could involve placing it into a state in which it can receive an instruction in a TAP instruction register (IR), or a state in which a TAP data register (DR) can be read from or written to. The sequences involved are shown in the state machine depicted in Figure 6.66, which contains a DR branch/pathway and an IR branch/pathway. In either case, the sequence is basically identical and starts with a *Capture* command, a number of iterations to *Shift* the information within the register, and then *Pause* or *Exit* commands as appropriate before an *Update* to the register at the end. Then a new sequence can be initiated (TMS = 1) or the idle state can be reasserted (TMS = 0). From any state, keeping TMS at a value of 1 for five clock cycles will allow a return to the reset state. The TMS signal is sent to all of the connected devices.

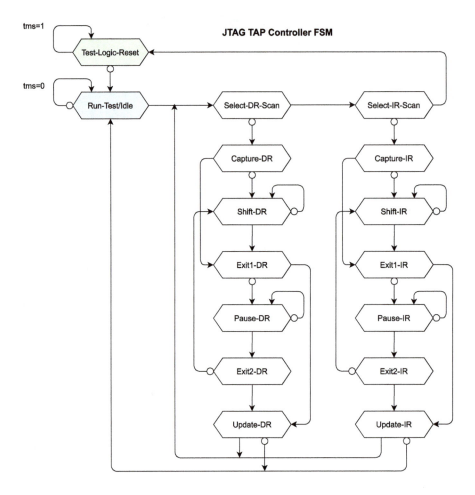

Figure 6.66 State machine for the JTAG interface (showing DR and IR pathways)

The data in the TAP (data or instruction) register is transferred serially bit by bit through the daisy-chained TDI-to-TDO bus with the *Shift* command. The operation of each state of the JTAG controller finite-state machine (FSM) is described in Table 6.19.

Table 6.19 JTAG controller FSM states

State	Description
Test-Logic-Reset	The test logic is disabled, enabling the normal operation of the IC. It can be reached with a maximum of 5 TCK cycles with TMS = 1. As such, the Test Reset (nTRST) pin is optional.
Run-Test/Idle	Some test logic in the IC is active only if certain instructions are present. It could be a self-test or specific instructions, which will be executed when the controller enters this state. Otherwise, the test logic in the IC is idle.
Select-DR-Scan	Controls whether to enter the Data Register pathway of the state machine (TMS = 0) or to go to the Select-IR-Scan state (TMS = 1).
Select-IR-Scan	Controls whether to enter the Instruction Register pathway (TMS = 0) or to return to the Test-Logic-Reset state (TMS = 1).

State	Description
Capture-IR	The shift register bank in the Instruction Register parallel-loads a pattern of fixed values on the rising edge of TCK. The last two significant bits must always be '01'.
Shift-IR	The Instruction Register is effectively connected into the TDI-to-TDO bus, and the captured pattern gets shifted across the bus to TDO bit by bit on each rising edge of TCK. The instruction placed on the TDI pin is shifted into the Instruction Register accordingly.
Exit1-IR	Controls whether to enter the Pause-IR state or Update-IR state.
Pause-IR	Allows the shifting of the Instruction Register to be temporarily halted.
Exit2-IR	Controls whether to re-enter the Shift-IR state or move to the Update-IR state.
Update-IR	The instruction in the Instruction Register is registered to the register bank of the Instruction Register on every falling edge of TCK, and becomes the current instruction once it is registered.
Capture-DR	The data is parallel-loaded into the Data Register selected by the current instruction on the rising edge of TCK.
Shift-DR / Exit1-DR / Pause-DR / Exit2-DR / Update-DR	These states operate just like their IR equivalents, described above, but for the Data Register instead of the Instruction Register.

Today, JTAG is used not only for testing in boundary scan devices (BSDs) but also for FPGA loading and debugging with internal logic analyzers, for downloading code to a microcontroller and debugging it, and for accessing internal registers and memories. Again, the basic approach is to send a command to select a register pathway, read it with a capture command, and then transfer the data out via TDO, at the same time as providing new data via TDI to replace the original, as illustrated in Figure 6.67. Some JTAG commands, such as BYPASS and IDCODE, are mandatory within these so-called TAP controllers, but many elements will be device/manufacturer-specific. The full set of information for any particular controller, assuming it is publicly available, must be obtained from the manufacturer.

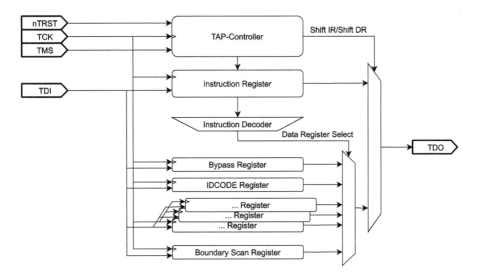

Figure 6.67 Internal view of a TAP controller and its registers in a JTAG interface

6.2.14.2 cJTAG

The compact JTAG (cJTAG) standard, defined in IEEE 1149.7, involves a reduced number of signals (two plus an optional reset) and permits a star configuration for the JTAG bus, in which some units may be deactivated or powered down (which isn't possible in the daisy-chained 4-pin JTAG bus). Figure 6.68 illustrates cJTAG connectivity, and the signals are as follows:

▪ TMSC (Test Serial Data)

▪ TCKC (Test Clock)

▪ nTRST (Test Reset) – optional, active low.

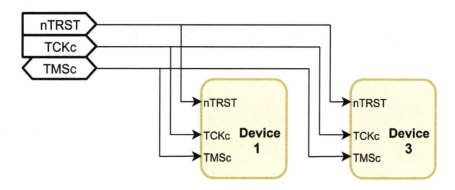

Figure 6.68 cJTAG configuration

It is possible to implement both standards on the same system, but in order to reproduce all of the functionality available within the 4-wire JTAG standard, the cJTAG protocol is considerably more complex.

6.2.14.3 SWD

Pin counts are a significant space consideration in SoC-based microcontrollers and, therefore, not all manufacturers of ARM processors have chosen to implement the 4-wire JTAG "extension" on their chips. Furthermore, the 2-wire cJTAG has not been widely adopted. For these reasons, in its ARM Debug Interface v5, Arm defined the 2-pin Serial Wire Debug (SWD) that provides similar high-level functionality to JTAG but is aimed at debugging rather than testing. SWD supports a star-based topology (like cJTAG), makes use of the existing ground connection, and involves two signals:

▪ SWCLK (Serial Wire Clock)

▪ SWDIO (Serial Wire Data In/Out).

Depending on the ARM processor family, JTAG and/or SWD will be available on specific devices; for example, the Cortex-M0 supports JTAG for boundary scanning and SWD for debugging, which can be configured to support up to four breakpoints and two watchpoints. JTAG cannot be used for debugging purposes in this family.

In the Cortex-M0, the nRESET pin selects between a JTAG boundary scan, available when the global signal nRESET = 0, and SWD debug (when nRESET = 1). This means that a boundary scan is feasible only when the processor is in the reset state, and debugging only when the processor is running. The SWD debug port is disabled while the processor (e.g. NXP UM10518) is in the reset state. The following steps should be followed to perform boundary scan testing:

1. Erase any user code residing in flash memory.

2. Power up the device with the nRESET pin pulled HIGH externally (placing the TAP controller in Run-Test/Idle mode).

3. Wait for at least 250 µs.

4. Pull the nRESET pin LOW externally to activate the TAP controller's Test-Logic-Reset state (POR or BOD reset will have the same effect).

5. Perform boundary scan operations.

6. Once boundary scan operations are complete, assert the nTRST pin to enable SWD debug mode and release the nRESET pin (pull it HIGH again).

6.2.14.4 JTAG/SWD Connectors

Many techniques exists to download microcontroller code and to debug it. One such technique makes use of the capability of some processors to incorporate a piece of program code in internal ROM memory called a **loader**. If a specific sequence of signals is supplied when the Reset pin is activated, the loader will look for new code being provided either via a UART interface or a USB interface, depending on the specific microcontroller.

This technique can be useful for remote downloading of new code onto a microcontroller. In the earlier stages of debugging, a better approach is the use of the standardized protocols described above: JTAG or SWD. Many development boards incorporate a standardized connector that can be linked to debugging adaptors in support of testing and programming. In practice, there a variety of connectors and pin arrangements in use, depending on the manufacturer of the board and the debugging tool. The connectors on the board are typically male, and have two rows of pins with a gap between them of 2.54 mm (0.1") or 1.27 mm (0.05"); Figure 6.69 shows a few examples. The same connector can support both standard JTAG and SWD signals, although not simultaneously: the development tools need to confirm which protocol is to be used. A female connector is plugged into this connector, with a flat cable leading to the debugging adaptor; ULINK2 and SEGGER J-Link are commonly used examples. On the other side of the adaptor, a USB connection enables connection to a PC that hosts the user debugging software.

Some development kits directly incorporate such adaptors on the development board: an inexpensive development tool can be acquired by severing this and using it independently of the target microcontroller.

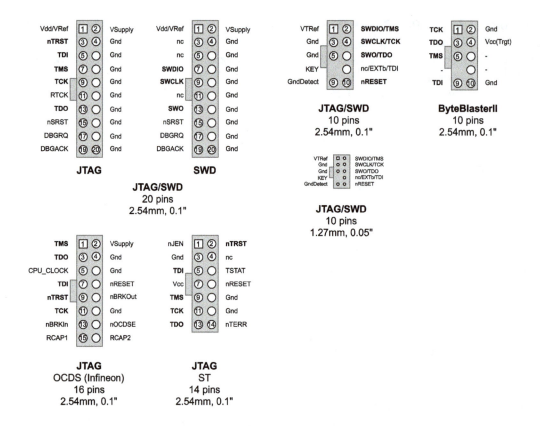

Figure 6.69 Examples of different onboard debug/test connectors for JTAG and/or SWD

Figure 6.70 shows three kinds of connections available on different microcontrollers. The upper parts of the figures represent the connections for the (SWD or JTAG) debugging signals. An additional capability is that of tracing data access or program execution, with the requisite connections shown in the lower parts of the figures. The simplest of these (e.g. ARM Cortex-M CoreSight) uses only one pin (SWO), or there may be four pins of data accompanied by a Trace Clock.

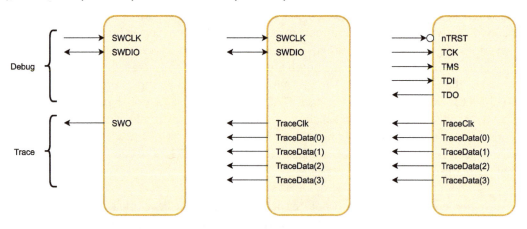

Figure 6.70 Debug and trace component pins for SWD and JTAG interfaces

6.2.15 LVDS

Low-voltage differential signaling (LVDS) does what its name suggests: it operates at low power and uses differential signaling on two lines (typically in a twisted-pair) for data transmission at very high rates of up to 3 Gbit/s. It is a physical/electrical standard rather than a protocol and was originally developed in 1994 by National Semiconductor and specified in TIA/EIA-644.

LVDS was designed as a unidirectional point-to-point link, with one transmitter and one receiver, as represented in Figure 6.71. The absolute voltage is between 1.0 V and 1.4 V, and the differential voltage between the two lines is small, at around ±350 mV. The drivers should provide ±3.5 mA of current on a 100 Ω termination resistor.

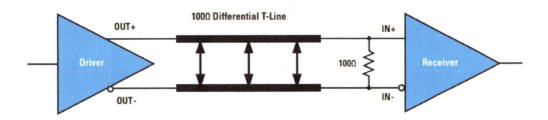

Figure 6.71 Point-to-point LVDS, from National Semiconductor (source: https://www.ti.com/interface/lvds-m-lvds-pecl/overview.html LVDS_ OwnersManual_snla187.pdf Fig 2.1 Reproduced with permission from Texas Instruments.)

Although intended as a point-to-point link, demand grew for support of multiple receivers ("multi-drop"), and the standard was revised to support up to 32 receivers (so-called "Bus LVDS"), in the form of TIA/EIA-644-A. A "multi-point" version, M-LVDS, involving multiple transmitters as well as receivers in a bidirectional, half-duplex configuration, has subsequently been defined via the TIA/EIA-899 specification.

The target application of LVDS was the high-speed transfer of video data over distances of a few meters, in support of video displays, cameras, and so on. A variety of communication protocols in this realm now use it as their foundation, and it is also used to support general-purpose computer buses. The first and best-known of these protocols is Flat Panel Display Link (FPD-Link), developed by National Semiconductor in 1996, and now used in most laptops, tablets and flat-screen monitors/TVs to move data from a graphics processing unit to the display controller.

As indicated in Figure 6.72, the theoretical maximum transfer rate for LVDS is 1.923 Gbit/s, and for M-LVDS is 500 Mbit/s. Higher rates are possible but not within the published standards.

In the first instance, data is transferred serially on the differential lines. The next step involves taking parallel-bus input data supplied synchronously with a clock and transferring it serially over several metres at high speed. Depending on the overlying communications protocol, the number of bits serialized (and then deserialized at the receiver, hence the term "SerDes") can change. The single differential bus of the TI/National Semiconductor DS92LV18 SerDes chip is represented in Figure 6.73. The 18-bit parallel bus input ("LVTTL" in the figure) is serialized onto the differential LVDS two-wire line, least-significant-bit first. The absence of a separate clock signal transmission means that synchronization between transmitter and receiver has to be accomplished via the data line, aided by a 'high' start bit (C1) and 'low' stop bit (C0) placed around every 18-bit word. Thus, synchronization of a SerDes transmitter/receiver pairing is achieved by the receiver's detection of rising edges on the data line of either specific synchronization patterns or the repeating low-to-high transition (marked in red in the figure) of consecutive stop and start (clock) bits in the "random" data stream.

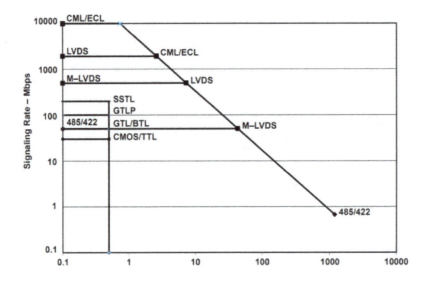

Figure 6.72 Data rate vs transfer distance [m] for various technologies (source: https://www.ti.com/lit/ug/slld009/slld009.pdf Fig 1.1 Reproduced with permission from Texas Instruments.)

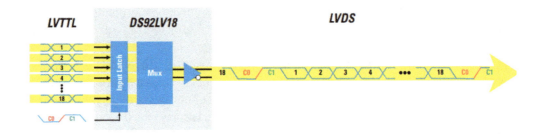

Figure 6.73 LVDS serializer with clock function embedded in the differential data line from National Semiconductor (source: https://www.ti.com/interface/lvds-m-lvds-pecl/overview.html LVDS_OwnersManual_snla187.pdf Fig 3.2 Reproduced with permission from Texas Instruments.)

The FPD-Link protocol enables the transfer of 18-bit RGB video data over LVDS by using **four** differential twisted-pair lines: three for data and one for an LVDS clock signal, which is processed through a phase-locked loop (PLL) device at the transmitter and receiver ends to implement the necessary frequency and phase conversions. Figure 6.74 illustrates this transfer (as performed by a TI/National Semiconductor DS90CR217 transmitter chip), with the 21-bit parallel input (18 RGB bits plus 3 control bits; "LVTTL" in the figure) serialized into three 7-bit outputs on each clock cycle, making the LVDS bit rate 21 (i.e. 3 × 7) times that of the input clock, that is, a clock rate of 85 MHz produces a transfer rate of 1.785 Gbit/s. The PLL-processed LVDS clock is asymmetric, with 2 bit periods high, then 3 low, followed by 2 more high (giving it an overall 7-bit cycle duration).

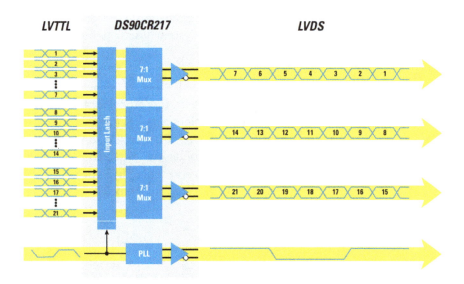

Figure 6.74 Parallel-to-serial LVDS-based data transmission using three data lines plus clock from National Semiconductor (source: https://www.ti.com/interface/lvds-m-lvds-pecl/overview.html LVDS_OwnersManual_snla187.pdf Fig 3.1 Reproduced with permission from Texas Instruments.)

Figure 6.75 shows a more detailed timing diagram for the transfer described above. The 21 bits of data are sent least-significant-bit first, with bits 0 to 6 on TxOUT0, bits 7 to 13 on TxOUT1, and bits 14 to 20 on TxOUT2. As previously indicated, TxClk_OUT is asymmetric, at '1' for the first two bits of the transfer, at '0' for the next three bits, and then at '1' again for the last two bits.

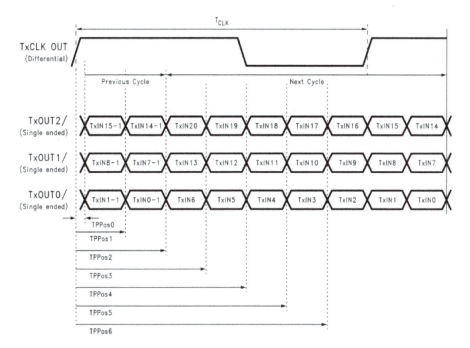

Figure 6.75 Timing diagram for the LVDS output lines (TI/NS DS90CR217) (source: https://www.ti.com/lit/ds/symlink/ds90cr217.pdf Fig.12 Reproduced with permission from Texas Instruments.)

Other popular video connector protocols, such as DVI (Digital Visual Interface) and HDMI (High-Definition Multimedia Interface), use an almost identical system based on the very similar transition-minimized differential signaling (TMDS).

6.2.16 Aurora

Xilinx, the inventor of the FPGA, has developed a data link layer protocol for high-speed point-to-point serial communication called Aurora, which combines a multi-channel serialization and deserialization approach similar to that described above for FPD-Link/LVDS, and the application of 8b/10b (or 64b/66b) paired disparity encoding. An array of higher-level communication protocols (e.g. Ethernet, TCP/IP, AXI4-Stream) can make use of Aurora (represented in Figure 6.76), which enables transmission data rates of 2.5 Gbit/s and is offered by Xilinx as an IP block for its FPGAs.

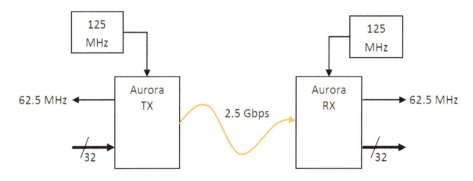

Figure 6.76 Aurora communication

6.3 Networks

Networks allow many computers to communicate with one another. In the simplest terms, they usually either connect together computers in a limited geographical area, generating a **local area network** (LAN), or they do so over a much larger geographical area: producing a **wide area network** (WAN). The **Internet** connects many of these independent networks together into a planetary network (a network of networks or, indeed, a giant WAN) that has the potential to interconnect everyone in the world.

Physical network connections frequently depend, in the first instance, on the buildings in which the computers are located; a densely populated office block will have larger and more sophisticated connections than a domestic dwelling. These local connections are interconnected to form WANs through large network routers and servers, typically provided by third parties in dedicated communications hubs.

At a LAN level, usually within the confines of a single building or campus, connection technologies can be divided into two:

- wired connections (e.g. Ethernet)

- wireless connections (e.g. Wi-Fi).

Over larger distances, a few kilometers for example, connections are achieved via:

▨ fiber-optic or copper cables (i.e. physical media)

▨ wireless radio frequency (RF) communications (e.g. 3G, 4G, 5G).

Today, almost every LAN-connected computer can have access to the Internet through a network gateway and router, with the majority of computer systems being connected together at some level. This trend looks set to continue with the advent and rapid advance of the Internet of Things (IoT), which is seeing more and more devices (not just computers) being interconnected.

Such devices need a way to handle data acquisition, manipulation, and transmission, for which a microcontroller is usually essential. Increasingly specialized microcontroller versions are being developed and made available, and this is the principal area of application of ARM architectures and, especially, the Arm Cortex-M microprocessor family.

6.3.1 LANs

6.3.1.1   Wired LANs

During the course of recent decades, almost all computer systems have become interconnected. For reasons of reliability and speed, cabled connections have been a must, although the increasing capacity and reliability of wireless technologies means that this is starting to change. Over the years, a large variety of LAN technologies have been developed, with a range of different topologies; for example:

▨ single-cable bus-type system with all computers/equipment connected to it, terminated at each end, as depicted in Figure 6.77; it might be a few hundred meters in length

▨ a "star"-shaped system, in which point-to-point connections with every computer spread out from a central hub of some sort, as represented in Figure 6.78

▨ a ring-shaped bus in which every computer is directly linked to two others.

Figure 6.77 Single-wire connection with coaxial cable

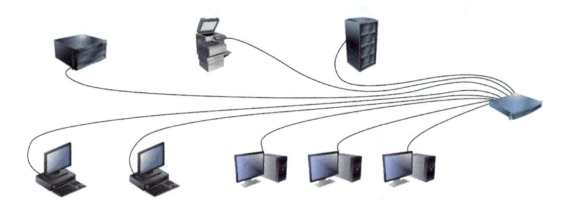

Figure 6.78 Star connection on a gateway/concentrator

The first and earliest of these topologies, the single-cable bus-type connection, typically uses either a single wire (e.g. coaxial cable) or a differential pair and is characterized by a single communication medium. If this is broken at any point, all the nodes on the network fail, making for very poor reliability. Nevertheless, it was widely used in the early implementations of Ethernet and many other network protocols, including AppleTalk, and remains in use in I²C topologies and the CAN bus. A further constraint of the topology is that a node cannot start a communication if another node is already transmitting. The bandwidth of the medium is shared by all and drops rapidly for each node as more are added to the network.

The second topology in common use is the star arrangement in which all nodes have their own direct point-to-point connection to a central hub that routes data between them. Nowadays, this is the most common topology for Ethernet-based LANs, using differential twisted-pair lines and RJ-45 connectors in the connections to the global router. It can involve far more cable than the single bus topology described above, but failure of one node or connection has no effect on the others, and there is no contention on the individual connections, making it much faster overall and more reliable (as long as the hub does its job).

It is, perhaps, slightly ironic that, in the days before PCs, this was the topology used to connect hundreds of so-called "dumb" terminals with RS-232-based cables. The volumes of wires involved eventually giving rise to the idea of using a single interconnecting coaxial cable instead. History often repeats itself!

The third main network topology used is the ring network; arguably, a variant on the single-cable bus-type network that suffers from some of the same reliability and contention issues. Each node has two connections – input and output – and all of the nodes are connected on a ring that runs from one node to the next. To improve reliability, some implementations involved a second ring, with communication flowing in both directions. To improve problems caused by contention, some higher-level protocols introduced tokens or slots to make access to the ring more efficient. Data is removed from the ring on two conditions: the recipient of the message removes it, or the original sender receives the message as input and therefore removes it on the grounds that it has passed around the ring without finding a recipient. Ring networks retain some niche applications but are no longer very widely used.

6.3.1.2 Wireless Networks

Many LAN-based communications today make use of wireless technology instead of cables. A variety of wireless networks exist, which operate at different frequencies and have differing ranges as a consequence, from just a few metres to hundreds of kilometers. Wireless communications are subject to many constraints and regulations, and many of these can vary according to the country of use. Some of the most significant (LAN and WAN) wireless systems include:

- Low-power, medium-range sub-gigahertz RF wavebands in the ranges of 433 MHz, and 800 to 950 MHz, depending on the country of use and the specific protocol — LoRa is a good example, and has a maximum communication distance of 15 km

- Wi-Fi (IEEE 802.11), which operates primarily in the 2.4, 5 and 6 GHz wavebands, and has a typical range of 20 to 50 meters

- Bluetooth, a short-range standard that also operates in the 2.4 GHz waveband but at lower power levels than Wi-Fi, giving a maximum range of about 10 meters

- 3G/4G/5G cellular networks that are aimed at mobile device (e.g. smartphone) communications. Prior to 5G, these operated in the sub-6 GHz waveband over distances of up to 15 km; 5G introduces a 24–52 GHz frequency range that offers higher data rates but only over much shorter distances (~300 m).

There are integrated circuits available in support of all of these interfaces/protocols, often in specialized modules keyed to the particular protocol stack, and it is an area that is in constant and rapid development as protocols increase in number and complexity. As quasi-autonomous processors, they are often connected to a main processor and run in parallel in a heterogenous multiprocessor system. Communication with such modules is typically achieved via USB, UART, SPI or I²C interfaces, and the Cortex-M microprocessor family provides a good basis for such communication modules.

6.3.2 Ethernet

The most commonly used **wired** network today is Ethernet. It was developed by Xerox in the mid-1970s with a data rate of 1 Mbit/s, and quickly came to dominate the market in 10 and 100 Mbit/s configurations, now supporting speeds of 1 Gbit/s or even 10 Gbit/s. It was standardized in 1983 as IEEE 802.3. The method of physical connection has changed over the years. At the outset, Ethernet LANs involved a common backbone with a few dozen nodes connected on the same coaxial cable. This suffered from the two main problems identified above for single-wire bus-type connections, unreliability and contention:

- Sharing the same backbone meant that if one node short-circuited the cable or did not relinquish active mode, no other nodes could access the media and the system would be blocked.

- Contention for the media was (and still is) arbitrated via a system termed Carrier Sense Multiple Access/Collision Detection (CSMA/CD). In this regime, which in many ways defines Ethernet, a sender first looks on the wire to see if another transmission is running; if it is, the would-be sender waits until the end of the transmission, waits a further random interval and then tries to transmit.

If the wire is free, the first packet of its transmission can be sent. If two nodes start transmitting at the same time, both should detect that another node is transmitting, transmit a few packets of "dirty" data to ensure that no other node will detect and accept any part of its transmission, and then halt transmission. Both nodes then wait for a random interval before retrying transmission, in the hope that the interval difference enables one of them to take control of the circuit. Obviously, if many nodes want to transmit at the same time, the network rapidly becomes very congested and inefficient.

In the first instance, the *cabling* evolved, giving rise to two different 10Mbit/s Ethernet forms:

- **Thick Ethernet**, 10BASE5, uses a thick, inflexible and relatively expensive coaxial cable (often colored yellow). Up to 100 nodes with a minimum spacing of 2.5 m (to avoid signal reflection phasing) can be connected on a cable of 500 m maximum length. Repeaters can be used to extend the reach. Small box-shaped transceivers called MAUs (Medium Adapter Units) were needed at every node to achieve physical connection to the backbone cable, which had to be terminated at each end with a 50 Ω resistor. Until MAUs started to be incorporated directly into computers, a 15-pin Attachment Unit Interface (AUI) cable was often required to connect the two, and involved three differential pairs (signals RxD +/-, TxD +/-, and Control +/-, plus Gnd, and +12 V) and a maximum length of 50 m.

- **Thin Ethernet**, 10BASE2, started to displace "thicknet" in the mid-1980s, and made use of a thinner, cheaper and far more flexible RG-58 coaxial cable. The maximum length of a backbone segment was just under 200 m, which could accommodate up to 30 nodes, with a minimum spacing of 0.5 m between nodes, and it had to be terminated with a 50 Ω resistor. Devices were frequently equipped with network interface cards that had transceivers built-in, making separate MAUs and AUI connections redundant: instead, a T-shaped BNC connector linked the device straight into the main 10BASE2 backbone.

Thereafter, the *topology* evolved, with the introduction of Ethernet switches enabling a hub-based star topology that also allowed even cheaper **twisted-pair**, 10BASE-T, cabling to be used. Every node has its own connection to the switch, meaning more cabling is required, but the switch routes a transmission directly to its target and the only collisions that can occur are if a node and its switch connection try to initiate a communication with each other at the same time. Overall transfer speeds increased accordingly, typically to 1 Gbit/s, and to 10 Gbit/s in some implementations. The reliability issues associated with a shared backbone cable were also addressed by this topology change.

Data transmitted over Ethernet is packaged in blocks of 46 to 1,500 bytes of data, plus header, synchronization and CRC components. Up to 10 Mbit/s, the encoding is of the Manchester type, with 8b/10b paired disparity encoding used for higher speeds. The header consists of three fields: a 48-bit (six byte) destination address, a 48-bit source address, and a 16-bit control or length field. The address of a node, known as the MAC (media access control) address, is designed to be unique in the world and is typically represented as six groups of two hexadecimal digits, separated by hyphens or colons (e.g. 0E-AB-31-FE-4D-89).

6.3.3 Wi-Fi

Wi-Fi communications are defined by the set of IEEE standards starting IEEE 802.11, first published in 1997, with one- or two-letter suffixes defining the precise standard in use (see Table 6.20). The Wi-Fi Alliance was formed in 1999 to promote this wireless LAN (WLAN) technology and establish and enforce compatibility and interoperability standards: Wi-Fi is designed to be fully interoperable with wired Ethernet LANs (every Wi-Fi device has a MAC address), and to support the Internet Protocol (IP). The Alliance renamed the most popular of the 802.11 standards to make them more consumer-friendly, giving them generation numbers (1 to 6; see column 2 of Table 6.20). The evolution in the protocols and specifications of the hardware enable increasingly better performance and lower power consumption.

Table 6.20 Summary of Wi-Fi specifications (most recent first, not exhaustive)

IEEE 802.11xx name	Simplified name	Frequency range (GHz)	Bandwidth (MHz)	Data rate (Mbit/s)	Modulation[1]	Range (Indoor/ Outdoor)	Comment	Year
bb	"Li-Fi"	60–790		>10,000 ?	OOK, CSK, VPPM, Optical OFDM	Short	Light-based comms using LEDs; expected Jul 2022	2022
az	NGP (Next Generation Position- ing)						Location- based apps; expected Mar 2021	2021
ba	WUR (Wake-Up Radio)	2.4 / 5	4.06	62.5 / 250 kbit/s	OOK		Low power for IoT; expected Mar 2021	2021
ay	WiGig	60	8,000	20,000	OFDM	10 m/ 100m	Extension of 802.11ad; expected Mar 2021	2021
ax	Wi-Fi 6	2.4 / 5 / 6	20 / 40 / 80 / 160	1,147/ 2,294/ 4,804/ 9,608 (max)	MIMO- OFDM	30 m/ 120m	Draft format; expected Feb 2021	2021
aj		45 / 60	540/ 1,080	15,000 (max)	OFDM		China Millimeter Wave	2018
ah	Wi-Fi HaLow	0.7 / 0.8 / 0.9	1–16	0.3–347		1 km	For IoT Region- dependent	2016

IEEE 802.11xx name	Simplified name	Frequency range (GHz)	Bandwidth (MHz)	Data rate (Mbit/s)	Modulation[1]	Range (Indoor/ Outdoor)	Comment	Year
-2016	Includes ae, aa, ad, ac & af						Most recent roll-up standard	
af	"Super Wi-Fi"	0.054–0.790	6–8	568.9 (max)	MIMO-OFDM		TV white-space spectrum	2014
ac	Wi-Fi 5	5	20 / 40 / 80 / 160	346.8 / 800 / 1,733 / 3,466 (max)	MIMO-OFDM	35 m /?		2013
ad	WiGig	60	2,160 (6 channels)	6,757 (max)	OFDM	3.3 m	Gigabit wireless	2012
-2012	Includesk, n, p, r, s,u, v, w, y & z						Roll-up standard	
p		5.9	10	3–27	OFDM	1 km	Vehicular comms	2010
n	Wi-Fi 4	2.4 / 5	20 / 40	288.8 / 600 (max)	MIMO-OFDM	70 m/ 250m		2009
y		3.65	5 / 10 / 20	6–54(@ 20MHz)	OFDM	5 km	High power	2008
-2007	Includes 1997 and a, b, d, e, g, h, i & j						Roll-up standard	
j		4.9–5	10 / 20	3–27 / 6–54	OFDM	?	Japan only	2004
g	Wi-Fi 3	2.4	5 / 10 / 20	6–54(@ 20MHz)	DSSS, CCK, PBCC OFDM, DSSS-OFDM	38 m/ 140m		2003
a	Wi-Fi 2	5	5 / 10 / 20	6–54(@ 20MHz)	OFDM	35 m/ 120m		1999
b	Wi-Fi 1	2.4	22	1 / 2 / 5.5 / 11	DSSS, CCK, PBCC	35 m/ 140m		1999
-1997		2.4	22	1 / 2	DSSS, FHSS	20 m/ 100m	Original specification	1997

[1] CCK – Complementary Code Keying; CSK – Color-Shift Keying; DSSS – Direct-Sequence Spread Spectrum; FHSS – Frequency-Hopping Spread Spectrum; MIMO – Multiple-Input, Multiple-Output; OFDM – Orthogonal Frequency-Division Multiplexing; OOK – On-Off Keying; PBCC – Packet Binary Convolutional Coding; VPPM – Variable Pulse Position Modulation.

The majority of commonly used Wi-Fi protocols operate in the 2.4, 5, 6 and 60 GHz frequency bands. The specific frequencies in use are dependent on the regulatory environments of different countries. Each frequency band is divided into a number of channels, typically 5 MHz apart. Channels can be bonded together for greater bandwidth. In practice, channels will overlap and interfere with one another if there is not adequate separation between them. The modulation regime will have a bearing on this latter. Thus, in 802.11b, which uses DSSS modulation, the minimum channel separation in the 2.4 GHz frequency band is defined as 22 MHz for 802.11b.

Figure 6.79 shows the central frequencies of the 14 channels of the 2.4 GHz frequency band, spaced 5 MHz apart (except for Channel 14). To maintain appropriate channel separation in 802.11b (i.e. 22 MHz), only Channels 1, 6 and 11 can be used by a station, but different countries may have different regulations about how much separation is acceptable. Thus, in 802.11g networks, which use OFDM modulation, Europe permits the use of channels 1, 5, 9 and 13, but North America does not.

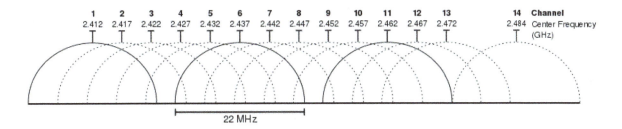

Figure 6.79 2.4 GHz Wi-Fi channels (802.11b, 802.11g)

In general, the range of Wi-Fi communication is quite short and is increased by lowering the carrier frequency: the lower the frequency, the greater the propagation distance (and vice versa).

6.3.4 Bluetooth

Bluetooth (BLT) is a short-range RF communication technology that was invented in 1989 at Ericsson Mobile. Following co-development with IBM it was made an open technology under the auspices of the Bluetooth Special Interest Group (SIG) in 1998, with the first consumer device launched a year later. The principal idea was to dispense with RS-232-style connecting cables and create a Personal Area Network (PAN). The range is typically between 10 m (for most mobile devices) and 100 m (for industrial uses; up to 400 m with version 5). Bluetooth uses the same 2.4 GHz frequency band as Wi-Fi (2.402–2.480 GHz) but at lower power.

This Bluetooth frequency forms part of the short-range ISM (industrial, scientific and medical) 2.4 GHz RF band. It consists of 79 channels of 1 MHz width. Transmissions are split into packets and then sent one at a time with a change of channel each time, using a frequency-hopping algorithm that the receiver also knows, at a rate of 1,600 frequency hops per second. This serves to minimize narrowband interference, and the risk of interception or jamming. Bluetooth now uses an adaptive form of this frequency-hopping spread spectrum (FHSS) modulation technique to avoid noisy/busy channels.

Bluetooth 4.0 incorporated a separate very-low-power protocol, originally developed by Nokia, as Bluetooth LE (Low Energy), and this consists of 40 channels, each of 2 MHz width. Both sets of channels are illustrated in Figure 6.80.

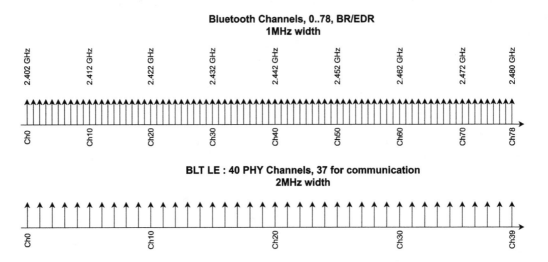

Figure 6.80 Bluetooth Classic (BR/EDR) and Bluetooth LE channels

At the outset, Bluetooth used a signal modulation based on Gaussian frequency-shift keying (GFSK), which allowed a data rate of 1 Mbit/s, referred to as Basic Rate (**BR**). Additional modulations in the form of π/4-DQPSK and 8-DPSK (differential [quadrature] phase-shift keying) were introduced with version 2, providing for Enhanced Data Rates (**EDR**) of 2 and 3 Mbit/s, respectively. Transmission is always initiated in BR mode (using GFSK) before switching to EDR. Figure 6.81 shows the basic formats of the packets in BR and BR/EDR transmissions. Note that Apple has defined a further High Data Rate (HDR) extension that provides a data rate of up to 8 Mbit/s.

BR: Basic Rate packet Format

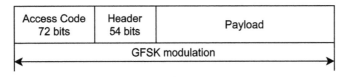

EDR: Enhanced Data Rate packet Format

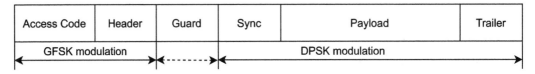

Figure 6.81 Bluetooth packet formats in BR and EDR modes

Bluetooth communication is based on a master–slave architecture, with one master able to service up to seven slaves in a "**piconet**", represented in Figure 6.82. Each slave is assigned a 3-bit Active Member

Address (AMA); more slaves (to a total of 255) can join the same piconet, being assigned an 8-bit Passive Member Address (PMA), but only seven slaves can be active at any one time.

In general, a master communicates with only one slave at a time, in a "round-robin" fashion; there is a broadcast mode but it is rarely used. Slaves cannot communicate with each other directly, the master must act as a relay. However, masters and slaves can switch roles.

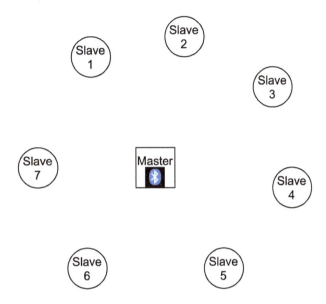

Figure 6.82 Bluetooth master–slave piconet

Packet exchange within a Bluetooth piconet is driven by the master's 28-bit counter or clock, which has a period of 312.5 µs, with two clock ticks representing a single "slot" of 625 µs. The master sends in "even" slots and receives in "odd" slots, but a packet can have a length of 1, 3 or 5 slots, and a slave must listen in each slot in which it might receive a packet. The *potential* transmission frequency changes every slot, but the *actual* transmission frequency only changes with each fresh packet. This regime is depicted in Figure 6.83.

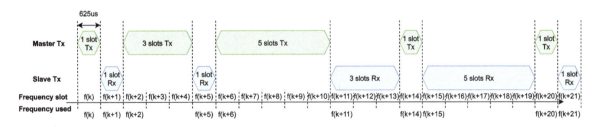

Figure 6.83 Bluetooth time-slot-based packet exchange and frequency hopping

Every Bluetooth device should be allocated a unique 48-bit Bluetooth Device Address (BD_ADDR), which must be in accordance with IEEE standard 802-2014. The address must be obtained through the IEEE Registration Authority.

Bluetooth defines five power classes, which have differing ranges in consequence (see Table 6.21). It is a low-power protocol and quite heavily affected by environmental conditions, so the practical range is often only around half of those shown in the table. Bluetooth specifies minimum permissible ranges but not maximum ones; higher-specification devices can be tuned to deliver significantly longer-range communication.

Table 6.21 Bluetooth power classes

Class	Power (mW)	Typical range (m)
1	100	100
1.5	10	20
2	2.5	10
3	1	1
4	0.5	0.5

Bluetooth is still evolving. It has been the subject of an IEEE specification, but the Bluetooth SIG takes the lead in defining the standards associated with each new version, each of which is designed to be backwards compatible. Table 6.22 provides a brief summary of its history to date.

Table 6.22 Summary of Bluetooth version history

Bluetooth version	Data rate	Modulation	Comment	Date
1.0, 1.0B	BR	FHSS, GFSK	Many issues	1998
1.1			Addressed version 1.0 problems	2002
1.2	721 kbit/s	Adaptive FHSS	L2CAP flow control and retransmission modes IEEE Standard 802.15.1–2005	2005
2.0 + EDR	EDR → 2 Mbit/s / 3 Mbit/s	π/4-DQPSK / 8-DPSK		2004
2.1 + EDR			Simpler, enhanced device pairing	2007
3.0 + HS			AMP (Alternative MAC and PHY): Negotiation of alternative high-speed (HS) data link over co-located 802.11 (Wi-Fi) connection	2009
4.0			Incorporation of Bluetooth Low Energy (BLE)	2010
4.1			Improved user experience	2013
4.2			IoT support	2014
5			Further IoT-oriented improvements Introduction to BLE of error correction via Forward Error Correction (FEC)	2016
5.1			Angle of Arrival (AoA) and Angle of Departure (AoD) for device tracking BLE many-to-many mesh-based networking models for sensors, building automation, etc.	2019
5.2			BLE isochronous channels and power control Enhanced Attribute (EATT) protocol	2019

6.3.4.1   Architectural Layering

The Bluetooth specifications are overseen by the Bluetooth SIG and regularly updated by Bluetooth SIG Working Groups. The SIG is the definitive source of information on this protocol, and the central document is the "Core Specification", with the most recently published version, as of 2020, being that of v5.2, which runs to well over 3,000 pages. It, and many other Bluetooth reference documents, are available on the bluetooth.com website.

Bluetooth defines a layered architecture, defined by a series of protocols akin to the OSI layers described earlier in this chapter. Bluetooth also defines sets of profiles, each profile stipulating how a given device is mapped onto, or makes use of, the various facilities made available by the protocol layers. Thus two different devices will use the same protocol layers in very different ways. This relationship is illustrated in Figure 6.84, and Table 6.23 outlines some of the key Bluetooth protocols.

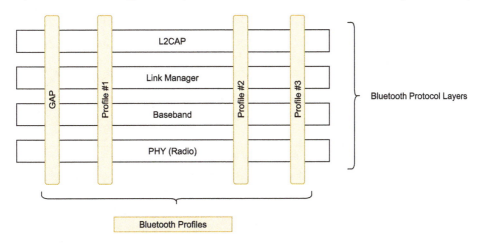

Figure 6.84 View of Bluetooth profiles and protocol layers

Table 6.23 Significant Bluetooth protocols

Protocol	Description
Core System Protocols	
PHY (Radio)	The PHY (physical layer) is responsible for transferring packets of data on the physical channel. The protocol determines the associated timing and frequency carrier.
LMP (Link Manager Protocol)	Classic (BR/EDR) only. Allows the creation of new logical links and logical transports between devices, as well as the control of associated attributes. The Link Controller is responsible for the encoding and decoding of the data payload into Bluetooth packets (i.e. it manages the baseband protocol).
LL (Link Layer Protocol)	BLE only. Similar functions to LMP outlined above.
AMP PAL (Alternative MAC & PHY Protocol Adaptation Layer)	The MAC (Medium Access Controller) layer sits between the PHY and PAL layers and provides addressing and channel control services. The AMP PAL maps host commands to and from the MAC and supports channel management, traffic flow and power efficiency.

Protocol	Description
L2CAP (Logical Link Control and Adaptation Protocol)	Allows connection-oriented or connectionless data services to use upper-layer protocols, supporting protocol multiplexing. Enables up to 64 KiB of information transfer, and handles segmentation and reassembly, flow control and error control. Allows logical channels to be multiplexed over one or more logical links.
AMP (AMP Manager Protocol)	Allows a device to request information from the AMP Manager of another device via a dedicated L2CAP signaling channel. Following initial discovery of a remote AMP Manager, they can communicate directly via AMP physical links.
Core Service Layer Protocols	
SDP (Service Discovery Protocol)	Allows devices to discover the services available from other devices and their characteristics, typically in the form of associated profiles. A service is uniquely identified by a 128-bit Universal Unique Identifier (UUID), but Bluetooth profiles are assigned a short-form 16-bit identifier.
ATT (ATTribute Protocol)	BLE only. Implements peer-to-peer host–client exchange of attribute data over a dedicated L2CAP channel.
SMP (Low Energy Security Manager Protocol)	BLE only. Peer-to-peer protocol used for pairing and transport of encryption and identity keys. It uses a dedicated L2CAP channel. In a Classic (BR/EDR) system, this functionality resides in the LMP Link Controller.
Other Protocols	
RFCOMM (Radio Frequency Communications)	An RS-232 (serial port) style of transmission can be emulated on Bluetooth using the RFCOMM protocol on top of L2CAP. Sixty channels can be emulated simultaneously, including control signals such as RTS, CTS, DTR, DSR, DCD, and RI.
BNEP (Bluetooth Network Encapsulation Protocol)	Specifies how the Ethernet protocol can be transferred on Bluetooth. A full Ethernet payload can be transported through a L2CAP packet using this protocol.
HCI (Host Controller Interface)	Allows standardized communication between a host, such as a microcontroller, through serial communication links (e.g. USB, SDIO, UART) to a Bluetooth master or slave. Different transport layer implementations are available accordingly.
MCAP (Multi Channel Adaptation Protocol)	Specifies the method of data connection establishment between two devices. It is a versatile L2CAP-based protocol that provides a control channel to create and manage a plurality of data channels.

For two Bluetooth devices to successfully communicate with one another, they must both comply with a given profile. For example, Bluetooth LE 4.0 specifies a set of dedicated profiles with which all such devices must be compliant in order to interoperate. Each profile will specify a minimum of information, such as:

- specific parts of each Bluetooth protocol layer used by the profile

- dependencies on other formats/external protocols (e.g. TCP/IP, PPP, WAP)

- suggested user interface formats.

Bluetooth defines two core profiles as follows:

- Generic Access Profile (GAP): All Bluetooth systems implement this mandatory profile. It specifies what must be included in terms of protocol functionality for the differing profiles of the Classic (BR/EDR) and Low Energy (BLE) Bluetooth systems.

- Generic Attribute (GATT) profile: BLE only; makes use of the ATT protocol and provides profile service discovery for LE devices, supporting the interfaces for discovering, reading, writing, and reporting of service characteristics and attributes.

6.3.5 Other Wireless Communications

Many other wireless systems exist on the market. They are typically specified in terms of their communication distance, data rate, power consumption, and topology. Some of the most significant are briefly highlighted below.

6.3.5.1   Near-Field Communication (NFC)

Over short distances of less than 10 cm and with power supply transfer, this specification, derived from RFID, allows contactless reading and writing of passive information stores (NFC tags) in debit and credit cards. To this end, NFC is typically incorporated into smartphones or data/card readers, although some smartphones can emulate a bank card or act as a reader.

An NFC tag is a small integrated circuit with a nonvolatile memory of a few kilobytes, associated with an antenna. It can be powered via RF in order to exchange (usually read-only) information with a reader. The transfer uses a 13.56 MHz carrier frequency, for a data rate of between 106 and 424 kbit/s. The NFC protocol is standardized in the form of ECMA-340 and ISO/IEC 18092.

6.3.5.2   Zigbee

Zigbee is a small Wireless Personal Area Network (WPAN), intended as a simpler and cheaper alternative to similar systems such as Bluetooth. It operates in the same short-range ISM (industrial, scientific and medical) 2.4 GHz RF band as Bluetooth, with a typical range of 10 to 20 meters, and a data rate of 250 kbit/s. Like Bluetooth LE, is supports mesh networking, which extends its range. Its development is overseen by the Zigbee Alliance, formed in 2002, and it follows the IEEE 802.15.4 specifications.

6.3.5.3   LoRa and LoRaWAN

Where long-range communication is required involving relatively low data rates, the LoRa network has seen rapid growth across the world. LoRa is a sub-gigahertz network that operates in the 868 or 915 MHz ranges, and provides a good basis for IoT solutions.

The communication range can exceed 10 km in good, line-of-sight conditions. Dependent on the configuration of its proprietary modulation technique, it can achieve a data rate of up to 27 kbit/s.

Following an acquisition, Semtech is now the principal developer of LoRa. LoRa itself specifies the low-level technology components, while LoRaWAN (Long Range Wide Area Network) defines the higher-level technologies and protocols.

The LoRa Alliance was formed in 2015 to support LoRaWAN interoperability, and its 500-plus members include Amazon (its Alexa and Ring products make use of LoRa) and Swisscom, which operates a countrywide LoRa network in Switzerland.

6.3.5.4   Sigfox

Sigfox is a direct counterpart to LoRa, operating in the same category of communication in terms of waveband and IoT target. Thus, Sigfox is a French network operator that builds networks on a global basis that are aimed at connecting low-power smart objects that need to exchange small amounts of data, such as smart meters and smartwatches, into a low-power wide area network (LPWAN). The communication standard used by Sigfox supports up to 12 bytes of data per message, at rates of up to 100 bit/s (600 bit/s in North America).

6.3.5.5   Cellular Networks

Cellular networks deploy a network of geographically based communication "cells" to enable local wireless connectivity over much larger territories, with most human habitation on the planet now served by one or more such networks, typically operated by large global telecom companies. The obvious examples are 2G/3G, 4G/LTE and 5G networks, and the operators of these networks are now looking to support the rapidly growing IoT market with a standardized narrowband LPWAN, called **NB-IOT**, that is designed to make use of these existing cellular networks.

6.4 Summary

This chapter is dedicated to connections with the external world, which is to say, ways of transferring data between SoCs and other computing systems, or humans using computer systems.

Some bit coding systems were described, as well as ways to packet the data.

We saw many protocol connections with the major links available on a SoC. Some examples are UART, SPI, I²C, 1-Wire, I²S, USB, CAN, and both wired and wireless networks.

All of the protocols described are very common in many designs today.

Chapter 7

Peripherals

In Chapters 4, 5 and 6, we have studied the internal interconnects and external connections that a microprocessor must handle in its role at the heart of a system-on-a-chip. In this chapter, we bring these subjects together to provide an overview of the IP peripherals most commonly deployed in a SoC, considering their main characteristics and internal compositions, as well as the interconnects and external signals though which they link the CPU with the outside world. We conclude with a real-world example of a Cortex-M1 SoC, as it might be implemented on a (Xilinx) FPGA using Arm's DesignStart rapid prototyping tool. The questions we will answer include:

1. What is the role of a peripheral in a SoC?

2. Which peripherals will commonly be present in a SoC?

3. How are peripherals connected to the CPU?

4. What do each of these common peripherals do?

5. What signal interface is associated with each of these peripherals?

6. How is each of these peripherals managed by the CPU?

7. What is the real-world application of each of these peripherals?

Note: In this chapter, and often in documentation, the term "peripheral" is used in place of "programmable interface". Strictly speaking, a peripheral is an external device connected through a programmable interface in a SoC. A peripheral in this sense is typically a device such as a disk drive, a mouse, a keyboard, or an LCD display. However, the term "peripheral" is commonly used in a more general fashion.

7.1 Role of Peripherals

Chapter 2 introduced the concept of IP blocks: the additional modules, with their inherent intellectual property, that must be placed around a microprocessor to create a SoC. In Chapter 6, we looked in considerable detail at the many forms of connection that SoCs in embedded devices might need to support in order to interact with the external world. Here, we bring these two things together to consider the "peripheral" IP blocks used by a microprocessor to implement these connections. The resulting interfaces can be digital or analog, and their number can vary according to the type and purpose of the SoC. Typically, the majority of such interfaces are digital, with very few being analog. The main reason for this relates to the applications themselves, which today involve far more digital interfaces than analog ones. In addition, the integration of analog interfaces requires extra effort in terms of design and manufacturing costs, partly due to the different sensitivity and noise elimination needed in the silicon substrate. Some of the most common IP peripherals used to support digital interfaces are GPIOs (general-purpose input/outputs), UARTs (universal asynchronous receiver/transmitters), and SPI (Serial Peripheral Interface) controllers; examples of IP peripherals for analog interfaces are ADCs (analog-to-digital converters) and DACs (digital-to-analog converters). In this chapter, we will see how these peripherals can be integrated into a SoC, and how they communicate with both the CPU and the external world. The information provided in this chapter does not refer to any specific IP block of any vendor; the idea is to provide the reader with a basic grasp of the concepts needed to work with a general-purpose IP peripheral. However, in the final section, we will consider the use of specific IP peripherals (from Xilinx) to show how they are instantiated and implemented in a real-life example.

7.1.1 High-level Architecture

Although IP peripherals (often shortened to "IPs") can be very different in terms of internal composition and functionality, the high-level architecture for their integration is common to almost all of them. The interfaces involved can be of two types: those on the CPU-facing side, by which the IP communicates with the CPU that will manage and control its behavior, and those on the externally facing side, where the IP presents the signals needed to accomplish its function, which usually means driving a digital or analog electrical signal to the outside world as necessary. On the CPU-facing side, peripherals exchange information through a bus interconnection, following the principles described in Chapter 4. Typical buses, therefore, will be members of the AMBA interconnect family, such as AHB, APB, and AXI. The bus front-end provides the protocol and signals for the interface, and supports the CPU in writing and reading values in the IP's internal registers to control and monitor the peripheral's behavior. This basic architecture is depicted in Figure 7.1.

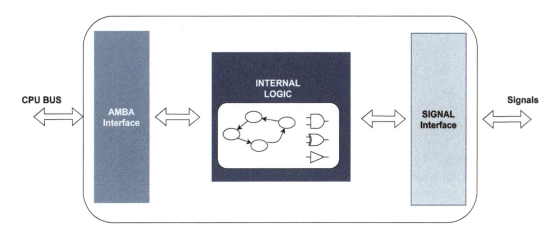

Figure 7.1 Generic IP peripheral architecture

In the sections that follow, we will look in turn at the most commonly used IP peripherals, considering the external interface and signals that each supports, and the registers they make available to the CPU for their control, with the AHB bus being used on the CPU-facing side.

7.2 GPIOs

7.2.1 Description

The general-purpose input/output (GPIO) module is one of the most fundamental and simplest IP peripherals of a SoC, supporting digital connections with the outside world. In essence, it consists simply of a set of digital pins, each of which can assume only two possible values, low or high. The basic exercise for a software programmer of making "Hello World" appear on a computer screen has its equivalent in the SoC world in the form of making an LED blink, which is done through the GPIO.

7.2.2 Mode of Operation

GPIO pins can be configured as inputs or outputs. This configuration is done through software, usually during the initialization stage, but it is not entirely forbidden to do this dynamically at runtime if required by the user application and permitted by the underlying hardware. At a hardware level, the connections incorporate bidirectional drivers, with a control signal that allows the polarity of the pin (input or output) to be controlled accordingly.

7.2.3 Component Diagram

Figure 7.2 shows the internal components of a GPIO IP. It consists of configuration and data registers, a bank of buffers, and the bus interface, which in this case supports the AHB bus.

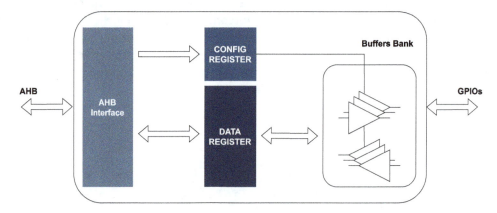

Figure 7.2 GPIO IP internal components

The functional design and operational detail of the AHB bus has been explained in Chapter 5. Here we focus attention on the aspects of the GPIO IP that are specific to its IP peripheral function. The role of the configuration register is to enable the CPU to control the behavior of the IP. As we have indicated, each pin can be configured for input or output. In addition, a pin may be configured to use a pull-up resistor to prevent floating electrical conditions. The data registers store the values from the I/O, and can be accessed in read or write mode, depending on configuration assigned by software. Finally, the bank of buffers is needed to interface electronically with the physical pins on the exterior of the chip.

7.2.4 Registers

Table 7.1 shows the internal registers for a GPIO IP. These registers do not reflect any specific custom nor any particular commercial IP. As for most of these IPs, there is a control register through which to define the behavior of the peripheral and a status register to monitor its internal state.

Table 7.1 GPIO IP registers

Register offset	Register name	Access (Read/Write)	Register description/function
0x00	Control	Write	Program the interfaces
0x04	Data	Read/Write	Write/read digital values to/from the input/outputs

Table 7.2 shows a typical GPIO **control register** used for configuration. In this example, the I/O is 16 bits in width, and for each I/O it is possible to select its direction and the use of a pull-up resistor. In software, these values can be singularly managed, for reading and writing, using bit-wise operations.

Table 7.2 GPIO IP control register bit functions

Bit position	Bit name	Possible value	Bit description/function
[15..0]	Direction [15..0]	0 – Input 1 – Output	Assign the I/O as input or output
[31..16]	Pull-up [15..0]	0 – Disabled 1 – Enabled	Enable/disable the pull-up

The **data register** (see Table 7.3) holds the data for the GPIO peripheral, that is, the values presented at the input pins.

Table 7.3 GPIO IP data register bit function

Bit position	Bit name	Possible value	Bit description/function
[15..0]	Value [15..0]	0x0000 to 0xFFFF	GPIO data

7.3 AHB UART

7.3.1 Description
After the GPIO IP, the next most common peripherals in embedded SoCs are UARTs (universal asynchronous receiver/transmitters). These peripherals provide a SoC with its serial communication to and from the outside world. A UART often finds application in the console port of an embedded system, allowing the end-user to access and communicate with the device, or as an interface for machine-to-machine communications.

7.3.2 Mode of Operation
As a serial communication peripheral, the main function of a UART is to serialize and deserialize transfer of data over a communication channel. Hence, a UART can operate in different ways, depending on the application. Chapter 6 provided considerable detail of UART communication parameters and protocols. To recall a few of these, a typical transmission can consist of 5, 6, 7, or 8 bits per character, have 1, 1.5, or 2 stop bits, and have odd or even parity applied for transmission error detection.

7.3.3 Component Diagram
Figure 7.3 shows the internal components of a generic UART IP. Besides the CPU-facing AHB interface, it consists of control and status registers, reception and transmission FIFO buffers, circuitry to control the transmit and receive signals, and a baud rate generator that produces the timing signal that controls the speed of the transmission.

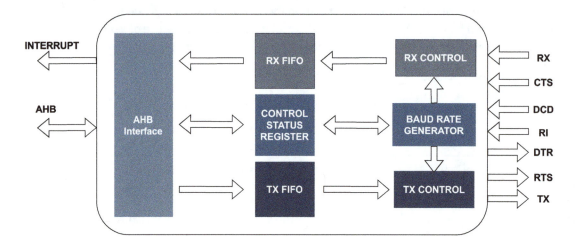

Figure 7.3 UART IP internal components

The roles of the control and status registers are common to all IPs. The main difference between a peripheral such as a GPIO and a serial communication peripheral is the presence of FIFO buffers. The role of these buffers is to temporarily store data actively in reception and transmission, immediately before or after being processed by the CPU. The components that control the signals in transmission and reception (TX Control and RX Control) are the ones implementing the different UART-supported protocols, such as RS-232 or RS-485/RS-422.

7.3.4 Registers

Table 7.4 describes the internal registers of a UART IP. These registers do not reflect any specific custom or commercial IP. Besides control and status registers, the list includes registers for transmission and reception buffers, and for the control and status reporting of line configuration and modem signal configuration. We provide a brief description of each of these registers below.

Table 7.4 UART IP registers

Register offset	Register name	Access (Read/Write)	Register description/function
0x00	Control	Write	Program the interfaces
0x04	Status	Read	Write/read digital values to the input/outputs
0x08	RX Buffer	Read	Read last character present in the FIFO
0x0C	TX Buffer	Write	Write last character to insert in the FIFO
0x10	Line Control	Write	Control the line configuration
0x14	Line Status	Read	Read the status of the line
0x18	Modem Control	Write	Control the modem configuration
0x1C	Modem Status	Read	Read the status of the line

The **control register** (see Table 7.5) provides for the basic control of the UART peripheral. Thus, it is possible to enable or disable the peripheral, reset it, or reset the FIFO buffers.

Table 7.5 UART IP control register bit functions

Bit position	Bit name	Possible value	Bit description/function
0	Enable	0 – Disable 1 – Enable	Enable/disable the UART controller
1	RST	0 – Disable 1 – Enable	Reset the IP
2	TX FIFO RST	0 – Disable 1 – Enable	Reset the transmission FIFO
3	RX FIFO RST	0 – Disable 1 – Enable	Reset the reception FIFO

The **status register** (see Table 7.6) stores information about the internal state of the IP. Examples of such information are the presence of error in the state machine, the receiving FIFO being full, or the transmitting FIFO being empty. Note that there is no reference to any of the output signals in this register; all the information regarding external signals is stored in the more specific registers that follow.

Table 7.6 UART IP status register bit functions

Bit position	Bit name	Possible value	Bit description/function
0	ERROR	0 – Non-active 1 – Active	Error detected
1	RX FULL	0 – Non-active 1 – Active	Provides information about the reception FIFO
2	RX EMPTY	0 – Non-active 1 – Active	Provides information about the reception FIFO
3	TX FULL	0 – Non-active 1 – Active	Provides information about the transmission FIFO
4	TX EMPTY	0 – Non-active 1 – Active	Provides information about the transmission FIFO

The UART **line control register** (see Table 7.7) is designed to enable control of the basic line communication parameters, such as the number of bits per character, the number of stop bits, and the parity mode used for error detection.

Table 7.7 UART IP line control register bit functions

Bit position	Bit name	Possible value	Bit description/function
[1..0]	Word Length	00 – 5 bits 01 – 6 bits 10 – 7 bits 11 – 8 bits	Define the word length in number of characters
2	Stop	0 – 1 1 – 2	Define the number of stop bits (1 or 2) used in the communication
3	Parity EN	0 – Non-active 1 – Active	Enable/disable the parity bits
4	Parity Mode	0 – Even 1 – Odd	Define the parity type

The **line status register** (see Table 7.8) stores information about the state of the communication line; examples include the presence of new data in the reception FIFO, the overrunning of the FIFO, and the existence of parity or framing errors.

Table 7.8 UART IP line status register bit functions

Bit position	Bit name	Possible value	Bit description/function
0	Data Ready	0 – Non-active 1 – Active	Indicates the presence of new data in the RX FIFO
1	Overrun	0 – Non-active 1 – Active	A new character has been received and the buffer has not been cleared by a previous read
2	Parity Error	0 – Non-active 1 – Active	The parity check has detected an error
3	Framing	0 – Non-active 1 – Active	The reception of the last character was not correct

Through a UART's **modem control register** (see Table 7.9), the programmer can manually control the output modem signals, DTR (Data Terminal Ready) and RTS (Ready To Send).

Table 7.9 UART IP modem control register bit functions

Bit position	Bit name	Possible value	Bit description/function
0	DTR	0 – DTR low 1 – DTR high	Data Terminal Ready
1	RTS	0 – RTS low 1 – RTS high	Request to Send

The complement to this modem control register is the **modem status register** (see Table 7.10), which stores information about the modem signals input to the UART. Furthermore, it provides useful information in terms of detecting the receipt of new characters and the presence of an entry call. The descriptions and behaviors of these modem signals were described in the RS-232 section of Chapter 6.

Table 7.10 UART IP modem status register bit functions

Bit position	Bit name	Possible value	Bit description/function
0	DCTS	0 – Non-active 1 – Active	Delta Clear To Send: set when CTS state changes
1	DDSR	0 – Non-active 1 – Active	Delta Data Set Ready: set when DSR state changes
2	TERI	0 – Non-active 1 – Active	Trailing Edge Ring Indicator
3	DDCD	0 – Non-active 1 – Active	Delta Data Carrier Detect: set when DCD state changes
4	CTS	0 – Non-active 1 – Active	Clear To Send
5	DSR	0 – Non-active 1 – Active	Data Set Ready

Bit position	Bit name	Possible value	Bit description/function
6	RI	0 – Non-active 1 – Active	Ring Indicator
7	DCD	0 – Non-active 1 – Active	Data Carrier Detect

7.4 AHB Timer

7.4.1 Description
The timer peripheral is another fundamental IP commonly present in SoC devices. It is the basic element behind the synchronization of system operation.

7.4.2 Mode of Operation
Timer operation and features can vary significantly, depending on the implementation and the vendor. In general, timers work in one of three different modes: generate, capture, or pulse-width modulation (PWM). In generate mode, the timer is initialized and configured for counting mode, either counting up or counting down. If and when the timer reaches a predefined upper value (or zero, when counting down) without being reset, it normally raises an interrupt. In capture mode, the timer is configured to be sensitive to a particular input, storing its value when the input occurs. In PWM mode, the timer runs continuously (free-running). In this case the timer is typically using two values (period and pulse width) to determine the duty cycle of a device (e.g. a motor or an LED) connected to the timer.

7.4.3 Component Diagram
Figure 7.4 shows the internal components of a generic timer IP. This peripheral is mainly composed of counters: logic modules able to count in binary. A timer usually hosts multiple counters, which can run independently of one another.

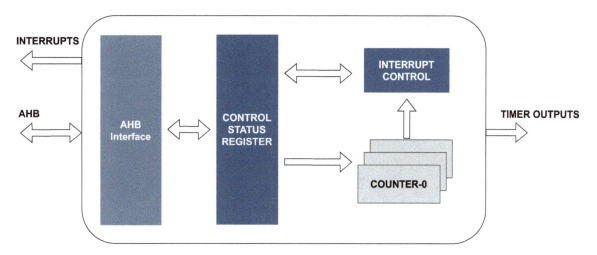

Figure 7.4 Timer IP internal components

415

In generate mode, the role of a counter module is to increment or decrement a value, as determined by the control registers. It is possible to start, stop, and reset counters via the same control registers. The status register makes it possible to check the current value of the count and/or whether it has reached its lower or upper limit (as appropriate). The role of the interrupt control module is to manage the interrupt outputs, if configured, when a count thus expires.

7.4.4 Registers

The register map of a timer IP can be very different depending on the implementation. A timer IP peripheral can support multiple counters/timers, and for each one there are usually four registers: control, status, load, and counter. For this reason, the number of internal registers can sometimes be very large, depending on the number of individual timers included in the IP. Table 7.11 shows an example of a register map for a timer IP with three internal counters/timers.

Table 7.11 Timer IP registers

Register offset	Register name	Access (Read/Write)	Register description/function
0x00	Control 0	Write	Program the interfaces
0x04	Status 0	Read	Status register
0x08	Load 0	Write	Load the initial value to the counter
0x0C	Counter 0	Write	Set the final count value to the counter
0x10	Control 1	Write	Program the interfaces
0x14	Status 1	Read	Status register
0x08	Load 1	Write	Load the initial value to the counter
0x0C	Counter 1	Write	Set the final count value to the counter
0x20	Control 2	Write	Program the interfaces
0x24	Status 2	Read	Status register
0x28	Load 2	Write	Load the initial value to the counter
0x2C	Counter 2	Write	Set the final count value to the counter

The **control register** (see Table 7.12) determines the working mode of the timers. Through the control register, it is possible to enable or disable each individual timer, set its mode to capture or generate, and set its counting mode to up or down. Furthermore, it is possible to configure a timer to raise an interrupt when its countdown (or count-up) completes.

Table 7.12 Timer IP control register bit functions

Bit position	Bit name	Possible value	Bit description/function
0	Enable	0 – Disable 1 – Enable	Enable/disable the timer
1	Mode	0 – Generate 1 – Capture	Set the timer mode
2	Up	0 – Down 1 – Up	Set the counting mode up or down
3	Generate	0 – Disable 1 – Enable	Enable Generate mode

Bit position	Bit name	Possible value	Bit description/function
4	Capture	0 – Disable 1 – Enable	Enable Capture mode
5	Reload	0 – Disable 1 – Enable	Auto-reload timer after count/capture
6	Interrupt	0 – Disable 1 – Enable	Enable Interrupt
7	PWM	0 – Disable 1 – Enable	Enable Pulse-Width Modulation mode

The **status register** (see Table 7.13) contains, for each individual timer, the internal status. Examples of internal status are the activation state of the timer, whether it is counting, whether it has completed its count, and whether an interrupt has been detected.

Table 7.13 Timer IP status register bit functions

Bit position	Bit name	Possible value	Bit description/function
0	ACTIVE	0 – Non-active 1 – Active	Timer is active
1	COUNT	0 – Non-active 1 – Active	Timer is counting
2	DONE	0 – Non-active 1 – Active	Timer has ended the count
3	INT	0 – Non-active 1 – Active	Interrupt detected

7.5 AHB SPI

7.5.1 Description
SPI (Serial Peripheral Interface) is a serial, full-duplex synchronous interface. As we saw in Chapter 6, it involves a master–slave architecture with one master and one or more slaves connected to a 4-wire serial bus, which uses four signals for communication: MOSI (Master Out, Slave In), MISO (Master In, Slave Out), SCK (Serial Clock), and CS (Chip Select; also known as Chip Enable [CE]). SPI is used to connect on-board chips, such as high-speed ADCs or DACs, or full-duplex communication interfaces such as network or memory chips.

7.5.2 Mode of Operation
As a SoC peripheral, an SPI IP is normally used as a master unit; it is very rare that it is used as a slave peripheral in this context, but it can have this role where the SoC is not the main controller of a complex system. Depending on whether the SPI peripheral is in master or slave mode it can be configured for alternative clock polarities and phases, which together determine clock-edge sensitivity (falling or rising) in the course of data transmission. The four possible combinations of these and the resulting SPI operational modes are captured in Table 7.14. Further details can be found in Chapter 6.

Table 7.14 SPI operational modes

SPI mode	Clock Polarity CPOL	Clock Phase CPHA	Clock Edge CKE/nCPHA
0	0	0	1
1	0	1	0
2	1	0	1
3	1	1	0

7.5.3 Component Diagram

Figure 7.5 shows a simplified component diagram for an SPI IP peripheral. As a serial communication interface, the SPI IP contains reception and transmission FIFO buffers and a clock rate generator, configured through the control register. Because the SPI IP is a full-duplex interface, in which transmission and reception can be simultaneous, the reception and transmission control units are implemented as separate modules, and can function independently. A shift register is also present in each of these modules, providing the ability to deserialize the payload data in the case of receipt and serialize it in the case of transmission.

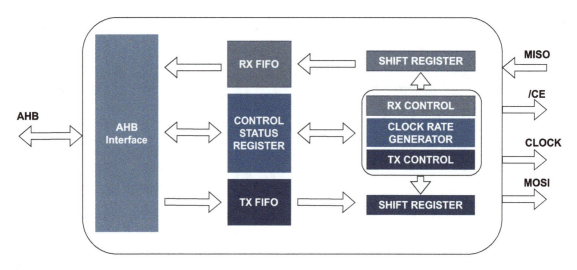

Figure 7.5 SPI IP internal components

7.5.4 Registers

Table 7.15 describes the internal registers of an SPI IP. Besides control and status registers, the list includes registers for transmission and reception buffers, and an address register for those occasions when the peripheral is configured as a slave device.

Table 7.15 SPI IP registers

Register offset	Register name	Access (Read/Write)	Register description/function
0x00	Control	Write	Program the interfaces
0x04	Status	Read	Write/read digital values to the input/outputs

Register offset	Register name	Access (Read/Write)	Register description/function
0x08	RX Buffer	Read	Read last character present in the FIFO
0x0C	TX Buffer	Write	Write last character to insert in the FIFO
0x10	Slave Address	Write	Define the address in case of slave mode

For the SPI peripheral, the **control register** (see Table 7.16) provides access to the configuration of the IP. Besides the clock configuration described above, it is possible to enable or disable the peripheral, and set its operating mode as master or slave. It is also possible to reset the reception and transmission FIFO buffers and, in this example, define whether the most- or least-significant bit is transmitted first.

Table 7.16 SPI IP control register bit functions

Bit position	Bit name	Possible value	Bit description/function
0	Enable	0 – Disable 1 – Enable	Enable/disable the SPI controller
1	Master	0 – Slave 1 – Master	Define the operational mode of the SPI controller
2	Clock Polarity	0 – Low 1 – High	Define the polarity of the SPI controller
3	Clock Phase	0 – High 1 – Low	Define the phase of the SPI controller
4	Clock Edge	0 – High 1 – Low	Define the operational edge of the SPI controller
5	TX FIFO RST	0 – Disable 1 – Enable	Reset the transmission FIFO
6	RX FIFO RST	0 – Disable 1 – Enable	Reset the reception FIFO
7	LSB FIRST	0 – MSb first 1 – LSb first	Define the endianness of the transmission: if '1', the least-significant bit is transmitted as first character; if '0', it is transmitted last

The main information about the SPI IP is stored in its **status register** (see Table 7.17). This provides information about the status of the reception and transmission FIFO buffers, such as whether they are empty or full, and also indicates the detection of an error.

Table 7.17 SPI IP status register bit functions

Bit position	Bit name	Possible value	Bit description/function
0	ERROR	0 – Non-active 1 – Active	Error detected
1	RX FULL	0 – Non-active 1 – Active	Provides information about the reception FIFO
2	RX EMPTY	0 – Non-active 1 – Active	Provides information about the reception FIFO

Bit position	Bit name	Possible value	Bit description/function
3	TX FULL	0 – Non-active 1 – Active	Provides information about the transmission FIFO
4	TX EMPTY	0 – Non-active 1 – Active	Provides information about the transmission FIFO

7.6 AHB I²C

7.6.1 Description

I²C (Inter-Integrated Circuit) is another serial synchronous communication bus, but is slower and simpler than SPI, only involving two wires and providing half-duplex operation. Again, this peripheral is widely present in embedded systems as a communication interface for on-board chips, in this case connecting low-throughput communication devices and data converters.

7.6.2 Mode of Operation

When deployed within a SoC, this peripheral commonly functions as a master interface, able to control multiple slave devices. The details of I²C slave addressing and signaling protocols are described in Chapter 6.

7.6.3 Component Diagram

Figure 7.6 shows the internal components of a simple I²C peripheral. In contrast to the SPI IP presented in the previous section, the I²C IP only supports half-duplex communication, where the transmission and reception pins are effectively time-multiplexed. Thus, unlike the SPI IP, in the I²C IP there is just one communication control unit and communication can switch from transmission to reception, as a function of the control registers.

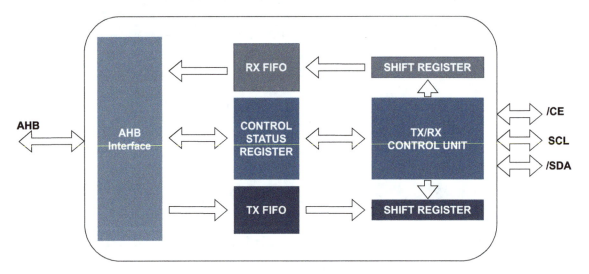

Figure 7.6 I²C IP internal components

7.6.4 Registers

The high-level register set of the I²C peripheral is very similar to that of the SPI peripheral, but in this instance also contains interrupt configuration and status registers, as shown in Table 7.18.

Table 7.18 I²C IP registers

Register offset	Register name	Access (Read/Write)	Register description/function
0x00	Control	Write	Program the interfaces
0x04	Status	Read	Write/read digital values to the input/outputs
0x08	RX Buffer	Read	Read last character present in the FIFO
0x0C	TX Buffer	Write	Write last character to insert in the FIFO
0x10	Slave Address	Write	Define the address in case of slave mode
0x14	Interrupt Control	Write	Configure the interrupts
0x18	Interrupt Status	Read	Read the interrupt status

Just as for the SPI module, the I²C **control register** (see Table 7.19) controls the behavior of the IP. Through the control register it is possible to enable or disable the peripheral, set master or slave operating mode, reset the FIFO buffers, and set transmission-related flags, such as the transfer mode (transmission or reception).

Table 7.19 I²C IP control register bit functions

Bit position	Bit name	Possible value	Bit description/function
0	Enable	0 – Disable 1 – Enable	Enable/disable the I²C controller
1	Master	0 – Master 1 – Slave	Define the operational mode of the I²C controller
2	TX Reset	0 – Non-active 1 – Active	Reset the FIFO buffer
3	TXRX MODE	0 – TX 1 – RX	Select the transfer mode: reception or transmission
4	Acknowledge	0 – Non-active 1 – Active	Set/unset the acknowledge send after the transmission

The **status register** (see Table 7.20) of the I²C peripheral contains information about the status of the reception and transmission FIFO buffers, as well as other useful information regarding the communication. More specifically, the presence of an enquiry from the bus, when the address matches with the slave address of the peripheral, or simply the presence of traffic on the bus, in order to avoid collision.

Table 7.20 I²C IP status register bit functions

Bit position	Bit name	Possible value	Bit description/function
0	ERROR	0 – Non-active 1 – Active	Error detected
1	Call	0 – Non-active 1 – Active	When the address selected on the bus matches the slave address of the peripheral
2	Busy	0 – Non-active 1 – Active	Detect the presence of traffic on the bus
3	Slave Read/Write	0 – Read 1 – Write	In slave mode, provides information as to whether the peripheral is writing to or reading from the bus
4	RX FULL	0 – Non-active 1 – Active	Provides information about the reception FIFO
5	RX EMPTY	0 – Non-active 1 – Active	Provides information about the reception FIFO
6	TX FULL	0 – Non-active 1 – Active	Provides information about the transmission FIFO
7	TX EMPTY	0 – Non-active 1 – Active	Provides information about the transmission FIFO

7.7 Analog Peripherals: ADC and DAC

7.7.1 Description
The ADC (analog-to-digital converter) and DAC (digital-to analog-converter) are the two peripherals usually involved in any form of analog-based interface. Their presence defines an embedded SoC as a "mixed-signal" SoC. An ADC converts the information from an electrical voltage into a digital number, such that it can then be processed by the CPU in terms of computation and analysis. The complementary unit, the DAC, converts a digital value into an electrical voltage. ADCs are used to interface analog sensors, that is, those detecting measures such as temperature or electrical current/voltage; DACs are used to drive analog devices such as motors and speakers.

7.7.2 Mode of Operation
Depending on its internal architecture, an ADC peripheral can work in different modes. However, here we will consider the simplest and most common working modes, of which there are three: single acquisition mode, auto-trigger mode, and free-running mode. In single acquisition mode, the ADC is programmed to perform a specific conversion from an analog signal to a digital one. The digital value is then stored in the register. In auto-trigger mode, the start of conversion is triggered independently of the CPU and by another peripheral, such as a timer. In free-running mode, the ADC is continuously acquiring data and updating the register. In this case, the end of conversion is notified to the CPU using an interrupt. Sometimes, in some applications, ADCs will have direct access to memory via a DMA controller.

In comparison to ADCs, DACs usually involve fewer features and operating modes. The digital-to-analog conversion is done as a single operation managed by the CPU. Nevertheless, there are, again, specialized situations in which a DAC will be able to fetch data directly from memory via a DMA controller.

7.7.3 Component Diagram

A component diagram for an ADC IP is depicted in Figure 7.7. Unsurprisingly, the ADC includes some special analog modules, in the form of the ADC itself, a sample and hold unit, and an analog multiplexer. The ADC unit that performs the conversion of an electrical analog signal into a numerical value can have different performance in resolution, conversion time, and signal-to-noise ratio. Depending on the architecture, it can be very expensive in terms of die area and manufacturing cost. Therefore, in a SoC, an ADC IP will usually only support single-channel conversion, meaning that only one conversion at a time can be executed. To provide the capability to connect multiple external pins and thereby acquire multiple analog signals, the ADC peripheral incorporates an analog multiplexer in its front-end. Then, even if the IP only provides single-channel ADC, it can perform analog acquisition on a time-multiplexed basis. The third analog module in the peripheral is the sample and hold unit. A detailed account of analog acquisition principles is beyond the scope of this book, but let us first assume that analog-to-digital conversion is not an instantaneous process. Depending on the architecture of the ADC, the conversion time can vary from tens of nanoseconds up to several microseconds. During this period, the input analog signal must be stable in order not to incur conversion errors. Because fluctuations in the input signal are not predictable, the role of the sample and hold unit is to "store" the analog value for as long as is necessary for the conversion. In this way, regardless of the precise nature of the input signal, the conversion can be performed without errors.

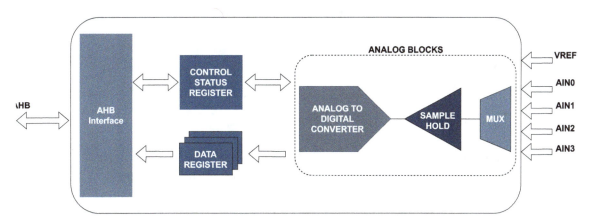

Figure 7.7 ADC IP internal components

A DAC IP functions as a complement to the ADC peripheral, converting a digital value into an electrical voltage (see Figure 7.8). Like the ADC peripheral, the DAC peripheral contains analog modules, but in this case they are the DAC unit itself (again, typically single-channel) and an output buffer. The function of the output buffer is to amplify the voltage and the current in order to drive the output load. However, the deliverable power will only be in the order of magnitude of milliwatts. Hence, to drive larger loads such as speakers or motors, a power amplifier must always be connected to the output pins of the peripheral/SoC.

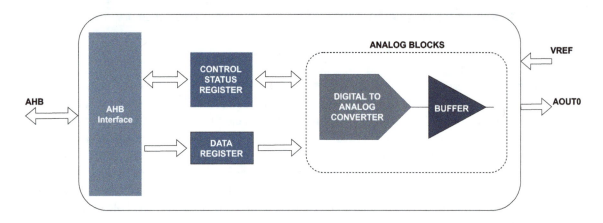

Figure 7.8 DAC IP internal components

7.7.4 ADC Registers

In the case of an ADC peripheral, the number of registers (see Table 7.21) can vary depending on the IP implementation. For our purposes, we will focus on the simplest version of an ADC IP that can work in a SoC.

Table 7.21 ADC IP registers

Register offset	Register name	Access (Read/Write)	Register description/function
0x00	Control	Write	Program the interfaces
0x04	Status	Read	Write/read digital values to the input/outputs
0x08	Data – CH0	Read	Read last data acquired on channel 0
0x0C	Data – CH1	Read	Read last data acquired on channel 1
0x10	Data – CH2	Read	Read last data acquired on channel 2
0x14	Data – CH3	Read	Read last data acquired on channel 3

In an ADC peripheral, the **control register** (see Table 7.22) makes it possible to program the acquisition mode and start/stop the acquisition and conversion of a fresh data sample.

Table 7.22 ADC IP control register bit functions

Bit position	Bit name	Possible value	Bit description/function
0	Enable	0 – Disable 1 – Enable	Enable/disable the ADC controller
[2..1]	Mode	00 – None 01 – Single 10 – Auto-trig 11 – Free	Define the operational mode of the ADC controller; possible values are single-mode acquisition, auto-triggered, and free-running
3	Start of conv	0 – Stop 1 – Start	Start a new conversion

Bit position	Bit name	Possible value	Bit description/function
4	Auto-trig source	0 – Timer	If running in auto-trigger mode, select the source of trigger
		1 – Ext source	
[6..5]	Source	00 – CH0	Select the acquisition channel
		01 – CH1	
		10 – CH2	
		11 – CH3	

Through the **status register** (see Table 7.23), the programmer can check the status of the ADC peripheral, whether a conversion is in progress or if it has terminated. In addition, there is usually a field present that indicates the channel selected for the acquisition.

Table 7.23 ADC IP status register bit functions

Bit position	Bit name	Possible value	Bit description/function
0	ERROR	0 – Non-active	Error detected
		1 – Active	
1	End of conv	0 – Non-active	Indicate the end of conversion
		1 – Active	
2	Busy	0 – Non-active	Indicate that the conversion is in progress
		1 – Active	
[4..3]	Channel	00 – CH0	Indicate the channel selected for the acquisition
		01 – CH1	
		10 – CH2	
		11 – CH3	

7.7.5 DAC Registers

The register map (see Table 7.24) of a DAC peripheral is similar to that of the ADC peripheral and, indeed, those presented for the other IPs; thus, we find control, status and data registers.

Table 7.24 DAC IP registers

Register offset	Register name	Access (Read/Write)	Register description/function
0x00	Control	Write	Program the interfaces
0x04	Status	Read	Write/read digital values to the input/outputs
0x08	Data – CH0	Write	Write the output data

For the DAC IP, the **control register** (see Table 7.25) makes it possible to enable or disable the peripheral, and activate or deactivate its output. In some cases, it is also possible to program the gain amplifier.

Table 7.25 DAC IP control register bit functions

Bit position	Bit name	Possible value	Bit description/function
0	Enable	0 – Disable	Enable/disable the DAC controller
		1 – Enable	

Bit position	Bit name	Possible value	Bit description/function
1	Output enable	0 – Disable 1 – Enable	Enable/disable the output
[3..2]	Gain	00 – Level0 01 – Level1 10 – Level2 11 – Level3	Set the gain

The **status register** (see Table 7.26) for the DAC peripheral is not complex: the programmer can check the error status of the peripheral, and whether its conversion has completed.

Table 7.26 DAC IP status register bit functions

Bit position	Bit name	Possible value	Bit description/function
0	ERROR	0 – Non-active 1 – Active	Error detected
1	Output	0 – Non-active 1 – Active	Indicate the end of conversion

7.8 AHB Static Memory Controller

7.8.1 Description

Today's SoCs integrate large memories of varying types and technologies. As described in Chapter 2, embedded memory is one of the factors affecting the final price of a SoC, because it involves a fairly direct relationship with silicon area. Sometimes, for reasons related to the market for the target application, it is more convenient to configure this memory as an external component. There may be other reasons too, related to the application itself, which might, for example, be required to store data even if the system reboots or, by using a backup battery, to recover data after power-off. One of the main advantages of using SRAM rather than flash memory for storing data, besides the lower cost, is its higher read/write speeds, as well as its avoidance of the limitation in number of writing cycles associated with flash technology.

A static memory controller (SMC) is the peripheral that allows a SoC to interface to off-chip memory, either SRAM or NOR flash technology, thereby extending the overall memory available. In this section, we introduce the main concepts and characteristics of an SMC IP peripheral. However, this type of IP can vary significantly depending on the implementation and the vendor.

7.8.2 Mode of Operation

An SMC can work in single-access mode or in burst mode. In the former, the controller performs an access for reading or writing to a specific location. Alternatively, in burst mode, the controller provides sequential access to memory locations, starting from a specific address for a predefined length. The maximum length is determined by the size of the read and write FIFO buffer present in the IP. Moreover, the timing access can be different depending on the external memory, whether SRAM or flash, and can be further tuned to a limited extent as a function of the external chip connected. The majority of SMC IPs embedded in a SoC also include a feature to operate in low-power mode, but we will not go into further details of this mode here.

7.8.3 Component Diagram

The component diagram of a static memory controller is shown in Figure 7.9. This IP, from an abstract high-level perspective, can be positioned as the bridge between the on-chip bus and an off-chip bus, with the internal bus connected to the CPU and the external bus connected to a memory. Besides the standard status and control registers, the SMC must implement the logic to interface to the external bus, respecting the timings needed to interact correctly with the bus-connected memory. These timings will differ from those used in the internal AHB bus and are programmable through the configuration registers. Furthermore, different memory types may have different timing requirements. Such timings are generally predefined and incorporated into the SMC peripheral, and a list of the memories with which it is compatible will usually be provided in its datasheet.

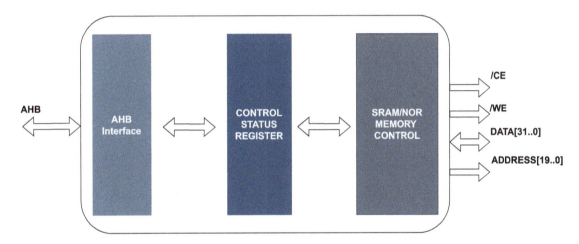

Figure 7.9 SMC IP internal components

7.8.4 Registers

Table 7.27 shows an example of a register map for an SMC IP. The main difference with respect to the other peripherals described in this chapter is the presence of command and cycle registers, which define the commands and timing required for accessing the external memory. Note that these registers do not reflect any particular SMC IP.

Table 7.27 SMC IP registers

Register offset	Register name	Access (Read/Write)	Register description/function
0x00	Status	Read	Indicate the status of the memory controller
0x04	Control	Write	Configure the memory controller
0x08	Command	Write	Command register to interface the memory
0x0C	Data	Read/Write	Payload data
0x10	Cycle	Write	Configure the cycles
0x14	Timing	Write	Configure the timing

The **status register** (see Table 7.28) contains the usual type of information about the status of the IP, such as whether it is enabled or disabled, and the existence of an interrupt. Complex SMC IPs can provide additional status information, about the last memory access, for example, or the parity information used for error correction.

Table 7.28 SMC IP status register bit functions

Bit position	Bit name	Possible value	Bit description/function
0	Enable	0 – Disabled 1 – Enabled	Provide the status of the SMC
1	Interrupt Enable	0 – Disabled 1 – Enabled	Provide information about the interrupt
2	Interrupt Status	0 – Not active 1 – Active	Provide the interrupt activation status

Through the **control register**, it is possible to program the parameters of the SMC, such as the memory type (SRAM or NOR flash), the number of memory chips connected to the interface, and the width of the data bus. An example of a typical SMC control register is shown in Table 7.29.

Table 7.29 SMC IP control register bit functions

Bit position	Bit name	Possible value	Bit description/function
[1..0]	MemType	00 – None 01 – SRAM 10 – NOR 11 – None	Define the memory type to interface
[3..2]	MemChips	00 – 1 01 – 2 10 – 3 11 – 4	Define the number of memory chips
[5..4]	MemWidth	00 – 8 01 – 16 10 – 32 11 – None	Define the memory width in bits

The **command register** manages the type of transaction used to access the external memory. In the simple and generic example shown in Table 7.30, the information required to access SRAM is as follows: address, mode, and the chip to which the access should be directed.

Table 7.30 SMC IP command register bit functions

Bit position	Bit name	Possible value	Bit description/function
[19..0]	Add	/	Define the address for the memory access
[21..20]	Command type	00 – AsyncRead 01 – AsyncWrite 10 – SyncRead 11 – SyncWrite	Define the access mode

Bit position	Bit name	Possible value	Bit description/function
[24..22]	Chip Select	00 – Chip0	Define the chip to which access is directed
		01 – Chip1	
		10 – Chip2	
		11 – Chip3	

The **data register** (see Table 7.31) holds the data to be written to or read from the external memory. This register is designed to be large enough to handle 32-bit data. In the case of the memory interface exposing fewer bits, only the least-significant bits will be considered as valid data.

Table 7.31 SMC IP data register bit function

Bit position	Bit name	Possible value	Bit description/function
[31..0]	Data	/	Payload data

The **timing register** (see Table 7.32) aims to define the cycles required to interface with the memory. These values are specific to each type of memory, so they can change as a function of the device connected. Correct tuning of these timings is critical to error-free, high-speed memory access. The read and write cycle times represent the time between assertion of the Chip Enable (CE) signal and the time when the associated data can be considered ready/valid. The chip-enable delay is the delay between the CE-driven chip selection and the activation of the internal circuitry of the memory. The write-enable (WE) assertion delay is the time that the memory requires between the activation of the WE signal and the data being ready for writing. The page cycle and turnaround times concern special characteristics of synchronous RAM. For the purposes of this book, we do not need to go into the details of these parameters; for detailed information about SRAM-specific timing parameters we recommend that you refer to an appropriate device datasheet.

Table 7.32 SMC IP timing register bit functions

Bit position	Bit name	Possible value	Bit description/function
[3..0]	TRC	0x0 to 0xF	Read cycle time
[7..4]	TWC	0x0 to 0xF	Write cycle time
[10..8]	TCEOE	0x0 to 0x7	Chip-enable delay/Output-enable delay
[13..11]	TWP	0x0 to 0x7	Write-enable assertion delay
[16..14]	TPC	0x0 to 0x7	Page cycle time
[19..17]	TPR	0x0 to 0x7	Turnaround time

7.9 Case Study: IP Peripheral Integration with Cortex-M1

The intent of this section is to show how the theoretical information presented in the preceding sections can be applied in a real situation. The vehicle for this is the Cortex-M1 processor, a "soft-core" software implementation of a Cortex-M microprocessor, designed to be loaded into an FPGA chip.

Arm provides a prototyping tool, known as DesignStart FPGA, that allows a Cortex-M1-based SoC to be designed rapidly through the use of proven IP integrations. The tool must operate with an FPGA design tool provided by one of Arm's DesignStart FPGA partners, currently Xilinx or Gowin. Here, our target is Xilinx's Arty A7 FPGA development board.

7.9.1 Clock Generation, Reset, and Start

So far in this chapter, we have focused on the IP peripherals that allow a SoC to communicate with the external world. However, to work at all, our CPU needs some additional fundamental circuitry, in the form of clock and reset functions. What happens when a processor starts? First, it is powered up and has a Reset signal activated. In almost all cases, this signal is active low. Note that it is good practice on a schematic to label this signal as nRST, RST_n, RST#, /RST, or nReset, in order to avoid misunderstandings as to the polarity of the signal.

Many SoCs automatically generate a Reset at power-up; this is a cold reset and its purpose is to initialize the system in a known state. It is typically referred to as a **power-on reset** (POR). Once a processor is up and running, other sources can instigate a reset function. These could include an external signal activating the nReset pin, such as a push-button, an external test pin, or a power supply monitor. In this last case, activation usually occurs when the power supply voltage is detected to have dropped below a certain level, and is termed a **brownout** reset. Alternatively, a reset may be instigated by the internal timeout of a specific counter, known as a **watchdog** reset. Similarly, a reset may be triggered if an oscillator (typically used to drive a clock) is not oscillating correctly, or be generated by software with a specific programming interface. There can be many other sources depending on the processor and the board.

Furthermore, once the processor starts the boot process, it is necessary to have a valid clock running and ensure that the initialization software activates this input clock accordingly. A common error is to activate a clock based on a quartz oscillator, but find that on the specific board the oscillator is not mounted or connected. Thus, when starting development with a new board, it is highly recommended that you search the documentation of the clock module component for the block diagram schematic of the board in use, then cross-reference information about the processor with the datasheet of the component as necessary.

Thus, before we go any further, we need to add a Clocks_and_Resets module (illustrated in Figure 7.10) to our baseline Cortex-M1 core in DesignStart FPGA.

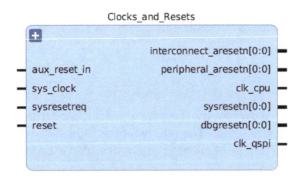

Figure 7.10 Arm DesignStart Cortex-M1 – Clocks and Resets module

7.9.2 Bus Interconnect

As we saw in Chapter 4, the bus interconnect can vary depending on the SoC implementation and final target. In the case of DesignStart FPGA targeted at Xilinx's Arty A7 development board, the internal bus is the AXI interconnect, and so an AXI interconnect module (see Figure 7.11) will be added to our Cortex-M1 core to connect all of the external interfacing peripherals to the CPU. The width of the bus is then dependent on the interfaces instantiated to the external world.

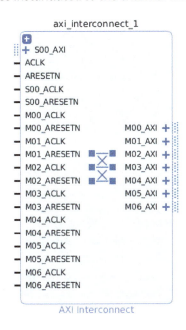

Figure 7.11 Arm DesignStart Cortex-M1 – AXI Interconnect module

7.9.3 IP Peripherals

The IPs present in the DesignStart reference design allow the Cortex-M1 soft-core CPU to connect with the external interfaces present on the Arty A7. Among these IPs, we can find the following bus-specific peripherals that we can incorporate into our target SoC design to provide interfacing facilities similar to those described in the earlier part of this chapter: AXI-GPIO, AXI-UART, AXI-QSPI, and AXI-BRAM.

In the following subsections, we will briefly explain the function of each of these IP peripherals together with their connections to the external pins of the FPGA. For detailed information about DesignStart and the specific characteristics of these Xilinx-based IPs we refer the reader to the original vendors' documentation.

7.9.3.1   AXI-GPIO

This GPIO IP peripheral is used to connect to the LEDs, DIP switches, RGB-LEDs, and push-buttons of the development board. As we have already seen, GPIOs represent the simplest IP interfaces in terms of connections and register descriptions. This IP can be easily configured to handle variable numbers of GPIOs, depending on the specifics of each interface. For our Cortex-M1-based SoC solution, we have implemented two GPIO IPs, as illustrated in Figure 7.12.

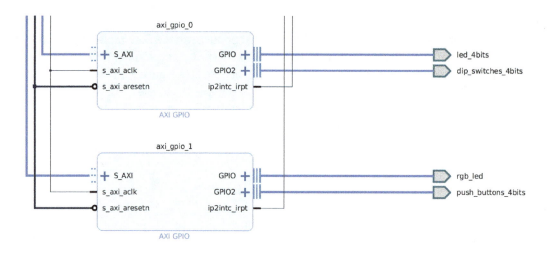

Figure 7.12 Arm DesignStart Cortex-M1 – AXI-GPIOs

7.9.3.2 AXI-UART

In comparison with the (AHB) UART IP previously described in this chapter, the AXI-UART version used in the DesignStart reference is much simpler, presenting only transmission (TX) and reception (RX) signals and none of the flow control signals. Furthermore, in this instance the output pins are connected via a special component used for debug purposes, the DAP (Debug Access Port), because the debug port effectively shares the same interface.

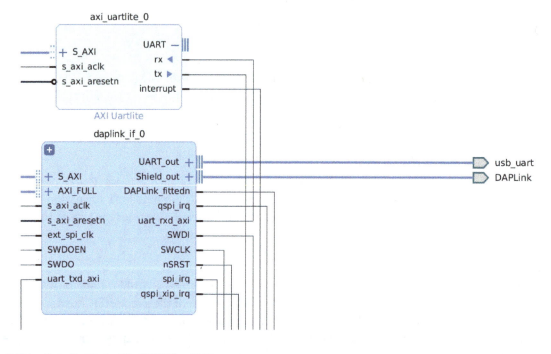

Figure 7.13 Arm DesignStart Cortex-M1 – AXI-UART and DAP

7.9.3.3 AXI-QSPI

The AXI-QSPI peripheral is used to connect the external flash memory present on the board with the FPGA. This memory could be used for firmware storage, for example, or used at runtime as nonvolatile memory, to store data to be recovered following a power-off event. Quad SPI is a variant of SPI, and is briefly described in Chapter 6. The working principles are similar to those of SPI but faster transfer speeds are achieved by using more I/O signal lines.

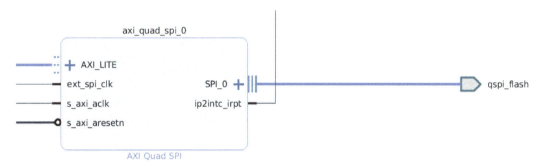

Figure 7.14 Arm DesignStart Cortex-M1 – AXI-QSPI

7.9.3.4 AXI-BRAM

The AXI-BRAM IP provides the CPU with access to memory. In an FPGA environment, block RAM (BRAM) represents the equivalent of internal SRAM. The AXI-BRAM controller supports memory sizes up to a maximum of 2 MB. However, this limit is imposed by the BRAM available on the target FPGA, which in some cases may be lower than 2 MB.

Figure 7.15 Arm DesignStart Cortex-M1 – AXI-BRAM

7.9.4 Putting It All Together

This small section is intended to summarize what has been presented in the immediately preceding chapters. Besides the CPU itself, a SoC must contain peripherals that enable the CPU to function in the most basic terms, and to interact with the external world. Thus, clock and reset circuitry, bus interconnects, memory interfaces, and, finally, the presence of IPs for the management of external communication interfaces all play a fundamental role in the functionality of a system-on-a-chip.

The combination of all of these IPs allows a fully functional FPGA-based Arm SoC prototype to be created.

Chapter 8

Memory System

We have referred constantly to memory throughout the preceding chapters, unsurprisingly, given that no computer could function without it. In this chapter, we finally get around to studying it in detail, starting with a look at how SoCs make use of the different types of memory, exploring memory caches and the organizational and policy complexities involved in their use, and finishing with a survey of the many different forms of memory available, volatile and nonvolatile, their potential applications, and the mechanisms involved in accessing them. In the course of the chapter, we will address a large array of questions, of which the following are just a few:

1. *What are the specific considerations when it comes to memory on a SoC?*

2. *What are the memory requirements for an OS or kernel on a SoC?*

3. *What is a cache and where is it located?*

4. *How are caches implemented?*

5. *How does cache implementation affect performance?*

6. *What are the pros and cons of using a cache?*

7. *When should caches be avoided and how can a cache be bypassed?*

8. *What types and sizes of cache are included on recent SoCs?*

8.1 Introduction

8.1.1 On-chip versus Off-chip Memory

In a computer system, memory can be organized into different levels and types. A standard approach to the representation of this is the pyramid view shown in Figure 8.1. At the top of the figure is the memory that needs to provide the fastest access to information. This memory level will also be the smallest in physical terms, typically measured in kilobytes. At the base of the figure is the slowest and physically largest level of memory, which can be measured in exabytes.

In a processor, the memory represented at the top of Figure 8.1 consists of its internal **registers**. Such registers typically consist of D ("data", or, sometimes, "delay") flip-flops, integrated circuits that can be driven to one of two possible states, representing a '0' or a '1', to store a single bit of data; they permit simultaneous read and write access.

Next in the pyramid are the internal "**cache**" memories, which we will describe in more detail later in this chapter. Depending on the particular processor, several levels of cache may be available. Having separate data and instruction caches can be advantageous to a processor because they can function in parallel and thus be more efficient. We have already seen this Harvard architecture (in Chapter 1), although it is not our principal interest here. The cache nearest the registers of the processor is called level-one (L1) cache. It is very fast but expensive in terms of memory size and cost. In Cortex-M processors, there is generally only one level of cache memory. In more complex processor systems, a second level of cache, called L2 cache, and even a third (L3) may be available on the same die. Multiprocessor systems often implement L3 caches. Again, as we progress down the pyramid (from L1 to L3), the caches get bigger and slower. Caches are traditionally based on SRAM technology.

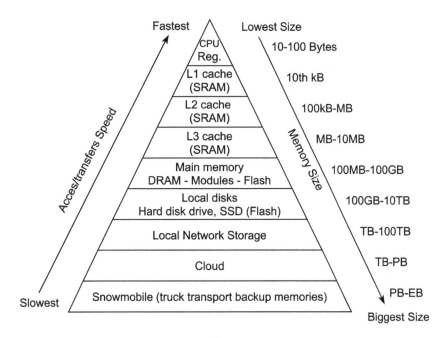

Figure 8.1 Memory hierarchy

The next level down the pyramid takes us outside the chip into **main memory** that uses DRAM-based technology, such as SDRAM or DDRx, to provide access to volatile data. Access is carried out in two phases: line selection and column selection. When cached memory is in use, the access to main memory is done by burst transfers that read or write data on the same line of main memory into or out of cache. We will describe this mechanism in more detail in due course. At this level, we can also find nonvolatile memory in the form of flash memory being used for program storage, either internal to the microcontroller or outside the chip. The access time for main memory is around 50 to 200 ns, depending on the technology.

Underpinning main memory is disk-based storage, most commonly in the form of external hard disk drive (HDD) devices. These consist of rotating disk platters offering high-density nonvolatile magnetic storage and capacities measured in terabytes. HDDs are now being replaced by more expensive but better-performing solid-state drives (SSDs), based on large numbers of NAND-based flash memories in an external device packaged in a similar way to HDDs. On embedded systems, flash memories based on SD cards or USB are often used.

Many years ago, CD and DVD arrays were provided on servers to store programs or data on a permanent basis. Likewise, digital cassettes and tapes were used to provide very high-density magnetic storage, albeit only with sequential access. Today, cloud-based storage is becoming commonplace, giving access to gigabytes, terabytes or even petabytes of information stored on large servers. This is a big change from the previous generation, mainly because of ever faster network communications and increasing system interconnectivity.

At the very bottom of our "memory" pyramid is bulk data storage, not found in every system, and representing huge amounts of data. Some companies manage this on massive servers to service the level immediately above in the pyramid. Backing up an exabyte (EB; 1000^6 bytes) of data over a 10 Gbit/s network would take more than 25 years! Amazon Web Services offers the *Snowmobile*, a container-based backup system towed by a truck, which can capture/transfer 0.1 EB in "a few weeks" (excluding transport time): faster but still not that fast [1].

8.1.1.1 On-chip Memory

Memory can be integrated into the same physical chip as the processor, as we saw in Chapter 1, to produce a microcontroller or SoC. But not all of the necessary memories can be integrated on the same die. In some systems, the integrated circuits are mounted together on a support and enclosed in a case: to the external user, it appears to be a single integrated circuit. This 3D approach can provide a good solution for implementing DRAM memories with a CPU or GPU. Alternatively, the integrated circuits may be welded one on top of another; for example, the Raspberry Pi in which the (SDRAM) memory is welded on top of the microcontroller (see Figure 8.2).

Figure 8.2 Memory on top of microcontroller (Raspberry Pi)

Why use such an approach? Mainly, it depends on the compatibility of the technologies used by the different units needed in the system. The manufacturing processes of the different parts may be incompatible when it comes to incorporating them into a single die. For example, the minimum size of the elements (e.g. transistor size) may not be compatible, or an analog element might generate too much noise for a digital component to be placed nearby. Alternatively, it might give the designer of the embedded system more freedom when it comes to the amount of memory that can be included in the SoC, and/or it could shorten the wire lengths required to connect to memory in comparison to those required for a regular connection to a memory module on the PCB (reducing the overall die area too).

Thus, depending on need and the technologies available, different techniques exist to provide for memory to be co-located with a processor:

▪ Everything is integrated on the same chip, both processor and memory. This approach is used for the majority of microcontrollers involving limited memory size (as determined by the technology available at any given time), and is generally the preferred solution for the user, keeping the PCB architecture simple. In general, SRAM, (NOR-based) flash memory or a variant of these are used. DRAMs are not usually integrated on the same die in this way.

▪ Similar restrictions apply to nonvolatile memory: co-location on the same die is only possible for relatively modest memory sizes (kibibytes to mebibytes) and extension is mandatory for larger amounts.

▪ New technologies are in development for 3D stacking of chips, but these are not widely available yet.

▪ Having the appropriate interfaces available on the processor to handle co-located memory can be a factor:

  ☐ Parallel bus for better performance

  ☐ Serial bus for data storage memory and transfers to internal SRAM.

8.1.2 Access to Memory

The mechanisms used by a CPU to access memory are closely linked to the architecture and topology of its incorporation into the system; for example, whether it is on-chip or off-chip.

8.1.2.1　Direct Addressing

When a processor can provide a memory address directly to memory either through its address bus or an interconnect such as AMBA, it is referred to as direct addressing. Data and instructions are passed between the memory and the processor through the processor's data bus. Depending upon the architecture, a transfer via cache memory may also be possible. For control signals, a specific controller/decoder may be used. In this scenario, the most widely used memory is SRAM: it is fast but will be limited in size, up to a few megabytes. This is the configuration most commonly implemented in microcontrollers.

For **dynamic memory**, the use of a multiplexer is necessary on the address bus because the address is provided in two steps: a line address first in the form of the highest part of the address, then the lower part of the address specifies the column. A specific controller is needed because the sequence of operation is quite complex. Dynamic memory is always external to the chip because the technology used is different to that of the processor itself and rarely directly compatible.

NOR-based **flash memory** can be adapted for direct addressing in terms of read access, but not for writing. Either a specialized memory controller is required or a special protocol is needed involving a specific algorithm to be executed by the processor. This solution is available in almost all microcontrollers for boot and program storage.

Some other nonvolatile memories also support direct addressing, such as FRAM, MRAM, and EEPROM. In general, these are of limited size and quite expensive, but are as easy to use as SRAM. However, their nonvolatility makes them useful for systems that must support very low power modes, allowing the power supply to be cut and data to still be available.

8.1.2.2 Block Access

When a microcontroller needs access to larger amounts of memory, typically nonvolatile, this can be made available via specific buses/interfaces of the sort described in Chapter 6; for example, SPI, QSPI, I²C, 1-Wire, USB or MMC/SD card. These forms of memory then need a specific programmable interface in the microcontroller to access them: an appropriate software driver, controlled by the processor, handles transfers to or from this external memory and SRAM, either byte by byte or in data blocks.

The size of such memory can range from a few kilobytes to many gigabytes. It can either be incorporated onto the board or be removable via the use of USB or MMC/SD card interfaces. The memory used is generally NAND-based flash memory, which offers very large capacities but is not as reliable as NOR-based flash. Some data error detection and correction are mandatory, often directly incorporated into the memory device itself. The integrity of the memorized data is not reliable beyond a given number of cycles, which might equate to periods in excess of ten years. Thus, backups are obligatory and read-rewrite of the data is recommended. The number of write accesses is limited to a few hundred thousand, but read access is unlimited.

Some manufacturers, mainly of SSD drives, offer interfaces similar to those of DDR memory modules, providing almost direct access to the memory involved.

8.2 SoC Memory

Given the smartphones of today, a SoC often needs access to many gigabytes of memory to store data such as pictures, videos, and third-party applications. This will be nonvolatile memory, mainly in the form of flash memory, which will either be incorporated into the main PCB or, sometimes, be available as an extension via an external connector, depending on the smartphone manufacturer.

Inside the chip itself, a few hundred kilobytes of memory must be available for the boot of the system and the core applications. In terms of RAM, the ever-increasing size and sophistication of smartphone operating systems and applications means that the more RAM the better.

For fast systems, such as those supported by the Cortex-A microprocessor family, the processor needs cache memory inside the chip with at least one level of cache hierarchy and possibly more. Even if we limit ourselves to the Cortex-M class of processors, more powerful and memory-hungry applications are emerging as the technology permits.

This can cause challenges for application designers at development time. Writing in high-level programming languages means that the application designer needs more memory at their disposal. A typical application may involve camera devices, where it is necessary to capture large video frames, compress them, and then save them to, for example, an SD card. Once it has been established that such an application will run on the SoC hardware it is essential to profile the minimum amount of memory that will be required to support it, before starting a board design!

8.2.1 Operating System Memory

As we have briefly discussed in previous chapters and will discuss further in Chapter 10, a SoC microcontroller can operate either without (i.e. bare metal) or with some form of operating system, even if it consists only of a kernel for time management and appropriate hardware drivers.

Where some form of operating system is used, there are two main levels of complexity:

1. A small OS/kernel in which the memory size (footprint) is limited, and an MMU is not necessary.

2. A large OS such as Linux in which larger amounts of memory are mandatory and an MMU is almost essential.

As we have indicated before, the latter case lends itself perfectly to the Cortex-A microprocessor family, and the small OS case is a good fit for the Cortex-M processor class. In this instance, nonvolatile memory is essential to contain the boot code and, in most cases, the application itself.

The application can be updated through various means, including the use of loaders and specific JTAG/SWD interface instructions to download from an external system on a serial (UART) connection and, best of all, autonomously by the processor itself, reading the new code from an external memory or a particular communication medium such as USB or Wi-Fi. In this latter case, the code must be temporarily loaded into volatile memory and the processor will then make a copy in nonvolatile memory to displace the existing software. Another method, mainly used for first-time development of bare-metal software, is the direct use of JTAG/SWD with an IDE to download and test the software. Two principal update cases exist:

1. kernel modification

2. application modification.

Ensuring that, in particular, the first of these is conducted safely is absolutely critical. If the system crashes (power failure, reset button pressed) during a kernel update and the new code has only partially replaced the previous code, it's unlikely that the system will be able to start again! It seems obvious, but the first time you have to program this feature, it is not something that is necessarily given much thought: until the system crashes! In this event, you will be pleased if you know of another way to program your processor.

In the case of application reprogramming, things are less critical because the system should still be able to boot, and it will just be part of the flash memory that needs to be erased and reprogrammed.

In either case, it is important to determine where the newly downloaded code will go. At least some buffering will be necessary before programming the flash, involving at least one block of flash; this will depend on the microcontroller manufacturer and the relevant documentation needs to be studied beforehand. It is also very important to verify that the update is both received and deployed accurately, which means that some form of error detection code will be required for verification purposes. Implementing a protocol that provides such control of code downloads is essential, and many simple protocols have been designed for this purpose during the past half-century, incorporating length indicators and checksum tests.

Another alternative involves new application code being loaded into external nonvolatile memory. When it needs to be executed, it is loaded into internal RAM.

8.3 Cache

This section introduces cache as a mechanism to speed up memory access. In order to execute an application, a SoC needs to access memory to fetch instructions, read data and store the results. Access to memory is a bottleneck in most processors because it is much slower than executing instructions. To mitigate this issue a system is composed of different types of memory as described above: some, like the cache, are small and fast and some are big and slow, like hard disk drives. Figure 8.3 shows typical access times, which are affected by several factors. The first of these is the processor clock speed; indeed, the access time is often given in number of clock cycles. In Figure 8.3, we have assumed a CPU clock speed of 1 GHz, which is quite high for a microcontroller but makes for simplicity in that one clock cycle is then 1 ns. Accessing information stored in the registers of the processor does not take more than one clock cycle, which means that the faster the clock, the quicker the access.

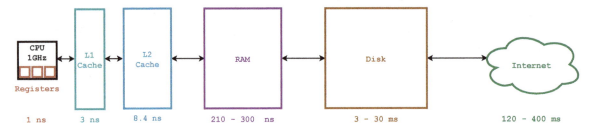

Figure 8.3 Time to access different memories

The second aspect that influences the memory access time is the physical distance between the CPU and the memory. How far away can the memory be on a microcontroller? A few centimeters at most? How can this distance influence the access time? The time that an electron takes to travel from one point to another is called the propagation time. In copper, we can assume that electrons propagate at the speed of light, which means that during 1 ns an electron can travel 30 cm at most. At a human scale, the propagation delay does not seem to be a big deal but at computer scale this is non-negligible. This factor is also independent of the clock speed, such that the propagation delay exerts more and more weight, proportionately, on the performance of the processor as the clock speed increases. Thus, if the propagation delay between the CPU and the memory is 1 ns, this is equivalent to one clock cycle at 1 GHz but 3 clock cycles at 3 GHz.

A third aspect that limits the speed of access to memory is the amount of time required to physically load a value from/to the memory. This factor depends on the technology used by the memory to store information. Furthermore, depending on this technology, it may take more time to access information in a large memory than in a small one. This is the case with a hard disk, for instance: the larger the disk, the longer is the access time.

Finally, memory is always linked to the CPU by a bus of some form , as explained in Chapter 4. If this bus can be used by other peripherals, memory access can be delayed. The arbitration protocols that exist among peripherals to manage the use of resources can introduce further delays in memory access over such a shared bus.

Caches were designed to address these issues, as far as possible, and improve CPU access to data and instructions.

The next subsection briefly revisits the different types of memory to better illustrate the main idea behind caches, and the following sections present the architecture of the cache, the different kinds of cache, and the mechanisms that need to be implemented to use a cache in a single- or multiple-processor environment.

8.3.1 Memory Review

For most computer systems, primary storage takes the form of a hard disk drive (HDD) or a solid-state drive (SSD), in which large amounts of data (gigabytes or terabytes) can be stored in a nonvolatile way. In the embedded world, this function is more likely to be instantiated in flash memory in the form of an SD card. However, an embedded system could also be connected to a larger drive to accommodate more data.

Volatile memory brings the data closer to the processor but, unlike nonvolatile storage, it requires the power to be on to retain the data therein; once the power is turned off, the data is lost. Two kinds of volatile memory can be distinguished: dynamic RAM (DRAM) and static RAM (SRAM). DRAM provides much faster access than primary storage and is often used to provide the central memory for a processor. When someone talks about the RAM modules of a computer, it is DRAM to which they are referring. Large embedded systems may have several gigabytes of DRAM while smaller systems will typically have megabytes of DRAM. The downside of this technology is that it must be refreshed at frequent intervals to maintain its data, which increases the overall power consumption of the board. Although such DRAM is physically closer to the CPU than the primary storage, it is still external to the SoC.

SRAM allows very fast memory access and does not require periodic refreshes, making it ideal for use as a memory cache. However, SRAM memory cells are composed of more transistors than DRAM cells, making SRAM memory bigger and more expensive than DRAM, and limiting the maximum size of the SRAM-based cache that can be placed directly on a SoC to a few kilobytes.

In resource optimization exercises, the Pareto principle (or the 80/20 rule) is frequently applied, which observes that 80% of the overall consequences (resources consumed) can be attributed to just 20% of the potential causes (operations) [2]. This principle has been adapted to software development, where Amdahl's law states that in a typical application, for 90 percent of the time, only 10 percent of the code and data are accessed. This is because an application usually repeats its instructions (for example, in a loop) and accesses the same memory regions most of the time. The fundamental idea behind a cache is therefore to have a smaller memory that contains the data and instructions that are in current use, and are therefore likely to be, by definition, in most frequent use. This means that memory can be quite small and still contain most of the information required.

Thus, caching works by maintaining a local copy of the data currently being used by the processor immediately next to the processor, and making sure that the underlying memory technology gives the fastest possible access to that data, as illustrated in Figure 8.4.

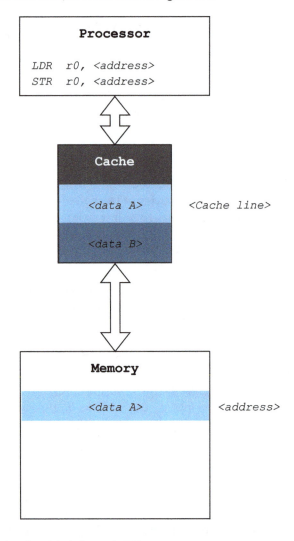

Figure 8.4 Duplication of data into the cache to bring it closer to the CPU

8.3.2 Caching Policies

When a processor is provided with a cache, it looks for the relevant data or instruction there before going to standard memory to fetch it. If the required data is currently duplicated in the cache, it is termed a **hit**, and otherwise a **miss**. As indicated above, the processor duplicates some of the data that is currently held in memory in its cache. Because there is a fixed (and relatively small) amount of storage capacity in the cache, it cannot store everything currently held in memory. How does the processor determine which information is most useful and worth keeping closer in this way? Once the cache is full, a new line must displace an older one, which is said to be evicted. Thus, two policies need to be defined and implemented: a cache storing policy to determine which data is stored in the cache, and a cache replacement policy to determine which data is evicted when there is no more available space.

In practice, we find that there are two types of data that are worth caching:

- **Temporal** locality data (giving rise to a time-based policy): information that has been used recently has a higher probability of being used again (the Pareto principle).

- **Spatial** locality data (giving rise to a proximity-based policy): information that is close to a piece of information that has been used recently is more likely to be used. For instance, this is often the case with arrays or instructions. When data is loaded from one address, it is likely that data from the next (adjoining) address is going to be loaded next.

Loops are great examples of temporally and spatially driven data access. A small set of instructions are executed multiple times and the loop counter can be used to access data sequentially (for example, to populate an array), as depicted in Figure 8.5, which features a single loop in which the letters stored in an array are shifted one by one.

```
char array[129] = "Hello World\n";

// Shift letter in the array
for (size_t i = 0; i < sizeof(array) - 1; i++)
{
   array[i] = array[i+1];
}
printf("New array: %s", array);
// Should print "New array: ello World"
```

Figure 8.5 Simple C code loop to move the characters in an array to the left.

In this code sample, the variable *i* is a good example of temporal data: it is reused in every loop cycle, where it is read and updated. Keeping a copy of this data in the cache allows quick access to it. The *array* construct is a good example of both spatial and temporal data: in the first loop, *array*[0] is written and *array*[1] is read; in the second loop, *array*[1] is accessed again (being written this time) and the adjacent *array*[2] is accessed too (being read), and so on.

Within the memory, *array*[0], *array*[1], … *array*[N] are stored contiguously, and we say that they are spatially close. If, when *array*[0] is loaded into the cache, *array*[1] and *array*[2] are loaded too, then when *array*[1] is required in the next code loop, it will already be available in the cache and there should be no need to retrieve it from memory and cache it. Thus, if we follow a temporal caching policy, we should store the variable *i* in the cache the first time it is used because, if it is used once, it is likely to be used multiple times within a short lapse of time. If we follow a spatial caching policy, we should store *array*[1], *array*[2], and so on, in the cache when *array*[0] is first used because it follows that *array*[1], *array*[2], and so on, will probably also be used in rapid succession.

```
        mov    r3, #0
        str    r3, [fp, #-8]
        b      .L2
.L3:
        ldr    r3, [fp, #-8]
        add    r3, r3, #1
        sub    r2, fp, #4
        add    r3, r2, r3
        ldrb   r3, [r3, #-132]
        lsl    r3, r3, #24
        asr    r1, r3, #24
        sub    r2, fp, #136
        ldr    r3, [fp, #-8]
        add    r3, r2, r3
        mov    r2, r1
        strb   r2, [r3]
.L2
        ldr    r3, [fp, #-8]
        add    r3, r3, #1
        str    r3, [fp, #-8]
        ble    .L3
```

Figure 8.6 Compiled instructions of the simple code loop of Figure 8.5

We have seen how the variables of the code sample in Figure 8.5 can take advantage of the cache to accelerate code execution. Another part of the code can also exploit the cache: the instructions. Figure 8.6 shows an assembler-based view of part of the compiled code that implements the logic of the sample in Figure 8.5. The instructions required to implement the for-loop are in blue and the instructions that implement what is inside the for-loop are in red. These instructions are stored sequentially in memory. In the case of the instructions, we can see that both spatial and temporal caching policies offer potential. Indeed, it is very likely that immediately after the execution of one instruction, an instruction very close to it in memory will be executed next. In addition, because it is a loop, each instruction is executed several times. Therefore, to minimize cache misses, we should store in the cache each instruction that is executed and some of its neighbors.

In the same manner, following compilation, the *printf()* function (shown in orange in Figure 8.5) can be broken down into multiple assembler instructions that need to be fetched by the processor when the function is called. If there is no cache, the CPU must retrieve the corresponding instruction from main memory for each instruction. If there is a cache, several instructions will be present at any given time. Because the time to access the cache is shorter than that to access main memory, the overall time taken to execute the *printf* function will be shorter.

If the *array* construct is reused later in the code, then if the data is still in the cache, the main memory is not accessed.

8.3.3 Cache Hits and Misses

Figure 8.7 illustrates a processor looking in the cache for some data. The first data item is found in the cache: a hit. The second instruction generates a miss because the data is not available in the cache, and needs to be retrieved from memory instead.

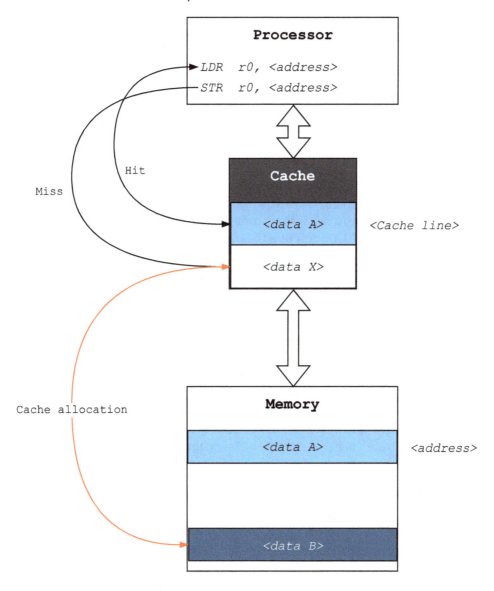

Figure 8.7 Hit and miss of data location in the cache

While the miss rate should be as low as possible, some level of misses cannot be avoided. These are termed **compulsory misses**. Following a reset, the cache will be empty, and the first load will be a compulsory (or "cold") miss. The same can happen when there is a branch to a new instruction or if an access is made to a data array that has not been accessed previously.

To keep the number of misses low and the number of hits high, the caching parameters need to be well-chosen. For instance, how many further instructions should be preloaded when the first instruction is loaded into the cache? It is hard to determine the ideal parameters because they may work well for some applications and not for others.

Adding a cache to a system can also have its drawbacks. When a cache miss occurs, there is an overhead in clearing the data stored (i.e. cache eviction) and fetching the new data from the next level of memory hierarchy. The time spent looking for the data in the cache is wasted. For some code, operating a cache with a low hit-to-miss ratio results in slower code execution overall. Furthermore, the presence of a cache reduces the predictability of the overall system because the time to read some information can vary quite considerably depending on this hit/miss ratio.

Finally, in some cases, incorporating a cache can increase power consumption, adds a new layer of complexity to memory access, and can create data incoherence between different actors trying to share the same memory. The approaches that are used to address such issues (such as preloading, hit ratios, and coherence mechanisms) are described below.

> Note: Only the largest class of Cortex-M processors has integrated caches: for example, the M7 and M33. For the smaller Cortex-M cores, the caches are external to the system. According to the Arm documentation [3]: "The Cortex-M0, Cortex-M0+, Cortex-M1, Cortex-M3 and Cortex-M4 processors do not have any internal cache memory. However, it is possible for a SoC design to integrate a system-level cache." In order to make writing of data to external memory more efficient (less time-consuming), some microcontrollers, including the mid-range Cortex-M processors (e.g. M3, M4 and M7), incorporate a "**write buffer**" (or "**store buffer**") in their internal bus system to assemble more bytes of data (up to 64 bits and a 32-bit address in each entry) before it is either written to cache RAM (if appropriate) or to main memory. Thus, a data write can be executed within a single clock cycle even if the underlying transfer will eventually consume several clock cycles on the memory bus.

8.3.4 Cache Hierarchy

Until now, we have been considering the use of one small cache in a system. Data is either available in the cache or in memory. When data is not present in the cache, a miss occurs, and the data needs to be retrieved from the more remote and slower RAM. The idea behind a cache hierarchy is to add a further level of cache between the first cache and memory. This second-level (L2) cache is larger than the first cache and can therefore contain more data. When a miss occurs at the first level of cache, instead of looking in the memory, the processor searches in the second level of cache to see if the data is present there. The access time for the second cache is longer than that of the first but is still much quicker than going to memory. As with the original cache, policies need to be determined to decide which data are worth storing in the second level of cache and when it should be evicted.

If we can have two levels of cache, what is to stop us adding another level, and another, and so on? Well, caches are expensive in terms of cost, space, and complexity, so it is not feasible, nor efficient, to add too many levels of caching.

Typical systems have up to three levels of cache, as depicted in Figure 8.8. The associated hierarchy involves the L1 cache being the closest to the core and not shared with others; L2 cache is outside the chip, as is L3 cache. The differences between L2 and L3 are in their sizes, with L3 being bigger, and in the number of cores linked to them: in a multiprocessor system, L3 is shared with all of the cores that access the main memory. The subsequent section on cache coherence describes the mechanisms that must be implemented when caches are used in a multiprocessor SoC.

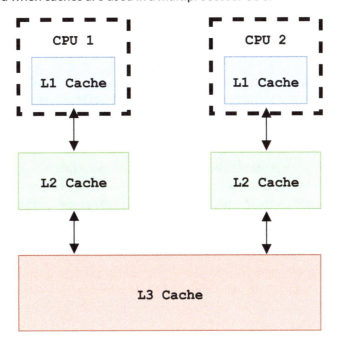

Figure 8.8 Cache hierarchy

8.3.5 Cache Addressing and Placement Policies

When something is loaded into the cache it is not enough to load the raw data or the instruction from the original memory address. Metadata needs to be stored alongside the data to indicate what is in the cache and its status. The details of this metadata are implementation-specific; however, it usually includes the following:

▪ a tag used to identify the cache line corresponding to a given address – combined with the cache line number, it is used to retrieve the full address

▪ a validity bit that indicates whether the cache line is valid

▪ a security bit indicating whether the cache line has been loaded from secure memory.

Other bit fields may exist and be used in some architectures. For instance, a specific bit field may be useful in a multi-processor architecture to indicate whether the cached data can be shared between the processors.

Under normal conditions, data is associated with an address corresponding to its position in memory. In software, pointers are typically used to retrieve data from memory, but the address of the data in memory will not correspond to the address of the data when copied into the cache, not least because the cache is much smaller than the memory, so there cannot be any one-to-one mapping. When data is cached, a cache address is associated with it, but the process is transparent to a programmer, who does not know whether the data is being accessed from the memory or the cache. Remember, too, that implementation of a spatial caching policy means that several blocks of contiguous data are typically preloaded into the cache when the first data item is loaded. So how does cache addressing make data addresses transparent to the programmer?

When placed in the cache, the address of the data is derived from its memory address. The relationship between cache and memory is referred to in terms of their **associativity**. The way the new cache address of the data is constructed depends on the **placement policy** of the cache. There are three types:

▪ **Direct-mapped cache**. In simple terms, in this type of cache, each cache line is effectively pre-assigned to a proportionate fraction of memory. Thus, for example, if there are 64 lines of cache available, the main memory is split up (into 64 "sets") on a modulo-64 basis and multiple lines of it will notionally be assigned to the same cache line (although the cache can only represent one of these lines at any time).

To manage this mapping, the memory address is split into three parts: a tag, an index, and an offset (or block). The number of bits assigned to the offset or block depends on the number of blocks preloaded into each cache line: if four blocks are loaded into each cache line, then two offset/block bits are required to indicate which of the four blocks is of interest. The number of bits assigned to the index depends on the number of lines the cache can contain: if it can contain 64 lines, then six ($2^6 = 64$) index bits will be required to indicate which cache line is of interest. Finally, the remaining bits of the memory address form the tag address.

As illustrated in Figure 8.9, when the cache receives a memory address, it extracts the index bits from it to identify a line within the cache, and it then compares the tag address in that cache line with the tag component of the memory address. If they match (a hit), the offset bits are used to extract the appropriate block from the cache line; if they don't match (a "conflict" miss), then the relevant memory address must be accessed and used to populate the cache line instead, updating the tag value therein. The main advantages of this type of cache are that it is simple and does not require a lot of additional hardware (one comparator, one AND-gate and a tri-state buffer). The downside of this type of cache is that whenever a data item has the same index value as another data item already present in the cache, the latter will be overwritten in the cache by the former, which is not very efficient.

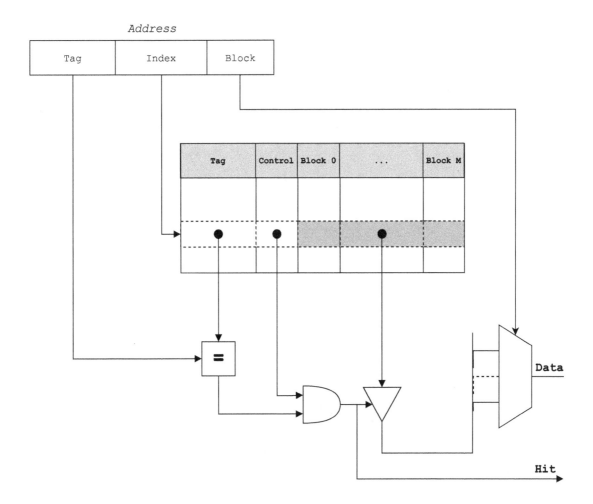

Figure 8.9 Direct-mapped cache

- **Fully associative cache**. In this type of cache, illustrated in Figure 8.10, the memory address is split into just two components, a tag and an offset (block); the index component is subsumed into the tag, and no longer affords the cache the ability to compare just one cache line in the search for a potential hit (meaning that memory is now treated as a single "set"). Instead, all of the lines of the cache must be compared to the tag (albeit in parallel). However, there is no preassigned mapping to constrain where a memory line must be stored within the cache (it can be placed in the next unused cache line), which significantly reduces the risk of overwriting existing data unless the cache is full (when an eviction policy must be invoked), and means that the cache is relatively efficient. However, here the inconvenience relates to the amount of hardware that is required to manage the search for the relevant item in the cache. Whereas direct-mapped cache requires one comparator, one AND-gate and one tri-state buffer, a fully associative cache requires one comparator, one AND-gate and one tri-state buffer for *every* cache line, as well as a very big OR-gate with one input per cache line too, as partially represented in Figure 8.10.

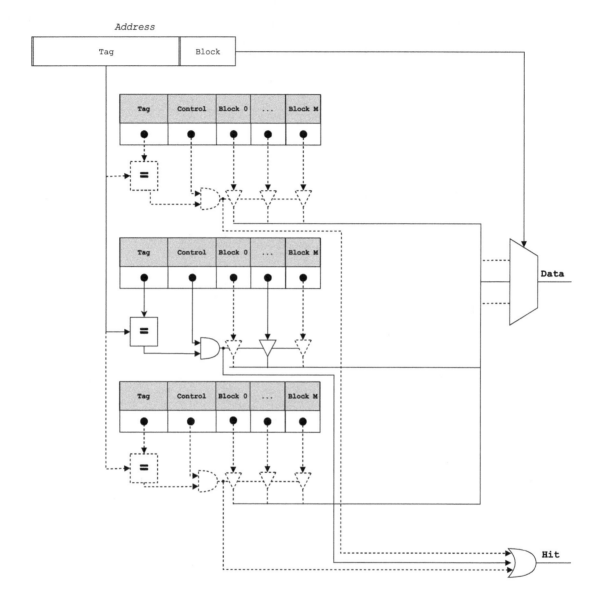

Figure 8.10 Fully associative cache

- **N-way set-associative cache.** This type of cache sits somewhere between fully associative and direct-mapped caches. The memory address is once again decomposed into a tag, an index and an offset, as shown in Figure 8.11. The cache is separated into N sets (where N is typically 2 or 4). As in a direct-mapped cache, when data is loaded into the cache, it will be placed in the cache line associated with its index in the first set. However, if this location is already populated, the cache will attempt to load the data into the equivalent cache line in the second set, and so on until all of the sets have been exhausted; only then will eviction/overwriting occur, reflecting some of the flexibility of the fully associated cache. When the cache receives a memory address, it need only search for a matching tag in one cache line in each of the N sets, rather than searching the entire cache. This placement policy reduces the number of collisions that would be encountered were we using a direct-mapped cache, but not as efficiently as in a fully associative cache (where collision only occurs if the entire cache is full). In an N-way set-associative cache, a collision occurs only if there are already N data items loaded for a given index. The hardware required to manage this type of cache is slightly more than is required for a direct-mapped cache and will depend on the value of N. You may have already noticed that a direct-mapped cache is effectively a 1-way set-associative cache, and a fully associative cache with 64 lines is effectively a 64-way set-associative cache.

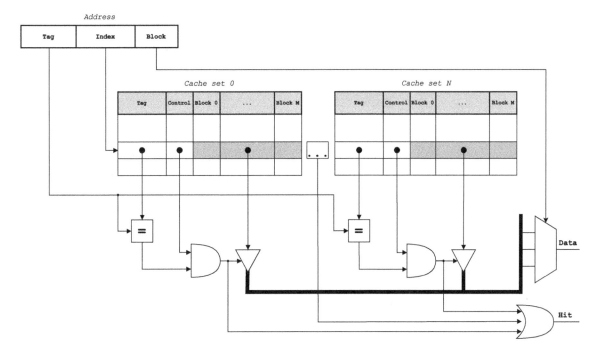

Figure 8.11 N-way set-associative cache

Let us consider a cache of 64 kB with a block number of 32, each block being a word of 32 bits (4 bytes): data will have a 32-bit memory address. In order to address the 32 blocks of a cache line, the offset (block) part of the address will consist of 5 bits ($2^5 = 32$). This will not be affected by the type of cache that is implemented. The number of lines that the cache will contain is 64 kB/(32 × 4 B) = 512:

■ For a fully associative cache, the tag will be all of the remaining bits of the address after removing the 5-bit offset, meaning that the tag will be 27-bits long (32 – 5).

■ For a direct-mapped cache, the index needs to be large enough to address each of the 512 lines, meaning that it must be 9-bits long ($2^9 = 512$), and the tag will be the bits remaining after removing this index and the 5-bit offset, making it 18-bits long (32 – 5 – 9).

■ For an 8-way set-associative cache, the 512 lines of cache will be separated equally into 8 sets of 64 lines each. The index needs to be large enough to address these 64 lines, meaning that it must be 6-bits long ($2^6 = 64$), and the tag will be 21 bits in length (32 – 5 – 6).

In some cases, cache performance can be heavily impacted when a block is replaced by another if the evicted line will be required again in a few cycles' time. In such cases, the cache removes line A, fetches new line B, uses new line B, and must then restore the original line A. The new line B might be used just once, or multiple times when it will cause line A to be moved back and forth between memory and cache. In this instance, increasing the associativity of the cache will help, but it might not be enough if there are other addresses that also clash.

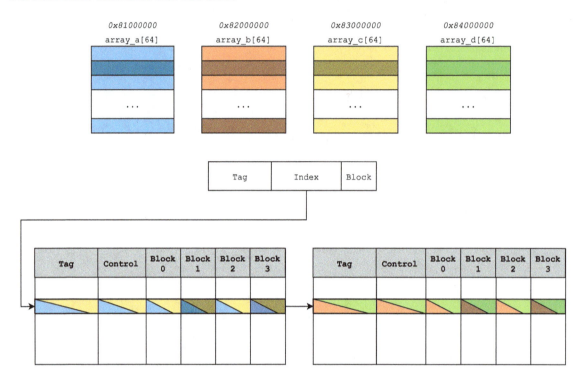

Figure 8.12 Cache eviction issue

To illustrate this, let us consider four arrays sharing the same index in a 2-way set-associative cache and imagine the following scenario, as depicted in Figure 8.12:

1. At the start of the program, the cache is empty.

2. *array_a*[0] is read. Because the cache is empty, there is a compulsory miss. The value is retrieved from memory instead, and is then added in the appropriate empty slot of the first set, along with *array_a*[1], *array_a*[2] and *array_a*[3] as part of a spatial caching policy.

3. *array_b*[0] is read. It also produces a cache miss. Because it has the same index as *array_a*[0], and the latter is already occupying the corresponding index slot in the first set, *array_b*[0] is placed in the equivalent slot in the second set of the cache, along with the following immediately proximate values of *array_b*.

4. *array_c*[0] is read. It has the same index as *array_a*[0] and *array_b*[0], which are already occupying the associated cache lines in both available sets, meaning that a conflict miss is raised. The cache line

that contains array_a[0], *array_a*[1], *array_a*[2] and *array_a*[3] is evicted and the four initial values of *array_c* are stored in the first set of the cache instead.

5. *array_d*[0] is read. The same pattern seen in step 4 repeats itself and *array_d* ends up replacing array_b in the second set of the cache.

6. *array_a*[1] is read. It is a (conflict) miss again! Indeed, *array_a*[1] had been loaded into the cache (in step 2) but has since been evicted to store *array_c*[1] instead (in step 4). The line that contains *array_c*[1] must be evicted and *array_a*[1] stored in its place.

If we continue with this program, we will have nothing but cache misses! Such continuous cycles of fruitless cache population and eviction are sometimes referred to as "cache pollution". However, if we were using a 4-way set-associative cache, this issue would not arise because each of the four sets of the cache could accommodate data from one of the four arrays.

Table 8.1 summarizes the pros and cons of the three types of cache, when it comes to associativity.

Table 8.1 Summary of pros and cons for cache associativity

Cache type	Pros	Cons	Cache parameters

Direct-mapped	Easy and inexpensive	Cache lines can be overwritten too frequently according to the index carried within the address	Address size: *A* bits
			Cache size: *C* bytes
			Line size: *L* bytes
			# Lines = *C* / *L*
			Index = $\log_2$(# Lines)
			Offset = $\log_2$(Line size)
			Tag = (*A* – Index – Offset)

N-way set-associative	Balanced combination of a direct-mapped and fully associative cache	Need to identify a "good" associativity number to get the best benefit from this cache; this depends on the application	Address size: *A* bits Cache size: *C* bytes # Sets: *N* Line size: *L* bytes # Lines = *C* / *L*

			# Lines per Set = (# Lines / *N*)
			Index = $\log_2$(# Lines per Set)
			Offset = $\log_2$(Line size)
			Tag = (*A* – Index – Offset)

Fully associative	Cache lines are fully used and there is no specific assignment for an address	Inspecting all cache lines requires lots of comparators and lots of hardware	Address size: *A* bits
			Cache size: *C* bytes
			Line size: *L* bytes
			# Lines = *C* / *L*
			Offset = $\log_2$(Line size)
			Tag = (*A* – Offset)

8.3.6 Cache Properties

We can see that there are several different parameters that need to be taken into consideration when we are designing a cache for our SoC. We have already touched on the following:

- Cache size: the number of bytes/words that can be stored.

- Cache line size: the number of bytes/words per line of cache.

- Addressing regime: whether a cache address relates to a word or a byte in the memory.

A further consideration that we have raised but not discussed in detail is the cache **replacement policy**, which determines how to replace a line when there is not enough space to add new data into the cache. There are many possible approaches to optimization of this policy; three of the simplest approaches are:

- **First-In, First-Out** (FIFO): effectively, remove the line in the cache that is the oldest (was populated first). Implementation of this policy requires the existence of metadata to indicate at what time a line was added. It does not, of course, indicate that the data is no longer required, and the approach runs the risk that the data removed may be needed again within a few more cycles.

- **Least Recently Used** (LRU): remove the line in the cache that has been used the least. Again, this approach implies the presence of metadata for each line to track its usage, and is based on the notion that something that has been used recently is more likely to be used again in the near future.

- **Random**: remove a line in the cache to make space for a new line on an entirely random basis. This approach has the advantage of not requiring metadata to decide which line to evict. In practice, the implementation of true randomness is not that easy.

Another consideration, that we have not discussed at all, is the **write policy** for the cache. When the cache is used as a shortcut to *read* a memory value, things are simple; the variable involved will have the same value in both the cache and the memory. However, when the cache is used to update this variable in a write operation, the value in the cache will no longer be the same as that in memory. The value in the cache is the "good" one, the one in memory is out-of-date. A mechanism is required to synchronize the two, referred to as the write policy, and there are different approaches available, the two most basic of which are illustrated in Figure 8.13:

- **Write-Back**: In this approach, no immediate attempt is made to update the memory to be consistent with the modified cache value, meaning that the change is only available in the cache. The main memory is not coherent with the cache and has different values. The cache uses a special "dirty" bit to remember that the cache line has updated values. Only when the associated line is evicted from the cache will its modified content be "written back" to main memory. The advantage is that the memory bus may be used less; the cached value may be updated several times before it finally gets copied back to memory. However, the approach also decreases the determinism of a program, because the number of writes to memory cannot be known in advance for certain.

- **Write-Through**: In this approach, when data is modified in the cache, the update is applied to the memory at the same time. This makes memory management simpler, but the bus is likely to experience more traffic. The write is also slower because an application must wait until the data has been written to memory before it can continue.

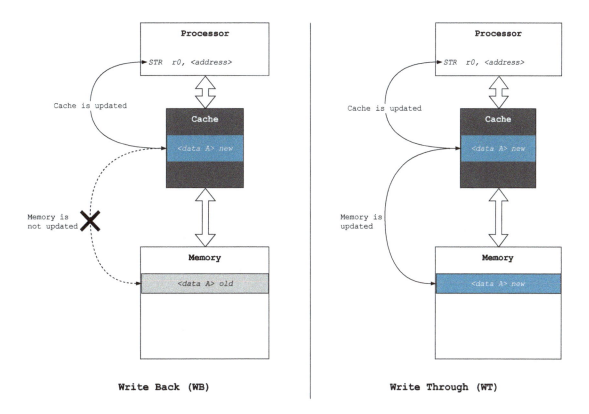

Figure 8.13 Write-back and write-through cache writing policies

Another approach adopts a slightly different philosophy:

▪ **Write-Around**: In this approach, the update occurs only in the main memory if the data is not already mapped in the cache. Otherwise, it is similar to a write-through. This can be of value in situations where data is unlikely to be re-read after it has been written/updated. This is to avoid cache pollution by not using a cache line for data that will not be reused.

Up until now we have considered situations in which a cache stores both instructions and data, in which case we describe the cache as "**unified**". Because instructions and data are usually not related to one another, they are often placed in separate caches, giving rise to a "**split**" cache: an instruction cache (I-cache) and a data cache (D-cache). The main advantage of a split cache is that the D-cache and I-cache can each be placed physically closer to where they will be most frequently used. Furthermore, in a pipelined processor, both the instruction fetch and the data access steps require concurrent access to the cache to load instructions and data. A split cache allows these accesses to occur in parallel. With a unified cache, arbitration is required to sequentialize the accesses. Finally, instructions and data are used in very different ways. Unlike data, instructions are mostly (although not always) read-only. A split cache allows the selection of different replacement and write policies for each cache, which may improve their overall performance. However, deciding how to apportion the available cache between the D-cache and I-cache is not straightforward and can result in a suboptimal solution. Retaining a unified cache is simpler and keeps hardware resources low.

Typically, a SoC might have a split L1 cache and a unified L2 cache. Cache IPs can be used to simplify the creation of a SoC cache. A typical example is the system cache IP from Xilinx, in which the cache size and associativity, among other parameters, can be configured. It uses an LRU cache replacement policy [4].

8.3.7 Cache Coherence

If a SoC has several processors that share data, a new issue emerges in the context of caching. Figure 8.14 illustrates the problem: CPU 1 reads a shared variable from memory into its local L1 cache, having the value 0xCAFE; CPU 2 loads the same variable into its L1 cache and then updates its value to 0xCOFFEE. If a write-through write policy has been adopted, then the value of the variable in memory is updated with 0xCOFFEE, but its value in the cache of CPU 1 is not updated. If no mechanism is implemented to address this, the next time CPU 1 reads the variable it will see 0xCAFE rather than 0xCOFFEE. The cache of CPU 1 and the memory are said to be in an "incoherent" state. It should be obvious that adding a third CPU into the equation will just compound the potential problems if, for example, one CPU is reading and two CPUs are writing the same variable: the order in which a variable is written needs to be perceived by all of the processors in the same way.

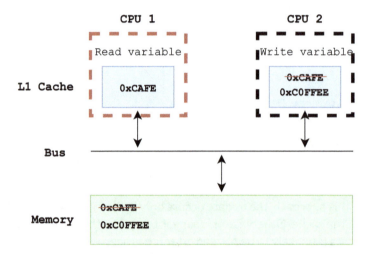

Figure 8.14 Cache coherence issue

Thus, cache coherence concerns itself with solving two issues:

- **Write propagation:** A write conducted in any cache needs to be propagated to all other caches. The value of a memory location read by a processor always needs to be the last value written for that location, whether in a cache or in memory.

- **Write serialization:** Reads and writes from and to a memory location need to be perceived as happening in the same order by all of the processors that might be involved.

Two basic mechanisms exist to maintain cache coherence, a **directory-based** protocol and a **snooping** protocol.

Directory-based coherence involves the use of a directory that maintains information about the cache lines of all the processor caches. Then, when loading data into its cache, a processor consults this directory and if that data is already present in another cache, the directory either invalidates or updates the data in the relevant cache(s). Because every processor must access this directory, it can become a bottleneck. One solution is to use distributed directories for systems that have high numbers of processors. Because such systems are not our focus in this book, we will concentrate on the snooping protocol instead.

In a snooping coherence protocol, the actions of each cache are broadcast on the bus and the other caches must listen to what is being done. Then, when data is written two actions are possible:

▓ **Write-invalidate:** Caches that already contain a copy of the data invalidate their copy, removing any risk of using out-of-date data.

▓ **Write-update:** The updated data is broadcast on the bus too, and the caches use this to directly update their copy of the data.

Because both of these approaches require the broadcast of some level of data to every cache, snooping does not scale to large systems. Furthermore, the greater amounts of data that must be broadcast to fulfill a write-update approach means that it is not often used.

Snooping solves the problem of write serialization by using the bus, which cannot be used concurrently, as a broadcast communication system with built-in arbitration: nothing else need be added to determine what action is performed first.

Several low-level protocols exist to maintain coherence and can be implemented regardless of the broader mechanism used for cache coherence (i.e. snooping or directory-based):

▓ Modified – Shared – Invalid (MSI)

▓ Modified – Owned – Shared – Invalid (MOSI)

▓ Modified – Exclusive – Shared – Invalid (MESI)

▓ Modified – Exclusive – Owned – Shared – Invalid (MEOSI).

We will study the first of these, MSI, because it forms the basis from which the other protocols are derived. We will do this by considering the finite state machines (FSMs) that each processor operates for every cache line when it comes to data reads and data writes under this protocol. Thus, Figure 8.15 shows the FSM for a read under the MSI protocol, in which data can be in one of three states:

▓ **Invalid** (I): The data is either not in the cache or has been invalidated by a write.

▓ **Shared** (S): The data is in the cache of one or more processors. However, only read accesses are made to the data.

■ **Modified** (M): The data in the cache has been modified. The memory no longer contains the correct value and needs to be updated when an eviction occurs.

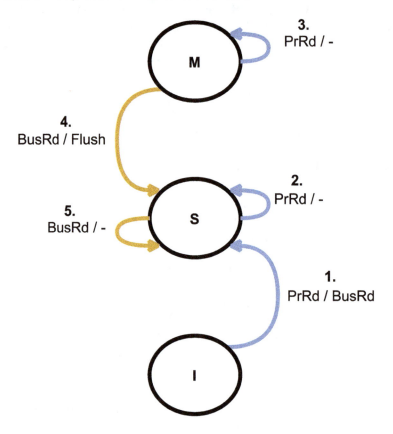

Figure 8.15 Finite state machine of MSI protocol for reads

The state transitions in Figure 8.15 can be explained as follows:

1. The processor reads a data value in the cache but it is invalid. This means that the data must instead be loaded into the cache from memory. A bus read (BusRd) signal is output to the other processors to inform them of this request. The freshly loaded data transitions to a shared state, indicating that it may be read by other processors too.

2. In this shared state the data can be read, either by the local processor or another processor; no output signal is required.

3. If the local processor has a data value in a modified state, it can read it without sending any output signal because it is the only one to have access to the data.

4. If, however, the data is in a modified state and the local processor receives a BusRd signal, it indicates that another processor wants to read the data. The modified data needs to be written

back to the memory such that the processor that wants to read it can obtain the latest value; this is done by flushing the data. Because another processor will now have loaded the latest value into its local cache, that cache line can transition to a shared state.

5. If the processor receives a BusRd while the data is in a shared state, it indicates that another processor wants to read the data. This is not a problem, and no signal need be output.

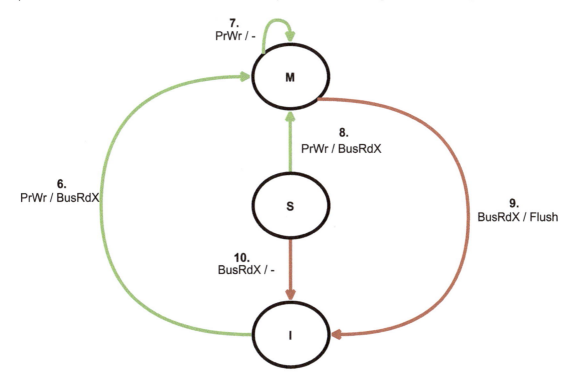

Figure 8.16 Finite state machine of MSI protocol for writes

Figure 8.16 represents the FSM for a cache line when a write is required. The green arrows are the state transitions for the local processor; the red arrows are the state transitions that are involved when another processor wants to write the data (aka a BusRdX signal is incoming from the bus). The state transitions in Figure 8.16 can be explained as follows:

6. The local processor wants to write a data value but the data is in an invalid state (probably not yet in the cache) and must be retrieved from memory. To indicate to the other processors that this processor is going to update the data, the BusRdX signal is output on the bus, and the data state transitions to 'Modified'.

7. Once the data is in the modified state, the local processor can update it again without sending any message to the other processors because it has already established that it is the only processor to have a valid copy of the data.

8. If the data is in a shared state, which means the processor had previously read the value, but the processor now wants to update it, the processor must notify the other processors by outputting a BusRdX signal, and the state of the data transitions to 'Modified'.

9. If the data is in the modified state and the processor receives a BusRdX signal, indicating that another processor wants to update it, the local processor must update the memory with the new value of the data, by means of a flush, after which the state of the local copy of the data is rendered 'Invalid'.

10. If the data is in a shared state, which means the processor had previously read the value, and a BusRdX signal is received, it means another processor wants to update the data. The copy of the data held in the local cache is therefore no longer correct, and its state transitions to 'Invalid'.

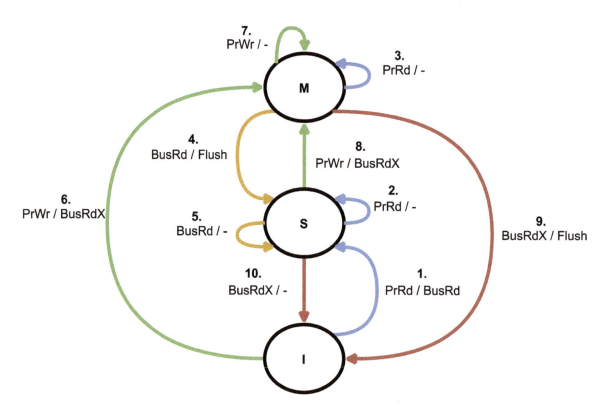

Figure 8.17 Finite state machine for MSI protocol

Figure 8.17 depicts the entire FSM, incorporating the transitions for both reading and writing data. Note that the MOSI, MESI and MOESI protocols require two additional states to be added to the basic MSI protocol:

■ **Exclusive** (E): A processor has exclusive access to a piece of data, and the data is not shared with others. In this case, it is safe for the processor to read or write it without any signaling to other processors, reducing the amount of broadcast communication required on the bus.

■ **Owner** (O): The owner indicates that the last written data value is in its local cache. This allows other processors to directly read the new data from the cache of this processor instead of reading it from the memory. The processor that owns the latest data is not required to write the data back to memory until such time as another processor wants to update (rather than read) it, when it takes over ownership after obliging the original owner to flush the value to memory. In some transaction sequences, this additional state can reduce the overall number of main memory writes.

Finally, because coherence mechanisms add significant complexity to a system, some systems dispense with them altogether. In this case, to avoid coherence issues, any data that is shared between several processors should not be cacheable, meaning that any access (read or write) to such data must be performed via the highest level of shared memory.

8.3.8 Cache Control Instructions

In an ideal world, the implementation of caching should be invisible to the programmer. However, in some situations it may be necessary to **bypass** the cache to ensure the correct operation of an application. For example, the Cortex-M microprocessor can support direct memory-mapped locations that point to physical registers for peripherals (as described in Chapter 3 in relation to the Memory Protection Unit). If caching is used with a write-back policy, then when an update occurs, it will only take effect in relation to these registers when the cache line is evicted. This can give rise to undesired behaviors if the programmer is expecting the data to be written directly, for example, for a UART output buffer. The same issue might occur if incoming data is cached. A program reading the memory location will always read the same value that was previously loaded into the cache rather than the fresh data. Thus, address ranges used for accessing peripherals such as DMA controllers and UARTs should be set as non-cacheable locations to avoid such behaviors. At a software level, this can be done in C, for example, via use of the keyword *volatile*, which forces any write of a data value to be directly stored in the memory.

In addition, the **MCR** instruction of the Arm instruction set can be used to clean or flush regions of the I-cache and D-cache. We recommend that use of this instruction be reserved for expert programmers, because it can lead to unexpected results in inexperienced hands.

8.3.9 Real-world Caches

Which parameters are used in real-world caches? The cache architectures of specific SoCs are often proprietary and manufacturers do not want to reveal them. It is, therefore, not always easy to gather information about the state-of-the-art of industrially produced cache. Nevertheless, 8.2 presents some specifications of caches that can be found in some current SoCs.

Table 8.2 Examples of caches used in SoCs

SoC	Vendor	Cortex	Instruction cache	Data cache
STM32F7xx [5]	ST	M7	16 KiB 32-byte cache lines 2-way set-associative	16 KiB 32-byte cache lines 4-way set-associative
KV5x [6]	NXP	M7	16 KiB	8 KiB
ATSAM4 [7]	Atmel	M4	Unified cache 2 KiB 16-byte cache lines 4-way set-associative	
EFM32GG [8]	Silabs	M4	512 bytes 64-byte cache lines 4-way set-associative	None

8.4 Volatile Memory

8.4.1 Introduction

Computer systems always seem to require more memory. Processors are becoming more and more efficient and routinely have 32-bit address lines and often more. Applications are making use of more and more of this memory. To make it possible to achieve relatively short access times, random-access memory (RAM) is required (as opposed to the mass memory provided by disks, for example). To load programs and data, such memory must support reads and writes. Two main types of RAM exist, and they represent the two main forms of volatile memory (i.e. requiring power to maintain it) in use today:

- Static random-access memory or SRAM

- Dynamic random-access memory or DRAM.

The advantages of static RAM are its speed and its ease of implementation; although volatile, SRAM does not need to be periodically refreshed, whereas dynamic RAM does. However, dynamic RAM has one big advantage: at any given time, its information density (effective capacity) is typically four times that of static RAM. This is due to the differences in internal architecture and operating principles. Whereas a static RAM memory cell consists of four transistors to store information and two for its selection, a dynamic RAM cell only requires one storage transistor (technically, a capacitor) and one selection transistor. Hence the ratio of 4:1 in relation to the storage component of the two memory types. In addition, dynamic RAM uses address multiplexing to enable smaller packaging and fewer lines to route on a printed circuit board (PCB).

In this section, we describe the main characteristics of volatile memory, principally in the context of DRAM: its principles of operation, its address-bus multiplexing, its read and write cycles, and its refresh cycles. Many variants have been created and some are briefly described before we continue to the later generations as represented by, for example, SDRAM and DDR.

Many different forms of volatile memory have been proposed in recent times in order to provide faster access to information. Some of them are touched on below, such as VRAM, EDO DRAM, SDRAM, DDR, etc. Not all of them have survived or are likely to survive, because the market does not demand such variation. Nevertheless, a large amount of research effort continues to be invested in the field of memory to increase its capacity and shorten access times.

In this section, some older and almost redundant memory types are described. Why? Because, in fact, inside the latest forms, the heart of the memory itself does not change very much, adhering to many common concepts and principles. The big improvements are typically technology-based, involving size reduction and/or synchronous access, and so study of some of these older forms serves to promote better understanding of the next generations of memory.

8.4.2 Basic DRAM Cell

Metal–oxide–semiconductor (MOS) technology forms the basis for building dynamic memory. The idea is to have one transistor as the selection element of a memory cell, with the memorization element realized by a capacitor, usually in the form of a real capacitor but sometimes through the use of the natural capacitance of a MOSFET transistor, which provides a capacitance between its gate and the substrate. The capacitor can store charge for a limited time, which is used to represent a binary value: charged (a logic '1') or uncharged (a logic '0'). When the transistor makes a pass-through connection to the capacitor, or selects it, the charge level of the capacitor can either be sensed ("read") or it can be changed ("written"). Figure 8.18 illustrates the principle of a basic cell of a dynamic memory, in which the transistor provides the selection element and the capacitor provides the memorization element.

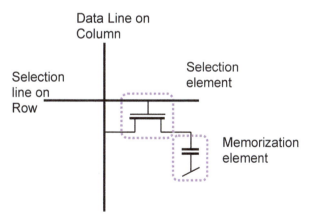

Figure 8.18 Memorization cell in DRAM

Over time, capacitors discharge and thereby lose the information stored. To counteract this, they must be recharged regularly by a specific cycle of dynamic refreshment (the JEDEC[1] standard for the current generation of DRAM is every 64 ms or less), which is why this form of memory is termed dynamic. The cell is selected and the charge is regenerated with an appropriate voltage level such

---

[1] JEDEC (www.jedec.org) develops open standards and publications for the microelectronics industry, especially in relation to memory.

that the cell value is rewritten. To reduce the overall number of transistors, some manufacturers have suggested using multiple levels of charge per cell and thus encoding more than one bit in each cell (four distinct levels could encode two bits of information) but this multi-level cell approach needs more complex technology to protect against the smaller margins for error that are involved when reading the cell's value.

8.4.3 Basic DRAM Architecture

A dynamic memory takes the form of a huge square matrix or array; for example, 1024 rows of 1024 columns for a memory of 1 mebibit. To select a point in this matrix, it is first necessary to define the address of the line (row) of interest, and then the address of the relevant column. Two signals, called nRAS (Row Address Strobe) and nCAS (Column Address Strobe), are used to validate the selected addresses. A fundamental aspect of DRAM architecture is address multiplexing, which reduces the number of address pins that a DRAM chip or circuit must show to the outside world, taking up less space on the die. Thus, although 20 bits are required to uniquely address a cell in a 1-Mibit memory, only 10 lines are needed (the address is cut in half, and the two halves are applied to the address pins on two separate cycles).

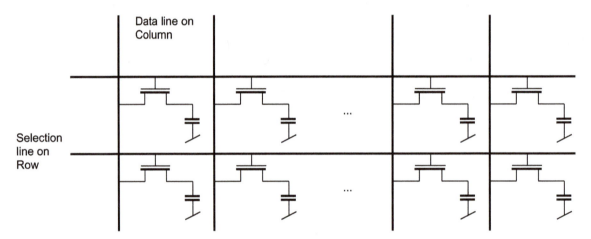

Figure 8.19 Two partial line of elements on a DRAM

As represented in Figure 8.19, when a specific row in the array is selected (driven high), all of the transistors on that row connect their associated capacitors to the vertical data or bit-lines. Thus, on each row access, all of the data in the row is "selected". Charge will be transferred from a capacitor to its adjacent bit-line if the stored value was a '1', and from the adjacent bit-line to the capacitor if the stored value was a '0'. The small change in voltage that results on each bit-line is sensed using an amplifier. This is used to amplify the small voltage value sensed to a logic level that can be interpreted as a 0 or 1 by the logic outside the row. The value of every cell in the row is then latched. The column address is then used to transfer the appropriate bit from the latch onto the external data bus.

Two immediate consequences arise from this system: first, the capacitors have effectively lost their value in the course of the read operation; second, if we imagine a column of 1024 bits in our array, the capacitance of the associated bit-line will be huge in comparison to the one used for memorization at cell level, yet connection of such a cell must be able to change the bit-line or column voltage consistently. To address these issues:

▪ Each time a row is selected and read, amplifiers on the columns recharge the capacitors in the storage cells and regenerate their previous memorization levels.

▪ Before a row is accessed, all of the columnar bit-lines are precharged to a known intermediate voltage level, such that a minimum of charge transfer from a cell is required to change the value read from a column.

▪ When a read is done the capacitor level value is compared to this middle voltage level to determine the '0' or '1' value read.

Figure 8.20 provides a component view of DRAM, together with the signals used to control it. The multiplexed address feeds into two registers that store the address supplied, the row address being memorized on the falling edge of the nRAS signal, and the column address on the falling edge of the nCAS signal, as represented in Figure 8.21. As we have already described, all of the cells in a row are activated with the row address, and an implicit refresh of that row is performed simultaneously. All of the corresponding bit values for that row of cells are passed to the column selector, which determines which specific cell is to be read or written to. The nWE (Write Enable) signal indicates whether the cell is to be read (high) or written to (low).

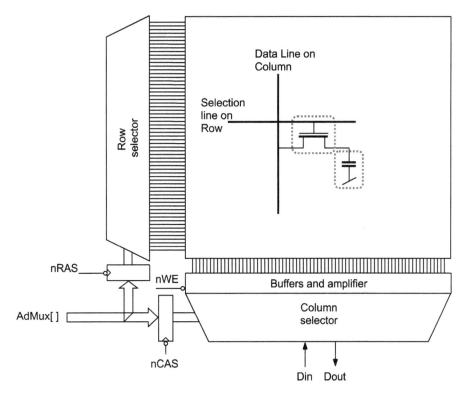

Figure 8.20 DRAM component diagram

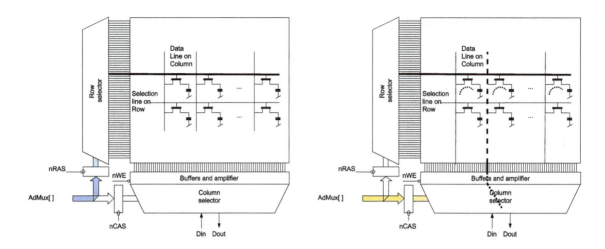

Figure 8.21 Use of nRAS and nCAS for row and column activation/selection

At their outset, DRAMs had a data width of just 1 bit; D_{in} and D_{out} buses were separate, and a single control signal (nWE) was used for read/write selection. Subsequently, as more data bits were made available on a single chip (e.g. 4, 8), the separate in and out data buses were combined into a shared tri-state bus, often referred to as DQ[ ], and a new control signal was introduced in the form of nOE (Output Enable; again, active low) to control output to the data pins. Once the width of the data bus grows to 16 bits, it is necessary to be able to make a selection in relation to the two (8-bit) bytes of the bus, and the nCAS signal must be split into two: nUCAS (Upper CAS) for selection of DQ[15..8], and nLCAS (Lower CAS) for selection of DQ[7..0]. Again, both signals are active low. These three configurations are depicted in Figure 8.22.

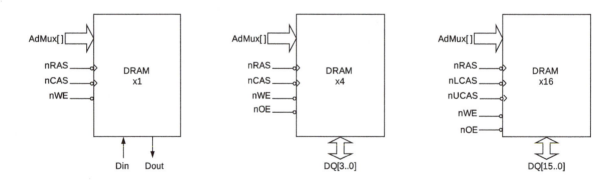

Figure 8.22 1-, 4- and 16-bit-wide DRAMs with associated control signals

Microprocessors typically have buses that are 8-, 16-, or 32-bits wide, and sometimes 64-bits wide. To match these bus widths, if we are using 1-bit wide DRAM chips, we will need a "bank" of 8, 16, 32 or 64 DRAMs. Similarly, in the case of 4-bit-wide DRAM chips, we will need 2, 4, 8 or 16 DRAMs to match these bus widths, and so on. All of the DRAMs will receive the incoming address. Because DRAM circuits must receive multiplexed addresses as input, they must be multiplexed from a normal, non-multiplexed microprocessor bus.

Figure 8.23 shows the principle of dynamic memory connection for an 8-bit processor with a multiplexer for the addresses. The sequencer takes care of the generation of the nRAS, nCAS, and nWE (shown as nWR in the figure) signals and the multiplexer control. It also takes care of performing periodic refresh cycles.

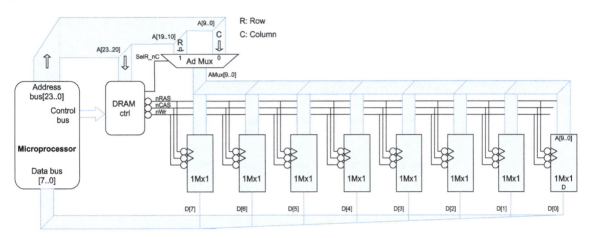

Figure 8.23 Connection of an 8-bit processor with eight 1-bit-wide DRAMs

8.4.4 DRAM Cycles

As we have seen above, the use of DRAM involves three basic forms of access: a read cycle, a write cycle, and a refresh cycle. Other more specialized cycles can be implemented for specific applications. Please note that in the remainder of this chapter the signal names nWE and nWR are used interchangeably to represent the Write Enable signal.

8.4.4.1 Read Cycle

A read cycle is characterized by the Write Enable signal being held inactive (i.e. high) for the entire duration of the transfer. The nOE signal is activated to make the data available as output. The read cycle for DRAM is depicted in Figure 8.24 and the sequence can be broken down as follows:

▧ The address of the row of interest is placed on the address lines of the DRAM memory chip.

▧ The nRAS signal is activated as a falling edge, causing the desired line to be selected.

▧ The address lines change as the address of the column of interest is provided.

▧ The nWR signal must be inactive at high level.

▧ The nCAS signal is activated low, providing a falling edge and causing the address of the desired column to be recorded.

▧ The data is supplied by the memory on the D_{out} pin within a given access time. Manufacturers specify a variety of parameters in relation to their DRAM chips. For example, t_{RAC} is the maximum time from nRAS activation to data output, and t_{CAC} is the maximum time from nCAS activation to data output.

■ For a memory chip that is more than 1-bit wide, nOE must be activated too.

■ After the data has been read, nRAS and nCAS are both deactivated, the data is removed from the bus by the memory, and the data line reverts to the Z state after tOFF or TOEZ (high impedance).

■ Before a new cycle can start, it is necessary to wait a certain amount time after the deactivation of nRAS, referred to as the **precharge time** (t_{RP}).

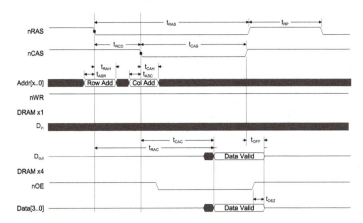

Figure 8.24 Read cycle

8.4.4.2 Write Cycle

The basic DRAM write cycle offers significant latitude in terms of when the data value actually gets stored in the memory cell. This gave rise to two different modes – early and delayed – which suited different kinds of processor and DRAM timing specifications.

The signaling involved in the two options is illustrated in Figure 8.25. In the early or advanced mode, the nWR signal is activated (i.e. driven low) early, before the address and data validation signal. During write cycles in general, writing to memory takes place on the falling edge of nWR or nCAS, whichever is last active. In each of the options, the data must be valid sufficiently early (i.e. before nCAS or nWR goes low, determined by data set-up time, t_{DS}) and remain long enough after the active falling-edge (data hold time, t_{DH}). We need to ensure that the nOE signal is not activated during a write cycle.

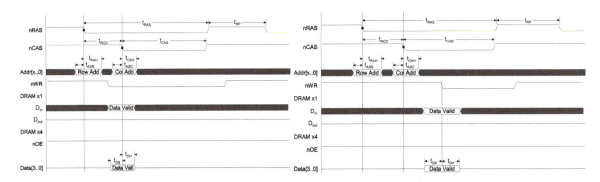

Figure 8.25 DRAM write cycle options: early (left) vs delayed (right)

8.4.4.3   Read-Modify-Write Cycle

Some microprocessors can take advantage of DRAMs that have been designed to allow a single indivisible read-modify-write cycle in which a memory location is first read and then written to without a new address having to be supplied in between, although the overall cycle time is extended to allow both operations to occur. This is illustrated in Figure 8.26. In the first step the data is read, then modified by an external device (e.g. the processor) and written back to the same memory position. No other access to the device can occur during this sequence.

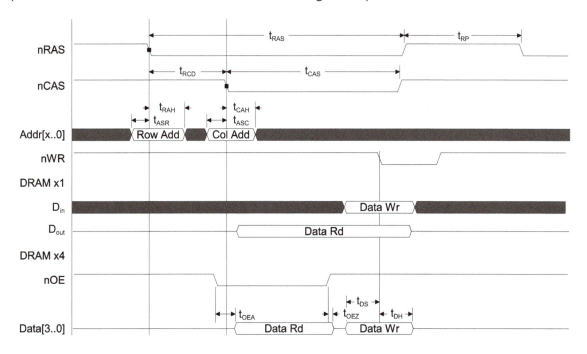

Figure 8.26 Read-modify-write cycle

8.4.4.4   Refresh Cycles

As we have previously indicated, dynamic memory only functions at all if it is almost continuously refreshed, and for a device in standby mode, DRAM refreshment can account for as much as 30 percent of the power consumed (DRAM currently accounts for about 25 percent of data center power consumption). Understandably, finding ways to refresh DRAM more efficiently, with less power and at less frequent intervals, has been and continues to be a major focus for manufacturers and a variety of refresh cycles have been developed, which have often served to define different versions of DRAM, as we shall see below. Despite the complexity that the need for refresh cycles introduces to DRAM design, the physical simplicity and information density of the DRAM cell has established its longevity. The necessary refresh interval depends on the model: smaller, earlier DRAM chips needed to be refreshed every 8 ms or so; for the latest generation of chips it is every 64 ms.

Reading from or writing to a line in DRAM memory is "destructive" and the line is always refreshed thereafter, but this is obviously not sufficient to ensure that every line in memory is regularly refreshed, so separate refresh cycles are also required. In its early days, the CPU would drive these refresh cycles using a counter as appropriate, but this function was subsequently delegated to memory controllers and now DRAM chips may be self-refreshing through the use of internal counters.

8.4.5 DRAM Versions

8.4.5.1 RAS-only Refresh

The original method of DRAM refreshment, dating back to the late 1960s, was to cycle through each row of memory on the basis of repeatedly activating the nRAS signal (i.e. driving it low) and using an external counter to increment the row address each time, as illustrated in Figure 8.27; no other signals are involved. The disadvantage of this method is that it depends on a counter that is external to the memory.

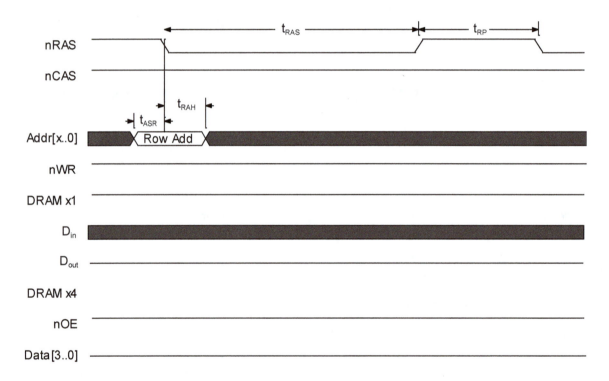

Figure 8.27 RAS-only refresh cycle

8.4.5.2 CAS Before RAS Refresh

It was not long before the refresh counter was incorporated into the memory chip itself (see Figure 8.28), providing the standard for DRAM ever since. If nCAS is activated before nRAS, which would not normally happen, then the chip ignores the usual address inputs (which are not powered up, saving energy) and instead uses an automatically incrementing internal counter to perform a refresh cycle, known as "CAS before RAS" and illustrated in Figure 8.29.

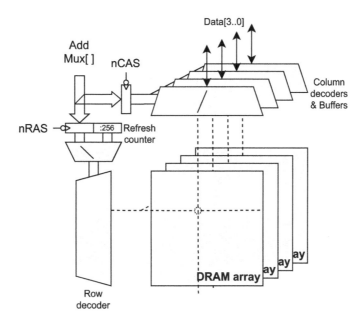

Figure 8.28 Internal DRAM architecture with a refresh counter, x4 memory

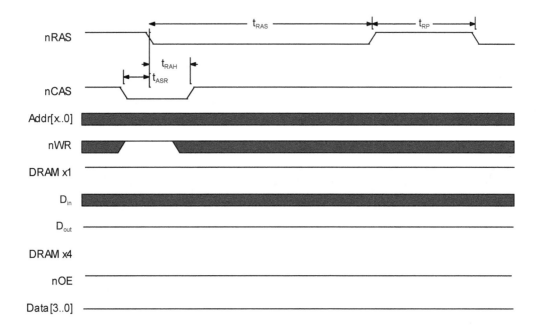

Figure 8.29 CAS before RAS refresh

It was further realized that if the nCAS signal was kept activated and the nRAS signal was then pulsed (i.e. deasserted and then reasserted), a CAS-before-RAS refresh cycle could be performed at the same time as a normal read (or write) transfer/output occurred, earning this latter the title of **hidden refresh**.

8.4.5.3   DRAM Burst Modes

When processors use DRAM as an internal memory cache, the memory is typically used in such a way that data is read or written to consecutive positions on the same row. Each row selection might involve a minimum of 50 to 100 ns, but column access is then much faster at around 10 to 50 ns, depending on the device. Eliminating the row selection step from multiple reads or writes within the same row can dramatically improve DRAM-based cache performance. A variety of such burst-based modes have been developed, some of which are described in the next few sections. In the associated signal timing diagrams, only read cycles are depicted, but write cycles (both early and delayed) and read-modify-write cycles are also available. However, it should be noted that support of these different forms of burst mode was not a programmable capability but was device-specific.

8.4.5.4   Page-mode DRAM and Fast Page-mode DRAM

Page-mode DRAM is a variation of the original DRAM signal interface in which multiple column accesses (reads or writes) can be made to the same row without the overheads of precharging and row selection each time. This is achieved by holding nRAS active and pulsing nCAS, with the target column address saved on each falling edge of nCAS. Although there is, theoretically, no limitation on the number of such nCAS cycles, they must not last longer than 100 µs to allow the next refresh cycle to be executed.

A further minor enhancement gave rise to **fast page-mode DRAM**, in which the target column address could be supplied before nCAS was activated and would propagate through the address data path, reducing latency (specifically in relation to t_{CAC}, the maximum time from nCAS activation to data output). Both modes are illustrated in Figure 8.30.

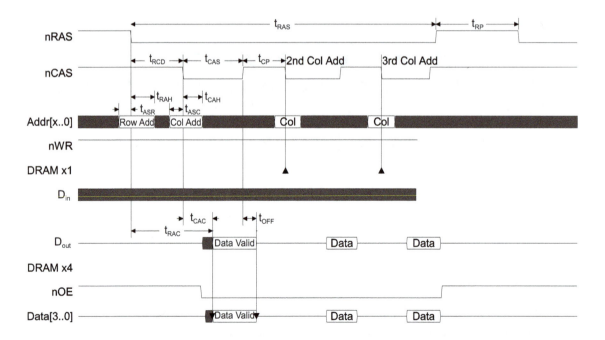

Figure 8.30 DRAM burst read: page-mode/fast page-mode

8.4.5.5   Nibble Mode

Nibble mode is another burst-based variant of page-mode DRAM, again designed to be more efficient for some situations. Nibble mode allows four consecutive locations (columns) on the same row to be read or written as nCAS is pulsed with nRAS held active. Only the first column address needs to be provided as input and the subsequent addresses are generated internally by incrementing the two lowest address bits, as represented in Table 8.3 and depicted in Figure 8.31.

Table 8.3 DRAM nibble mode address incrementation

First column address [1..0]	Next column address [1..0]	Sequence
00	01	0 → 1
01	10	1 → 2
10	11	2 → 3
11	00	3 → 0

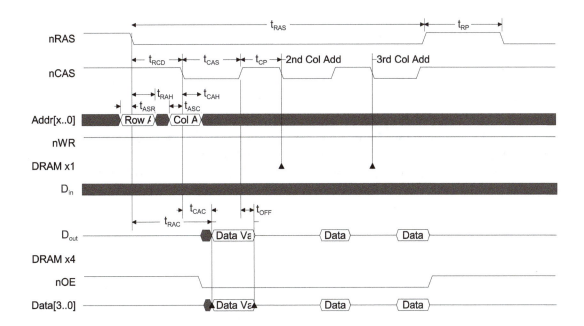

Figure 8.31 DRAM burst read: nibble mode

8.4.5.6   Static Column Mode

Static column mode is yet another burst-based variant of page-mode DRAM in which flow-through latches were used in the column address path, allowing the column address to be changed externally without pulsing the nCAS signal. Thus, the column address change was fed directly to the column address decoder, the outputs were prevented from going into the Hi-Z state on a change of column address, and the corresponding data was output almost immediately thereafter. The underlying mechanism involves a copy of an entire row of dynamic memory being generated in a static memory construct upon nRAS activation, from which data can be output just by changing the column address.

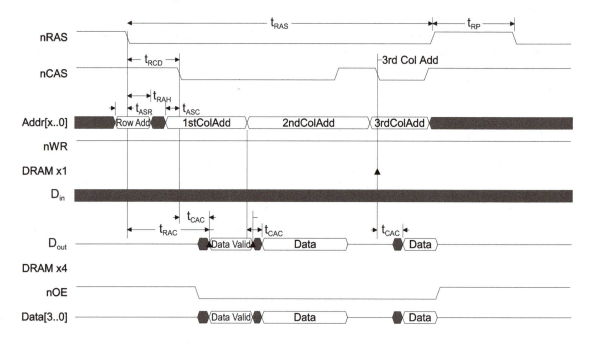

Figure 8.32 DRAM burst read: static column mode

8.4.5.7 EDO DRAM

Extended data-out (EDO) DRAM is, in essence, a further variation on fast page-mode DRAM. In the DRAM burst modes described thus far, the read data bus reverts to a tri-state when the nCAS signal is deactivated, even if the nOE signal is active. By contrast, in EDO DRAM, data output continues even when nCAS is deactivated (i.e. goes high), and if nCAS is reactivated a new column can be selected. The associated signal cycle is illustrated in Figure 8.33. The extended time that data output remains valid gives the processor more flexibility in terms of when to read the data, making memory operations considerably more efficient.

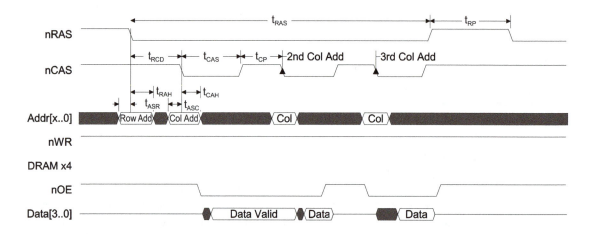

Figure 8.33 DRAM burst read: EDO mode

When EDO DRAM first went on the market, in the mid-1990s, it was very successful, heavily used in L2 caches and often displacing the far more expensive Video RAM (see below) from video cards. Further evolutions of EDO DRAM were arguably superior to the Synchronous DRAM (SDRAM) that was starting to come to the fore at the same time and which marked the end for what became known, retrospectively, as "asynchronous" DRAM.

8.4.6 Video RAM

To drive video output to a screen, some applications need to access large areas of memory at contiguous addresses very quickly. To meet this need, a specialized variant of DRAM was patented by IBM and introduced in the mid-1980s. Video RAM, or VRAM, was very similar to traditional DRAM but with one very significant difference: beside the standard DRAM port it introduced a separate data port (so is sometimes referred to as "dual-ported DRAM"). When a row is accessed and its contents are latched, the entire row is transferred into a separate row buffer (or shift register) from which the data bits can be serially streamed to a video display through the read-only data port.

Thus, VRAM also introduced a serial register for each bit of the data bus, meaning that a 4-bit-wide VRAM data bus (the first to be introduced, by Texas Instruments) had four registers, producing a local instance of sequential-access memory (SAM). The basic VRAM architecture adheres to classical DRAM operation with a multiplexed data bus, nRAS and nCAS selection signals, and an nWE write signal. However, the nOE pin now has a dual function: output enable and data transfer (nDT), from RAM to SAM, as depicted in Figure 8.34.

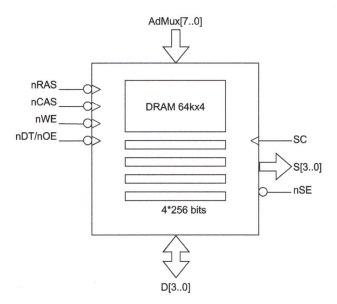

Figure 8.34 VRAM ports and signals

Soon afterwards, the need for memory capable of *capturing* continuous serial information – as, for example, in a camera buffer – gave rise to a second generation of VRAM (see Figure 8.35), in which the serial register took on a multiplexed bidirectional function associated with a counter. The starting address for outputting or capturing serial data is then selectable via a specific transfer cycle.

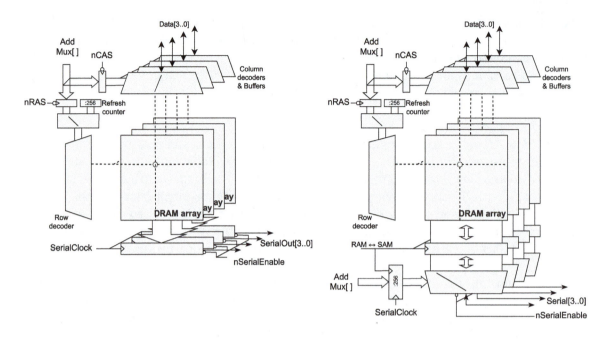

Figure 8.35 VRAM architecture component diagram, first (left) and second (right) generations

The emergence of fast, low-cost SDRAM (see below) means that this form of DRAM-based VRAM has largely become obsolete, although the generic term "video RAM" clearly lives on.

8.4.7 Static RAM vs Dynamic RAM

As already indicated, volatile memory comes in two basic forms, dynamic RAM and static RAM (SRAM). We have described the former in some detail in the preceding sections. We described the basic architecture of SRAM in Chapter 1, and provided further detail of its operation in the context of the static memory controller described in Chapter 7.

SRAM circuits started with data widths of 4 or 8 bits, before 16-bit data widths became commonplace, requiring the addition of two extra control signals (nLB and nUB) to select the lower or upper 8-bit byte, as depicted in Figure 8.36, which provides a comparative view of the lines/signals employed by the three most commonly used forms of volatile memory. Activation of both control signals indicates a 16-bit transfer. Where a 32-bit bus (DQ[31..0]) is in use, then four active-low Byte-Wide selection lines are required: nBW3, nBW2, nBW1 and nBW0. Currently, the largest commercially produced asynchronous SRAM on a single chip is a 16-bit-wide 64-Mibit memory (4Mx16).

Unlike DRAM, SRAM doesn't use address multiplexing, making data access straightforward, and to allow even easier interfacing with microprocessors, synchronous, clock-driven forms of SRAM have been developed and often supplant asynchronous SRAM, providing a range of automatic address-incrementation capabilities. The current maximum memory capacity of synchronous SRAM circuits is 288 Mibit (16Mx18). Eighteen? Yes, 8 bits per byte plus 1 bit per byte for parity or other functionality.

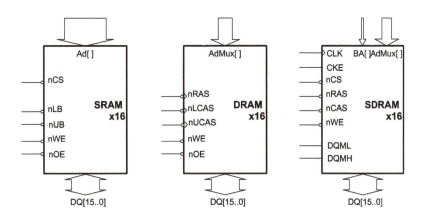

Figure 8.36 SRAM, DRAM and SDRAM signals

SRAM also doesn't need refreshing in the same way as DRAM, thanks to its internal architecture of (usually) six MOSFET transistors per cell. These consume more power than the single transistor of a DRAM cell except when idle, when the absence of any refresh requirement confers very low power overheads.

In terms of the signal comparisons shown in Figure 8.36, the address multiplexing of DRAM demands two control signals, to select the row and column, and the column selection signal must be doubled up (nUCAS and nLCAS) for memories with data bus widths of more than 8 bits to provide upper- and lower-byte selection, as previously described.

A clock-driven, synchronous form of DRAM was also introduced, SDRAM (see below), and is now the dominant form of volatile memory in computers. Its interface signals, shown on the right-hand side of Figure 8.36, include a clock (CLK) and a Clock Enable signal (CKE) to validate clock use. An nCS signal is also included in support of Chip Select.

8.4.8 Synchronous DRAM (SDRAM)

The DRAM management signals described to date are asynchronous and do not depend on a clock signal. Instead, a large number of manufacturer-specified timings must be respected in order to operate these components. As external processor buses became fully synchronous, it was easier in terms of the electrical interface to have synchronous memories too; hence the development of Synchronous DRAM (SDRAM). Then, for interaction with an SDRAM controller, only four (non-clock) timings need be taken into consideration, as represented in Figure 8.37:

▪ The Command Set-up (t_{CMS}) and Hold (t_{CMH}) times in relation to the clock edge (almost always the rising edge).

▪ The Access time (t_{AC}), the time between the rising clock edge and the data being available on the data bus (very important).

▪ The Output Hold time (t_{OH}), the length of time the SDRAM will hold the output data stable on the data bus.

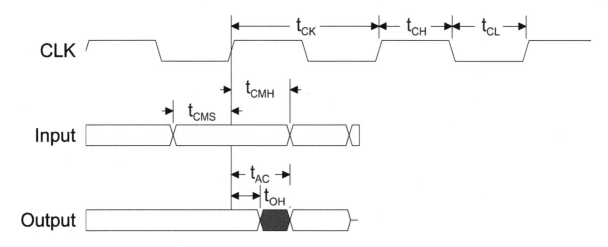

Figure 8.37 Principal timing parameters for an SDRAM controller

The typical clock frequency for SDRAM is approximately 100 MHz (t_{CK} = 1/f = 10 ns). The initial size of SDRAM, in the early 1990s, was around 16 Mibit (2M × 8). However, the most significant feature of SDRAM is that it can incorporate several (two, most commonly four, but sometimes eight) separate "banks" of memory within the same memory chip. Thus a 512-Mibit SDRAM chip might contain four separate 16-MiB banks, each consisting of an 8,192 × 16,384 array. The operation of these banks can be *interleaved*, by means of a 2- or 3-bit bank address (BA) bus, to invoke a significant degree of pipelining or operational concurrency through "hiding" of the associated precharge times. This increased efficiency is what has given SDRAM its latter-day dominance of the volatile memory market.

Aside from the two clock-related signals outlined above (CLK and CKE), the signals used to control SDRAM have considerable overlap with those of asynchronous DRAM:

▨ $A_n..A_0$, or A[n..0], used to specify row and column addresses, which are generally non-symmetrical, as in the example of the array above

▨ A_{11}, or A(11), used to indicate the bank address, later renamed BA, and extended to two bits for four banks, to BA[1..0], and by three bits for eight banks, to BA[2..0]

▨ nRAS, nCAS, and nWE are repurposed as command bits, supporting 8 (2^3) different commands, while nOE acquires a new role as a byte-level data input/output signal

▨ nCS, a new Chip Select signal

▨ DQ[7..0] for an 8-bit-wide data bus, DQ[15..0] for a 16-bit-wide data bus, and DQ[31..0] for a 32-bit-wide data bus

▨ DQMx byte-mask signals; when high, the corresponding byte is disabled. An 8-bit-wide data bus will have one such signal, a 16-bit-wide data bus will have two, and a 32-bit-wide data bus will have four.

We can see that the ideas behind the external connections of SDRAM are fairly universal. For the designer of the controller used to access SDRAM memory, matters are much simpler because it lends itself to a state-machine-driven design that makes use of synchronous logic.

In the decades before SDRAM, this kind of interface was provided via programmable logic, external to the processor. Now, the manufacturers of microprocessors and SoCs must provide a programmable interface that will give access to this type of memory controller, and this will have to be configured. This is not always an easy job, especially when it comes to double data rate (DDR) SDRAM (see below), and it is necessary to understand how the memory works to program the controller correctly. Later in this chapter, we will study a few timing diagrams to better grasp the principles of SDRAM control.

For example, a particular 512-Mibit SDRAM consists of four banks and uses BA[1..0] to select one accordingly. Address lines A[12..0] provide 13 lines for row selection, supporting 8,192 (2^{13}) rows, as well as mode register values, which we will discuss shortly. Ten of these address lines, A[9..0], are used for column selection, supporting 1,024 (2^{10}) columns, each of which contains a 16-bit word.

8.4.8.1 SDRAM Commands

All the transfers to and from SDRAM are synchronous with the rising edge of the CLK signal. Table 8.4 shows the signal levels required for the different commands that can be executed by the SDRAM. Note that timing diagrams for some of these functions can be found below.

Table 8.4 SDRAM commands (from Integrated Silicon Solution, Inc.)

Command	CKE n−1	CKE n	nCS	nRAS	nCAS	nWE	BA1	BA0	A10	A12, A11, A9–A0
Device deselect (DESL)	H	×	H	×	×	×	×	×	×	×
No operation (NOP)	H	×	L	H	H	H	×	×	×	×
Burst stop (BST)	H	×	L	H	H	L	×	×	×	×
Read	H	×	L	H	L	H	V	V	L	V
Read with auto precharge	H	×	L	H	L	H	V	V	H	V
Write	H	×	L	H	L	L	V	V	L	V
Write with auto precharge	H	×	L	H	L	L	V	V	H	V
Bank activate (ACT)	H	×	L	L	H	H	V	V	V	V
Precharge select bank (PRE)	H	×	L	L	H	L	V	V	L	×
Precharge all banks (PALL)	H	×	L	L	H	L	×	×	H	×
CBR auto-refresh (REF)	H	H	L	L	L	H	×	×	×	×
Self-refresh (SELF)	H	L	L	L	L	H	×	×	×	×
Mode register set (MRS)	H	×	L	L	L	L	L	L	L	V

Key: H = V_{IH} (high-level input voltage); L = V_{IL} (low-level input voltage); × = V_{IH} or V_{IL}; V = Valid data.

A state machine to send the commands to SDRAM for the different functions will show that an activate (ACT) command starts a Read or Write sequence, single or burst (BST), and then after every group of Read or Write commands a precharge is mandatory to ensure that all of the columns in the memory array are at the appropriate intermediate voltage, ready for the next cycle (just as in asynchronous DRAM).

8.4.8.2   SDRAM Mode Register and Initialization

The original SDRAM chips incorporated a programmable 10-bit mode register that configures their operation. Subsequent SDRAM versions extended this register to 13 bits (e.g. DDR2) and introduced additional "extended" mode registers. The mode register controls SDRAM features such as burst length, burst type, CAS latency, and write burst mode.

Following power-up, the SDRAM mode register must be configured, but before this can happen the data columns of all the internal banks must be precharged and a number of auto-refresh commands, interspersed with NOP (No operation) commands, must be issued to this end, as represented in Figure 8.38.

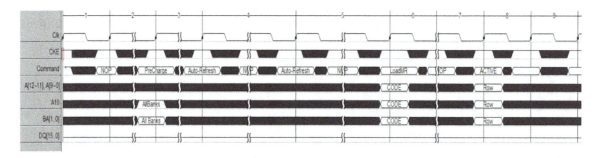

Figure 8.38 SDRAM initialization phase

After precharging, the mode register can be programmed with a Mode Register Set command (**MRS**; shown as LoadMR in Figure 8.38). To transfer the appropriate settings into the 10-bit register, the information is placed on address lines A[9..0] (additional address and bank address lines are used for the larger/extended registers of subsequent SDRAM versions) and a read operation is performed. Many **NOP** commands have to be inserted within this initialization sequence to give the SDRAM sufficient time to implement it, typically at least 100 μs.

In the example shown in Figure 8.38, the SDRAM has four banks, selected by BA[1..0]. Specifying a '1' in address A[10] indicates that all banks have to be precharged; alternatively, specifying a '0' in address A[10] indicates that only the bank selected via BA[1..0] has to be precharged. Because we want to auto-refresh all of the banks, the correct level ('1') has to be provided on A[10].

Figure 8.39 illustrates how the "address" loaded into address lines A[9..0] is used to configure the ten bits, M[9..0], of the mode register in terms of the SDRAM functionality. These functions are then invoked by different combinations of the six signals – nCS, nRAS, nCAS, nWE, BA1 and BA0 – as shown in Table 8.4 above. As previously observed, the design engineers of 30 years ago retained the DRAM signal names and didn't trouble themselves with the introduction of more germane or generic ones.

In the SDRAM example shown in Figure 8.39, we can see that different **burst lengths** (1, 2, 4 or 8) can be configured, and that the **burst type** can be defined as either sequential or interleaved: sequential mode increments addresses contiguously, whereas the interleaved mode is more complex and depends on the way some processors replenish their internal caches.

CAS latency specifies how long, in number of clock cycles, the data bus must wait before providing the data following a read command. It is technology-dependent and must be adapted on the basis of the period of the clock being used. For the example SDRAM device represented in Figure 8.39, CAS latency can be configured to be either 2 or 3 clock cycles.

BA1	BA0	A12	A11	A10	A9	A8	A7	A6	A5	A4	A3	A2	A1	A0
					M9	M8	M7	M6	M5	M4	M3	M2	M1	M0
Reserved Should be '0'					Write Burst	Operating Mode		CAS Latency			Burst Type	Burst Length		

Burst Length (M2, M1, M0):

M2	M1	M0	M3 =0	M3 =1
0	0	0	1	1
0	0	1	2	2
0	1	0	4	4
0	1	1	8	8
1	0	0	-	-
1	0	1	-	-
1	1	0	-	-
1	1	1	Full	-

Write Burst (A9 / M9):

	M9
Programmed Burst Length	0
Single Location	1

Burst Type (M3):

M3	
0	Sequential
1	Interleaved

CAS Latency (M6, M5, M4):

M6	M5	M4	
0	0	0	Reserved
0	0	1	Reserved
0	1	0	2
0	1	1	3
1	0	0	Reserved
1	0	1	Reserved
1	1	0	Reserved
1	1	1	Reserved

Operating Mode (M8, M7):

M8	M7	
0	0	Standard Operation
-	-	Reserved

Figure 8.39 Mode register specification

8.4.8.3   SDRAM Read and Burst-read Transfers

Read transfers start with an activate (ACTIVE) command, followed by several NOPs to respect the minimum t_{RCD} (the necessary delay between sending a row address and sending a column address), after which the read (or write) command can be issued, as illustrated in the timing diagram of Figure 8.40.

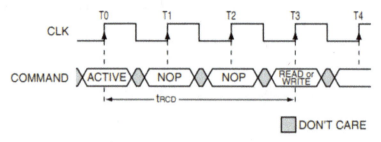

Figure 8.40 Timing diagram for SDRAM read (or write) transfer

If a read is being performed, then a further delay that reflects the CAS latency, in this case either two or three clock cycles, must be sustained using more NOP commands, after which the data should be available on the data port, as depicted in the timing diagram of Figure 8.41.

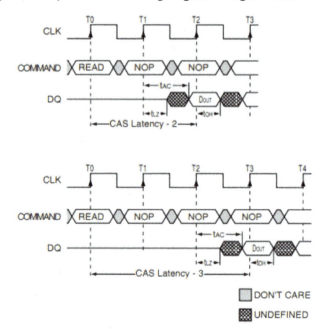

Figure 8.41 Timing diagram showing SDRAM post-read CAS latency of 2 or 3 CLK cycles

For a burst-read transfer, once the first data value has been made available, an address auto-increment gives rise to a new data value with each new clock cycle, with the length of the burst being determined by the value configured during mode register initialization. Figure 8.42 illustrates this sequence, in relation to two separate columns, for the same two CAS latencies as before.

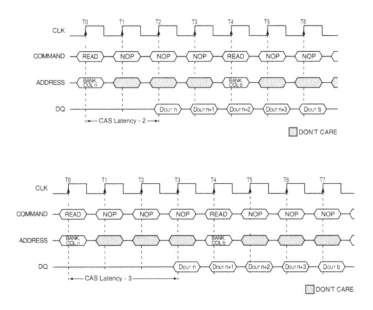

Figure 8.42 Timing diagram for SDRAM burst-read transfers showing CAS latency effect (burst length = 4)

Figure 8.43 shows the timing involved in two consecutive burst transfers, the first a burst-read of length 4, the second a burst-write, also of length 4. CAS latency is 2 CLK in each case. In this example, in the burst-read access, the output of $D_{out}(n+2)$ is disabled by the deactivation (driving high) of the DQMx byte-mask *two clock cycles before* the data would normally be output; similarly, the writing of $D_{in}(m+1)$ is also disabled with the DQMx byte-mask (at '1'), but in this instance it is done *at the same time* as the data would normally be provided. We can see an asymmetry between the read and write cycles.

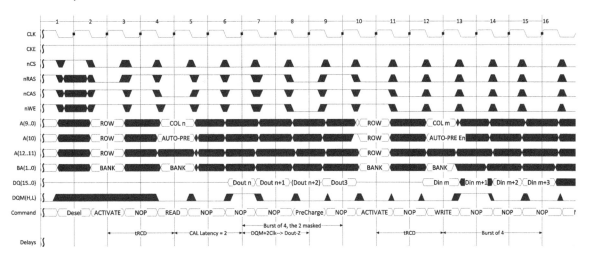

Figure 8.43 Timing diagram for SDRAM burst-read and burst-write transfers with byte-masks applied (burst length = 4)

For other transfer types, careful study of the datasheet of the specific SDRAM chip is essential.

8.4.9 Rambus DRAM (RDRAM) and Enhanced Synchronous DRAM (ESDRAM)

Rambus DRAM (RDRAM) was a form of synchronous DRAM developed in the late-1990s by Rambus, a company that was not a circuit manufacturer but specialized in interface technologies. It proposed a new memory architecture based on the principle of data transfer over a single bus in which address, control, and up to 256 bytes of data information were combined together in packets. Both transitions (rising and falling edges) of the processor clock are used, such that a 250 MHz clock could transfer 500 MB/s over a "narrow channel" 8-bit bus. Particular care has to be taken over the electrical interface and the printed circuit to achieve these characteristics.

To transfer data, the master (processor) transfers a request packet of 6 bytes, containing the address (36 bits), the number of bytes to transmit (in 8 bits), and control information. The memory responds with an acknowledgment when the requested data is ready for transmission (a read) or can be received (a write), after which the transfer can be carried out.

In 1997, Intel announced that it would license only RDRAM for its future motherboards, making RDRAM well-placed to dominate the memory marketplace, but it subsequently lost out to DDR SDRAM (see below) in a cost- and litigation-driven standards war, and the RDRAM design and its successors have since seen little take-up by memory manufacturers/fabricators.

At a similar time, the mid-1990s, Enhanced Synchronous DRAM (ESDRAM) was a development of the asynchronous EDRAM developed by a subsidiary of a different company, Ramtron, better known for its work on FeRAM/FRAM (see below). Using a similar principle to that seen in the static column mode of DRAM (described above), EDRAM and ESDRAM involved the dramatic acceleration of DRAM performance by means of incorporating a small SRAM cache (e.g. 256 bytes) on the DRAM chip, a technique also referred to as Cached DRAM (CDRAM). The SRAM cache is searched first and only then does a wide, fast bus pass the request on to the DRAM element. Such devices were used on high-performance computers rather than low-cost PCs, let alone SoCs!

8.4.10 Double Data Rate (DDR) SDRAM and DDR2, DDR3, DDR4 and DDR5

In a DRAM chip, in the course of a read access, there is a well-established delay between the selection of a row and the data being made available for output on the bus. The situation in an SDRAM chip is little different, in terms of the delay between the activate command and data availability. However, once the data from a row has been made available, access to data on the same row (i.e. in a different column) can be very fast: in SDRAM, following the CAS latency time, it can occur (for a burst-read) on the rising edge of every subsequent clock cycle, as we have seen.

However, access times could still be improved. One approach would be to increase the clock frequency, but a better solution is to use both clock edges for burst data transfers (also known as "double pumping"), effectively doubling the data transfer rate for bursts (although single word access is not significantly improved). This is the basis of double data rate (DDR) SDRAM.

The first commercial DDR chip was launched in 1998 by Samsung. Subsequent DDR generations have revised the protocol, in terms of both signaling and closer regulation of voltages and timings, to allow the external data bus to be operated at increasing multiples of the internal clock frequency.

Similarly, a prefetch buffer of increasing burst depth has enabled interleaved access and even better performance, with the result that the DDR SDRAM family is the most prevalent form of volatile/dynamic RAM in use today. A comparison of the DDR versions is shown in Table 8.5, with the original SDRAM retrospectively referred to as "single data rate" (SDR). The first DDR5 DRAM chip was launched in October 2020.

Table 8.5 DDR generation comparison

SDRAM generation	Voltage $V_{DD}/V_{DD}Q$ (V)	Chip standard name (~Mb/s)	Module	Chip CLK (MHz)	f_{mult}	Prefetch buffer depth	Data bus CLK (MHz)
SDR	3.3			100 → 166	1	1n	100 → 166
DDR	2.5 / 2.6	DDR-200 → DDR-400	PC-1600 → PC-3200	100 → 200	1	2n	100 → 200
DDR2	1.8	DDR2-400 → DDR2-1066	3200 → 8533	100 → 266	2	4n	200 → 533
DDR3	1.5 / 1.35	DDR3-800 → DDR3-2133	6400 → 17066	100 → 266	4	8n	400 → 1066
DDR4	1.2 / 1.05	DDR4-1600 → DDR4-3200	12800 → 25600	200 → 400	4	8n	800 → 1600
DDR5	1.1	DDR5-3200 → DDR5-8400				8/16n	

The ability to take advantage as often as possible of the high-speed burst transfers offered by external DDR-based memory is one of the main reasons that SoCs incorporate local cache memories.

Given the high clock and bus frequencies involved, DDR SDRAM is quite complex to interface and calibration is required for precise timing adjustment. The main protocols in terms of commands for row activation and read and write transfers are similar but not identical across the DDR generations, and care is needed in their interfacing, particularly if you want to implement your own controller but even if you only want to configure one from a manufacturer or third party. For example, voltages alter with each generation, DDR3 introduced a new nRESET pin, while DDR5 involves up to 256 configuration registers! Close study of the specific documentation, as well as the JEDEC standards, is essential.

Figures 8.44 through 8.47 (see also Table 8.5) illustrate the different depths of prefetch buffer (respectively, n, 2n, 4n and 8n) and the external clock speed multiples for SDR SDRAM (where SDR stands for single data rate; only the rising edge of the CLK is used for data transfers), and the DDR, DDR2 and DDR3 variants (from [9]). For an easier timing comparison, the internal bus frequency remains constant (at 133 MHz) but the available data transfer rate per clock cycle doubles with each new generation.

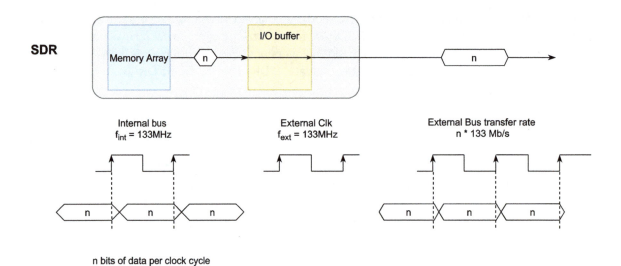

Figure 8.44 Standard, single data rate (SDR) SDRAM: same external clock speed as internal bus, data on rising edge only (source: inspired by Elpida, User's Manual E0437E40)

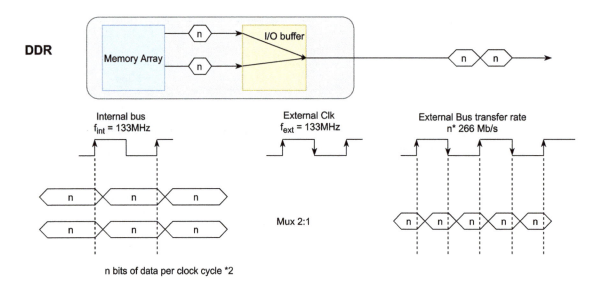

Figure 8.45 DDR SDRAM: same external clock speed as internal bus, data on rising and falling edges (source: inspired by Elpida, User's Manual E0437E40)

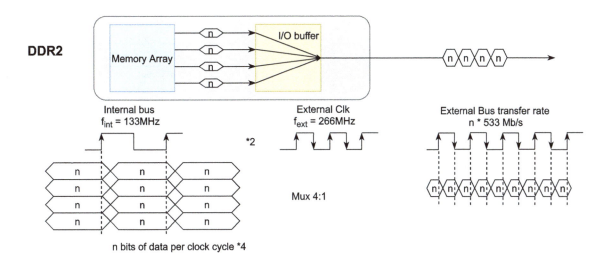

Figure 8.46 DDR2 SDRAM: external clock speed twice that of internal bus, data on rising and falling edges (source: inspired by Elpida, User's Manual E0437E40)

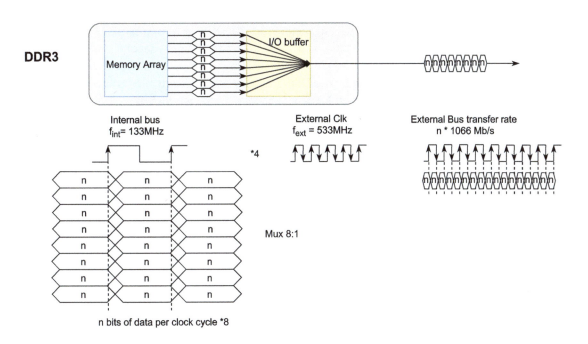

Figure 8.47 DDR3 SDRAM: external clock speed four times that of internal bus, data on rising and falling edges (source: inspired by Elpida, User's Manual E0437E40)

DDR memory is available in the form of an integrated circuit, typically in a ball grid array (BGA) package that can better support circuits with many pins, or as a "rank" (not bank) of standardized DIMMs on a PCB, which makes memory upgrades easier. In the case of the latter, the DDR generations are electrically and physically incompatible, having a specific mechanical indicator (or "notch") to prevent the wrong generation of DDR DIMM being placed in a given DIMM socket, as illustrated in Figure 8.48.

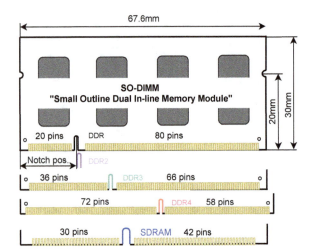

SO-DIMM					
Mem Type	Nb Pins	Pitch [mm]	Notch pos. [mm]	Size [mm]	H [mm]
DDR	200	0.6	15.35	67.6	~30
DDR2	200	0.6	16.25	67.6	~30
DDR3	204	0.6	24.8	67.6	~30
DDR4	260	0.5	38.3	69.6	~30
SDRAM	144	0.8	29	67.6	~25.4

Figure 8.48 DIMM configurations for different DDR generations (note varying notch locations)

8.4.10.1 DDR Data Synchronization

As noted above (see Figure 8.47), the external clock speed of DDR3 can easily be 533 MHz or higher, and that of DDR4 in excess of 1 GHz, giving a clock cycle of less than 1 nanosecond, and a high signal for less than half of this. This gives the receiver of a signal a tiny window in which to detect its value. If the length of the physical circuit between the DDR memory and the controller is also factored in (a signal might travel 15 cm in a nanosecond) , there is an increasing risk with each subsequent DDR generation that the receiver will no longer sample the external data signal at the correct point of the signal cycle, particularly in the case of reads, where the synchronizing clock signal must travel several centimeters from the controller to the memory and the data must then be returned and sampled against the same signal. The implicit delay gives rise to "clock skew" and this becomes a limiting factor in implementing higher data rates.

For this reason, DDR2 introduced a new data synchronization signal in the form of a differential strobe pair termed **DQS** and **nDQS** (or DQS and /DQS). This serves as a reference clock for the I/O data: it is a bidirectional signal and is transmitted with the data by whichever unit (i.e. memory or memory controller) is sending. Thus it is completely synchronous with the data, experiencing an identical propagation time and providing a reliable basis on which to sample the data and so eliminate clock skew.

8.4.10.2 DDR On-die Termination (ODT)

As we have discussed elsewhere, signal reflection in a wire causes noise and disrupts signal quality. In the high-speed buses involved in DDR communication, particularly when several DDR modules are connected into a common "rank", signal reflection is a significant issue. Starting with DDR2 memories, a function has been added to allow dynamic enabling of internal termination on each of the data bus (DQ) pins and the associated DQS, nDQS and RDQS, nRDQS strobe pins within the DRAM. This on-die termination (ODT) allows activation of a resistor between V_{TT} (the tracking termination voltage) and the DQ and data strobe lines to eliminate, or at least attenuate, reflection of electrical signals. The value of the resistor is configured in the DRAM chip via the DRAM controller using a mode register, as 50 Ω, 75 Ω or 150 Ω.

Before ODT, such termination resistors had to be mounted on the motherboard, adding to its complexity and without the capability of enabling/disabling them.

8.5 Nonvolatile Memory

8.5.1 EEPROM
EEPROM (electrically-erasable programmable read-only memory) has been around since the 1970s, and was the first commercial form of nonvolatile memory that could also be erased and rewritten electronically. It offers similar access times to that of SRAM memory, but relatively small memory capacities. Nevertheless, this made EEPROM very useful for microcontrollers where access was predominantly read-based, in terms of kernel or OS code for example, and only a small number of parameters needed to be written or configured.

EEPROM has, to a very large extent, been superseded by flash memory (see below), which offers much higher speeds and memory densities than EEPROM (typically tenfold), although the better endurance of EEPROM in terms of erase/write cycles (also typically tenfold), and EEPROM's support of byte-level erasure, mean that EEPROM still finds niche application in the microcontroller world.

8.5.2 Flash Memory
Flash memory has, as noted above, become the most commonly used form of nonvolatile memory, and is gradually displacing many of the other forms such as hard disk drives, as well as EEPROMs. Although some other alternative nonvolatile memory technologies exist – as we shall see, briefly, below – none has yet matched the capacity and cost-effectiveness of flash.

Flash memory is a form of EEPROM that was invented and developed in the 1980s at Toshiba. It is distinguished from EEPROM by the fact that erasure is carried out at block rather than byte or bit level. This is achieved via in-circuit wiring that allows an electrical field to be applied to the entire memory chip or predetermined sections of it (blocks), making the pre-write erasure process much quicker and large write operations much faster. The high-voltage energy discharge required for block-based erasure is said to have inspired the designation of "flash" (as in camera flash), and involves resetting every bit in the block to a binary 1 (the only mechanism by which to do so: programming/writing can only generate binary 0s). This block-based erasure also allowed the chips to be simpler and thus cheaper, with further economies of scale deriving from flash's subsequent popularity.

As previously indicated, there are currently two main forms of flash memory, which differ in terms of their cell architecture: NOR- and NAND-based flash are so named because the connections resemble a NOR logic gate in one and a NAND logic gate in the other. The arrangements have a bearing both on the way in which the two types are erased, written and read, and on their relative densities and storage capacities.

Thus, once erased at the block level, NOR-based flash supports writes one byte at a time whereas NAND-based flash writes a page (or a part-page in newer chips) at a time, affording it write speeds that are typically six times faster than NOR flash. By contrast, the byte-level addressing of NOR-based flash allows it much faster read access (typically, threefold) than NAND flash, except where large sequential reads are required, which hand the advantage back to NAND. Further, the much larger size of a NOR memory cell limits its capacity relative to NAND flash, enforcing lower densities and making NOR flash more expensive. On the other hand, the high densities of NAND flash, as well as its cell architecture, contribute to a much higher incidence of bit failure; NAND devices build in quite high levels of CRC-managed redundancy and the associated drivers and controllers (such as USB and SSD) must incorporate protocols, such as error correction and wear-leveling, to handle this.

It should be stressed that these are general principles; a variety of protocols and controllers have been used to improve the flexibility afforded by the basic architectures of the two forms. Nevertheless, overall, they lend themselves to different types of application. Thus, NOR flash is best-suited to situations in which a limited amount of data will be written but most access will be read-based: the operating systems of embedded and mobile devices, including smartphones, being good examples. NAND flash is well-suited to situations in which large files will be frequently written and replaced: digital cameras, MP3 players and USB memory sticks, among others.

Different types of flash memories exist as memory extensions for microcontroller systems. Parallel NOR flash incorporates an SRAM interface with enough address lines to address the entire chip and thus enable byte-level addressing, which means that processors can retrieve code directly from NOR flash and execute it in place (XIP) without first having to copy it to RAM. In terms of the number of pins, the largest chips are those providing access in parallel to both addresses and data, as illustrated in Figures 8.49 and 8.50.

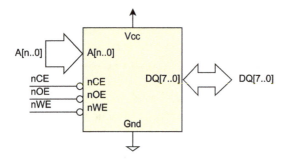

A[n..0]	Addresses	In	
DQ[7..0]	Data Rd/Wr	InOut	
nCE	Chip Enable	In	active low
nOE	Output Enable	In	active low
nWE	Write Enable	In	active low
Vcc	+ Power Supply	Power	+5V
Gnd	Ground		0V

Ex: SST39SF010A / SST39SF020A / SST39SF040

Figure 8.49 NOR-based 8-bit flash memory with parallel address and data access (from Microchip Technology, Inc.)

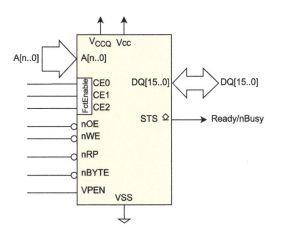

A[n..0]	Addresses	In	A0 used only in x8 mode
DQ[15..0]	Data Rd/Wr	InOut	
CE[2..0]	Chip Enable	In	Special Function
nOE	Output Enable	In	active low
nWE	Write Enable	In	active low
nWP	Write Protect	In	active low
nRP	Reset	In	active low
STS	Status: - Ready - nBusy	Out Open Drain	active high / active low
nBYTE	BYTE mode	In	x8 or x16 mode
VPEN	Program/Erase Enable	In	active high
Vcc	+ Power Supply	Power	+2.7 - +3.6V
VCCQ	I/O Power Supply	Power	+2.7 - +3.6V
Gnd	Ground		0V

Ex: Numonyx Embedded Flash Memory (J3 65 nm)

Figure 8.50 NOR-based 16-bit flash memory with parallel address and data access (from Micron Technology, Inc.)

In some other flash memories, such as that shown in Figure 8.51, the interface dispenses with a separate address bus (to reduce the number of pins) and instead uses the data bus to transfer in the starting address of the data to access in an initial phase controlled by the Address Latch Enable (ALE) command signal. In a second phase, the same data lines are used for the data transfer itself.

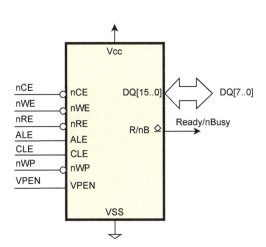

nCE	Chip Enable	In	Special Function
nRE	Read Enable	In	active low
nWE	Write Enable	In	active low
nWP	Write Protect	In	active low
ALE	Address Latch Enable	In	active high
CLE	Command Latch Enable	In	active high
DQ[7..0]	Data Rd/Wr	InOut	active high/ tri-state
R/nB	Ready/nBusy	In	active high/active low
VPE	Volatile Protection Enable	In	active high
Vcc	+ Power Supply	Power	+2.7 - +3.6V
Vss	Ground	Power	0V

Ex: SkyHigh Memory S34ML04G3

NAND Flash Interface

Figure 8.51 Flash memory with parallel data and serial control/address protocol

Serial NOR flash, typically accessed via SPI or I²C interfaces, involves fewer pins and is therefore cheaper to manufacture. If the serial NOR chip incorporates a buffer, then a page can be read into it, modified and written back to the NOR memory; otherwise, the entire page has to be exported from the chip, modified and then written back to the chip. For microcontroller-based systems in which the external memory does not need to be very fast for data transfers, but where the size of the external components is critical, an SPI-based solution is a good option, with the number of pins reduced to just eight (see Figure 8.52) and most microcontrollers incorporating SPI support, making interfacing straightforward. In terms of operation, pins SI and SO (equivalent to MOSI and MISO) provide the 1-bit serial data path, SCK is the serial clock, and nCS (CS# in the figure) enables communication when driven low.

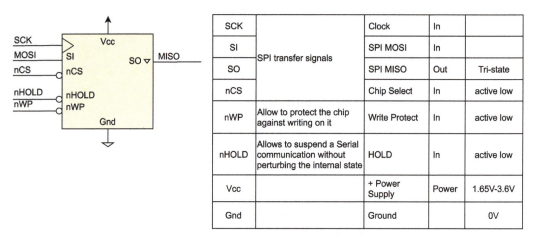

			Clock	In	
SCK			Clock	In	
SI	SPI transfer signals		SPI MOSI	In	
SO			SPI MISO	Out	Tri-state
nCS			Chip Select	In	active low
nWP	Allow to protect the chip against writing on it		Write Protect	In	active low
nHOLD	Allows to suspend a Serial communication without perturbing the internal state		HOLD	In	active low
Vcc			+ Power Supply	Power	1.65V-3.6V
Gnd			Ground		0V

Ex: AT25DF041B

Figure 8.52 Flash memory with SPI interface

Access to NAND flash is almost invariably serial, external address and data buses having been removed to keep size and cost down, and typically also involves an I²C or SPI interface of 8 pins on which will be transmitted sequential control, address and data information.

Figure 8.53 illustrates the signal timings for a single read access in flash memory: valid data is available once the addresses are stable, CE# and OE# are both activated (i.e. driven low), and WE# is deactivated. As soon as one of these CE or OE signals is deactivated, the read cycle completes, as indicated by the red ellipse in the figure, and the data line returns to high impedance.

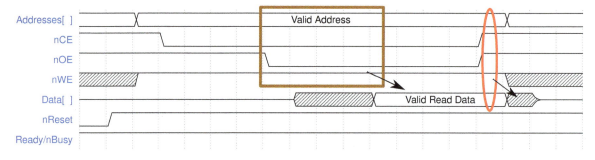

Figure 8.53 Timing diagram for single read access in flash memory

Figure 8.54 illustrates a burst-read in which the control signals are held in an active state and the address is changed sequentially, the constraint being that the addresses must be within the same page.

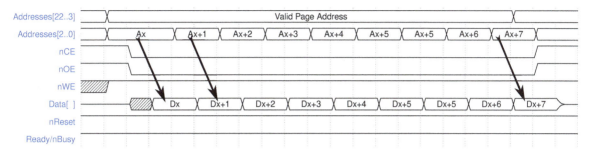

Figure 8.54 Timing diagram for burst-read access in flash memory

Erasing and then writing data in flash memory is slower and more complex, and a specific sequence is required to write a byte/word. A follow-up status or verification read operation is typically implemented to check that the write operation has been successful, as shown in the blue rectangle in Figure 8.55.

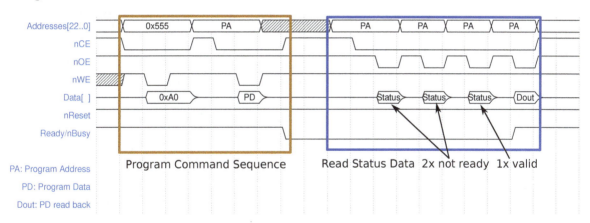

Figure 8.55 Timing diagram for program (write) operation in flash memory, with follow-up status read

Figure 8.56 presents a 3D view of a typical flash memory matrix. It contains a scratchpad RAM area, shown at the top of the figure, that acts as a data cache or page buffer. A read access transfers a block of data into this area from the flash memory, from which it is then transferred out to the external world. To modify data in the flash memory, a copy of the relevant flash memory block is transferred into the buffer where it can be updated; the relevant block in the flash memory is then erased and the updated content in the buffer can then be written back into the flash memory.

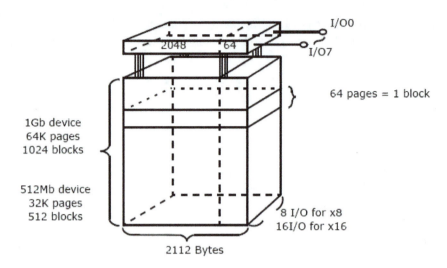

Figure 8.56 Flash memory with serial access (control/addresses) and parallel (8-bit) data bus (from Kioxia)

With this type of memory, data transfer to and from the external world is done by burst transfers. Figure 8.57 shows the operational sequence for a read operation. In the first part of the read phase (all of which is shown in the figure by the red rectangle), the Command Latch Enable (CLE) signal is used to indicate that the information on the data bus is a command, in this instance to specify that a starting address is to be sent: nCE (CE#) and nWE (WE#) must be activated at the same time. The next part involves specification of the starting address on the data bus sequentially, using four write accesses with Address Latch Enable (ALE) activated. A flash-specific command (0x30/30h in the figure) indicates what to do next, which is to initiate a transfer from the memory array to the page buffer. In the next phase (shown in the figure by the blue rectangle) the read is performed by transfers with nCE (CE#) and nRE (RE#) both activated (driven low).

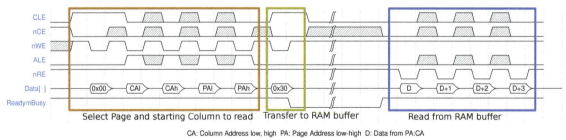

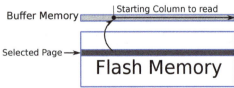

Figure 8.57 Read operation sequence in serial flash memory

Figure 8.58 shows the same initial sequence as Figure 8.57, but also includes an intermediate change in the column to be read within the page already loaded into the buffer. Thus, the second red rectangle highlights a command (0x05/05h in the figure) to specify the starting point of the new column from which to read, with the data following in the next blue sequence.

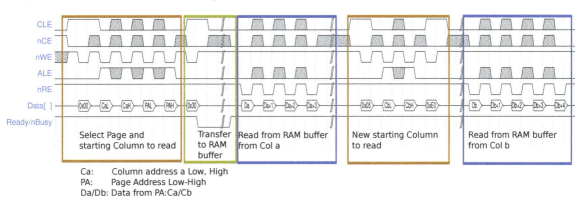

Ca: Column address a Low, High
PA: Page Address Low-High
Da/Db: Data from PA:Ca/Cb

Figure 8.58 Random column read operation sequence in serial flash memory

8.5.3 Ferroelectric RAM (FRAM)

Ferroelectric RAM (F-RAM or FeRAM or FRAM) does not, as its name might imply, contain any ferrous material. A ferroelectric material is one in which electrical polarization can be reversed by the application of an external electrical field. The resulting behavior resembles that previously seen in ferromagnetic materials in magnetic fields; hence the historical and rather misleading name.

In construction and operation, FRAM looks quite similar to DRAM. FRAM memory cells involve a capacitor and a transistor, but the dielectric used in a FRAM capacitor incorporates a ferroelectric material (typically lead zirconate titanate [PZT]), such that application of an electrical field can create one of two polarizations in the cell, generating logical ones and zeros (see Figure 8.59). Unlike the DRAM charge that leaks away, the FRAM electrical polarization is nonvolatile and does not need to be refreshed, although reading the state of an FRAM cell is, as in DRAM, destructive and requires the cell to be rewritten thereafter.

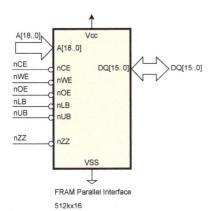

nCE	Chip Enable	In	Special Function
nWE	Write Enable	In	active low
nOE	Output Enable	In	active low
nLB	Lower Byte Control	In	active low
nUB	Upper Byte Control	In	active low
DQ[15..0]	Data Rd/Wr	InOut	active high/ tri-state
nZZ	Sleep Mode	In	active low
Vcc	+ Power Supply	Power	+1.8V - +3.6V
Vss	Ground	Power	0V

Ex: FujitsuMB85R8M2T

FRAM Parallel Interface
512kx16

Figure 8.59 FRAM architecture

FRAM offers much faster write times than flash memory, much lower power consumption and will endure many more write cycles (~10^{14} vs 10^6 for flash memory), but is not yet able to compete in terms of memory density or cost. FRAM is typically interfaced in a similar way to SRAM, with SPI- and I²C-based chips (as well as Quad SPI) available from several manufacturers (as illustrated by Tables 8.6 and 8.7 and Figure 8.60).

Table 8.6 FRAM device manufacturers

Manufacturer	Size range (bits)	Parallel	SPI	SPI/QSPI	I²C
Cypress Semiconductor → Infineon	4 kib → 8 Mib	x	x	x	x
Fujitsu	4 kib → 8 Mib	x	x	x	x
Ramtron → Cypress Semiconductor	4 kib → 4 Mib	x	x		
Rochester Electronics	4 kib → 2 Mib	x	x		
ROHM (LAPIS Semiconductor)	32 kib → 256 kib		x		

Table 8.7 FRAM memory availabilities

Size (bits)	Size (x8)	Size (x16)	Parallel	SPI	I²C
4 kib	0.5 kiB			x	x
16 kib	2 kiB			x	x
32 kib	4 kiB			x	
64 kib	8 kiB		x	x	x
128 kib	16 kiB			x	x
256 kib	32 kiB		x	x	x
512 kib	64 kiB			x	x
1 Mib	128 kiB	64 kiW	x	x	x
2 Mib	256 kiB	128 kiW	x	x	
3 Mib		256 kiW (x12)	x		
4 Mib	512 kiB	256 kiW	x	x	
8 Mib	1 MiB	512 kiW	x	x	

FRAM category (ex. Fujitsu)								
Size bits	i^2c 1.8V	i^2c 3.3V	i^2c 5V	SPI 1.8V	SPI 1.8V-3.3V	SPI 5V	Parallel 1.8V	Parallel 3.3V
4ki								
16ki								
64ki								
128ki								
256ki								
512ki								
1Mi								
2Mi								
4Mi								
8Mi								

Figure 8.60 Fujitsu FRAM range

The materials used in FRAM manufacture are not instantly compatible with those used in standard CMOS-based chips (flash memory even less so) but Texas Instruments has embedded FRAM into one family of its microcontrollers to provide on-chip nonvolatile memory, and Freescale (now NXP) has done similar.

8.5.4 Resistive RAM (ReRAM)

Resistive RAM (or ReRAM) is a form of nonvolatile memory in which a pulse voltage is applied to a solid dielectric material, typically in the form of a thin film of metal oxide, to create resistance changes that can represent ones and zeros, giving rise to what is sometimes termed a "memristor". The cell structure is relatively simple, making for a simple manufacturing process. Combined with fast writes and very low power consumption, ReRAM was initially seen as the eventual replacement for flash memory. Although new dielectric materials have resurrected research interest in ReRAM, its benefits have not yet been sufficient for the chip industry to invest in it wholesale. At least one product is commercially available, from Fujitsu (see Table 8.8), which promotes its use in low-power applications such as hearing aids and IoT devices such as sensors and meters, and claims that its ReRAM memory cells can be rewritten up to 1 million times.

Table 8.8 ReRAM memory availability

Size (Mibit)	Size (x8)	Size (x16)	Parallel	SPI	I²C
8	1 MiB			x	

8.5.5 Magnetoresistive RAM (MRAM)

Magnetoresistive RAM (or MRAM) is another form of nonvolatile memory that has been touted as a successor to flash memory. With echoes of the magnetic-core memory that was dominant in the 1950s and 1960s (and the read-heads of modern disk drives), it is based on measuring the electrical resistance of a memory cell to determine the magnetic orientation of two ferromagnetic plates separated by a thin layer of insulation (a "magnetic tunnel junction"), which is then interpreted as a one or a zero accordingly. Initially, the magnetic orientation of the writable plate was created with an electrical current, but a more energy-efficient approach makes use of polarized electrons to induce magnetic torque in the plate through a process referred to as "spin-transfer torque" (STT). The advent of STT led in 2006 to the first commercially available MRAM chip, and a number of manufacturers now produce such chips, including Everspin, Renesas and Samsung (see Table 8.9).

Table 8.9 MRAM memory availabilities

Size (Mibit)	Size (x4)	Size (x8)	Size (x16)	Parallel	SPI	SPI/QSPI	ST-DDR3/4
0.25		32 kiB		x	x		
1		128 kiB	64 kiW		x		
4	1 Mi nibble	512 kiB	256 kiW		x		
8		1 MiB				x	
16	4 Mi nibble	2 MiB	1 MiW			x	
256		32 MiW	16 MiW				x
1024		128 MiW	64 MiW				x

Ongoing challenges for MRAM include relatively large cell sizes (with lower densities than DRAM) and the size of the write currents needed to ensure high-speed access and almost "infinite" retention times (and endurance of 10^{16} write cycles), which otherwise give MRAM a huge advantage over flash memory.

8.6   Processor–Memory Interaction

The code executed by a processor and the data that it processes have to be fetched from memory.

Some microcontrollers contain highly local tightly-coupled memory (or "scratchpad RAM") embedded on the chip, typically in the form of SRAM. This memory is mapped to the address space of the processor and, unlike a cache, is software-controlled and can be directly addressed, offering a zero wait state for memory access and proving very useful for storing small routines such as interrupt functions or very frequently used data. As well as offering faster access than cache, it can offer savings on power consumption, die area and overall runtime. The downside is the additional effort needed to program this compiler-managed memory.

As we have seen, a system can have caches of memory at several different levels, particularly if an application is memory-hungry. For a lot of Cortex-M-based systems, this is not the situation, and they can operate successfully with the limited memory available on the chip, without caches. However, in higher performance systems that do use caches, when a cache does not contain the required data, it must be requested from the next level of cache or, ultimately, from main memory. In general, as we have seen, the caching system will perform multiple transfers using a burst of contiguous addresses to populate a cache line in anticipation of the next request.

We have already highlighted the issue of incoherence within caches that can arise when multiple masters (such as DMA controllers) have to share the same addresses. Some simple guidelines should be followed accordingly:

- Use the MPU/MMU to mark the regions of common access as shareable and prevent their use in D-cache(s).

- Routinely clear or invalidate the cache whenever software passes control to another processor or DMA controller. There are functions available within the CMSIS library that can do this.

- Use a write-through cache writing policy for write-only memory buffers where the CPU is the producer of the data.

References

[1]   *AWS Snowmobile*. [Online]. Available: aws.amazon.com/snowmobile/

[2]   B. Wescott, *The Every Computer Performance Book*, 2013, Chapter 3: Useful laws.

[3]   Arm, *ARM Cortex-M Programming Guide to Memory Barrier Instructions: Application Note 321*, 2012, p. 18.

[4]   Xilinx, *System Cache v4.0. LogiCORE IP Product Guide (PG118)*, 2017. [Online]. Available: www.
        xilinx.com/support/documentation/ip_documentation/system_cache/v4_0/pg118-system-cache.
        pdf.

[5]   ST, *STM32F7 Series.* [Online]. Available: www.st.com/en/microcontrollers-microprocessors/
        stm32f7-series.html.

[6]   NXP, *KV5x: Kinetis® KV5x-240 MHz, Motor Control and Power Conversion, Ethernet, MCUs based on
        Arm® Cortex®-M7.* [Online]. Available: www.nxp.com/products/processors-and-microcontrollers/
        arm-microcontrollers/general-purpose-mcus/kv-series-cortex-m4-m0-plus-m7/kinetis-
        kv5x-240-mhz-motor-control-and-power-conversion-ethernet-mcus-based-on-arm-cortex-
        m7:KV5x.

[7]   Atmel, *SAM4CM Series. Smart ARM-based Flash MCU. Datasheet.* [Online]. Available: ww1.
        microchip.com/downloads/en/DeviceDoc/Atmel-11203-32-bit-Cortex-M4-Microcontroller-
        SAM4CM32-SAM4CM16-SAM4CM8-SAM4CM4.pdf.

[8]   Silabs, *EFM32GG Reference Manual.* [Online]. Available: www.silabs.com/documents/public/
        reference-manuals/EFM32GG-RM.pdf.

[9]   Elpida, *User's Manual*: How To Use DDR2 SDRAM (Document No. E0437E40 [Ver. 4.0]), 2007.

Chapter 9

FPGA SoC Architecture

We finished Chapter 7 with a case study that considered how peripherals can be connected to a SoC microcontroller in practical terms, using an FPGA chip and a soft-core implementation of a Cortex-M microprocessor, and we have frequently referred to FPGAs throughout this book, particularly with reference to their function as a basis for SoC prototyping. In this chapter we will look at FPGAs, or field-programmable gate arrays, in more detail, providing a basic knowledge of the implementation of an Arm Cortex-M as a soft-core processor in an FPGA, and an appreciation of the advantages and disadvantages of an FPGA-based SoC compared to the classical approach of an ASIC (application-specific integrated circuit) implementation. Thus, we will consider the use of FPGAs beyond the realm of prototyping, and will also briefly review the more recent SoC-FPGA hybrids that look set to play an increasingly significant role in the future of the SoC. In the course of the chapter, we will address the following questions, among others:

1. What is the difference between ASICs and FPGAs in relation to SoCs?

2. What are the benefits of using an FPGA?

3. How can I implement a Cortex-M processor on an FPGA?

9.1 FPGA Basics

9.1.1 What is an FPGA?
An FPGA is a silicon chip containing an array of programmable digital logic blocks, typically in the form of logic gates. This can be described as a "sea-of-gates" architecture, in which the logical functions of the gates on the chip are not assigned during the manufacturing process but can be configured afterwards by the designer, according to their needs. This represents a remarkably flexible and powerful architecture: almost any digital circuit implementable using the standard digital chip design flow can also be implemented on an FPGA, with the advantage that it is configurable rather than fixed at manufacturing time. Of course, this is not a "free lunch", and there are both advantages and disadvantages associated with the adoption of an FPGA-based solution rather than the traditional ASIC-based approach, as we shall see. However, after a brief history lesson, we will start by describing how an FPGA is built and how it works.

Xilinx, the company credited with the invention of FPGA technology, currently leads the FPGA market. Three former Zilog employees, Ross Freeman, Jim Barnett, and Bernie Vonderschmitt, founded Xilinx as a startup in 1984 after Freeman came up with the idea of building a reprogrammable architecture but could not persuade Zilog to invest in it. The notion was to create the equivalent of a single chip of transistor-rich silicon that could be configured to meet the needs of almost every customer, during a period in which the semiconductor business was growing exponentially on the back of ASIC technology. After the first successful experiment using reprogrammable logic, Bill Carter, one of the first engineers hired to work on the development, called Freeman and Vonderschmitt to report that Xilinx "had successfully created the world's most expensive inverter"! Xilinx subsequently announced (in 1985) the birth of the world's first FPGA, the XC2064, referred to as a "Logic Cell Array".

9.1.2 FPGA Architecture

Among the list of FPGA vendors today we can find both large companies such as Xilinx (currently valued at ~\$35 billion in its ongoing purchase by AMD), Intel (having purchased Altera), Microsemi (now part of Microchip Technology), and Lattice Semiconductor, and smaller companies that cover specific markets, such as Achronix, Menta, and Flex Logix in relation to embedded FPGAs (eFPGAs), and NanoXplore, which specializes in space applications of FPGAs. While each company started with different basic structures, over the years they have converged toward a similar architecture. Thus, each company uses its own terminology but the underlying principles and the overt functionality are very similar.

The basic element present in an FPGA is the configurable logic block (CLB); Intel FPGAs use the acronym ALM (adaptive logic module) to describe their module. CLBs effectively fulfill the function served by a transistor in a regular ASIC, and contain three elementary components: lookup tables (LUTs), flip-flops, and multiplexers, as represented in Figure 9.1. A LUT is a special combinatorial component, able to represent any logic function, that generates an output as a logical function of two or more inputs, as configured by the designer. Thereafter, the multiplexer determines whether or not the output is registered, bypassing the flip-flop as appropriate.

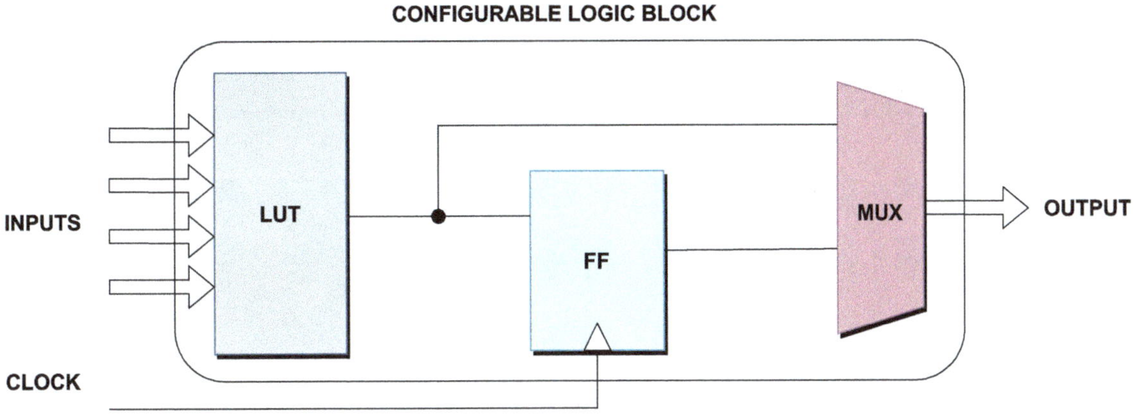

CONFIGURABLE LOGIC BLOCK

Figure 9.1 Configurable logic block of FPGA

The elementary structure of an FPGA consists of an array of CLBs, surrounded by I/O "pads", all interconnected by routing channels on which sit configurable switch boxes (SBs), as illustrated in Figure 9.2. These latter provide routing resources and enable the FPGA to create sequential or combinatorial circuits capable of executing digital logic functions.

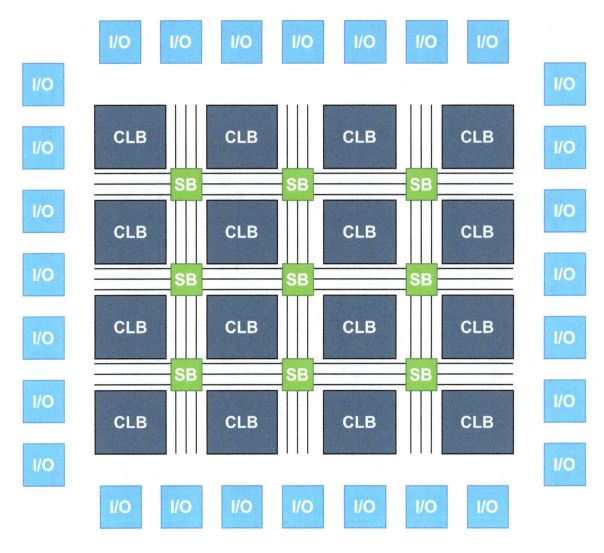

Figure 9.2 Elementary FPGA structure

In practice, modern CLB architectures are far more complex than the ones presented in the figures above. Thus, a single CLB usually contains a LUT with 5 or 6 inputs, and multiple flip-flops and multiplexers. Xilinx's Ultrascale CLB, for example, integrates two flip-flops in order to harness the same logic function to drive multiple outputs, optimizing the associated routing resources and the total area required to implement a specific circuit. Beyond the basic configurable elements, today's FPGAs will typically also contain a set of primitives, such as DSP (digital signal processing) units, BRAM (block RAM), input/output transceivers, and (PLL-based) clock management units. Of course, DSP and RAM functions could be implemented by making use of the CLBs themselves, but such components have become such common elements of FPGAs that it is more efficient to integrate them within the FPGA fabric as native components in order to maximize device integration and performance, as depicted in Figure 9.3.

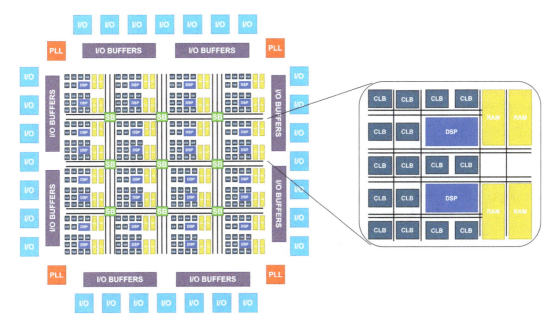

Figure 9.3 Typical FPGA structure

The research and development of new and more efficient FPGA architectures is still evolving. The FPGAs of the 1980s nowadays find application in small custom circuits and low-end devices. The latest FPGAs integrate plenty of hard IP components, as well as input/output transceivers and memory controllers. As the technology shrinks, the routing between components has started to become a limiting factor in performance. CLBs can be utilized as pipelining registers to accelerate performance but this approach is afflicted by the same issue. To address the problem, the most recent Intel devices, such as the Agilex and Stratix 10 FPGAs, implement a so-called Hyperflex architecture, which includes additional registers, called Hyper-Registers, throughout the FPGA fabric, as represented in Figure 9.4. The purpose of these registers, which are bypassable, is to enable circuits to be retimed to eliminate critical paths, and to implement pipeline registers that don't depend on CLBs (ALMs) and thus diminish routing delays.

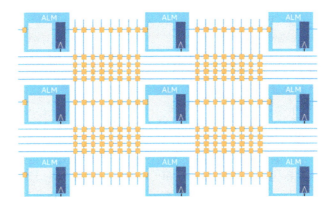

Figure 9.4 Intel Hyperflex FPGA architecture showing Hyper-Registers (in orange) (source: https://www.intel.la/content/www/xl/es/products/ programmable/fpga/stratix-10/features.html Copyright © Intel Corporation).

9.1.3 ASIC versus FPGA

A SoC is essentially a chip designed for a specific function, something that is traditionally referred to as an ASIC (application-specific integrated circuit). However, SoCs, in terms of their final implementation, can be customized to specific functions too, creating an additional level of ASIC definition/categorization. Sometimes, SoCs are also included in the category of ASSPs (application-specific standard products), a special subset of ASICs that can be used in a wide spectrum of applications. An FPGA plays a slightly different role, effectively merging the concepts of general-purpose and application-specific use. In practice, an FPGA allows the creation of a customized hardware circuit by means of a predefined programmable general-purpose structure.

Performance-wise, the flexibility offered by an FPGA has a price, typically providing poorer performance than would a customized ASIC-based solution (see Figure 9.5). To provide an example in terms of order of magnitude, a SoC implemented on an ASIC might run at 1 GHz, but the same SoC implemented on an FPGA will operate at around one-quarter of that frequency. Of course, this ratio can change as a function of the target FPGA and the CPU itself. This gulf in performance is largely due to the nature of the internal interconnections in an FPGA, which introduce delay between the components, as we have already highlighted. Nevertheless, given the increased flexibility conferred by programmability and the extremely high development costs typically associated with an ASIC, FPGAs still have a significant role to play in the SoC marketplace.

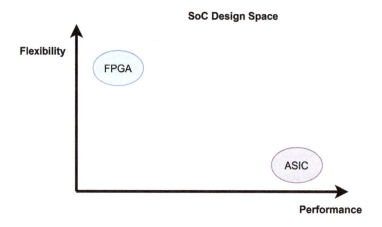

Figure 9.5 SoC design space: performance vs flexibility trade-off

Another important aspect in evaluating the most appropriate implementation of a SoC – either FPGA or ASIC – is the number of units expected to be sold. Although the initial design of the two forms of implementation can be the same, in the form of hardware description language (HDL) and/or pre-implemented IP, the design flows in the backend are typically more complex and involve more moving parts in the case of an ASIC-based solution. This implies a higher overall development cost in comparison to an FPGA implementation. Besides this development cost, the ASIC design flow also requires the chip to be manufactured, whereas an FPGA chip is available to buy off-the-shelf from an appropriate vendor. As depicted in Figure 9.6, there will be a crossover point that determines which of the two solutions offers the better cost-effectiveness (with lower sales volumes favoring FPGAs and higher sales volumes tipping the balance in favor of ASICs).

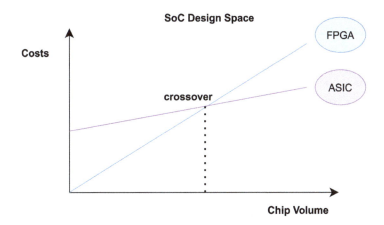

Figure 9.6 SoC design space: sales volume vs cost trade-off

Very often, the FPGA plays the role of prototyping platform for a SoC, with the final target being an ASIC. In this way, designers can prove the functionality and effectiveness of a chip-based implementation, provided that the gap in performance referred to above does not affect the core functionality of the chip itself. Table 9.1 summarizes the trade-offs involved.

Table 9.1 ASIC–FPGA trade-offs

ASIC	FPGA
High performance	Lower performance
Complex and expensive development process	Less complex development process
Hardwired circuit	Programmability

9.2 CPUs on FPGAs

9.2.1 Soft-core IP
When a CPU is implemented in a FPGA, it is termed a soft-core CPU. The main difference between a soft-core and a classical hard-core microprocessor is, as already indicated, the operating frequency and hence the overall performance. On the other hand, the implementation of a soft-core CPU does provide considerable flexibility in terms of area and performance. In addition, FPGAs allow development of application-specific instruction set processors (ASIPs), in which application-specific instructions can be incorporated into the existing instruction set, compiled, and executed by a custom hardware unit designed and implemented on the FPGA fabric.

Over the years, FPGA vendors have built up tools and methods to facilitate access to and use of soft-core CPUs. Every FPGA vendor offers their own soft-core solution, which in most instances can be acquired free of charge in non-optimized versions. In the case of Intel's FPGA, originally developed by Altera, the soft-core CPU is named Nios II and exists in three different versions, /f, /s, and /e. The first is optimized for performance, the last for area, and the middle one represents a compromise between the two.

In the case of Xilinx, its soft-core CPU is called MicroBlaze. It also exists in three different preset implementations, characterized by their levels of OS support: the Microcontroller runs bare-metal code; the Real-Time Processor runs an RTOS; and the Application Processor runs a Linux kernel. Many other soft-core CPUs exist in the marketplace, including ARC from Synopsys, LatticeMico32 from Lattice Semiconductor, and LEON from CAES, not to mention the soft-core CPU offered by Arm, the Cortex-M1.

9.2.2 Arm Cortex-M1

Arm's Cortex-M1 is specifically designed for embedded applications that require a small processor integrated into an FPGA.

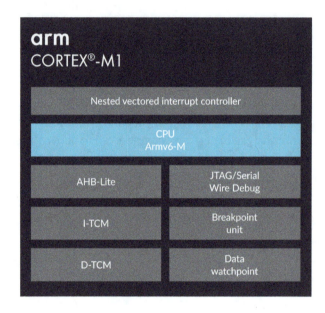

Figure 9.7 ARM Cortex-M1 Block Diagram (source: Reproduced with permission from Arm Ltd)

As represented in Figure 9.7, the Cortex-M1 soft-core encompasses the CPU itself, a nested vectored interrupt controller (NVIC), a JTAG/SWD interface, tightly coupled memories for both instructions and data, and an AHB-Lite bus interface. The characteristics of the microprocessor can be summarized as follows:

■ Arm v6-M architecture: a Thumb instruction set architecture (ISA) that also includes the 32-bit Thumb-2 BL, MRS, MSR, ISB, DSB, and DMB instructions.

■ Operating System (OS) extension option. If implemented, functionality within the processor is enabled that is capable of running an OS, including the SVC instruction, a banked stack pointer register, and an integrated system timer (SysTick).

■ System exception model.

■ Handler and Thread modes.

- Stack pointers: one stack pointer is always present; if the OS extension option is implemented, two stack pointers are present.

- Thumb state only.

- BE-8/LE support: data endianness is configurable; however, instructions and system control registers are always little-endian (LE), and if the processor has debug, debug resources and debugger accesses are always little-endian too.

- No hardware support for unaligned accesses.

The NVIC is closely integrated with the processor to achieve low-latency interrupt processing and includes the following features:

- 1, 8, 16 or 32 configurable external interrupts

- 2 priority bits, providing four levels of programmable interrupt priority

- Automatic saving and restoration of processor state on interrupt entry/exit, with no instruction overhead.

The M1 is available without debug support or with full and reduced debug options that provide:

- Access to all memory and registers in the system, including the processor register bank when the core is halted

- A Debug Access Port (DAP)

- A BreakPoint Unit (BPU) for implementing breakpoints

- A Data Watchpoint (DW) unit for implementing watchpoints.

Finally, the M1 offers a 32-bit hardware multiplier, configurable either as the standard multiplier or a smaller, lower performance implementation.

9.2.3 Arm DesignStart: Cortex-M1 on FPGA

We previously described how an FPGA could serve as a prototyping platform for SoC design. To speed up the prototyping process and facilitate access to existing, proven IPs, Arm created the DesignStart rapid prototyping tool, which we introduced in Chapter 7's case study. DesignStart gives designers access to design resources that can be integrated with Arm IPs to create custom SoCs. In this section, we introduce the process for implementing a soft-core Arm Cortex-M1 on an FPGA, summarizing the main steps involved. However, this is not a substitute for the reference guide, which should be consulted for more detailed information [1]. The DesignStart example provided by Arm and outlined below targets the Arty A7 or S7 boards from Digilent, which include a Xilinx XC7A100TCSG324-1

FPGA. More information about the board can be found online [2]. For the sake of simplicity, in this book we use the Arty A7 board.

9.2.3.1   Setup and Initial Design

Because we are using DesignStart to implement a Cortex-M1-based SoC using a Xilinx FPGA as our target, we will need Xilinx development tools, specifically Vivado, a software suite for HDL-based design. We also need to download DesignStart (from Arm) before we can begin.

In the Vivado Block Design editor (see Figure 9.8), create a new project and install the IP for the Cortex-M1: in the *IP Catalog tab*, right click and select *Add Repository*. Select the *DesignStart* folder containing the Cortex-M1 processor for Xilinx. In *packaging options*, select *Package*, specify a directory, and start a new block diagram.

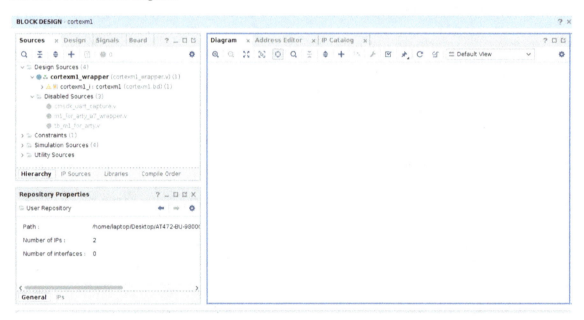

Figure 9.8 Vivado Block Design editor

Adding the Cortex-M1 block can be done by looking in the IP Catalog or searching for it via the + button. This should result in the Cortex-M1 representation depicted in Figure 9.9 being displayed in the Vivado Block Design diagram.

This Cortex microprocessor can have up to 32 interrupts, which explains the 32-bit size of the IRQ bus, corresponding to one bit per interrupt. There is also an NMI signal for non-maskable interrupts. Depending on the configuration of the IRQ bus, the external interrupts defined in the interrupt vector will be called. The CM1_AXI3 bus (top right in Figure 9.9) is an AXI master that needs to be connected to a slave AXI interconnect; the associated IP block (see Figure 9.10) must be selected and incorporated into the on-screen design diagram.

Figure 9.9 Arm Cortex-M1 component representation in Vivado Block Design diagram

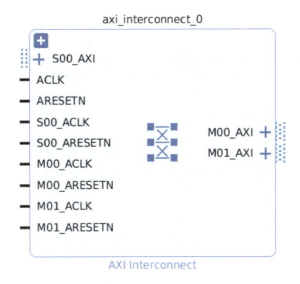

Figure 9.10 AXI interconnect component representation in Vivado Block Design diagram

By default, as illustrated, the AXI interconnect component has only one slave and two master bus connections. For our particular design, we will need controllers for block RAM, Quad SPI, a UART and a GPIO, meaning at least four master bus connections will be required, one for each of these slave components. The configuration of the interconnect block can be updated accordingly, as illustrated for one such component in Figure 9.11. To complete the design, a Clocks_and_Resets module must be added, as previously described in the case study of Chapter 7, as well as the block RAM memory controller and the local block RAM memory itself (also described in Chapter 7's case study).

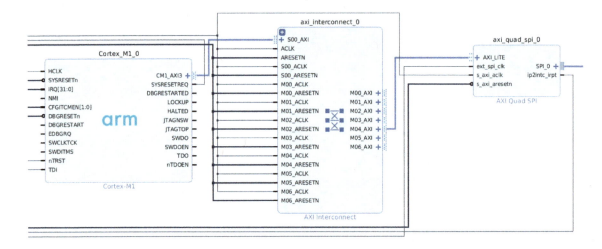

Figure 9.11 Arm DesignStart connection example

9.2.3.2   Customizing the Cortex-M1 Processor

Having incorporated the CPU into the design, the Cortex-M1 can be customized according to user and application needs. For the purpose of this book, as an introduction, we will present the options associated with each of the four main customization tabs for the processor, as illustrated in Figure 9.12, starting with the *Configuration* tab. Again, for detailed information, we recommend that the reader consults the official documentation.

Configuration

- Number of interrupts: 1, 8, 16 or 32.

- OS Extensions: to allow the Cortex-M1 to be implemented on small FPGAs, functions such as the SysTick timer, **SVC** instruction and shadow stack pointer are disabled by default and must be enabled with this option.

- Small Multiplier: gives the option to implement a smaller version of the integer multiplier, saving hardware resources in the FPGA fabric.

- Big Endian: gives the capability to change the byte order in memory, the default being little-endian.

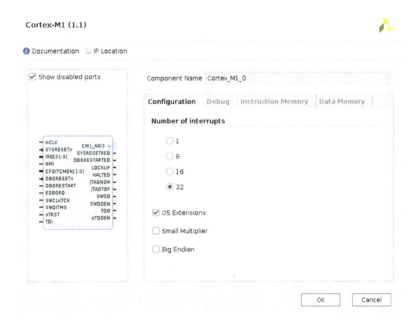

Figure 9.12 Arm Cortex-M1 customization – Configuration tab

Debug

In the *Debug* tab (see Figure 9.13), it is possible to configure the processor to support JTAG, Serial Wire Debug, or both. It is also possible to select a "Small Debug" option to reduce the resource utilization of the debug unit.

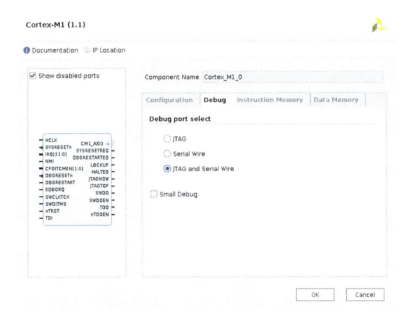

Figure 9.13 Arm Cortex-M1 customization – Debug tab

Instruction Memory

In the *Instruction Memory* tab (see Figure 9.14), the size of the tightly-coupled memory used for instructions (ITCM) can be configured by the developer, in a range from 8 kB to 1 MB, depending on the target FPGA and the program size. This will be implemented in the FPGA fabric as block RAM. This memory can then be initialized using a pre-compiled program, which in this case is the file *bram_a7.hex*.

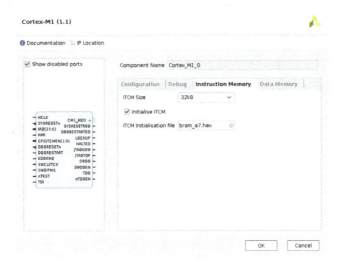

Figure 9.14 Arm Cortex-M1 customization – Instruction Memory tab

Data Memory

The *Data Memory* tab (see Figure 9.15) provides similar configuration facilities for data-oriented tightly-coupled memory (DTCM), with the same size range available (8 kB to 1 MB).

Figure 9.15 Arm Cortex-M1 customization – Data Memory tab

9.2.3.3   Synthesis and Implementation

Once the CPU and peripherals have been incorporated and configured, the design is ready to be synthesized and implemented on the FPGA. In Vivado, the synthesis process can be launched either by using the green Run button within the GUI (see Figure 9.16) or by using the command line.

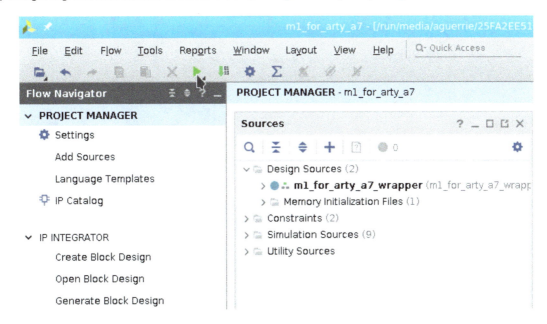

Figure 9.16 Vivado run button (green arrow) for FPGA synthesis

Synthesis and implementation reports are generated during the respective processes. Resource utilization, timing closure, and power consumption estimations can be analyzed in order to assess the quality of the design. For example, following implementation, the resource utilization report for the reference design is shown in Figure 9.17.

Utilization   Post-Synthesis | **Post-Implementation**

Graph | **Table**

Resource	Utilization	Available	Utilization %
LUT	7830	20800	37.64
LUTRAM	201	9600	2.09
FF	8495	41600	20.42
BRAM	30	50	60.00
DSP	3	90	3.33
IO	51	210	24.29
BUFG	4	32	12.50
MMCM	1	5	20.00

Figure 9.17 Vivado report: Post-Implementation Resource Utilization

Timing information is very important in designing with FPGAs. In technical terms, the process of analyzing such timing information is called Static Timing Analysis, or simply STA. For our DesignStart example, the frequency of the Arm Cortex-M1 CPU, indicated by cpu_clk, is 100 MHz. Other peripherals, such as the QSPI, work at 50 MHz. A clock summary report is shown in Figure 9.18.

Timing × Design Runs | Clock Networks |

Q ⤧ ⇕ **Clock Summary**

Name	Waveform	Period (ns)	Frequency (MHz)
SWCLK	{0.000 25.000}	50.000	20.000
slow_out_clk	{0.000 50.000}	100.000	10.000
⌄ sys_clock	{0.000 5.000}	10.000	100.000
clkfbout_m1_for_arty_a7_clk_wiz_0_0	{0.000 5.000}	10.000	100.000
cpu_clk	{0.000 5.000}	10.000	100.000
⟩ qspi_clk	{0.000 10.000}	20.000	50.000

Figure 9.18 Vivado report: Clock Summary

During the timing analysis, the timing constraints for the given hardware design can be checked to provide information about the integrity of the design. Besides the detailed information, a final message may be displayed to the effect that "All user-specified timing constraints are met", as represented in Figure 9.19. Where the timing constraints are not met, it will be necessary to reanalyze the critical path of the design and, where it is not possible to add pipeline stages to overcome the timing constraints, reduce the clock operating frequency accordingly.

Design Timing Summary

Setup		Hold		Pulse Width	
Worst Negative Slack (WNS):	0.186 ns	Worst Hold Slack (WHS):	0.017 ns	Worst Pulse Width Slack (WPWS):	3.000 ns
Total Negative Slack (TNS):	0.000 ns	Total Hold Slack (THS):	0.000 ns	Total Pulse Width Negative Slack (TPWS):	0.000 ns
Number of Failing Endpoints:	0	Number of Failing Endpoints:	0	Number of Failing Endpoints:	0
Total Number of Endpoints:	19998	Total Number of Endpoints:	19498	Total Number of Endpoints:	8817

All user specified timing constraints are met.

Figure 9.19 Vivado report: Design Timing Summary

In addition, Vivado offers the ability to display the FPGA layout and highlight the resource utilization of specific components, as illustrated in Figure 9.20. In this instance, it is the Arm CPU core that is being highlighted (in white).

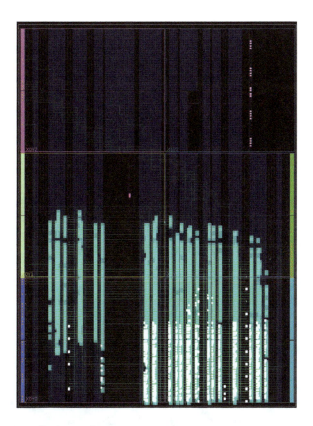

Figure 9.20 Vivado report: FPGA resource utilization mapping

9.2.3.4 Bitstream Generation and Board Test

The final step of the hardware design involves generation of the bitstream, which is the file containing the configuration information for the FPGA; in other words, your circuits. Once the bitstream has been successfully generated, it can be downloaded onto the FPGA. The easiest way to achieve this, in this case, is to use the *Hardware Manager* available from Vivado.

Once the bitstream has been downloaded onto the board, opening a serial terminal (e.g. Minicom emulator) will cause the Arm Cortex-M1 to print the message shown below, this being part of the software (*bram_a7.hex*) included in the BRAM during the synthesis and implementation process:

```
*************************************
Arm Cortex-M1 Revision 0 Variant 1

Example design for Digilent A7 board

V2C-DAPLink board not detected
Use DIP switches and push buttons to
control LEDS
 Version 1.1
*************************************
Bram readback correct
Base SPI readback correct
```

Your first Arm Cortex-M1 is now running on the FPGA as a soft-core microcontroller! The example software provided in the reference design allows control of the LEDs present on the board via the push-button and the DIP switches (see Figure 9.21). The software runs on bare-metal, the level closest to the hardware. No RTOS examples are provided in the DesignStart tool, which focuses its attention on the implementation of an Arm Cortex-M1 on an FPGA, as in this chapter. For more information on how to compile the software, and build more complex software applications, we refer the reader to the official documentation.

Figure 9.21 Arm Cortex-M1 running on FPGA

9.3 FPGA and Microcontroller Integration: The Best of Both Worlds?

As demands for increased performance and improved efficiency continue apace, a hybrid solution that embeds a hard-core Cortex-style microprocessor within a configurable FPGA has become increasingly significant, bridging the gap between full FPGA-based customization and the power and size/energy efficiency of a general-purpose hard-core CPU. Various FPGA vendors, including Intel, Xilinx, and Microchip, now offer integration of Arm CPUs in their FPGA chips in hard-core rather than soft-core form. For example, Microchip has targeted low-power applications by incorporating a Cortex-M3 microcontroller into its Microsemi SmartFusion and SmartFusion2 SoCs. Given the focus of this book on the Cortex-M family, we present a brief account of the SmartFusion architecture below, even though it is relatively mature (SmartFusion2 was released in 2012), as a representative example of this trend.

9.3.1 SmartFusion

SmartFusion was originally designed to address the needs for hard-core CPU performance, FPGA design flexibility and analog signal processing in a single chip. It was the first of its kind, and was aimed at the world of IoT and low-power portable applications. Embedding an Arm Cortex-M3 microprocessor allowed SmartFusion SoCs to offer low power consumption, low gate counts, low and predictable interrupt latency, and low-cost debug. SmartFusion uses AHB as its main bus, with a bridge to APB to connect low-power peripherals, some of which are also incorporated as hard IP blocks, such as timers, UARTs, and SPI and I²C interfaces. The SoC designer can implement their own custom function(s) on the FPGA in the form of an AHB peripheral, which can then be interfaced with the CPU using the same interface as used for the other, hard peripherals.

The SmartFusion chip is effectively partitioned into three main blocks: the microcontroller subsystem (MSS), the FPGA fabric, and the programmable analog components. The MSS contains the Cortex-M3, including common digital peripherals/functions such as JTAG, NVIC, SWD, SysTick, and an MPU. The FPGA fabric is based on Microsemi's ProASIC3 architecture, with up to 500,000 system gates and 350 MHz system performance. It also contains embedded FIFOs, embedded SRAMs with variable aspect ratio and dual-port support, and up to 128 FPGA I/Os supporting LVDS, PCI, PCI-X and LVTTL/LVCMOS standards. The programmable analog block provides ADC and DAC conversions and analog signal-conditioning blocks (SCBs) with voltage, current and temperature monitors, offloading these functions from the CPU.

9.3.2 The State of the Art

Most SoC-FPGA integrations target the application-level market, making the Cortex-A family more suitable for the purpose. Thus, the Intel Arria 10 and Cyclone V SoC FPGAs integrate a Cortex-A9 CPU, while the new Intel Stratix 10 SoC FPGA incorporates a Cortex-A53. Similarly, the Xilinx Zynq integrates a dual-core Cortex-A9, while the Xilinx UltraScale MPSoC integrates a quad-core Cortex-A53 plus a dual-core Cortex-R5.

These hybrid solutions appear to signal the future for FPGA computing: general-purpose processing units in the form of hard IP, surrounded by the programmable logic provided by an FPGA fabric. Thus, the latest devices from Xilinx, based on its Adaptive Compute Acceleration Platform (ACAP) architecture, include application-level processors such as Arm Cortex-A- and Cortex-R-class CPUs, software-programmable accelerators, and AI cores, all on the same die.

Announcing these devices in 2018, Xilinx's CEO, Victor Peng, declared that "Xilinx is not an FPGA company; Xilinx is a platform company", which represents something of a departure for the inventor of the FPGA. The new device families, given the name Versal (VERSatile universal; see Figure 9.22), are focused on application-level hardware acceleration. Besides Xilinx's FPGA "Adaptable Engines" fabric, they include many other computing elements; for example:

- "Scalar Engines", based on Arm Cortex-A72 application processors and Cortex-R5 real-time processors

- "Intelligent Engines", consisting of massively parallel AI engines based on hundreds of purpose-built, networked and programmable SIMD processors, and DSP engines enhanced with floating-point extensions

- hard IP blocks for a range of standard interface and memory protocols, including Ethernet, PCIe, CCIX and SDRAM controllers

- high-speed SerDes ports, from 32 to 112 Gbps, and programmable I/O

- on-chip memory distributed all over the device as local RAM for the scalar and AI engines, and also embedded within the FPGA fabric

- a network-on-chip (NoC) implementation that links the engines to the large number of on-chip memories

- a software-controlled processor, the Platform Management Controller (PMC), which manages the entire device, including booting, configuration, dynamic reconfiguration, encryption, authentication, power management, and system monitoring.

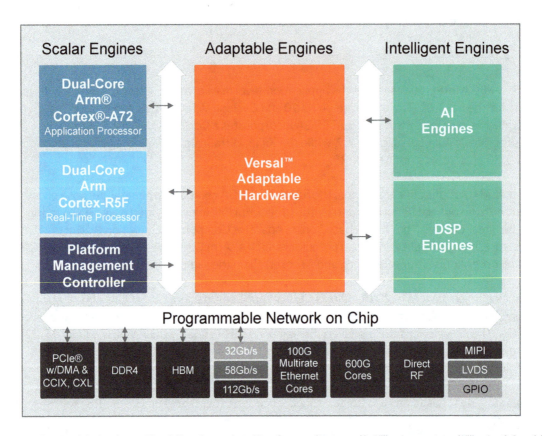

Figure 9.22 Xilinx Versal platform (source: Material based on or adapted from figures and text owned by Xilinx, Inc., courtesy of Xilinx, Inc. © Copyright Xilinx 2020)

References

[1]   Arm, *Arm DesignStart*. [Online]. Available: developer.arm.com/ip-products/designstart

[2]   Digilent, *Arty A7*. [Online]. Available: reference.digilentinc.com/reference/programmable-logic/arty-a7/start

Chapter 10

Software for SoCs

In our final chapter, having covered all of the hardware-related aspects of SoCs, we turn our attention to some of the software aspects, particularly those that might differ significantly from regular software development. Thus we consider the process of software development when working with SoCs, and the different approaches, such as bare-metal programming and the use of real-time operating systems, that programming a SoC may involve. We conclude with a brief sortie into the subject of scheduling algorithms, needed to ensure that your SoC can actually fulfill the real-time functions that are typically required of it. In the course of the chapter, we will address the following questions, among others:

1.   *What is a software development toolchain?*

2.   *What elements are involved in this toolchain?*

3.   *How do I apply this toolchain?*

4.   *What is meant by "bare-metal"?*

5.   *What are the advantages and disadvantages of using a bare-metal approach?*

6.   *How do we run an operating system on a small SoC?*

7.   *What do we mean by "real-time" and what is a real-time operating system (RTOS)?*

8.   *How does an RTOS differ from a traditional operating system?*

9.   *What are the advantages and disadvantages of using an RTOS on a SoC?*

10. *What is a scheduling algorithm and why do we need one?*

11. *What is the difference between a static- and a dynamic-priority scheduling algorithm?*

12. *How can I decide which scheduling algorithm is the best for my application?*

10.1 Toolchain Basics

In software engineering, the term toolchain is used to indicate the collection of software tools needed to build a software application. The term comes from the fact that these tools are usually employed in a sequential fashion, where the output of one tool becomes the input to the next, although the term does not refer exclusively to a set of tools deployed in this consecutive manner.

Of all the components of a toolchain, the main elements are a compiler, a linker and a debugger. Each of these can involve sets of libraries that represent various proven and/or specialized functions, some of which may eventually become incorporated into the relevant elements of the toolchain themselves.

10.1.1 Compilation

Compilation refers to the process of transforming a high-level programming language such as C/C++ into the machine-level instructions or code that a processor will be able to understand and execute on the target hardware. In the case of Arm Cortex-M processors, compiling the software application means transforming the high-level source code into a binary file that will be executable by the given target, specifically an "ELF" (executable and linkable format) file. The process is depicted in Figure 10.1.

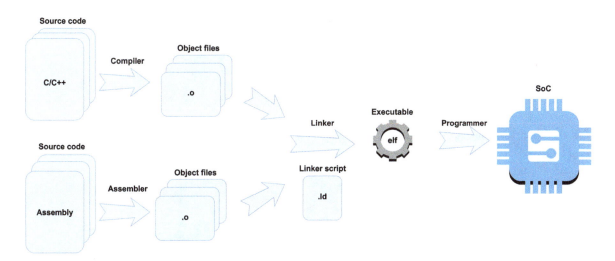

Figure 10.1 Compilation flow

The first step in the process is the transformation of the high-level code, which may often take the form of assembly language ("assembler") instructions too, into a set of so-called object files (having a .o suffix). These object files contain machine-level code, although this code is not yet ready to be executed by the CPU. Instead, following the generation of the entire set of object files, a linker must link these together to build a single executable file of binary instructions for the target, in this case the Arm CPU. The resulting file, having the suffix *.elf*, can then be downloaded (or programmed) into the nonvolatile memory of the SoC (e.g. EEPROM or flash memory), ready to be executed by the CPU. This final step of the process is sometimes referred to as "flashing" the binary onto the target.

10.1.1.1 Cross-compiler

A cross-compiler is the form of compiler required to compile applications for embedded systems. In simple terms, a cross-compiler simply refers to a compiler that runs on a different platform to that on which the target code will run, meaning that each has its own distinct instruction set. Thus, a standard compiler operating on a desktop machine will generate executable code for the same machine, but if the target is an Arm CPU, then a cross-compiler will be needed, as illustrated in Figure 10.2 (in which the HOST system is a desktop machine similar to that at bottom left).

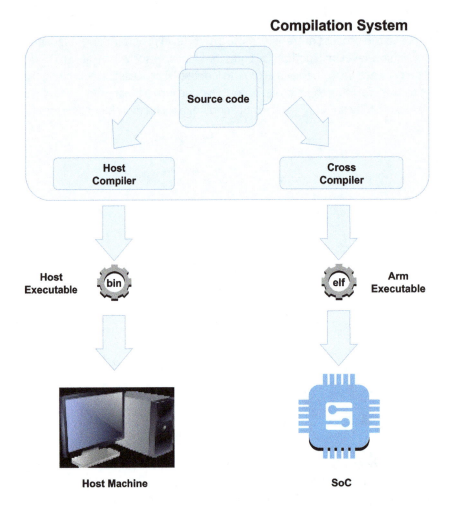

Figure 10.2 Cross-compilation principles

10.1.1.2 Linking

A software application is usually composed of multiple source files, which are respectively compiled into object files. As described above, the linker must build the individual object files into a single executable file. Within this process, it has to incorporate code from object libraries that is referred to within the main object files, and must also resolve cross-references between object files, which may include memory locations where code and data can be found, for example, relocating relative address jumps, loads, and stores.

In order to do this, the linker needs information about the memory layout of the target CPU, in terms of where the code must be loaded, the area to be used for data, and the area(s) available for the stack and the heap, all of which is provided via a linker script.

The object files to be linked contain different segments that indicate the different types of data that must be accommodated in memory. Thus, the text segment contains executable code, the data segment contains initialized static variables, and the bss (block starting symbol) segment contains uninitialized static variables (i.e. declared but without an assigned value), as represented in Figure 10.3.

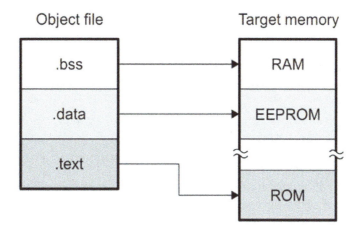

Figure 10.3 Object file data types and target memory assignment

C compilers generate similar sections for the compiled code too, which may be initialized with data or instructions or left uninitialized to create placeholders for the variables without assigning initial values, as for the stack.

10.1.2 Debugging

Debugging an application running on an embedded target is not straightforward. The difficulties arise less from the software debugging itself, and more from the complexity of all of the components involved in the end-to-end process, represented in Figure 10.4.

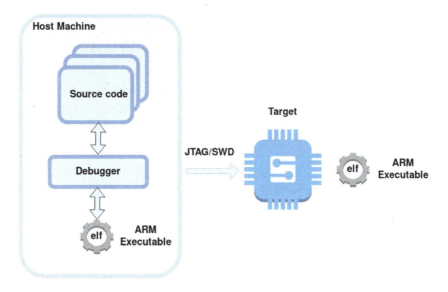

Figure 10.4 Embedded debug overview

Compared to the classical debugging process, where the code is frequently executed on the same machine as that performing the debug, in the embedded world the code is being executed on a foreign target, implying a continuous exchange of information between the host and the target, which is usually performed via a communication interface such as JTAG or SWD. Furthermore, the debugger application must handle the fact that the symbols being returned by the target processor's instruction set at run-time will be different to those returned by the local host during execution, and must be read and interpreted accordingly. The complexity of the debugging framework is usually smoothed with the support of an integrated development environment (IDE).

10.2 Programming Approaches

10.2.1 Bare-metal Coding

Bare-metal is a programming approach that involves the execution of the application software at the closest possible level to the hardware. Thus, in a bare-metal programming scenario, there is no operating system involved and the software runs as a single thread on the CPU. The main advantage of this approach is execution efficiency: a bare-metal application can run on an embedded processor without incurring expensive memory requirements. However, the downside of the approach is that all of the hardware resources, such as peripherals and communication interfaces, must also be managed by the application programmer, increasing the development complexity. The programming language typically used in bare-metal coding is C or C++, and the code, once compiled for the embedded CPU target, can be downloaded into the nonvolatile memory of the embedded system.

As implied above, one of the principal limitations of bare-metal coding is single task execution: multitasking is not possible. As well as the management of task execution, timings, interrupt management and operations all fall under the programmer's remit. On the other hand, if well designed, bare-metal coding can make it easier to satisfy hard real-time constraints and execution deadlines. In summary:

▪ **Advantages**: full control of the hardware resources; small memory footprint

▪ **Disadvantages**: single-thread execution; no driver support.

Note that, sometimes, bare-metal application software may be referred to as firmware.

10.2.2 SoC with RTOS Kernel

How can an operating system run on a small SoC like the Cortex-M? As anticipated in preceding chapters, a real-time operating system (RTOS) is a lightweight operating system that is designed to provide more deterministic control of system resources than is afforded by regular operating systems (such as Linux) and thus make it easier to meet the execution timings/deadlines demanded of real-time applications. From a high-level perspective, and in terms of a concept already explained, the RTOS can be regarded as a bare-metal program that offers methods and services to the developer through which to manage multi-task applications. Thus, an RTOS kernel is compiled at the lowest level possible for the specific SoC. Although the adoption of an RTOS can present several advantages to the developer, it represents a significant overhead in execution time compared to bare-metal application coding and an overhead in code memory utilization as well. In summary, in comparison to bare-metal programming, the use of an RTOS on a SoC provides:

- **Advantages**: multi-thread support; wide range of device drivers

- **Disadvantages**: overheads in memory utilization; overheads in execution time.

10.2.2.1 RTOS Portability and Hardware Abstraction Layers

One of the most basic issues when developing software for a SoC is related to the portability of the code, by which we mean the capability of the software to run on a different target, in this case a different embedded SoC. This is a fundamental issue for any organization that wants to invest in developing an RTOS, which is only likely to have a commercial existence if it can run on multiple embedded SoC platforms without significant effort and development expense. In such a scenario, the goal is to make the software as abstract as possible in respect to the underlying hardware. To this end, in all RTOSs, and, indeed, more generally in all operating systems, the concept of a hardware abstraction layer (HAL) has been developed, consisting of a series of methods that allow the virtualization of the execution environment, enabling the software in the layer above it to be compatible with multiple target platforms.

10.3 Real-time Operating Systems

A real-time operating system is a collection of hardware and resource management software that runs on a CPU in support of application software, with the main characteristic being that its timing is predictable, and thus tasks can be executed and will adhere to a given deadline. To do this, the delays and latencies associated with the richer facilities of a traditional operating system have to be eliminated or tightly controlled. An RTOS can usually run on CPUs of different sizes and for different purposes, from embedded processors to desktop CPUs. Examples of RTOSs include Arm Mbed OS, FreeRTOS, µC/OS-II, QNX, VxWorks, Windows CE, and RTEMS.

10.3.1 Characteristics

An RTOS can be event-driven or timing-driven. In the former, the tasks are scheduled and executed as a function of inputs/outputs or interrupts. In the latter, the scheduling policies are managed by timing events, such as task deadlines or timers.

On the basis of the level of tolerance allowable in meeting the defined deadlines, real-time systems can be classified into three different categories: soft, firm and hard. In a hard real-time system, all the deadlines must be satisfied in order to meet the system functionality. In a soft real-time system, deadlines can occasionally be missed, within a certain limit, without any consequent system issue. In a firm real-time system, missing a deadline can lower the quality level of the system, which may, for example, have commercial consequences, but does not imply a fault as such.

Some of the most significant characteristics of real-time operating systems are:

▪ **Preemption**. The capability to suspend a process and swap it for another with higher priority, after which the execution of the previous process will be resumed from precisely the state in which it was halted.

▪ **Context switching**. This is a key function of any (multitasking) operating system, and refers to the detailed procedure and mechanisms used to swap the thread of execution in the processor from one process or task to another (e.g. in support of preemption).

▪ **Board support package**. This represents the main element that makes an RTOS compatible with a specific SoC.

▪ **File system**. An RTOS typically supports simple file systems of the sort normally used in embedded and flash memories, such as FAT16 or FAT32.

10.3.2 Architecture

The main components of an RTOS are the kernel, device drivers, a file system, network stacks, and various input/output utilities, as represented in Figure 10.5. An RTOS is responsible for providing the developer with all of the mechanisms necessary for task instantiation, synchronization, and communication, such as semaphores, mutexes (or locks), and mailboxes. We will consider these in more detail below. Tasks, also defined more closely below, do not have direct access to the underlying target hardware. All of the operations that involve the hardware are managed by the kernel, which in turn uses device drivers to handle and manage the physical device(s).

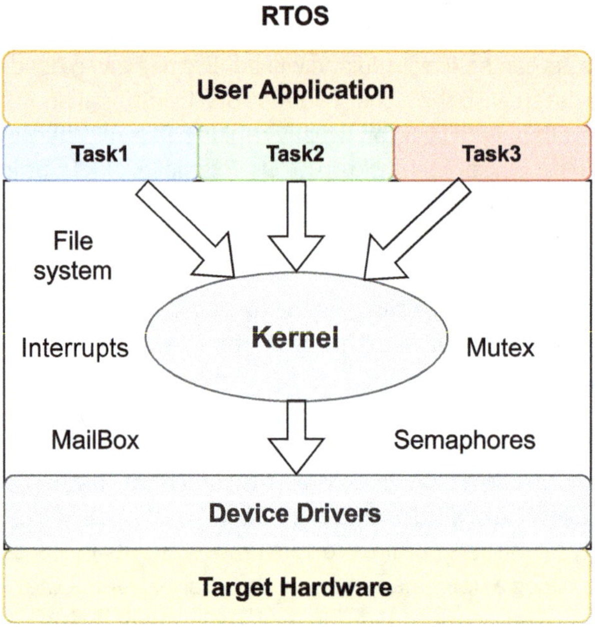

Figure 10.5 RTOS structure

10.3.3 Kernels

The kernel is the core component of an RTOS or any other operating system. It is the part of the operating system program that is always resident in memory and controls everything else in the system, providing the abstraction and overseeing the underlying connectivity between the user applications, running in user space, and the hardware. Thus, it provides all of the services that the tasks running on the system require in order to be executed and to run concurrently with other tasks. Depending on their internal architecture, kernels can be classified into three types:

- **Microkernel**. Only provides the most essential services for process execution, such as process management, inter-process communication and memory protection. Other traditional OS functions, such as device drivers, I/O utilities, and file systems, are separated out and run in user space. Because these latter are typically subject to more historical variation, their exclusion from the "protected" space of the kernel means that a microkernel is often seen as more reliable than a monolithic one.

- **Monolithic kernel**. Consists of a single program that contains all of the code necessary to perform all kernel functions. It handles all services, such as memory protection and inter-process communication, and also provides the abstractions of the hardware (covering device drivers, I/O utilities, etc.). A monolithic kernel is usually faster than a microkernel, in part because there is no overhead from context switching and message passing between protected kernel space and user space.

- **Hybrid kernel**. As might be expected, this is a hybrid of the two preceding types, potentially combining the best of them. In practice, it is difficult to define a hybrid kernel very precisely and it has been dismissed by some as a marketing term. However, in essence, a hybrid kernel adopts the structure of a microkernel, but runs the functions that a microkernel relegates to user space in protected space, just like a monolithic kernel does. In these terms, Windows NT, which still forms the basis of many of the most recent Windows operating systems (e.g. Windows 10, Windows Server 2019), is an example of a hybrid kernel (although it is not an RTOS).

10.3.4 Tasks

A task, or process, refers to the user application hosted by the operating system and running on the CPU. Each exists within a pool of tasks, which are scheduled and executed by the CPU depending on the priority assigned to them by the user. The RTOS contains an internal structure that describes the parameters associated with each task. The scope of these attributes defines the task in terms of its processing by the system, and the principal parameters are outlined in Table 10.1.

Table 10.1 RTOS task parameters

Parameter	Description
Task ID	The task identifier, enabling different tasks within the pool to be identified; also commonly referred to as a TID or, in more complex operating systems, a PID (Process ID)
Task State	Represents the current state of the task

Parameter	Description
Task Stack Pointer	Points to the memory address within the stack that is being used for the task
Task Priority	The priority of the task; the scheduler uses this information to assign task execution order
Task Program Counter	The counter for the program
Task Stack	This resides in RAM and is accessed via the task stack pointer
Task Routine	The program code for the task
Task Control Block	TCBs are data structures residing in RAM, accessible only by the RTOS, and used to maintain information about a task in support of context switching

10.3.4.1 Task Classification

Tasks can generally be categorized into two types: I/O-bound processes and CPU-bound processes. Unsurprisingly, the former are tasks that spend the majority of their time performing input/output processing (e.g. a task that reads data from a serial port on a UART and logs the traffic in a text file), whereas the latter spend the majority of their time performing CPU computation (e.g. a task that takes a small input key and uses it to drive several mathematical computations in support of a crypto-algorithm). A well-balanced system will support a good combination of I/O-bound and CPU-bound tasks.

10.3.5 Task Management

A task represents the user code executed by a CPU. From a timing perspective, a task presents with three main characteristics: its release or issue time (when it arrives for execution), its deadline (by when it must be completed) and its execution time (the time required by the processor to perform the task). These parameters will be useful later for evaluating whether a given set of tasks are schedulable by a specific type of scheduler.

A task can assume different states, which represent the status of the process in respect to all the other tasks in a system. For example, in a single-CPU system, only one task can be in the "running" state at a time. While this task is "running", all other tasks must, by definition, be in a different state. A brief description of the possible states that a task can assume follows, and Figure 10.6 is a state diagram in which the direction of the arrows indicates transitions between such states:

- **New** – The task is inserted into the queue of the scheduler.

- **Ready** – The task is ready for execution and is waiting for CPU resource to be made available.

- **Execution** – The task is currently executing on the CPU.

- **Waiting** – The task is waiting for a resource, which may be the CPU or I/O.

- **Termination** – The task completes its activity and is removed from the scheduler queue.

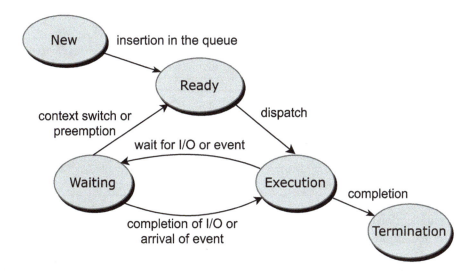

Figure 10.6 Task state transition diagram

During the execution of an application program, individual tasks are continuously switching from one state to another. However, in a single-core machine, only one task will be in the running state (i.e. given control of the CPU) at any point of the execution. In situations where CPU control is switched from one task to another, the context of the to-be-suspended task must be saved while the context of the to-be-executed task must be retrieved; thus "context switching" as previously described.

10.3.6 Inter-task Communication and Synchronization

A task is a sequence of instructions, typically related to a specific and self-contained function of the system. However, a task cannot have full control of a SoC because it is running on a time-sharing basis with all of the other tasks on the same hardware. For this reason, each task must synchronize its operation with the other tasks, and, moreover, it needs to exchange data with the rest of the system. If an RTOS is running on the SoC, it will handle peripherals such as memory and timers to service task operation, and the communication and synchronization between tasks happens via shared memory, managed by the RTOS. The RTOS offers the task developer various functions, termed APIs (application programming interfaces), through which to control aspects of task communication and synchronization. Before explaining inter-task communication and synchronization in more detail, some basic definitions are provided in Table 10.2.

Table 10.2 Inter-process communication/synchronization terms

Definition	Description
Critical section	A critical section is a portion of task code that operates on data or a hardware resource that is shared with another task; in this context, tasks should behave appropriately and protect the critical section to avoid compute errors or, in the worst case, a system crash
Deadlock	A particular condition in which two or more tasks are simultaneously waiting for resources from one another to complete their operations; the result is that none of the tasks is actually able to run and all are in wait states indefinitely

Definition	Description
Livelock	A form of deadlock in which the tasks involved in waiting for shared resources continuously change their state relative to one another but are still unable to progress; it is a special case of starvation
Mutual exclusion	Also known as mutex, it is the condition that must be imposed to protect a critical section and prevent a race condition
Race condition	A situation that occurs when two or more tasks are reading or writing shared data and the outcome varies according to their relative execution timings (i.e. which of them finishes first)
Starvation	A situation in which a task that is ready for execution is never run by the CPU (i.e. it is starved of a shared resource, in this case the CPU)

Inter-task communication refers to the mechanisms that allow tasks to exchange information with other tasks. These methods vary, and they change as a function of the operating system, the latency requirements, and the amount of information that must be exchanged. Furthermore, tasks must have ways to synchronize their operations with one another in order to avoid deadlocks, livelocks and race conditions, and to protect access to critical sections of the code. The mechanisms for task synchronization also vary, in terms of performance and characteristics. Some of the most common inter-task mechanisms are:

- **Mailboxes**. A method by which two or more processes can communicate with each other. The working principle is akin to a physical mailbox: a process can send a message by placing it in a box; the receiving process then accesses the same box to retrieve the message sent.

- **Message queues**. An inter-process communication method based on the exchange of messages. The main distinction from a mailbox is one of capacity: while a mailbox normally contains one message, a message queue contains multiple messages.

- **Semaphores**. A synchronization mechanism used to avoid shared-resource conflicts. Semaphores can be binary (unavailable/available) or counting semaphores. Similarly to a traffic light, a semaphore gives access to a shared resource: if the light is green, the process can continue; if red, it should wait (until another process releases the semaphore).

- **Mutexes**. Mutually exclusives, also referred to as locks, are a subset of (binary) semaphores that allow access to a portion of code by only one task at a time. When a mutex is active no other process can access that portion of code. Following the code's execution, a mutex should be released by the same process that locked it; if not, a deadlock condition can occur.

10.3.7 Interrupts

Interrupts play a key role in software programming, and are even more important in RTOSs. The technical definition of an interrupt is the interruption of sequential software execution to service a particular function, causing a temporary departure from the normal flow of execution. The function thus invoked is referred to as an interrupt service routine (ISR). When an interrupt occurs, the system saves the status of the task currently being executed and passes control of the CPU registers to the ISR, which after execution restores control of the system to the original sequential flow.

In an RTOS environment, all of the execution deadlines and execution timings should be predictable, even if an interrupt occurs. Indeed, the latency associated with handling interrupts is a fundamental element of real-time systems.

10.4 Scheduling Algorithms

10.4.1 Characteristics

A scheduling algorithm is the basis used by an operating system to dispatch (send for processing) a task for execution on the CPU. In computer science, a variety of scheduling algorithms have been developed over the years, each with its own characteristics and performance. The simplest example of a scheduling algorithm is first come, first served (FCFS). A scheduler implementing this type of algorithm simply processes the tasks in the order in which they are requested. Each request is inserted into a queue and dispatched as soon as the CPU becomes free. Another simple type of scheduling algorithm is called shortest job first (SJF). A scheduler implementing this algorithm prioritizes the waiting task with the shortest execution time, with the aim of reducing the overall turnaround time. The clear downside derives from the fact that, if short tasks continue to appear, some longer tasks may never be dispatched (a starvation condition). To overcome some of the issues associated with these simpler algorithms, one solution is to assign a priority level to each task, independent of its order of insertion into the queue or its execution time. In this book we do not attempt to provide details of all of the myriad scheduling algorithms that have been described in the literature. Our goal is merely to introduce the basic concepts and principles behind real-time scheduling algorithms, for which we need some definitions (see Table 10.3) if we are to understand the scope and policies involved.

Table 10.3 Scheduling parameters

Definition	Description
CPU utilization	The fraction of the processor's time actually spent in executing the set of tasks (rather than being idle or waiting for I/O)
Throughput	Number of processes completed per unit of time
Turnaround time	Represents the time between the submission (release) of a process and the time of its completion
Waiting time	The period spent waiting in the ready queue
Response time	Time either required or experienced between the submission of a request and production of the first response (to the request)
Fairness	Provision to each task of an equal amount of CPU time
Schedulability	Condition in which a set of tasks can be hosted by the system such that their execution deadlines are met/respected

The goals of a good scheduler are to maximize CPU utilization, throughput and fairness, and to minimize turnaround time, waiting time and response time. Last but not least, a scheduling algorithm should enable a system to meet its design deadlines, that is, to confer "schedulability".

A scheduling algorithm can be described as static or dynamic. In the static scenario, each task is assigned a deadline and a priority, and the scheduler just ensures that the tasks are executed sequentially following the predefined order of priority. However, in the dynamic scenario, the scheduler can reorder the tasks as a function of their priorities and deadlines, acknowledging that events can occur that can necessitate a change to the original order.

10.4.2 Real-time Scheduling Algorithms

Real-time scheduling algorithms can also be static or dynamic in terms of assigning task priority. In order to guarantee the functionality of a system and its ability to meet its real-time constraints, the developer must analyze, a priori, the schedulability of the likely pool of tasks, and identify one or more specific algorithms that can confer schedulability on this pool. To analyze this system schedulability requires solving some first-order mathematical equations, explained in the following sections. For example, some systems may be capable of respecting task deadlines using one particular scheduling algorithm, but not another. Worst-case scenarios have to be modeled and investigated accordingly; for instance, when a task instance is submitted at the same time as all of the other high-priority instances.

10.4.2.1 CPU Utilization Calculation

In the previous subsection, we defined what we meant by CPU utilization (see Table 10.3); now we will see how to calculate it. Starting with a single task T with an execution time C and an execution deadline D, its CPU utilization (U) can be simply expressed as its execution time divided by its execution deadline (assumed to be the same as its period):

$$U = \frac{C}{D}$$

For a set of n tasks, $T_1, T_2, T_3, \ldots T_n$, with execution times $C_1, C_2, C_3, \ldots C_n$, and execution deadlines $D_1, D_2, D_3, \ldots D_n$, the CPU **utilization factor**, U, is defined as the sum of each individual task's CPU utilization:

$$U = \frac{C_1}{D_1} + \frac{C_2}{D_2} + \frac{C_3}{D_3} + \cdots + \frac{C_n}{D_n}$$

For a set of n tasks with fixed priority assignment, the lowest upper bound of this processor utilization factor is defined by the following relation, which is associated with **static-priority** scheduling (and tends to a value of 0.693 as n approaches infinity):

$$U = n \cdot (2^{\frac{1}{n}} - 1)$$

10.4.3 Rate-monotonic Scheduling (RMS)

We start by considering one of the simplest static-priority scheduling algorithms, termed rate-monotonic scheduling or RMS. In this algorithm the priority of a task is assigned as a function of its period (which is the time between repeating instances of a task, such as capturing and processing a sequence of readings from some form of monitor, effectively defining its execution deadline), where a task with a shorter period (i.e. execution deadline) automatically acquires a higher priority.

Using the relation above, we can say that a real-time system will be schedulable using RMS if the following condition is satisfied:

$$\sum U_i \leq n \cdot (2^{\frac{1}{n}} - 1)$$

Furthermore, RMS is also an "**optimal**" scheduling algorithm for static-priority scheduling, meaning that if any static-priority algorithm can confer schedulability on a set of tasks, RMS can.

Thus, if the RMS algorithm cannot satisfy the condition above for the set of tasks that must be processed, we have to conclude that there is no static-priority assignment that can possibly produce a feasible schedule.

Let us, for example, consider the set of tasks in the table below:

Task	Execution Time	Execution Deadline
T1	2	6
T2	1	5
T3	2	12

The CPU utilization factor will be:

$$U_i = \frac{2}{6} + \frac{1}{5} + \frac{2}{12} = 0.33 + 0.20 + 0.17 = 0.70$$

and the upper bound of the utilization factor will be:

$$U = 3 \cdot (2^{\frac{1}{3}} - 1) = 0.78$$

Hence, we can say that this pool of tasks will be schedulable using an RMS algorithm, because 0.70 is less than 0.78. In simple terms, the processor utilization for this set of tasks scheduled using RMS would look like Figure 10.7.

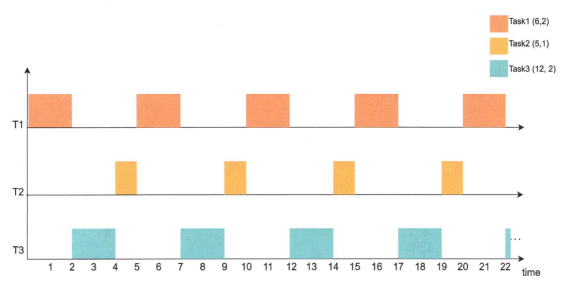

Figure 10.7 Example of static-priority RMS algorithm application

As a further example, let us analyze another set of tasks, as shown below:

Task	Execution Time	Execution Deadline
T1	2	5
T2	4	10
T3	1	8

In this instance, the CPU utilization factor for these three tasks will be:

$$U_i = \frac{2}{5} + \frac{4}{10} + \frac{1}{8} = 0.4 + 0.4 + 0.125 = 0.925$$

and the upper bound of the utilization factor for three tasks will again be:

$$U = 3 \cdot (2^{\frac{1}{3}} - 1) = 0.78$$

Hence, we conclude that this particular set of tasks will NOT be schedulable using an RMS algorithm, because 0.925 is not less than or equal to 0.78, and we must further conclude that there is no static or fixed priority assignment that can produce a feasible schedule for this particular trio of tasks. How can we do better? The only option is to try a dynamic-priority scheduling algorithm instead.

10.4.4 Earliest Deadline First Scheduling

Earliest deadline first (EDF) is a scheduling algorithm in which each task is assigned a priority on a **dynamic** basis, with the task with the most imminent deadline being assigned the highest priority. EDF is also an "optimal" scheduling algorithm for independent tasks on a preemptive single processor, which is to say that if any algorithm can confer schedulability on such tasks, EDF can.

For tasks that have execution deadlines equal to their periods, the utilization bound of 0.78 seen for three tasks in a static-priority regime increases to 1 in all cases under the dynamic-priority EDF regime, representing the upper bound achievable:

$$\sum U_i \leq 1$$

Applying the EDF scheduling algorithm to the example that we failed to successfully schedule with RMS in the previous section again produces a CPU utilization factor of 0.925, but because this is less than 1, we can say that this set of tasks will be schedulable using the dynamic-priority EDF algorithm, as represented in Figure 10.8.

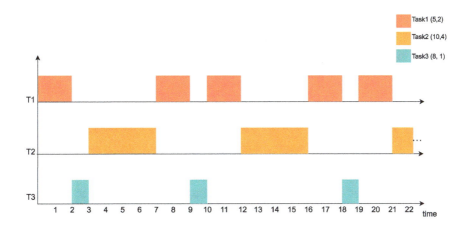

Figure 10.8 Example of dynamic-priority EDF algorithm application

10.4.5 Round-robin Scheduling

The round-robin scheduling algorithm distributes an equal amount of time in turn to each task, sometimes referred to as "time-slicing", as illustrated in Figure 10.9. Recalling one of the scheduling parameters introduced previously (see Table 10.3), round-robin is the scheduling algorithm that maximizes fairness. Hence, if there are *n* tasks, each is assigned 1/*n* of the CPU time. In practice, the timing of the round-robin algorithm is based on interrupts, which determine the swap time of a task, and enforce preemption by definition.

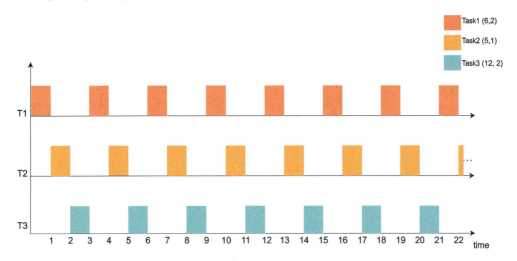

Figure 10.9 Example of round-robin time-slicing algorithm application

Because of its simplicity, round-robin is one of the most widely adopted scheduling algorithms, even though it is not the most efficient from the perspective of CPU utilization. Typically, in a real-time system, a time slice of 1 ms will be applied.

10.4.5.1 Priority Inversion

Priority inversion is a phenomenon that can occur in real-time kernels. It refers to a situation in which a lower priority task inadvertently blocks the dispatch of a higher priority task, inverting the standard priority regime, and typically involves inconsistencies in resource contention between a minimum of three tasks. An example serves to illustrate this best.

Imagine three tasks, identified as H (high priority), M (medium priority), and L (low priority). If L is already running and has a mutex on a specific resource (or critical section) that H also requires, H will be blocked until L releases the resource. However, if M, which does not rely on the same resource, becomes runnable it can be dispatched without any constraints, preempting L and preventing it from releasing the resource required by H, leaving H blocked and effectively displaced from its position in the queue for the processor by M, completely inverting the intended priority regime.

Almost needless to say, although priority inversion is generally to be avoided, there are some scenarios where the phenomenon can be put to profitable use to avoid particular deadlock conditions or other priority-related side effects that might otherwise compromise a system.

10.5 Summary

In this chapter we have seen the basic principles of software for SoCs. We introduced how different programming approaches can affect performance and flexibility, such as bare-metal for single-task memory-constrained applications or multitasking with the support of RTOS for more complex ones. We introduced the benefits and limitations of both approaches. For a more comprehensive understanding of the basic concepts presented here, we suggest the reader consults the software examples provided with this book.

Nevertheless, in this chapter we just scratched the surface of the domain of software for SoCs. Further relevant aspects, such as technical details of software compilation, optimization techniques, debugging, and profiling of a real application for a SoC have not been discussed as they are outside the scope of this chapter. For specific details of these aspects, we direct the reader to advanced books.

The software ecosystem surrounding SoCs is much wider and more powerful than the basic concepts we touched on in this chapter. For example, IDEs and board support packages, along with software libraries, design examples, and efficient compilers, all contribute to the success of a SoC, reducing time to market and development costs. From the perspective of the SoC designer, the software programmer can be seen as a sort of end user. The role of software programmers is fundamental to widespread adoption of the chip. The community of programmers is wider, the variety of use-cases broader, and the available examples more numerous, leading to a generally more efficient use of the SoC. For this reason it is crucial, from the perspective of the SoC vendor, to make the software ecosystem as programmer-friendly, as open, and as accessible to everyone as possible.

APPENDIX

Prerequisites

A1.1 Bases & Arithmetic

When we are talking about numbers, the decimal system is used by most people, with numbers based on decimal digits from 0 to 9, also referred to as "base 10". Combining these digits allows the formation of any integer (whole number).

▨ Base 10 is the one used by humans because we have 10 fingers: it's easier to do calculations with their help!

▨ Any positive number can be represented by a concatenation of digits: $d_n d_{n-1} d_{n-2} \ldots d_1 d_0$

▨ Each term in this concatenation has an implied meaning, thus:

$$d_n d_{n-1} d_{n-2} \ldots d_1 d_0 = (d_n \times 10^n) + (d_{n-1} \times 10^{n-1}) + (d_{n-2} \times 10^{n-2}) + \ldots + (d_1 \times 10^1) + (d_0 \times 10^0)$$

▨ As an example:

$$2017_{base(10)} = (2 \times 10^3) + (0 \times 10^2) + (1 \times 10^1) + (7 \times 10^0)$$
$$= (2 \times 1000) + (0 \times 100) + (1 \times 10) + (7 \times 1)$$

▨ This can be generalized to any base, replacing base(10) with any number. Thus:

$$number_{base} = (d_n \times base^n) + (d_{n-1} \times base^{n-1}) + (d_{n-2} \times base^{n-2}) + \ldots + (d_1 \times base^1) + (d_0 \times base^0)$$

where $d_i \in [0, \ldots, (base-1)]$.

☐ Base = 2	(binary)	→	$d_i \in [0, 1]$
☐ Base = 8	(octal)	→	$d_i \in [0, 1, 2, 3, 4, 5, 6, 7]$
☐ Base = 10	(decimal)	→	$d_i \in [0, 1, 2, 3, 4, 5, 6, 7, 8, 9]$
☐ Base = 16	(hexadecimal)	→	$d_i \in [0, 1, 2, 3, 4, 5, 6, 7, 8, 9, A, B, C, D, E, F]$

A1.1.1 Binary

In the binary system, only two digits are used (0 and 1) and are termed **bits** (short for **bi**nary digi**t**). Applying the principle described above:

$$b_7 b_6 b_5 b_4 b_3 b_2 b_1 b_0 \rightarrow (b_7 \times 2^7) + (b_6 \times 2^6) + (b_5 \times 2^5) + (b_4 \times 2^4) + (b_3 \times 2^3) + (b_2 \times 2^2) + (b_1 \times 2^1) + (b_0 \times 2^0)$$

Thus, to convert a specific binary number to its decimal equivalent:

$$1\ 1\ 0\ 0\ 1\ 0\ 0\ 1 \rightarrow (1 \times 2^7) + (1 \times 2^6) + (0 \times 2^5) + (0 \times 2^4) + (1 \times 2^3) + (0 \times 2^2) + (0 \times 2^1) + (1 \times 2^0)$$
$$b_7 b_6 b_5 b_4 b_3 b_2 b_1 b_0 \rightarrow 128\ +\ 64\ +\ 0\ +\ 0\ +\ 8\ +\ 0\ +\ 0\ +\ 1$$
$$\rightarrow 201$$

A1.1.2   Hexadecimal

In the hexadecimal, base(16) system, the digits run from 0 to 9 followed by the letters A to F to provide 16 distinct digits. Thus to convert a specific "hex" number to its decimal equivalent:

$$h_1\,h_0 \;\rightarrow\; C9_{hex} \;\rightarrow\; (C_{hex} \times 16^1) + (9_{hex} \times 16^0) \;\rightarrow\; (12 \times 16) + (9 \times 1) \;\rightarrow\; 192 + 9 \;\rightarrow\; 201$$

Conversions between these three dominant base systems (decimal, binary and hexadecimal) are illustrated in Table A1.

Table A1 Base conversion for 4-bit numbers

Decimal	Binary	Transformation Binary → Decimal	Hexadecimal
0	0000	0 + 0 + 0 + 0	0
1	0001	0 + 0 + 0 + 1	1
2	0010	0 + 0 + 2 + 0	2
3	0011	0 + 0 + 2 + 1	3
4	0100	0 + 4 + 0 + 0	4
5	0101	0 + 4 + 0 + 1	5
6	0110	0 + 4 + 2 + 0	6
7	0111	0 + 4 + 2 + 1	7
8	1000	8 + 0 + 0 + 0	8
9	1001	8 + 0 + 0 + 1	9
10	1010	8 + 0 + 2 + 0	A
11	1011	8 + 0 + 2 + 1	B
12	1100	8 + 4 + 0 + 0	C
13	1101	8 + 4 + 0 + 1	D
14	1110	8 + 4 + 2 + 0	E
15	1111	8 + 4 + 2 + 1	F

A1.1.3   Binary-coded Decimal

Binary-coded decimal (BCD) is a way to represent a decimal number simply by grouping together the four-bit binary translations for each of the decimal digits and concatenating them, for example:

$$2017 = 0010\ 0000\ 0001\ 0111\ (BCD)$$

BCD was heavily used in early computing, and remains in frequent use for simple displays (e.g. in portable calculators or electricity meters) where it is simpler to populate each segment of a seven-segment display if the digits are encoded in BCD form than to manipulate a pure binary representation to populate the segments with an appropriate decimal digit.

A1.1.4   Unsigned/Signed Numbers

Inside a computer, by which we really mean in its registers and in memory, all values are stored and manipulated in binary form, with only '0' and '1' values, assembled together into groups of 8, 16, 32 or more bits. It is the responsibility of the program to manipulate those bits and assign meaning to them. Performing operations on the contents of registers may or may not activate various "flags", most commonly Negate, Zero, oVerflow or Carry. It is when the program code executes a test of these flags that the full meaning of the data comes into effect.

If "unsigned" numbers are manipulated, then all of the bits available are used to represent a **positive** value. If we are using binary values of 8 bits, then the value can range from $0000\ 0000_2$ to $1111\ 1111_2$ → 00_{16} to FF_{16} → 0_{10} to 255_{10}.

Many different computer architectures have been developed over the years, with many different ways of manipulating numbers arising as a consequence. We will look at four different ways of representing "signed" numbers below.

A1.1.4.1   Sign and Magnitude

We humans generally represent "signed" numbers with a minus (−) sign before a number if it is negative, and a + sign or nothing at all before a number if it is positive (we will ignore the convention sometimes used in which a negative number is represented by enclosing it in parentheses such that "(1234)" is the equivalent of −1234).

We can adopt a similar approach in a computer by using the most significant bit (MSb) of the data to represent this sign, such that a '1' in this position indicates a negative value for the subsequent "absolute" bits, and a '0' in the MSb position indicates a positive value. Thus, in an 8-bit representation:

- **0**000 0000 to **0**111 1111 → 0_{10} to 127_{10}

- **1**000 0000 to **1**111 1111 → -0_{10} to -127_{10} .

This is referred to as the **sign and magnitude** (or sign and absolute value) representation. It is relatively easy for a human to comprehend such numbers, but less easy for a computer to manage them. For example, in this system, there are two different representations of zero, a positive value and a negative one (referred to as "signed zero"). Some functions have a discontinuity at zero, and having negative and positive signed zeros can produce unexpected results from some operations if adjustments are not made accordingly. In contrast, it is very easy to flip from a positive to a negative number and back: just change the MSb.

A1.1.4.2   Ones' Complement

Another way to represent a negative number is to take its positive version, in which the MSb is always '0', and to invert every single bit of the number, producing its "ones' complement".

Again, the MSb of any negative number will always be a '1'. Thus, in an 8-bit ones' complement representation:

■ 0000 0000 to 0111 1111 → 0_{10} to 127_{10}

■ 1111 1111 to 1000 0000 → -0_{10} to -127_{10}.

Again, as with the previous representation – sign and magnitude – there are two representations of the number zero and so, again, when operations traverse the boundary between positive and negative, adjustments can be required; for example, equivalence to zero requires two comparisons rather than just one. A few computers have been implemented using this number representation for arithmetic operations.

A1.1.4.3 Two's Complement

Complements are used in computing as a means of ensuring that an arithmetic addition operation will work consistently whether an integer value is positive or negative. However, we have seen that a ones' complement operation throws up an issue in terms of two signed zeros. A two's complement operation is able to address this: in simple terms, we effectively say that the binary 1111 1111 no longer means −0 (negative zero) but represents −1. Thus, to represent the negative of a positive number, we can simply take its ones' complement and add 1. To represent the positive equivalent of a negative number, we can do the same.

In mathematical terms, the two's complement of an n-bit number is its complement in relation to 2^n. Thus, for a 3-bit number, 101, its two's complement is 8 (i.e. 2^3) minus 101, which is 011. If we invert the bits (101 → 010) and add 1, we get the same result (011).

Two's complement is the representation used for signed numbers in most modern computer systems.

A1.1.4.4 Offset Binary

Offset binary (also known as biased representation) is a system designed such that the lowest negative value will be represented by all bits being set to 0, and the highest positive value by all bits being set to 1. In order to achieve this, an offset (or bias) needs to be applied to the counting scheme, the typical value being 2^{n-1} for a scheme of n bits. The middle value of the range will represent 0_{10} and will take a form in which all bits are set to 0 except the MSb, which will be set to 1. Thus, for 8-bit numbers, using an offset of 128 (2^7):

■ 1111 1111 → $+127_{10}$

■ 1000 0000 → 0_{10}

■ 0000 0000 → -128_{10}

On this basis, offset binary can be converted to two's complement simply by inverting the MSb.

A1.1.4.5 Other Representations

Clearly, any base can be used in theory to represent a set of integers. An alternative binary representation makes use of −2 instead of +2 as a base, throwing up an asymmetric range of positive and negative number representations depending on whether an even or odd number of bits is used. It represents more of an intellectual exercise than a system that is actually implemented in practical terms.

A1.1.5 Review of Binary Representation

Table A2 captures comparative representations of the application of the foregoing schemes.

Table A2 Number representations in 8 bits

Decimal	BCD A	Unsigned	Sign/Mag	Ones' Comp	Two's Comp	Offset (+128)
+256	N/A	N/A	N/A	N/A	N/A	N/A
+255	N/A	1111 1111	N/A	N/A	N/A	N/A
+254	N/A	1111 1110	N/A	N/A	N/A	N/A
...						
+128	N/A	1000 0000	N/A	N/A	N/A	N/A
+127	N/A	0111 1111	0111 1111	0111 1111	0111 1111	1111 1111
...						
+99	1001 1001	0110 0011	0110 0011	0110 0011	0110 0011	1110 0011
+98	1001 1000	0110 0010	0110 0010	0110 0010	0110 0010	1110 0010
...						
+1	0000 0001	0000 0001	0000 0001	0000 0001	0000 0001	1000 0001
+0	0000 0000	0000 0000	0000 0000	0000 0000	0000 0000	1000 0000
−0	N/A	N/A	1000 0000	1111 1111		
−1	N/A	N/A	1000 0001	1111 1110	1111 1111	0111 1111
−2	N/A	N/A	1000 0010	1111 1101	1111 1110	0111 1110
...						
−126	N/A	N/A	1111 1110	1000 0001	1000 0010	0000 0010
−127	N/A	N/A	1111 1111	1000 0000	1000 0001	0000 0001
−128	N/A	N/A	N/A	N/A	1000 0000	0000 0000
...						
−255	N/A	N/A	N/A	N/A	N/A	N/A

A1.1.6 Gray Code

Counters (for example, in timers) are fundamental to most computer systems. With a standard binary code, including any of those discussed above, more than one bit will change in the representation as we increment a counter. For example, in going from 3_{10} to 4_{10}, three bits have to be changed ("011" to "100"). In computing terms, this can represent a significant overhead: if these bits are individually switched, three switches have to change position to reflect an increment of one, incurring not just a power consumption penalty but also running the risk of the switch change not being simultaneous and an intermediate switch configuration being decoded by mistake. To address this, in 1947, Frank Gray issued a patent for a device that used a "reflected binary code" for non-negative integers that involved just one change in the binary coding as the decimal number it represented was incremented. This system subsequently became known as Gray code, and there are now numerous variations of it.

The logical function to convert from binary code to simple Gray code, for values of n from 0 to that of the MSb−1, is:

$$b(n+1) \text{ XOR } b(n) \rightarrow g(n)$$

For the final MSb bit, there are two functions that can be used:

$$b(MSb) \rightarrow g(MSb) \quad \text{or} \quad b(MSb) \text{ XOR '0'} \rightarrow g(MSb)'$$

To convert from Gray code to binary code, the logical function is:

$$b(n) \leftarrow g(MSb) \text{ XOR } \dots g(n+1) \text{ XOR } g(n)$$

or, starting the conversion from the MSb:

$$b(n) \leftarrow b(n+1) \text{ XOR } g(n)$$

Tables A3 and A4 illustrate these respective conversions, and show the decimal and hexadecimal equivalents. Figure A1 demonstrates that an 8-bit Gray-based counter involves far less "switching" (change in the eight digit positions) than a binary-based one.

Table A3 Binary to Gray conversion

binary				Gray				binary dec	binary hex
b3	b2	b1	b0	g3	g2	g1	g0		
0	0	0	0	0	0	0	0	0	0
0	0	0	1	0	0	0	1	1	1
0	0	1	0	0	0	1	1	2	2
0	0	1	1	0	0	1	0	3	3
0	1	0	0	0	1	1	0	4	4
0	1	0	1	0	1	1	1	5	5
0	1	1	0	0	1	0	1	6	6
0	1	1	1	0	1	0	0	7	7
1	0	0	0	1	1	0	0	8	8
1	0	0	1	1	1	0	1	9	9
1	0	1	0	1	1	1	1	10	A
1	0	1	1	1	1	1	0	11	B
1	1	0	0	1	0	1	0	12	C
1	1	0	1	1	0	1	1	13	D
1	1	1	0	1	0	0	1	14	E
1	1	1	1	1	0	0	0	15	F

B1 XOR b0 ──────────────────┘

B2 XOR b1 ─────────────────┘

B3 XOR b2 ───────────────┘

'0'   XOR b3 ────────────┘

Table A4 Gray to binary conversion

binary					Gray				binary dec	binary hex
b3	b2	b1	b0		g3	g2	g1	g0		
0	0	0	0		0	0	0	0	0	0
0	0	0	1		0	0	0	1	1	1
0	0	1	0		0	0	1	1	2	2
0	0	1	1		0	0	1	0	3	3
0	1	0	0		0	1	1	0	4	4
0	1	0	1		0	1	1	1	5	5
0	1	1	0		0	1	0	1	6	6
0	1	1	1		0	1	0	0	7	7
1	0	0	0		1	1	0	0	8	8
1	0	0	1		1	1	0	1	9	9
1	0	1	0		1	1	1	1	10	A
1	0	1	1		1	1	1	0	11	B
1	1	0	0		1	0	1	0	12	C
1	1	0	1		1	0	1	1	13	D
1	1	1	0		1	0	0	1	14	E
1	1	1	1		1	0	0	0	15	F
			▲	XOR	⊥	⊥	⊥	⊥		
		▲		XOR	⊥	⊥	⊥			
	▲			XOR	⊥	⊥				
▲				XOR	⊥					

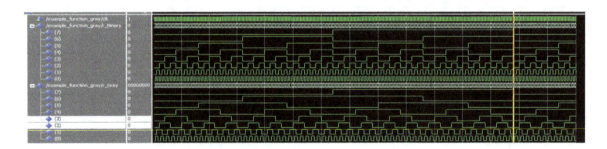

Figure A1 Comparison of counter simulations for binary (top) and Gray (bottom) systems

A1.1.7 ASCII Codes

The American Standard Code for Information Interchange (ASCII) code was introduced in 1963 to allow the coding of characters in a binary form of 7 or 8 bits (see Table A5). The first 32 characters provided control characters for telecommunication protocols and the formatting of data on a screen or printer. There have since been many updates and expansions; for example, an 8-bit encoding to capture the accented characters (diacritics) used in many European languages (ISO 8859, ISO 8859-1 and ISO Latin 1). In the mid-1980s, Microsoft created a superset of ISO 8859-1, known as CP-1252 (code page 1252), which has since become the most widely used single-byte encoding system.

Table A5 ASCII coding in 7 bits

Hex	Code	Hex	Code	Hex	Code	Hex	Code	Hex	Code	Hex	Code	Hex	Code	Hex	Code
00	NUL	10	DLE	20		30	0	40	@	50	P	60	`	70	p
01	SOH	11	DC1	21	!	31	1	41	A	51	Q	61	a	71	q
02	STX	12	DC2	22	"	32	2	42	B	52	R	62	b	72	r
03	ETX	13	DC3	23	#	33	3	43	C	53	S	63	c	73	s
04	EOT	14	DC4	24	$	34	4	44	D	54	T	64	d	74	t
05	ENQ	15	NAK	25	%	35	5	45	E	55	U	65	e	75	u
06	ACK	16	SYN	26	&	36	6	46	F	56	V	66	f	76	v
07	BEL	17	ETB	27	'	37	7	47	G	57	W	67	g	77	w
08	BS	18	CAN	28	(	38	8	48	H	58	X	68	h	78	x
09	HT	19	EM	29	)	39	9	49	I	59	Y	69	i	79	y
0A	LF	1A	SUB	2A	*	3A	:	4A	J	5A	Z	6A	j	7A	z
0B	VT	1B	ESC	2B	+	3B	;	4B	K	5B	[	6B	k	7B	{
0C	FF	1C	FS	2C	,	3C	<	4C	L	5C	\	6C	l	7C		
0D	CR	1D	GS	2D	–	3D	=	4D	M	5D	]	6D	m	7D	}
0E	SO	1E	RS	2E	.	3E	>	4E	N	5E	^	6E	n	7E	~
0F	SI	1F	US	2F	/	3F	?	4F	O	5F	_	6F	o	7F	DEL

- Control code
- Character code, printable
- Character code, printable, number
- Character code, printable, letter

A1.1.8   Base64 Encoding

Some telecommunication systems are designed around the transfer of textual content and do not readily support communication of binary-encoded material; the World Wide Web and SMTP email attachments are prime examples. It then becomes necessary to encode the binary material in a textual form.

Base64 encoding achieves this by first grouping three 8-bit bytes into a 24-bit number, which is then sliced into four 6-bit words (2^6 = 64), each of which can be represented by a single ASCII character (see Figure A2 and Table A6). To support its use on the Internet, the associated RFC 4648 standard replaces the + and / characters with – (minus/hyphen) and _ (underline) to generate a URL-specific form of Base64 (as shown in Table A6).

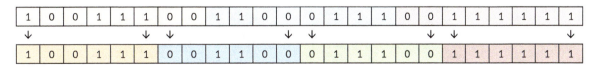

Figure A2 Bit correspondence in Base64 transformation of three 8-bit bytes to four 6-bit characters

Table A6 Base64 encoding of 6-bit binary to ASCII character

6-bit binary						Base64 ASCII	Base64url ASCII	Hex
0	0	0	0	0	0	A		41
0	0	0	0	0	1	B		42
0	0	0	0	1	0	C		43
0	0	0	0	1	1	D		44
0	0	0	1	0	0	E		45
0	0	0	1	0	1	F		46
0	0	0	1	1	0	G		47
0	0	0	1	1	1	H		48
0	0	1	0	0	0	I		49
0	0	1	0	0	1	J		4A
0	0	1	0	1	0	K		4B
0	0	1	0	1	1	L		4C
0	0	1	1	0	0	M		4D
0	0	1	1	0	1	N		4E
0	0	1	1	1	0	O		4F
0	0	1	1	1	1	P		50
0	1	0	0	0	0	Q		51
0	1	0	0	0	1	R		52
0	1	0	0	1	0	S		53
0	1	0	0	1	1	T		54
0	1	0	1	0	0	U		55
0	1	0	1	0	1	V		56
0	1	0	1	1	0	W		57
0	1	0	1	1	1	X		58
0	1	1	0	0	0	Y		59
0	1	1	0	0	1	Z		5A
0	1	1	0	1	0	a		61
0	1	1	0	1	1	b		62
0	1	1	1	0	0	c		63
0	1	1	1	0	1	d		64
0	1	1	1	1	0	e		65
0	1	1	1	1	1	f		66
1	0	0	0	0	0	g		67
1	0	0	0	0	1	h		68
1	0	0	0	1	0	i		69
1	0	0	0	1	1	j		6A

6-bit binary						Base64 ASCII	Base64url ASCII	Hex
1	0	0	1	0	0	k		6B
1	0	0	1	0	1	l		6C
1	0	0	1	1	0	m		6D
1	0	0	1	1	1	n		6E
1	0	1	0	0	0	o		6F
1	0	1	0	0	1	p		70
1	0	1	0	1	0	q		71
1	0	1	0	1	1	r		72
1	0	1	1	0	0	s		73
1	0	1	1	0	1	t		74
1	0	1	1	1	0	u		75
1	0	1	1	1	1	v		76
1	1	0	0	0	0	w		77
1	1	0	0	0	1	x		78
1	1	0	0	1	0	y		79
1	1	0	0	1	1	z		7A
1	1	0	1	0	0	0		30
1	1	0	1	0	1	1		31
1	1	0	1	1	0	2		32
1	1	0	1	1	1	3		33
1	1	1	0	0	0	4		34
1	1	1	0	0	1	5		35
1	1	1	0	1	0	6		36
1	1	1	0	1	1	7		37
1	1	1	1	0	0	8		38
1	1	1	1	0	1	9		39
1	1	1	1	1	0	+	-	2B / 2D
1	1	1	1	1	1	/	_	2F / 5F

A1.1.9 Fixed-point Numbers

When it is necessary to represent a real number rather than a simple integer, the simplest convention is to adopt a format in which the position of the radix point (akin to a decimal point) is deemed to be fixed. The most prevalent way to describe this uses the Q notation for signed fixed-point numbers, where Q$m.f$ represents a signed number with m integer (or magnitude) bits and f fractional bits, plus 1 bit for the sign, if the full number is in two's complement. For example, Q7.8 has 1 sign-bit + 7 bits for the mantissa and 8 bits for the fractional part on a 16-bit number.

UQ is used to indicate an unsigned number in Q format..

An alternative notation uses the form **fxm.b** to specify m integer/magnitude bits and b as the word length or total number of bits; thus, the number of fractional bits is $(b - m)$.

A1.1.10 Floating-point Numbers

The obvious alternative to the fixed-point representation of a real number is one in which the radix point can move around; hence floating-point numbers. In general terms, a floating-point number resembles the format typically found in scientific notation, involving a significand (or mantissa), a base and an exponent, for example:

$$1.2345 \times 10^{-4}$$

where 1.2345 is the significand, 10 is the base and −4 is the exponent.

The binary representation of floating-point numbers used in computers was defined by the IEEE in 1985 in the IEEE 754 standard. The value of the base is taken as implicit and the internal representation consists of a sign bit, a number of exponent bits, and a number of significand bits, which vary depending on the "precision" involved. When stored in binary format, a "normalizing" offset or bias is applied to the exponent portion of the representation such that it is stored in an unsigned format. Further, in these circumstances, the leading '1' bit of a significand is not actually stored and is referred to as the "implicit" or "hidden" bit, affording an additional bit's worth of precision, as illustrated in Table A7, which summarizes the two most commonly implemented IEEE 754 floating-point precision formats.

Table A7 *IEEE 754 binary floating-point precision formats*

IEEE 754 precision	Sign bit(s)	Exponent bits	Significand bits	Total bits	Exponent offset	Binary precision (bits)	Decimal precision (no. of digits)
Single	1	8	23	32	127	24	~7.2
Double	1	11	52	64	1023	53	~15.9

A1.1.11 Word Size

Binary notation is used in computers because it is easily represented in the hardware components from which computers are constructed; thus, current or no current, two-level voltages, charged or uncharged, switches on or off, lights on or off, and so on.

To represent more "normal" number forms, bits are assembled in groups to form **bytes** and **words**, and the size of these has varied and grown in accordance with the evolution of computer hardware. The modern de facto standard of an 8-bit byte dates from an ISO standard of 1993. By contrast, word lengths are determined by the size of the unit of data that a given computer routinely handles within its instruction set, with word lengths of 16, 32 or 64 bits being most prevalent today. This variation means that we must be careful to check the precise frame of reference when discussing word-related sizes (and bytes when much older systems are involved). Table A8 captures some common naming conventions.

Table A8 Common word size naming conventions

No. of bits	Name	16-bit word system	32-bit word system
4	Nibble		
8	Byte	Byte	Byte
16	Doublet	Word	Half-word
32	Quadlet	Double Word (or Long Word)	Word
64	Octlet	Quad Word (or Long Long Word)	Double Word
128	Octoword	Octo Word	Quad Word

A1.1.12 Multiple-byte Units

Over the years, much confusion has arisen around the precise meaning of the term "kilobyte". Under the longstanding International System of Units (SI) convention, the prefix "kilo-" refers to one thousand (10^3). However, within the binary world of computing, particularly with reference to memory, the use of "kilobyte" was adopted as a convenient shorthand for 2^{10} bytes, which is, of course, 1024 bytes, rather than 1000 bytes. Clearly, the two are not equivalent.

In an attempt to eliminate this confusion and provide a more precise definition of large binary numbers, in 1998 the IEC devised a naming scheme for the latter and the two schemes are laid out together for comparison in Table A9.

Table A9   Prefixes for units of bytes

	Binary			Decimal			
IEC prefix	Power of 2 (2^{power})	Power of 1024 (1024^{power})	IEC unit	SI prefix	Power of 10 (10^{power})	Power of 1000 (1000^{power})	SI unit
	2^0	1024^0	B		10^0	1000^0	B
kibi	2^{10}	1024^1	KiB	kilo	10^3	1000^1	kB
mebi	2^{20}	1024^2	MiB	mega	10^6	1000^2	MB
gibi	2^{30}	1024^3	GiB	giga	10^9	1000^3	GB
tebi	2^{40}	1024^4	TiB	tera	10^{12}	1000^4	TB
pebi	2^{50}	1024^5	PiB	peta	10^{15}	1000^5	PB
exbi	2^{60}	1024^6	EiB	exa	10^{18}	1000^6	EB
zebi	2^{70}	1024^7	ZiB	zetta	10^{21}	1000^7	ZB
yobi	2^{80}	1024^8	YiB	yotta	10^{24}	1000^8	YB

Adapted from: en.wikipedia.org/wiki/Pebibyte

The tebibyte (TiB), along with the gibibyte (GiB), mebibyte (MiB), and kibibyte (KiB), are the standard units currently of most relevance in the fields of data processing and transmission.

As can be seen from Table A9, the two sets of prefixes and units are quite similar, which means that they are quite often treated, and not always intentionally, as synonyms for each other; for example, 1 tebibyte is 2^{40} or 1,099,511,627,776 bytes, while 1 terabyte is 10^{12} or 1,000,000,000,000 bytes, representing a difference of almost 10 percent, which is significant. Table A10 captures some similar comparisons.

Table A10 IEC/SI comparisons

Name	Unit	No. of bytes	
One mebibyte	1 MiB	2^{20}	1,048,576
One megabyte	1 MB	10^6	1,000,000
One gibibyte	1 GiB	2^{30}	1,073,741,824
One gigabyte	1 GB	10^9	1,000,000,000
One tebibyte	1 TiB	2^{40}	1,099,511,627,776
One terabyte	1 TB	10^{12}	1,000,000,000,000

For commercial purposes, most vendors still use the decimal form of naming, but this often means that if you connect a new "5.0 TB (terabyte)" hard drive to your computer, the OS may inform you that the drive's capacity is "4.547 TB", by which it really means 4.547 TiB (tebibytes).

A1.2 IC Digital Signals

A1.2.1 Logic Levels

In the digital world, we are generally concerned with two-level logic, in which signals are interpreted as either a binary '0' or a binary '1'.

But how are these '0' and '1' interpretations determined? In practice, it all depends on the specific physical system in use. Most digital systems employ "positive logic" and define a logic level of '0' (or Low) as a voltage of around 0 V, and a logic level of '1' (or High) as a higher voltage, most obviously that associated with the power supply to the system, commonly referred to as V_{CC} (where CC refers to common collector, or the positive-voltage power rail to which the collector pin of each transistor in a circuit was connected).

For many years, V_{CC} was standardized for TTL circuits at +5 V, but as IC power consumption has been driven down through far more efficient CMOS technology, then so too has the value of V_{CC} (remember $P = V^2/R$), first to 3.6 V, and then progressively lower to just 0.8 V or even less inside some ICs.

Thus, on a board it is quite common to have two, three or even more different values of V_{CC} in use; for example, 3.3 V for I/O and 1.8 V for the internal logic of a microprocessor or an FPGA. Sometimes, level-adapters or level-shifters are required to adapt incompatible voltage levels accordingly.

Even though we are talking about logical levels, in reality we are dealing with analog voltage signals and, in any digital integrated circuit, four voltage levels are defined in recognition of the inherent variation in such signals:

- V_{IH} High-level input voltage, representing the minimum input voltage associated with a logical '1'

- V_{IL} Low-level input voltage, representing the maximum input voltage associated with a logical '0'

▧ V_{OH} High-level output voltage, representing the minimum output voltage associated with a logical '1'

▧ V_{OL} Low-level output voltage, representing the maximum output voltage associated with a logical '0'.

Some ICs, such as the Texas Instruments SN74LV1T126, can be used for level adaptation ("voltage translation") between different technologies, as illustrated in Figure A3; this particular device supports four different TTL/CMOS voltage levels, and also provides an illustration of the four I/O voltage levels defined above.

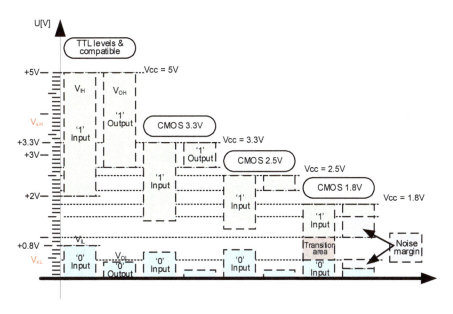

Figure A3 Logic voltage levels (SN74LV1T126 from Texas Instruments)

Almost every FPGA or CPLD can handle different I/O technologies and is well adapted for inter-technology compatibility. Figures A4 and A5 provide examples of ICs specifically designed for the purpose.

▧ DIR = '0'   A ← B

▧ DIR = '1'   A → B

▧ V_{CCA} Voltage for the A side, including DIR level

▧ V_{CCB} Voltage for the B side

▧ for adaptation of standard power voltages of 1.8, 2.5, 3.3 & 5.0V

▧ can be any voltage from 1.65 V to 5.5 V

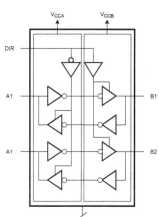

Figure A4 A two-bit buffer with voltage-level adaptation

■ up translation:

☐ 1.2 V to 1.8 V @ V_{CC} = 1.8 V

☐ 1.5 V to 2.5 V @ V_{CC} = 2.5 V

☐ 1.8 V to 3.3 V @ V_{CC} = 3.3 V

☐ 3.3 V to 5.0 V @ V_{CC} = 5.0 V

■ down translation:

☐ 3.3 V to 1.8 V @ V_{CC} = 1.8 V

☐ 3.3 V to 2.5 V @ V_{CC} = 2.5 V

☐ 5.0 V to 3.3 V @ V_{CC} = 3.3 V

■ 5 V tolerant inputs.

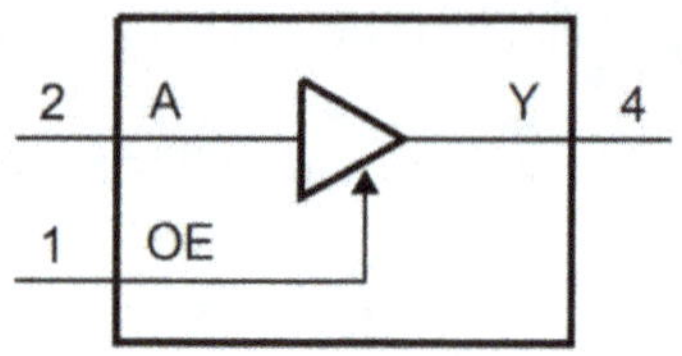

Figure A5 SN74LV1T126: single signal-level adaptor and buffer with Output Enable (source: 74LV1T126 Single supply translating buffer/line driver; 3-stateRev. 2 – 3 December 2019 https://assets.nexperia.com/documents/data-sheet/74LV1T126.pdf © Nexperia B.V. 2019. Reproduced with permission. All rights reserved. For more information, please visit: http://www.nexperia.com)

Some voltage translators are specialized for particular buses:

■ The bidirectional IP4856CX25, from Nexperia, used for SD/MMC card readers

■ The bidirectional PCA9306, used for I²C interfaces.

A1.2.2   CMOS Transistors

The most basic element in electronics, providing the basis for all digital and analog circuits, is the transistor. In simple terms, a transistor consists of four electrical terminals with a semiconducting material between them. The application of a small voltage across the semiconductor between one pair of terminals changes its conductivity and effectively allows a current to flow through it between the other pair of terminals, typically producing a higher voltage than that used for the input. In this way, the transistor can function either as a switch that is normally in the off or open position until a voltage is applied, or it can function as an amplifier, producing a larger output voltage than that input. For the purposes of this book, it is the transistor's switching function that is of interest.

Many forms of transistor have been developed since its invention in the 1940s. However, transistors can be divided into two basic types, bipolar and unipolar transistors, depending upon whether they make use of two charge carriers to generate their semiconductor-based effect, or just one charge carrier. The charge carriers involved are either electrons or "electron holes" (often referred to just as "holes"). Electron holes exist in an atomic (semiconductor) lattice that is lacking electrons in positions within the atoms therein where electrons could normally be expected to exist. Whereas electrons bear a negative electrical charge, the absence of an electron confers a positive charge on an electron hole. (The concept of a "hole" having charge and moving around may seem strange, but a fuller explanation would take us into the realms of nuclear physics and/or quantum chemistry and is beyond the scope of this book.)

Unipolar transistors, which are more commonly referred to as field-effect transistors (FETs), are nowadays based on a three-layer metal–oxide–semiconductor (MOS) structure, although the metal component has largely been superseded by a polycrystalline form of silicon for ease of manufacture. MOS-based transistors that use electrons as charge carriers are referred to as using negative-type MOS (nMOS) technology, and those that use holes as using positive-type MOS (pMOS) technology. Bipolar transistors, which use both forms of charge carrier, can be configured as either PNP or NPN types.

The voltage behaviors of pMOS and nMOS transistors effectively mirror one another: a high positive voltage will cause an nMOSFET to conduct and a pMOSFET not to conduct, while a high negative voltage reverses this. Pairing them together in a symmetrical, complementary manufacturing process (hence complementary MOS or CMOS) leads to a dramatic reduction in power consumption (~7 times lower than nMOS-based logic circuits and 100,000 times lower than bipolar TTL circuits). Unsurprisingly, CMOS is now the dominant form of transistor technology and our primary focus here.

A variety of techniques (e.g. planar, FinFET, silicon-on-insulator or SOI) have been developed to optimize and miniaturize CMOS transistors, and there are plenty of microelectronics textbooks that describe these in great detail. For our simplified, high-level view, the necessary information is outlined below.

Although we have described a transistor as involving two pairs of electrical terminals, most representations dispense with the body, or base, terminal (on the substrate, "opposite" the gate terminal) and concentrate on the other three terminals:

■ **Source** or S terminal, where the incoming signal is provided: typically, V_{cc} for a pMOS, Gnd for a nMOS (in simplified terms)

■ **Drain** or D terminal, where the outgoing signal is detected when the transistor is activated

■ **Gate** or G terminal, where the signal to control the transistor is applied.

The **Body** (or Base or sometimes Bulk) or B terminal is often connected to the Source terminal in discrete components, while in integrated circuits a common "bulk" connection is used for all transistors to ensure that the voltages of their gates relative to the body (substrate) can be controlled.

Figure A6 presents five types of symbolic representation of pMOS and nMOS transistors.

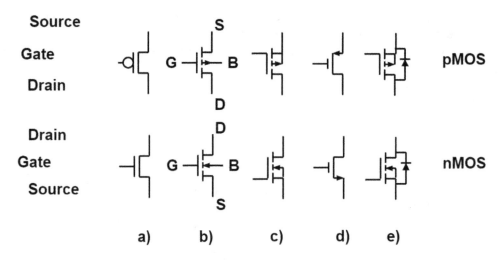

Figure A6 Symbolic representations of pMOS (top) and nMOS (bottom) transistors

Considering each representation in turn:

a) This view represents the simplified symbols for logical use. The circle on the pMOS gate indicates that it is activated by a logic level '0'; the lack of a circle on the nMOS gate reflects its activation by a logic level '1'.

b) This view represents a full depiction of the two transistors; each representation is completely symmetrical and the Drain and Source terminals could be interchanged, although would not be available in this form as a discrete component. The Body/Bulk connection is made to the back of the conductive channel (between D and S); the arrowhead, which always points from positive to negative, will point in to this channel in an nMOS transistor, and out from the channel in a pMOS transistor.

c) This view depicts the usual connection, already mentioned, of the Body to the Source terminal (meaning that, unlike the depiction in b), the transistor is now asymmetric, and D and S terminals cannot be interchanged if this representation is used). Note that the gate has an L-shape, with its (horizontal) input leg being closer to whichever is the Source terminal, appearing at the top in the pMOS representation, and at the bottom in the nMOS representation.

d) This view is a simplified version of that in c), dispensing with an explicit indication of the Body connection. In these representations, the arrowhead indicates the direction of the current (again, from positive to negative) in the Source connection.

e) This view is a full representation of the transistors with an internal diode, making it explicit that if the transistor is incorrectly connected (i.e. S and D are reversed) a short circuit will occur through the diode. The direction of the arrowhead on the Body-to-Source connection and the orientation of the L-shaped gate representation are, as in c), important in differentiating the transistor type (nMOS or pMOS).

Figure A7 uses the representation from Figure A6 a) to show the cases of switch control logic for pMOS and nMOS transistors: applying a logical '0' at the gate turns a pMOS switch On (closes it) and an nMOS switch Off (opens it), and vice versa for the application of a logical '1'.

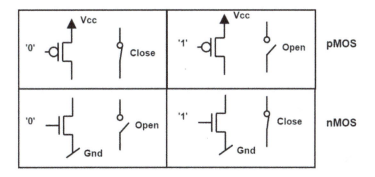

Figure A7 pMOS and nMOS transistors in On/Off switch model

This simplified view of pMOS and nMOS transistors should give us a better understanding of the operation of more complex transistor-based circuits. We'll start by looking at the output of one of the most basic integrated circuits in the digital world.

A1.2.3   Push–Pull Output (Digital)

The output from bipolar or CMOS technologies is based on transistors passing a logic level '1' or '0' to the external world of an integrated circuit.

Figure A8 represents the most basic logical gate, the logic NOT gate, sometimes called an inverting buffer or just an inverter. The logical symbol for this gate is in the middle of the figure and its basic behavior is illustrated on the right-hand side: inputting a logical '0' results in the output of a logical '1'; inputting a logical '1' results in the output of a logical '0'. The left-hand side of the figure shows how this logic element can be realized with two CMOS transistors; the upper transistor (T_{pMOS}) is a pMOS, and the lower transistor (T_{nMOS}) is an nMOS.

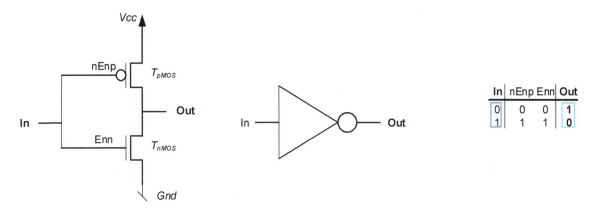

Figure A8 CMOS inverter, push–pull output

To understand how these two transistors work together to realize this logical function, we need to study them in more detail. Figure A9 shows a cross-sectional view of the two transistors as they are entrenched in a global p-type silicon substrate, as required by an nMOS transistor. Because a pMOS transistor requires an n-type substrate to function, an n-type well is created in the global substrate to accommodate this.

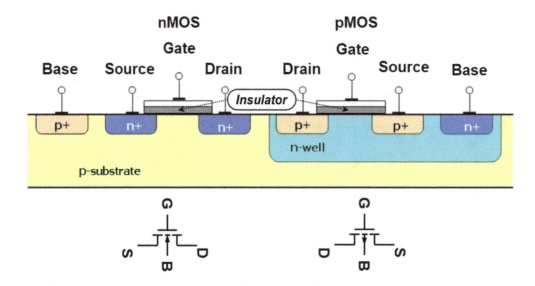

Figure A9 Cross-sectional view of CMOS (from Wikipedia)

The p-type substrate is created by introducing electron-depleted or electron-accepting impurities (such as boron) into the silicon semiconductor (a process known as doping) to increase the proportion of positively charged electron holes in it. By contrast, an n-well is created by doping the semiconductor with an electron-rich or electron-donating impurity such as phosphorus to ensure that it is rich in negatively charged electrons. Base terminal connections are created in the substrates of both transistors by doping them even more heavily (as indicated by the + symbol; it is not an indication of charge): an n+ region in the n-well and a p+ region in the p-substrate.

Then, for the nMOS, the terminals for the Source (of the charge carriers) and the Drain (where the charge carriers leave the channel) are connected to two heavily doped n+ regions, and an insulator is layered over the body between the two, with the Gate terminal on top of this. A very similar arrangement exists for the pMOS transistor, except that its Source and Drain terminals are connected to two heavily doped p+ regions.

In Figure A10, the connections required to generate our inverter circuit are now overlaid on our basic CMOS construct. Thus, the red arrow indicates connection to the supply voltage, V_{cc}, and in both transistors the Base terminal is connected to its respective Source terminal: thus, in the pMOS (on the right) the Source is connected to V_{cc}, and in the nMOS (on the left) it is connected to Gnd. The Drain terminals of the two transistors are connected together. So too are the two Gate terminals, which will receive the signal that will ultimately control the On/Off status of the two transistors.

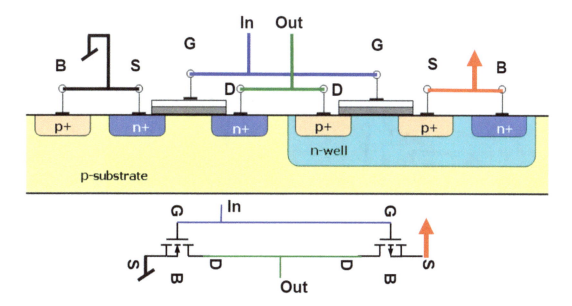

Figure A10 Cross-sectional view of CMOS with connections for inverter function

In the nMOS transistor, as the voltage on the Gate terminals increases (becomes more positive relative to the Source and Body), the positively charged holes in the p-substrate are "repelled" from the upper surface of the substrate immediately below the Gate, creating a region of "depletion" into which the negatively charged electrons from the substrate will be attracted. At a sufficiently high "threshold" voltage (V_{TH}), this upper surface of the p-substrate undergoes an "inversion" and an "n-channel" of negatively charged electrons forms between the n+ Source and Drain terminals through which a current can now flow, causing the voltage at the Drain terminal to drop to that of the Gnd-connected Source, that is, logical '0'.

In the pMOS transistor, a similar process occurs but opposite polarities of charge and voltage are involved. Thus, the application of an increasingly negative voltage on the Gate terminals relative to the Source (and Body) repels the negatively charged electrons in the upper surface of the n-well body immediately below the Gate, creating a depletion region into which positively charged electron holes effectively migrate. Eventually, at a sufficiently negative threshold voltage, an inversion layer is generated in this upper surface of the n-substrate that forms a "p-channel" of positively charged electron holes between the p+ Source and Drain terminals through which current can flow, causing the voltage at the Drain terminal to rise to that of the V_{CC} connected to the Source, that is, logical '1'.

In Figure A11, we illustrate what happens within this system when a logical '1' value, in the form of V_{CC}, is applied to the Gate terminals. As described above, the high positive voltage at the Gate terminal relative to the Source and Body of the nMOS transistor creates an n-channel through which current flows to reduce the Drain voltage to that of the Gnd-connected Source. By contrast, this high positive voltage has no effect on the pMOS transistor; there is no flow of current and, in switch terms, it remains open (Off). Thus, our combined circuit outputs a logical '0', the Gnd voltage, and a logical inversion has been achieved.

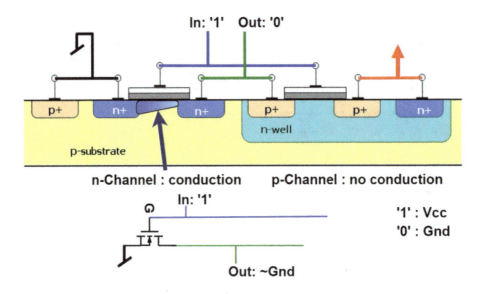

Figure A11 Cross-sectional view of a CMOS inverter circuit with logical '1' input

In Figure A12, we illustrate what happens within this same system when a logical '0' value, provided by Gnd, is applied to the Gate terminals. In this case, because this voltage is close to that already applied at the Source and Body terminals of the nMOS, nothing happens within it; there is no current flow because an n-channel does not form and, in switch terms, it remains open (Off). However, in the pMOS transistor, the Gnd voltage at the Gate terminal is highly negative relative to the V_{cc} voltage at its Source and Body terminals and a p-channel is induced in the n-well substrate below the pMOS Gate, allowing current to flow to increase the Drain voltage to that of the V_{cc}-connected Source. This time, our combined circuit outputs a logical '1', again producing a logical inversion.

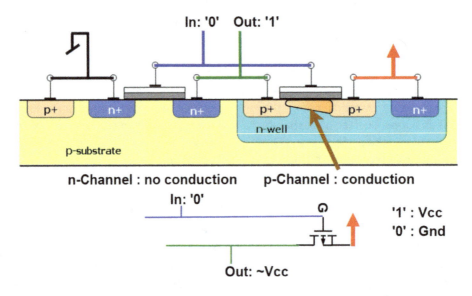

Figure A12 Cross-sectional view of a CMOS inverter circuit with logical '0' input

The path between Drain and Source terminals in an nMOS or pMOS presents an infinite resistance when there is no conduction; when one or other is conducting, the path still presents a residual resistance equivalent to anything from a few milliohms to a few ohms, and the voltage levels used to drive the circuit need to take account of this.

This type of circuit, in which a pair of active devices work together to either supply current to, or absorb current from, a connected load, is referred to as a push–pull output.

A1.2.4   Tri-state Output

We frequently connect multiple devices to a common output line, or set of lines in the case of a bus. This presents the risk of a short circuit if two devices are using different levels and, if the overall current flowing in the circuit is not limited, can destroy the transistors providing the outputs. To address this issue, serial resistors can be added to the circuit to limit the current that can flow, or transistors can be used that provide a current-limiting capability.

However, a more measured solution is to remove a device from the circuit when it is not actively communicating and, furthermore, to allow only one device to output at a time by using an explicit control signal.

The first aspect of this is to introduce an additional high-impedance, or "Hi-Z", state into a circuit alongside the existing high ('1') and low ('0') logic levels. By adopting a high-impedance state on its I/O pins, a device effectively removes itself from the circuit. Of course, this could mean that the device would no longer know when another device wanted to communicate with it. For this reason, we also introduce an additional control signal, **Output Enable** (OE), typically active low (so nOE), to indicate to the device whether it should drive its output as usual or adopt the high-impedance Z state, also described as "floating" (neither high nor low). The result is termed three-state or "**tri-state**" logic ("Z" is the standard symbol for impedance and is often used in HDLs to indicate a tri-state configuration), summarized in Table A11.

Table A11 Tri-state outputs

State	Electrical level	CMOS transistor states
'0'	Gnd	T_{pMOS} = Off; T_{nMOS} = On
'1'	$+V_{CC}$	T_{pMOS} = On; T_{nMOS} = Off
'Z'	High impedance	T_{pMOS} = Off; T_{nMOS} = Off

Figure A13 shows the CMOS logical inverter of the preceding section with tri-state control applied to it, represented by a schematic, its logical symbol, and its truth table:

- nEnp represents the active-low enabling (control) signal for the pMOS transistor. When activated, the pMOS transistor conducts and V_{CC} (level '1') is output (to Out).

- Enn represents the active-high enabling (control) signal for the nMOS transistor. When activated, the nMOS transistor conducts and Gnd-level voltage (level '0') is output (to Out).

▪ OE is an active-high Output Enable signal; when this is deactivated (i.e. '0'), both transistors are deactivated and the output (Out) is placed in the high-impedance "Z" state.

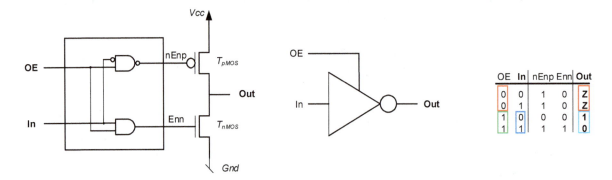

OE	In	nEnp	Enn	Out
0	0	1	0	Z
0	1	1	0	Z
1	0	0	0	1
1	1	1	1	0

Figure A13 *CMOS logical inverter with tri-state control*

Note that the nEnp and Enn signals cannot be activated at the same time. Otherwise, a short circuit would be produced between V_{CC} and Gnd. This combination is not possible with the internal logic illustrated here.

A1.2.5   Open-collector/Open-drain Output

A commonly used alternative to tri-state logic is the use of open-collector outputs, in which a transistor moderates the output signal, behaving like a switch that is either disconnected (allowing the output to float, with high impedance) or is connected to ground (driving the output low). Where a MOSFET transistor is used instead of a bipolar transistor, it is termed an open-drain output, but the principle is identical. Thus, there are only two output states involved (rather than three).

The Hi-Z output from the transistor is typically connected to a resistor, usually of a few kOhms (kΩ), which moderates the voltage such that receivers will perceive a high, logical '1' level (denoted as 'H' for VHDL purposes). Figure A14 depicts some common open-collector configurations, including a representative I/O truth table.

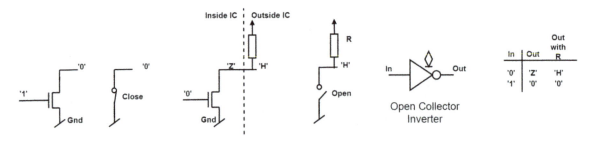

In	Out	Out with R
'0'	'Z'	'H'
'1'	'0'	'0'

Figure A14 *Open-collector electronics with CMOS (nMOS) and symbolic representation of an inverter*

When an open-collector output is pulled active low, current passes through the resistor and energy is dissipated, contributing to significant levels of power consumption in such devices. The value of the resistor used therefore needs to strike a balance between being high enough to minimize power consumption at such times, but low enough to allow the line to return promptly to the 'H' state (i.e. pull it up) when it is no longer being driven low by the device. The higher the operating speed required, the faster this "**pull-up**" must occur (i.e. the shorter the signal rise time), which means the lower the value of the "pull-up resistor" must be.

The open-collector arrangement allows more than one open-collector output to be connected to a single line. This is useful in situations in which many devices expect to be able to activate the line, such as:

- an interrupt request line shared by many sources (nINT)

- a data line shared by many sources (as in the 1-Wire and I²C communication protocols)

- a clock shared in support of serial communication (as in I²C communications).

If all of the connected outputs are in the high-impedance (Hi-Z) state, the pull-up resistor will hold the line at a high, logical '1', level. However, when one device drives its output active low to the ground state, it pulls the shared line to ground, driving it without interference from the other, inactive devices. This is the physical basis for several communication protocols, such as I²C, although an arbitration system must operate on top of it to handle situations where more than one device attempts to control the line at the same time.

When several open-collector devices are connected to a circuit, its overall capacitance, referred to as its equivalent capacitance, C_{equ}, will increase and acts as an increasing drag on the pull-up function; internal pull-up resistors may be used within devices to enable more granular management as necessary.

Let us connect a few open-collector outputs together, as shown in Figure A15, with all outputs deactivated (in the high-impedance Z state): the external pull-up resistor will raise the line to around V_{CC} level (i.e. 'H') through its resistance R.

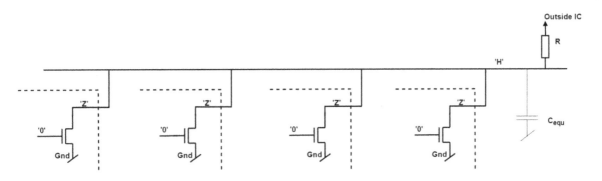

Figure A15 Open-collector outputs deactivated and connected together

If all of the outputs are deactivated, the common line will be at 'H', effectively implementing an AND function. If one of the outputs is now activated ('0' level), as shown in Figure A16, the common line will be forced to Gnd level ('0') too. It's a form of active-low OR gate: if one or more gate outputs go to '0', the line will go low too.

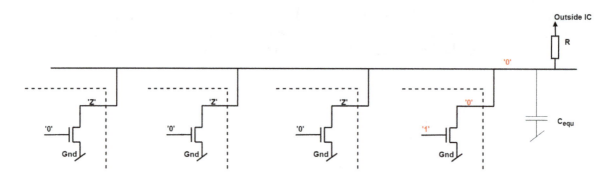

Figure A16 Open-collector outputs connected together with at least one activated at '0'

It is necessary to be careful with this kind of connection if the distance between the outputs is large (tens of centimeters): there is a risk of "ground bouncing" as the transistors switch on (the local ground potential gets inadvertently raised to the extent that the transistor perceives it as higher than its base voltage and so shuts down again; as the local potential dissipates, the transistor turns on again, and this cycle can occur several times).

In high-speed electronics, it is also important to consider the "rise time", the length of time it takes a signal to change from a specified low value to a specified high value, as illustrated in Figure A17 for an open-collector output in relation to a standard CMOS V_{CC} of 3.3 V.

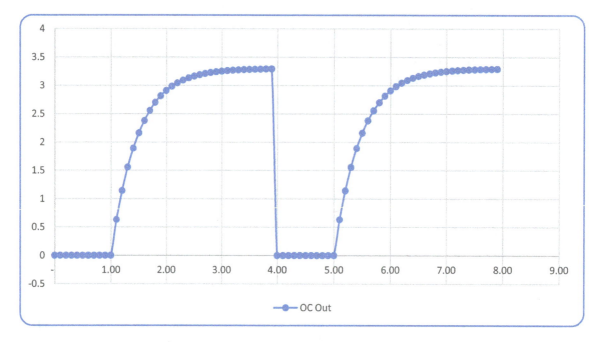

Figure A17 Open-collector output rise time

The time taken to effect a change of voltage in an RC (resistor–capacitor) circuit is determined by its capacitance and resistance. The RC time constant τ (or tau) provides an indication of how long it takes to raise the charge of a capacitor, through a resistor, from an initial voltage of zero to ~63% of the value of the voltage applied (or to discharge the same capacitor through the same resistor to ~37% of its initial charge voltage):

$$\tau = R \times C$$

As we described above, in a shared output line, all of the wires and the connected devices together confer an equivalent capacitance upon it. For a standard CMOS V_{CC} of 3.3 V, using a 4.7 kΩ resistor as the pull-up, and assuming that the circuit has an equivalent capacitance C_{equ} = 100 pF (which is a lot), the voltage will evolve as:

$$V_{out} = V_{CC} \times (1 - e^{-t/\tau}).$$

From this equation, the value of t can be deduced by measuring the time between the start of the rise in the V_{out} signal and when it reaches a voltage of $V_{CC} \times (1 - e^{-1})$ = 3.3 × 0.63212 = 2.1 V, which happens to be around the voltage level at which a TTL input will detect a '1'. This time delay is illustrated in Figure A18, and corresponds well to the calculated value of t for our example, using R = 4.7 kΩ and C_{equ} = 100 pF:

$$\tau = 4.7 \times 10^3 \times 100 \times 10^{-12} = 470 \times 10^{-9}\,s = 0.47\ \mu s.$$

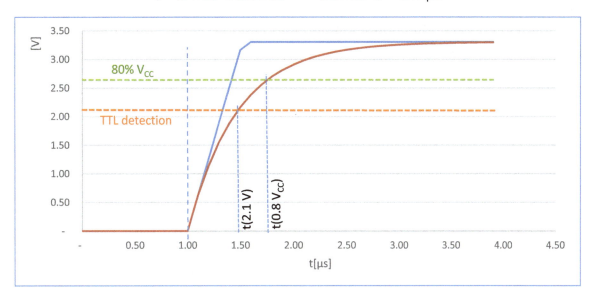

Figure A18 Detection delays for an open collector outputting a logic level '1' (V_{CC} = 3.3 V, R = 4.7 kΩ, C = 100 pF)

As we can observe from Figure A18, if we have a CMOS input instead, level '1' detection is guaranteed at 80% of V_{CC} → 2.64 V. The detection delay can be derived from:

$$V_{out} = V_{CC} \times (1 - e^{-t/\tau}) \rightarrow t = -t \times \ln(1 - (V_{out}/V_{CC}))$$

which tells us that for V_{out} = 2.64 V, the detection delay t = 0.75 µs (which, again, corresponds well to the observed delay shown in Figure A18).

When a MOSFET open-drain output transistor is activated, the delay will be very low because the equivalent resistor of the T_{nMOS} is less than an ohm as compared to the several kΩ of the external pull-up resistor.

A1.3 Logic Systems

In a computer, all operations are performed by logical circuits. The basic elements of these are transistors. Connected together in a specific way, they realize basic logical functions referred to as **gates**, the most basic being NOT, AND, NAND, OR, XOR and XNOR. Combinations of these basic gates realize more complex functions such as multiplexers, drivers, and arithmetic logic unit (ALUs).

The next thing we need in a computer is a way to memorize information. The simplest element for this purpose is a D (data or, sometimes, "delay") flip-flop (DFF), a simple circuit that can be driven to one of two possible states, representing a '0' or a '1', to store a single bit of data, and also sometimes termed a latch (although fine distinctions are made between the two, as we shall see below). Other forms of flip-flop (e.g. T, SR, JK) have been used in the past, but with the advent of VLSI chips and FPGAs, DFFs are used almost exclusively.

Once we have gates and DFFs available to us, we can realize more complex synchronous functions, such as counters, parallel registers, and shift registers.

A1.3.1   Basic Logical Elements

The next few subsections review the basic gates, describing their logical equations, the truth tables that represent their outputs in relation to the logical input levels of '0' and '1', and the logical symbols used for them in schematics and block diagrams.

A1.3.1.1 NOT Function (Inversion)

VHDL: Out = **NOT** (In)
Verilog: Out = ~ (In)

In	Out
0	1
1	0

A1.3.1.2 AND Function

VHDL: Out = InA **AND** InB
Verilog: Out = InA & InB

InA	InB	Out
0	0	0
0	1	0
1	0	0
1	1	1

Both inputs must be at level '1' for the output to be '1'; if either of the inputs is at level '0', the output will be '0'.

A1.3.1.3 NAND Function

VHDL: Out = InA **NAND** InB
Verilog: Out = ~ (InA **&** InB)

InA	InB	Out
0	0	1
0	1	1
1	0	1
1	1	0

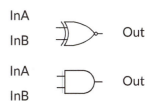

Both inputs must be at level '1' for the output to be '0'; otherwise, the output will be '1'.

A1.3.1.4 OR Function

VHDL: Out = InA **OR** InB
Verilog: Out = InA **|** InB

InA	InB	Out
0	0	0
0	1	1
1	0	1
1	1	1

At least one of the inputs must be at level '1' for the output to be '1'; both inputs must be at level '0' for the output to be '0'.

A1.3.1.5 XOR (Exclusive OR) Function

VHDL: Out = InA **XOR** InB
Verilog: Out = InA **^** InB

InA	InB	Out
0	0	0
0	1	1
1	0	1
1	1	0

For the output to be '1', one input must be at level '1' and the other at level '0'. If both inputs are at the same level, the output will be '0'.

A1.3.1.6 XNOR (Exclusive NOR) or Identity Function

VHDL: Out = InA **XNOR** InB
Verilog: Out = InA **^~** InB

InA	InB	Out
0	0	1
0	1	0
1	0	0
1	1	1

If both inputs are at the same level, the output will be '1'; otherwise, it will be '0'. For this reason, the XNOR gate is sometimes referred to as the "equivalence" or "identity" function.

A1.3.2 Multiplexers

If one signal must be chosen from among several, a multiplexer is used. It receives as input the set of signals from which to choose (e.g. In0, In1, In2 and In3), as well as, in the case shown below, a 2-bit indication (Sel1..Sel0) of the signal to select. The multiplexer output will be the onward transmission of the selected signal.

Sel1	*Sel0*	Out
0	0	In0
0	1	In1
1	0	In2
1	1	In3

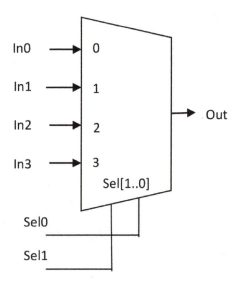

Samples of VHDL and Verilog code to implement the 4:1 multiplexer represented above are shown in the two boxes below.

```
VHDL:
-- Conditional affectation
Out <= In0 when Sel = "00" else

        In1 when Sel = "01" else
        In2 when Sel = "10" else

        In3;
-- OR
-- Process with case
Process (In0, In1, In2, In3, Sel)
Begin
        Case  Sel is
                When "00" => Out <= In0;
                When "01" => Out <= In1;
                When "10" => Out <= In2;
                When "11" => Out <= In3;
                When others => null;
        End case;
End process;
```

```
Verilog:




-- Process with case
always @(Sel[1:0] or In0 or In1 or In 2
or In3);
begin
        case (Sel)
                2'b00: Out = In0;
                2'b01: Out = In1;
                2'b10: Out = In2;
                2'b11: Out = In3;
        endcase
end
```

A1.3.3 Adders

The addition operation (ADD) takes two binary inputs and provides two outputs, the sum (Sum) and the "carry" (C_{out}).

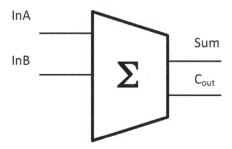

To perform calculations on several bits, the ADD operations are chained, and it is necessary to include an additional term, the "carry in", C_{in}, which will be the C_{out} from the previous operation.

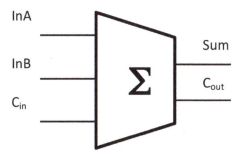

Two binary inputs without carry in, or entry with C_{in} = '**0**', produce the following truth table:

InA	InB	C_{out}	Sum
0	0	0	0
0	1	0	1
1	0	0	1
1	1	1	0

Two binary inputs with carry in, C_{in} = '**1**', produce the following truth table:

C_{in}	InA	InB	C_{out}	Sum
1	0	0	0	1
1	0	1	1	0
1	1	0	1	0
1	1	1	1	1

It is obviously possible to chain operations bit by bit to create an *n*-bit adder, which is very simple to design but quite costly in terms of operations; there are several variations on the basic *n*-bit adder that manipulate the output in two-bit form (bit 1 = C_{out}; bit 0 = Sum) in conjunction with C_{in} to implement more efficient addition operations.

Adders are typically used in the arithmetic logic units (ALUs) of processors.

A1.3.4 Data Registers: Flip-flops and Latches

To store data in a logical system, two types of circuit can provide this function:

- A flip-flop (typically a D flip-flop, but there are other less-used variants: T, SR and JK flip-flops)
- A latch.

Both memorize a single bit of data (although it should be noted that the term latch is sometimes used to describe a device that registers many bits of data upon a single trigger). The principal difference between the two is one of timing, in terms of **when** the input data is actually memorized in the storage element. Thus, a D flip-flop is defined as a synchronous device: it captures the value of the *D* input at a specific part of a clock cycle (such as the clock's rising edge or falling edge); the captured value becomes its *Q* output, which only changes on the next clock cycle transition.

By contrast, a latch is essentially asynchronous and is designed to be transparent; that is, a change in the *D* input signal causes an immediate change in the *Q* output. The latch is acting as a simple buffer. Such transparency is not always desirable, giving rise to the gated latch, in which an additional signal, Latch Enable, is required before an input signal will be registered. This is the basis on which flip-flops are sometime defined as "edge-triggered" whereas latches are "level-triggered".

Figure A19 compares the ways a D flip-flop (DFF) and a gated latch work.

Figure A19 Functional timings of D flip-flop (top) and gated latch (bottom)

We can see that the two controlling signals, Clk and LE (Latch Enable), have the same shape. Similarly, the input signals to both, D[] and DL[], are identical. However, the output signals, Q[] and QL[], are not the same, specifically when the input signal (D[]/DL[]) changes while the controlling signal (clk/LE) is at a high level ('1'):

- In the case of the D flip-flop, the output signal only changes on the next rising clock edge, for example, when the current input signal is "g", which is memorized by the flip-flop and becomes its next output on Q[] after "d".

- In the case of the gated latch, because the LE signal is high when the input signal changes from "d" to "e", and from "e" to "f", both of these values ("e" and "f") are transferred ("e") when LE = 1 and "f" is memorized when LE goes low.

Figures A20 and A21 show, respectively, the symbols for a D flip-flop and its register form, and for a latch and its register form. Most processor registers are formed from D flip-flops rather than latches; a register of 8 flip-flops can store a byte of data.

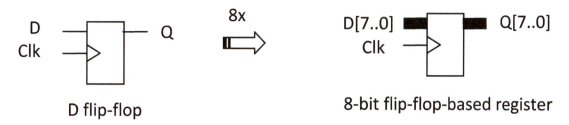

Figure A20 D flip-flop and register symbols

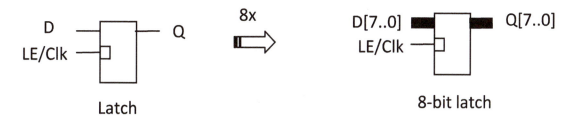

Figure A21 Latch and latch register symbols

In the D flip-flop symbol, the triangular element of the Clk input is indicative of it being edge-triggered. A latch often makes use of a Clk signal to drive its operation instead of an explicit Latch Enable signal, but the signal will still be interpreted in terms of its level rather than its rising (or falling) edge.

In an FPGA, the presence of a latch is frequently the consequence of a design error. The use of latches can cause issues in terms of synchronization, memorization and glitch generation and, although they have their uses, they are generally best avoided. Nevertheless, even D flip-flops can be afflicted by timing-related issues, as we shall see below.

A1.3.4.1 Metastability

When a flip-flop (or a latch) samples the incoming digital signal (D), there is a risk that if this signal is not held steady for the duration of the potential sampling, its value will be misinterpreted and an unrepresentative value will be passed to the output (Q). Datasheets for the devices in question will, to this end, specify periods before and after the clock edge during which the data must be held steady (and valid), referred to respectively as the setup time (t_{su}) and the hold time (t_h), as represented in Figure A22.

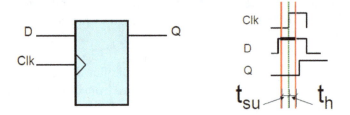

Figure A22 D flip-flop and setup and hold times

But what happens if this timing is not respected, as can be the case when a real-time signal is being sampled by a D flip-flop (DFF) in a digital system? This signal will be independent of the clock and can come at any time, in violation of the DFF timing constraint. In Figure A23, the red "columns" denote the periods around the rising clock edge, as defined by t_{su} and t_h, when the data input should be valid and stable. We can see that in all but the first instance, a change in the input data occurs during these periods, violating the timing constraints, and leading to a very significant degree of indeterminacy in the output value. This issue is one of **metastability**.

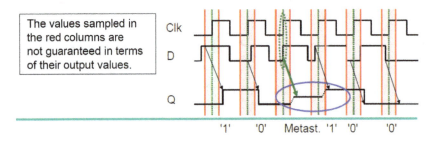

The values sampled in the red columns are not guaranteed in terms of their output values.

'1'   '0'   Metast. '1'   '0'   '0'

Figure A23 Illustration of metastability within D flip-flop

Indeed, in one instance in Figure A23 we can see that the result is an intermediate value in the output signal. If this is passed as input to another device in the circuit, will it be treated as a '0' or a '1'? It will depend on the device. Likewise, if the output signal is passed to more than one device, some may treat the signal as a '1' and some as a '0', throwing the entire state machine into chaos! An example of such a metastable output is shown in the oscilloscope trace for the D flip-flop memorization of thousands of samples, shown in Figure A24.

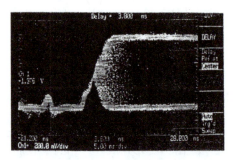

Figure A24 Oscilloscope trace of D flip-flop sample memorization showing metastability

It proves logically impossible to build a perfectly metastability-proof flip-flop. However, the problem can be marginalized by chaining two or more D flip-flops together in series, as depicted in Figure A25, exponentially reducing but never completely eliminating the probability of a metastable output being propagated. Without adopting this approach, sooner or later a metastable signal will manifest and be very, very difficult to track down.

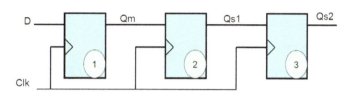

Figure A25 Chaining of D flip-flops to reduce metastability propagation

A1.3.5   Logic Design and Finite State Machines

To design any form of moderately complex system, the use of some form of design methodology is essential. The main view of a digital system can be seen as a **data path** in which many parallel signals propagate information in the form of data or addresses. Another kind of signal are the **control signals** that specify what operations are to be performed and when. The data path incorporates components such as buffers, ALUs, counters, and registers.

The design of the logic for the control signals is done using **finite state machines** (FSMs). These consist of two main parts:

▨ Combinational element

▨ Register element.

Figure A26 presents a generalized schematic of such an FSM.

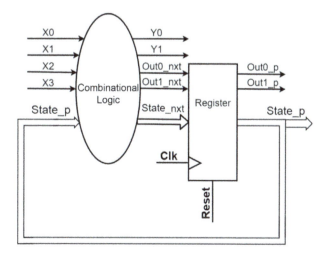

Figure A26 Generalized view of an FSM

The entire system needs to be synchronized with a global **clock** (**Clk**). More than one clock can exist within a system but this needs very specialized and careful design for it to work successfully and ensure that the resulting **clock domains** are synchronized correctly, typically requiring comprehensive analysis. The other signals shown in the figure can be described as follows:

- *X0..X3*: input signals

- *Y0..Y1*: combinational output signals

- *Out0_nxt..Out1_nxt*: next synchronous output

- *Out0_p..Out1_p*: present synchronous output

- *State_nxt*: next state

- *State_p*: present state

- *Reset*: reset signal to the register to initialize the FSM to its starting state.

Depending on the basis on which the outputs are generated, different kinds of FSM are defined. In all cases, the next state of the FSM, *State_nxt*, is dependent on the present state of the FSM, *State_p*, and the input vector *X*:

$$State\_nxt = f(State\_p, X).$$

A1.3.5.1 Medvedev FSM

The simplest form of FSM is often referred to as a Medvedev FSM. This is represented in Figure A27 and is characterized by the absence of any output logic: in other words, the output changes synchronously with the state of the machine (*Y* = *State_p*) and, in practical terms, the flip-flops of the state register would be connected directly to the output.

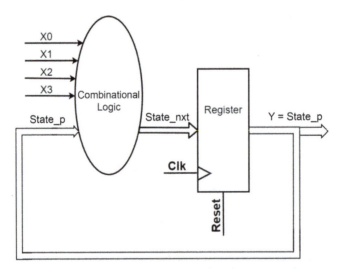

Figure A27 Medvedev FSM block diagram

A1.3.5.2 Moore FSM

In a Moore FSM, the output logic involves a combinational function that depends ONLY on the present state, that is, $Y = f(State\_p)$, as represented in Figure A28. There is no dependency on the input vector X.

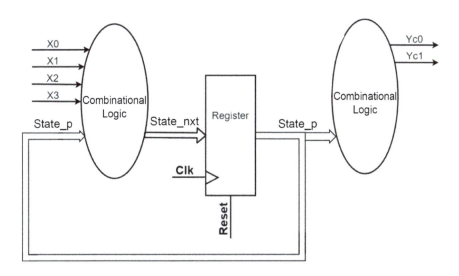

Figure A28 Moore FSM block diagram

A1.3.5.3 Mealy FSM

In contrast to a Moore FSM, the output logic of a Mealy FSM involves a combinational function that also depends on the input vector X as well as on the present state, that is, $Y = f(State\_p, X)$. This is represented in Figure A29.

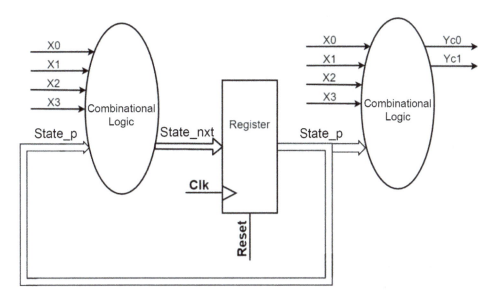

Figure A29 Mealy FSM block diagram

Generally, in circuit design, a Medvedev FSM, lacking any output logic, is too simplistic for common use. Moore and Mealy FSMs can be more or less applicable to different situations. Mealy FSMs are harder to design and typically involve more hardware to implement, but react more quickly to inputs, largely because Moore FSM output is typically driven only synchronously, on the next clock cycle following state change. Without this, a Moore FSM will propagate a state change to the output almost instantly, creating the potential for glitches (see section on metastability above). However, in a Mealy FSM, a change of input can trigger an almost immediate change in output, which is asynchronous and so can generate issues of its own. Thus, close control of output timing is crucial to both Moore and Mealy FSMs.

A1.4 Endianness: Big and Little

Within a computer register, in what order are the bits arranged? In what order are the bytes in a computer word stored in memory?

In 1726, Jonathan Swift published the satirical novel *Gulliver's Travels*, in which the eponymous traveler finds himself in a country called Lilliput with two small islands that are at civil war with one another. Why? Because the King of Lilliput introduced a law that required that people break open their soft-boiled eggs at the same end as him, the "little end". Those used to doing so at the "big end" rebelled and fled to the nearby island of Blefescu, setting the "Little-Endians" and the "Big-Endians" at permanent odds with one another.

This episode is widely understood to be a satirical commentary on the religious conflict between the Protestant Church of England and the Roman Catholic church in France, which informed so many of the historical wars between the two countries during the preceding centuries, and in 1980, the computer scientist Danny Cohen used it to make a plea for *consistency* in the order in which bits were communicated – either always the small end (the least-significant bit) first or always the large end (the most-significant bit) first – while noting that the question of the underlying order itself was essentially just as trivial as the Lilliputian dispute.

It's fair to say that his plea did not bring eternal peace to the subject of "endianness", and partisans of the two approaches still debate it avidly, while everyone else that works at bit-level with networks and computers must appreciate the distinctions and consequences, as described below.

A1.4.1 Bit Numbering

What exactly is endianness? Let's start by defining some terms and associated abbreviations:

- Most-significant byte – MSB

- Most-significant bit – MSb

- Least-significant byte – LSB

- Least-significant bit – LSb

We can define how to number the bits in a computer register. Figure A30 depicts a 32-bit register, Rx. In the figure, the bits are numbered from right to left, starting at 0. We describe the bit number as the **rank** of the bit, and we can define the **weight** of that bit as base^{rank}, where the base in this example is obviously 2 because we're dealing with a binary register.

Thus, for the bit numbered 8, its rank is 8, and its weight is $2^8 = 256_{10}$, which is also the value of the register if a '1' is placed in this position alone.

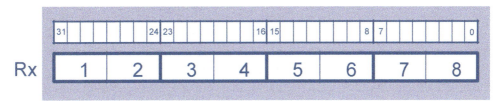

Figure A30 Little-endian bit numbering

This is the convention of **little-endian** bit numbering; the smallest weight is at the lowest ranked position in the register. It's also the direction used in writing and reading Arabic script, but here we're concerned with numbers rather than text. Thus, in a 32-bit little-endian register, the MSb is bit31 and the LSb is bit0.

The obvious alternative, shown in Figure A31, is to number the bits in the same register from left to right, in the order that we write Latin/Roman script (i.e. as used in English and most other Western European languages). This is **big-endian** bit numbering.

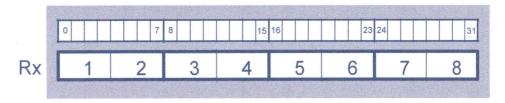

Figure A31 Big-endian bit numbering

Unlike the little-endian system, there is no elegant relationship between the rank and weight of a bit under this system and its representation of an actual value, except by virtue of an arithmetic operation:

$$bitRank = MaxBitNumber - bitValue.$$

In a 32-bit big-endian register, the MSb is bit0 and the LSb is bit31.

At this point, it becomes a matter of opinion as to which system is better, and it becomes a question of convention as to which representation is used by any given processor. Implementations of both systems can be found, but the majority of processors nowadays use little-endian bit numbering. For the figures in the rest of this section, we adopt a little-endian representation, with the MSb on the left with the highest index and the LSb on the right with the lowest (0) index.

A1.4.2   Byte Numbering

Now, let's consider what impact such a bit-numbering approach might have when it comes to byte numbering, when a number is in the internal register, such as Rx, of a processor. This register could be 8, 16, 32, or 64 bits in width, or even more. However, the same principles will apply whatever the size, and for our examples below we will use a 32-bit-wide register.

We define an address in memory as being a **byte address** (although the real world will always throw up an exception to this). How do we go about representing this memory? Needless to say, some representations will show memory addresses being incremented downwards, as shown in the upper half of Figure A32, and some will show memory addresses being incremented upwards, as in the lower half of the figure. Within this book, both representations are used, depending on the topic. In the next few figures, the downward representation is used.

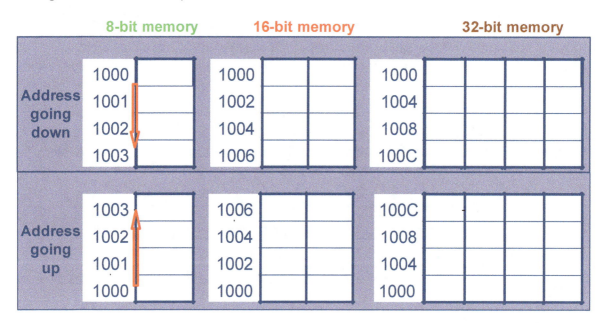

Figure A32 Representations of different memory widths showing addresses incrementing downwards (top) or upwards (bottom)

We need to study what happens when one or more bytes of an internal 32-bit processor register are transferred into memory of various widths under little-endian and big-endian regimes. We will see that the results are not the same, which has implications for any programmer working at this level on a system.

Figure A33 shows what happens when the least-significant byte (LSB) of our internal processor register, Rx, is transferred into memory of different widths under each of the regimes. The hexadecimal value of this byte is 0x78, as shown, and the 16-bit-wide and 32-bit-wide memories show the respective memory offsets (+0, +1, etc.) from the base address indicated to the left. In each transfer we have to STORE the register data starting at address 0x1000.

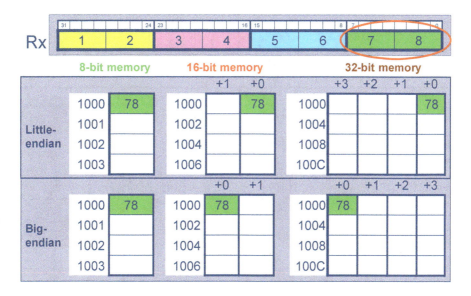

Figure A33 8-bit transfer from register to different memory widths under little- and big-endian regimes

As we can see in the figure, the data will end up in a different part of the memory under the two regimes if the size of the transfer is not the same as the width of the memory. Figure A34 depicts a similar situation for a two-byte (16-bit) transfer (of 0x5678) from Rx to memory; again, the data ends up in a different part of memory under each regime if the size of the transfer does not match that of the target memory. In the big-endian regime, the MSB (0x56) is written into the lowest address, but in the little-endian regime, the LSB (0x78) is written to this address. The same behaviors are visible in the four-byte (32-bit) transfer (of 0x12345678) shown in Figure A35.

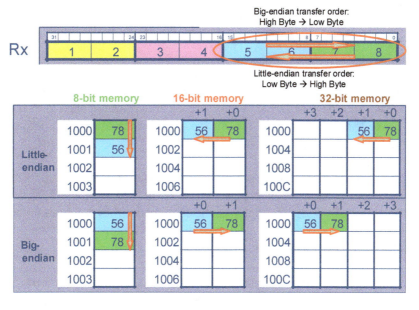

Figure A34 16-bit transfer from register to different memory widths under little- and big-endian regimes

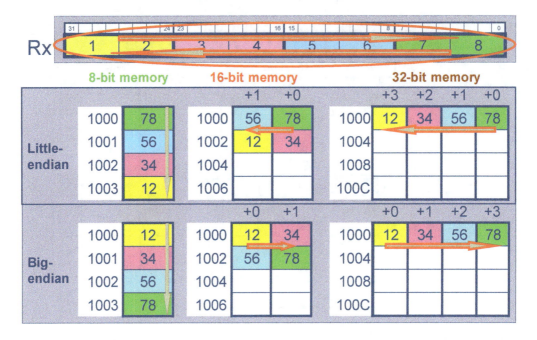

It is not hard to imagine the difficulties of mixing devices with different endianness in the same SoC design. Clearly, it is not impossible, and some processors incorporate instructions to support the necessary reversals during transfers, but it will require appropriate care and consideration.

So, is it little-endian or big-endian for the Arm processor? Well, the default is typically little-endian but both are available depending upon the specific manufacturer of the processor, such that endianness may be hard-selected in the design, may be a start-up configuration, or could be determined by software at run-time.

A1.4.3 Unaligned Transfers

Endianness also has a significant bearing on another issue: that of unaligned transfers. Thus, what happens when a transfer is required to a memory address that does not align to the size in bytes of the transfer; for example, the transfer of a 32-bit word to a memory location that does not start from a multiple of 4, that is, it crosses a four-byte word boundary.

The first question that must be answered is whether the processor will even support such an unaligned transfer. Many processors will throw an error upon such a request. Even where a processor will accept such transfers, they are inherently inefficient because they will typically require two bus transfers to complete, one to update the last part of the first affected word in memory, and the second to update the first part of the next affected word in memory.

Assuming that our processor does support unaligned transfers, we will consider the transfer of a 32-bit word to a non-aligned memory address starting at 0x1001, as depicted in Figure A36, under both endianness regimes for three different memory widths. As we saw above, the lowest address holds the MSB (0x12) in the big-endian regime, and it holds the LSB (0x78) in the little-endian regime, and the two regimes present dramatically different memory arrangements in consequence.

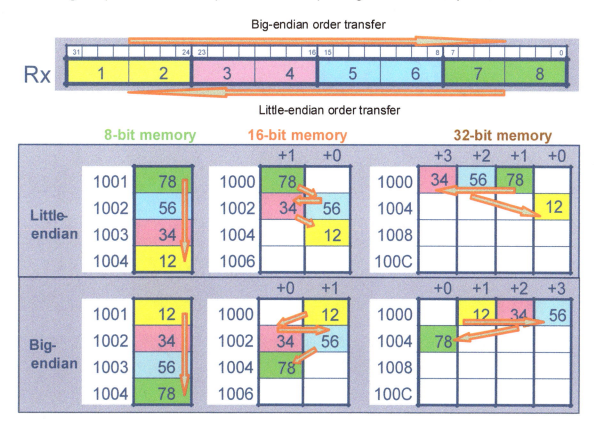

Figure A36 Unaligned 32-bit transfers in little- and big-endian regimes

A1.5 Summary

In this appendix, we have explained number base representations, microelectronics, logic and endianness as basic elements for a better understanding of the concepts explained in this book on SoCs. We think they will help the reader to understand more advanced concepts within the wonderful world of computers.

Glossary of Abbreviations

µC	micro-Controller, microcontroller
ACE	AXI Coherency Extensions
ADC	Analog-to-Digital Converter
AES	Advanced Encryption Standard
AHB	Advanced High-performance Bus
ALU	Arithmetic Logic Unit
AMBA	Advanced Microcontroller Bus Architecture
AP	Access Port
APB	Advanced Peripheral Bus
ARM	Advanced Risc Machine
AS	Address Strobe
ASB	Advanced System Bus
ASCII	American Standard Code for Information Interchange
ASIC	Application-Specific Integrated Circuit
ASIP	Application-Specific Instruction set Processor
AXI	Advanced eXtensible Interface
bit	binary digit
BNEP	Bluetooth Network Encapsulation Protocol
BOD	Brown Out Detection
BSD	Boundary Scan Device
BSDL	Boundary Scan Description Language

CAN	Controller Area Network
CDM	Charged-Device Model
CD-ROM	Compact Disc – ROM
CEC	Consumer Electronics Control
CHI	Coherent Hub Interface
CMOS	Complementary Metal–Oxide–Semiconductor
CPU	Central Processing Unit
CRC	Cyclic Redundancy Check
CS	Chip Select
CS_n	Chip Select, active low (also nCS or CS#)
DAC	Digital-to-Analog Converter
DAP	Debug Access Port
DDC	Data Display Channel
DDR	Double Data Rate (SDRAM)
DFF	Data (or Delay) Flip-Flop
DMA	Direct Memory Access
DP	Debug Port
DRAM	Dynamic RAM
DS	Data Strobe
DTS	Debug and Test System
DUT	Device Under Test
DVD	Digital Versatile Disc

DVI	Digital Visual Interface
EDA	Electronic Design Automation
EDF	Earliest Deadline First
EDO	Extended Data-Out
EDRAM	Enhanced Dynamic Random Access Memory
eDRAM	Embedded DRAM
EMI	Electro Magnetic Interference
EOF	End Of Frame
EOP	End Of Packet
ESD	Electro Static Discharge
ESDRAM	Enhanced Synchronous DRAM
ETM	Embedded Trace Module
FMC	FPGA Mezzanine Card
FPGA	Field-Programmable Gate Array
FPU	Floating-Point Unit
GPIO	General-Purpose Input/Output
GPU	Graphics Processing Unit
HBM	Human Body Model
HDL	Hardware Description Language
HDMI	High-Definition Multimedia Interface
HPD	Hot Plug Detect
HPS	Hard Processor System

HW	Hardware
I/F	Interface
I²C	Inter-Integrated Circuit
I²S	Inter-IC Sound, Integrated Interchip Sound
IC	Integrated Circuit
IEEE	Institute of Electrical and Electronics Engineers
IO *or* I/O	Input/Output
IoT	Internet of Things
IP	Intellectual Property
IP	Internet Protocol
IRC	Internal RC
IrDA	Infrared Data Association
IRQ	Interrupt ReQuest
ISA	Instruction Set Architecture
JTAG	Joint Test Action Group, norms IEEE 1149.1
L2CAP	Logical Link Control and Adaptation Protocol
LAN	Local Area Network
LCD	Liquid Crystal Display
LIN	Local Interconnect Network
LoRa	Long-Range Communication Network
LR	Link Register
LSB	Least-Significant Byte

LSb	Least-Significant bit
LSW	Least-Significant Word
LVDS	Low-Voltage Differential Signaling
MAC	Media Access Control
MAU	Medium Attachment (or Access) Unit
MEM-AP	MEMory Access Port
MEMS	Micro Electro Mechanical Systems
MGT	Multi-Gigabit Transceiver
MIIM	Media Independent Interface Management
MISO	Master In, Slave Out
MMU	Memory Management Unit
MOSI	Master Out, Slave In
MPU	Memory Protection Unit
MSB	Most-Significant Byte
MSb	Most-Significant bit
MSW	Most-Significant Word
MTB	Micro Trace Buffer
MTBF	Mean Time Between Failures
MTU	Maximum Transmission Unit
NA *or* N/A	Not Available/Applicable
NC	Not Connected
nMOS	negative-type Metal–Oxide–Semiconductor

nMOSFET	negative-channel Metal–Oxide–Semiconductor Field-Effect Transistor
NOC	Network On Chip
NU	Not Used
OHCI	Open Host Controller Interface
OSI	Open Systems Interconnection
OTG	On-The-Go
PAN	Personal Area Network
PCB	Printed Circuit Board
PCIe	Peripheral Component Interconnect Express
PI	Programmable Interface
PHY	Physical Layer
PLL	Phase-Locked Loop
pMOS	positive-type Metal–Oxide–Semiconductor
pMOSFET	positive-channel Metal–Oxide–Semiconductor Field-Effect Transistor
PMSA	Protected Memory System Architecture
PMU	Power Management Unit
PSR	Program Status Register
PWM	Pulse-Width Modulation
QSPI	Quad Serial Peripheral Interface (or Queued Serial Peripheral Interface)
RAM	Random-Access Memory
RIT	Repetitive Interrupt Timer
RMII	Reduced Media Independent Interface

RMS	Rate-Monotonic Scheduling
ROM	Read-Only Memory
RTL	Register Transfer Layer
RTOS	Real-Time Operating System
SCB	System Control Block
SCS	System Control Space
s/w	Switch
SD-Card	Secure Digital Card
SDRAM	Synchronous Dynamic RAM
SE0	Single-Ended 0 (Zero)
SFP	Small Form-factor Pluggable
SOF	Start Of Frame
SoC	System on a Chip
SOM	System On Modules
SP	Stack Pointer
SPI	Serial Peripheral Interface
SSI	Synchronous Serial Interface
SSP	Synchronous Serial Port
SW	Software
SWD	Serial Wire Debug
SysClk	System Clock
TB	Test Bench

TBC	To Be Confirmed
TBD	To Be Determined/Defined
TCM	Tightly-Coupled Memory
TMDS	Transition-Minimized Differential Signaling
TS	Target Systems
TTL	Transistor–Transistor Logic
UAL	Unified Assembly Language
UART	Universal Asynchronous Receiver/Transmitter
USB	Universal Serial Bus
VESA	Video Electronic Standards Association
VGA	Video Graphics Array
VHDL	VHSIC Hardware Description Language
VHSIC	Very High Speed Integrated Circuit
VLSI	Very Large Scale Integrated circuits
VMSA	Virtual Memory System Architecture
VRAM	Video Random Access Memory
WAN	Wide Area Network
WD	Watch-Dog

Index

The Arm Education Media Story

Did you know that Arm processor design is at the heart of technology that touches 70% of the world's population - from sensors to smartphones to super computers.

Given the vast reach of Arm's computer chip and software designs, our aim at Arm Education Media is to play a leading role in addressing the electronics and computing skills gap; i.e., the disconnect between what engineering students are taught and the skills they need in today's job market.

Launched in October 2016, Arm Education Media is the culmination of several years of collaboration with thousands of educational institutions, industrial partners, students, recruiters and managers worldwide. We complement other initiatives and programs at Arm, including the Arm University Program, which provides university academics worldwide with free teaching materials and technologies.

Via our subscription-based digital content hub, we offer interactive online courses and textbooks that enable academics and students to keep up with the latest Arm technologies.

We strive to serve academia and the developer community at large with low-cost, engaging educational materials, tools and platforms.

We are Arm Education Media:
Unleashing Potential

Arm Education Media Online Courses

Our online courses have been developed to help students learn about state of the art technologies from the Arm partner ecosystem. Each online course contains 10-14 modules, and each module comprises lecture slides with notes, interactive quizzes, hands-on labs and lab solutions.

The courses will give your students an understanding of Arm architecture and the principles of software and hardware system design on Arm-based platforms, skills essential for today's computer engineering workplace.

For more information, visit www.arm.com/education

Available Now:

Professional Certificate in Embedded Systems Essentials with Arm (on the edX platform)

Efficient Embedded Systems Design and Programming

Rapid Embedded Systems Design and Programming

Internet of Things

Graphics and Mobile Gaming

Real-Time Operating Systems Design and Programming

Introduction to System-on-Chip Design

Advanced System-on-Chip Design

Embedded Linux

Mechatronics and Robotics

Arm Education Media Books

The Arm Education books program aims to take learners from foundational knowledge and skills covered by its textbooks to expert-level mastery of Arm-based technologies through its reference books. Textbooks are suitable for classroom adoption in Electrical Engineering, Computer Engineering and related areas. Reference books are suitable for graduate students, researchers, aspiring and practising engineers.

For more information, visit www.arm.com/education

Available now, in print and ePub formats:

Embedded Systems Fundamentals with Arm
Cortex-M based Microcontrollers:
A Practical Approach, FRDM-KL25Z EDITION
by Dr Alexander G. Dean
ISBN 978-1-911531-03-6

Embedded Systems Fundamentals with Arm
Cortex-M based Microcontrollers:
A Practical Approach, NUCLEO-F09IRC EDITION
by Dr Alexander G. Dean
ISBN 978-1-911531-26-5

Digital Signal Processing using Arm Cortex-M
based Microcontrollers: Theory and Practice
by Cem Ünsalan, M. Erkin Yücel and H. Deniz Gürhan
ISBN 978-1911531-16-6

Operating Systems Foundations with Linux
on the Raspberry Pi
by Wim Vanderbauwhede and Jeremy Singer
ISBN 978-1-911531-20-3

Modern System-on-Chip Design on Arm
by David J. Greaves
ISBN 978-1-911531-36-4

System-on-Chip with Arm Cortex-M Processors
by Joseph Yiu, Distinguished Engineer at Arm
ISBN 978-1-911531-19-7

Arm Helium Technology
M-Profile Vector Extension (MVE) for Arm
Cortex-M Processors
by Jon Marsh
ISBN: 978-1-911531-23-4